# Transportation systems in buildings

CIBSE Guide D: 2005

**CIBSE**

© September 2005 (3rd edition) The Chartered Institution of Building Services Engineers London

Registered charity number 278104

ISBN-13: 978-1-903287-61-3
ISBN-10: 1-903287-61-8

Typeset by CIBSE Publications Department

Printed in Great Britain by Page Bros. (Norwich) Ltd., Norwich, Norfolk, NR6 6SA

## Note from the publisher

This publication is primarily intended to provide guidance to those responsible for the design, installation, commissioning, operation and maintenance of building services. It is not intended to be exhaustive or definitive and it will be necessary for users of the guidance given to exercise their own professional judgement when deciding whether to abide by or depart from it.

Cover illustration: design sketch for the London Bridge Tower by Renzo Piano (courtesy of Renzo Piano Building Workshop)

# Foreword

This CIBSE Guide D: *Transportation systems in buildings* is now in its third edition representing a commitment for well over a decade by the Institution and the CIBSE Lifts Group to provide professional guidance for its members and industry in general.

This new edition of the Guide is very comprehensive covering the whole spectrum of interior circulation, planning and design, selection of lift equipment and performance, computer programs, types of systems, legislation, fire and safety, requirements for the disabled, lift components and installation also drives and controls, lift traffic control, escalators and moving walks (passenger conveyors), electrical systems and environmental conditions.

Chapter 1 includes a very useful section indicating to readers the main changes and additions since the previous edition of this Guide.

The very important subject of energy consumption and efficiency is well covered including remote monitoring and alarms to enable management to deal with the continuing safe and efficient use of the various transportation systems.

Whilst the design and installation phases are very important, commissioning, testing and thorough examination must be a major consideration before handover to the end user and this section should not go unheeded.

During the daily use of any transportation system management have a very clear responsibility to ensure the safe and efficient use, preventative maintenance and periodic thorough examination of all systems, which should include any future modernisation or refurbishment. Estate managers and those responsible for the facilities management of transportation systems should find those sections very useful.

The section covering legislation, standards and codes of practice is a very useful source of reference.

In conclusion it is important that people, goods and equipment are moved safely and efficiently — I believe this new edition of Guide D: *Transportation systems in buildings* will help meet those objectives.

Peter Day
*Founder chairman, CIBSE Guide D Steering Committee*

# Guide D Steering Committee

John Bashford (Chairman) (J Bashford & Associates)

Dr Lutfi Al-Sharif (Al-Sharif-VTC)
Dr Gina Barney (Gina Barney Associates)
Jerry Brace (Axess4All)
Dennis Burrell (TVC Monitoring)
John Carroll (Hoare Lea)
David Cooper (LECS (UK) Ltd.)
Dr Richard Peters (Peters Research Ltd)
Simon Russett (Hoare Lea)
Charles Salter (ACE Lifts Ltd.)
Adrian Shiner (KONE plc)
Derek Smith (Otis Ltd.)
John Snowball (Steven Morris Associates)
Ken Butcher (Secretary) (CIBSE)

# Principal authors and contributors (3rd edition)

Dr Lutfi Al-Sharif (Al-Sharif-VTC), Dr Gina Barney (Gina Barney Associates), John Bashford (J Bashford & Associates), Jerry Brace (Axess4All), Dennis Burrell (TVC Monitoring), John Carroll (Hoare Lea), David Cooper (LECS (UK) Ltd.), Peter Day (engineering consultant), John Inglis (Amron Resources), Dr Richard Peters (Peters Research Ltd), Simon Russett (Hoare Lea), Charles Salter (Artisan Control Equipment), Adrian Shiner (KONE plc), Derek Smith (Otis Ltd.), John Snowball (Steven Morris Associates)

## Authors and contributors (1st and 2nd editions)

Guide D is a continuing publication and each successive edition relies on material provided for previous editions. The Institution acknowledges the material provided by previous authors and contributors, including: Dr Lutfi Al-Sharif (Al-Sharif-VTC), Roy Bailey (Watkins Payne and Partners), Paul Baker (Otis Ltd), Dr Gina Barney (Gina Barney Associates), Jerry Brace (Otis Handling), Ish Buckingham (*Elevation*), Ken Butcher (CIBSE), Bob Challans (Faber Consulting Engineers), Chris Chapman (Trend Control Systems Ltd.), David Cooper (LECS (UK) Ltd.), Peter Day (engineering consultant), P Eagling (Kone Lifts Ltd.), Stuart East (John Noad (Building Environment) Ltd.), John Gale (*Elevator World*), Simon Gray (Geoffrey Wilkinson (City) Ltd.), Gerald Honey (The Gerald Honey Partnership), Roger Howkins (Arup), Paul Johnson (Mitsubishi), Peter Jones (PJ Lift Consultancy), Michael Ling (deceased) (Alimak Ltd.), Patrick Moore (BSC Consulting Ltd.), Stuart Morgan (Hann Tucker Associates), Anthony Neighbour (Schindler Ltd.), John Newbold (SVM Lift Consult Ltd.), Craig Pearce (Arup Australia), Dr Richard Peters (Peters Research Ltd.), D Rich (Schindler Ltd.), Adrian Shiner (KONE plc), Derek Smith (Otis Ltd.), Dr Albert So (City University of Hong Kong), Steve Taylor (SVM Lift Consult Ltd.), E Studer (Telefuni-AG), Barry Wheeler (Otis Ltd.)

## Acknowledgements

The Institution is grateful to the panel of reviewers who provided valuable feedback during the drafting of this Guide. Members of the review panel included the following: Mike Bottomley (Lerch Bates & Associates), Alex Carmichael (Bureau Veritas), Roy Cooper (KONE plc), Peter Day, Henry Dunbar, Mike Goddard (ETL), Miller Hannah (Hoare Lea Fire Engineering), Lionel Hutt (Magnetek-UK Ltd.), Ian Jones (Otis Ltd.), Phil Jones (Building Energy Solutions), Bob Lee (LEIA), P R Horton (Consultant), Nick Mellor (Pickerings), Dr Bruce Powell (The Bruce Powell Company Inc.), Michael Savage (Schindler Ltd.), Vincent Sharpe (ACE), Dr Marja-Liisa Siikonen (Kone, Finland), Ian Simpson (Health & Safety Executive), Dr Tony Sung (University of Manchester), Diana Williamson (BSI Consumer Council).

Chapter 18 is based on guidelines to the CDM Regulations produced by the Lift and Escalator Industry Association. The CIBSE gratefully acknowledges the LEIA for permission to reproduce these guidelines in full.

Appendix A1 is reproduced from the *Elevator and Escalator Micropaedia* by G C Barney, D A Cooper and J Inglis, published by the International Association of Elevator Engineers. The CIBSE gratefully acknowledges the IAEE for permission to reproduce this glossary in full.

## Technical editor

Dr Gina Barney (Gina Barney Associates)

## Editor

Ken Butcher

## CIBSE Publishing Manager

Jacqueline Balian

# Contents

1    **Introduction**     **1-1**

   1.1    Purpose of Guide D     1-3

   1.2    Recent developments     1-3

   1.3    Contents of Guide D     1-3

   1.4    Other sources of information     1-4

2    **Interior circulation**     **2-1**

   2.1    Introduction     2-3

   2.2    General considerations     2-3

   2.3    Human factors     2-4

   2.4    Circulation elements     2-4

   2.5    Circulation in shopping centres     2-8

   2.6    Circulation in other types of buildings     2-11

   2.7    Location and arrangement of transportation facilities     2-13

   2.8    Facilities for persons with disabilities     2-16

   References     2-16

3    **Traffic planning and selection of equipment and performance**     **3-1**

   3.1    Introduction     3-3

   3.2    Review of traffic design     3-3

   3.3    Passenger design     3-4

   3.4    Lift system performance     3-6

   3.5    Calculation of the round trip time     3-7

   3.6    Assumptions made in the derivation of the round trip time equation     3-10

   3.7    Other factors to be considered in the evaluation of the round trip time equation     3-11

   3.8    Matching passenger demand to handling capacity during up-peak     3-12

   3.9    Passenger waiting, transit and journey times and time to destination during up-peak traffic demand     3-12

   3.10    Traffic conditions other than up-peak     3-13

   3.11    Selection of equipment with respect to lift function     3-14

   3.12    Selection of equipment with respect to building form     3-15

   3.13    Selection of equipment with respect to building function     3-17

   References     3-19

   Appendix 3.A1: Table of $H$ and $S$ values     3-20

   Appendix 3.A2: Example calculations     3-21

4    **Advanced planning techniques and computer programs**     **4-1**

   4.1    Introduction     4-3

   4.2    Up-peak calculation using computer software     4-3

   4.3    General Analysis     4-6

   4.4    Simulation of lift systems     4-7

   4.5    Measuring traffic     4-11

   4.6    Describing traffic     4-13

   References     4-14

   Appendix 4.A1: Symbols and formulae     4-14

   Appendix 4.A2: Standard templates     4-16

| | | |
|---|---|---|
| **5** | **Types of transportation systems** | **5-1** |
| 5.1 | Introduction | 5-3 |
| 5.2 | Passenger and goods/passenger lifts | 5-4 |
| 5.3 | Goods lifts | 5-11 |
| 5.4 | Observation lifts | 5-15 |
| 5.5 | Service lifts | 5-19 |
| 5.6 | Motor vehicle lifts | 5-21 |
| 5.7 | Rack and pinion lifts | 5-23 |
| 5.8 | Lifts for other purposes | 5-25 |
| 5.9 | Future concepts | 5-29 |
| | References | 5-30 |
| | Appendix 5.A1: Car, well, headroom, pit and machine room sizes | 5-31 |
| | | |
| **6** | **Firefighting lifts and evacuation lifts for people with disabilities** | **6-1** |
| 6.1 | Introduction | 6-3 |
| 6.2 | Need for firefighting lifts | 6-3 |
| 6.3 | Firefighting lifts: design considerations | 6-6 |
| 6.4 | Firefighting lifts: inspection, testing and maintenance | 6-8 |
| 6.5 | Evacuation lifts for people with disabilities | 6-8 |
| | References | 6-10 |
| | | |
| **7** | **Lift components and installation** | **7-1** |
| 7.1 | Introduction | 7-3 |
| 7.2 | Electric traction drives | 7-3 |
| 7.3 | Hydraulic drives | 7-9 |
| 7.4 | Controller cabinet | 7-13 |
| 7.5 | Guide rails | 7-13 |
| 7.6 | Counterweight | 7-15 |
| 7.7 | Lift car | 7-16 |
| 7.8 | Door operators | 7-17 |
| 7.9 | Door configurations | 7-19 |
| 7.10 | Overspeed governors | 7-22 |
| 7.11 | Safety gear | 7-22 |
| 7.12 | Buffers | 7-24 |
| 7.13 | Uncontrolled upward movement device | 7-25 |
| 7.13 | Ropes | 7-25 |
| 7.14 | Roping systems | 7-27 |
| 7.15 | Car and landing fixtures | 7-29 |
| | References | 7-30 |
| | | |
| **8** | **Lift drives and controls** | **8-1** |
| 8.1 | Introduction | 8-3 |
| 8.2 | Lift controllers | 8-4 |
| 8.3 | Controller technology | 8-5 |
| 8.4 | Control of lift drives | 8-6 |
| 8.5 | DC motor control techniques | 8-8 |
| 8.6 | AC motor control techniques | 8-11 |
| 8.7 | Control of hydraulic drives | 8-13 |
| 8.8 | Control of door operators | 8-14 |
| | References | 8-15 |

| | | |
|---|---|---|
| **9** | **Lift traffic control** | **9-1** |
| 9.1 | The need for lift traffic control | 9-3 |
| 9.2 | Single lift traffic control | 9-3 |
| 9.3 | Purpose of group traffic control | 9-4 |
| 9.4 | Types of traffic control algorithms | 9-5 |
| 9.5 | Advanced group traffic control features | 9-8 |
| 9.6 | Other group traffic controller features | 9-10 |
| 9.7 | Effect of the traffic control algorithm on traffic design | 9-12 |
| 9.8 | Case studies | 9-13 |
| | References | 9-15 |
| | | |
| **10** | **Escalators and moving walks** | **10-1** |
| 10.1 | Introduction | 10-3 |
| 10.2 | Definitions, commonly available equipment and duty | 10-4 |
| 10.3 | Principal components | 10-4 |
| 10.4 | Installation planning | 10-6 |
| 10.5 | Drive systems, energy usage and safety devices | 10-8 |
| | References | 10-10 |
| | | |
| **11** | **Transportation facilities for persons and persons with disabilities** | **11-1** |
| 11.1 | Access for everyone | 11-3 |
| 11.2 | Disability or impairment? | 11-3 |
| 11.3 | Disability Discrimination Act 1995 | 11-3 |
| 11.4 | Building Regulations Approved Document M | 11-4 |
| 11.5 | Equipment selection to meet user needs | 11-4 |
| 11.6 | Environmental conditions | 11-5 |
| 11.7 | Equipment provision | 11-6 |
| 11.8 | Escalators and moving walks | 11-9 |
| 11.9 | Egress for persons with disabilities | 11-9 |
| 11.10 | Selection of lifting device | 11-10 |
| | References | 11-11 |
| | Appendix 11.A1: Principal requirements of BS EN 81-70 | 11-12 |
| | | |
| **12** | **Electrical systems and environmental conditions** | **12-1** |
| 12.1 | Introduction | 12-3 |
| 12.2 | Lift power supplies | 12-3 |
| 12.3 | Protection of supplies | 12-4 |
| 12.4 | Standby power | 12-4 |
| 12.5 | Isolating switches, lighting and socket outlets | 12-5 |
| 12.6 | Harmonic distortion | 12-5 |
| 12.7 | Harmonic interference | 12-6 |
| 12.8 | Cabling and wiring | 12-6 |
| 12.9 | Machine room environment | 12-8 |
| 12.10 | Lift well environment | 12-10 |
| 12.11 | Lift car environment | 12-11 |
| 12.12 | Human comfort considerations | 12-11 |
| 12.13 | Environment for maintenance | 12-12 |
| | References | 12-13 |
| | Appendix 12.A1: Schedules for electrical system requirements | 12-15 |

**13    Energy consumption of lifts, escalators and moving walks**    **13-1**

13.1    Energy consumption and energy efficiency    13-3

13.2    Energy consumption of lifts    13-4

13.3    Factors affecting lift energy consumption    13-4

13.4    Estimating the energy consumption of lifts by calculation    13-6

13.5    Estimating the energy consumption of lifts by measurement    13-7

13.6    Estimating the energy consumption of lifts by modelling    13-8

13.7    Estimating the energy consumption of escalators    13-8

13.8    Measuring the energy consumption of lifts and escalators    13-9

13.9    Measures to conserve energy    13-9

References    13-10

**14    Remote monitoring and alarms**    **14-1**

14.1    The reason for monitoring and alarms    14-3

14.2    General features of lift monitoring systems    14-3

14.3    Benefits of remote monitoring    14-4

14.4    Definitions    14-5

14.5    Estate management    14-5

14.6    Group systems    14-7

14.7    Interfacing with building management systems (BMS)    14-8

14.8    Remote alarms    14-9

14.9    Communications systems and interconnection protocols    14-11

14.10    Escalators and moving walks    14-11

References    14-11

**15    Commissioning, preventative maintenance, testing and thorough examination of lifts, escalator and moving walks**    **15-1**

15.1    Introduction    15-3

15.2    Commissioning    15-3

15.3    Preventative maintenance    15-6

15.4    Thorough examination of escalators and moving walks    15-8

15.5    Documentation    15-11

References    15-11

**16    Modernisation of lift installations**    **16-1**

16.1    Introduction    16-3

16.2    Life cycle considerations    16-3

16.3    Influencing factors to upgrading    16-3

16.4    Relevant legislation, standards and codes of practice    16-4

16.5    Undertaking modifications to an existing lift installed before 1 July 1999    16-4

16.6    Undertaking modifications to an existing lift installed after 1 July 1999    16-4

16.7    Important considerations when undertaking modifications to existing lifts    16-5

16.8    Improving the safety of existing lifts    16-6

16.9    Step-by-step approach to improving the safety of existing lifts    16-6

16.10    Tests and records    16-7

References    16-7

**17      Legislation, standards and codes of practice          17-1**

    17.1      Legislation                                              17-3

    17.2      Standards and Codes of Practice                          17-7

    References                                                   17-8

**18      Construction (Design and Management) Regulations 1994    18-1**

    18.1      Introduction                                            18-3

    18.2      Definitions                                             18-3

    18.3      General                                                 18-4

    18.4      Requirements of the CDM Regulations                     18-5

    18.5      Compliance with the CDM Regulations in relation to lift and    18-7
           escalator work

    18.6      Roles and responsibilities                              18-8

    18.7      Penalties for failure to observe the CDM Regulations    18-12

    References                                                  18-12

    Bibliography                                                18-12

**Appendices                                                       A-1**

    A1: Glossary of terms                                       A-1

    A2: Lift kinematics                                         A-29

    A3: Legislation and standards related to lifts, escalators and moving walks    A-33

**Index**
                                                                 I-1

# 1  Introduction

## Principal author

John Bashford (Chairman) (J Bashford & Associates)

## Chapter contents

1.1    Purpose of Guide D                          1-3

1.2    Recent developments                         1-3

1.3    Contents of Guide D                         1-3

1.4    Other sources of information                1-4

# 1     Introduction

## 1.1     Purpose of Guide D

The purpose of CIBSE Guide D: *Transportation systems in buildings* is to provide guidance to practitioners involved in such systems. Guide D should also be of interest to architects and surveyors, and also facilities and building managers who may not be directly concerned with the design and installation of lifts and escalators but need to understand the advice offered to them by specialists. Not least, the Guide should be of value to students embarking on a career in mechanical, electrical or building services engineering and those already practising in these disciplines who wish to enhance their knowledge through a programme of continuing professional development.

## 1.2     Recent developments.

Many technological advances have occurred in recent years, the most far-reaching being the introduction of the machine room-less (MRL) lifts, which are explained, in greater detail in Chapter 5. MRL lifts have been welcomed by architects and developers alike as they have removed the need for separate machine rooms and allowed greater use of the available floor space, which in turn provides a greater financial return. The original machine room-less lifts were of the traction drive type and designed to be installed in purpose made lift shafts. These early designs have however been re-engineered to allow them to be used in existing lift shafts and have been especially useful in replacing hydraulic lifts where intensive traffic use is required. The manufacturers of hydraulic lifts have, however, taken up the challenge and have come up with their own version of machine room-less lifts which has given the end user a greater choice of lift types. Other advancements in lift design have also seen the introduction of two lifts in one shaft and a counterweight-less traction drive lift and hall call destination control which eliminates the need for destination floor push buttons inside the lift cars. These new developments may only have a limited use but demonstrate that the vertical transportation industry is still striving to provide a wider range of products.

The coming years will see greater emphasis on energy conservation, especially with the threat of global warming and its subsequent consequences, see Chapter 13. The lift and escalator manufacturers are meeting this challenge with the aid of modern technology. The use of gearless driven VVAC motors has reduced the starting and running currents, which has also reduced the operating costs for building owners. More advanced control systems have also improved the efficiency of lifts by reducing the number of unnecessary stops, especially during the morning and evening peak periods.

There is also more emphasis on accommodating people with disabilities, see Chapter 11. The needs of people with particular disabilities can no longer be ignored and suitable provision has to be made in all modern buildings. Fortunately the industry has made great strides in this area and new products are appearing which address these needs.

## 1.3     Contents of Guide D

The design of any lift or escalator system must commence with a consideration of the traffic flows through the building for which the system is intended. The relevant factors, along with guidance on the location and arrangement of lifts and escalators within buildings are discussed in Chapter 2. Many of the conclusions have been drawn for the observations recorded in different types of buildings.

The assessment of demand and the fundamental principles of traffic planning and selection of lift equipment are considered in Chapter 3. Two models are used considered, one uses a calculation method and one uses digital simulation of the building.

Chapter 4 covers advanced planning techniques and the use of computer programs which should greatly reduce the possibility of errors compared to manual methods. However, it is important that the input and output data are checked by experienced designers.

Chapter 5 presents an overview of the various types of lifting systems and provides advice on the planning and design. The chapter also examines the standard traction drive and hydraulic drive lifts, including the recently introduced motor room less lifts.

Firefighting lifts and escape lifts for people with disabilities are particularly important categories. For this reason these are treated separately in Chapter 6, which explains the basic requirements for lifts that are intended to be used in fire situations.

The principal components of lifts, including both electric traction and hydraulic drives, are described in Chapter 7. Many variations of these basic arrangements are possible but the component parts are fundamentally the same.

Lift drive and control techniques are considered in Chapter 8. It provides an unbiased guide to controls and drives to allow a better understanding for users and specifiers to ensure they select the correct system for their particular application.

Lift group traffic control is outlined in Chapter 9. It provides guidance on the traffic control of single lifts and for groups of lifts through legacy systems, based on relay logic, to modern day systems, utilising microcomputers.

Chapter 10 discusses escalators and moving walks (formerly known as 'passenger conveyors'), including their safety considerations. Escalator applications range from low-rise installations to accommodate a small change in level within a story of a building to high-rise installations in deep underground stations.

Transportation systems in buildings should provide independent and equal access for everyone. Chapter 11 provides guidance on the types of disability and design issues that need to be considered along with the standards and regulations that are applicable.

Electrical systems and environmental conditions are discussed in Chapter 12. This chapter examines the provision of power supplies for the whole building and guidance on key environment conditions, which must be considered during the design process.

Increasing awareness of global warming means it is important to consider lift and escalator energy efficiency and consumption. These are discussed in Chapter 13, which addresses how energy consumption can be minimised through good design, selection and control of the transportation equipment.

Chapter 14 offers some guidelines on remote monitoring and remote alarms and suggests ways in which the resulting data can be used to improve the efficiency of vertical transportation systems and interfacing with other automation systems within the building.

The proper commissioning, thorough examination, inspection and preventive maintenance of lifts and escalators is critical to ensure that they are safe and the capital value of these assets are maintained. These important issues are dealt with in Chapter 15.

Typically, lift installations require upgrading after 15–20 years of service. Chapter 16 examines the reasons for upgrading, which can range from improving the performance in terms of its traffic handling, ride quality or energy consumption or to improve the equipment. This chapter also includes easy to read tables for upgrading existing traction and hydraulic drive lifts.

It is fortunate that safety rules for the construction and installation of lifts and escalators, specifications, codes of practice, commissioning recommendations and safe working are all covered by an extensive range of British and European Standards and International codes. Chapter 17 provides an overview of these important documents.

The Construction (Design and Management) Regulations 1994 signalled a clear message to all those working in the construction industry that safety needed to be improved and Chapter 18 provides a guide to the impact of the Regulations on lifts and escalators. CIBSE is indebted to the Lift and Escalator Industry Association (LEIA) for permission to reproduce its guidance document.

Appendix A1 provides an extensive glossary of terms. This is not limited to the terms used within this Guide, but also includes definitions of many of the terms likely to be encountered when dealing with lift and escalator systems. CIBSE is indebted to the International Association of Elevator Engineers for permission to reproduce this valuable glossary.

Finally, a comprehensive index is provided.

Table 1.1 gives a summary of the main changes from the previous edition of Guide D.

## 1.4 Other sources of information

It is hoped that this third edition of CIBSE Guide D: *Transportation systems in buildings* will provide an invaluable reference source for those involved in the design, installation, commissioning, operation and maintenance of transportation systems in buildings. However in cannot be, and does not claim to be, exhaustive. The various chapters contain many references to other sources of information, particularly British Standards and associated standards and codes of practice (see Chapter 17), which should be carefully consulted in conjunction with this Guide, together with relevant trade and professional publications.

**Table 1.1** Summary of changes from the 2000 edition

| Chapter | Changes from 2000 edition |
|---|---|
| 1 Introduction | Revised to reflect new content. |
| 2 Interior circulation | Guidance updated in line with current thinking. Number of building types considered increased from 7 to 12 (also referenced in Chapters 3 and 5). Escalator and passenger conveyor sections amended to include circulation on landings. Section added on facilities for people with disabilities. |
| 3 Traffic planning and selection of lift equipment and performance | Guidance updated in line with current thinking. Better presentation of passenger loading. Number of building types considered increased from 7 to 12 (also referenced in Chapters 2 and 5). Examples link to Chapter 4. |
| 4 Advanced planning techniques and computer programs | Most of mathematics removed. Appendices 4.A3 and 4.A.4 removed. Lift kinematics moved to become Appendix A2. Presents computerisation of the manual calculations given in Chapter 3. Presents general analysis and its limitations. Revised to include simulation techniques with examples. Examples link to Chapter 3. Sections added describing measuring and describing traffic. New Appendix 4.A2 describing standard templates. |
| 5 Types of lift | Brought up-to-date. Additional figures. Introduction extended to include conventional and MRL lifts. Lift/Machinery Directives discussed. Revised order of lift types to reflect likely numbers installed in UK. Common format adopted for lift type subsections. Summary descriptions of firefighting and evacuation lifts added. Applications cover the 12 building type and link to Chapters 2 and 3. |
| 6 Firefighting lifts and escape lifts for people with disabilities | Updated to current standards. BS 5588 changes indicated. |
| 7 Lift components and installation | Updated to current equipment and requirements. Revised presentational order. New items include upward safety gear, MRLs. BS EN 81-28 requirements added. |
| 8 Lift drives and controls | Revised layout. Updated particularly with regard to VVVF. Several new figures added. |
| 9 Lift traffic control | Completely revised. Review of classical methods; nearest car, static sectoring, dynamic sectoring. Review of computer-based methods: ETA, stochastic, HCA, ETD. Other features and facilities. Design and installation case studies added. |
| 10 Escalators and moving walks | Chapter expanded, with additional figures. Updated to reflect BS 5656-2 and BS 7801. Safe use extended. |
| 11 Transportation facilities for persons and persons with disability | New chapter. Discussion of disabilities and the legal framework surrounding disabilities (Machinery and Lifts Directives), Building Regulations Part M, BS 8300, Disability Discrimination Act). Review of equipment provision and relevant standards (BS EN 81-70, BS ISO 9386-1/2). Egress of disabled persons added. BS 5588-8. Summary selection table added. |
| 12 Electrical systems and environmental conditions | Combines two sections of 2000 edition in a revised format. Electrical systems extended. Reference to BS 5655-6: Section 8 added. Cable sizing considered. Electromagnetic compatibility considered (BS EN 12015 and 12016). Safety of electrical personnel. Machine environment section revised together with heat dissipation. Ride quality (BS ISO 18738) added. |
| 13 energy consumption of lifts, escalators and moving walks | Chapter considerably extended to reflect current practice. Hong Kong and ISO energy material referenced and discussed. Link to CIBSE Guide F. Measures to conserve energy given. Energy modelling added. |
| 14 Remote monitoring and alarms | Chapter completely revised in line with current practice. Major manufacturer systems and independents systems. Includes monitoring, management, interfacing and modern communication systems. |
| 15 Commissioning, preventative maintenance, testing and examination | Chapter considerably expanded and divided into three main sections: commissioning, preventative maintenance and thorough examination and testing. Includes references to BS 5655: Part 10, PAS 32, BS 5656: Part 1. Consultant/owner/developer tests. Maintenance section includes check lists to BS EN 13015. Example certificates provided. |
| 16 Undertaking modifications to existing lifts | Reviews practice for modernisation. Include information from BS 5655: Parts 11 and 12. Guidance to BS 5655: Part 6 added. Reviews progressive safety requirements to BS EN 81-80. |
| 17 Legislation, standards and codes of practice | Updates legislation. Detailed list of legislation and standards moved to become Appendix A3. |
| 18 Construction (Design and Management) Regulations 1994 | Unchanged from 2000 edition. |
| A1 Glossary of terms | Content unchanged but format revised. |
| A2 Lift kinematics | Format revised. Worked example included. |
| A3 Legislation and standards related to lifts, escalators and moving walks | Up-to-date detailed list of relevant legislation and standards. |

# 2 Interior circulation

## Principal author

Dr Gina Barney (Gina Barney Associates)

## Chapter contents

| | | |
|---|---|---|
| 2.1 | Introduction | 2-3 |
| 2.2 | General considerations | 2-3 |
| | 2.2.1 Basic factors | 2-3 |
| | 2.2.2 Design factors | 2-3 |
| | 2.2.3 Coordination factors | 2-3 |
| | 2.2.4 Efficiency factors | 2-4 |
| 2.3 | Human factors | 2-4 |
| | 2.3.1 Human physical dimensions | 2-4 |
| | 2.3.2 Human personal space | 2-4 |
| | 2.3.3 Interpersonal distances | 2-4 |
| 2.4 | Circulation elements | 2-4 |
| | 2.4.1 Corridor capacity | 2-5 |
| | 2.4.2 Portal capacity | 2-6 |
| | 2.4.3 Stairway capacity | 2-6 |
| | 2.4.4 Escalator handling capacity | 2-7 |
| | 2.4.5 Moving walks handling capacity | 2-8 |
| | 2.4.6 Handling capacity of lifts | 2-8 |
| 2.5 | Circulation in shopping centres | 2-8 |
| | 2.5.1 General considerations | 2-8 |
| | 2.5.2 Factors affecting circulation in shopping centres | 2-9 |
| | 2.5.3 Practical levels of shopper movements | 2-9 |
| | 2.5.4 Factors affecting shopping centre circulation | 2-11 |
| 2.6 | Circulation in other types of buildings | 2-11 |
| | 2.6.1 Airports | 2-11 |
| | 2.6.2 Car parks | 2-12 |
| | 2.6.3 Department stores | 2-12 |
| | 2.6.4 Entertainment centres, cinemas, theatres, sports centres, stadia and concert halls | 2-12 |
| | 2.6.5 Hospitals | 2-12 |
| | 2.6.6 Hotels | 2-12 |
| | 2.6.7 Offices | 2-12 |
| | 2.6.8 Railway stations | 2-12 |
| | 2.6.9 Residential buildings | 2-13 |
| | 2.6.10 Residential care homes and nursing homes | 2-13 |
| | 2.6.11 Shopping centres | 2-13 |
| | 2.6.12 Universities and other education buildings | 2-13 |
| 2.7 | Location and arrangement of transportation facilities | 2-13 |
| | 2.7.1 General | 2-13 |
| | 2.7.2 Stairs | 2-14 |
| | 2.7.3 Escalators and moving walks | 2-14 |
| | 2.7.4 Lifts | 2-14 |
| | 2.7.5 Lifts versus escalators | 2-14 |
| 2.8 | Facilities for persons with disabilities | 2-16 |
| | References | 2-16 |

# 2    Interior circulation

## 2.1    Introduction

This chapter provides general guidance regarding the movement of people in buildings. Because it deals with people, many of the recommendations are based on empirical data acquired by observation and the experience gained in their application. Much of what follows cannot be proved theoretically and many of the conclusions have been drawn from the observations made. Reasons are given for the conclusions so that if new evidence comes to hand (or opinions change) the results can be modified. National and local regulations may also affect the circulation design, such as Fire and Safety codes and these must be taken into account. Readers are referred to Adler[1], Barney[2] and Fruin[14] for details, fuller expositions and case studies.

Whilst the reader may apply the guidance given here, specialist design assistance may be needed for complex or unusual situations. Throughout the chapter people are called pedestrians when on foot, and called passengers when being mechanically transported.

*Warning*: all the tables in this chapter give empirical values and should be considered to be average values only.

## 2.2    General considerations

### 2.2.1    Basic factors

The circulation of people in the interior of buildings is a complicated activity (Dober, 1969)[13] and is affected by a number of basic factors:

(*a*)    *Mode*: horizontal and vertical movement

People generally move horizontally, except where they are using inclined moving walks (previously known as 'passenger conveyors'), they will then change to vertical movement to reach a higher or lower level. To change mode they will use stairs, escalators or lifts.

(*b*)    *Movement type*: natural or mechanically assisted

People are moving naturally when walking along corridors and through portals and are mechanically assisted when using escalators and lifts.

(*c*)    *Complications*: human behaviour

The movement of people around a building is complex because people are complex. Individuals have their concepts of route; their purpose for travel; their level of urgency; their personal characteristics of age, gender, culture, handicaps etc. There is always an unpredictability in human behaviour.

### 2.2.2    Design factors

A number of design factors affect the interior circulation in a building:

—    *Consider all circulation routes*: these include principal and secondary circulation areas, escape routes, service routes and areas.

—    *Provide clear and obvious routes*: pedestrians should be able to see the route to take and be assisted by good signage and open vistas.

—    *Ensure that the circulation patterns are rational*: an example is the avoidance of pedestrians passing through a lift lobby, where other persons are waiting.

—    *Ensure that incompatible types of circulation do not coincide*: this would apply to pushing goods trolleys across a pedestrian mall in a shopping centre.

—    *Minimise the movement of people and goods*: the location of related or associated activities is essential e.g. sales and marketing, and personnel and training in an office building.

### 2.2.3    Coordination factors

The design and location of portals (defined here as: entrances, doorways, gates etc.), corridors, stairs and mechanical handling equipment (horizontal and inclined pedestrian conveyors, escalators, lifts) must be coordinated:

—    *The free flow of people, goods and vehicles*: levels of occupancy and density of usage should be such as to permit the free movement of people and goods.

—    *The occupation of the minimum space*: a building owner/tenant wishes to maximise the area in which people may occupy.

—    *Prevention of bottlenecks*: a bottleneck will reduce the free movement of people and goods.

It is important to size each circulation element. Thus the handling capacities of corridors, which lead to stairs, which in turn lead to a lift should be adequately sized for their anticipated load. The term 'handling capacity' is used here for passive (non-mechanical) building elements in the same way as it is applied to the mechanical elements. The term 'load' is used to indicate the level of usage.

Another consideration is the requirement to provide space for the movement of shopping trolleys and retailers carts in a shopping centre. In offices, it may be necessary to make provision for the occasional movement of equipment, plant and refurbishment materials.

### 2.2.4        Efficiency factors

The efficiency of interior circulation is dependant on building shape. Tall/slender and low/squat buildings are generally inefficient. The ideal shape is 'compact'. Efficiency is also affected by a number of other factors:

—        the relative location of rooms;

—        the relationship of major spaces with entrances and mechanical people handling equipment;

—        the importance of the journey undertaken (e.g. hospital theatre traffic);

—        the separation of different traffic types (e.g. clean/dirty);

—        the need to group some spaces together;

—        the conflict of vertical and horizontal circulation modes.

## 2.3        Human factors

### 2.3.1        Human physical dimensions

The physical dimensions of the human body vary widely. Without being politically incorrect, females are generally smaller than males. The space an individual occupies depends on the clothing worn and what they might be carrying. To allow for all these factors and other circumstances such as body sway it is recommended that the typical occupancy template be considered to be an ellipse of dimensions 600 mm by 450 mm and covering an area of 0.21 m². (See Figure 2.1) This is a typical value mainly specific to European and North American people. It can be used where pedestrians or passengers are not standing in a confined space.

Note the actual body template of the individual does not fill the ellipse.

If the typical occupancy template is used to represent the average individual, then the larger males and females will be compensated for by smaller males and the females who may be present.

There is no doubt that over the last few decades more European and North American people have become bigger and taller. Some have become overweight, obese and clinically obese as evidenced by changes in their body mass index (BMI). The average used in this chapter follows Figure 2.1 with the average person considered to weigh 75 kg.

Adler[1] devotes a complete chapter to anthropomorphic factors.

### 2.3.2        Human personal space

Humans value personal space. This is measured by a personal buffer zone around each individual. The actual size of the buffer zone varies according to an individual's culture, age, status, gender, handicaps, etc. It has been observed that individual female subjects are comfortable with a personal buffer zone of 0.5 m² (circle of 0.8 m diameter) and individual male subjects with a personal buffer zone of 0.8 m² (circle of 1.0 m diameter). To visualise these sizes, a woman's umbrella occupies an area of approximately 0.5 m² and a man's umbrella occupies approximately 0.9 m².

These factors must be borne in mind when designing pedestrian waiting areas. When considering bulk queues, i.e. where people are waiting for an event, the occupation densities shown in Table 2.1 are typical.

When considering linear queues, where people are waiting in line for a service, assume two persons per metre length of space. Where a queue is unrestrained it is necessary to assume that they occupy a width of at least 1.5 m width. A control barrier, which should be at least 600 mm in width can used to restrain the queue width.

### 2.3.3        Interpersonal distances

The spatial separation of humans is also important: its origins, however, are lost in antiquity. Hall[15] (1966) classified interpersonal distances with characteristics based on the sensory shifts of sight, smell, hearing, touch and thermal receptivity as summarised in Table 2.2

## 2.4        Circulation elements

The discussion in this section is mainly applicable to office buildings, where a number of factors effect pedestrian movement. They include:

—        pedestrian dimensions;

—        pedestrian velocities;

—        unidirectional/bidirectional flow;

—        cross flows;

—        patterns of waiting;

—        site and environmental conditions;

—        statutory requirements.

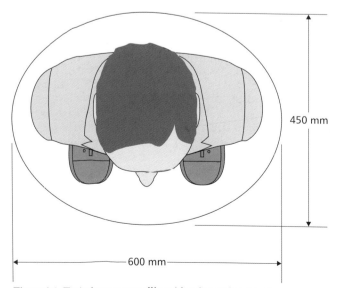

**Figure 2.1** Typical occupancy ellipse (showing male subject)

450 mm

600 mm

**Table 2.1** Summary of density of occupation of a space

| Level of occupancy | Density (person/m²) | Characteristics |
|---|---|---|
| Desirable | 0.4 | Allows individuals to walk more or less where they wish to go or stand without any interference from other individuals. |
| Comfortable | 1.0 | Allows individuals to walk with some deviations necessary where they wish to go and for individuals to stand without any interference from other individuals. |
| Dense | 2.0 | Individuals who are walking must now take care not to collide with other persons and persons waiting are aware that other individuals are present. |
| 'Crowding' | 3.0 | It is only possible to walk at a shuffle and with care at the average rate of the crowd. There is no or little chance of a contra-flow. Individuals waiting are very aware of other individuals. |
| Crowded | 4.0 | Walking is almost impossible. Individuals waiting are unhappy to be so close to other individuals. This density is only possible, where persons are placed in a confined space, such as a lift car, or a rapid transit train. |

**Table 2.2** Interpersonal distances

| Interpersonal spacing | Distance (m) | Classification | Useage |
|---|---|---|---|
| Public distance (far) | > 7.5 | Flight zone | |
| Public distance (near) | 3.6–7.5 | | |
| Social distance (far) | 2.1–3.6 | Zone of potential vulnerability | Formal meetings |
| Social distance (near) | 1.2–2.1 | | Casual meetings |
| Personal distance (far) | 0.75–1.2 | Circle of trust | Waiting |
| Personal distance (near) | 0.45–0.75 | | Queuing |
| Intimate distance | < 0.45 | Touch zone | Enclosed spaces |

*Notes*: 'Flight zone': where an individual can take evasive or defensive action; 'Zone of potential vulnerability': could be the 'en garde' distance of sword fighting; 'Circle of trust': an individuals interpersonal spacing found in a spacious waiting area; 'Touch zone': touching situation found, for example, when travelling in a lift car.

## 2.4.1  Corridor capacity

The term corridor is defined here to include: passageways, walkways, subways etc., i.e. areas whose main function is to provide a connection between major spaces and operational areas. They do not include areas where waiting can occur, such as shopping malls. These will be dealt with in section 2.5.

The capacity of a straight corridor can be given as:

$$C_c = 60 \, v \, D \, W_c \qquad (2.1)$$

where $C_c$ is the corridor handling capacity (person/min), $v$ is average horizontal pedestrian speed (m/s), $D$ is the average pedestrian density (person/m²) and $W_c$ is the effective corridor width (m).

Equation 2.1 is an empirical relationship with a number of qualifications. Pedestrian speed and density are not independent of each other. For densities below 0.3 persons per square metre pedestrians can walk freely, called free flow design. When densities increase above 0.5 persons per square metre there is an approximately linear decrease of average walking speed up to a density of about 3.0 persons per square metre, when walking is reduced to a shuffle. The throughput peaks at densities of about 1.4 persons per square metre, called 'full flow' design. Walking speeds vary systematically (statistically) with type of population (age, gender, grouping, purpose), ability (fitness, handicap), gradient, flow direction, air temperature, floor finish etc. Within each group there will be variations in average speed. Table 2.3 indicates the empirically derived average values, as guidance.

Table 2.3 shows the possible horizontal pedestrian flows in persons per minute and persons per hour, and typical pedestrian speeds in metres per second (m/s) for a free flow design density of 0.3 person/m² and a full flow design density of 1.4 person/m².

**Table 2.3** Possible horizontal pedestrian flow rates with grouping

| Type of traffic | Pedestrian design density | | | | | |
|---|---|---|---|---|---|---|
| | 0.3 person/m² | | | 1.4 person/m² | | |
| | Speed (m/s) | Flow rate* (people/min) | | Speed (m/s) | Flow rate* (people/min) | |
| Commuters, working persons | 1.5 | 27 | (1620) | 1.0 | 84 | (5040) |
| Individual shoppers | 1.3 | 23 | (1380) | 0.8 | 67 | (4020) |
| Family groups, tourists | 1.0 | 18 | (1080) | 0.6 | 50 | (3000) |
| School children | 1.1–1.8 | 18–32 | (1080–1920) | 0.7–1.1 | 59–92 | (3540–5520) |

* Flow rate in person/hour shown in parentheses

The flows assume a corridor width of one metre. The corridor must be at least 900 mm wide and is assumed to be one metre. Equation 2.1 allows for the flow rate to increase/decrease as the corridor width increases/decreases. This factor must be used with great care as small changes in corridor width will have little or no effect.

Table 2.4 presents the minimum straight widths of corridors, which have been found to be suitable for different purposes and shows the minimum width of corridors to accommodate various types of traffic. Some compensation can be allowed for mixed two way traffic situations, e.g. a 3.0 metre wide corridor would allow most traffic types to be accommodated.

Traffic can only flow freely along unrestricted routes. Corridors are rarely free of obstructions. For example a row of seated persons will reduce the effective width of a corridor by 1.0 m. Table 2.5 indicates the effect of a number of obstructions. The table shows the reduction in metres of the effective corridor width caused by obstructions.

**Table 2.4** Minimum corridor widths

| Usage | Minimum width (m) |
|---|---|
| One-way traffic flow | 1.0 |
| Two-way traffic flow | 2.0 |
| Two men abreast | 1.2 |
| Man with bag | 1.0 |
| Porter with trolley | 1.0 |
| Woman with pram | 0.8 |
| Woman with pram with child alongside | 1.2 |
| Man on crutches | 0.9 |
| Wheelchair | 0.8† |

† Wheeled vehicles require extra width in order to turn at junctions, especially if they are very long, e.g. hospital trolleys

**Table 2.5** Reductions in corridor width

| Obstruction | Reduction in width (m) |
|---|---|
| Ordered queue | 0.6 |
| Unordered single queue | 1.2–1.5 |
| Row of seated persons | 1.0 |
| Coin operated machine: | |
| — one person | 0.6 |
| — queue | 1.0 |
| Person waiting with bag | 0.6 |
| Window shoppers | 0.5–0.8 |
| Small fire appliance | 0.2–0.4 |
| Wall-mounted radiator | 0.2 |
| Rough or dirty wall surface | 0.2 |

## 2.4.2 Portal capacities

Portals, which are called by various names, i.e. gate, door, entrance, turnstile etc., form a division between two areas, for reasons of privacy, security, access control etc. They represent a special restriction in corridor width. Their main effect is to reduce pedestrian flow rates. Table 2.6 indicates probable flow rates for a possible range of pedestrian flows in persons per minute and persons per hour through an opening of 1 m. Note that this table indicates flows through a portal of 1.0 m. Most domestic

**Table 2.6** Possible portal flow rates

| Portal type | Flow rate (person/min) | Flow rate (person/h) |
|---|---|---|
| Gateway | 60–110 | 3600–6600 |
| Clear opening | 60–110 | 3600–6600 |
| Swing door | 40–60 | 2400–3600 |
| Swing door (fastened back) | 60–90 | 3600–5400 |
| Revolving door | 25–35 | 1500–2100 |
| Waist-high turnstile: | | |
| — free admission | 40–60 | 2400–3600 |
| — cashier | 12–18 | 720–1080 |
| — single coin operation | 25–50 | 1200–1800 |
| — card/detector operation | 20–30 | 1200–1800 |

doors are less than this width (approximately 750 mm) and the flow rates would be likely to be the lower values in the range shown. Doors in non-domestic buildings may be slightly wider than 1.0 m and would permit the higher values in the range shown to be possible.

## 2.4.3 Stairway capacity

Stairways impose a more stylised and disciplined form of movement on pedestrians. For instance pace length is restricted by tread depth (going). More accurate cones of vision are required for step placement and assistance is often required by the use of handrails. The movement is more regular, as disciplined by the steps, permitting higher densities than are possible on the flat. Whereas for free movement during walking on the flat a pedestrian requires an area of some 2.3 m$^2$ (0.4 persons per square metre) to account for body sway etc., a stair walker only needs to perceive two vacant treads ahead (and room for body sway) and occupies an area of some 0.7 m$^2$. Thus free flow design is possible at a density of 0.6 persons per square metre and full flow design is possible at a density of 2.0 persons per square metre.

The speed along the slope is about half that on the flat, but this is compensated by the increased densities possible. Speed, however, is very much dependent on the slowest stair walker owing to the difficulty in overtaking under crowded conditions. Higher walking speeds are generally not possible in the down direction owing to the need for greater care. Speed is also affected by the angle of inclination and step riser height.

The energy consumed walking on stairs is related to the riser height. To enable comfortable walking on a stair a rule of thumb has been to match the average adult stride (on a stairway) of about 600 mm with the sum of twice the riser (rise) height plus the tread (going) depth. This results in a range of riser heights of 100 mm to 180 mm and treads of 360 mm to 280 mm, and a range of possible inclinations from 15° to 33°. A domestic stair often has a rise of 180 mm and a going of 240 mm. An efficient inclination has been found to be 27°.

Stairway handling capacity is 83% of that for a corridor, i.e:

$$C_s = 0.83 \, (60 \, v \, D \, W_s) \tag{2.2}$$

**Table 2.7** Stairway pedestrian flows per metre width of stair

| Type of traffic | Pedestrian design density | | | | | |
|---|---|---|---|---|---|---|
| | 0.6 person/m$^2$ | | | 2.0 person/m$^2$ | | |
| | Speed (m/s) | Flow rate (person/min) | Flow rate (person/h) | Speed (m/s) | Flow rate (person/min) | Flow rate (person/h) |
| Young/middle aged men | 0.9 | 27 | 1620 | 0.6 | 60 | 3600 |
| Young/middle aged women | 0.7 | 21 | 1260 | 0.6 | 60 | 3600 |
| Elderly people, family groups | 0.5 | 15 | 900 | 0.4 | 40 | 2400 |

where $C_s$ is the stairway handling capacity (person/min), $v$ is average pedestrian speed on the slope (m/s), $D$ is the average pedestrian density (person/m$^2$) and $W_s$ is the effective stair width (m).

Table 2.7 shows the possible pedestrian flow rates in persons per minute and persons per hour, and typical pedestrian stairway speeds along the slope in metres per second (m/s) for a free flow design density of 0.6 persons per square metre and a full flow design density of 2.0 persons per square metre for each one metre width of stairway.

## 2.4.4 Escalator handling capacity

Escalators provide a mechanical means of continuously transporting pedestrians from one level to another. Except for deep underground systems escalators provide for short range movement. They are found in offices, stores, shopping centres, railway stations, hospitals, museums etc. Speed, step widths, inclination and the size of boarding and alighting areas are factors that affect their handling capacity.

Escalator speed is measured in the direction of the movement of the steps. The most common speed is 0.5 m/s, although speeds of 0.65 m/s and 0.75 m/s are available. Most escalators run at one speed only, although some heavy duty escalators can switch to a higher speed during heavy traffic. Speeds of 0.75 m/s are used on the London Underground and speeds of 0.9–1.0 m/s are used on deep systems in Russia and Ukraine.

Step widths of 600 mm, 800 mm and 1000 mm for escalators are available, the latter allowing two columns of passengers to be carried. The usable width at hip level is measured between the skirting panels and is typically 200 mm wider than the step width. Hence the actual width available to passengers on an escalator with a 1000 mm step width is some 1200 mm (enough for two people to pass each other).

The inclination of an escalator is usually 30°, but can be 35° provided the maximum speed is 0.5 m/s and it serves a maximum rise of 6 m. For escalators the step tread (going) is 400 mm and thus the step rise is fixed by the inclination to a rise of some 210 mm. When the stair rule for comfortable walking is applied (see section 2.4.3) this gives a value of 820 mm. This is in excess of the assumed stair walkers average stride of 600 mm, and accounts for how much harder it is to walk on an escalator.

It takes less than one second (0.8 s) for a step to appear at a boarding point of a 0.5 m/s escalator, which is too fast for most people to get onto each vacant step. In order to encourage pedestrian confidence and to assist the efficient and safe boarding and alighting of escalators, it is recommended in BS EN 115: 1995[3] that at least two to three flat steps are provided on light duty escalators and at least three to four flat steps are provided on heavy duty escalators, dependant on the rated speed and rise. In locations where it is anticipated that the escalators may be used by persons with impaired mobility additional flat steps should be considered. The definitions of duty are given in BS 5656-2: 2004[8].

The theoretical handling capacity of an escalator is given by:

$$C_e = 60\,V\,k\,s \qquad (2.3)$$

where $C_e$ is the escalator handling capacity (person/min), $V$ is speed along the incline (m/s), $k$ is average density of people (person/escalator step) and $s$ is number of escalator steps per metre.

For the usual case where the step depth is 400 mm, then $s = 2.5$ and equation 2.3 becomes:

$$C_e = 150\,V\,k \qquad (2.4)$$

The density factor $k$ allows consideration of the step occupancy levels and experience has shown this depends on step width. BS EN 115: 1995[3] suggests that there can be two persons per 1000 mm step ($k = 2.0$), one and one half persons per 800 mm step ($k = 1.5$) and one person per 600 mm step ($k = 1.0$). These theoretical values of $k$ are never seen in practice.

Observations on the London Underground, which has probably the most intense traffic levels in the world, showed that each 1000 mm step of a moving escalator is occupied by one passenger. This gives a standing person a space of some 500 mm by 800 mm in which to stand, which is an area of 0.4 m$^2$. This is a density of occupation of 2.5 persons/m$^2$, which Table 2.1 defines as between dense and crowding. The BS EN 115: 1995 occupancy levels are too optimistic and practical occupancy levels are usually half (50%) of these values, i.e:

— 1000 mm: one person every step, $k = 1.0$ (density = 2.5 persons/m$^2$);

— 800 mm: three persons every four steps, $k = 0.75$ (density = 2.3 persons/m$^2$);

— 600 mm: one person every two steps, $k = 0.5$ (density = 2.1 persons/m$^2$).

Table 2.8 gives guidance to the practical escalator handling capacities based on these assumed densities in persons per

**Table 2.8** Practical escalator handling capacity (BS 5656: Part 6: 2004[8])

| Speed (m/s) | Handling capacity (person/min)* for given step width | | | | | |
|---|---|---|---|---|---|---|
| | 1000 mm | | 800 mm | | 600 mm | |
| 0.50 | 150 | (9000) | 113 | (6750) | 75 | (4500) |
| 0.65 | 195 | (11 700) | 146 | (8775) | 98 | (5850) |
| 0.75 | 225 | (13 500) | 169 | (10 125) | 113 | (6750) |

* Handling capacities in person/hour shown in parentheses

minute and persons per hour and horizontal speeds in metres per second (m/s).

The practice in the UK of one stationary column and one walking column will not increase an escalator's mechanical handling capacity, but will increase the passenger flow rate and decrease an individual passenger's travelling time.

### 2.4.5 Moving walks handling capacity

Moving walks (previously known as 'passenger conveyors') can either be horizontal or be inclined. Horizontal moving walks are typically used for medium/long range travel in airports, exhibition centres and railway stations. Inclined moving walks are typically used for short range travel in shopping centres, stores and railway stations.

Inclinations range from 6° to 12°, although the safest maximum inclination is generally 10°. The running speeds for horizontal moving walks are 0.5 m/s, 0.65 m/s and 0.75 m/s. The permitted running speed for an inclined moving walk is 0.5 m/s. The speed is again measured in the direction of movement of the pallets.

Nominal widths for moving walks up to an inclination of 6° are 800 mm, 1000 mm and 1400 mm and above 6° are 800 mm and 1000 mm. A width of 1400 mm allows two columns of passengers and the possibility for some passengers to walk along the moving walk.

The practical density of passengers assumed for an escalator is 2.5 person/m² (one passenger per 1000 mm step). A moving walk should permit denser concentrations of passengers than an escalator as the space is defined by pallets not steps. In practice it is likely that the maximum density will be about 2.0 person/m² (dense level of occupancy). Table 2.9 indicates handling capacities in persons per minute and persons per hour assuming a density of 2.0 person/m², using equation 2.1, but substituting the equipment speed for pedestrian speed.

**Table 2.9** Handling capacities of moving walks and ramps

| Inclination (degree) | Speed (m/s) | Nominal handling capacity (person/min)* for given width | | | | | |
|---|---|---|---|---|---|---|---|
| | | 800 mm | | 1000 mm | | 1400 mm | |
| Horizontal moving walks: | | | | | | | |
| 0 | 0.50 | 48 | (2880) | 60 | (3600) | 84 | (5040) |
| 0 | 0.63 | 60 | (3600) | 76 | (4536) | 106 | (6350) |
| 0 | 0.75 | 72 | (4320) | 90 | (4050) | 126 | (7560) |
| Inclined moving walks: | | | | | | | |
| 6 | 0.50 | 48 | (2880) | 60 | (3600) | 84 | (5040) |
| 10 | 0.50 | 48 | (2880) | 60 | (3600) | — | — |
| 12 | 0.50 | 48 | (2880) | 60 | (3600) | — | — |

* Handling capacity in person/hour shown in parentheses

### 2.4.6 Handling capacity of lifts

Lifts cannot handle the traffic volumes handled by other facilities and have a considerable 'throttling' effect on pedestrian movement. For example the most efficient 8-car group comprising 21-person capacity cars serving 14 office floors can only provide a handling capacity of 50 person/min (3000 person/h). This is less than a flight of stairs can provide. And a 3-car group comprising 10-person cars serving 8 floors can only manage 16 person/min (960 person/h). Thus the recommendation to use escalators in bulk transit systems is proven. Fortunately the high volumes found in bulk transit systems do not occur when populating or emptying a building.

Considerable care must be taken in sizing a lift system to accommodate the worst passenger demands. The method of sizing a lift is given in Chapter 3 and will not be further discussed here.

## 2.5 Circulation in shopping centres

### 2.5.1 General considerations

A shopping centre is unlike the old-fashioned high street, where shops line each side of the road, with shoppers on pavements at the sides and vehicular traffic passing along the middle of the street. A shopping centre is usually a purpose built building, where all shoppers are protected from the weather in a climatically controlled environment and segregated from vehicular traffic. The shops line each side of the malls with several floors of malls above and below. No two shopping centres have the same structure, population or circulation patterns. Generally shopping centres are on one, two or three floors. Two floors are generally considered as much as the average shopper is prepared to contemplate. Centres with three floors often have food courts at the upper or lower floors to form an attraction and a contrast to the main sales areas. There are places set aside for rest, sustenance and amusement.

This section looks at the aspects of circulation in shopping centres in contrast to circulation in office buildings. It presents, in general terms, observations made by researchers and discusses how they may be applied to shopping centres. It is concerned with the two main circulatory aspects: horizontal traffic flows along malls and through entrances and vertical movement between the different floors in the shopping centre. This section is not concerned with:

— the estimation of external traffic flows into a shopping centre;

— the estimation of peak flows down malls;

— shopping centre design, except where it impinges on circulation;

— in-store circulation.

Readers will find Barney[2] (2003), Beddington[10] (1982) and Fruin[14] (1971) knowledgeable on some of these matters.

Shoppers do not populate a shopping centre to the high levels (in density terms) found in other public places, e.g. railway stations. Two traffic conditions can be observed:

— a low level of shopper occupancy (uncrowded–free flow);

— a peak value of shopper occupancy (crowded–full flow).

Also although the walking speeds vary widely, they are generally less than the natural (comfortable) speed of 1.3 m/s (3 mph). Contrast these values with those given in section 2.4.

There are three types of shopper: quarter-mastering, technical and leisure. The first type replenishes supplies, e.g. food; the second type obtains specific items, e.g. a TV; and the third type shops for pleasure! A shopper spends a large percentage of the time in a shopping centre walking and browsing and the lower density levels are necessary so that shoppers feel comfortable. The ambulant shoppers' primary (and preferred) means of transfer from one floor to another is by using an escalator. The secondary means of transfer from one floor to another is a stairway and an additional means of transfer from one floor to another is a lift. Where shoppers have disabilities or are encumbered with purchases or with children and pushchairs, their primary means of transfer from one floor to another is a lift.

In a shopping centre some of the good design criteria set out in earlier sections may be intentionally violated, as they are not necessarily conducive to the selling of goods. For instance having attracted shoppers into a store, the exit routes from the store may not be clearly marked (emergency exits excepted). The free flow of people may be deliberately reduced by the introduction of display stands along the route offering goods for sale to encourage impulse buying. Circulation may be designed to be irrational, but not obviously so. For instance, escalator layouts may cause shoppers to walk some distance around a floor, in order to reach the next escalator, thus presenting merchandise to prospective shoppers.

## 2.5.2 Factors affecting circulation in shopping centres

The general intention behind the design of a shopping centre or mall is to encourage shoppers to enter the centre, then to stop and browse and hopefully to purchase goods on impulse. The malls should provide a modulated sequence of conditions through side malls, a range of linking corridors, to central squares and features. The purpose is to create a feeling of bustle, excitement, sparkle, competition and a variety of experiences within an organised framework, whereby the shopper has a retreat from the effects of the weather and the motor car and is cocooned within a relatively safe environment. There are many factors which will affect and 'ease' pedestrian movement in a shopping centres.

— Simple layouts are best. The ability for a shopper to find their way in, through and out of a centre are prerequisites of good design. Simple floor plans overcome the problems of shoppers' unfamiliarity with a centre.

— Standard mall designs rely on 'magnet' or 'anchor' stores to draw shoppers past secondary stores, which provide convenience goods and encourages impulse buying opportunities.

— The length of malls is important with 200 m being the maximum distance a shopper is likely to walk. The introduction of bends makes a mall appear longer than it really is. The use of magnet stores at each end of a long mall increases the attraction and reduces the apparent length.

— A shopping centre should be able to be explored in one trip, so pause points need to be cleverly placed. Additional breaking up of the mall by the use of courts and squares for public space, rest and recreation areas help to reduce the apparent mall length.

— Mall widths should be narrow enough not to discourage shoppers from crossing over to shop on the other side.

— Escalators and lifts need to be carefully sited to invite shoppers onto other levels.

— The positioning of vertical circulation elements requires great care to avoid 'dead-ends' and 'double-back' circulation. The elements should be provided in the natural circulation path of shoppers.

— Visual stimulation and variety should be provided by the shop fronts themselves. The size of every shop front affects its trading potential (and hence its revenue/m² and its rental).

— Design should centre around a series of primary nodes, which include landmarks such as intersecting malls and transfer points such as parking, entrances and exits. Nodes are activity areas where pathways (malls) meet and people relax.

— Points of conflict should be minimised to allow shoppers to concentrate on shop displays. For example cross-flows, counter-flows and right angle bends all cause conflicts. People in a minor flow will alter pace and timing to fit the gaps in the major flow. Ideally shoppers should be able to pick their own speed and direction.

— Malls are often 'landscaped' by the introduction of street furniture, planters and displays to break up and reduce the perception of space in the mall.

— Shoppers have to enter and leave a shopping centre by means of entrances. These entrances interfere with the flow as they often have either a swing door or an automatic sliding door, and because the shopper may be adjusting to the new environment and even looking at a store directory.

## 2.5.3 Practical levels of shopper movements

### 2.5.3.1 Entrances

Walking speeds reduce to 0.7 m/s, when shoppers pass through entrances, otherwise the shopper flows remain similar to those given in Table 2.6.

### 2.5.3.2    Malls

— The density of shoppers in uncrowded conditions is 0.2 person/m² and 0.45 person/m² during crowded conditions. The density can increase to 1.0 person/m² at pinch points (areas where the mall size is inadequate, e.g. at a food court).

— The walking speed of shoppers in uncrowded conditions is generally 1.3 m/s and in crowded conditions is generally 1.0 m/s.

— Counterflows reduce mall capacity by 15% compared to unidirectional flows.

— The effective mall width reduces (equal to actual mall width minus street furniture and window shoppers), as the condition changes from uncrowded to crowded. This results from more stationary shoppers looking into shop windows.

— Mall widths should be of the order of 68 m wide as a compromise between too wide to cross and too narrow to pass along.

**Table 2.10**  Actual mall pedestrian flow rates per metre width of mall

| Traffic type | Uncrowded (0.2 person/m²) | | Crowded (0.45 person/m²) | |
|---|---|---|---|---|
| | Speed (m/s) | Flow rate (person/h) | Speed (m/s) | Flow rate (person/h) |
| All shoppers | 1.3 | 936 | 1.0 | 1620 |

### 2.5.3.3    Stairs

— Uncrowded density on stairs is found to be approximately 0.4 person/m² and crowded density on stairs reaches 0.8 person/m².

— Shoppers' speeds when using stairs varies according to traffic type.

— The stair capacity under uncrowded conditions and under crowded conditions varies according to traffic type.

— There is a tendency for more down traffic than up traffic in the ratio 60/40.

— A minor contraflow will reduce a major flow by effectively reducing the stairway width by some 750 mm.

**Table 2.11**  Stairway pedestrian flows per metre width of stair

| Traffic type | Speed (m/s) | Uncrowded (0.4 person/m²) | Crowded (0.8 person/m²) |
|---|---|---|---|
| Men | 0.8 | 960 | 1920 |
| Women | 0.7 | 840 | 1680 |
| Elderly men | 0.5 | 600 | 1200 |
| Elderly women | 0.6 | 720 | 1440 |
| Children | 0.8 | 960 | 1920 |
| Push chairs | 0.5 | 600 | 1200 |

### 2.5.3.4    Escalators and moving walks

— About 80% of shoppers will use the escalators to quickly reach other floors in a shopping centre, as they will rarely have to wait.

— The 800 mm escalators (commonly used) have a theoretical step utilisation of $k = 1.5$. However, shopping centre escalators are observed to load to only $k = 0.5$ step utilisation under uncrowded

conditions and to $k = 1.0$ step utilisation under very crowded conditions. The width of an 800 mm step is not large enough to accommodate two adult people side by side. To achieve this a 1000 mm is required, when a higher step utilisation can be achieved.

— There is a tendency for stores and shopping centres to install inclined moving walks, which allows shoppers to keep their purchases with them as they circulate. For safety, the conveyors should be designed to accept trolleys that lock onto the pallets.

**Table 2.12**  Actual escalator handling capacity

| Speed (m/s) | Handling capacity (person/h) for 800 mm step | |
|---|---|---|
| | Uncrowded | Crowded |
| 0.50 | 2250 | 4500 |

### 2.5.3.5    Lifts

Observation (scenic) lifts, pram lifts, car park and other lifts are provided in shopping centres, but not in sufficient quantities to serve more than a fraction of the shoppers. They are mainly used by the elderly, infirm, disabled, mothers with children and push chairs, and people with heavy packages. Observation lifts are sometimes installed as a feature to provide a visual impact in retail complexes. They do contribute to the circulation aspects of a shopping centre, but can not be considered as a major handling capacity provider as passengers often use one simply for the ride.

Lifts cannot handle the traffic volumes handled by other facilities and have a considerable throttling effect on pedestrian movement. For example a group of two, 16-person, observation lifts, serving two retail levels and two car park levels, probably has a possible handling capacity of only about 300 persons per hour. This is due to the need to have long door dwell times, the slow motion dynamics, the slowness of passenger loading/unloading and the low levels of occupancy owing to the presence of prams, push chairs and baggage. Thus it is recommended to install as many escalators as possible in shopping centres, in order to provide for the large volumes of traffic.

Bearing in mind that the building of low-rise, out-of-town, shopping centres is now considered detrimental to town centres by many planning authorities, it is likely that in-town shopping centres will be the norm comprising six, or more, storeys. Probably these will be two/three level shopping arcades, with parking provided above and/or below the arcades on several levels.

These developments will throw an increased emphasis onto the provision of additional lifts, as the elderly and the very young in wheel chairs and push chairs must be accommodated. Push chairs are not permitted on escalators, as it is very unsafe, again requiring more lifts to be provided.

A problem is that a push or wheel chair occupies more space in a lift than ambulant passengers. This space can be equivalent to three standing persons. The means that larger lifts than the conventional 17-person car are recommended in these circumstances. See the discussion in section 2.6.1 regarding baggage handling in airports.

Thus in the future the number of lifts in the higher rise shopping centres should be substantially increased. Even the ambulant shoppers baulk at walking several floors when laden with the week's shopping. The lifts should be at least 26-person and have wide doors to permit easier entry and exit for mixed loads of passengers and shopping trolleys and push chairs. Observation lifts should be provided as a feature and not a primary transportation element.

### 2.5.4      Factors affecting shopping centre circulation

Below is given some guidance as to good practice.

—    Malls should be designed to avoid 'pinch points'.

—    Stairs should have a minimum width of 2.5 m.

—    Stairs should be divided into channels by use of a separating rail, which aids movement (particularly for persons with mobility problems) and can separate the up and down flows

—    Stairs should always be located near to escalators to form a secondary means of vertical circulation. (Important when an escalator is out of service.)

—    To ease flows, stair risers should be less than 180 mm and with a slope less than 30°.

—    All stairs with flights of more than 16 steps should have intermediate landings for resting and pedestrian safety.

—    Adequate clear areas should be provided at access points to stairs to allow queuing and safe movement.

—    Adequate clear areas should be provided at boarding and alighting points of escalators to allow queuing and safe movement, perhaps with barriers to discipline users.

—    There should be at least two escalators at each location to serve two traffic flows.

—    Escalators should be located in a parallel arrangement, probably on a slight offset.

—    The maximum rise for an escalator should be less than 6 m.

—    Escalator step widths of 1000 mm are preferred, not necessarily to permit passengers to stand side by side but to allow shopping to be carried.

—    Maintenance of escalators should be carried out when the centre is closed.

—    The reliability of escalators is important and comprehensive maintenance agreements must be in place with a competent service company to reduce breakdowns to a minimum.

—    Car operating panels within lifts should be simple in layout and operation and comply to BS EN 81-70[6] to permit access for all.

—    Maintenance of lifts should be carried out when the centre is closed.

—    All stairs, escalators and lifts should be adequately illuminated.

—    All stairs, escalators and lifts should be readily visible.

—    All stairs, escalators and lifts should be easily identified and well signed.

## 2.6      Circulation in other types of building

*Important note*: this section is concerned with the circulation of people in twelve different types of buildings. Reference to the corresponding sub-sections of section 3.13, which deals with the selection of equipment and those sub-sections of Chapter 5, which deal with the application of different types of lifts, should also be consulted.

### 2.6.1      Airports

Most airports are arranged on two main levels with the arrival level below the departure level. There may then be other levels above and below providing various services (e.g. baggage handling, catering) and facilities (offices). Another common characteristic is an adjacent, underground or elevated railway station.

Passengers at airports, with any significant baggage, will use the trolleys provided. Most airports have sufficiently large halls and corridors and no problems should arise, when used on one level. However, when the passenger requires to move from one level to another, e.g. to reach a railway station, then difficulties can arise.

Generally each baggage trolley will be attended by two persons plus their baggage. The weight of the baggage is generally restrained by the 20 kg allowance most (economy) passengers are allowed plus some 5 kg of hand luggage. Thus a loaded trolley will weigh (including its own weight) some 75 kg, i.e. equivalent to one person. However, it will occupy the space taken by three or four persons. Thus the total weight of two passengers and their trolley will be some 225 kg and occupy the space of some five people. This space requirement must be considered, when designing the circulation.

It becomes particularly awkward when considering the part lifts play in circulation. Consider a nominal 50-person rated capacity (rated load 3750 kg) lift. According to BS EN 81-1: Table 1.14, the maximum available car area for an electric traction lift must then be 7.0 m². According to the body template (Figure 2.1) only 33.3 passengers can be accommodated. They will weigh only 2500 kg, some 67% of the rated load.

If each pair of passengers and their baggage trolley occupy 1.05 m² (5 human spaces) then the nominal 50-person lift can accommodate 13.4 passengers and 6.7 trolleys. The total load will be 1500 kg. This is 40% of the rated load. Thus it can be seen that lifts in these circumstances are unlikely to be overloaded.

If the lift were to be a nominal 50-person rated capacity, 3750 kg rated load, hydraulic lift then the platform area from BS EN 81-2: Table 1.15 would be exactly the same. However BS EN 81-2: Table 1.1A, which can be used 'when there is a low probability of the car being overloaded', allows a maximum area of 13.6 m². It is then possible to accommodate 26 passengers and 13 trolleys. This is a load of 2925 kg, which is some 80% of rated load. This would indicate that hydraulic lifts are most suitable for this environment and their poorer dynamic performance would not be a significant disadvantage.

## 2.6.2    Car parks

Car parks can be attached to shopping centres, offices, airports, railway stations etc. They are often multi-storey, although those at shopping centres and out-of-town railway stations may be a single or at most two levels. The circulation requirements are more likely to be constrained by the entry and exit ramp handling capacities.

For offices the peak demand is often in the evening when occupants are attempting to reach their cars. The office lifts, which may not serve the car parking levels will bring large numbers of people to the lobby. Those with cars will then make a significant demand on any lifts serving the car park levels. Once the occupants have reached their cars they may then spend some time before reaching the exit. Another factor is the car occupancy, which for offices is likely to be about 1.2 persons per car, unless car pools are in operation. The car park lifts must be designed to meet the demand efficiently.

For shopping centres the car occupancy will be much higher with at least 2.0 persons per car. Large lifts should be installed in shopping centres where a large food store is situated in order to provide an adequate service.

## 2.6.3    Department stores

This category applies to large departmental and chain stores. These stores will have many entrances, some of which may open to a main street whilst others open into shopping centre mall areas. The opportunity therefore exits for 'leakage' into and out of shopping centres. Many stores will own lifts and escalators inside their demise. These facilities may be used by shopping centre shoppers to move between mall areas. Thus store facilities enhance those provided by a centre to the mutual advantage of both.

## 2.6.4    Entertainment centres, cinemas, theatres, sports centres, stadia and concert halls

This category of building types often accommodate large numbers of people attending public events. Large theatres have many levels and their circulation must be designed to permit the rapid build-up of patrons prior to performances. Usually these entry routes are not large enough for a rapid departure, but this is not usually a problem.

Other buildings in this category are generally lower rise although stadiums can also have many levels and accommodate many tens of thousands of attendees.

Circulation in these buildings needs to be properly considered at the design stage to ensure that entrances are wide enough and of sufficient number to permit entry and exit. Corridors, stairs and any vertical transportation in addition to that provided for people with disabilities should be sized adequately.

## 2.6.5    Hospitals

These are mainly designed in Britain on the 2–3 storey low-rise principle, although many city hospitals have high-rise elements. In the main the principal corridors are sized to accommodate bed and trolley movements and therefore present no difficulties when handling pedestrian movements. Lifts are provided mainly as a means of moving bed bound patients from floor to floor. The use of lifts as a primary circulation element in high rise hospitals is vital, particularly for theatre traffic, where special arrangements must be made.

## 2.6.6    Hotels

Lifts play an important part in the circulation of guests and service staff in a hotel. It is recommended that there should be at least one lift per 100 guests in a medium quality hotel and at least one goods lift per two passenger lifts. Escalators should be employed for short range movements e.g. to connect function levels with the lobby.

## 2.6.7    Offices

There are significant numbers of lifts installed in offices and without them most office buildings would be untenable. Some locations may also include escalators. The guidance of section 2.2 should be followed and some is repeated here.

The interior circulation in a building must be designed to consider all principal and secondary circulation areas, escape routes, service routes and areas. Pedestrians should be able to see the route to take, assisted by good signage. Circulation patterns should be rational, e.g. avoid pedestrians passing through a lift lobby, where other persons are waiting. Ensure that incompatible types of circulation do not coincide, e.g. tenants and goods traffic. Minimise the movement of people and goods by locating similar activities close to each other, e.g. sales and marketing, and personnel and training.

Consider the levels of occupancy and density of usage so as to permit the free movement of people and goods. Prevent bottlenecks. Consider the relationship of major spaces, e.g. meeting and seminar rooms, with entrances and the people handling equipment. Consider the importance of the journey undertaken, e.g. rapid access to trading floors.

The capability of the various circulation elements is given in detail in section 2.4 and their location is given in section 2.7.

## 2.6.8    Railway stations

Railway stations may be served mainly by stairs, although the deeper ones will use escalators. The main problem is that when a train arrives many hundreds of people can alight. Obviously it would be expensive to install vertical transportation equipment to serve this peak demand. Thus the demand must be spread out in some way. A method of achieving this is to place the stairs/escalators at one end of the platform thus producing a more even demand on the facility. Distractions can be provided along the way such as shops and kiosks etc. The width of the platform will be determined more by safety rather than circulation requirements and will thus be adequately sized for its purpose.

Railway stations suffer from the same problems as airports (see section 2.6.1) with respect to baggage trolleys. Inclined moving walks may be installed to assist these movements.

## 2.6.9 Residential buildings

Residential buildings include flats (local authority and private), university, college and hospital residencies. Circulation is not normally a problem except in high rise flats, where insufficient lifts may be installed.

## 2.6.10 Residential care homes and nursing homes

Residential care homes and nursing homes do not usually present any circulation problems as they are not densely populated and do not experience peak traffic conditions.

## 2.6.11 Shopping centres

The circulation of shopping centres has been dealt with in detail in section 2.5.

## 2.6.12 Universities and other education buildings

Most university buildings can be classified as institutional buildings, where the occupants receive a service. A university campus will often have a mixed collection of lecture blocks, office type buildings, halls of residence, catering services and factory-like units containing teaching and research equipment (reactors, high voltage laboratories, telescopes). Where universities occupy city sites many have tall buildings (10–20 stories) and even those on out-of-town sites follow suit in order to reduce land use and keep a compact campus. The office type buildings can be treated in the same way as detailed earlier in section 2.4. The halls of residence can be treated in a similar way to hotels, although perhaps at lower levels of demand and performance. The catering services can be attached to either the office type buildings or halls of residence and should be treated as office facilities or hotel facilities. The factory like buildings will probably be low rise and be subject to special movement provisions associated with the equipment installed i.e. barriers to radioactive areas.

The main feature of the university campus is the lecture changeover periods. There are hourly cycles of 10 minutes of demand after each 50 minute lecture, tutorial or seminar finishes. In between the peaks the activity levels are low. To install lifts in a tall building to suit this demand is not cost effective. (And universities do not have large capital budgets.) A better solution is to try to re-arrange the activities in the building to reduce the load on the lifts. An example in Adler[1] illustrates the relationship chart in a small firm. A set of relationships can be formed for a university building. It would be possible to reduce the demands made for 10 minutes every hour by:

—   Placing lecture facilities in the lower levels, say basement, ground and three to four floors above the entrance level. Students can be encouraged to use stairs if they are wide, well lit and visible.

—   Laboratory, bulk service facilities (computer clusters, libraries) and student administration (registrars, bursars, careers advisory etc. can be placed from the fourth floor upwards. These are either used for periods longer than one hour (laboratories), shorter than one hour (administration) or randomly (libraries).

—   Offices should be placed at the top of the building. Their occupants will generally use the lifts on a more random basis.

## 2.7 Location and arrangement of transportation facilities

### 2.7.1 General

Having discussed the various passive circulation elements (corridors, stairs, portals, etc) and the active circulation elements (moving walks, escalators and lifts) in the previous sections it is now necessary to consider their location and arrangement, which should take account of:

(a)   the location of entrances and stairs;

(b)   the location of lifts, escalators and moving walks;

(c)   the distribution of the occupants in the building;

(d)   safe circulation.

The main principles, as given in section 2.2, to bear in mind here are:

—   to minimise the movements of people;

—   to minimise the movements of goods;

—   to prevent clashes between people and goods;

—   to prevent bottlenecks.

Ideally all circulation activities should be centralised in a main core of a building.

This is clearly not always possible when access into a building is considered. Sometimes the main lobby is close to the main entrance and sometimes the main lobby is some distance into the building. This latter case requires occupants and visitors to walk some distance in order to reach the transportation facilities. However, it may be better for occupants to walk to the centre of a building to access stairs and lifts, since their central location during the day may outweigh the comparative inconvenience during arrival and departure. Generally the maximum distance to a lift or stair from an occupant's work place should not exceed 60 metres with a distance of less than 45 metres being preferred. Emergency escape routes are usually closer, but do not necessarily form part of the normally used circulatory routes.

## 2.7.2     Stairs

Stairs should not lead directly off corridors, but be accessed from landing and lobby areas, where people may congregate without obstructing a circulation route. Thus the vertical and horizontal modes of circulation can be allowed to merge smoothly. If it is the intention to encourage the use of stairs for short journeys to/from adjacent floors (interfloor movement), then the stairs should be of sufficient size, clearly visible, adequately signed and encountered before reaching the lifts. Although stairs provide an always available facility their attraction diminishes with the number of floors a person travels. Peters et al.[16] (1996) provides an indication of this characteristic as summarised in Table 2.13.

**Table 2.13** Stair usage

| Floors travelled | Usage up (%) | Usage down (%) |
|---|---|---|
| 1 | 80 | 90 |
| 2 | 50 | 80 |
| 3 | 20 | 50 |
| 4 | 10 | 20 |
| 5 | 5 | 5 |
| 6 | 0 | 0 |

## 2.7.3     Escalators and moving walks

Escalators and moving walks should be placed in an obvious circulation path. They should only be accessed from adjacent corridors/walkways, landing and lobby areas, where people do not obstruct other pedestrian circulation routes. Space should be available to accommodate queuing at the boarding point. Again the intention is to ensure that the vertical and horizontal modes of circulation can merge smoothly.

It is especially important that the boarding and alighting areas adjacent to an escalator or moving walk are not part of another circulation route, in order to provide a safe area for passengers to board and alight. This obligation is required by clause 5.2.1 of BS EN 115: 1995[3], which requires a sufficient unrestricted area be available to accommodate passengers at the landings. The area of this space is defined as the distance between the handrails multiplied by a depth of from 2.0 metres to 2.5 metres, dependant on the configuration of the escalator or moving walk. The unrestricted area has to be considered as part of the whole traffic function and sometimes needs to be increased (Barney: 2003, Chapter 3[2]).

Figure 2.2 illustrates clause 5.2.1 with option 1 being a 2.5 m landing depth and option 2 being a 2.0 m landing depth.

An interpretation has been made by the BS EN 115 committee that when successive escalators[8] are installed each successive escalator, or moving walk, must have its own unrestricted area and is not allowed to share them.

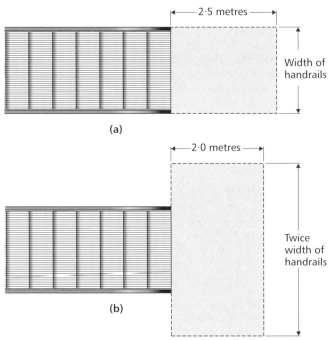

**Figure 2.2** Illustration of unrestricted free space according to BS EN 115[3]

Escalators occupy more space than stairs in order to accommodate their inclination. There are several standard escalator arrangements as shown in Figure 2.3. Types (a) and (b) provide efficient circulation by providing the shortest transition path and time from one escalator and the next. Type (b) requires a larger structural opening than types (a) and (c) and presents users with a higher risk of falling into the void. Type (c) is typical of a store as it allows the store to lengthen the circulation route past goods for sale. This configuration also takes up less space.

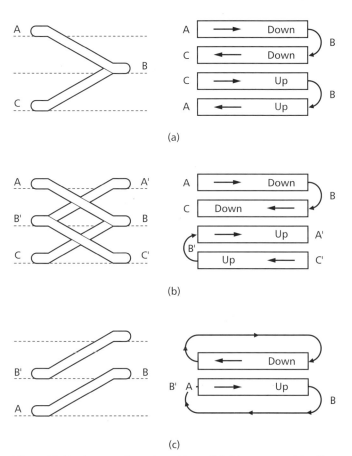

**Figure 2.3** Escalator configurations; (a) parallel, (b) cross-over, (c) walk round

Escalators are typically used for short range movement between adjacent floors (the underground railway systems excepted). They are found in offices between principal levels, in shops between trading floors, in shopping centres between malls and elsewhere such as railway stations, hospitals, museums etc. They are usually sited in an obvious circulation path making it easy for pedestrians to board them.

Some escalators and moving walks are adapted to receive and lock-on shopping/baggage trolleys. In these cases the unrestricted area at the landings should be increased to at least five metres and the number of flat/horizontal steps at the boarding and alighting points increased (see section 10.4.5). The most significant effect is the increased footprint required for the equipment.

### 2.7.4 Lifts

The grouping of passenger lifts is particularly important where they provide the main means of vertical transportation within a building. Lifts should always be placed together, rather than distributed around a building. This will provide a better service (shorter intervals), mitigate against the failure of one car (availability of adjacent cars) and lead to improved traffic control (group systems). Eight lifts are the maximum number of lifts that should be grouped together, especially if large lifts are used (>2000 kg). This allows passengers to determine when a lift arrives (from the lantern and gong signals), to walk to the car (across the lobby) and to enter it before the lift doors start to close. The distance across a lobby is usually $1\frac{1}{2}$ to 2 times the car depth. If the lobby is any larger, passengers have too far to walk and the closure of the car doors has to be delayed (increased door dwell time) to accommodate the increased walking time.

Lift lobbies should not be part of a through circulation route, either to other lifts, or other areas in the building. Lobbies should be provided that are dedicated to passengers waiting for the lifts. The ideal lobby size would be one which could accommodate one full car load of passengers waiting and permit the simultaneous disembarkation of one full car load of arriving passengers. This area can be calculated using the density information given in section 2.2.2 at between comfortable and dense (say 1.4 person/m²).

BS 5655: Part 6[7] gives recommended layouts and limitations for groups of lifts. The preferred arrangements of between two and four lifts arranged in line are given in Figure 2.4, and between two and eight lifts arranged opposite each other are shown in Figure 2.5. Note all the lobbies (indicated L) are waiting areas with no through circulation.

Where a building layout cannot accommodate these arrangements the following factors should be considered to optimise the accessibility and visual links to all lifts within a group to the passengers:

— lobby size;

— location of push buttons;

— location and type of landing indicators;

— walking distances to lift entrances in a lift lobby.

It is suggested that the position of any central lift core should be towards the centre of the building and that actual walking distances should be no greater than 45 metres from any point in the building.

### 2.7.5 Lifts versus escalators

In general lifts are used for travel over a large number of floors and escalators for travel over a small number of floors. A judgement is made by the passenger with respect to the waiting time for a lift versus the length of time walking (and walking effort) with respect to escalators.

Low rise structure such as shopping centres, sports complexes, conference and exhibition centres, railway stations, airports, hospitals, etc. are good examples of buildings where the provision of escalators considerably aids circulation (and is used by the visitors/passengers).

In office environments the usefulness of escalators is lessened, although they can be a advantageous where (say) a heavily populated trading floor(s) must be assessed. They are also very useful for access to car parks, relieving the lifts of travelling below the main terminal, and may be used for access to double-deck lifts. Table 2.14 indicates some guidance as to the division of traffic between lifts and escalators.

**Table 2.14** Likely division of traffic between lifts and escalators

| Floors travelled | Escalator (%) | Lift (%) |
| --- | --- | --- |
| 1 | 90 | 10 |
| 2 | 75 | 25 |
| 3 | 50 | 50 |
| 4 | 25 | 75 |
| 5 | 10 | 90 |

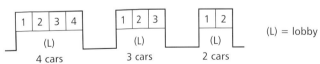

(L) = lobby

**Figure 2.4** Preferred arrangement for 2 to 4 lifts: in line

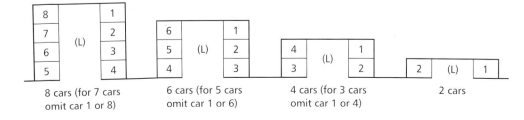

8 cars (for 7 cars omit car 1 or 8)

6 cars (for 5 cars omit car 1 or 6)

4 cars (for 3 cars omit car 1 or 4)

2 cars

**Figure 2.5** Preferred arrangement for 2-8 lifts: facing

## 2.8 Facilities for persons with disabilities

The discussion so far has assumed that all persons circulating in a building are fully able bodied. However, a large proportion of the population are disadvantaged in some way. The BS EN 81-70: 1999[6] categorises disabilities into physical, sensory and intellectual. BS 8300: 2001: *Design of buildings and their approaches to meet the needs of disabled people*[9] gives some guidance for facilities within buildings. The Disability Discrimination Act: 1995[12] lays down various provisions, regulations and penalties for non conformance. Approved Document M[11] to the UK Building Regulations provides guidance to compliance in the UK.

Generally, arrangements made to allow persons with disabilities to make use of circulation elements, assist the able-bodied and should be implemented wherever possible. Chapter 11 of this Guide discusses lifting facilities for the disabled.

## References

1    Adler D *Metric handbook* (London: Architectural Press) (1999)

2    Barney G C *Elevator traffic handbook* (London: Spon) (2003)

3    BS EN 115: 1995: *Safety rules for the construction and installation of escalators and passenger conveyors* (London: British Standards Institution) (1995)

4    BS EN 81-1: 1998: *Safety rules for the construction and installation of lifts. Electric lifts* (London: British Standards Institution) (1998)

5    BS EN 81-2: 1998: *Safety rules for the construction and installation of lifts. Hydraulic lifts* (London: British Standards Institution) (1998)

6    BS EN 81-70: 2003: *Safety rules for the construction and installation of lifts. Particular applications for passenger and goods passenger lifts. Accessibility to lifts for persons including persons with disability* (London: British Standards Institution) (2003)

7    BS 5655-6: 2002: *Selection and installation of new lifts* (London: British Standards Institution) (2002)

8    BS 5656-2: 2004: *Selection, installation and location of escalators and moving walks* (London: British Standards Institution) (2004)

9    BS 8300: 2001: *Design of buildings and their approaches to meet the needs of disabled people* (London: British Standards Institution) (2001)

10    Beddington N *Design for shopping centres* (Oxford: Butterworth) (1982)

11    Building Regulations 2000 Approved Document M: *Access to and use of buildings* (London: The Stationary Office) (2004)

12    Disability Discrimination Act 1995 (London: The Stationary Office) (2002)

13    Dober R P *Environmental design* (London: Van Nostrad Reinhold) (1969)

14    Fruin J J *Pedestrian planning and design* (Mobile AL: Elevator World)

15    Hall E T *The hidden dimension* (New York, NY: Doubleday) (1966)

16    Peters R D, Mehta P. and Haddon J Lift passenger traffic patterns *Elevator Technology* 7 (Stockport: IAEE Publications) (1996)

# 3 Traffic planning and selection of lift equipment and performance

## Principal author

Dr Gina Barney (Gina Barney Associates)

## Chapter contents

| | | |
|---|---|---|
| 3.1 | Introduction | 3-3 |
| | 3.1.1 General | 3-3 |
| | 3.1.2 Symbols | 3-3 |
| 3.2 | Review of traffic design | 3-3 |
| 3.3 | Passenger design | 3-4 |
| | 3.3.1 Traffic patterns | 3-4 |
| | 3.3.2 Estimation of passenger demand: quantity of service | 3-5 |
| | 3.3.3 Estimation of passenger demand: quality of service | 3-6 |
| 3.4 | Lift system performance | 3-6 |
| | 3.4.1 The round trip | 3-6 |
| | 3.4.2 Performance equations | 3-7 |
| 3.5 | Calculation of the round trip time | 3-7 |
| | 3.5.1 Average number of passengers ($P$) | 3-7 |
| | 3.5.2 Average number of stops ($S$) and average highest call reversal floor ($H$) | 3-8 |
| | 3.5.3 Single floor transit time ($t_v$) | 3-8 |
| |     3.5.3.1 Interfloor distance ($d_f$) | 3-8 |
| |     3.5.3.2 Rated speed ($v$) | 3-9 |
| | 3.5.4 Time consumed when stopping ($T - t_v$) | 3-9 |
| |     3.5.4.1 Single floor flight time ($t_f(1)$) and start delay time ($t_{sd}$) | 3-9 |
| |     3.5.4.2 Door closing time ($t_c$) and opening time ($t_o$) and advance (pre-) opening time ($t_{ad}$) | 3-9 |
| | 3.5.5 Passenger transfer time ($t_p$) | 3-10 |
| | 3.5.6 Performance time ($T$) as a quality indicator | 3-10 |
| | 3.5.7 Note on up-peak round trip time calculations | 3-10 |
| 3.6 | Assumptions made in the derivation of the round trip time equation | 3-10 |
| | 3.6.1 Passengers arrive uniformly in time | 3-10 |
| | 3.6.2 All lifts load to an average of 80% | 3-11 |
| | 3.6.3 All floors are equally populated | 3-11 |
| | 3.6.4 Rated speed is reached in a single floor jump and interfloor heights are equal | 3-11 |
| 3.7 | Other factors to be considered in the evaluation of the round trip time equation | 3-11 |
| | 3.7.1 Landing and car call dwell times | 3-11 |
| | 3.7.2 Lobby loading interval | 3-11 |
| | 3.7.3 The traffic controller is ideal | 3-11 |
| 3.8 | Matching passenger demand to handling capacity during up-peak traffic | 3-12 |
| 3.9 | Passenger waiting, transit and journey times and time to destination during up-peak traffic demand | 3-12 |
| | 3.9.1 Definitions | 3-12 |
| | 3.9.2 Average passenger waiting time (AWT) | 3-12 |
| | 3.9.3 Average passenger transit time (ATT) | 3-13 |
| | 3.9.4 Average passenger travel time to destination (ATTD) | 3-13 |
| | 3.9.5 Average passenger journey time (AJT) | 3-13 |

| | | |
|---|---|---|
| 3.10 | Traffic conditions other than up-peak | 3-13 |
| | 3.10.1 Down peak traffic condition | 3-13 |
| | 3.10.2 Interfloor traffic condition | 3-14 |
| | 3.10.3 Mid-day traffic condition | 3-14 |
| | 3.10 4 Review of all traffic conditions | 3-14 |
| 3.11 | Selection of equipment and lift function | 3-14 |
| | 3.11.1 Double deck lifts | 3-14 |
| | 3.11.2 Firefighting lifts | 3-14 |
| | 3.11.3 Goods lifts | 3-15 |
| | 3.11.4 Observation (glass/scenic) lifts | 3-15 |
| | 3.11.5 Shuttle lifts | 3-15 |
| 3.12 | Selection of equipment and building form | 3-15 |
| | 3.12.1 Basement service and floors served by only part of a lift group | 3-15 |
| | 3.12.2 Multiple entry levels | 3-15 |
| | 3.12.3 Entrance bias | 3-16 |
| | 3.12.4 Large floor plates | 3-16 |
| | 3.12.5 Stairs and escalators | 3-16 |
| | 3.12.6 Attractive building facilities | 3-16 |
| | 3.12.7 Lobby design | 3-16 |
| | 3.12.8 Tall buildings | 3-16 |
| | 3.12.9 Very tall buildings | 3-16 |
| 3.13 | Selection of equipment and building function | 3-17 |
| | 3.13.1 Airports | 3-17 |
| | 3.13.2 Car parks | 3-17 |
| | 3.13.3 Department stores | 3-17 |
| | 3.13.4 Entertainment centres, cinemas, theatres, sports centres, stadia and concert halls | 3-18 |
| | 3.13.5 Hospitals | 3-18 |
| | 3.13.6 Hotels | 3-18 |
| | 3.13.7 Offices | 3-18 |
| | 3.13.8 Railway stations | 3-18 |
| | 3.13.9 Residential buildings | 3-18 |
| | 3.13.10 Residential care homes and nursing homes | 3-19 |
| | 3.13.11 Shopping centres | 3-19 |
| | 3.13.12 Universities and other education buildings | 3-19 |
| References | | 3-19 |
| Appendix 3.A1: Table of $H$ and $S$ values | | 3-20 |
| Appendix 3.A2: Example calculations | | 3-21 |

# 3 Traffic planning and selection of lift equipment and performance

## 3.1 Introduction

### 3.1.1 General

This chapter provides a general guide to UK and European practice, which may differ from North American practice (Strakosch: 1998)[11]. It is recommended that Barney (2003)[2] be consulted for the detailed theory and an extensive list of references. The various terms encountered are generally explained in the text, but fuller definitions are to be found in the glossary (Appendix A1 to this Guide).

Two models are used for traffic design calculations and analysis. One model uses a calculation method based on mathematical formulae. This classical model has been used for nearly 75 years and results in a satisfactory solution for 90–95% of designs. The second model, which has been used for over 30 years, is based on a discrete digital simulation of the building, its lifts and the passenger dynamics. This simulation model allows very complex situations to be analysed. This section deals with the classical model based on calculation and chapter 4 deals with the simulation model.

The formula-based method sizes a lift system to serve the demands of a building's occupants by matching the demands for transportation with the handling capacity of the installed lift system for the worst five minute period during the morning up-peak traffic condition. It thus provides the means of calculation and analysis for the planning and selection of lifts mainly for office buildings and the procedures to determine their likely performance. This procedure should also result in an economic solution.

All the calculations in this chapter are based on average values derived from mathematical models of experimental data. There will never be an average system and therefore the results may not represent the performance gained from an actual installation. The calculations do in 90–95% of cases provide a sufficient traffic design. For unusual arrangements and a more accurate indication of performance, simulation techniques as described in chapter 4 must be used.

### 3.1.2 Symbols

| | |
|---|---|
| AC | Actual capacity (persons) |
| $A_d$ | Average down-peak passenger arrival rate (persons/5-minutes) |
| $A_i$ | Average interfloor passenger arrival rate (persons/5-minutes) |
| $A_r$ | Average up-peak passenger arrival rate (persons/5-minutes) |
| AJT | Passenger average journey time (s) |

| | |
|---|---|
| ATTD | Passenger average travel time to destination (s) |
| ATT | Passenger average travel time to destination (s) |
| AWT | Up-peak passenger average waiting time (s) |
| CA | Car area (m²) |
| CC | Rated (contract) capacity (persons) |
| CF | Capacity factor |
| $d_f$ | Average interfloor height (m) |
| DNPAWT | Down-peak passenger average waiting time (s) |
| $H$ | Average highest reversal floor |
| $H_M$ | Average basement reversal floor |
| IFAWT | Interfloor passenger average waiting time (s) |
| INT | Average interval with defined car load (s) |
| $L$ | Number of lifts |
| MIDAWT | Mid-day passenger average waiting time (s) |
| MIDINT | Mid-day average interval (s) |
| $N$ | Number of served floors above the main terminal |
| $P$ | Average number of passengers (persons) |
| %POP | Percentage population |
| RTT | Average round trip time (s) |
| RTTD | Average down-peak round trip time (s) |
| RTTM | Average mid-day round trip time (s) |
| RL | Rated load (kg) |
| $S$ | Average number of stops |
| $S_M$ | Average number of basement stops |
| SRT | System response time (s) |
| $T$ | Floor to floor cycle time (s) |
| $T_M$ | Basement floor to floor cycle time (s) |
| $t_{ad}$ | Advance door opening time (s) |
| $t_c$ | Door closing time (s) |
| $t_{cyc}$ | Cycle time (s) |
| $t_e$ | Main terminal to express zone terminal flight time (s) |
| $t_f(1)$ | Single (1) floor flight time (s) |
| $t_f(n)$ | Time to jump $n$ floors (s) |
| $t_l$ | Passenger loading time (s) |
| $t_o$ | Door opening time (s) |
| $t_p$ | Average passenger transfer time (entry or exit) (s) |
| $t_{sd}$ | Start delay time (s) |
| $t_u$ | Passenger unloading time (s) |
| $t_v$ | Time to transit two adjacent floors at rated speed (s) |
| $t_{vm}$ | Time to transit two adjacent basement floors at rated speed (s) |
| $U$ | Effective building population (persons) |
| UPPHC | Average up-peak handling capacity (persons/5-minutes) |
| UPPINT | Average up-peak interval with 80% car load (s) |
| $v$ | Rated (contract) speed (m/s) |

## 3.2 Review of traffic design

The whole subject of the planning and selection of transportation equipment is a very involved one. Although the basic calculations are relatively simple, the theory on which they are based is complex. The results obtained need to be always tempered with a great deal of working experience of existing buildings, in order to ensure a satisfactory design results.

The transportation capacity of the lift group in a building is a major factor in the success or failure of a building as a place to work, to live or to receive a service. Building occupants expect lifts to be available and easy to use without a second thought. Unfortunately this is not always the case and speculative building often results in the installation of an imperfect lift system.

The difficulty in planning a lift installation is not in calculating its probable performance, but in estimating the passenger demand that is likely to occur. Quite often the building has yet to be built and estimates have to be based on the experience gained with previous similar structures. Existing buildings can be surveyed, by observation, or by means of an attached data logger, to determine the current activity. However, even this is prone to error, as the building's population may have adapted to a poor (or good) lift performance. It is essential, therefore, that all the parties involved in the planning of a lift installation have a clear understanding of the basis for the planning. For example it is important that the architect or planner establishes the lift system required at a very early stage and not after the rest of the building has been designed, as often has happened in the past.

A design, which is tightly planned, may prove inadequate once a new building becomes fully occupied. Alternatively, floors in a building may become vacant, thus reducing demand on an undersized lift system. It is important to remember that the distribution and size of the population of any large building can alter regularly, as tenants change. To understand the effect of any of these changes on a building, it is essential to document the design criteria and the reasons for decisions taken at all stages of a design.

Two key factors affect the demand that a building's occupants will make on a lift system: the quantity of service and the quality of service required. The quantity of service factor — how many people will use the lift system over a defined period of time — is represented by the handling capacity. The quality of service factor — how well must the lift system deal with its passengers — is represented by passenger waiting time, and lobby queuing. Both factors are interrelated. Both factors depend, amongst other things, on the type of building and its use, and on the type of occupier. This makes the design task very difficult for buildings of a speculative nature.

Section 3.3 identifies methods to measure passenger demand and section 3.4 provides a calculation method to determine lift system performance. The analysis is mainly relevant to commercial office buildings.

## 3.3    Passenger demand

### 3.3.1    Traffic patterns

Figure 3.1 illustrates a classical traffic pattern of passenger demand in an office building as would be seen from the main terminal, or main access, floor. It shows the number of up landing calls and down landing calls registered during the working day. Today this pattern is rarely observed exactly as shown, as many companies have

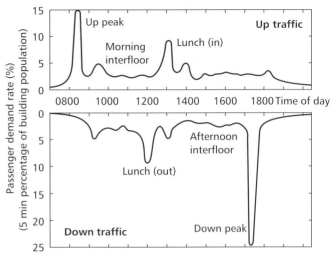

**Figure 3.1** Passenger demand for an office building

adopted a 'flexitime' attendance regime. It does, however, serve as a model for discussion.

There are four distinct classical traffic patterns:

— At the start of the day there are a larger than average number of up landing calls. This demand is due to the building's occupants arriving to start work. This traffic pattern is called the morning up-peak. Industry practice is to size a lift installation to handle the number of passengers requesting service during the heaviest five minutes of the up-peak traffic condition. This is a sound recommendation. To size the lift system to handle the actual peak would require too large a system, which would be very expensive and much of the equipment would be under utilised during large periods of the working day.

The duration of the classical up-peak traffic condition is five minutes.

— Late in the day there is a larger than average number of down landing calls. This demand is due to the building's population leaving at the end of the working day. This traffic pattern is called the evening down peak. The profile of the down-peak traffic is larger in size and longer in duration than the up-peak profile. Fortunately a lift system inherently possesses about 60% more handling capacity, during down-peak, than during up-peak. During down-peak a lift fills at three to five floors and then makes an express run to the main terminal. This reduction in the number of stops allows the lift to serve other waiting passengers more quickly.

The duration of the classical down-peak condition is 10 minutes.

— In the middle of the day there may be one, or two, separate sets of up and down-peaks. This represents a situation where the occupants of the building take one, or two, distinct lunch periods. This pattern is called mid-day traffic. Today this traffic pattern can be very intense often more demanding than, either the up-peak, or the down-peak, with strong patterns of simultaneous up and down traffic.

This traffic condition may exist for one to two hours dependent on the arrangements for the mid-day break.

— During the rest of the day the numbers of up and down landing calls are much smaller than during the up-peak and down-peak periods, but are similar in size and over a period of time are equally balanced. This traffic pattern is called interfloor traffic, sometimes qualified as balanced interfloor traffic.

The interfloor traffic condition exists for most of the working day and is thus very important.

If the lift system is sized correctly for the up-peak traffic pattern, generally, all other traffic patterns will be adequately served. There are exceptions to this comment. These include hotels, where meal times clash with check-in/check-out; hospitals at visiting times; buildings with trading floors (insurance and stock markets), which open at specified times; buildings where restaurants are high in the building; and residential buildings.

### 3.3.2 Estimation of passenger demand (quantity of service)

Passenger demand is dependent on the population of a building. The size of the demand is measured, either in terms of the arrival rate of either, a specified number of persons/5-minutes, or a specified percentage of the building population assumed to arrive in the peak 5-minutes. The traffic design should select a lift system to meet this quality of service criterion.

The size of the intended population should be obtained, either from the building owner or from the proposed occupier. If the population numbers are not available, or the building is a speculative one, then an estimation must be made using floor areas[15].

Most estimates start from a knowledge of the net usable area (NUA), that is, the area which can be usefully occupied. The NUA excludes circulation space (stairs, corridors, waiting areas, escape routes), structural intrusions (steelwork, space heating, architectural features,

ductwork), and facilities (training rooms, smoking rooms, kitchens, toilets, cleaners' areas etc.). The net internal area (NIA), sometimes called the 'rentable area', is larger than the usable area as it includes tenant's facilities such as kitchens and cleaners' cupboards and some of the circulation space. The gross internal area (GIA) is the area generally within the internal face of the perimeter walls. The gross external area (GEA) is generally the area measured outside the perimeter walls (the footprint).

Experience in the UK and USA[1] has shown that the following relationships can also be employed in initial calculations, although it is wise to obtain actual net usable areas from the owner or developer:

— rentable area (NIA): 90–95% of GEA

— usable area (NUA): 75–80% of GEA.

These ratios would suggest that the ratio of usable area to rentable area might be 80–85%.

The number of people occupying the usable area will vary according to:

— the purpose of the building (residential, commercial or institutional);

— the quality of the accommodation (prestigious, standard, speculative);

— the type of occupancy (for office buildings: single/multiple tenanted).

The British Council of Offices' *Best practice in the specification of offices* (2000)[7] suggests that good UK practice for conventional occupancy should assume between 12 $m^2$ and 17 $m^2$ per person of NIA. The BCO guide further suggests that for task based activities (e.g. trading desks and call-centre workstations) the space per person may range from 4 $m^2$ to 6 $m^2$ and for enclosed (cellular) offices 15 $m^2$ or more per person.

Table 3.1 gives guidance to population estimation for a number of building types based on surveys and experience of the population which may need to be accommodated.

**Table 3.1** Estimation of population

| Building type | Estimated population | Arrival rate (%) | Interval (s) |
|---|---|---|---|
| Hotel | 1.5–1.9 persons/room | 10–15 | 30–50 |
| Flats | 1.5–1.9 persons/bedroom | 5–7 | 40–90 |
| Hospital | 3.0 persons/bedspace★ | 8–10 | 30–50 |
| School | 0.8–1.2 $m^2$ net area/pupil | 15–25 | 30–50 |
| Office (mixed, multiple tenancy): | | | |
| — standard | 11–14 $m^2$ NIA/person | 11–14 | 25–30 |
| — prestige | 12–17 $m^2$ NIA/person | 12–15 | 20–25 |
| Office (sector, multiple tenancy)†: | | | |
| — standard | 10–13 $m^2$ NIA/person | 12–14 | 25–30 |
| — prestige | 11–16 $m^2$ NIA/person | 13–16 | 20–25 |
| Office (single tenancy): | | | |
| — standard | 8–10 $m^2$ NIA/person | 12–15 | 25–30 |
| — prestige | 10–14 $m^2$ NIA/person | 13–17 | 20–25 |

★ excluding patient

† 'sector, multiple tenancy' applies to tenants involved in the same activity

The passenger arrival rate can be expressed as a percentage of a building's total population. The percentage of a building's population, which will require transportation to the higher floors of a building during the morning five minute up-peak, will vary dependent on:

— the type of building occupancy (different business interests or single tenant);

— the starting regime (unified or flexitime);

— the distance to bulk transit facilities such as buses and trains.

In many buildings it is unlikely that all the total population is present on any day. The former Greater London Council[11] in one study measured the attendance at 84%. A 1997 study by RICS[13] indicates that 93% of organisations have at least 60% of a building's occupants present at any one time. The 1999 RICS study[14] shows a daily staff presence of 84–89% in the period 09.00–12.00. 'Hot desking' and home working is now considered significant. Thus in design calculations the total building population can be reduced by 10–20% to account for:

— persons working at home,

— persons away on holiday;

— persons away sick;

— persons away on company business;

— vacant posts;

— persons who arrive before or after the peak hour of incoming traffic;

— hot desking.

Table 3.1 gives guidance of the probable percentage peak arrival rates of the remaining occupants for a number of building types. The BCO guide[7] (2000) gives a broad-brush recommendation of 15% for offices, which is only suitable in a few cases.

### 3.3.3 Estimation of passenger demand (quality of service)

The quality of service criterion is represented by the average passenger waiting time. The intended average passenger waiting time should be obtained from the building owner or the developer. If this is not available a judgement will need to be made and documented by the traffic designer.

Actual average passenger waiting time, i.e. the time period between when a passenger either registers a landing call, or joins a queue, until the responding lift begins to open its doors at the boarding floor, would be the best indicator of the quality of service that an installed lift system could provide. The shorter the average passenger waiting time the better the service. Unfortunately, average passenger waiting times cannot be easily measured, owing to the difficulty of determining the exact arrival instant for each passenger. However, the time the lift system takes to respond to the landing call registered by the first arriving passenger can be measured. During up-peak traffic this time is called the interval and is the average period of time between successive arrivals of the lift, or lifts, at the main terminal.

*Important note*: some lift companies define the lift arrival time to be when the arrival signal is given (lantern/gong) or call registration cancellation. This will give optimistic performance results as this signal can be as much as eight seconds (to allow for deceleration and levelling) before the lift arrival.

Some designers use the interval of car arrivals at the main terminal as an estimation of the quality of service. Interval is part of the evaluation of handling capacity, which represents the quantity of service of a lift system. Table 3.1 shows the range of interval values recommended for a number of building types. Table 3.2 expands the value of interval to represent a quality of service criterion for office buildings. The BCO guide[7] (2000) gives a broad-brush recommendation of 30 seconds for offices, which is only suitable in a few cases.

These values are similar to those given in BS 5655-6: 2002[10].

**Table 3.2** Probable quality of service in office buildings

| Interval (s) | Quality of service |
|---|---|
| <20 | Excellent system |
| 25 | Very good system |
| 30 | Good system |
| 40 | Poor system |
| >50 | Unsatisfactory system |

Caution must exercised, when using the interval as a quality indicator as passenger waiting time depends on car occupancy, i.e. the number of passengers in the lift. Statistical analysis indicates that the average passenger waiting time is 85% of the calculated interval at an average car occupancy of 80% of actual lift capacity (cf. Table 3.3). If cars are allowed to load above 80% then the average passenger waiting time increases substantially and rapidly becomes unacceptable.

The following is a useful rule of thumb for the general level of service provided by a single lift serving several floors:

— excellent service: one lift per 3 floors;

— average service: one lift per 4 floors;

— below average service: one lift per 5 floors.

These rules of thumb may be need to be ignored in order to achieve, for example, either a specified interval, or a specified handling capacity.

See Example 3.1 in Appendix 3.A2 for an illustration of this calculation.

## 3.4 Lift system performance

### 3.4.1 The round trip

Once the passenger demand has been determined a lift system needs to be designed to meet this demand. The performance of a lift system can be determined by a simple calculation.

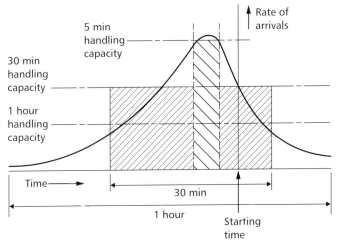

**Figure 3.2** Detail of a round trip for a single lift during peak up-peak traffic

Figure 3.2 shows that a lift round trip is characterised by passengers arriving at the main terminal for transportation to the upper floors. The lift travels around the building making stops to allow passengers to alight eventually reaching the highest requested floor when the lift reverses direction and then travels non-stop back to the main terminal floor. A lift system with more than one lift brings the lifts successively to the main terminal to load the passengers and take them to their destinations. A lift group presents each lift, successively, at the main terminal separated in time by the average interval.

The calculation method involves determining the round trip time for a single lift. A number of lifts are then selected to provide the specified up-peak interval. The up-peak handling capacity can then be calculated and a value determined for the percentage of the building population served.

### 3.4.2 Performance equations

The round trip time (RTT) of a single lift is defined as the average period of time for a single car trip around a building, during the up-peak traffic condition, measured from the instant the car doors start to open at the main terminal until the instant the car doors start to reopen at the main terminal, when the car returns to the main terminal after its trip around the building.

The round trip is characterised by the numerical values for average number of stops ($S$) made; the average highest call reversal floor ($H$) visited during the trip; and the average number of passengers carried ($P$) on each trip. A simple formula can be derived (Barney, 2003[2a]):

$$\text{RTT} = 2Ht_v + (S+1)(T - t_v) + 2Pt_p \tag{3.1}$$

where the number of time components in the round trip time equation are defined as follows:

$$t_v = d_f/v$$

$$T = t_f(1) + t_{sd} + t_c + t_o - t_{ad}$$

$$t_p = 0.5(t_l + t_u)$$

All symbols are defined in section 3.1.1.

The performance time ($T$) (sometimes called 'door-to-door' time) is important and is defined as the time from when the doors start to close until the doors are 800 mm open at the next adjacent floor.

*Caution*: some lift companies define the performance time ($T$) to be the time from the instant the doors start to close until the instant the doors start to open even if the lift is still moving.

*Important note*: of the three terms in the round trip time equation, the central term is the most influential. Saving one second on the value of $T$ can increase the handling capacity by about 5%.

In an installation of only one car the up-peak interval (UPPINT) is equal to the round trip time (RTT), but in a system of $L$ cars the up-peak interval is given by:

$$\text{UPPINT} = \frac{\text{RTT}}{L} \tag{3.2}$$

The up-peak handling capacity of a lift system is defined as the number of persons that can be transported from the main terminal to the upper floors of a building during the worst (heaviest) five minutes (300 seconds) of up-peak activity. This is calculated by determining the number of trips made by the lifts, which occur over the worst five minute period and then multiplying it by the average number of passengers ($P$) carried in that five minutes. The up-peak handling capacity (UPPHC) is thus given by:

$$\text{UPPHC} = \frac{300\,P}{L} \tag{3.3}$$

The percentage of building population that can be handled (%POP) is obtained by dividing the UPPHC value by the building's effective population ($U$).

$$\text{\%POP} = \frac{\text{UPPHC} \times 100}{U} \tag{3.4}$$

## 3.5 Calculation of the round trip time

In order to calculate lift system performance it is necessary to evaluate the six parameters: $H, S, P, T, t_v, t_p$, in the round trip time equation (equation 3.1).

### 3.5.1 Average number of passengers ($P$)

The average number of passengers assumed to load into a lift during an up-peak traffic condition is important as it affects any calculation (or simulation) significantly. Traditionally, lifts have been assumed to load, on average, to 80% of their rated capacity. This is the loading factor. Thus $P$ has been taken as 80% of the rated capacity (CC) of a lift in persons, i.e:

$$P = 0.8 \times \text{CC} \tag{3.5}$$

Industry experts and consultants state that many lifts, particularly the larger ones, are not observed to fill with passengers to the numbers suggested by equation 3.5. Why is this?

The value for CC, column 2 of Table 3.3, can be obtained from Table 1.1 of BS EN 81-1/2: 1998[8], or by dividing the rated load (RL) in kilograms (column 1 of Table 3.3) by 75 (and rounding down). The assumption is that the average weight of a person is 75 kg. Although this relationship between rated load and rated capacity is obviously linear, the relationship between rated load and the platform area (CA) of lift cars (column 3 of Table 3.3) is non-linear. For example, a 450 kg lift has a rated capacity of six passengers and a platform area of 1.3 m², whereas a 2500 kg lift has a rated capacity of 33 passengers and a platform area of 5.0 m². Thus for a 450 kg lift, BS EN 81-1/2 allocates each passenger a platform space of 0.21 m², whereas in a 2500 kg lift each passenger is only allocated a platform space of 0.15 m². The maximum actual capacity of all but the smallest lifts is therefore smaller than the value given by the rated capacity.

Section 2.3.1 indicated that a 75 kg person might occupy an area of 0.21 m². Dividing the maximum platform area (CA) by 0.21 gives the maximum actual capacity of a lift (AC), (column 4 of Table 3.3). If the maximum actual capacity is divided by the rated capacity, then a capacity factor (CF) can be determined as shown in column 5 of Table 3.3. The value for P, which should be used in all calculations, shown in column 6 of Table 3.3, is then 80% of the maximum actual capacity in persons, i.e:

$$P = 0.8 \times \text{CC} \times \text{CF} \tag{3.6}$$

Column 7 of Table 3.3 gives the car loading factor to be assumed when carrying out simulations.

In other parts of the world a different value is used to represent the average weight of a single passenger. In Singapore it assumed to be 65 kg and in Australia to be 68 kg. Although it is assumed to be 75 kg in Europe, this may need revision in the future as people are getting heavier. The capacity factor remains the same regardless of the assumed average weight, if it is assumed that the area occupied by a person changes in the same proportion.

### 3.5.2 Average number of stops ($S$) and average highest call reversal floor ($H$)

The two parameters $H$ and $S$ are dependent on $P$ (the number of passengers carried in the lift), and $N$ (the number of floors served above the main terminal floor).

The average highest call reversal floor was determined by Schroeder (1955)[16] using simple statistical theory as:

$$H = N - \sum_{i=1}^{N-1} \left( \frac{i}{N} \right)^P \tag{3.7}$$

The average number of stops was determined by Basset Jones (1923)[6] using simple statistical theory as:

$$S = N \left( 1 - \left( 1 - \frac{1}{N} \right)^P \right) \tag{3.8}$$

Table 3.A1.1 (Appendix 3.A1) gives values of $H$ and $S$ for the variable ($P$) for a range from 5 to 20 persons.

### 3.5.3 Single floor transit time ($t_v$)

This is made up of the two variables: interfloor distance ($d_f$) and rated speed ($v$).

#### 3.5.3.1 Interfloor distance ($d_f$)

The interfloor distance can be taken as the average interfloor distance and is determined as the total travel divided by the number of possible stopping floors above the main terminal floor. For domestic dwellings this averages to around 3.0 m and for commercial buildings the range is from 3.3 m upwards. Commercial buildings often introduce a mixed floor pitch for a number of reasons. Some floors have increased heights, e.g. lobby/main terminal floors, service floors, special floors (restaurant, lecture, conference, VIP suite). Some floors are not

**Table 3.3** Car capacity

| (1) Rated load (RL) / kg | (2) Rated capacity (CC) (persons) | (3) Max area (CA) (m²) | (4) Actual capacity (AC) (persons) | (5) Capacity factor (CF) (%) | (6) Value of $P$ to be used in calculations | (7) Loading factor (LF) (%) |
|---|---|---|---|---|---|---|
| 320 | 4 | 0.95 | 4.5 | 100 | 3.6 | 80 |
| 450 | 6 | 1.30 | 6.2 | 100 | 4.9 | 80 |
| 630 | 8 | 1.66 | 7.6 | 95 | 6.3 | 76 |
| 800 | 10 | 2.00 | 9.5 | 95 | 7.6 | 76 |
| 1000 | 13 | 2.40 | 11.4 | 88 | 9.1 | 70 |
| 1275 | 17 | 2.90 | 13.8 | 81 | 11.0 | 65 |
| 1600 | 21 | 3.56 | 16.9 | 81 | 13.5 | 65 |
| 1800 | 24 | 3.92 | 18.6 | 78 | 14.9 | 62 |
| 2000 | 26 | 4.20 | 20.0 | 77 | 16.0 | 62 |
| 2500 | 33 | 5.00 | 23.8 | 72 | 19.0 | 58 |

*Notes*: (1) rated load (RL) range taken from BS ISO 4190-1[9]; (2) maximum car area values (CA) taken from BS EN 81-1/2[8], Table 1.1; (3) rated car capacity (CC) calculated by dividing the value for RL by 75 as BS EN 81-1/2, clause 8.2.3 and rounded down; (4) actual capacity (AC) calculated by dividing the value for CA by 0.21; (5) capacity factor (CF), in per cent, calculated from CF = (CA/CC)× 100; (6) loading factor (LF), in per cent, calculated by multiplying CF by 0.8

available for alighting during some periods of the day, e.g. first (and sometimes the second) floor above the main terminal during up-peak, service floors, security floors etc.

### 3.5.3.2 Rated speed (v)

The value of the rated speed is usually supplied by the lift maker, who will select it to meet various engineering requirements (gear ratio, sheave, rope speed, drive controllers, product line, etc.) and duty. For instance, goods lifts are generally slower than passenger lifts. Speed, however, is not a dominant factor in equation 3.1. It does become significant, however, if the served floors are in an upper zone, when a higher speed will permit the unserved floors to be rapidly traversed.

Where no value for rated speed is available it must be chosen by the traffic designer.

The minimum value of rated speed might be taken from the requirement for a firefighting lift, whose speed shall be sufficient to enable it to run from the fire access level to the furthest floor of the building in less than 60 s. This is not a realistic speed for very tall buildings where higher speeds are required to reduce passenger travel times. There is no theoretical upper limit to lift rated speed and speeds of 17 m/s have been installed. At very high speeds passenger comfort may be affected. Speed is limited by practical factors such as maximum sheave diameter, rope bending radius (fatigue), rope wear, safety aspects (over-travels, etc.) etc.

Section 6 of BS 5655: Part 6[10], Table 4, recommends rated speeds in relation to the total time to travel between terminal floors for several types of building. These speeds can be translated into a nominal travel time (without allowance for acceleration/deceleration/levelling/start delays) to travel at rated speed between the highest and lowest floors (the terminal floors), as shown in Table 3.4.

Table 3.5 gives guidance for office buildings for the selection of the speed of a lift on the basis that the total time to travel the distance between the terminal floors at rated speed should only take 20 s.

### 3.5.4 The time consumed when stopping $(T - t_v)$

The time consumed when stopping was given in the description of equation 3.1 as:

$$T = t_f(1) + t_{sd} + t_c + t_o - t_{ad}$$

The components of performance time $(T)$ need to be carefully selected in order to achieve the correct handling capacity for the lift installation. The lift maker should be contracted at the tender stage to provide them at the

specified values and the maintenance contractor should be required to keep them at the contract values throughout the life of the lift installation. Failure to do this will invalidate any traffic design. Taking each term in turn.

### 3.5.4.1 Single floor flight time ($t_f(1)$) and start delay time ($t_{sd}$)

The single floor flight time is the time taken from the instant that the lift doors close until the lift is level at the next adjacent floor. It is dependent on the rated speed, the rated acceleration and the jerk value. This latter unscientific sounding parameter (sometimes called 'shock') is the name given to the rate of change of acceleration. The relationships between distance travelled, velocity, acceleration and jerk are complex and are given in detail in Appendix A1 at the end of this Guide. Using the equations of motion given in Appendix A1, flight times can be obtained for any distance, or number of floors, travelled. Fortunately for designers of lift drives there are limits to the maximum values of acceleration and jerk. These constraints are imposed by the physiology of the human body. Passengers are uncomfortable, when subjected to values of acceleration greater than about one sixth of the acceleration due to gravity (that is about 1.5 m/s²). There is a similar constraint on the maximum value of jerk at about 2.2 m/s³.

In the past the numerical value for maximum jerk was twice the numerical value of maximum acceleration (i.e. rated acceleration reached in 0.5 s), but nowadays a 'softer' ride is expected and it is never more than 1.5 times the numerical value for acceleration.

Table 3.5 indicates the likely range of acceleration and jerk values and single floor flight times for an interfloor distance of 3.3 m. The single floor flight times are slightly larger than those given by a theoretical calculation, in order to allow for start delay time (tsd). The start delay time includes the times for the doors to lock on closure, the motor field build-up, brake release, levelling, etc.

### 3.5.4.2 Door closing time ($t_c$) and opening time ($t_o$) and advance (pre-) opening time ($t_{ad}$)

Door operating times are dependent on door width, weight and type. The three most common standard door widths of 800, 1100 and 1300 mm. Narrow doors of 800 mm width are fitted to lifts up to 10-person rated capacity and wider doors thereafter. Wider doors of 1300 mm width are fitted on goods lifts and hospital lifts. There are two basic door types: side opening and centre opening (see section 7.9). Side opening doors have to open and close over the whole width of the doorway, which will take more time. Where centre opening doors can be fitted,

**Table 3.4** Total time to travel between terminal floors in different types of building

| Building type | Travel time (s) |
|---|---|
| Large offices, hotels, etc. | 17–20 |
| Small offices, hotels, etc. | 20 |
| Hospitals, nursing/residential homes, etc. | 24 |
| Residential buildings | 20–30 |
| Factories, warehouses, shops, etc. | 24–40 |

**Table 3.5** Typical lift dynamics

| Lift travel (m) | Rated speed (m/s) | Acceleration (m/s²) | Jerk (m/s³) | Single floor flight time (s) |
|---|---|---|---|---|
| <20 | <1.00 | 0.4 | 0.6 | 8.0 |
| 20 | 1.00 | 0.4-0.7 | 0.75 | 7.0 |
| 32 | 1.60 | 0.7-0.8 | 0.9 | 6.0 |
| 50 | 2.50 | 0.8-0.9 | 1.0 | 5.5 |
| 63 | 3.00 | 1.0 | 1.25 | 5.0 |
| 100 | 5.00 | 1.2 | 1.5 | 4.7 |
| 120 | 6.00 | 1.2 | 1.8 | 4.5 |

faster door operation is achieved and the symmetrical reaction against the car frame will reduce lift sway.

The door closing time $(t_c)$ is the time taken from the instant the lift doors start to close until they are locked-up. Because a door is a moving object it can gather considerable kinetic energy. To protect passengers from injury the BS EN 81[8] standard requires the maximum energy to be limited to 10 joules. The maximum energy constraint limits the maximum values of door speed, when closing. The weight of the door is determined by many factors such as fire resistance, height, width, type etc. Typically, a 150 kg door has a maximum speed of 0.23 m/s and a 500 kg door has a maximum speed of 0.13 m/s.

The door opening time $(t_o)$ is the time from the instant that the lift doors start to open at a landing, until the instant that the doors are 800 mm open at the next floor. Door opening time is not subject to energy constraints. However, as the same door operator will be used for both directions of movement, opening times may not be significantly faster.

An improvement in the door operating times can be achieved by overlapping the levelling operation with the first part of the opening of the doors. This is called advanced door opening $(t_{ad})$. This is permitted within the door zone (BS EN 81 specifies the door zone as $\pm 200$ mm from floor level). There will be no tripping hazard if, when the lift stops, the doors are only 600 mm open.

Table 3.6 gives initial design values for the two door types, two door sizes, with and without advanced opening. See Table 7.1 for the times for a wider range of door times and operators.

### 3.5.5 The passenger transfer time $(t_p)$

The passenger transfer time is the average time a single passenger takes to enter or leave a car. This parameter is the vaguest of all the components of equation 3.1 principally because it is dependent on human behaviour. The passenger transfer time can vary considerably and is affected by the shape of the car, the size and type of car entrance, environment (commercial, institutional, residential), type of passenger (age, gender, agility, purpose), car loading. General rules can be suggested. If the car door width is 1000 mm, or less, assume passengers enter or exit in single file. For door widths over 1000 mm assume the first six passengers enter or exit in single file and the remainder in double file. For offices consider 1.0 s to be the average passenger transfer time. Where passengers have no reason to rush or are elderly, the transfer times should be increased to about 2.0 s.

### 3.5.6 Performance time $(T)$ as a quality indicator

The performance time $(T)$ has the most effect on the round trip time, see equation 3.1. As indicated earlier reducing the value of $T$ by one second increases the handling capacity by about 5%. This indicates that the quality of service can be judged by the value selected for $T$. For an interfloor height of 3.3 m, Table 3.7 gives the values of $T$ that indicate the probable performance of an installed lift system.

See Example 3.2 in Appendix 3.A2 for an illustration of this calculation.

Table 3.7 Performance time $(T)$ as an indicator of quality of service

| Value of $T$ (s) | Comment |
| --- | --- |
| 8.0–9.0 | Excellent system |
| 9.0–10.0 | Good system |
| 10.0–11.0 | Average system |
| 11.0–12.0 | Poor system |
| >12.0 | Consider system replacement |

### 3.5.7 Note to up-peak round trip time calculations

The up-peak traffic pattern is well defined, but it is never as pure as has been suggested by Figure 3.1. Often, there will be some down travelling and interfloor traffic during the up-peak period. Some designers attempt to include these in their calculations, but with the variety of possible assumptions no general benchmark condition can be defined. It is recommended that all up-peak calculations are 'pure' with no other traffic considered. Then the calculation can be used as a benchmark to compare different designs and different competitive offers in a tender situation.

See standard templates in chapter 4, Appendix 4.A1.

## 3.6 Assumptions made in the derivation of the round trip time equation

A number of assumptions are made in order to derive the round trip time equation (equation 3.1). These can place limits on the validity of the method. It is important for a designer to be aware of these limitation, especially when using computerised design methods, in order to ensure a correct design.

### 3.6.1 Passengers arrive uniformly in time

Basset Jones[6] and Schroeder[16] statistically derived the formulae for $S$ and $H$ (equations 3.7 and 3.8) assuming that passengers arrived at a lift system for transportation, according to a rectangular probability distribution

Table 3.6 Typical door closing and opening times†

| Door type | Closing and opening times (s) for given door width | | | | | |
| --- | --- | --- | --- | --- | --- | --- |
| | Closing | | Closing (no advanced opening) | | Opening (with advanced opening) | |
| | 800 mm | 1100 mm | 800 mm | 1100 mm | 800 mm | 1100 mm |
| Side | 3.0 | 4.0 | 2.5 | 3.0 | 2.0 | 1.5 |
| Centre | 2.0 | 3.0 | 2.0 | 2.5 | 1.0 | 1.5 |

† see Table 7.1 for fuller range of door types and times

function (PDF), in order to simplify the mathematics. This means the periods of time between successive passenger arrivals are assumed to be equal for a constant arrival rate and to change linearly for varying arrival rates. However, it is more likely that the arrival processes will be according to a Poisson PDF, which is one of a family of exponentially related PDFs. In the Poisson PDF the passenger inter-arrival periods are related nonlinearly even for a constant arrival rate. Does this affect the design method?

It has been shown[2b] that values for $S$ and $H$ derived using the Poisson PDF are always smaller than with a rectangular PDFs. Also it can be shown that other PDFs (e.g. Erlangian) produce results between the rectangular and the Poisson. Thus the use of formulae based on the rectangular PDF produces slightly conservative designs when compared to designs using formulae derived from other PDFs.

## 3.6.2 All lifts load to an average of 80%

Equations 3.7 and 3.8 can be used to calculate values for $S$ and $H$ for any number of passengers ($P$) carried. In the round trip time calculation the lifts are assumed to fill to 80% of the actual capacity (see Table 3.3). This has been shown[2c] to be a reasonable statistical assumption and allows some lifts to fill to capacity and others to lower values, in order to average 80%. If a higher loading factor than 80% is used, queues develop and poor performance results. This is a valid design assumption.

## 3.6.3 All floors are equally populated

Generally the floors of a building are not equally populated. It is possible[2d] to derive quite complex formulae for $S$ and $H$. Would the use of such formula improve the accuracy of the design?

If calculations are carried out for a building where most of the population occupies the higher floors then it is found that the value for $H$ rises and the value for $S$ falls. Conversely, if most of a building's population occupies the lower floors of a building the value for $H$ falls significantly and the value for $S$ also falls. The effect in both cases compared to a building with each floor being equally populated is that the value for the round trip time falls. Therefore the effect of an unequal population is generally favourable to the conservative sizing of a lift system.

## 3.6.4 Rated speed is reached in a single floor jump and interfloor heights are equal

These two commonly made assumptions are related. For lifts with speeds greater than 1.6 m/s the first assumption is not valid. Most buildings have irregular interfloor distances, e.g. main entrance floors, service floors, conference floors, making the second assumption invalid. Are these errors significant?

It has been found[2e], that if the flight time to travel the average interfloor distance is determined and this time is used as $t_f(1)$ in the round trip time calculation, then an error in the calculation of a few percent occurs.

## 3.7 Round trip time: other factors to be considered

### 3.7.1 Landing and car call dwell times

Some door control systems cause the lift doors to (dwell) open for a fixed length of time after a lift arrives at a floor. Passengers can then leave a lift (for a car call), or board a lift (for a landing call), without the doors closing on them.

Typical office building door dwell times are 2.0–3.0 seconds for a car call stop and 3.0–4.0 seconds for a landing call stop. The longer landing call dwell times allow waiting passengers to walk across a large lobby to the allocated lift. Where passenger detection systems are fitted, these times can be automatically shortened to 0.5 s once the first passenger crosses the threshold. This is called differential door timing. The lift doors will then close only when the threshold is clear of passengers. Where disabled access is required the dwell time is set at 5.0 seconds minimum. In residential buildings it is common to set dwell times to 7.0 seconds to allow for prams and bicycles to be manoeuvred into and out of the lift. Good control systems will reduce the dwell times on a car call being registered, or re-registered, or when the door close button is operated.

Where a door dwell time is longer than the assumed passenger transfer time the round trip time equation needs to be adjusted to account for this. This introduces the concept of a lift system cycle time ($t_{cyc}$). This time is defined as the period of time between the instant the lift doors begin to close until the instant the lift doors begin to close again at the next adjacent floor. The cycle time can be applied to the round trip time equation by deleting the term $2Pt_p$ and adding the value of the dwell time to the value of the performance time ($T$)

### 3.7.2 Lobby loading interval

Many control systems operate a loading interval at the main terminal floor during up-peak. This prevents the lift closing its doors and moving away with only one passenger, once that passenger has entered and registered a car call. The loading interval is set to be equal to the time for a reasonable number of passengers to board the car. Thus the loading interval should be set to the time it would take for the car to become about 60% loaded. There will then be no effect on the round trip time calculation due to the loading interval.

### 3.7.3 The traffic controller is ideal

The traffic control system (dispatcher) is assumed to be ideal. During up-peak the controller is programmed to bring the cars to the main terminal floor immediately after the last passenger exits from the car at the highest demanded floor ($H$). On older scheduled (timed) systems, it is possible for the wrong control algorithm to be switched on for the prevailing traffic pattern, e.g. the down-peak program during up-peak. The round trip time equation cannot be expected to accommodate this error.

The older scheduled controllers used a despatch interval to maintain a headway between cars leaving the main terminal. This was designed to space cars equally around the building, but during up-peak it has the effect of reducing the handling capacity by delaying the departure of loaded cars from the main terminal. The despatch interval was often set at the theoretical value of the UPINT, say 30 s, so its effect can be significant. With this type of controller it is recommended that the round trip time be increased by 15%.

The more modern on-call traffic controllers utilise load and direction detection systems to determine the prevailing traffic pattern. The difficulty is that sometimes the change of traffic pattern is detected too late to be effective. Some designers add 10% or 15% to the round trip time to account for this inefficiency. This is a reasonable correction, provided it is added to all prospective designs and the value used is known to all parties to a design.

Up-peak performance can be boosted by traffic control techniques such as up-peak zoning, up-peak sectoring, landing call allocation and landing call allocation with up-peak sub zoning (see section 9.7).

## 3.8 Matching passenger demand to handling capacity during up-peak traffic demand

### 3.8.1 Iterative matching of demand with lift handling capacity

The round trip time equation assumes that cars will load to 80% of the actual capacity (AC). The value obtained for UPPHC also makes the same assumption. But this is only correct if the arrival rate ($A_r$) exactly equals UPPHC. If too few, or too many, passengers arrive to load the cars the car load will not be 80% and the values for $S$, $H$, RTT and the interval will alter. It is possible to make a calculation to determine the interval and passenger load for a defined passenger arrival rate.

It is a common practice for a lift designer to select a desired value for the interval (INT). If the passenger arrival rate ($A_r$) is in persons per second then the number of passengers ($P$) in a lift is:

$$P = A_r \text{INT} \tag{3.9}$$

where the interval (INT) does not assume an 80% lift car loading.

For specified values of $t_v$, $t_s$ and $t_p$ it is necessary to obtain values for $H$ and $S$, so that a value for the round trip time can be calculated. Table 3.A1.1 (Appendix 3.A1) gives values of the variable ($P$) for a range from 5 to 20 persons.

By selecting a suitable number of cars ($L$), the round trip time and then the interval can be calculated. Should this value for interval differ from the one initially selected in value for 3.9, then a new value for it should be selected, equation 3.9, until the initial and final values converge.

This is an iterative procedure commonly used to solve two-point boundary problems, where the start and finish values are known. With an iterative procedure a rule for the next trial has to be defined. A suitable one here is to subtract twice the difference between the first and final values from the first value:

$$\text{INT}_{\text{new}} = \text{INT}_{\text{first}} - 2 \times (\text{INT}_{\text{first}} - \text{INT}_{\text{final}}) \tag{3.10}$$

See Example 3.3 in Appendix 3.A2 for an illustration of this calculation.

## 3.9 Passenger waiting, transit and journey times and time to destination during up-peak traffic demand

### 3.9.1 Definitions

The generally accepted definitions[3–5] are:

— *Passenger waiting time*: time from when a passenger either registers a landing call, or joins a queue, until the responding lift begins to open its doors at the boarding floor.

*Note 1*: the passenger waiting time continues if a passenger does not enter the responding lift, e.g. it is full.

*Note 2*: the passenger waiting time is zero, if the responding lift doors are open, when a passenger arrives.

— *Passenger transit time*: time from when a responding lift begins to open its doors at the boarding floor until the doors begin to open again at the destination floor.

*Note*: the passenger transit time commences, if the responding lift doors are open, when a passenger arrives.

— *Passenger time to destination*: time from when a passenger either registers a landing call, or joins a queue, until the responding lift begins to open its doors at the destination floor.

— *Passenger journey time*: time from when a passenger either registers a landing call, or joins a queue, until the passenger alights at the destination floor.

*Note*: a passenger is deemed to have alighted, when any passenger detection device is interrupted or the passenger physically crosses the door sills.

Figure 3.3 illustrates the relationship between these definitions.

### 3.9.2 Average passenger waiting time (AWT)

Having sized a lift system to meet the anticipated up-peak traffic demand, the designer would then like to know the likely average passenger waiting times. Many lift companies state this to be half the interval. Others using

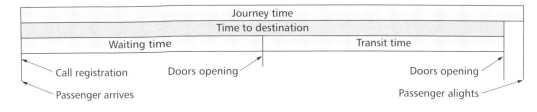

**Figure 3.3** Illustration of definitions

logged data state incorrectly that the average passenger waiting time is the time for the lift to respond to a first landing call registered (system response time).

System response time (SRT) is defined as the time between a passenger registering a call at a landing and the subsequent cancellation of that call by the traffic controller. These times are often inaccurate as some lift companies cancel the call registration as much as eight seconds before the lift actually starts to open its doors at a landing.

Passenger average waiting time (AWT) is the sum of all the individual passenger waiting times divided by the number of calls. Average waiting time is not dependent solely on the interval, but is also affected by the average car load and the arrival probability distribution function (PDF). Figure 3.4 shows the relationship of performance expressed as AWT/INT against car load is exponential in shape.

An equation can be derived for the passenger average passenger waiting time[2f] shown in Figure 3.4. For car loads from 50% to 80% the AWT is given by:

$$\text{AWT} = [0.4 + (1.8 \times \text{CC} / 100 - 0.77)^2] \, \text{INT} \qquad (3.11)$$

For car loads less than 50% the AWT is 40% of the interval (INT). Car loads above 80% are not considered.

### 3.9.3 Average passenger transit time (ATT)

This has been defined as the time from when a responding lift begins to open its doors at the boarding floor until the doors begin to open again at the destination floor. It is useful to know the average time it would take for an average passenger to reach their destination floor (assumed to be half way up the building zone being served) after their allocated lift is ready for boarding with its doors opening.

An estimate of how long it takes the average passenger to reach their destination is to calculate ATT to the midpoint of the local travel for any group of lifts. This implies travel for a distance of $H/2$ with the number of stops being $S/2$

and a transfer of $P$ passengers boarding the lift and $P/2$ passengers alighting before the average passenger alights. The formula is:

$$\text{ATT} = 0.5 \, H \, t_v + 0.5 \, S \, t_s + 1.5 \, P \, t_p \qquad (3.12)$$

### 3.9.4 Average passenger travel time to destination (ATTD)

It is also useful to know the average time it would take for an average passenger to reach their destination floor. This is obtained by adding the primary physiological consideration of passenger average waiting time (AWT) to the secondary physiological consideration of passenger average transit time (ATT) to give a passenger average time to destination (ATTD), see Figure 3.3.

$$\text{ATT} = 0.5 \, H \, t_v + 0.5 \, S \, t_s + 1.5 \, P \, t_p + \text{AWT} \qquad (3.13)$$

### 3.9.5 Average passenger journey time (AJT)

Using the definition above for average passenger journey time, this is longer than the average passenger travel time to destination by the time to open the lift doors and the passenger to cross the threshold.

## 3.10 Traffic conditions other than up-peak

### 3.10.1 Down-peak traffic condition[2g]

During down-peak traffic there may be some up-peak and interfloor activity. Formulae for a pure down-peak traffic condition can be obtained in the same way as for up-peak. The car movements are characterised by a down staircase pattern of floor stops. The cars stop less often than during up-peak and the interval at the main terminal is smaller. A formula for the down-peak round trip time (RTTD) can be derived as:

$$\text{RTTD} = N \, t_v + (0.5 \, S + 1) \, t_s + 2 \, P \, t_p \qquad (3.14)$$

The underlying down-peak handling capacity can then be calculated from the value of RTTD. Using simulation techniques a formula for down-peak average passenger waiting time (DNPAWT) can be obtained in terms of the up-peak interval (UPPINT), up-peak handling capacity (UPPHC) and the number of passengers arriving during the down-peak period ($A_d$):

$$\text{DNPAWT} = 0.85 \, A_d \, \frac{\text{UPPINT}}{\text{UPPHC}} \qquad (3.15)$$

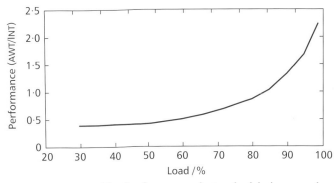

**Figure 3.4** Relationship of performance against car load during up-peak traffic

The control algorithms available to deal with down-peak traffic exhibit different properties. The main generic types are fixed and dynamic sectoring, estimated time of arrival, self tuning, landing call allocation (see chapter 9). There is no clear best down-peak traffic control algorithm, as some algorithms work well at low demands others at high demands. The choice requires a study of all the circumstances by simulation (see section 4).

## 3.10.2  Interfloor traffic condition[(2h)]

A true interfloor activity will be completely random (no obvious pattern of calls) and balanced, so that no floor gains or loses population over the period of several hours. Because there is no discernible pattern of movements during interfloor traffic, the concept of an interval has no meaning during interfloor traffic as round trips do not always pass through the main terminal. However, using simulation techniques a formula for interfloor average passenger waiting time (IFAWT) can be obtained in terms of the up-peak interval (UPPINT), up-peak handling capacity (UPPHC) and the number of passengers arriving during the interfloor period ($A_i$):

$$\text{IFAWT} = \text{UPPINT} \, (0.22 + 1.78 \, A_i \, / \, \text{UPPHC}) \qquad (3.16)$$

The traffic controller is an important influence on interfloor traffic performance. However, at interfloor demands equivalent to 3% up-peak arrival rates (typical of a busy system) the differences are only a few percentage points. The actual performance requires a study of all the circumstances by simulation (see chapter 4).

## 3.10.3  Mid-day traffic condition[(2i)]

The mid-day traffic condition is probably the busiest the lift system must serve. This traffic condition exists at mid-day and presents a very complex traffic condition. During the lunch time traffic condition there is a combination of up and down traffic to and from the main terminal. There will also be interfloor traffic in buildings with drinks machines, sandwich bars, restaurants, leisure facilities and meeting rooms. It is most likely that all lifts visit the main terminal floor during each trip. This allows a formula for the mid-day round trip time (RTTM) to be developed for mid-day traffic as:

$$\text{RTTM} = 2 H t_v + 2 S t_s + 4 P t_p \qquad (3.17)$$

The underlying mid-day handling capacity can then be calculated from the value of RTTM. Passengers will during mid-day traffic probably have to wait a little longer for a lift as a result of the simultaneous up and down demand that exists. An estimate of the average passenger waiting time (MIDAWT) can be made from:

$$\text{MIDAWT} = 0.85 \, \text{MIDINT} \qquad (3.18)$$

This traffic condition can present the most severe demand on the lift system and may be the one for which the lift system should be sized. The only reliable way to study this would be determined would be by simulation (see chapter 4).

## 3.10 4  Review of all traffic conditions[(2j)]

The primary traffic condition for design is pure up-peak. It is analytic and formula can be derived. The pure down-peak and mixed mode, mid day traffic patterns are usually satisfied by the sizing carried out for the up-peak traffic pattern. Both of these patterns are analytic if assumptions are made. The interfloor traffic pattern can be analysed mathematical but it is very complex. Fortunately interfloor demands are very modest compared to the other three traffic patterns.

The up-peak design method provides a measure of the underlying handling capacity of a lift system. This in turn sets the performance of the three other major traffic conditions of down-peak, interfloor and mid-day traffic. With up-peak considered to be unity, the underlying ratios for these conditions can be shown to be:

—     up-peak:      1.0
—     down-peak:  1.6
—     mid-day:     1.3
—     interfloor:   1.4.

The underlying interfloor handling capacity is generally never utilised, as the typical demand is about one fifth of the up-peak demand.

It is important to obtain the correct up-peak sizing if the other traffic patterns are to be satisfactory.

## 3.11  Selection of equipment and lift function

### 3.11.1  Double deck lifts

There are some 500 double deck lifts installed world wide, mostly in the USA, with only 20 in Europe. They are used mainly in very tall buildings and comprise two passenger cabs one above the other connected to one suspension/drive system. The upper and lower cabs can serve two adjacent floors simultaneously. During peak periods the cabs are arranged to serve even and odd floors respectively with passengers guided into the appropriate cab for their destination. Special arrangements are made at the lobby for passengers to walk up/down a half flight of stairs/escalators to reach the lower or upper main lobby.

The advantage for double deck lifts is that the shaft handling capacity is improved as effectively there are two lifts in each shaft. The disadvantage is for the passengers during off peak periods, when one cab may stop for a call with no equivalent call required in the other cab. Special control systems are available such as only using one deck during off peak periods. Formulae for double deck analysis have been developed[(2k)]. The use of double deck lifts is rare in the UK and their traffic design is a specialised procedure.

### 3.11.2  Firefighting lifts

Firefighting lifts are discussed in detail in chapter 5 and are usually single lifts situated around the floor plate.

Their rated load is often only 630 kg and their rated speed sufficient only to reach the highest occupied floor in 60 s. Therefore their handling capacity is low. They do provide a small but useful addition to the vertical transportation services of a building, especially those with large floor plates. Where a firefighting lift is part of a group, extra precautions are made to protect it, i.e. fire-protected stairways, through-car doors etc. These precautions may affect the traffic handling of these lifts and this should be taken into account when calculating the handling capacity of such a group.

### 3.11.3 Goods lifts

The need for goods lifts has increased substantially in recent years. Despite the computer revolution the amount of paper in and scrap paper out has increased. Also it is quite common to find in any type of building one or more floors under refurbishment, with the requirement to bring in equipment and to remove rubbish and debris. All buildings should be served by an adequate number of goods lifts of a suitable size. This will ensure that the passenger lifts are used for their designed purpose and not used as goods transporters to the detriment of the passenger service. It is recommended that all office buildings contain at least one dedicated goods lift for usable floor areas up to 30 000 m². For larger buildings, an additional goods lift should be provided for each additional 40 000 m² gross floor area. Dedicated goods lifts should have a minimum rated capacity of 1600 to 2000 kg. Where passenger lifts are used as goods lifts, either generally, or in an emergency, the interiors should always be protected.

### 3.11.4 Observation (glass/scenic) lifts

Observation lifts are often installed in hotels and shopping complexes to provide a feature or visual impact. They will, naturally, draw a large percentage of pleasure riders. They contribute to the vertical transportation system of a building. Generally they have longer flight and door times, which reduces their traffic handling performance. Also the car interiors are shaped for aesthetic and viewing purposes rather than easy circulation in the car. They should be considered to be occupied at a reduced occupancy of (say) 60% in comparison to the 80% used for a conventional lift.

### 3.11.5 Shuttle lifts

Shuttle lifts generally serve two stops, such as at a railway station, underground station or in a tall building, which are divided into zones with service direct from the main lobby to an upper lobby. Calculation of their traffic performance is relatively easy as they only serve two floors. When installed in tall/very tall buildings shuttle lifts are usually quite large and fast and are an important transportation facility. Here their traffic design is a specialised procedure as they often transport passengers to/from a sky lobby, where further groups of lifts serve another section of the building.

## 3.12 Selection of equipment and building form

### 3.12.1 Basement service and floors served by only part of a lift group

Buildings are often designed with car parks or with a service facility, such as restaurant or leisure area, below the main terminal at basement levels. Often not all floors below the main terminal floor will be served by all lifts in a group. While this saves capital expenditure, it is not recommended as it contradicts the general rule that all lifts in a group should serve the same floors. Passengers will experience difficulty in selecting the correct lifts out of a group, which serve a basement, unless special signalling arrangements are made. In the event that only one lift out of a group serves all floors, the wait experienced by passengers will be long. It may be better to provide such basement service to the main terminal floor by a separate lift or lifts. This solution will avoid seriously detracting from the traffic handling capabilities of the main group.

During interfloor traffic there will not be an appreciable deterioration in service. The effect on serving floors below the main terminal has an effect on the up-peak, down-peak and mid-day traffic patterns. An effect of service to the basement area during up-peak is that cars arrive at the main terminal already partly full, causing confusion. The time penalty to be added to the round trip time can be between 15 s to 30 s. Designers will need to take account of these factors, when sizing an installation with served levels below the main terminal.

It is possible to calculate the effect of basement service[21] by considering it to be an up-peak in reverse. A calculation of the probable stops ($S_M$) and reversal floor ($H_M$) can be carried out in a similar way to the upward service. The resulting additional time can then be added to the normal round trip time. The round trip, equation 3.1, is modified to become:

$$\text{RTT} = 2H t_v + (S + 1)(T - t_v) + 2P t_p$$
$$+ 2H_M t_{vm} + S_M(T_M - t_{vm}) \qquad (3.19)$$

where transit time $t_{vm}$ and the performance time $T_M$ are evaluated for the basement interfloor distance.

### 3.12.2 Multiple entry levels

Some buildings may be designed with their main entry points at more than one level. The presence of more than one main terminal level for the lift system does not lead to efficient circulation and, where possible, buildings should not be designed in this way. Means should be provided to bring the two entrance routes together at a single lift lobby. Except in special cases it is recommended that the main terminal floor should be used as an interchange for the different circulation modes. Service to/from basement levels should be by well designed stairways, escalators or short rise lifts (perhaps hydraulic). If this is not possible then the lift system sizing should take into account the extra times incurred stopping and loading at multiple entry floors.

### 3.12.3 Entrance bias

Some buildings have more than one main entrance (at a common level) and each entrance may be served by its own group of lifts. Or there may be a large lobby area with two groups of lifts on either side serving the same floors. The difficulty here is deciding whether the building population will use these entrances (and their associated group of lifts) on a 50/50 basis or not. In the absence of any guidance the solution is to assume an entrance bias of 60/60 and size the lift groups to meet this demand.

### 3.12.4 Large floor plates

Some floor plates are the size of football fields. Ideally all circulation activities should be centralised in a main core of a building. This is clearly not always possible when access into a building is considered. Sometimes the main lobby is close to the main entrance, sometimes the building design places the main lobby some distance into the building. This latter case involves occupants and visitors in a long walk to reach the transportation facilities. However it may be better for occupants to walk to the centre of a building to access stairs and lifts, since their usage during the day may outweigh the comparative inconvenience during arrival and departure. Generally the maximum distance to a lift or stair from an occupant's work place should not exceed 60 m with a distance of less than 45 m being preferred. Emergency escape routes (see chapter 5) are usually closer, but do not necessarily form part of the normally used circulation routes.

### 3.12.5 Stairs and escalators

In general, lifts are used for travel over a large number of floors and stairs or escalators for travel over a small number of floors. A judgement is made by the passenger with respect to the waiting time for a lift versus the walking time (and walking effort) with respect to stairs and escalators. Low rise structures such as shopping centres, sports complexes, conference and exhibition centres, railway stations, airports, hospitals etc. are good examples of buildings, where the provision of stairs and escalators considerably aids circulation. In office environments the usefulness of stairs and escalators is lessened, although they can be a advantageous where (say) heavily populated trading floors must be accessed. They are also very useful for access to car parks, relieving the lifts of travelling below the main terminal, and may be used for access to double deck lifts.

Peters (1996)[12] provides guidance on stair usage for off peak periods, see Table 3.8. In general during a peak period in an office building between 5% and 15% of passengers might use the stairs for one or two floor movements.

Table 3.9 provides some guidance to the division of passenger demand between lifts and escalators. The use of

**Table 3.8** Stair usage

| Floors travelled | Usage up (%) | Usage down (%) |
|---|---|---|
| 1 | 10 | 15 |
| 2 | 5 | 10 |

**Table 3.9** Lifts and escalators: division of traffic

| Floors travelled | Escalator (%) | Lift (%) |
|---|---|---|
| 1 | 90 | 10 |
| 2 | 75 | 15 |
| 3 | 50 | 50 |
| 4 | 25 | 75 |
| 5 | 10 | 90 |

escalators is mainly inhibited by the length of time travelling. The provision of well signed and positioned stairs and escalators can considerably lessen the demands made on the lifts. Designers must take these factors into account.

### 3.12.6 Attractive building facilities

There may be facilities in buildings which will distort traffic movements. Examples are restaurants (positioned at the top of the building, in the basement, even half way up the building), drinks and sandwich machines, leisure club facilities (swimming pools, gymnasia), facilities floors (bank, travel agent, shops), toilet facilities, post rooms, trading floors etc. These floors will provide a powerful attraction at different times of the day and must be considered in the traffic design.

### 3.12.7 Lobby design

The design of lift lobbies, especially at the main terminal, where there is most activity is a neglected area. Very often the design of a lift lobby is considered against the requirements of aesthetic design, security, noise limitation, smoke penetration and fire precautions, rather than the movement of people. If a lift lobby becomes too crowded, especially during up-peak, then intending passengers often reach a lift and cannot board it because it is too full, or cannot reach it and it leaves partially empty. The latter event reduces the handling capacity and the former may delay the despatch of the lift as passengers may need to leave as it has become not only crowded, but also overloaded. The shape of lobbies is most important. For example, a group of lifts whose doors are fitted to a convex shaped lobby would be most inefficient, whereas if the doors were fitted to a concave shaped lobby the lobby design would be nearly perfect.

The lobby design has an effect on the round trip equation. If lifts are served from large lobbies then the lobby door dwell time may need to be increased. Or an increase in the passenger transfer time (tp) used in Equation (3.1) by 10% could be considered to account for the inefficiency. In severe situations some designers add 10% to the round trip time.

### 3.12.8 Tall buildings

Examination of Table 3.4 indicates that for a specified size of car the number of stops ($S$) increases as the number of served floors ($N$) increases. As the round trip time in equation 3.1 is dominated by the central term, which includes $S$, the effect is to increase the round trip time, which in turn increases UPPINT, the passenger waiting time and the passenger journey time. A similar deterioration of performance occurs for the other traffic conditions. The solution is to limit the number of floors served by the lifts. A rule of thumb is to serve a maximum of 15–16 floors with a lift or a group of lifts. This introduces the concept of zoning. Zoning is where a building is divided so that a lift or group of lifts is constrained to serve a designated set of floors. There are two forms of zoning: interleaved and stacked.

An interleaved zone is where the whole building is served by lifts, which serve either even floors or odd floors. This was a common practice in local authority housing. The technique reduces the capital costs because there are fewer openings and landing doors to install. The service to passengers, however, is poorer than with a duplex serving all floors. Interleaved zoning is not recommended today.

A stacked zone building is where a tall building is divided into horizontal layers. This in effect stacks several buildings on top of each other, with a common footprint, in order to save ground space. It is a common and recommended practice for office and institutional buildings. Each zone can be treated differently with regard to shared, or separate, lobby arrangements, grade of service etc.

The number of floors in a zone, the number of lifts serving a zone and the length of the express jump all affect the round trip time. The round trip time equation can be adjusted by adding a time equal to the time taken to pass the unserved floors in both directions.

$$\text{RTT} = 2Ht_v + (S+1)(T-t_v) + 2Pt_p + 2(t_e - t_f(1))$$

$$(3.20)$$

where $t_e$ is the flight time from the main terminal to the express zone terminal (sky lobby) (s).

Where it is required that each zone receives the same grade of service, either the number of floors, or the number of lifts, in each zone is adjusted to achieve this. It is usually easier to adjust the number of floors per zone, than the number of lifts per zone, as there are more of them.

Zoning a building requires more space at the main terminal level. The positioning of the groups is important. Adequate signs should be provided to quickly and simply direct the passengers to the correct group.

### 3.12.9 Very tall buildings

Very few very tall buildings, i.e. over 40 stories high, are built in the UK at the moment. It is not proposed to discuss the traffic design of such buildings, the use of sky lobbies, shuttle lifts, top/down service and double deck lifts etc. as this is a very specialised procedure.

## 3.13 Selection of lift equipment and building function

*Important note*: this section is concerned with the selection of equipment for twelve different types of buildings. Reference to the corresponding subsections of section 2.6,

which deals with the circulation of people and those subsections of chapter 5, which deal with the application of different types of lifts, should also be consulted.

### 3.13.1 Airports

Many airports are arranged on two main levels with the arrival level below the departure level. There may then be other levels above and below providing various services (e.g. baggage handling, catering) and facilities (offices). Another common characteristic is an adjacent, underground or elevated railway station. As with shopping centres, the movement of baggage trolleys from one level to another is a problem. A solution to this problem is to install moving ramps and this greatly improves circulation. Lifts, however, are the main means of vertical movement.

Generally each baggage trolley will be attended by two persons plus their baggage. A trolley may weigh (including its own weight) some 75 kg but will occupy the space taken by three or four persons. Thus the total weight of two passengers and their trolley will be some 225 kg and occupy the space of some 5 people. This occupancy and loading requirement must be taken into account. In these circumstances lifts are very unlikely to be overloaded.

There are no changes required to equation 3.1, but care will need to be taken in the assumptions of car occupancy levels.

### 3.13.2 Car parks

Car parks can be attached to shopping centres, offices, airports, railway stations etc. They are often multi-storey, although those at out of town shopping centres and railway stations may be at a single level. The pedestrian demand is more likely to be restrained by the vehicle entry and exit ramp handling capacities. A factor is the vehicle occupancy, which is likely to be 1.2 persons per car for office car parks and two persons per car elsewhere.

For offices the peak demand is often in the evening, when building occupants are attempting to reach their cars. The office lifts, which may not necessarily serve the car parking levels, will bring large numbers of people to the lobby. Those persons with cars will then make a significant demand on any lifts serving the car park levels. The demand on the car park lifts is similar to that experienced by the main lifts during the morning peak period, but this demand is downwards and to fewer floors.

The traffic design should use equation 3.1 if the car park lifts are separate to the main lifts and equation 3.19 if the lifts are part of a basement service.

### 3.13.3 Department stores

This category applies to large departmental and chain stores. These stores will have many entrances, some of which may open to a main street whilst others open into shopping mall areas. The opportunity therefore exists for 'leakage' into and out of shopping centres. Many stores will own lifts and escalators inside their occupancies.

These facilities may be used by shopping centre shoppers to move between mall levels.

### 3.13.4 Entertainment centres, cinemas, theatres, sports centres, stadia and concert halls

Buildings providing these functions can specialise in one of the activities or many of them. Many sports centres are low rise and do not require lifts. Town centre buildings such as cinema complexes, concert halls and theatres will be of higher rise. Such complexes generally use escalators as the main vertical transportation element. Lifts provided in these circumstances do not have to meet a large demand and may only have to satisfy the requirements for the handicapped and firefighting.

### 3.13.5 Hospitals

The building form is important, i.e. whether the building has a small footprint and is tall (US practice) or has a large footprint and is low rise (UK practice). In the former case, where lifts are used as a primary circulation element, their proper operation is vital, particularly when dealing with operating theatre emergencies. In Britain most hospitals are designed on a 2–3 storey low rise principle, although many city hospitals have high rise elements. Lifts are provided mainly as a means of moving bed bound patients from floor to floor.

The traffic designer will need to understand the modus operandi of the hospital before finalising a design. Factors to be considered include numbers of staff and shift patterns, numbers of visitors and visiting hours, location of theatres, X-ray facilities etc., distribution and deliveries of food, beverages, supplies, waste disposal, patient emergency evacuation, porterage etc. It is important that patient bed lifts are separate from the visitor and staff lifts, to avoid cross infection.

### 3.13.6 Hotels

Lifts play an important part in the circulation of guests and service staff in a hotel. Escalators should be employed for short range movements, e.g. to connect function levels with the lobby.

The traffic patterns in hotels are complex, and are not comparable to the morning and afternoon peaks in an office. The most demanding times are at check-out (08:00 to 10:00) and check-in (17:00 to 19:00). At these times heavy two-way traffic occurs with guests going to and from rooms, restaurants and in and out of the hotel. Calculations should therefore assume equal numbers of up and down stops at these times.

At most times lifts are unlikely to load to more than 50%. However, the lift sizes should be at least 17-person, in order to accommodate luggage and provide guests with uncrowded travel conditions. As a rule of thumb assume one lift for every 90–100 keys and there should be one passenger/goods lift for every two passenger lifts. This rule must be used with care as it would not be suitable for a low rise hotel with 30% of its rooms at the entrance level.

Neither would it be suitable for a high rise hotel with a small footprint. There are also differences between the operational needs of 'transit' hotel near to airports etc., where guests stay one night, and hotels used by longer term and holiday guests.

### 3.13.7 Offices

Much of this chapter is concerned with lifts in commercial office buildings, except section 3.13. Reference should be made to these sections for detailed guidance.

### 3.13.8 Railway stations

Railway stations may be served mainly by stairs and pedestrian ramps, although some, particularly the deeper underground stations, will use escalators. Generally railway stations, whether above or below ground, have poor provision of lifts. This will change as the requirements to assist persons with limited mobility are applied.

When passengers require to move from one level to another with hand baggage, difficulties arise. When baggage trolleys are used these difficulties increase. Escalators should not be used. As with shopping centres (section 3.13.11) a solution to this problem is to install moving ramps and this also greatly improves circulation.

### 3.13.9 Residential buildings

The estimation of the population in a residential building is usually based on the number of bedrooms and the occupancy per bedroom. Suitable rules of thumb for the number of persons occupying a flat are given in Table 3.10.

The commonly used design period for a residential building is the afternoon 5-minute, two-way traffic condition, which is considered the most demanding traffic period. During this period of time, people are both entering and leaving the building. The lifts are loading passengers at the main lobby, distributing these passengers to various upper floors, reversing at the uppermost hall call, stopping in the down direction for additional passengers and transporting them to the main lobby. In low income housing, where many children and adults are leaving for school and work at the same time, the morning down-peak may also be very heavy. Table 3.11 gives guidance.

Often in residential and low income (local authority) flats one passenger lift is generally arranged to allow furniture movement and stretchers and to handle other service needs. Luxury flats may include a separate goods lift for furniture, tradespeople and domestic help. These goods lifts are usually 'hospital shaped' with capacities of around 2000 kg.

**Table 3.10** Occupancy factors for residential buildings

| Type | Luxury | Normal | Low income |
|------|--------|--------|------------|
| Studio | 1.0 | 1.5 | 2.0 |
| 1-bedroom | 1.5 | 1.8 | 2.0 |
| 2-bedroom | 2.0 | 3.0 | 4.0 |
| 3-bedroom | 3.0 | 4.0 | 6.0 |

**Table 3.11** Design criteria: residential buildings (5-minute, two-way)

| Type | Luxury | Normal | Low income |
|---|---|---|---|
| Interval (s) | 45–50 | 50–60 | 50–70 |
| Two-way handling capacity | 8% | 6–8% | 5–7% |

There are also requirements that each flat shall have access to an alternative lift during maintenance or out-of-service conditions. This has often been achieved in the past for low income blocks of flats, by using two simplex lifts operating on an interleaved (skip stop) basis. This solution is not recommended today. Another solution for low income residential blocks is high level walkways to an alternative lift.

### 3.13.10 Residential care homes and nursing homes

Homes generally have a low traffic requirement, which can be catered for by a single lift. Larger homes might acquire a second lift giving security of service in the event of break down or maintenance.

### 3.13.11 Shopping centres

Shopping centres are often built with two or three levels of retail and several levels of car parking above or below. Lifts do not play a major part in the transportation arrangements, which are usually centred on escalators. Lifts should always be located in pairs and not singly in order to provide a reasonable interval of 40–60 s and security of service during breakdowns and maintenance. Often scenic lifts are provided not only for transportation, but as an enjoyable experience.

In multi-level shopping complexes provision must be made for the movement of shopping trolleys, push chairs and persons with mobility problems from one level to another. A commonly applied solution to this problem is to install moving ramps. Where lifts are used it is unlikely that they fill to more than 50%.

The use of car park lifts is determined mainly by the maximum rate of entry of vehicles and the average occupancy of each vehicle. These values are usually determined from an associated (road) traffic study.

### 3.13.12 Universities and other education buildings

University buildings can be classified as institutional buildings, where the occupants receive a service. Where universities occupy city sites many have tall buildings (10–20 stories) and even those on out-of-town sites follow suit in order to reduce land use and keep a compact campus. Most buildings are mixed function: lecture rooms, laboratory and offices, although some buildings may specialise as lecture blocks. There are hourly cycles of 10 minutes of demand before and after each 50 minute lecture, tutorial or seminar session. In between the peaks the activity levels are low.

Often a university campus will have a mixed collection of office type buildings, halls of residence, catering services and factory like units containing teaching and research equipments. The office type buildings can be treated as detailed above. The halls of residence can be treated as hotels, although perhaps at lower levels of demand and performance. The catering services can be attached to either the office type buildings or halls of residence and should be treated similarly to those provided in office facilities or hotel facilities. The research buildings will probably be low rise and be subject to special movement provisions associated with the equipment installed.

## References

1   ANSI: Z65.1-1980: *Standard method for measuring floor area in office buildings* (Washington DC: American National Standards Institute) (1980)

2   Barney G C *Elevator traffic handbook* (London: Spon Press) (2003)

    (2a, ibid. p98; 2b, ibid. p163; 2c, ibid. p105; 2d, ibid. p149; 2e, ibid. p156; 2f, ibid. p312; 2g, ibid. ch.13; 2h, ibid. ch.14; 2i, ibid. ch.15; 2j, ibid. p354; 2k, ibid. p174; 2l, ibid. p188)

3   Barney G C, Peters R D, Powell B and Siikonen M-L Towards agreed traffic design definitions *Elevatori* **34** (1) (Jan/Feb 2005)

4   Barney G C, Peters R D, Powell B and Siikonen M-L Towards agreed traffic design definitions *Elevator World* (February 2005)

5   Barney G C, Peters R D, Powell B and Siikonen M-L Towards agreed traffic design definitions *Elevation* **42** (Winter 2004/5)

6   Basset Jones The probable number of stops made by an elevator *GE Review* **26** (1923).

7   BCO: *Best practice in the specification for offices* (London: British Council for Offices (2000)

8   BS EN 81-1: 1998: *Safety rules for the construction and installation of lifts. Electric lifts*; BS EN 81-2: 1998: *Safety rules for the construction and installation of lifts. Hydraulic lifts* (London: British Standards Institution) (1998)

9   BS ISO 4190-1: 1999: *Lift (US: Elevator) installation. Class I, II, III and VI lifts* (London: British Standards Institution) (1999)

10  BS 5655-6: 2002: *Code of practice for the selection and installation of new lifts* (London: British Standards Institution) (2002)

11  GLC: *Traffic generation: users guide and review of studies* (London: Greater London Council) (date unknown)

12  Peters R D, Mehta P. and Haddon J Lift passenger traffic patterns: applications, current knowledge and measurement *Elevator Technology* 7 (Stockport: IAEE Publications) (1996)

13  RICS: *Report of a study of office occupational densities* (London: Royal Institution of Chartered Surveyors) (1997)

14  RICS: *Report of a study of office occupational densities* (London: Royal Institution of Chartered Surveyors) (1999)

15  RICS: *Code of measuring practice* (4th edn.) (London: RICS Books)

16  Schroeder J Personenaufzuege *Foerden und Heben* **1** (1955)

17  Strakosch G. (ed) *The vertical transportation handbook* (Chichester: John Wiley) (1998)

# Appendix 3.A1: Table of values of *H* and *S*

**Table 3.A1.1** Values of *H* and *S* with respect to number of passengers carried in car (*P*)

(*a*)  For 5 to 12 passengers per trip

| Number of served floors, *N*, above MT | *H* and *S* values for stated average number of passengers per trip (*P*) | | | | | | | | | | | | | | | |
|---|---|---|---|---|---|---|---|---|---|---|---|---|---|---|---|---|
| | 5 | | 6 | | 7 | | 8 | | 9 | | 10 | | 11 | | 12 | |
| | *H* | *S* | *H* | *S* | *H* | *S* | *H* | *S* | *H* | *S* | *H* | *S* | *H* | *S* | *H* | *S* |
| 5 | 4.6 | 3.4 | 4.7 | 3.7 | 4.8 | 4.0 | 4.8 | 4.2 | 4.9 | 4.3 | 4.9 | 4.5 | 4.9 | 4.6 | 4.9 | 4.7 |
| 6 | 5.4 | 3.6 | 5.6 | 4.0 | 5.7 | 4.3 | 5.7 | 4.6 | 5.8 | 4.8 | 5.8 | 5.0 | 5.9 | 5.2 | 5.9 | 5.3 |
| 7 | 6.3 | 3.8 | 6.4 | 4.2 | 6.5 | 4.6 | 6.6 | 5.0 | 6.7 | 5.3 | 6.7 | 5.5 | 6.8 | 5.7 | 6.8 | 5.9 |
| 8 | 7.1 | 3.9 | 7.3 | 4.4 | 7.4 | 4.9 | 7.5 | 5.3 | 7.6 | 5.6 | 7.7 | 5.9 | 7.7 | 6.2 | 7.8 | 6.4 |
| 9 | 8.0 | 4.0 | 8.2 | 4.6 | 8.3 | 5.1 | 8.4 | 5.5 | 8.5 | 5.9 | 8.6 | 6.2 | 8.7 | 6.5 | 8.7 | 6.8 |
| 10 | 8.8 | 4.1 | 9.0 | 4.7 | 9.2 | 5.2 | 9.3 | 5.7 | 9.4 | 6.1 | 9.5 | 6.5 | 9.6 | 6.9 | 9.6 | 7.2 |
| 11 | 9.6 | 4.2 | 9.9 | 4.8 | 10.1 | 5.4 | 10.2 | 5.9 | 10.3 | 6.3 | 10.4 | 6.8 | 10.5 | 7.1 | 10.6 | 7.5 |
| 12 | 10.5 | 4.2 | 10.7 | 4.9 | 11.0 | 5.5 | 11.1 | 6.0 | 11.2 | 6.5 | 11.3 | 7.0 | 11.4 | 7.4 | 11.5 | 7.8 |
| 13 | 11.3 | 4.3 | 11.6 | 5.0 | 11.8 | 5.6 | 12.0 | 6.1 | 12.1 | 6.7 | 12.3 | 7.2 | 12.3 | 7.6 | 12.4 | 8.0 |
| 14 | 12.1 | 4.3 | 12.5 | 5.0 | 12.7 | 5.7 | 12.9 | 6.3 | 13.0 | 6.8 | 13.2 | 7.3 | 13.3 | 7.8 | 13.4 | 8.2 |
| 15 | 13.0 | 4.4 | 13.3 | 5.1 | 13.6 | 5.7 | 13.8 | 6.4 | 14.0 | 6.9 | 14.1 | 7.5 | 14.2 | 8.0 | 14.3 | 8.4 |
| 16 | 13.8 | 4.4 | 14.2 | 5.1 | 14.5 | 5.8 | 14.7 | 6.5 | 14.9 | 7.0 | 15.0 | 7.6 | 15.1 | 8.1 | 15.2 | 8.6 |
| 17 | 14.6 | 4.4 | 15.0 | 5.2 | 15.3 | 5.9 | 15.6 | 6.5 | 15.8 | 7.1 | 15.9 | 7.7 | 16.0 | 8.3 | 16.1 | 8.8 |
| 18 | 15.5 | 4.5 | 15.9 | 5.2 | 16.2 | 5.9 | 16.5 | 6.6 | 16.7 | 7.2 | 16.8 | 7.8 | 16.9 | 8.4 | 17.1 | 8.9 |
| 19 | 16.3 | 4.5 | 16.8 | 5.3 | 17.1 | 6.0 | 17.4 | 6.7 | 17.6 | 7.3 | 17.7 | 7.9 | 17.9 | 8.5 | 18.0 | 9.1 |
| 20 | 17.1 | 4.5 | 17.6 | 5.3 | 18.0 | 6.0 | 18.2 | 6.7 | 18.5 | 7.4 | 18.6 | 8.0 | 18.8 | 8.6 | 18.9 | 9.2 |
| 21 | 18.0 | 4.5 | 18.5 | 5.3 | 18.8 | 6.1 | 19.1 | 6.8 | 19.4 | 7.5 | 19.6 | 8.1 | 19.7 | 8.7 | 19.8 | 9.3 |
| 22 | 18.8 | 4.6 | 19.3 | 5.4 | 19.7 | 6.1 | 20.0 | 6.8 | 20.3 | 7.5 | 20.5 | 8.2 | 20.6 | 8.8 | 20.8 | 9.4 |
| 23 | 19.6 | 4.6 | 20.2 | 5.4 | 20.6 | 6.2 | 20.9 | 6.9 | 21.2 | 7.6 | 21.4 | 8.3 | 21.5 | 8.9 | 21.7 | 9.5 |
| 24 | 20.5 | 4.6 | 21.1 | 5.4 | 21.5 | 6.2 | 21.8 | 6.9 | 22.1 | 7.6 | 22.3 | 8.3 | 22.5 | 9.0 | 22.6 | 9.6 |

(*b*)  For 13 to 20 passengers per trip

| Number of served floors, *N*, above MT | *H* and *S* values for stated average number of passengers per trip (*P*) | | | | | | | | | | | | | | | |
|---|---|---|---|---|---|---|---|---|---|---|---|---|---|---|---|---|
| | 13 | | 14 | | 15 | | 16 | | 17 | | 18 | | 19 | | 20 | |
| | *H* | *S* | *H* | *S* | *H* | *S* | *H* | *S* | *H* | *S* | *H* | *S* | *H* | *S* | *H* | *S* |
| 5 | 4.9 | 4.7 | 5.0 | 4.8 | 5.0 | 4.8 | 5.0 | 4.9 | 5.0 | 4.9 | 5.0 | 4.9 | 5.0 | 4.9 | 5.0 | 4.9 |
| 6 | 5.9 | 5.4 | 5.9 | 5.5 | 5.9 | 5.6 | 5.9 | 5.7 | 6.0 | 5.7 | 6.0 | 5.8 | 6.0 | 5.8 | 6.0 | 5.8 |
| 7 | 6.9 | 6.1 | 6.9 | 6.2 | 6.9 | 6.3 | 6.9 | 6.4 | 6.9 | 6.5 | 6.9 | 6.6 | 6.9 | 6.6 | 7.0 | 6.7 |
| 8 | 7.8 | 6.6 | 7.8 | 6.8 | 7.9 | 6.9 | 7.9 | 7.1 | 7.9 | 7.2 | 7.9 | 7.3 | 7.9 | 7.4 | 7.9 | 7.4 |
| 9 | 8.7 | 7.1 | 8.8 | 7.3 | 8.8 | 7.5 | 8.8 | 7.6 | 8.8 | 7.8 | 8.9 | 7.9 | 8.9 | 8.0 | 8.9 | 8.1 |
| 10 | 9.7 | 7.5 | 9.7 | 7.7 | 9.8 | 7.9 | 9.8 | 8.1 | 9.8 | 8.3 | 9.8 | 8.5 | 9.8 | 8.6 | 9.9 | 8.8 |
| 11 | 10.6 | 7.8 | 10.7 | 8.1 | 10.7 | 8.4 | 10.7 | 8.6 | 10.8 | 8.8 | 10.8 | 9.0 | 10.8 | 9.2 | 10.8 | 9.4 |
| 12 | 11.6 | 8.1 | 11.6 | 8.5 | 11.6 | 8.7 | 11.7 | 9.0 | 11.7 | 9.3 | 11.7 | 9.5 | 11.8 | 9.7 | 11.8 | 9.9 |
| 13 | 12.5 | 8.4 | 12.5 | 8.8 | 12.6 | 9.1 | 12.6 | 9.4 | 12.7 | 9.7 | 12.7 | 9.9 | 12.7 | 10.2 | 12.8 | 10.4 |
| 14 | 13.4 | 8.7 | 13.5 | 9.0 | 13.5 | 9.4 | 13.6 | 9.7 | 13.6 | 10.0 | 13.7 | 10.3 | 13.7 | 10.6 | 13.7 | 10.8 |
| 15 | 14.4 | 8.9 | 14.4 | 9.3 | 14.5 | 9.7 | 14.5 | 10.0 | 14.6 | 10.4 | 14.6 | 10.7 | 14.6 | 11.0 | 14.7 | 11.2 |
| 16 | 15.3 | 9.1 | 15.4 | 9.5 | 15.4 | 9.9 | 15.5 | 10.3 | 15.5 | 10.7 | 15.6 | 11.0 | 15.6 | 11.3 | 15.6 | 11.6 |
| 17 | 16.2 | 9.3 | 16.3 | 9.7 | 16.4 | 10.2 | 16.4 | 10.6 | 16.5 | 10.9 | 16.5 | 11.3 | 16.6 | 11.6 | 16.6 | 11.9 |
| 18 | 17.2 | 9.4 | 17.2 | 9.9 | 17.3 | 10.4 | 17.4 | 10.8 | 17.4 | 11.2 | 17.5 | 11.6 | 17.5 | 11.9 | 17.6 | 12.3 |
| 19 | 18.1 | 9.6 | 18.2 | 10.1 | 18.2 | 10.6 | 18.3 | 11.0 | 18.4 | 11.4 | 18.4 | 11.8 | 18.5 | 12.2 | 18.5 | 12.6 |
| 20 | 19.0 | 9.7 | 19.1 | 10.2 | 19.2 | 10.7 | 19.3 | 11.2 | 19.3 | 11.6 | 19.4 | 12.1 | 19.4 | 12.5 | 19.5 | 12.8 |
| 21 | 19.9 | 9.9 | 20.0 | 10.4 | 20.1 | 10.9 | 20.2 | 11.4 | 20.3 | 11.8 | 20.3 | 12.3 | 20.4 | 12.7 | 20.4 | 13.1 |
| 22 | 20.9 | 10.0 | 21.0 | 10.5 | 21.1 | 11.1 | 21.1 | 11.5 | 21.2 | 12.0 | 21.3 | 12.5 | 21.3 | 12.9 | 21.4 | 13.3 |
| 23 | 21.8 | 10.1 | 21.9 | 10.7 | 22.0 | 11.2 | 22.1 | 11.7 | 22.2 | 12.2 | 22.2 | 12.7 | 22.3 | 13.1 | 22.3 | 13.5 |
| 24 | 22.7 | 10.2 | 22.9 | 10.8 | 22.9 | 11.3 | 23.0 | 11.9 | 23.1 | 12.4 | 23.2 | 12.8 | 23.2 | 13.3 | 23.3 | 13.8 |

# Appendix 3.A2: Example calculations

## Example 3.1

Suppose an office building is to be built for an occupancy of 837 persons. A 15% arrival rate at an interval of 25–30 seconds is specified. What handling capacity is required?

Assuming 10% of the total occupants are absent, i.e. a daily population of 753 persons (0.9 × 837), then 113 persons (0.15 × 753) arrive in the peak 5-minutes.

The lift system specification would be for a system with a 5-minute handling capacity of 113 persons/5-minutes, at an interval of 25–30 seconds.

## Example 3.2

What would be the values for the round trip time, interval, handling capacity and percentage population served for a 10 floor building (4.0 m interfloor distance) served by four lifts of rated capacity 16-persons and rated speed of 2.5 m/s. (Assume $t_p = 1.0$ s.) The given lift dynamics are: $t_f(1) = 5.5$ s, $t_{sd} = 0.5$ s, $t_c = 3.0$ s, $t_o = 2.5$ s, $t_{ad} = 1.0$ s.

For CC = 16, $P = 16 × 0.86 × 0.8 = 11.0$ (from equation 3.7 and Table 3.3).

Then, for $N = 10$, $H = 9.6$, $S = 6.9$ (from Appendix 3.A1, Table 3.A1.1).

For $d_f = 4.0$ and $v = 2.5$, then $t_v = 1.6$ s.

Then:

$$T = 5.5 + 0.5 + 3.0 + 2.5 - 1.0 = 10.5 \text{ s}$$

and:

$$T - t_v = 8.9 \text{ s}$$

Then:

$$\text{RTT} = 2 × 9.6 × 1.6 + 7.9 × 8.9 + 2 × 11.0 × 1$$

$$= 30.7 + 70.3 + 22.0 = 123 \text{ s}$$

Then, UPPINT = 30.7 s and UPPHC = 108 persons/5-min.

This system would suit the specification in Example 3.1. Note that with practical traffic designs it is not necessary to precisely achieve either an interval less than 30 seconds (30.7 seconds is close enough), or a handling capacity of 113 persons per 5-minutes (108 persons/5 minutes is close enough).

## Example 3.3

Suppose for the system specified in Example 3.2 the passenger demand was 100 persons in 5 minutes. Determine the interval and loading factor.

The system of Example 3.2 has a handling capacity that is larger than the actual passenger demand of 100 persons/5-minutes, so the iterative balance method should be used.

A suitable initial value for the interval could be the 30.7 seconds obtained in Example 3.2.

The effect of eight fewer people arriving during the peak 5-minutes is to reduce the interval from 30.7 seconds to 28.6 seconds with a loading factor of 59%. Note that as 16-person lifts have been specified, Table 3.3 indicates that the maximum loading factor for optimal performance would be 69%. This design is 10% below this value and is satisfactory.

Example 3.3 shows that it is possible to match the specified arrival rate, exactly. When carrying out traffic calculations, it is recommended that the actual lift car loading and interval are determined.

**Example 3.3** Iterative calculation of interval (INT)

| Parameter | Trial 1 | Trial 2 |
|---|---|---|
| $\text{INT}_{first}$ (s) | 30.7 | 28.5 |
| $P$ | 10.2 | 9.5 |
| $H$ | 9.5 | 9.5 |
| $S$ | 6.6 | 6.3 |
| RTT (s) | 118.4 | 114.5 |
| Select value for $L$ | 4 | 4 |
| $\text{INT}_{final}$ (s) | 29.6 | 28.6 |
| Does value of $\text{INT}_{final}$ meet criterion? | No | Yes |
| New $\text{INT}_{first}$ | 28.5 | — |
| Loading factor | — | 59% of CC |

# 4     Advanced planning techniques and computer programs

## Principal author

Dr Richard Peters (Peters Research Ltd.)

## Section contents

| | | |
|---|---|---|
| 4.1 | Introduction | 4-3 |
| | 4.1.1 General | 4-3 |
| | 4.1.2 Symbols | 4-3 |
| 4.2 | Up-peak calculation using computer software | 4-3 |
| | 4.2.1 Basis of manual calculations | 4-3 |
| | 4.2.2 Flight time calculation | 4-4 |
| | 4.2.3 Average distance between stops | 4-4 |
| | 4.2.4 Express zones | 4-4 |
| | 4.2.5 Car loading | 4-5 |
| | 4.2.6 A computer based up-peak calculation | 4-5 |
| | 4.2.7 Beyond the up-peak calculation | 4-5 |
| 4.3 | General Analysis | 4-6 |
| 4.4 | Simulation of lift systems | 4-7 |
| | 4.4.1 Comparing round trip calculations and simulation | 4-7 |
| | 4.4.2 Running multiple simulations | 4-7 |
| | 4.4.3 Templates | 4-7 |
| | 4.4.4 Comparing simulation with round trip time calculations | 4-8 |
| | 4.4.5 Evaluating proprietary analysis software | 4-8 |
| | 4.4.6 Comparing results between different simulation programs | 4-8 |
| 4.5 | Measuring traffic | 4-11 |
| | 4.5.1 Why measure? | 4-11 |
| | 4.5.2 Automated traffic analysers | 4-11 |
| | 4.5.3 Manual passenger traffic surveys | 4-12 |
| 4.6 | Describing traffic | 4-13 |
| | References | 4-14 |
| | Appendix 4.A1: Formulae | 4-15 |
| | Appendix 4.A2: Standard templates | 4-16 |
| | 4.A2.1 Introduction | 4-16 |
| | 4.A2.2 Standard up-peak traffic template | 4-16 |
| | 4.A2.3 Standard down peak traffic template | 4-16 |
| | 4.A2.4 Standard interfloor traffic template | 4-16 |
| | 4.A2.5 Standard mid-day traffic template | 4-16 |
| | 4.A2.6 Performance measurement | 4-17 |

# 4 Advanced planning techniques and computer programs

## 4.1 Introduction

### 4.1.1 General

Chapter 3 indicated the procedure to carry out a manual calculation of lift traffic performance. A number of assumptions (see section 3.6) were indicated and the means to overcome other factors (see section 3.7) were given. The method provides a design based on statistical derivations using a rectangular probability distribution function (see section 3.6.1) and can only produce average design values. This average estimation of performance may not relate to the specific installation under consideration.

The use of computer methods greatly reduces the possibility of errors compared to manual methods and it is a simple matter to program the main equations (see equations 3.1 to 3.4). A number of such programs are available from consultants and most lift manufacturers will have a version. However, with any computer program, it is important that both the input data and the output data are checked by experienced designers and not simply accepted without question.

Implemented in software, lift traffic analysis calculations are quick and easy to do. Furthermore, because the computer carries out the calculations, the analysis can be made more sophisticated without making the program any more difficult to use.

This chapter discusses the implementation by software of a basic up-peak calculation. Advanced planning techniques, using the General Analysis theory and digital simulation are also considered. Such techniques are only practical because of the processing power of modern computers.

### 4.1.2 Symbols

| | |
|---|---|
| $a$ | Acceleration (m/s$^2$) |
| CC | Car rated (contract) capacity (persons) |
| $d$ | Travel distance (m) |
| $d_H$ | Distance to reach reversal floor $H$ excluding express zone (m) |
| $d_x$ | Total height of unserved floors in express zone (m) |
| $H$ | Average highest reversal floor |
| $h_i$ | height of floor $i$ (m) |
| $j$ | Jerk (m/s$^3$) |
| $L$ | Number of lifts |
| $l$ | Lowest reversal floor |
| $m$ | Average passenger mass (kg) |
| $N$ | Number of floors served above the main terminal |
| $P$ | Average number of passengers in car (persons) |
| RL | Rated load (kg) |

| | |
|---|---|
| RTT | Average round trip time (s) |
| $S$ | Average number of stops above main terminal |
| $T$ | Performance time (s) |
| $t_{ad}$ | Advanced door opening time (s) |
| $t_c$ | Door closing time (s) |
| $t_f(d)$ | Flight time for travel distance(s) |
| $t_l$ | Passenger loading time per person (s) |
| $t_o$ | Door opening time (s) |
| $t_p$ | Average passenger transfer time (entry or exit) (s) |
| $t_{sd}$ | Start delay time (s) |
| $t_u$ | Passenger unloading time per person (s) |
| $U$ | Effective building population (persons) |
| $U_i$ | Population of floor i (persons) |
| UPPHC | Up-peak handling capacity (persons/5-minutes) |
| UPPINT | Average up-peak interval with 80% car load (s) |
| $v$ | Rated (contract) speed (m/s) |
| %CF | Capacity factor (%) |
| %LOSS | Round trip time losses (%) |
| %POP | Percentage population served in up-peak 5-minutes (%) |

## 4.2 Up-peak calculation using computer software

### 4.2.1 Basis of manual calculations

Most lift designs are based on up-peak calculations, using equation 3.1:

$$\text{RTT} = 2 H t_v + (S - 1)(T - t_v) + 2 P t_p$$

where RTT is the average round trip time (s), $H$ is the average highest reversal floor, $t_v$ is the time to transit two adjacent floors at rated speed (s), $S$ is the average number of stops above main terminal, $T$ is the performance time (s), $P$ is the average number of passengers in car and $t_p$ is the average passenger transfer time (entry or exit) (s).

As discussed in section 3.14, the up-peak is not always the most appropriate choice of peak period for the analysis. Nevertheless, the up-peak calculation is important as an industry standard benchmark calculation, and provides a good starting point for assessing the handling capacity of a lift system.

Section 3.6 indicates the following assumptions:

(1) passengers arrive uniformly in time

(2) all lifts load to an average of 80%

(3) all floors are equally populated

(4) rated speed is reached in a single floor jump and interfloor heights are equal.

Section 3.7 indicates some other factors:

(5)    landing and car call dwell times

(6)    lobby loading interval

(7)    the traffic controller is ideal

The manual calculation can be enhanced to deal with some, but not all, of these factors.

## 4.2.2    Flight time calculation

In a manual calculation, most designers use a table to determine the time it takes for a lift to travel between floors. Some typical values are given in section 3.5.4.1, Table 3.5. This table is limited because the interfloor heights are assumed to be 3.3 m and fixed values for speed, acceleration and jerk (rate of change of acceleration) are used.

In software it is possible to write a program which accepts the dynamic parameters (speed, acceleration and jerk) and then calculates the transit time for any lift trip distance. Depending on these three parameters the lift may or may not reach full speed and full acceleration during any given trip. As shown in Table 4.1 there are four conditions, each of which yields different kinematics equations.

Peters[5] (1996) provides formulae to calculate transit time for all these conditions. These formulae are included in Appendix 4.A1 and should be applied in any software program in preference to using a table. A simplified form of the kinematic equations and examples of their use is given in Appendix A2, found at the end of this Guide.

This enhancement to the manual calculations partly deals with assumption 4 in section 4.2.1 above.

## 4.2.3    Average distance between stops

The conventional round trip time (RTT) equations assume that the lift reaches rated speed in the distance of a single floor jump and that there are no irregularities in floor heights (see section 3.6.4). This is not always the case. Peters[6] (1997) has provided formulae for the 'corrections' recommended in the 1993 edition of this Guide. This results in an improved value for the time consumed when stopping (given as $(T - t_\text{v})$ in equation 3.1). The approach is to:

(1)    Calculate the average distance to the highest reversal floor $(d_H)$ and the average number of stops $(S)$.

(2)    Calculate the average distance between stops $(d_H / S)$.

(3)    Determine the flight time $(t_\text{f}(d))$ for this average trip by using the flight time calculation above.

(4)    Add the door operating times and start delays, less any advanced door opening, $(t_\text{c} + t_\text{o} + t_\text{sd} - t_\text{ad})$.

(5)    Subtract the time to travel the average distance at the rated speed $(d_H / v)$

Equation 3.1 is thus modified to become:

$$\text{RTT} = \frac{2\,d_H}{v} + (S+1)\left(T^* - \frac{d_H}{vS}\right) + 2\,P\,t_\text{p} \qquad (4.1)$$

where $d_H$ is the distance to reach reversal floor $H$ excluding express zone (m), $v$ is the rated (contract) speed (m/s) and $T^*$ is given by:

$$T^\star = t_\text{f}(d) + t_\text{c} + t_\text{o} + t_\text{sd} - t_\text{ad}$$

where $t_\text{f}(d)$ is the flight time for travel distance $d$ (s), $t_\text{c}$ is the door closing time (s), $t_\text{o}$ is the door opening time (s), $t_\text{sd}$ is the start delay time (s) and $t_\text{ad}$ is the advanced door opening time (s).

The term $d_H / v$ is equivalent to $H\,d_\text{f} / v$ if all floors are of equal height $(d_\text{f})$.

The resulting mathematics associated with these corrections is shown in Appendix 4.A1. This approach may be applied to all calculations, not just those requiring correction.

This enhancement to the manual calculations completes dealing with assumption 4 in section 4.2.1 above.

## 4.2.4    Express zones

For completeness, express zones can be included in the round trip time equation as shown in equation 3.19. This can be expressed in distance terms as:

$$\text{RTT} = \frac{2\,d_H}{v} + (S+1)\left(T^* - \frac{d_H}{vS}\right) + 2\,P\,t_\text{p} + \frac{2d_\text{x}}{v} \qquad (4.2)$$

Table 4.1  Flight time calculation conditions

| Condition | Lift reaches rated acceleration? | Lift reaches rated speed? | Notes |
|---|---|---|---|
| A | Yes | Yes | The lift reaches full speed; this is typical of a low speed lift or a high speed lift making a multiple floor run. |
| B | Yes | No | The lift reaches full acceleration, but not full speed; typical for a single floor run for a high speed lift, where the distance travelled is not enough to accelerate up to, and decelerate down from full speed. |
| C | No | No | The lift does not reach full speed or acceleration; this is an unlikely scenario corresponding to very short trips. It can occur during re-levelling, or for a through lift that has two almost adjacent stops at opposite sides of the lift. |
| D | No | Yes | This condition corresponds to a nonsensical design, but is included for completeness. |

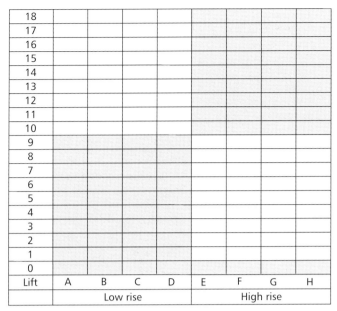

| | | | | | | | | |
|---|---|---|---|---|---|---|---|---|
| 18 | | | | | | | | |
| 17 | | | | | | | | |
| 16 | | | | | | | | |
| 15 | | | | | | | | |
| 14 | | | | | | | | |
| 13 | | | | | | | | |
| 12 | | | | | | | | |
| 11 | | | | | | | | |
| 10 | | | | | | | | |
| 9 | | | | | | | | |
| 8 | | | | | | | | |
| 7 | | | | | | | | |
| 6 | | | | | | | | |
| 5 | | | | | | | | |
| 4 | | | | | | | | |
| 3 | | | | | | | | |
| 2 | | | | | | | | |
| 1 | | | | | | | | |
| 0 | | | | | | | | |
| Lift | A | B | C | D | E | F | G | H |
| | Low rise | | | | High rise | | | |

**Figure 4.1** Arrangement of zones in high-rise and low-rise buildings

where $d_x$ is the sum of the heights of the un-served floors, i.e. the length of the express zone, (m).

For example, for the lift groups represented diagrammatically in Figure 4.1, $d_x$ would be zero for the low-rise group, and the sum of the floor heights of levels 1 to 9 for the high-rise group.

This approach is based on the assumption that the lift reaches full speed in its travel through the express zone (note the $2\, d_x/v$ term). If this is not the case, the RTT calculation will be optimistic, and a better approach would be to determine the actual flight time using the calculation described in section 4.2.1 or to use simulation.

## 4.2.5    Car loading

In a manual lift calculation, it is normally assumed that the lift fills with a fixed capacity factor (CF) of 80%. The calculation then enables the up-peak handling capacity (UPPHC) to be determined. If the calculated UPPHC is greater than passenger demand, the CF has to be reduced using an iterative procedure until the required UPPHC is achieved (refer to section 3.8 and Example 3.3). Using a computer, this iteration should be done automatically, so that the user enters the required value of UPPHC and the computer outputs the corresponding CF.

To determine the maximum practical loading of the car, divide the platform area by 0.21 m² per person (see Table 3.3).

This enhancement to the manual calculations deals with assumption 2 in section 4.2.1 above.

## 4.2.6    A computer based up-peak calculation

The complete up-peak calculation recommended for implementation in software is given in Appendix 4.A1. The same or similar calculations are implemented in a number of computer programs available commercially.

This enhancement to the manual calculations deals with Assumption 3 (unequal floor populations) in Section 4.2.1 above. Equation 4.13 in Appendix 4.A1 also suggests that Assumption 7 (traffic control not ideal) can be dealt with by increasing the round trip time by a percentage (LOSS) such as 5%–10%.

*Example 4.1*

Apply a computer program based on the discussion above to Example 3.3. For convenience the input data are repeated here.

Number of office floors ($N$) = 10; daily population (POP) = 753 persons; standard interfloor distance ($d_f$) = 4.0 m; number of lifts ($L$) = 4; rated capacity (CC) = 17 persons; rated speed ($v$) = 2.5 m/s; acceleration ($a$) = 0.7 m/s²; jerk ($j$) = 1.04 m/s³; $t_f(1)$ = 5.5 s; $t_{sd}$ = 0.5 s; $t_c$ = 3.0 s; $t_o$ = 2.5 s; $t_{ad}$ = 1.0 s; assume $t_p$ = 1.0 s.

Suppose for the system specified the passenger demand was 100 persons in 5 minutes what would be the interval and capacity factor?

The output results would be:

— Interval (INT) = 29.7 s

— Capacity factor (CF) = 58.3%

— Average number of passengers ($P$) in car = 9.9

— Average number of stops ($S$) = 6.5

— Average highest reversal floor ($H$) = 9.5

— Stopping time ($T^\star - d_H/v\,S$) = 9.2 s

— Standard performance time (see section 3.4.2) ($T$) = 10.5 s

This example design would be satisfactory for an office building as the interval is less than 30 seconds. As the capacity factor (car loading) is 58.3% the average passenger waiting times will generally be less than 25 seconds.

## 4.2.7    Beyond the up-peak calculation

The standard up-peak calculation is a valuable tool, but it is limited in its application. For example:

— The calculation considers only pure up-peak traffic, as discussed in section 3. This is not always the most demanding traffic flow in buildings. It is possible to extend the calculations to cope with other traffic conditions (see section 3.10), but these are of limited applicability.

— Up-peak traffic calculations are not directly applicable to many situations, e.g. in shopping centres, car parks, airports, hospitals, hotels and residential buildings.

— It presents an average solution rather than a design particular to specified installation.

— It relies on many simplifying and simplistic assumptions.

Two other methods are widely applied in computer programs: General Analysis[7] and simulation[8].

# 4.3 General Analysis

Alexandris et al.[1] (1979) considered the problem of analysing traffic patterns other than up-peak. Their approach was to model a multi-car system as a bulk service queuing problem. In order to do this they had to make a large number of assumptions. Peters[6] (1997) working from first principles has been able derive more plausible formulae. The mathematics is complex and was described in Appendix 4.A3 of the 2000 edition of this Guide.

General Analysis allows round trip time calculations to be performed for any peak traffic flow. This overcomes most of the limitations associated with conventional up-peak calculations. For example, General Analysis will allow assessment of:

— office buildings with car parks and basements

— hotel or residential buildings with two-way peak traffic

— shopping centres with heavy interfloor traffic

— offices with restaurants causing heavy peaks at lunch times

— double deck lifts.

The General Analysis technique can be programmed into a computer. A full implementation of the General Analysis method allows individual floor populations to be considered (assumption 3 in section 4.2.1) and for the specification of differing arrival rates at all floors. It is important to note, however, that all RTT calculations are designed to analyse 'peak' traffic situations, where there are traffic flows to and/or from the main terminal floor. If the traffic levels are low relative to the underlying handling capacity of the system being considered, the mathematical basis of the RTT calculation is no longer valid. Using the General Analysis method may result in low or zero results being obtained. This is a limitation of all round trip time calculations as non-peak traffic can only be analysed using simulation techniques.

General Analysis can be used to analyse up-peak, down peak and mid day traffic as these are heavy traffic conditions. The method provides improved results compared to the simple equations given in section 3.10.

*Example 4.2*

Repeat Example 4.1 using a program employing the General Analysis technique.

The results are shown in column 2 of Table 4.2. Column 3 shows the results for Example 4.1 and Column 4 the results for Example 3.3.

The results in Table 4.2 demonstrate that the interval and capacity factor calculated by the basic RTT method of section 3, the enhanced calculation method of section 4.2.6 and the General Analysis method (section 4.4.1) are very similar. The General Analysis results for $S$ and $H$ appear dissimilar. This is because in an up-peak analysis, the probability of the lift stopping at each of the upper floors is calculated. This provides a value for $S$. In the RTT equation, unity is added to $S$ to take into account the stop at the main terminal floor. In General Analysis it is not automatically assumed that the lift stops at the main terminal floor. It calculates the probability of the lift stopping at every floor. Thus, if analysing an up-peak traffic pattern using General Analysis, the value obtained for $S$ is greater by approximately one. Similarly for the value for $H$. The amended values are shown in parenthesis. When analysing other traffic conditions using the General Analysis technique, the actual number of stops will be presented, not simply those above the main terminal.

With General Analysis, the average lowest reversal floor ($l$) is also calculated. This is particularly important when analysing buildings with basements or other lightly used floors below the main terminal.

The results shown in Table 4.2 vary by a few percentage points for this particular example. Generally this is the case for all pure up-peak calculations. Thus, although the enhanced and General Analysis methods are more mathematically rigorous, the basic calculation method based on equation 3.1 is robust enough to give initial guidance for most design studies. Designers comparing different calculation programs and manual methods should not be unduly concerned when the results are not precisely the same.

**Table 4.2** Comparison of results

| Parameter | Example 4.2: General Analysis | Example 4.1: Enhanced computer-based calculation | Results from Example 3.3 |
|---|---|---|---|
| Interval (INT) | 28.7 s | 29.7 s | 28.6 s |
| Capacity factor (CF) | 56.3% | 58.3% | 59.4% |
| Average number of passengers in car ($P$) | 9.6 | 9.9 | 9.5 |
| Average number of stops ($S$) | 7.2 (6.2) | 6.5 | 6.3 |
| Average highest reversal floor ($H$) | 10.4 (9.4) | 9.5 | 9.5 |
| Lowest reversal floor ($l$) | 1.0 | N/A | N/A |
| Stopping time ($T^\star - d_H/v\,S$) | 9.2 s | 9.2 s | 8.9 s |
| Performance time ($T$) | 10.5 s | 10.5 s | 10.5 s |

## 4.4 Simulation of lift systems

### 4.4.1 Comparing round trip calculations and simulation

In simulation the whole process of passengers arriving at the landings, registering their landing call, boarding the lift when it arrives, registering their car call and then alighting at their destination is modelled.

Simulation has a number of advantages over round trip time calculations:

— Round trip time calculations simplify the analysis exercise in order to be able to formulate the problem in mathematical terms. Results are extrapolated from an 'average' trip in the 'average' round trip of a single lift. With simulation, every lift trip is modelled, thereby avoiding the need to work with average trips.

— Round trip time calculations give results in terms of the system 'interval', which is the average time between successive lift departures from the main terminal floor. Quality of service is better measured in terms of passenger waiting and transit times, which can be calculated by simulation.

— Simulation is visibly closer to 'real life' and therefore more intuitive. To the non-technical person, watching a simulation gives a far better understanding of the operation of the lift system. For example, an overloaded system in simulation will show queues forming at landings.

— Simulation can model the traffic control system (assumption 7 in section 4.2.1). Simulation programs normally have a range of control systems available and sometimes have an option for users to link in their traffic control algorithms. The choice of control system can significantly affect the results.

— Simulation can take account of system features such as dwell times (assumption 5), lobby times (assumption 6).

— The output results can be displayed in a wide range of tables and graphs.

Simulation can be used to analyse any peak traffic flow. In addition, it can be used to model:

— light (non-peak) traffic

— changing levels of traffic, e.g. the increasing levels of traffic as the work start time approaches in an office building

— mixed types of traffic, e.g. goods and passenger traffic using the same lifts.

With simulation, it is also possible to model unusual requirements, e.g. lifts in the same group with different speeds and sizes.

Simulation is not always appropriate. If a designer's brief is to select a lift installation for an office building using the design benchmarks (see section 3.3), e.g. 13% up-peak handling capacity and maximum 25-second interval, then the preferred approach would be to use a round trip time calculation. Introducing simulation can complicate a simple exercise. However, if the actual traffic flow is known, or can be estimated with some certainty, simulation will give a better indication of actual lift performance. Simulation is a particularly valuable modernisation tool, as actual lift performance and passenger traffic can be measured and modelled. This allows the benefits of modernisation to be assessed more realistically.

### 4.4.2 Running multiple simulations

If a simulation is to give the same results each time an analysis is run, the simulation must always generate the same list of passengers for the same input data. By running multiple simulations for the same data, simulation can mimic real life. This is because each simulation must generate a set of arriving passengers according to a random number sequence. With computers this sequence is provided by a pseudo random binary sequence number generator (PRBS). This sequence starts at a certain initial value, which can be changed by a process called 'seeding'. Thus when a number of multiple runs are carried out, with different seeds, different results are obtained. It is as if Monday, Tuesday, Wednesday, etc., simulations are being run. The results can then be averaged for all the simulations.

Without multiple simulations, this chance element in simulation means that changing a parameter, such as speed or door operating times can sometimes lead to performance results getting worse when it would be expected for them to improve (or vice versa). For example, consider two simulations with exactly the same data, except one simulation used lifts with a rated speed of 2.5 m/s and the other simulation used lifts with a rated speed of 1.6 m/s. In a single simulation with faster lifts, a group of passengers may miss a lift by less than a second, whereas in the simulation with the slower lifts they catch it. Sometimes the faster lifts perform less well than the slower lifts. The longer a simulation is run, the less effect this will have on the results. However, running multiple simulations is the best way to avoid counter-intuitive results.

When a simulation starts, the lifts are empty and have no calls. The lifts effectively have a 'head start'. It is possible to provide some 'conditioning' traffic prior to the analysis period, for example, by running the simulation for an extra five minutes and ignoring the results for the first five minute period. However, if the simulation is run for a sufficient length of time, for example, through the application of a template (see section 4.4.3), the effect of the head start becomes negligible.

### 4.4.3 Templates

Most simulation programs include templates to generate traffic for the common design profiles of up-peak, down peak, mid-day and interfloor traffic. This allows the designer to assess how the lift system performs against a specific building by referencing a table of preset percentages for traffic intensity and applying these to the building population entered by the designer. Templates provide a means to achieve this. Examples of the four major templates are described[4] in Appendix 4.A2.

Example 4.3 (Figure 4.2) shows a simulation using an up-peak template.

If the lifts cannot cope with the traffic defined, the longer the simulation run, the longer the passenger waiting times will become (as queue lengths will increase as time passes). If this is the case, the designer must consider whether this level of traffic will, in real life, be sustained for more than a short period. Example 4.4 (Figure 4.8) shows the simulation of an increasing traffic demand and the effect it has on performance.

### 4.4.4    Comparing simulation with round trip time calculations

When comparing round trip time calculations with simulations, it is important to note:

(1)    round trip time calculations make no allowance for door dwell times

(2)    round trip time calculations are based on averages and may be based on the assumption a car is loaded with say 9.9 persons; a simulation will only allow integer numbers of persons.

(3)    unless a round trip time inefficiency (%LOSS in Appendix 4.A1, equation 4.13) is used, round trip time calculations assume an ideal system with, for example, no bunching[2], door re-openings or other 'real life' delays.

To demonstrate consistency, it may therefore be necessary to marginally adjust variables in either the calculation or the simulation.

Also note that round trip time calculations are normally carried out to establish the maximum handling capacity of a system. Thus in simulation the modelling can be near or at the saturation point. When a simulation reaches saturation, long queues will form, with excessive waiting times, as will be seen in a real system.

### 4.4.5    Evaluating proprietary analysis software

Modern lift traffic analysis software packages provide engineers and designers with a powerful tool for determining the number of lifts required, their speed and the size of the cars. Programs available range from crude and very limited to sophisticated and complex. Thus it is important that a software evaluation exercise is carried out prior to making a purchase. It is recommended that answers to the following questions should be obtained as part of any software evaluation exercise:

—    Will the program run on the computer and operating systems intended to be used?

(*Note*: some programs require a particular version of a particular operating system, others will not run using that operating system.)

—    Is additional software needed to run the program, such as BASIC interpreter or spreadsheet program?

—    Does the program use round trip time formulae, simulation, or both?

—    Does the program use an iterative process to find the solutions for a level of passenger demand, e.g. 17% up-peak handling capacity, specified by the designer.

—    What traffic flows can the program analyse (e.g. up-peak, down peak etc.)?

—    Will the program analyse single and/or double deck lifts?

—    What are the inputs and outputs to the program?

(Compare these inputs and outputs with those discussed in sections 3 and 4 of this Guide. If the program omits some inputs it is important that the user is aware of, and satisfied with, the values used and/or assumptions made by the program. If the program omits some outputs, the user must be satisfied that these will not be required.)

—    Does the program provide spreadsheet and graphical output?

—    Does the program use a rigorous PRBS sequence?

—    Does the PRBS sequence provide a choice of probability distribution functions?

—    Does the program have an adequate random number generator to emulate floor demands?

—    Who are the authors?

—    What quality control procedures are in place to test the results are correct?

—    Is the program generally available?

—    What are the initial and on-going costs?

—    Is a detailed manual provided?

—    Is technical support available and, if so, from whom and at what cost?

—    Is the program copy-protected? If so, what form of protection is used?

—    Is user-training available and, if so, at what cost?

—    Is the source code available for review?

—    Are there future plans for upgrades, enhancements etc?

### 4.4.6    Comparing results between different simulation programs

When comparing the results of different simulation programs, note that there must be consistency between:

—    input parameters including traffic templates

—    definition of results

It should be possible to demonstrate consistency between lift simulation programs when 'like for like' analyses are being compared. Some benefits can be demonstrated by applying enhanced dispatching algorithms. However dramatic discrepancies should be examined closely and treated with caution.

Barney[3] (2003) has examined two commercially available simulation programs, one of which dates back to the early

1970s and the other to the 1990s. The graphical output data shown in Example 4.3 follows this examination.

## Example 4.3

Carry out a simulation against the data in Example 4.1 (section 4.2.7).

An up-peak template has been applied that rises and falls to the specified peak value of handling capacity, 13.3 % (100/753). A minimal door dwell time (0.5 s) has been used to provide some consistency with the RTT calculation, which does not take door dwell into account.

*Note*: to determine the maximum practical loading of the car, divide the platform area by 0.21 m² per person (see Table 3.3). This may be rounded to the nearest whole number. Depending on the simulation program being used, set the car size, passenger mass and capacity factor to allow this loading to be achieved. During the simulation it is acceptable for the maximum car load to be the maximum practical loading. However, it is preferable for the average load in any five minute period should not exceed 80% of the maximum practical loading.

The car size is 1275 kg. From Table 3.3, the platform area is 2.9 m², which divided by 0.21 m² per person yields 13.8 persons, i.e. 14 persons when rounded to the nearest whole number. (A simulation deals with integer numbers of passengers, thus the passenger values are rounded up.) If each passenger is assumed to weigh 75 kg and there are 14 persons in the car, the design capacity factor would be 83 % (14 × 75 / 1275). Then the average load would be 80% of 14 persons, i.e. 11 persons. It is preferable that the average load in any five minute period does not exceed this value.

The simulation is using a generic up-peak traffic controller (dispatcher). The simulation program has been run for ten separate simulations and the results presented are the average for the ten runs. The results are given below.

(*a*)    *Passenger demand*

See Figure 4.2.

(*b*)    *Spatial plot*

See Figure 4.3.

(*c*)    *Car loading*

See Figure 4.4.

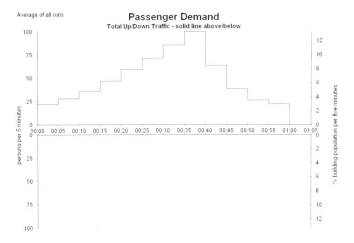

**Figure 4.2** Example 4.3: passenger demand through the application of a one hour up-peak template. The traffic rises to the peak value (13.3%) between 35 minutes and 40 minutes and then falls in 5-minute periods.

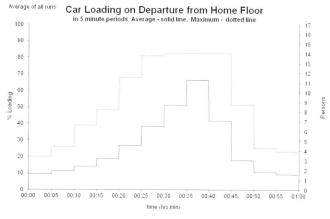

**Figure 4.4** Example 4.3: average and maximum car load when the car leaves the main terminal floor. Note that the car does load up to its maximum allowed load of 14 persons. But during the peak five minutes the average loading is close to 11 persons (80% of 14 persons is 11.2 persons).

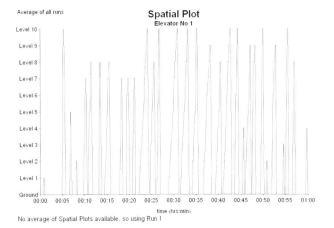

**Figure 4.3** Example 4.3: spatial plot of the movement of one lift during the one hour of activity. A typical staircase pattern can be seen, particularly around the busiest 5 minutes (35–40 minutes).

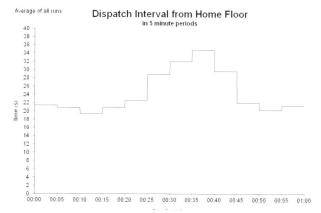

**Figure 4.5** Example 4.3: dispatch interval. It is calculated by counting the number of times a car is dispatched from the home floor in each five minute period. Then dividing this number into 300 seconds (i.e. five minutes).

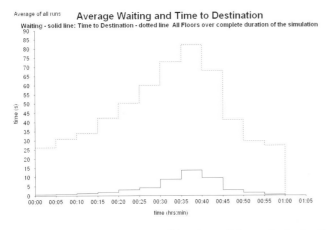

**Figure 4.6** Example 4.3: average waiting time and time to destination for each 5 minutes. The lower line is the average waiting time, peaking at 13.8 seconds, which is excellent service. The upper line is the average time to destination, peaking at 81.9 seconds. The difference between the two lines is the passenger travel time. The average time to destination is difficult to appreciate as it deals with the modal passenger's journey to half way up the building.

*(d)    Dispatch interval*

See Figure 4.5.

The dispatch interval corresponds directly to the interval calculated in round trip time calculations. It is measured in a simulation for each five minute period. It is calculated by counting the number of times a car is dispatched from the home floor in each five minute period. Then dividing this number into 300 seconds (i.e. five minutes). It will be noted that the calculation yielded an average interval of 28.5 seconds, whereas the simulation shows an interval of approximately 35 seconds. This is a reasonable correlation, as the simulation assumed an 'ideal' controller with 0% losses. In a simulation a good interval does not necessarily correspond to good performance. Conversely a poor interval does not imply a poor performance. For example, the interval may be 20 seconds, but if there are queues on the landing passengers may have to wait two or more intervals before there is enough space for them to get into a lift. Furthermore, in destination dispatch systems a good interval does not necessarily correspond to good passenger waiting times. This is because the passenger is not necessarily allocated to the next car to depart from the main terminal floor. To determine good performance it is necessary to examine passenger average waiting times as shown in Figure 4.6.

*(e)    Average waiting time and time to destination*

See Figure 4.6.

When applying a traffic template, it is important to monitor how the average passenger waiting and transit time varies over the period of analysis. Average results may hide a problem during the busiest period of the template. Figure 4.6 provides information about how long passengers wait for a lift and how long they take to reach their destinations.

Passenger waiting time is defined as the actual time a prospective passenger waits after registering a hall call (or entering the waiting queue if a call has already been registered) until the responding lift doors begin to open. If the responding lift doors are already open when a

passenger arrives, the waiting time for this passenger is taken as zero.

Passenger transit time is the time the responding lift doors begin to open to the time the doors begin to open again at the passenger's destination. If the responding lift doors are already open when a passenger arrives, the transit time for this passenger commences at the time the passenger arrived.

The time to destination is the passenger waiting time plus the passenger transit time.

*(f)    Distribution of passenger waiting times*

See Figure 4.7.

*Example 4.4*

Simulate an increasing traffic demand applied to the system described in Example 4.1 (section 4.2.7). This type of traffic template tests a lift installation through a range of demands. It is similar to the mathematical technique known as sensitivity analysis, where small perturbations (changes) are applied to a system under test to show its tolerance to those changes. An experienced designer can then determine the limiting values for the design. Figures 4.8 to 4.11 illustrate the design results.

*(a)    Passenger demand*

See Figure 4.8.

*(b)    Queue lengths*

See Figure 4.9.

*(c)    Car loading*

See Figure 4.10.

*(d)    Average passenger waiting and time to destination*

See Figure 4.11.

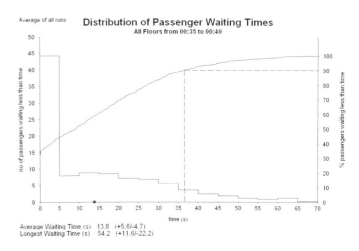

**Figure 4.7** Example 4.3: distribution of passenger waiting times for the peak five minutes (35-40 minutes). The average is 13.8, as stated above, and the ninety percentile is 37 seconds. This is a very reasonable distribution. The longest wait is 54.2 seconds.

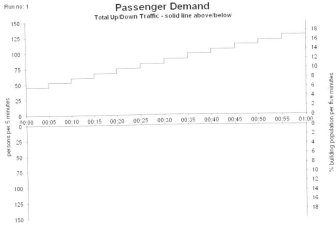

**Figure 4.8** Example 4.4: step profile showing an increasing passenger demand. The template represents an increasing up-peak demand from 6% to 17% in 1% increments. The underlying up-peak handling capacity from example 3.2 is 108 persons/5-minutes, i.e. with a population of 753 and a percentage demand of 14.3%. Thus the system should start to saturate at around 00:40 as it is presented traffic faster than it can take it away.

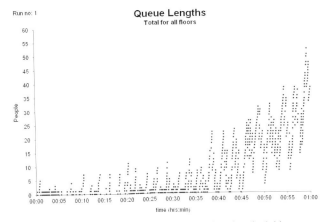

**Figure 4.9** Example 4.4: queue lengths showing that the lobby queue builds up as the demand increases

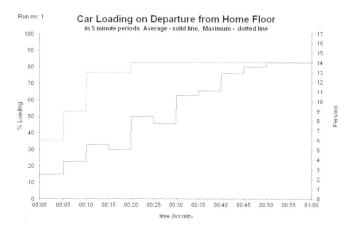

**Figure 4.10** Example 4.4: car loading on departure from the home floor. Once the system reaches saturation, every car leaves the main terminal full, thus the average and maximum loading converge.

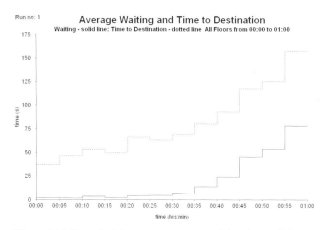

**Figure 4.11** Example 4.4: average passenger waiting time and time to destination; once the system reaches saturation the average passenger waiting times and times to destination increase rapidly to unacceptable values.

# 4.5 Measuring traffic

## 4.5.1 Why measure?

A pre-modernisation design exercise should begin with a traffic survey. All other input parameters to a calculation, or simulation, should also be measured on site. Simulation is an extremely powerful pre-modernisation tool, allowing designers to answer a number of 'what if' questions, such as:

— What is the effect of adding or removing cars from service?

— What will the performance be like during the modernisation when one or more cars are out of service?

— What benefit will increasing rated speed, door times, etc., have on waiting and transit times?

— Will improvement to the traffic control algorithm have any significant benefits?

Note the changes in dispatching algorithms may require the simulation of any faults in the existing systems, some of which may require input from the authors of the simulation program being applied, see section 4.6.3.

Simulation programs that allow for third parties to add their own dispatching algorithms can be applied to justify performance claims by suppliers.

In interpreting results, note the following:

— any differences between pre- and post- modernisation building populations

— modernisation may lead to a marginally increased demand on the system as people are more likely to take the lifts if the service is improved.

## 4.5.2 Automated traffic analysers

Simple traffic analysers are linked to the lift control system, and record the time every landing and car call is made and cleared. They analyse the data and provide a range of performance results and graphs. Modern control systems incorporate similar functionality. A range of traffic and performance measures can be determined, for example:

— average response time to landing calls by time of day

— distribution of response times

— distribution of car calls by floor.

These traffic analysers give an indication of a lift system's performance, but very limited information about the actual passenger traffic flow.

The main drawback of these simple systems is that they cannot identify all the peaks. This is because the analyser is counting up and down calls rather than the number of people using the lifts. In the morning there could be long queues in the lobby but the up landing button would only be pressed once for each carload. At other times of the day, and on other floors, a landing button could be pressed for just one passenger. For this reason, it is generally unreliable to use simple traffic analyser results to assess the demand on an existing system, or to evaluate the benefits of modernisation.

To provide really useful information, passenger traffic surveys must count or estimate the number of people transported as opposed to the number of calls registered.

To achieve this, some manufacturers have improved the technique by using information from passenger detection systems (light beams) and load weighing. Siikonen[10] presents an example of this for a multi-tenant office building in Paris. The survey results measured and stored by the group control system are reproduced in Figure 4.12. The lower section of the columns show the incoming traffic, the middle sections of the columns the interfloor traffic and the upper section of the columns outgoing traffic.

The lifts are busy throughout the working day. The results of the survey demonstrate predominately up traffic in the morning, a combination of heavy up and down traffic at lunchtime, and predominately down traffic in the evening. This is as expected for an office building. It should be noted that this traffic data has been collected in 15 minute (as opposed to 5 minute) intervals and that results are averages based on daily statistics. On a single day during the busiest 5 minutes, measured peaks could be higher.

Automated people-counting systems are not widely available, but new technology (infra-red, computer vision tracking systems) mean that a portable and cost effective system could be available in future years. In the meantime, most surveys will be manual.

### 4.5.3 Manual passenger traffic surveys

In manual surveys, observers count passengers in and out of the lifts. A manual survey requires at least one person at each main terminal floor and a person in at least one car.

Observers at the main terminal floor(s) should record the number of passengers loading/unloading the cars in five minute intervals. Observers in-car record the number of passengers loading and unloading the cars at each floor. Again, all data should be separated into five minute intervals. The main terminal count is required to count the main traffic flow accurately. The in-car count is required to sample the intensity of interfloor traffic.

Figure 4.13 shows the results of a traffic survey carried out during the lunch period of an office building. The lower section of the columns show the incoming traffic, the middle sections of the columns the interfloor traffic and the upper section of the columns outgoing traffic. In this survey the building management team advised that this was a quiet day owing to a forthcoming national holiday. Care must be taken to ensure that the basis of future designs is realistic. In practise this means surveying on more than one day, avoiding holidays, avoiding Mondays and Fridays, and preferably returning to the building at different times of the year.

The survey team should include a person able to identify faults and limitations in the existing system, for example:

— wasted stops due to the absence or failure of the load bypass system

— unnecessary stops due to more than one hall call riser in the system (e.g. people registering hall calls on both sets of buttons, resulting in two cars being sent to serve one person)

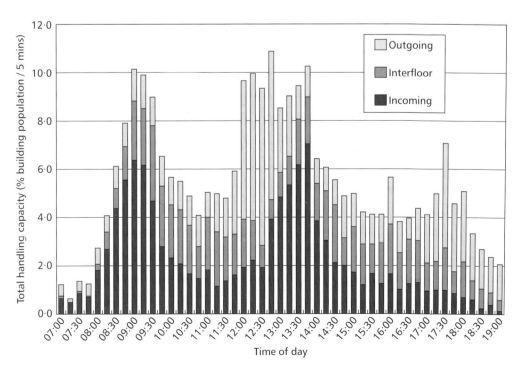

**Figure 4.12** Example automatic traffic measurements for a multi-tenant office building

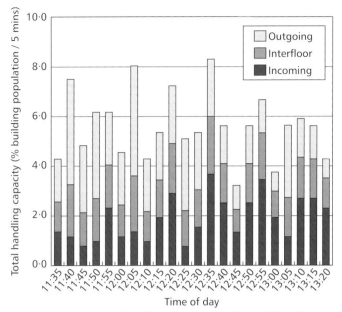

**Figure 4.13** Example results of a traffic survey in office building during the lunch period

— wasted car trips due to over active zoning systems continuously re-parking idle cars

— failure of systems to switch into an up-peak mode when there is predominant traffic from the main terminal floor; this can result in one or more cars being idle at upper floors, while at the same time there are queues forming at the main terminal

— failure of systems to switch into a down peak mode; this can result in lower floors in the building receiving no or very poor service during down peaks.

Additional important survey data are:

— net usable area

— nominal building population (current occupant numbers obtained from building management lists)

— design building population (from developer's brief)

— the actual building population on the day of the survey (from entry logs)

— existing lift handling capacity data (measured)

— design lift handling data (from installer's lift specification).

Useful background data are:

— gross and net lettable floor area of each floor

— attendance regime (fixed/flexitime)

— facilities in the building (restaurants, banks, shops etc.)

— proximity of mass transit transportation facilities (trains, buses, underground)

— nature of the accommodation (call centre, government office, commercial office, multinational company headquarters)

— type of occupant (single tenant, mixed sector, multiple tenancy).

— location (inner city, outer city, science park).

Before a survey is undertaken, it is important that observations or advice is taken to identify when the peak traffic flows occur. If it is intended to correlate different traffic conditions, e.g. up-peak to down peak, the surveys should be carried out on the same days.

If the surveys are to be credible it is also important that they are supervised by a person, who is experienced in carrying out research, has an understanding of lift systems.

Readers of this Guide are invited to submit their survey results to the CIBSE Lifts Group★ in the interests of improving the understanding of traffic in modern buildings, and to assist in improving future editions of this Guide. Survey forms and guidance will be offered for those prepared to share their survey results.

## 4.6    Describing traffic

In order to be able to input data into a simulation program it is necessary to consider ways in which complex lift traffic can described. Simple traffic is defined in terms of the percentage of the building population transported upwards or downwards in five minutes. Mixed traffic includes an element of people travelling to and from the main terminal floor, plus and element of interfloor traffic. This can be described by specifying a total arrival as a percentage of the building population over 5-minute periods. This total can then be split into three parts as follows:

— % up: the part of the total arrival rate that corresponds to passengers arriving at the main terminal, and travelling up the building (or down to any floors below the main terminal floor). Sometimes called 'entrance traffic'[9].

— % down: the part of the total arrival rate that corresponds to passengers arriving at floors above (or below) the main terminal floor, and travelling to the main terminal floor. Sometimes called 'exit traffic'[9]

— % interfloor: the part of the total arrival rate that corresponds to passengers travelling between floors other than the main terminal floor.

This approach is particularly useful for defining heavy traffic at mid-day. For example, the traffic in an office building could peak at 12% of the building population arriving over five minutes, with a split of 40% up, 40% down and 20% interfloor, i.e. 4.8%, 4.8% and 2.4% in terms of the up-peak handling capacity.

For complex traffic flows, a more sophisticated measure is needed and two further terms are required:

— the passenger arrival rate at floor $i$ (defined for each floor at which passengers may arrive

— the probability of the destination floor of passengers from floor i being the floor $j$ (defined for all possible values of $i$ and $j$).

This approach will result in a destination probability table similar to the example in Table 4.3 below.

★ www.cibseliftsgroup.org

**Table 4.3** Example arrival rate and destination probability table

| From/to | Arrival rate (persons per 5-minutes) | Destination probabilities for travel between stated levels (%) | | | | | | | |
|---|---|---|---|---|---|---|---|---|---|
| | | Level 0 | Level 1 | Level 2 | Level 3 | Level 4 | Level 5 | Level 6 | Level 7 |
| Ground | 25.2 | 0.0 | 14.3 | 14.3 | 14.3 | 14.3 | 14.3 | 14.3 | 14.3 |
| Level 1 | 2.4 | 50.0 | 0.0 | 8.3 | 8.3 | 8.3 | 8.3 | 8.3 | 8.3 |
| Level 2 | 2.4 | 50.0 | 8.3 | 0.0 | 8.3 | 8.3 | 8.3 | 8.3 | 8.3 |
| Level 3 | 2.4 | 50.0 | 8.3 | 8.3 | 0.0 | 8.3 | 8.3 | 8.3 | 8.3 |
| Level 4 | 2.4 | 50.0 | 8.3 | 8.3 | 8.3 | 0.0 | 8.3 | 8.3 | 8.3 |
| Level 5 | 2.4 | 50.0 | 8.3 | 8.3 | 8.3 | 8.3 | 0.0 | 8.3 | 8.3 |
| Level 6 | 2.4 | 50.0 | 8.3 | 8.3 | 8.3 | 8.3 | 8.3 | 0.0 | 8.3 |
| Level 7 | 2.4 | 50.0 | 8.3 | 8.3 | 8.3 | 8.3 | 8.3 | 8.3 | 0.0 |

# References

1  Alexandris N A *Statistical models in lift systems* PhD thesis (Manchester: University of Manchester Institute of Science and Technology) (1977)

2  Barney G C *Elevator Traffic Handbook* (section 12.6) (London: Spon Press) (2003)

3  ibid. ch. 16

4  Barney G C Traffic design — benchmarks standard templates *Elevator World* (February 2005)

5  Peters R D Ideal lift kinematics: derivation of formulae for the equations of motion of a lift *Int. J. of Elevator Engineers* **1** (1) (1996)

6  Peters R D *Vertical transportation planning in buildings* EngD thesis (Uxbridge: Brunel University) (1997)

7  Peters R D Lift traffic analysis: formulae for the general case *Building Serv. Eng. Res. Technol.* **11** (2) (1990)

8  Peters R D Simulation for control system design and traffic analysis (*Elevator Technology* 9) *Proc. ELEVCON '98* (International Association of Elevator Engineers) (1998)

10  Siikonen M-L On Traffic Planning Methodology (*Elevator Technology* 10) *Proc. ELEVCON 2000* (International Association of Elevator Engineers) (2000)

9  Powell B A Elevator Planning and Analysis on the Web (*Elevator Technology* 11) *Proc. ELEVCON 2001* (International Association of Elevator Engineers) (2001)

# Appendix 4.A1: Formulae

Rated capacity (CC):

$$CC = floor\left(\frac{RL}{m}\right) \tag{4.3}$$

where *floor* is a function meaning round down to the nearest whole number.

Number of passengers (*P*) in the lift:

$$P = \left(\frac{\%CF}{100}\right)CC \tag{4.4}$$

Effective building population (*U*):

$$U = \sum_{i=1}^{N} U_i \tag{4.5}$$

Highest reversal floor (*H*):

$$H = N - \sum_{j=1}^{N-1}\left(\sum_{i=1}^{j}\frac{U_i}{U}\right)^{P} \tag{4.6}$$

Probable number of stops (*S*):

$$S = N - \sum_{i=1}^{N}\left(1 - \frac{U_i}{U}\right)^{P} \tag{4.7}$$

Average passenger transfer time ($t_p$):

$$t_p = \frac{t_l + t_u}{2}$$

(4.8)

Travel distance to highest reversal floor ($d_H$):

$$d_H = \left( \sum_{i=0}^{\text{floor}(H-1)} h_i \right) + \left( H - \text{floor}(H) \right) h_{\text{floor}(H)}$$

(4.9)

Transit time function:

If: $\quad d \geq \dfrac{a^2 v + v^2 j}{j\,a}$ then: $\qquad t_f(d) = \dfrac{d}{v} + \dfrac{a}{j} + \dfrac{v}{a}$

(4.10)

If: $\quad \dfrac{2\,a^3}{j^2} \leq d < \dfrac{a^2 v + v^2 j}{j\,a}$ then: $\qquad t_f(d) = \dfrac{a}{j} + \sqrt{\dfrac{4d}{a} + \left( \dfrac{a}{j} \right)^2}$

(4.11)

If: $\quad d < \dfrac{2\,a^3}{j^2}$ then: $\qquad t_f(d) = \left( \dfrac{32\,d}{j} \right)^{\frac{1}{3}}$

(4.12)

Round trip time (RTT):

$$\text{RTT} = \left( \frac{2\,d_H}{v} + (S+1)\left( T^* - \frac{d_H}{vS} \right) + 2\,P\,t_p + \frac{2\,d_x}{v} \right)\left( 1 + \frac{\%\text{LOSS}}{100} \right)$$

(4.13)

where $T^* = t_f(d) + t_c + t_o + t_{sd} - t_{ad}$

Up-peak interval (UPPINT):

$$\text{UPPINT} = \frac{\text{RTT}}{L}$$

(4.15)

Up-peak handling capacity (UPPHC):

$$\text{UPPHC} = \frac{300\,P}{\text{UPPINT}}$$

(4.16)

Handling capacity expressed as percentage of building population (%POP):

$$\%\text{POP} = \frac{\text{UPPHC}}{U} \times 100$$

(4.17)

# Appendix 4.A2: Standard templates

## 4.A2.1    Introduction

The problem faced by most people when comparing traffic designs offered by lift companies, consultants, developers and others is that each design is based on different, often undeclared, criteria. The use of a set of agreed benchmarks would avoid this. Barney[4] has suggested a set of standard templates which can be used to describe the four major traffic patterns of up-peak, down-peak, mid-day and interfloor. These can be used to compare different designs and also to compare a before and after scenario in a modernisation and can be easily incorporated into most simulation programs.

## 4.A2.2    Standard up-peak traffic template

This template, see Figure 4.A2.1, represents the classical up-peak (see Figure 3.1) for a morning up-peak.

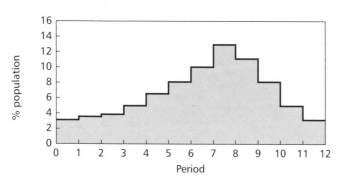

**Figure 4.A2.1** Standard up-peak traffic template

The template represents one hour in twelve 5-minute periods. It shows a rise in passenger arrivals from a low background level to a peak and then a fall back to the background level. The profile represents the arrival of 80% of the effective building population. Two-thirds (57%) are assumed to arrive before the peak and one-third (27%) after the peak. The peak occurs during the eighth 5-minute period. The value of the peak can be adjusted to meet the design value. The effect on the shape of the profile would be that a low arrival rate would result in a squatter profile and a high arrival rate would produce a sharper profile.

## 4.A2.3    Standard down-peak traffic template

This template, Figure 4.A2.2, represents the classical down peak (see Figure 3.1) for the evening outgoing traffic.

The template represents twelve 5-minute periods. It shows a rapid rise in passenger departures from a background level to a high demand, which then dies away. The profile represents 80% of the effective building population leaving during the peak hour. The peak is shown to occur at the third 5-minute period. The value of the peak can be

adjusted to represent the expected rate of departures. Normally this would be set to 1.6 times the design up-peak value. The effect on the shape of the profile would be that a low departure rate results in a squatter profile than a high departure, which would produce a sharper profile.

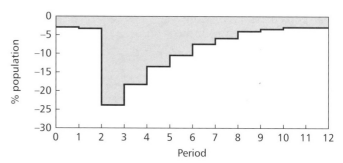

**Figure 4.A2.2** Standard down-peak traffic template

## 4.A2.4    Standard interfloor traffic template

See Figure 4.A2.3. There is no generally accepted interfloor profile. It has been considered that a 5-minute demand of 3% of the effective population is a busy system. This equates to a 36% demand over one hour, or one third of the effective building population using the lifts every hour.

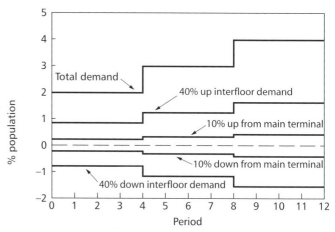

**Figure 4.A2.3** Standard interfloor traffic template

The template shows three levels of total demand in groups of four 5-minute periods. Periods 1–4 are at 2%, periods 5–8 are at 3% and the periods 9–12 are at 4%. The demand is a hybrid and is made up of 40% upward interfloor demand, 40% downward interfloor demand, 10% demand to the main terminal and 10% demand from the main terminal.

## 4.A2.5    Standard mid-day traffic template

See Figure 4.A2.4. There is no generally accepted mid-day traffic profile. The template proposed shows four 5-minute peaks. The strength of the four peaks are (respectively) equal to the up-peak design value, one and one third up-peak design value, one and two thirds up-peak design value and twice up-peak design value. The demand is a hybrid of 40% up demand, 40% down demand and 20% interfloor demand. In between the peaks the demand falls to a background level.

## 4.A2.6　Performance measurement

How is the performance determined? Using a simulation, the important parameter values of average interval, car load, average waiting time (AWT) and the ninety percentile (90-percentile) can be obtained and a judgement made. Table 4.A2.1 gives an indication of the parameters to be obtained. The values shown in the table are for illustration only.

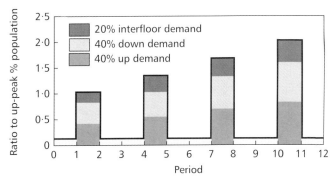

**Figure 4.A2.4** Standard mid-day traffic template

**Table 4.A2.1** Performance measurement (values for illustration only)

| Parameter | Traffic type | | | | | | |
|---|---|---|---|---|---|---|---|
| | Up-peak | Down-peak | Interfloor | Mid-day | | | |
| | Period 8 | Period 3 | Periods 1–12 | Period 2 | Period 5 | Period 8 | Period 11 |
| Interval (s) | 38 | 16 | N/A | N/A | N/A | N/A | N/A |
| Car load (%) | 100 | 62 | N/A | N/A | N/A | N/A | N/A |
| AWT (s) | 15 | 24 | 8 | 20 | 36 | 50 | 61 |
| 90-percentile (s) | 33 | 60 | 18 | 49 | 100 | 145 | 144 |

# 5 Types of lifts

## Principal author

John Carroll (Hoare Lea)

## Chapter contents

| | | |
|---|---|---|
| 5.1 | Introduction | 5-3 |
| 5.2 | Passenger and goods/passenger lifts | 5-4 |
| | 5.2.1 General | 5-4 |
| | 5.2.2 Applications of passenger and goods/passenger lifts | 5-5 |
| |    5.2.2.1 Airports | 5-5 |
| |    5.2.2.2 Car parks | 5-5 |
| |    5.2.2.3 Department stores | 5-5 |
| |    5.2.2.4 Entertainment centres, cinemas, theatres, sports centres, stadia and concert halls | 5-5 |
| |    5.2.2.5 Hospitals | 5-5 |
| |    5.2.2.6 Hotels | 5-6 |
| |    5.2.2.7 Offices | 5-6 |
| |    5.2.2.8 Railway stations | 5-6 |
| |    5.2.2.9 Residential buildings | 5-7 |
| |    5.2.2.10 Residential care homes and nursing homes | 5-7 |
| |    5.2.2.11 Shopping centres | 5-7 |
| |    5.2.2.12 Universities and other education buildings | 5-8 |
| | 5.2.3 Car size and payloads | 5-8 |
| | 5.2.4 Entrances, car fittings and finishes | 5-8 |
| | 5.2.5 Types of drive and operating speeds | 5-9 |
| |    5.2.5.1 Traditional electric traction drive | 5-9 |
| |    5.2.5.2 Hydraulic drive | 5-9 |
| |    5.2.5.3 Machine room-less (MRL) electric traction drive | 5-10 |
| | 5.2.6 Well | 5-10 |
| | 5.2.7 Machine rooms | 5-10 |
| |    5.2.5.1 Traditional electric traction drive | 5-10 |
| |    5.2.7.2 Hydraulic lifts | 5-10 |
| |    5.2.7.3 Machine room-less lifts | 5-11 |
| 5.3 | Goods lifts | 5-11 |
| | 5.3.1 General | 5-11 |
| | 5.3.2 Applications for goods lifts | 5-11 |
| |    5.3.2.1 Airports | 5-11 |
| |    5.3.2.2 Car parks | 5-11 |
| |    5.3.2.3 Department stores | 5-11 |
| |    5.3.2.4 Entertainment centres, cinemas, theatres, sports centres, stadia and concert halls | 5-11 |
| |    5.3.2.5 Hospitals | 5-11 |
| |    5.3.2.6 Hotels | 5-12 |
| |    5.3.2.7 Offices | 5-12 |
| |    5.3.2.8 Railway stations | 5-12 |
| |    5.3.2.9 Residential buildings | 5-12 |
| |    5.3.2.10 Residential care homes and nursing homes | 5-12 |
| |    5.3.2.11 Shopping centres | 5-12 |
| |    5.3.2.12 Universities and other education buildings | 5-12 |
| | 5.3.3 Car sizes and payloads | 5-12 |
| | 5.3.4 Entrances, car fittings and finishes | 5-13 |
| | 5.3.5 Types of drive and operating speeds | 5-13 |
| |    5.3.5.1 Electric traction drive | 5-13 |
| |    5.3.5.2 Hydraulic drive | 5-14 |
| |    5.3.5.3 Machine room-less electric traction drive | 5-14 |

|          | 5.3.6  | Well dimensions and construction | 5-14 |
|          | 5.3.7  | Machine room | 5-14 |
|          |        | 5.3.7.1  Traditional electric traction lifts | 5-15 |
|          |        | 5.3.7.2  Hydraulic lifts | 5-15 |
|          |        | 5.3.7.3  Machine room less lifts | 5-15 |
|          |        | 5.3.7.4  Rack and pinion lifts | 5-15 |
| 5.4      | Observation lifts | | 5-15 |
|          | 5.4.1  | General | 5-15 |
|          | 5.4.2  | Application of observation lifts | 5-16 |
|          |        | 5.4.2.1  Airports | 5-17 |
|          |        | 5.4.2.2  Car parks | 5-17 |
|          |        | 5.4.2.3  Department stores | 5-17 |
|          |        | 5.4.2.4  Entertainment centres, cinemas, theatres, sports centres, stadia and concert halls | 5-17 |
|          |        | 5.4.2.5  Hospitals | 5-17 |
|          |        | 5.4.2.6  Hotels | 5-17 |
|          |        | 5.4.2.7  Offices | 5-17 |
|          |        | 5.4.2.8  Railway stations | 5-17 |
|          |        | 5.4.2.9  Residential buildings | 5-17 |
|          |        | 5.4.2.10  Residential care homes and nursing homes | 5-17 |
|          |        | 5.4.2.11  Shopping centres | 5-17 |
|          |        | 5.4.2.12  Universities and other education buildings | 5-17 |
|          | 5.4.3  | Car size and payload | 5-17 |
|          | 5.4.4  | Entrances, car fittings and finishes | 5-17 |
|          | 5.4.5  | Types of drive and operating speeds | 5-18 |
|          | 5.4.6  | Well | 5-18 |
|          | 5.4.7  | Machine room | 5-18 |
| 5.5      | Service lifts | | 5-19 |
|          | 5.5.1  | General | 5-19 |
|          | 5.5.2  | Applications | 5-19 |
|          | 5.5.3  | Car size and payload | 5-19 |
|          | 5.5.4  | Entrances, car fittings and finishes | 5-19 |
|          | 5.5.5  | Types of drive and operating speeds | 5-20 |
|          | 5.5.6  | Well | 5-20 |
|          | 5.5.7  | Machine room | 5-20 |
| 5.6      | Motor vehicle lifts | | 5-21 |
|          | 5.6.1  | General | 5-21 |
|          | 5.6.2  | Applications | 5-21 |
|          | 5.6.3  | Car sizes and payloads | 5-21 |
|          | 5.6.4  | Entrances, car fittings and finishes | 5-21 |
|          | 5.6.5  | Types of drive and operating speeds | 5-22 |
|          | 5.6.6  | Well | 5-22 |
|          | 5.6.7  | Machine room | 5-23 |
| 5.7      | Rack and pinion lifts | | 5-23 |
|          | 5.7.1  | General | 5-23 |
|          | 5.7.2  | Applications | 5-23 |
|          | 5.7.3  | Car size and payload | 5-24 |
|          | 5.7.4  | Entrances, car fittings and finishes | 5-24 |
|          | 5.7.5  | Types of drive and operating speeds | 5-24 |
|          | 5.7.6  | Runway | 5-24 |
|          | 5.7.7  | Machinery location | 5-25 |
| 5.8      | Lifts for other purposes | | 5-25 |
|          | 5.8.1  | Firefighting lifts | 5-25 |
|          | 5.8.2  | Evacuation lifts | 5-26 |
|          | 5.8.3  | Passenger lifts for use by persons with disabilities | 5-26 |
|          | 5.8.4  | Lifting platforms for use by persons with disabilities | 5-27 |
|          | 5.8.5  | Stairlifts for use by persons with disabilities | 5-27 |
|          | 5.8.6  | Explosion protected lifts | 5-28 |
|          | 5.8.7  | Scissor lifts | 5-28 |
|          | 5.8.8  | Inclined lifts | 5-29 |
| 5.9      | Future concepts | | 5-29 |
| References | | | 5-30 |
| Appendix 5.A1: Car, well, headroom, pit and machine room sizes | | | 5-31 |

# 5 Types of lifts

## 5.1 Introduction

In the modern building, vertical transportation takes on an increasingly important role to ensure the efficient movement of all potential occupants is achieved. This is achieved by providing passenger lifts with adequate capacity and performance as well as additional lifts to provide goods service, firefighting and evacuation and other building servicing functions. Chapter 2 indicates the circulation requirements and Chapters 3 and 4 detail how the correct number and size of lifts are established for a building. This chapter looks at the different types of lifting systems and provides advice on the planning and design of each type.

Within the UK, lifts are typically provided for passenger service by using either an electric geared or gearless traction (see Figure 5.1) or hydraulic drive arrangement (see Figure 5.2). Rack and pinion drives (see Figure 5.7) offer an alternative, worthy of consideration, for some very large goods lifts or where the use of hydraulic or electric traction lifts are otherwise not practical. Paternoster systems, consisting of a number of open cars (no doors) moving continuously in a single well, are now obsolete. A few systems are still operating in the UK and no new systems have been installed for many years, the relevant British Standard having been withdrawn. For these reasons, paternoster systems are not considered in this Guide.

At the time of writing the 2000 edition of Guide D, the Lifts Regulations 1997[36] had only just (1 July 1999) become mandatory for new lifts. Today, all new passenger lift systems installed within the UK must satisfy the Essential Health and Safety Requirements (EHSRs) laid down in the Lifts Regulations 1997. This ensures the installation provides the necessary levels of safety. The EHSRs can be achieved by designing and installing the lift, either in accordance with harmonised standards such as BS EN 81-1[2] or BS EN 81-2[3], or by obtaining approval from a Notified Body for any parts of the design or installation which do not comply with these standards.

As well as the BS EN 81 series of harmonised European standards, some British Standards remain current (see section 17) and should be applied as necessary to installations in the UK. In particular, code of practice BS 5655 Part 6[19] provides useful guidance to the selection and installation of new lifts and BS 7255[24] is the primary standard for safe working on lifts.

The economic life cycle for the types of system depends upon the original design duty and standard of maintenance employed. Typically, a 20–25 year life span can be anticipated for traditionally engineered lift systems, whilst life spans of less than 15 years might be more realistic for package lifts that are mass produced using lightweight materials to keep down costs. During the normal life cycle of all types of lift systems, oil seals, suspension ropes, bearings and other components subject to wear will require maintenance and possibly replacement as part of an ongoing modernisation programme (see section 16).

The type, speed, load and layout of the lift system all contribute to the user's perception of the service provided. The lift car finishes need to suit the particular application to project the required impression, be it the strength and durability of a goods lift or various levels of refinement for passenger lifts. The design, however, must be practical from the users' point of view and pushbuttons and fixtures, for example, should be selected not only on the basis of appearance but also their practicality. Compliance with any relevant disabled access codes such as BS EN 81-

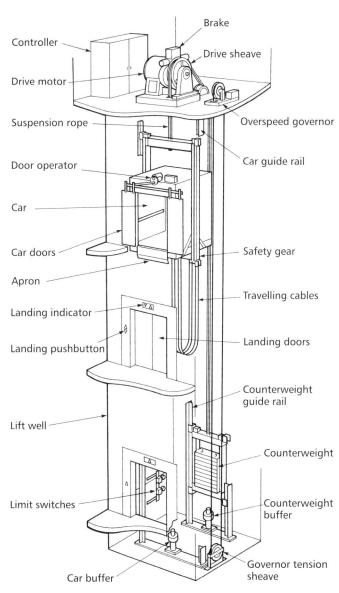

Controller

Drive motor

Brake

Drive sheave

Suspension rope

Overspeed governor

Door operator

Car guide rail

Car

Car doors

Safety gear

Apron

Landing indicator

Travelling cables

Landing pushbutton

Landing doors

Counterweight guide rail

Lift well

Counterweight

Limit switches

Counterweight buffer

Car buffer

Governor tension sheave

**Figure 5.1** Electric traction passenger lift; principal components

70[9] and Building Regulations Approved Document M[29] to ensure compliance with the Disability Discrimination Act 1995[33] must be considered from both the functional and aesthetic point of view, see section 11.

BS ISO 4190-1[14] for passenger lifts and BS ISO 4190-2[15] for goods lifts set out the recommended dimensions of cars and wells for lifts of various standard capacities and dimensional configurations. These sizes may be fine-tuned in negotiation with the lift supplier to suit the particular circumstances. Some manufacturers now offer lift cars with variable dimensions to satisfy non-standard lift dimensions, however non-standard arrangements generally incur higher design and production costs and should be avoided unless there are good reasons for deviating from the standard BS ISO 4190 dimensions.

Over recent years the range of machine room-less lifts (MRL) has expanded and all major manufacturers are now able to provide MRL products. MRL products and equipment is now available from component and package suppliers to enable independent companies to supply MRL lifts. The development of more compact, powerful drives and machines for MRL lifts mean they are now widely available for applications up to 1600 kg capacity and speeds of 1.75 m/s with some capable of 2000 kg capacity and 2500 kg for application in lower speed MRL goods lifts. Care should be taken when designing for MRL lifts as the accommodation of drives and control equipment within the lift well sometimes means the lift well dimensions need to be larger than those recommended by BS ISO 4190, whilst other dimensions may be smaller. Chapter 6 of BS EN 81-1[2] and BS EN 81-2[3] was amended in 2004 (Amendment 2) to update the requirements for machine spaces and machine rooms for MRL lifts.

The modern passenger lift appears, or should appear, to be a simple means of transport within a building. This apparent simplicity belies a complex and sophisticated mechanical, electrical and microelectronic system. Passengers and owners expect safe, comfortable, trans-portation, which is always in service.

—   *Safety*: the motion of the doors should be smooth and safety devices should be provided to ensure that passengers entering or leaving the lift car will not be injured if the doors start to close. The levelling of the car to the landing floor should not constitute a tripping hazard and should allow easy movement of any wheeled objects such as trolleys, wheelchairs or pushchairs etc.

—   *Comfort*: the ride between floors should have acceptable levels of acceleration and jerk (i.e. rate of change in acceleration) and vibration should be kept to a minimum. Quiet operation of the doors and noise levels during travel are important factors in overall passenger comfort. Noise levels emitted on to landings must also be kept to a minimum since some buildings do not have lift lobbies, see section 12.12.

—   *Service*: passengers regard waiting time as the appropriate measure of quality of service for a lift system. However, whilst this is becoming easier to predict using proprietary computer simulation software, most designers still adopt traditional calculations based on round trip time calculations to quantify performance levels in terms of a theoretical interval time, related to handling capacity, see sections 3 and 4.

Safety must be ensured at all times and this applies equally to passengers and to persons working on a lift, e.g. service personal, surveyors, consultants, inspectors, etc. It is also important that any goods transported, are safe from damage and that the lift does not degrade the environment in which it operates. Any alterations to suit particular or special circumstances must not jeopardise the provision of good, safe access to equipment after installation, since it will be necessary to carry out in-service maintenance and repairs to the equipment during the life of the installation. The final equipment layout must also take into account the space requirements for possible replacement of major components in the future. This is particularly important with MRL equipment where maintenance operations that would previously have occurred in a protected and nor-mally spacious machine room are carried out within the confines of the car top or from inside the car. In addition more activities may be required from landing levels where control, or emergency operating equipment, may be located.

The type of building and the potential traffic demand will determine the choice of control for the lift system. After consideration of any special client requirements or traffic patterns, the vertical transportation designer should select a suitable control system (e.g. single button, down collective, full collective or group control). In addition, the use of hall call allocation systems is becoming more wide spread and these too can be considered for non-public installations, see section 9.4.2.3.

The following sections offer guidance to the selection of the type of lift most suitable for the application being considered. Reference should be made to section 7, which describes individual components in detail.

## 5.2    Passenger and goods/passenger lifts

### 5.2.1    General

Lift suppliers offer ranges of products from 'pre-engineered' lifts to one-off systems tailored to individual requirements. Pre-engineered lifts offer a limited choice of options of styling and function but the production line methods used in manufacture help to reduce costs. Custom-tailored systems are appropriate for more complex applications in which a more sophisticated design is required. With custom or one-off designs, the price reflects the higher design and production costs and longer manufacturing and delivery times will be required.

With the introduction of modern, versatile micro-processor-controlled lift systems it is possible to tailor lift groups to different types of buildings. However, the lift drive, door control and group control must be correctly specified to ensure that the required quality of lift service and safety is provided for the customer and the passenger.

The main applicable standards for passenger lifts and goods/passenger lifts are BS EN 81-1[2] for electric traction lifts and BS EN 81-2[3] for hydraulic lifts. Passenger lifts are designed to carry passengers and although they may occasionally carry goods this is not their primary purpose. Goods/passenger lifts transport both passengers and goods. If used mainly for passenger service they may have fixings for drapes to protect the car interior, or may be more robustly fitted out. When goods/passenger lifts are part of a group they may also be provided with extra controls to enable goods service operation. This section deals with the transportation of passengers. Where lifts are designated specifically as goods lifts, with or without accompanying persons, then section 5.3 should be consulted.

## 5.2.2 Applications of passenger and goods/passenger lifts

Within the UK there are twelve main types of buildings, each with differing requirements for passenger lifts, (see also sections 2.6 and 3.13). These are listed alphabetically for easy reference and thus the order does not represent the relative number of lifts installed in a particular building type.

Where reference is made to disability requirements readers should refer to BS EN 81-70[9], the Disabilities Discrimination Act[33] and Part M of the Building Regulations[29]. Where reference is made to vandal resistance readers should refer to BS 5655: Part 13[20] and BS EN 81-71[10].

### 5.2.2.1 Airports

See also sections 2.6.1 and 3.13.1.

Airports are often low-rise structures, but lifts are essential for passengers with baggage and persons with disabilities. The size of the lifts should be as large as possible to cater for passengers with baggage and to provide space for other passengers. Lifts that can accommodate one or two baggage trolleys are not suitable. The recommended minimum size for a lift is 2000 kg, which will easily provide compliance with the recommendations of BS EN 81-70[9] for wheelchair access.

The major operational difference is likely to be in the control of the lift doors. These should have a door opened period (dwell time) sufficiently long to ensure that the doors do not close on passengers, or their baggage. However, long door times will detract from the efficiency of the lift system and this needs to be considered in determining the number, size and speed of the lifts.

As many of the people who visit an airport will be unfamiliar with the layout of the building, suitable signage must be provided, giving clear directions to the lifts and the stairs at all levels.

### 5.2.2.2 Car parks

See also sections 2.6.2 and 3.13.2.

Of all passenger lift types, car park lifts are probably subjected to the greatest misuse. Unlimited public access, combined with limited supervision, means that vandal resistant fixtures are essential. Passenger detection equipment is recommended to electronically control the doors owing to the significant use of shopping trolleys, prams, walking aids, etc. A reasonable number of lifts should provide facilities for disabled persons. Consideration should be given, to incorporating additional security such as anti-'surfing' devices that sound an alarm and prevent the movement of the lift, in the event of intruders accessing the lift car roof or the pit area.

### 5.2.2.3 Department stores

See also sections 2.6.3 and 3.13.3.

Department stores may be situated in high streets, where they must make independent provision, or in retail developments where they may rely on the lift provision of the shopping centre. The lifts will be used by people carrying shopping or pushing trolleys and also by people with pushchairs or wheelchairs. They should therefore be sized to carry a minimum of 13 persons (1000 kg) and preferably 17 persons (1275 kg) in order to provide adequate capacity for unattended wheelchair access in accordance with BS EN 81-70[9]. The design recommendations made in BS EN 81-70 to facilitate use by disabled persons should also be considered.

The finishes should provide a pleasant environment in keeping with the general surroundings whilst providing the necessary contrasting details to offer maximum usability to passengers with any visual impairment. The doors should be electronically controlled to ensure that the lifts are accessible to people with trolleys, push chairs and wheel chairs and incorporate full height, electronic, non-contact safety edges.

Larger department stores will incorporate a combination of lifts and escalators to provide an efficient transportation system.

### 5.2.2.4 Entertainment centres, cinemas, theatres, sports centres, stadia and concert halls

See also sections 2.6.4 and 3.13.4.

With the exception of stadia, this application generally makes little demand for passenger lift provision with lifts mainly provided to cater for disabled access.

Modern stadia, however, often incorporate extensive conference, banqueting and corporate entertaining facilities as well as large media centres. These facilities are often spread over a number of floors and lifts will be required to provide access from the entrance level for guests and visitors.

The nature of the events hosted within stadia, involves heavy traffic flows as people arrive and leave after events. Lifts should be supplemented with easily accessible stairs and consideration can be given to escalators to deal with the high volumes of people.

### 5.2.2.5 Hospitals

See also sections 2.6.5 and 3.13.5.

The passenger lifts in hospitals serve two distinct functions:

— transportation of patients (including those being moved on beds and trolleys)

— transportation of the staff and visitors.

The provision of dedicated lifts for each function is often not possible due to financial constraints and therefore a dual role can be achieved by incorporating special control features which allow the staff to call lifts out of normal passenger service to serve as bed lifts (priority control). The waiting time for lifts on bed service must be very short since this control mode will be required for emergencies.

The transportation of patients requires lifts that provide a smooth ride and, therefore, the acceleration and jerk (rate of change of acceleration) should be kept low. The operation of the doors must allow for the potentially slow movement of passengers into and out of the lift car. The lift door safety edges should be of the electronic (non-contact) type, as any contact with an infirm or elderly patient should be avoided. These considerations will affect the performance of these lifts and must be considered when determining the quantity, size and speed of lifts required for any particular project. The lift groups should be able to perform efficiently during visiting times where, depending on hospital visiting policy, the building population may double within a period of 30 minutes.

For the general public, the car interior should have clear and concise indication of floor and ward locations. Cars should also be designed to be easy to clean and vandal resistant, and incorporate the relevant recommendations of BS EN 81-70[9] for compliance with the Disability Discrimination Act 1995[33]. Lifts in hospitals should have suitable lobbies that are recessed from any walkways, corridors or streets to ensure that waiting passengers do not interfere with other traffic flows through the hospital.

Other lifts, in addition to the passenger lifts, will be required to provide hygienic and 'dirty' service paths, meal and housekeeping activities and general goods service. In addition to the BS ISO 4190-1/2[14,15], further information on lift car dimensions to suit the movement of beds and trolleys is available in Health Building Note HBN 40[34] and additional design information specific to lifts in hospitals is available in Health Technical Memorandum HTM 2024[35].

### 5.2.2.6    Hotels

See also sections 2.6.6 and 3.13.6.

The requirements of passenger lifts and goods/passenger lifts (used by guests with luggage and staff for service) for a hotel are different to those for offices and the company or hotel image will be reflected in the quality and design of the lifts.

The major operational difference is likely to be in the control of the lift doors. These may have a longer door opened period (dwell time) than other public lifts to ensure that the doors do not close on passengers, or their luggage, thereby giving the use of the lift a more relaxed image. The slower door systems will detract from the efficiency of the lift system and this needs to be considered in determining the number, size and speed of the lifts. In hotels, the level of service with regard to interval and waiting time is not expected to be as high as that in commercial buildings.

The sizing of guest lifts in hotels should be generous to cater for passengers with baggage and to afford the necessary comfort levels for guests. The minimum recommended car size for a hotel passenger lift is 1275 kg, which will also provide compliance with the recommendations of BS EN 81-70[9] for wheelchair access.

Since many of the people who visit a hotel will be unfamiliar with the layout of the building, suitable signage must be provided, giving clear directions to the lifts and the stairs at all levels.

### 5.2.2.7    Offices

See also sections 2.4 and 3.13.7.

The prime objective when providing lifts in a commercial office is to transport passengers quickly and efficiently to their places of work. The quality of service in terms of the lift interval and passenger waiting time should be high. The psychological effects of long waiting times on the user can be significant. Long waiting times will also result when large queues build up during peak periods which reflects badly on the building and can affect the marketability of the premises.

The number of lifts, car size, type, speed, type of drive, drive control and door control will all affect the efficiency of the lift system.

The aesthetic aspects of the lift system, e.g. call buttons, position indicators, car interiors and the ride comfort, reflect the company's image and must harmonise with the architecture. The design must also consider passengers with special needs in accordance with the recommendations of BS EN 81-70[9] for compliance with the Disability Discrimination Act 1995[33].

### 5.2.2.8    Railway stations

See also sections 2.6.8 and 3.13.8.

Surface railway stations are low-rise and usually provide access for persons with disabilities. The able-bodied are expected to use the stairs or escalators where provided. In addition to the primary lift safety standards, Train Operating Companies (TOCs) adopt special codes published by Network Rail which are designed to provide equipment with a minimum life span of 25 years and it will be found that model lifts are generally not suitable for use in railway environments.

Underground stations are often very deep and passenger lift provision is poor to non-existent with only recently constructed stations offering passenger lifts as a matter of course. New stations should incorporate lifts to provide compliance with BS EN 81-70[9], the Disabilities Discrimination Act[33] and Part M of the Building Regulations[29].

The underground environment of stations is very dusty and the confined conditions introduce additional risks in terms of safety and reliability. Underground train operators such as London Underground Limited or the New York City Transit Authority address the special requirements with prescriptive codes and standards and, again, model lifts will not normally be accepted for such applications.

The poor provision within many existing underground stations may have to change in order to assist the elderly and persons with disabilities, as required by the requirements of the Disabilities Discrimination Act. However the structural implications will make this very difficult and will limit the level of compliance that can be achieved.

### 5.2.2.9 Residential buildings

See also sections 2.6.9 and 3.13.9.

Modern architectural and design concepts demand careful consideration of the needs of the people using a building. This is particularly true for residential buildings, which should provide a pleasant and safe environment for the occupants.

A well-designed residential building ensures that its inhabitants can easily and safely move within the building. Parents with children and shopping, the elderly and especially those with special needs should be provided with a convenient and reliable means of transport.

The requirements of the Disability Discrimination Act 1995[33] mean that reasonable provision must be made to enable all people to be able to access residential premises. All new multi-storey residential developments should incorporate lifts or some other suitable means of access to upper storeys.

Therefore where a single lift will provide the necessary performance for the population levels and size of a particular residential building, consideration should be given to the height and demographics of potential residents to ensure that in the event of the only lift failing, residents could be reasonably expected to walk up to their respective accommodation levels. For this reason a single lift should only be considered in buildings with four or five levels above the entry level. Beyond this it may be considered unreasonable to expect all passengers to be able to walk up stairs in the event of a lift failure and two lifts should be considered in residential buildings above five storeys.

Where the layout of the building requires separate lifts, perhaps at each end of a long block, consideration should be given to linking these with a public corridor to provide redundancy in the event of lift failures.

The required performance and aesthetic appeal of lifts will vary according to the nature of the accommodation, e.g. luxury apartments or local authority housing.

If the access to the lifts is not restricted, as in the case of many local authority buildings, the car fixtures and fittings should be robust in design and vandal resistant. Consideration should also be given, to incorporating additional security such as anti-'surfing' devices that sound an alarm and prevent movement of the lift, in the event of intruders accessing the lift car roof or the pit area.

### 5.2.2.10 Residential care homes and nursing homes

See also sections 2.6.10 and 3.13.10.

The passenger lift requirements for care and nursing homes will vary greatly depending on the type of premises. Many homes are large, old properties converted from domestic housing stock that make them unsuitable for accommodating conventional lifts. In such cases, vertical transportation will be provided by lifting platforms and stairlifts.

Modern purpose-built care homes should be designed with conventional lifts where necessary and consideration should be given to providing 1000 kg (13-person) lifts capable of accommodating stretchers or beds.

Due to the likelihood of elderly and infirm passengers, designers should consider fitting folding seats and low level alarm pushes for passengers who may be prone to falling. In many homes, the alarm system within the lift car will be arranged to link into the emergency nurse call system normally provided in care and nursing homes.

### 5.2.2.11 Shopping centres

See also sections 2.5 and 3.13.11.

With the recent trend for large urban and suburban retail developments, there is a growing demand for lift installations in shopping centres. Often, modern shopping centres incorporate a mixture of conventional passenger lifts with observation lifts in large atria, to enhance the overall aesthetics of the centre. See also section 2.5.

Lifts in public shopping areas will be used by people carrying shopping or pushing trolleys and also by people with pushchairs or wheelchairs. They should therefore be sized to carry a minimum of 13 persons (1000 kg) and preferably 17 persons (1275 kg) in order to provide adequate capacity for unattended wheelchair access in accordance with BS EN 81-70[9]. The design recommendations made in BS EN 81-70 to facilitate use by disabled persons should also be considered.

Careful consideration should be given at the design stage to the finishes, which should be durable, and the fixtures and fittings, which need to be robust and vandal resistant. The finishes should also provide a pleasant environment in keeping with the general surroundings whilst providing the necessary contrasting details to offer maximum usability to passengers with any visual impairment.

The doors should be electronically controlled to ensure that the lifts are accessible to people with trolleys, push chairs and wheel chairs and incorporate full height, electronic, non-contact safety edges.

Shopping centres usually incorporate a combination of lifts and escalators to provide an efficient transportation system.

#### 5.2.2.12    Universities and other education buildings

See also sections 2.6.12 and 3.13.12.

Universities have a variety of building types from low-rise to tower blocks. The use of these building types varies from residential accommodation (halls of residence), conference facilities with hotel style accommodation, bars, restaurants, lecture blocks, laboratory areas and office accommodation. The need for passenger lifts should be assessed based on the building types considered in the previous sections.

### 5.2.3    Car size and payloads

BS EN 81-1/2[2,3] requires that all lift cars display a notice detailing the carrying capacity of the lift in terms of the number of passengers and the rated load in kilograms. These European standards assume each passenger has a mass of 75 kg for this purpose and Tables 1.1 and 1.2 in these standards are provided to ensure lift cars are rated according to the available floor area. The rated load of a hydraulic goods/passenger lift can be to Table 1.1A of BS EN 81-2, which permits a lower rated load/available car area ratio. This permits the drive system to be smaller in environments where it is known that the lift car will not fill to the rated load/available car area of Table 1.1. Examples include airports, where baggage trolleys take up significant space, and shopping centres, where shopping trolleys and pushchairs are carried.

BS ISO 4190-1[14] provides internationally recognised standard dimensions and standard lift configurations for passenger lifts and entrances for rated loads between 630 kg (8-person) and 2500 kg (33-person) capacities. BS ISO 4190-2[15] provides internationally recognised standard dimensions and standard lift configurations for goods/passenger lifts and entrances for rated loads between 630 kg (8-person) and 5000 kg (66-person) capacities.

BS EN 81-70[9] specifies the minimum size of lift car, suitable to accommodate a manual wheelchair only, as a 450 kg lift with internal dimensions of 1000 mm wide and 1250 mm deep. To accommodate a manual wheelchair with an accompanying person the minimum size required is the 630 kg (8-person) car with internal dimensions: 1100 mm wide by 1400 mm deep. The minimum size of lift to accommodate a stretcher is the 1000 kg (13-person) car. Where full manoeuvrability of the wheelchair is necessary a lift with a rated load of 1275 kg (17-person) car is required. See also section 5.8.3 and section 11.

BS ISO 4190-1 recognises a lift rated at 320 kg for residential use. This is unsuitable for use in a commercial or public environment since it would not provide sufficient room to accommodate a wheelchair and is below the minimum dimensions for compliance with the Disability Discrimination Act 1995[33]. This car size is not recommended for any public or commercial applications.

Even where an 8-person lift provides adequate capacity to achieve the required traffic handling performance (see section 3), there may be operational reasons for adopting larger cars such as the need to move furniture or coffins and stretchers in residential buildings, or the need to provide capacity and comfort for passenger with baggage in commercial or hotel environments.

### 5.2.4    Entrances, car fittings and finishes

Landing entrances are perhaps the most important aspect of a lift to the user, since they offer the first impression to a prospective passenger of the quality of the installation. For passenger lifts, entrances doors should be automatically operated and incorporate edge protection by way of non-contact electronic safety edges. The use of single beam detectors has reduced dramatically in recent years as technological advances and competition has made full height curtain protection the norm for all but the very cheapest of model lift packages.

Automatic doors for passenger lifts are available in either centre parting or side opening configurations. Centre parting doors offer improved operating (opening and closing) times and better aesthetics so are often preferred on higher quality installations such as those in commercial offices, hotels, shopping centres or luxury residential environments.

Side opening doors can be accommodated in smaller lift wells than the equivalent sized centre opening doors, however due to the reduced performance (longer opening and closing times) and the poorer aesthetics, side opening doors tend to be used on residential buildings where the usage is not intensive or in hospitals where larger opening widths can be achieved to provide access for beds and stretchers.

BS ISO4190-1[14] provides internationally recognised standard dimensions for entrance sizes as shown in Table 5.1.

For residential lifts, there are two series (A and B) for 800 mm and 900 mm entrances and for a small residential lift a 700 mm entrance is also indicated. However, this entrance size would not provide access for passengers with wheelchairs or pushchairs and should not be considered for general usage.

Three different series (A, B and C) are intended to cover the different entrance requirements of national regulations and localised markets around the world for general purpose passenger lifts. For intensive duty passenger lifts the entrance sizes should be larger at 1100 mm and 1200 mm.

The larger entrances (1100 mm, 1300 mm, 1400 mm) for hospital and health care applications are common on these larger lifts specifically designed to transport beds and stretchers.

**Table 5.1** BS ISO 4190-1[14] entrance sizes

| Class | Usage | Entrance sizes / mm |
|-------|-------|---------------------|
| I | Residential | 700, (A) 800, (B) 900 |
| I | General purpose | (A) 800, (B) 900, (C) 1100 |
| III | Health care | 1100, 1300, 1400 |
| VI | Intensive duty | 1100, 1200 |

Generally, all the configurations given above are available within the UK from most manufacturers standard product ranges.

## 5.2.5 Types of drive and operating speeds

For passenger lifts, electric traction and hydraulic drives can both be considered suitable (see section 8). Each has its own advantages and the final choice is likely to be determined by the specific application. An alternative drive exists in the form of rack and pinion (see section 5.7) although this is generally only used where a hydraulic or electric traction lift cannot be used.

### 5.2.5.1 Traditional electric traction drive

Traditional electric traction drives are suitable for passenger lifts of any capacity, and there are no significant travel or speed limitations. Generally long travel distances are avoided with passengers transferring at sky lobbies (see section 3.12.9). Rated speeds can be as low as 0.25 m/s and the current maximum speed in service is 17 m/s. The commonly used range is from 1.0 m/s to 6.0 m/s. Accurate levelling is achieved by modern solid state control and feedback position monitoring equipment. Single and two speed and to a lesser extent variable speed AC power systems and DC converter systems are now technologically obsolete and should not generally be considered for passenger lifts. Variable voltage variable frequency (VVVF) drives are now almost exclusively specified and provide good energy efficiency and speed control.

Re-levelling should be provided since the loading or unloading of lift cars can cause the lift to drop below, or rise above the floor level, particularly with long travel or larger capacity lifts.

The limitations of conventional electric traction drives are mainly concerned with the location of the machine room, available headroom and the possibility of high loads being applied to the building structure.

### 5.2.5.2 Hydraulic drive

Hydraulic drives, see Figure 5.2, are available for lifts up to a rated speed of 0.63 m/s although some manufacturers offer speeds of 1.0 m/s. The realistic maximum travel distance for a hydraulic lift is around 18 m.

Up to 1275 kg rated load, hydraulic drives can use a single side-acting cylinder unit supporting a cantilever car. This imposes a horizontal load to the supporting wall which must be considered during building design. Above 1275 kg capacity, the most common configuration is twin rams, located with one each side of the car (see section 7.3.2.3). This reduces the horizontal loading to a minimum.

The energy efficiency of hydraulic lifts is relatively poor since they typically have no balance weight. This is reflected in high heat outputs and maximum duty cycles of around 45 starts per hour before additional cooling becomes necessary. The use of hydraulic lifts therefore tends to be for installations with low traffic and light

usage or where the structural advantages of a hydraulic lift are necessary and the limited duty cycles and heat issues can be accommodated (see section 7.3).

More recently hydraulic systems have become available with variable voltage variable frequency drives and hydraulic accumulator systems that act as a hydraulic counterweight. These are able to offer much improved energy efficiency, lower heat outputs and increased duty cycles without the need for additional cooling and can be considered for more intensive use, but are unlikely to be selected in preference to electric traction lifts, unless there are other reasons for selecting a hydraulic lift, such as structural or aesthetic requirements

Starting currents will generally be higher than those for electric traction lifts and it is recommended that star-delta starting or a similar alternative means be used in order to limit the starting currents on hydraulic lifts. This may be critical if the capacity of the mains supply to the building is limited or where the lift may require powering from a standby generator and therefore must be considered early in the design process.

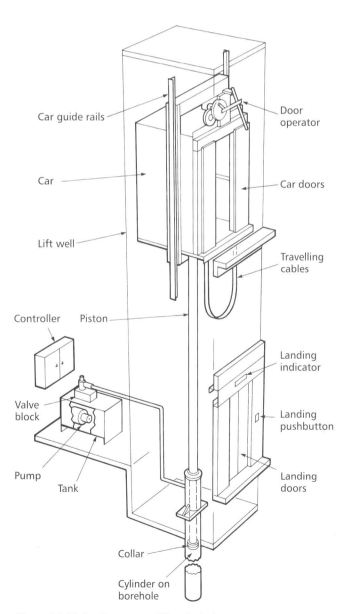

Figure 5.2 Hydraulic passenger lift; principal components

### 5.2.5.3 Machine room-less (MRL) electric traction drive

Standard machine room-less (MRL) passenger lifts are available currently with rated loads between 630 kg and 2000 kg at rated speeds of between 1.0 m/s and 1.75 m/s. Some manufacturers can now also achieve 2.0 m/s, but there is limited availability at the higher speed. Travel distances are much improved with modern machine room less lifts capable of travel distances up to 75 m. At these travel heights however, the existing speed limitations may make it preferable to consider conventional traction lifts with a higher speed.

The mounting of the drive machine in the lift well is achieved in different ways by the various manufacturers. Some mount the drive machine directly on the guide rails so that most of the vertical loads are transferred via the guide rails to the pit floor, in a way similar to that for hydraulic lifts. Others adopt a bedplate arrangement built into the structure for which adequate provision must be made in the construction design.

## 5.2.6 Well

The construction of the lift well must comply with BS EN 81-1/2[2,3], which require minimum safety clearances within the pit, the headroom and the lift well, in order to provide a safe lift installation and safe working conditions for maintenance and service personal. These clearances are required to enable the CE-marking to be applied to an installation.

BS ISO 4190-1[14] provides guidance on the minimum pit depth and headroom, but since the requirements may vary between different manufacturers and drive types, headroom and lift pit dimensions should be checked with lift manufacturers at an early stage of the design process.

Guidance on well sizes is provided in BS ISO 4190-1, although this standard only deals with lifts using automatic doors. Well dimensions for any given application will vary depending on the door type and configuration, the lift car size, the rated speed, the rated load and the type of drive. Thus, the space requirements should also be established with a lift manufacturer, particularly for non-standard lift sizes and arrangements, such as manual doors.

Appendix 5.A1 is a summary table[1] of the BS ISO 4190-1 requirements. Further extensive guidance regarding wells can be found in BS 5655: Part 6: 2002[19].

## 5.2.7 Machine rooms

The machine room or machine space must comply with BS EN 81-1/2[2,3]. All machine room doors and any personnel access doors must be lockable and able to be unlocked from the inside without a key. They should always open outwards.

All machine rooms should be heated and ventilated to control the temperature and remove smoke (see section 12) and lighting is required to a minimum of 200 lux at floor level.

Appendix 5.A1 indicates possible machine room sizes.

### 5.2.7.1 Traditional electric traction drive

Guidance on the size of the machine room is given in BS ISO 4190-1[14]. The sizes appear to be generous, when using modern equipment, and smaller machine rooms may be adequate but this should be checked with lift manufacturers. Depending on machine size, machine room heights at least 2000 mm, and possibly higher for large systems, will be required. In all cases a suitable lifting beam should be installed overhead to provide lifting facilities from the trap door to the approximate position of the machine.

For electric traction drives, the machine room is ideally located directly above the lift well (see section 7.2.5). Bottom and side drives are sometimes used, but can be costly, requiring special engineering for machine mountings and increased maintenance costs for reduced rope life caused by multiple and reverse bends introduced in potentially complicated roping arrangements (see section 7.15).

With bottom or side drive, an overhead pulley room is required which should be the plan size of the lift well with a minimum internal height of 1500 mm. A separate pulley room may not be required if an under slung car arrangement is employed (see section 7.15.1). Basement machine rooms must be adjacent to the lift well with a plan size to suit the equipment and to provide an adequate safe working area for maintenance. In such installations, the designer should refer to the lift supplier for guidance.

Access should be considered for the possible replacement of machine room equipment in the future. With top drive, trap doors in the machine room floor with suitably located lifting beams should be considered. Access to machine rooms of bottom drive electric traction lifts must be sufficient for the passage of lift equipment. This should be checked carefully when equipment is located in basements.

### 5.2.7.2 Hydraulic lifts

For hydraulic drives, the machine room is ideally located adjacent to the lift at the bottom level. However, if necessary the machine room can be located remote from the well but the distance between the machine and the hydraulic jack should not be greater than 6 metres. In these circumstances, the lift supplier should be consulted.

Guidance on the size of the machine room is given in BS ISO 4190-2[15], which recommend a minimum machine room size of the lift well width (or depth) by 2000 mm and at least 2000 mm high. This is usually adequate, except for very large capacity lifts requiring more than one tank unit. In such a case, if the machine room is on the short side of the well, it may be necessary to increase the 2000 mm dimension and advice should be sought from a manufacturer. The machine room height will need to be increased if a lifting beam is required. Access to machine rooms for hydraulic lifts must be provided for the passage of lift equipment.

Temperature control in hydraulic machine rooms can be a major issue due to the generally higher heat outputs of this type of lift. Oil coolers are often fitted to increase the lift duty cycle (typically quoted as the number of motor starts a lift can make in one hour without overloading the motor or drive unit) and maintain adequate performance during peak operating periods. However, the cooler is generally located in the machine room and therefore the output from the cooler has to be dissipated or ventilated away to prevent excessive temperatures in the machine room which would restrict the effectiveness of the cooler. In many cases, it is necessary to install cooling equipment by way of air conditioning units to maintain suitable ambient temperatures in hydraulic machine rooms.

Where direct acoustic communication between the lift well and the machine room is not possible, a maintenance intercom should be fitted between the machine room and the lift car.

### 5.2.7.3 Machine room-less lifts

The concept is that all equipment is located and accommodated within the lift well. The pit depth and over-runs on MRL lifts tend to be less than conventional lift installations and therefore additional space is not usually required external to the lift well for MRL lifts.

Solutions for accommodating drive machine or drive unit and controller equipment within the lift well have been achieved in a variety of ways. For electric traction lifts, arrangements are available with the drive machine located within the lift pit, the headroom of the well and in some cases even on the lift car itself (refer to section 7.2.5.4). For hydraulic lifts the drive unit may be placed in the pit area.

The controller cabinet is commonly located at either the top or bottom lift landing, within the front wall but can also be located within the lift well. Where the controller is located inside the lift well, a remote control panel is provided, that can be accessed from the landing, for carrying out emergency procedures.

The high efficiencies of modern traction gearless machines used for MRL lifts rarely requires additional ventilation however advice should be taken from the lift manufacturer on any additional requirements for ventilating the lift well to maintain suitable ambient temperatures around the control and drive equipment.

## 5.3 Goods lifts

### 5.3.1 General

Lifts designed for the movement of goods are generally not used to transport passengers (see section 5.2.1). They must comply with the Lifts Regulations[36], either by the use of the harmonised standards BS EN 81-1[2] for electric traction lifts and BS EN 81-2[3] for hydraulic lifts, or by certification by a Notified Body.

The width, depth and height of a goods lift is often a function of the nature of the goods carried and the way in which they are moved (e.g. on pallets of a known size or in containers). Where possible, the designer should select one of the standardised sizes given in BS ISO 4190-2[15] since lifts manufactured to these sizes are likely to be cheaper than 'one-off' designs.

Consideration should also be given to the transportation of items other than those for which the lift is normally used. For example, the goods lift may be the only means of transporting items such as office furniture and partitions between floors. Standard access doors are not always wide enough for such items.

For safe loading and easy access, goods lifts should be located in a position which provides adequate free space in front of the entrance. If wheeled trolleys or fork-lift trucks are to be used, adequate space to manoeuvre must be provided, with clear access to the loading area. Consideration must also be given to the effect of loading on the lift car sills and flooring. The installation of trolley 'bump rails' should be considered.

### 5.3.2 Applications for goods lifts

#### 5.3.2.1 Airports

Airports contain offices, restaurants, shops, cinemas, some sleeping accommodation etc. All these facilities require goods service. The use of airport passenger lifts for goods service should be avoided and dedicated goods lifts provided. Their specification will depend on their main purpose, as described in the following subsections.

#### 5.3.2.2 Car parks

The requirement for goods lifts in a car park are unlikely.

#### 5.3.2.3 Department stores

Single goods lifts may be provided in smaller department stores, but it is recommended where ever possible to install at least two units to allow for peak periods and lift breakdowns. They are usually placed adjacent to vehicle loading/unloading bays or lay-bys. Care must be taken to ensure sufficient units are provided. The rated load will depend on the nature of the stores business, but should be at least 2000 kg, except where specialised goods are being transported, when smaller rated loads might be appropriate.

#### 5.3.2.4 Entertainment centres, cinemas, theatres, sports centres, stadia and concert halls

A variety of activities can be found in this application area including offices, restaurants, bars, changing rooms, washrooms etc., all of which will require goods service. Dedicated goods lifts may not be necessary, provided goods/passenger lifts are available. Service lifts (see section 5.5) may be required to serve bars, restaurants and kitchens.

#### 5.3.2.5 Hospitals

In addition to passenger lifts, hospitals require facilities to support the facilities management (FM) teams to move trolleys of food, linen, goods and clinical equipment around the hospital. These lifts may be located on dedicated FM routes, although current trends for hospital design around a 'hospital street' make this less common. Hospital planning should try to minimise the number and intensity of these journeys by arranging deliveries and collections of different load types so they do not coincide.

In addition to BS ISO 4190-2[15], which provides recommended lift car and well sizes for hospital lifts, information specifically related to hospital trolley dimensions is available in Health Building Note HBN 40[34] and additional design information specific to hospitals is available in Health Technical Memorandum HTM 2024[35].

### 5.3.2.6    Hotels

Generally, service (goods) activity such as baggage transfers, room service, housekeeping, etc. should be separate to the guest lifts. Designers of lift systems for hotels should thus carefully consider the operational requirements of the hotel and incorporate dedicated goods lifts (and service lifts, see section 5.5) for the use of staff servicing the guest rooms as far as possible. The use of passenger lifts by cleaning or laundry staff will detract from the lift service available to guests.

Goods lifts should be located in an area not normally accessible to guests (i.e. 'back of house') and will need to be sized to cater for any cleaning or laundry trolleys that may be used. Since such lifts will be used for transporting large amounts of goods and refuse, they should have durable finishes and a minimum load of 1600 kg.

In addition to servicing the guest rooms, hotels with banquet and conference facilities may require additional goods lifts dedicated to these areas.

### 5.3.2.7    Offices

See section 3.11.3.

### 5.3.2.8    Railway stations

The requirement for goods lifts at railway stations is generally small, as most surface stations are single level and underground stations make other arrangements. Many stations where the platforms are above or below the access road employ ramps for passenger use and these can be used for the movement of goods. Where they are provided, passenger lifts can be used to transport goods provided passengers take priority and the cars are suitably protected.

An exception to this is in terminal stations where trains are prepared for journeys. Such preparation may involve the charging of water tanks, restocking of catering facilities and cleaning of the trains and therefore terminal stations will have a need for goods lifts. Some goods lifts may be of a special size to accept baggage trolleys or water tugs and will require early consultation with the station operators to establish the correct requirements.

### 5.3.2.9    Residential buildings

Most residential buildings are designed with dual purpose goods/passenger lifts. However, in some high quality, prestigious developments, it may considered necessary to incorporate dedicated goods lifts. These should be sized to accommodate large furniture items and any refuse

containers that might be transported in the lift. They may be located in a separate core to allow a separate passenger lobby to be provided with high quality decoration and finishes.

Where dual purpose lifts are used, the goods/passenger lift should permit the hanging of protective drapes and should be sized to accept stretchers or coffins as well as furniture and general goods, etc. The minimum size for dual purpose lifts should be a 13-person lift with internal dimensions of 1100 mm wide by 2000 mm deep. Where a dedicated goods lift is used, a 13-person lift should be the minimum size provided, however, larger cars of 1600 kg rated load should be considered to maximise the benefits of providing a dedicated goods lift.

### 5.3.2.10    Residential care homes and nursing homes

Goods service is unlikely to be required, unless the home is very large.

### 5.3.2.11    Shopping centres

Goods lifts provided in shopping centres are usually placed singly, or in pairs, adjacent to vehicle loading/unloading bays or lay-bys and along service corridors at the rear of retail units. Each lift or group of lifts will service a group of shops and stores, although some major store chains may have dedicated goods lifts and delivery areas. Care must be taken to ensure sufficient units are provided to allow for peak deliveries and lift breakdowns. Generally one goods lift for every 10 units should be provided. Goods should not be moved through the public malls and walkways. The rated load should be at least 2000 kg, except where specialised goods are being transported, when smaller rated loads might be appropriate.

### 5.3.2.12    Universities and other education buildings

Universities have a variety of building types from the low rise to tower blocks. The use of these building types varies from residential accommodation (halls of residence), conference facilities with hotel style accommodation, bars, restaurants, lecture blocks, laboratory areas and office accommodation. The need for dedicated goods lifts should be considered by reference to the previous sections for the specific use identified.

## 5.3.3    Car sizes and payloads

The first step, if possible, is to determine the specific type of goods to be moved, the overall dimensions and the weight, when selecting a goods lift. This enables the designer to calculate the volume and total weight expected to be moved at any one time. Additional space must be allowed for any personnel, who may be required to accompany the goods.

The recommended minimum internal width for lift cars is the overall width of the goods plus 600 mm. This allows goods to be stacked to one side whilst leaving an area for accompanying personnel. In the case of 'through cars', with entrances on opposite sides, this space is essential. It is possible that the attendant will have to unload the lift through the opposite entrance and therefore will require access to both entrances from inside the car.

When considering through cars fitted with folding shutter-type gates, it is important to check that the distance between the bunched leaves of the gate is adequate. Otherwise goods against the closed gate may encroach on the area required by the leaves of that gate when open.

Having determined the minimum size required, the nearest standard size given in BS ISO 4190-2[15] should be selected wherever possible.

When loading is carried out by fork-lift trucks or other vehicles, the carrying capacity of the lift must reflect the additional load imposed by the weight of any vehicle, which may enter the lift car. This does not necessarily require an increase in the size of the car, but consideration must be given to whether strengthened sills will be required to accommodate the localised high loads imposed by the vehicle wheels. It may also be necessary to consider additional stiffening for the car floor at the design stage.

### 5.3.4 Entrances, car fittings and finishes

Door configurations are dealt with in detail in section 7.9. Goods lift doors can be horizontal sliding, as used in passenger and goods/passenger lifts, and vertical sliding specifically for goods service. The latter type is not recommended for goods/passenger service. For horizontal sliding doors entrance widths of 1100 mm, 1300 mm, 1400 mm, 1500 mm, 1800 mm, 2100 mm and 2500 mm are available. For vertical sliding doors entrance widths of 1400 mm, 1500 mm, 1800 mm, 2100 mm and 2500 mm are available. The slide direction and entrance width will be dependent on the goods to be transported. Special width doors can be supplied by most manufacturers, but are likely to be expensive. Goods lifts need to be robust in service and it is sometimes necessary to fit entrance

protection to avoid damage to the doors and surrounding door frames.

Manual doors are specified for some goods lifts, particularly where heavy duty usage is required such as in retail or industrial applications. These should be arranged to give an opening equal to the full width of the car if possible, for maximum flexibility. Folding shutter gates are usually preferred since they require a minimum of well space and are easily adapted to suit varying entrance widths. The standardised heights of 2000 mm, or 2300 mm, should be selected wherever possible.

Power-operated shutter gates are available and offer a durable, robust solution to applications where tugs, or loading vehicles are used, avoiding the need for lift users to demount and manually open the lift gates. For general goods usage however, conventional horizontal sliding, automatic doors should be considered where manual doors are not required or suitable.

Good lifts should be rugged and the finishes should be easy to clean and repair, see Figure 5.3. Walls and roofs should be constructed in sections to allow easy replacement if damaged. Many materials and finishes are available but the most common are either steel with a cellulose or powder coated finish, or patterned stainless steel. While the latter is initially more expensive, its appearance is superior and it does not require maintenance after installation. For very light duty applications, laminate-faced panels may be used. The appearance is good but the surface is more prone to damage than steel panels.

In all cases it is desirable to fit some form of bumper rail in the car to provide a measure of protection for the walls. The rail should be mounted at a suitable height to absorb the impact of trolleys, loading pallets etc. Alternatively, a series of rails may be provided, spaced 100 mm apart up to a height of 1 m. However, bumper rails reduce the interior dimensions and this must be taken into account when calculating the required car size.

The flooring should be replaceable. Many goods lifts will have floors of patterned 'chequer plate' steel, but, for

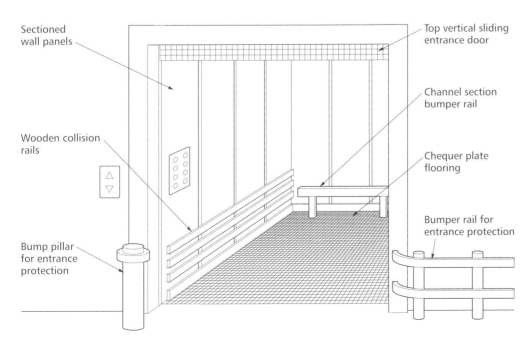

Sectioned wall panels

Top vertical sliding entrance door

Channel section bumper rail

Wooden collision rails

Chequer plate flooring

Bumper rail for entrance protection

Bump pillar for entrance protection

**Figure 5.3** Entrances, car fittings and finishes for a rugged goods lift lighter duty applications, surfaces such as aluminium chequer plate or vinyl may be preferred. In applications where corrosive fluids are carried, epoxy resin or terrazzo flooring may be required. Consideration must also be given to the consequences of washing-out or hosing-down the lift car if it is intended for a hospital or food preparation facility.

## 5.3.5 Types of drive and operating speeds

For conventional goods lifts, electric traction, hydraulic and rack and pinion drives can all be considered suitable (see sections 7.2, 7.3 and 5.7). Each has its own advantages and the final choice is likely to be determined by the specific application.

### 5.3.5.1 Electric traction drive

Electric traction drives are suitable for goods lifts of any capacity, and there are no travel or speed limitations. Goods lifts do not depend on travel speed for quality of service since loading and unloading consume the greatest time on the round trips. Typically speeds of 1.0 m/s or 1.6 m/s are satisfactory for a dedicated goods lift. It is unusual to apply speeds in excess of 2.5 m/s for dedicated goods lifts, even in tall buildings in the UK.

Accurate levelling can be achieved with variable speed and variable speed, variable frequency (VVVF) AC drives. Both types of drive can provide re-levelling, which should be provided since the loading or unloading of heavy loads can cause the lift to fall or rise at the landing floor, particularly with long travel lifts.

The limitations of electric traction drives are mainly concerned with the location of the machine room, available headroom and the possibility of high loads being applied to the building structure.

### 5.3.5.2 Hydraulic drive

Goods lifts do not depend on high travel speeds for quality of service since loading and unloading consume the greatest time on round trips. Therefore, the speed limitations of hydraulic drives, at 0.5 m/s or 0.63 m/s, are not important for goods applications, but the travel remains limited to 18 m.

Up to 1275 kg rated load, hydraulic drives use a single side-acting cylinder unit supporting a cantilever car. This imposes a horizontal load to the supporting wall which must be considered during the building design. Above 1250 kg capacity, the most common configuration is twin rams, located with one each side of the car (see section 7.3.2). This reduces the horizontal loading to a minimum. Single side-acting cylinders should not be considered for goods lifts where there may be heavy loading requirements, e.g. using fork-lift trucks or large trolleys etc.

Unless modern, and currently more costly, VVVF drive and accumulator balancing is used, (see section 8.7.4) heat outputs from large hydraulic lifts will be high and will require the use of oil coolers and machine room cooling to control the ambient machine room temperature. Starting

currents can also be higher than those for electric traction lifts and it is recommended that star-delta starting be used in order to limit the starting currents on large lifts. This may be critical, if the capacity of the mains supply to the building is limited and therefore must be considered early in the design process.

### 5.3.5.3 Machine room-less electric traction drive

Standard machine room-less goods/passenger lifts are also available with loads between 1000 kg and 2000 kg at speeds of 0.5 m/s and 1.0 m/s, up to a maximum travel of 20 m. The larger applications can utilise up to 4:1 roping ratios (see section 7.15) to minimise the power requirements. The drive and suspension is arranged to transfer most of the loading vertically via the guide rails to the pit floor, in a way similar to that for hydraulic lifts.

### 5.3.5.4 Rack and pinion drive

Refer to section 5.7 for details of rack and pinion drives.

## 5.3.6 Well dimensions and construction

The construction of the lift well must comply with BS EN 81-1/2[2,3], which require minimum safety clearances within the pit, the headroom and the lift well, in order to provide a safe lift installation and safe working conditions for maintenance and service personal. These clearances are required to enable the CE-mark to be applied to an installation.

The construction of the lift well must ensure that it will be strong enough to accept all the loads applied by the lift. This is particularly important where loading and unloading is to be carried out by fork-lift trucks or trolleys, or if the lift is of a cantilever design. In the case of lifts loaded using forklift trucks, large additional loads are temporarily applied to the stationary lift. This generates a turning moment with resulting reactions on the car guides, or mast assembly in the case of rack and pinion lifts. These loads are transferred to the building structure by the guide rail or mast fixings and the structure must be strong enough to accept these without degradation. While block work has a high compressive strength, it is not suitable for expanding bolts or other heavy-duty fixings. If necessary, steel or reinforced concrete sections should be used. At the very least, local areas of cast concrete blocks, suitably tied and bonded to the wall panel, should be used. It must be noted that lift installers cannot accept responsibility for the design of the building, or its structural strength.

Guidance on well sizes is provided in BS ISO 4190-2[15], although this standard only deals with lifts using automatic doors. Well dimensions for any given application will vary depending on the door type and configuration, the lift car size, the rated speed, the rated load and the type of drive. Thus, the space requirements should also be established with a lift manufacturer, particularly for non-standard lift sizes and arrangements, such as those with manual doors and manual shutter gates, as might be required in retail or industrial applications.

BS ISO 4190-2 also provides guidance on the minimum pit depth and headroom, but since the requirements may vary between different manufacturers and drive types, headroom and lift pit dimensions should be checked with lift manufacturers at an early stage of the design process.

Appendix 5.A1 is a summary table[1] of the BS ISO 4190-2 requirements. Further extensive guidance regarding wells can be found in BS5655: Part 6: 2002[19].

## 5.3.7 Machine room

All machine rooms and any personnel access doors must be lockable and able to be unlocked from the inside without a key. They should always open outwards.

All machine rooms should be heated and ventilated to control the temperature and remove smoke (see section 12) and lighting is required to a minimum of 200 lux at floor level.

Appendix 5.A1 indicates possible machine room sizes.

### 5.3.7.1 Traditional electric traction lifts

Guidance on the size of the machine room is given in BS ISO 4190-2[15]. The sizes appear to be generous, when using modern equipment, and smaller machine rooms may be adequate but this should be checked with lift manufacturers. The height of the machine room will depend on the machine size and the location of lifting beams or eyes etc. but should allow at least 2000 mm beneath the lowest part of the ceiling, lifting facilities or structure. In all cases suitable lifting facilities should be installed overhead to provide access between any trap doors and the approximate position of the machine.

For electric traction drives, the machine room is ideally located directly above the lift well (see section 7.2.5.1). Bottom and side drives are sometimes used, but can be costly, requiring special engineering for machine mountings and increased maintenance costs for reduced rope life caused by multiple and reverse bends introduced in potentially complicated roping arrangements (see section 7.15).

With bottom and side drive, an overhead pulley room is required which should be the plan size of the lift well with a minimum internal height of 1500 mm. A separate pulley room may not be required if an under slung car arrangement is employed (see section 7.15.1). Basement machine rooms must be adjacent to the lift well with a plan size to suit the equipment and to provide an adequate safe working area for maintenance. In such installations, the designer should refer to the lift supplier for guidance.

Access should be considered for the possible replacement of machine room equipment in the future. With top drive, trap doors in the machine room floor with suitably located lifting beams should be considered. Access to machine rooms of bottom drive electric traction lifts must be sufficient for the passage of lift equipment. This should be checked carefully when equipment is located in basements.

### 5.3.7.2 Hydraulic lifts

For hydraulic drives, the machine room is ideally located adjacent to the lift at the bottom level. However, if necessary the machine room can be located remote from the well but the distance between the machine and the hydraulic jack should not be greater than 6 metres. In these circumstances, the lift supplier should be consulted. Access to machine rooms for hydraulic lifts must be provided for the passage of lift equipment.

Guidance on the size of the machine room is given in BS ISO 4190-2[15], which recommends a minimum machine room size of the lift well width (or depth) by 2000 mm and at least 2000 mm high. This is usually adequate, except for very large capacity lifts requiring more than one tank unit. In such a case, if the machine room is on the short side of the well, it may be necessary to increase the 2000 mm dimension and advice should be sought from a manufacturer. The machine room height will need to be increased if a lifting beam is required. Access to machine rooms for hydraulic lifts must be provided for the passage of lift equipment.

Temperature control in hydraulic machine rooms can be a major issue due to the generally higher heat outputs of this type of lift. Oil coolers are often fitted to increase the lift duty cycle (typically quoted as the number of motor starts a lift can make in one hour without overloading the motor or drive unit) and maintain adequate performance during peak operating periods. However, the cooler is generally located in the machine room and therefore the output from the cooler has to be dissipated or ventilated away to prevent excessive temperatures in the machine room which would restrict the effectiveness of the cooler. In many cases, it is necessary to install cooling equipment by way of air conditioning units to maintain suitable ambient temperatures in hydraulic machine rooms.

Where direct acoustic communication between the lift well and the machine room is not possible, a maintenance intercom should be fitted between the machine room and the lift car.

### 5.3.7.3 Machine room-less lifts

The concept is that all equipment is located and accommodated within the lift well. The pit depth and over-runs on MRL lifts tend to be less than conventional lift installations and therefore additional space is not usually required external to the lift well for MRL lifts.

Solutions for accommodating drive machine or drive unit and controller equipment within the lift well have been achieved in a variety of ways. Electric traction arrangements are available with the drive machine located within the lift pit, the headroom of the well and in some cases even on the lift car itself (refer to section 7.2.5.4). For hydraulic MRL lifts the drive unit may be placed in the pit area.

The controller cabinet is commonly located at either the top or bottom lift landing, within the front wall but can also be located within the lift well. Where the controller is located inside the lift well, a remote control panel is provided, that can be accessed from the landing, for carrying out emergency procedures.

The high efficiencies of modern traction gearless machines used for MRL lifts rarely requires additional ventilation however advice should be taken from the lift manufacturer on any additional requirements for ventilating the lift well to maintain suitable ambient temperatures around the control and drive equipment.

#### 5.3.7.4 Rack and pinion drive

Refer to section 5.7 for details of rack and pinion machine room requirements.

## 5.4 Observation lifts

### 5.4.1 General

Refer to sections 3.11.4 and 5.2.1.

Observation lifts consist of a glazed, or partially glazed, lift car, running within a glazed or partially enclosed lift well, see Figure 5.4. They are referred to by various names including wall climber, scenic, panoramic, panorama and glass lifts. They are often installed as an architectural feature in a building within an atrium, or occasionally, external to the building. All the guidance offered for passenger lifts in section 5.2 is generally applicable, however, the following additional advice should be taken into account when considering, or designing, observation lifts.

All observation lifts must comply with the Essential Health and Safety Requirements (EHSRs) of the Lifts Regulations 1997[36]. This can be achieved by lifts complying fully with BS EN 81–1/2[2,3]. These standards contain specific clauses to cover the use of glass in and around the lifts and the screening requirements around partially enclosed wells.

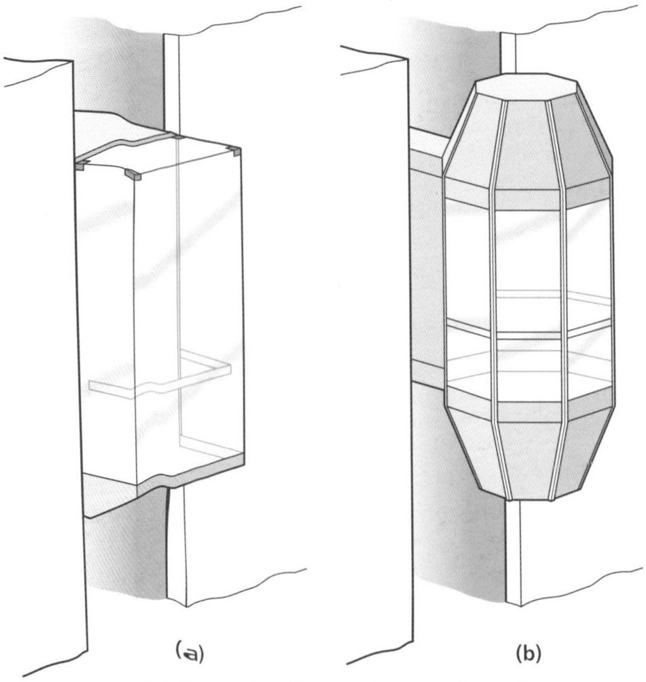

Most large lift manufacturers offer pre-engineered observation lift designs. These reduce costs and delivery times because the majority of the design work has already been carried out. Pre-engineered designs range from a normal lift car with a glass window in the back wall and a glass-sided lift well to very sophisticated designs, such as an octagonal car with a lobby area leading into the viewing area.

Observation lifts are often tailor-made to suit the particular building in which they are to be installed. For many applications, observation lifts will need to be specially engineered because of structural problems, or space limitations. An advantage of custom-designed lifts is that they can be designed to match building décor and other architectural requirements. However, it should be noted that the time required for design and manufacture will be greater than that for pre-engineered lifts. Special features, finishes and the need to obtain any approval in accordance with the Lifts Regulations 1997[36] will further increase delivery times. Therefore the detailed specification must be confirmed, and the lifts ordered, as soon as possible during the planning of the building to ensure that the lift is operational by the time the building is ready for occupation.

As discussed in sections 2.5.3 and 3.11.4 observation lifts do not provide the same handling capacity as conventional lifts of the same specification. There are many reasons for this. In public buildings they attract sightseers and joy riders and many passengers will wish to enjoy an unobstructed view through the glass. This problem does not occur to the same extent in offices, or apartments, where users become accustomed to the lifts and are more likely to use them in a conventional manner.

It is common in public places such as shopping malls, to position observation lifts individually around a development, to create a repeating architectural feature. Where

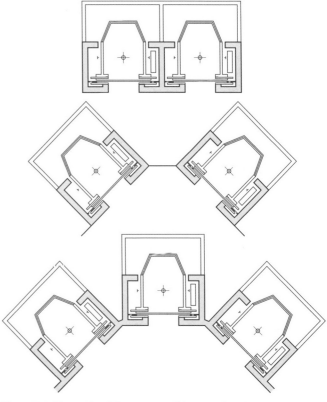

**Figure 5.4** Typical observation lift cars; (a) rectangular without mullions, (b) octagonal with mullions

(a)  (b)

**Figure 5.5** Observation lifts; some possible group layouts this is a consideration, the reduced handling capacity of the individual lifts must be considered within the system design to ensure that the likely traffic demands can be accommodated by individual lifts. Alternatively, they could be grouped together at a single point to maximise efficiency. Figure 5.5 shows some possible configurations.

Observation lifts can also be part of a mixed group with conventional lifts. The two types must be clearly distinguishable to passengers before they enter the lift, as some people may dislike glazed lifts and be reluctant to use them. There are also potential negative psychological effects on waiting passengers. Where glazed doors or fronts are used, passengers are able to observe lifts passing their floor. This can occur for traffic control reasons, or because the car is fully loaded. However, passengers may think the system is malfunctioning and may generate complaints about the lift performance.

## 5.4.2 Application of observation lifts

Refer to section 5.2.2 and its relevant subsection, the sequence of which is followed below.

### 5.4.2.1 Airports

Observation lifts are rare in airports.

### 5.4.2.2 Car parks

Observation lifts are not generally suitable for this environment, however some car park operating companies have a preference to include glass doors on lifts. This can provide enhanced security allowing the use of CCTV to monitor the lift. In such cases, the lifts do not tend to be considered as observation lifts and little attention is expected to the location and aesthetics of shaft equipment that becomes visible through the glass doors.

The provision of glass doors should be subject to due consideration of the location of the car park and the level of security and management provided  to avoid any increased likelihood of vandalism such as breakage of glass or attempted entry into the visible shaft, that might occur.

### 5.4.2.3 Department stores

Observation lifts are frequently used in department stores to provide a pleasing and leisurely environment. Their rated speed would usually be low in order to display the goods on sale for the maximum time.

### 5.4.2.4 Entertainment centres, cinemas, theatres, sports centres, stadia and concert halls

Observation lifts are generally not suitable for this environment. They may be found in some exhibition centres over a low rise.

### 5.4.2.5 Hospitals

Observation lifts are not suitable for this environment.

### 5.4.2.6 Hotels

Observation lifts play an important part in large top class hotels where they provide a spectacular feature in lofty atria. Their performance specification should be similar to that of an enclosed lift especially where the observation lifts form all or part of the primary vertical transportation.

### 5.4.2.7 Offices

Observation lifts can play an important part in prestige offices where they can provide a spectacular feature in lofty atria. Their performance specification should be similar to that of an enclosed lift especially where the observation lifts form all or part of the primary vertical transportation.

### 5.4.2.8 Railway stations

Observation lifts are not generally suitable for most railway station however they have been incorporated in some modern terminus stations where they tend to be architectural driven bespoke units. In such cases the lifts are provided as a feature, to supplement stairs and escalators which provide the main means of vertical circulation.

### 5.4.2.9 Residential buildings

Observation lifts are not suitable for this environment.

### 5.4.2.10 Residential care homes and nursing homes

Observation lifts are not suitable for this environment.

### 5.4.2.11 Shopping centres

Observation lifts are frequently used in shopping centres to provide a pleasing focal point. Their rated speed would usually be low in order to provide a leisurely environment.

### 5.4.2.12 Universities and other education buildings

Observation lifts are not suitable for this environment.

## 5.4.3 Car size and payload

Refer to section 5.2.3.

Although the BS ISO 4190-1[14] dimensions are still relevant they may not be applicable as the shape of the car platform may not be rectangular for aesthetic reasons. However, the rated load/available area requirements of Tables 1.1 of BS EN 81-1[2] and Tables 1.1 and 1.1A of BS EN 81-2[3] do apply. Generally the rated load of observation lifts ranges from 800 kg to 1600 kg.

If an observation lift is to be used by persons with disabilities, the design of the controls, signals and aesthetics must comply with BS EN 81-70[24].

### 5.4.4 Entrances, car fittings and finishes

Refer to section 5.2.4.

It is most likely that centre opening doors will be fitted as part of the aesthetic scheme. A suitable clear opening width would be 1100 mm.

Special consideration is required when using glass on doors to prevent friction levels creating a risk to children's hands that might be dragged along and pinched in between the door and any trims or architraves. Such protection is available by using coatings with a low coefficient of friction, reducing the running clearances between the doors and trims or by introducing mechanical or electrical sensors to detect the presence of hands or fingers etc. The method of protection will depend on the equipment supplied and should be discussed with the manufacturer. All glass should incorporate markings indicating the name of the supplier, the type of glass and the trade mark. These should remain visible when the glass is installed.

Care also needs to be taken when using glass to ensure that adequate contrast and visibility exists so that passengers with visual impairments are not inconvenienced in any way. This may require the use of visual manifestation on glass walls, doors and enclosures to aid passengers with visual impairments. Low level manifestation should be considered for glazed doors to provide modesty screening for passengers.

The car fit out is likely to be more elaborate than a conventional passenger lift. However, it is important that handrails, of a sturdy appearance, are fitted all round the glazed area to provide assistance and re-assurance to the passengers.

### 5.4.5 Types of drive and operating speeds

Refer to section 5.2.5.

The power system and drive chosen for any lift installation depends on the required speed, likely usage and desired comfort of ride. Observation lifts can utilise all the different types of drives and configurations appropriate to passenger lifts (see also section 7). However, observation lifts are often associated with prestigious installations and the quality of ride and levelling accuracy must be appropriate to the situation.

Lifts with modern variable speed AC, variable voltage variable frequency (VVVF) or gearless drives offer sophisticated control and high standards of levelling accuracy. Acceleration and deceleration are smooth, with a fast approach to floors. Overall, a smoother and more accurate ride results from the use of a system designed for intensive service.

Hydraulic drive systems also offer smooth and comfortable ride conditions with accurate floor levelling along with the ability to incorporate a remote machine pump room. They are, however, incapable of the short flight times and duty achieved by electric traction drives and

their travel is usually limited to a maximum of 18 metres, see section 7.3. Hydraulic drives in which the cylinder is installed in a borehole can make an attractive architectural feature. With this arrangement there are no problems with hiding ropes and pulleys as occur with suspended lift cars and the control equipment and pump unit can be located remote from the lift. However, the 'wall climbing' illusion is lost due to the visibility of the piston.

The available headroom, lift speed and required rise are important considerations when selecting the drive system. If there is sufficient headroom to accommodate a machine or pulley room above the lift, and the rise is more than 20 m, electric traction drive would be appropriate since the required lift speed is dependent on the rise.

In situations where headroom is limited, hydraulic lifts are often more suitable although their speed and maximum rise are limited (see section 7.3). Electric traction drives using an underslung configuration (see sections 7.2.5.2 and 7.2.5.3) or machine room-less lifts offer alternative solutions without the limitations on speed and rise that may apply to a hydraulic installation. With machine room-less lifts, the drive and control equipment may be visible as will the suspension ropes that run up the side of the car in the underslung arrangements adopted on many machine room less lifts.

The use of machine room-less lifts for observation lift applications may result in limited options for lift car design in terms of finishes or car dimensions. However product ranges are increasing at a pace and some manufacturers are able to offer variable lift car dimensions and improved drive machine technology can offer higher torque levels giving the ability to incorporate special lift car finishes.

The speed of travel of an observation lift is very important to the comfort of the passengers. Low speeds suitable for short travel lifts will give a leisurely journey, which enables passengers to observe the view and instils a sense of safety, whilst still providing the required service levels. With higher rises, speeds need to be higher to give good service, but this can only be achieved at the expense of a leisurely journey. There is also the possibility that people may feel less secure at higher speeds, as the walls, or structure, of the building pass by.

Historically, it was considered that the speed of observation lifts should be limited to a maximum of 1.6 m/s in situations where there is a close focal point for the passengers. Modern observation lifts however, particularly in offices or other private buildings, commonly travel at speeds up to 2.5 m/s. In Europe, there are partial observation lifts that travel at 6 m/s.

With the use of higher speeds, alternative enclosed lifts should be available for people who do not like to travel in high speed observation lifts.

### 5.4.6 Well

Refer to section 5.2.6.

Owing to the often non rectangular shapes of observation lift cars the provisions of BS ISO 4190-1[14] may not be applicable. As observation lifts are often installed with virtually no well structure it is important to prevent access to unauthorised persons. BS EN 81-1/2[2,3] requires screening to a height of 3.50 m on the entrance sides of a lift well. On the other sides, screens should be provided to a height of 2.50 m, where people would otherwise have access to the lift area. This dimension can be reduced progressively to a minimum of 1.10 m where the distance to any moving part is greater than 2.0 m.

Any glass used for lift well enclosures within reach of persons must be laminated. All glass should incorporate markings indicating the name of the supplier, the type of glass and the trade mark. These should remain visible when the glass is installed. Care also needs to be taken when using glass to ensure that adequate contrast and visibility exists so that all passengers can detect its presence. Low level manifestation should be considered for glazed doors or walls to provide modesty screening for passengers.

Since the essence of observation lifts is to provide a visually pleasing installation, it is essential that early discussions be held between the architect or designer and the lift manufacturers. These discussions should develop the original design concept, taking into account both the technical and visual limitations of the lift equipment required to provide the complete installation.

Consideration may be required to concealing switches in the lift well and to specially designed guide and switch support brackets. The use of roller guide shoes running on dry guide rails is recommended for all panoramic lifts. This will eliminate oil splatter onto glazed parts of the lift car or well and in the pit, which may occur if oiled or greased guide rails are used in conjunction with sliding shoes.

Due to the unusual layout of the lift wells associated with observation lifts, the space requirements are quite different to those of conventional lifts. The counterweight and travelling cables may be required to run in a screened-off area and the shape of the car may be unusual, thereby requiring a large pit area that will need to be screened.

In addition, safe and easy access for maintenance will have to be provided over the total travel and access to the exterior panels of the lift car will be required for cleaning. Consideration of the cleaning regime is required at an early stage in the design process to ensure that safe access is available and can be accommodated within the architectural and structural design.

External observation lifts will be exposed to the elements and considerable care is required to ensure that extreme temperatures will not affect the safety and reliability of the lift, and the comfort of passengers during its use. In the UK where frosts are expected, the use of trace heating should be considered on exposed equipment and, in particular, the guide rails, safety gear, buffers and door equipment. For glazed cars exposed to direct sunlight, the potential solar gain should be considered and air conditioning installed to provide cooling. This is particularly important where a glazed lift car is located in a glazed well and where there is a possibility of passenger entrapment. It would be unwise to rely on external observation lifts as the sole means of vertical transportation for a building without some form of weather shielding.

### 5.4.7 Machine room

Refer to section 5.2.7.

The machine room or machine space must comply with BS EN 81-1/2[2,3]. Its position, for an observation lift, may be constrained by aesthetic requirements. If space permits, for an electric traction lift the best position is above the well. An alternative is to use a bottom drive and place the machine room at the lowest level. This option however, presents problems in hiding or disguising the extra roping required. Hydraulic lifts provide an easier option as their machine spaces can be some distance away from the lift and even below it.

## 5.5 Service lifts

### 5.5.1 General

Service lifts, or 'dumb waiters', are designed for carrying goods only and their dimensions and designs are arranged to prevent their use for carrying persons. Service lifts can be provided conforming to BS EN 81-3[4], which contains many of the provisions of BS EN 81-1/2[2,3] and should ensure reliability and safety in operation. Alternatively, as persons are not to be transported, a suitable device under the Machinery Directive[30,32] enacted as the Supply of Machinery Regulations[37] (as amended) could be installed and is likely to be less expensive.

Much of what follows is particular to providing a service lift to BS EN 81-3. If a unit is supplied under the Machinery Directive specialist advice should be sought.

### 5.5.2 Applications

The main uses of service lifts is to transport books, documents, food and beverages, money, laundry, papers, post, retail stock, rubbish etc., so they find application in department stores, entertainment centres, cinemas, theatres, sports centres and concert halls, hospitals, hotels, offices, residential buildings, residential care homes and nursing homes, shopping centres, universities and other education buildings. Their principal area of use, however, is in kitchens and restaurants.

### 5.5.3 Car size and payload

Most manufacturers offer a range of standard car sizes, normally in 100 mm increments, with limitations on the maximum dimensions imposed by BS EN 81-3[4] as follows:

— maximum floor area = 1.0 m²

— maximum car depth = 1.0 m

— maximum height = 1.2 m

The maximum height may be more, subject to the use of a permanently fixed shelf that restricts the height of each compartment to less than 1.2 m.

The rated load is not based on the available floor area as required by BS EN 81-1/2 but is limited to a maximum of 300 kg by BS EN 81-3.

Within these limitations, the lift car dimensions must be appropriate for the size of the goods to be carried. Any containers to be used should be taken into account since these could affect the rated load.

## 5.5.4      Entrances, car fittings and finishes

When deciding on the size of load carrying unit (car) and its entrance, it is important to take into account the need for clear access for loading and unloading. The size of packaging and transportation containers must be considered as well as handling clearances.

For cars with adjacent (i.e. front and side) entrances, the width of the side entrance is normally less than that for the front entrance. When selecting such cars it is imperative to ensure that items loaded through the front entrance can be unloaded from the side entrance.

Car doors are required where there is a risk of goods being transported, coming into contact with the well walls. Where car doors are not provided, it may be necessary to include means of immobilising any loads that may be prone to movement during the lift journey.

Where no car doors are provided on service lifts with a through car arrangement, protection may be required in the lift well to prevent entanglement of goods with the lift well or landing door equipment during travel.

Where car entrance protection is provided, the clear entrance width is normally less than the full width of the lift car and this must be taken into account to ensure easy loading and unloading of the car.

Figure 5.6 shows a typical service lift installation. Entrance doors or gates may be either manual or power-operated.

Manual vertical operating shutters (bi-parting or 'rise and fall') are normally fitted at serving height on landings and may also be fitted to the car. Hinged doors for landings are sometimes provided at floor level as an alternative.

Open collapsible gates or roller shutters may be provided for car entrance protection. A drop-bar (barrier) or similar protection for cars is also available to ensure that goods are restrained during travel, but these methods are suitable only for service lifts which carry bulky items or containers.

Power-operated vertical shutters or automatic closing hinged doors may be provided. Full power operation for hinged doors can be provided but this is expensive and normally a self-closing mechanism is adequate.

Automatic loading and unloading systems are available which employ power-operated rollers in the car with non-powered rollers on the landings. For carrying items such as documents, the car may be fitted with tilting trays and collection boxes at each landing. In both cases power-operated entrances are required.

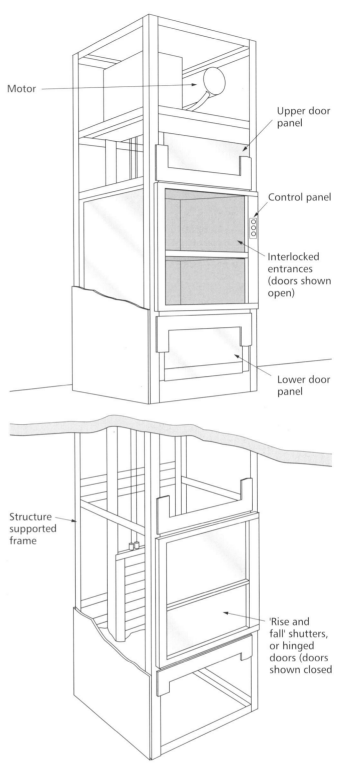

**Figure 5.6** Cutaway section of a typical service lift serving two levels

Side runners can be provided within the car to support serving trays etc. These remain permanently in place, and would need to be specified to suit a given size of tray. Alternatively, removable frame systems, custom made to requirements, can be provided.

For transporting food, heating panels can be fitted within the car. In this application, solid protection for car entrances is required and it is also advisable to specify smooth edges and corners within the car to enable easy cleaning.

### 5.5.5 Types of drive and operating speeds

Service lifts normally employ an electric traction drive, using either a drum, sprocket or counterweight arrangement. The ideal position for the drive is directly above the well and since the machines are relatively small they can often be accommodated within a normal room height to avoid the need for more costly locations to the bottom or side of the well.

Rated speeds are usually between 0.2 and 0.5 m/s but may be as high as 1.0 m/s, if required by the travel, or by special operational requirements.

### 5.5.6 Well

Most service lifts are supplied with their own structural frames to minimise builder's work. The lift and the frame is normally to the manufacturers standard details and therefore well sizes for service lifts are similar and can be based on the following guidance.

For initial layout purposes, the following well dimensions can be used:

— *well width*: car width plus 500 mm
— *well depth*: car depth plus 300 mm.

The actual overall sizes will be confirmed by the lift supplier who will take into account the lift arrangement, entrance details and any necessary space required for the enclosure.

The height of the soffit of the well (i.e. to the underside of the pulley or machine room floor) from the floor level of the highest floor served should be the height of the serving hatch plus the car height plus an allowance of between 500 and 1000 mm.

Where access to all serviceable parts is not possible from the landings, the lift must be designed to accommodate service personnel in the well with a clear height of 1800 mm above the top of the car at the top floor served. This is likely to cause the enclosure to penetrate the ceiling above the top floor served and should be avoided if possible.

For floor level service, a pit depth from 150 mm to 1000 mm is required, depending on car design and landing door arrangements. A pit is also required if the height of the serving hatch is such that there is insufficient height below the hatch to accommodate the landing shutters.

Where the pit is accessible for servicing, or maintenance, a minimum clear height of 1.8 m must be provided beneath the car by using a prop that is stored in the lift well.

### 5.5.7 Machine room

For electric traction service lifts with a machine room above, a minimum height of 600 mm is required for the machine room. The plan dimensions should be the same as the lift well. In some instances a separate area will be required to accommodate a control panel if this cannot be accommodated within the machine room itself.

For electric traction lifts with machine room adjacent or below, a pulley room is required above the well, which should have the same plan area as the well and a height of between 200 mm and 500 mm.

The machine room can be directly below the serving height of the lowest floor, positioned to either side of the well or within the well.

Items of equipment will need to be moved into and out of the machine room for installation, replacement and repair. A minimum access opening of 600 mm by 600 mm is normally recommended, but the final size depends on the equipment contained in the machine room. The area in front of the access door must be clear of ducting, piping, ceiling panels etc.

## 5.6 Motor vehicle lifts

### 5.6.1 General

There is currently no specific standard for vehicle lifts and they can be designed to BS EN 81-1/2[2,3] as heavy duty goods lift, if persons are to be transported with the vehicle. Vehicle lifts will, of necessity, have to provide a relatively large platform. The platform area is required to support at least 500 kg/m$^2$ (Table 1.1 of BS EN 81-1) for electric traction lifts and at least 333 kg/m$^2$ (Table 1.1A of BS EN 81-2) for hydraulic lifts. These loading requirements may be significantly in excess of the vehicle loads to be carried.

Where vehicles only are transported, the lift can be provided under the Machinery Directive[30,32], enacted as the Supply of Machinery Regulations[37] (as amended), which allows a more realistic loading requirement to be provided. If vehicles and persons are to be transported a lift complying with the Machinery Directive can still be installed, provided its rated speed is less than 0.15 m/s and it is operated by 'hold-to-run' controls. Provision of vehicle lifts under the Machinery Directive may only be made after a risk assessment has been carried out to determine the maximum loading.

It is unlikely that any supplier will be able to offer a suitable standard design and therefore consideration of the likely delivery time will be particularly important.

Special features for operation and signals are required for motor vehicle lifts, as detailed below.

### 5.6.2 Applications

The most common application for motor vehicle lifts is to gain access to restricted garage parking associated with commercial, office, institutional, residential buildings, and theatrical/entertainment premises. When considering this type of lift, it is important to allow adequate space for turning from the road and for manoeuvring within the garage area. Provision must be made for the removal of fumes from the lift car and well, in addition to their removal from the garage area itself.

### 5.6.3    Car sizes and payloads

Unless small vehicles only are to be carried, the lift car dimensions should be adequate to accommodate the largest standard production models. The lift car should be large enough to allow for driver errors in alignment and provide room to allow the driver to leave the vehicle in an emergency.

Special consideration may be required if there is a possibility of accommodating 'stretch' limousines and modern off-road vehicles, or vans, which may require additional length or height for the lift car and doors.

The recommended internal dimensions are:

— *width*: motor vehicle width plus 750 mm (375 mm clearance on each side)

— *depth*: motor vehicle length plus 500 mm (250 mm clearance at each end)

A lift car height of 2100 mm is satisfactory for most applications, but an increased height should be allowed if the lift is required to carry vehicles fitted with roof racks or commercial vans or lorries.

The rated load of any lift designed to carry passengers within the car must be in accordance with the relevant BS EN 81[2,3] standard.

### 5.6.4    Entrances, car fittings and finishes

The entrance does not need to be the full width of the lift car, but must be large enough for easy access including sufficient clearance for wing mirrors, roof racks etc. Entrances, particularly in basement areas, will usually require to be fire rated and it is important to advise the lift supplier accordingly.

If the entrance is exposed to external elements, consideration must be given to weather-proofing the equipment, including control stations and doors. Ramps should be provided in front of such entrances to prevent rainwater from entering the lift well.

Consideration should also be given to providing mechanical protection to the landing entrances by using bollards to avoid accidental impact damage from vehicles.

The simplest form of entrance doors are folding leaf shutters. They are inexpensive, reliable very durable and take up minimum well space but are not recommended because they are often unacceptable to users. The leaves intrude into the lift car and it will be necessary to increase the internal length accordingly. Folding leaf shutters require the driver to leave the vehicle on three occasions (four if the gates are to be closed after egress) and therefore may not be suitable for many vehicle lift applications.

Power operated doors with four, or even six panel, horizontal sliding, centre-opening doors provide a reliable and relatively inexpensive system. However, these doors can require considerable well space beyond the platform width and can prove less durable and require additional

mechanical protection to minimise damage caused by impact or misuse.

Vertical bi-parting door systems take up little plan well space, but are more expensive and require vertical clearance at the top and bottom entrances that can impact on the required pit and headroom dimensions. However, they are very heavy duty, making them particularly suitable for garage environments. A major negative aspect is the need for this type of door to be operated by continuous pressure control buttons. This can prove difficult for passengers using controls from within a vehicle.

Power-operated folding shutter gates are also available and offer a durable, robust solution for vehicle lift applications. The opening and closing times of these doors are not comparable with the quicker horizontal sliding doors and should not be considered in any applications where operational times may be critical to satisfactory performance.

Where automatic power-operated entrances are used, it is important to provide additional door closing protection to both the landing and the car entrances to ensure the doors cannot close on a vehicle. This protection should take the form of a light beam or series of beams in the landing architrave and car side wall (or front return where fitted). The beams can be connected to a traffic signal type system to indicate to the driver when the car is positioned correctly, similar to those fitted in many automatic car washes.

Control stations should be positioned to be within easy reach of the vehicle driver. Strip-type pushes, or a series of push buttons, fitted to both sides of the lift car will permit operation from within the vehicle.

Consideration will need to be given to protecting the entrances, car floor and walls. Reference should be made to the latter paragraphs of section 5.3.4 for guidance.

### 5.6.5    Types of drive and operating speeds

For travels up to four floors (i.e. approximately 12 m) twin-ram hydraulic systems, with speeds in the range 0.2 m/s to 0.3 m/s, are the most suitable. A direct-acting central piston provides an economic solution, where ground works permit the required borehole. However, the cost savings resulting from the simpler system will be offset by the additional costs of providing the borehole and also the need for future inspection of a borehole mounted cylinder must not be overlooked.

Travels in excess of 12 m are better served by electric traction drives with speeds up to 0.5 m/s. The ideal drive position is directly above the well. In view of the high payloads it is common to use rope factors up to 4:1 to reduce the load on the drive. In the past, floor levelling was an important consideration but, with modern control systems, floor levelling to an accuracy of ±6 mm should be possible.

Twin mast rack and pinion lifts can also be used with the same benefits indicated in section 5.7 and at speeds up to 0.3 m/s.

### 5.6.6        Well

In the absence of specific guidance in any standards, the dimensions in Table 5.2 are offered as guidance for initial space planning purposes, based on lift cars with front and rear entrances, for both hydraulic and electric traction motor vehicle lifts.

Note that electric traction lifts with bottom drive and without a pulley room require the well widths to be increased by 500 mm.

All dimensions should be checked with the lift installer before construction commences to avoid costly remedial works.

For initial planning of electric traction and hydraulic lifts, the headroom for a 2100 mm high lift car, should be based on 4200 mm from the top floor served to the underside of the pulley or machine room floor. The headroom will increase by 100 mm for each additional 100 mm of car height. For rack and pinion lifts the requirements will depend upon the location of the drive motors and should be checked with the lift manufacturer.

For electric traction and hydraulic lifts with horizontal sliding doors, the typical minimum pit depth required is 1800 mm. If vertical bi-parting doors are required, the pit depth will depend upon the configuration of the doors and should be checked with the lift manufacturer. For rack and pinion lifts the requirements will depend upon the location of the drive motors and should be checked with the lift manufacturer.

**Table 5.2** Well sizes for vehicle lifts

| Door type | Well width / mm | Well depth (mm) |
|---|---|---|
| Manual folding leaf | Lift car width plus 900 mm | Lift car depth plus 600 mm (including bunched lift car doors) |
| Power operated vertical | Lift car width plus 900 mm | Lift car depth plus 500 mm |
| Power operated horizontal, centre opening | Lift car width plus greater of either 900 mm or 1.5 × clear door opening width | Lift car depth plus 800 mm |

### 5.6.7        Machine room

The machine room requirements will be the same as those for goods lifts and are given in section 5.3

## 5.7        Rack and pinion lifts

### 5.7.1        General

The basic components of a rack and pinion drive are a continuous length of machine-cut toothed bar (rack) and a

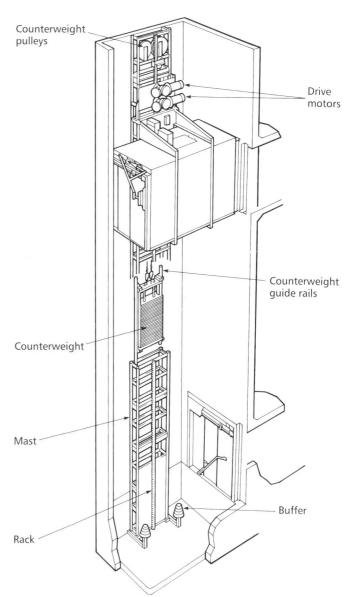

**Figure 5.7** General arrangement of rack and pinion lift

pinion, or pinions, which are held in permanent mesh with the rack mounted on a mast or masts, see Figure 5.7. Due to the ease of erection of the mast from the car roof (a practice developed over many years of experience with construction hoists) there is no need for a scaffold to be erected in the well during installation of the lift.

The virtually unlimited travel available with minimal loading on the building fabric, is a major benefit. Travel distances are largely unlimited; the tallest known installation at the time of publication is 640 m.

British Standard DD 222: 1996[12] gives recommendations for rack and pinion lifts and European standard prEN 81-7[5] is under development, which mainly relies on clauses from BS EN 81-1. Floor call systems, alarms, telephones, car-top control and landing levelling accuracy are all as for normal lift practice.

### 5.7.2        Applications

The main applications for rack and pinion lifts are in factories, warehouses and retail buildings where goods, heavy duty goods and vehicle service is required. There are occasional applications for their use in general purpose passenger lifts for loads up to 2000 kg using a single mast with a cantilevered car. Rack and pinion lifts are particularly suited to situations where the lift is installed without a well as with lifts exterior to a building. There is no requirement for the erection of accurately plumbed and parallel guide rails. In addition the speed of installation and the possibility for external application makes rack and pinion lifts suitable for temporary lifting facilities e.g. in residential buildings where an existing lift is being repaired or modernised.

Rack and pinion drive has been widely applied to the vertical transportation of passengers and goods in the construction and mining industries since about 1960. The ease of initial erection and subsequent extension as building work progresses has led to the rack and pinion lift replacing the rope hoist for passenger transportation on building sites in the UK. The height of travel can be increased or decreased by the addition or removal of mast sections. Relocation of the lift, as may be required when reorganising a factory, is also readily achieved. By jacking-up the mast, sections may be inserted into or removed from the base of the installation if there is any change in the level of the lowest landing served.

In recent years, the use of rack and pinion drives has been extended to include special installations where the use of a pre-formed rack can enable the lift car to follow a curved travel whilst being retained in a vertical position. This application is particularly suitable for high chimneys and off-shore platforms where the constructions do not always lend themselves to lifts that are mounted vertically in a straight run.

Rack and pinion drives are being used increasingly for heavy duty applications. They can be used with a single mast supporting a cantilever car on lifts with a capacity up to 2000 kg, or with a double mast for larger installations. The single mast arrangement imposes a horizontal load to the supporting wall, which must be considered during building design. Twin mast arrangements transfer the loading to the pit floor thus minimising any horizontal loading on the structure.

Rack and pinion drives are also commonly used for funicular railways and inclined lifts (see section 5.8.8), where the directional flexibility is again important.

In addition to the general applications already mentioned special applications include:

—    TV and radio masts

—    chimneys

—    cranes

—    grain silos

—    offshore exploration/production platforms.

### 5.7.3        Car size and payload

The load rating of the lift is dependent upon the available car area as defined in BS EN 81-1/2[2,3]. The range of rated loads and car sizes are as given in BS ISO 4190-1[14] or BS ISO 4190-2[15].

Smaller cars, for loads down to 200 kg, are available for special applications such as warehouses or tower cranes

where they can be located within the tower section to provide access to cabins at high level.

The car, which is fitted into the sling, is of similar construction to those found in electric traction or hydraulic lifts. The car can be cantilevered from a single guide mast, so making possible applications where building support can be offered from one side of the lift only, as with some types of observation lift and installations without a well. For applications with a rated load in excess of 2000 kg a twin mast arrangement should be considered, which eliminates the high loading imposed on the building support in cantilevered applications.

### 5.7.4        Entrances, car fittings and finishes

Car doors, landing doors, well and pit clearance dimensions are all to the appropriate parts of BS EN 81-1/2[2,3]. Doors may be manual or power-operated, however, due to the potential deflection of masts, particularly on single mast installations, special attention is required to ensure that automatic doors will operate reliably and provide correct alignment of the car and landing doors under all operating conditions. Modern solutions can incorporate automatically driven landing doors with no mechanical linkage to car doors to eliminate this problem.

### 5.7.5        Types of drive and operating speeds

The operation of a rack and pinion drive requires a pinion or pinions to be held in permanent mesh with the rack, see Figure 5.8. The pinions are driven by individual motors (usually electric but may be hydraulic, petrol or diesel) through reduction gearing. In order to simplify the range of components and to maintain constant motor and pinion sizes, high payload requirements are often met by using one, two or three drive units, each unit having an identical motor, gear box and pinion. The drive units are usually mounted on the lift frame, above the car.

The mechanical nature of rack and pinion drive, provides the ability to maintain floor level position during loading and unloading of heavy loads, without the need for

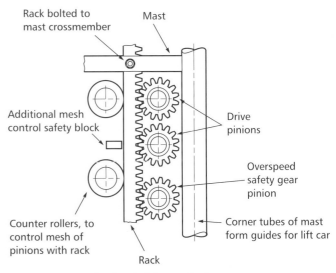

**Figure 5.8** Detail of rack and pinion mechanism

locking devices such as safety pawls, making it particularly beneficial for goods lifts applications.

The noise levels generated by the mechanical meshing of the pinion with the rack and the location of the motors on the lift car frame can be unacceptable in some instances. The noise levels can be greatly reduced by employing lower speeds and by reducing the module size which provides a finer mesh pitch between the rack and the pinions.

The speed of rack and pinion lifts whilst available up to 1.5 m/s is generally considered to be more acceptable at less than 0.5 m/s due to the excessive noise generated by high speed units. Speeds above 0.5 m/s tend to be used on building site hoists where fast journey times are important to the efficient operation of the site and passenger comfort is not a priority. If noise is considered a nuisance then rack and pinion lifts should only be considered at speeds up to 0.3 m/s with a reduced module size.

### 5.7.6 Runway

A rack and pinion lift does not run in a conventional well, but up a mast, or masts. The rack is bolted to a rigid mast section, the rack and the mast normally being produced in standard 1.5 m lengths. These are bolted together to give the required lifting height. The mast forms the guide rails and also provides the structural support for the complete lift. The mast sections may be preformed so that the lift can follow a varying radius of curvature, as may be found in offshore platform support legs, cooling towers, etc, the car being restrained to remain vertical. The corner tubes of the mast are enclosed by the guide rollers and the car is thus cantilevered from the mast and restrained to follow the path set by the mast. At various intervals, generally between 3 m and 12 m, the mast is laterally restrained by ties to the building. These ties can be adjusted to accommodate discrepancies in building verticality.

The single mast arrangement imposes a horizontal load to the supporting wall similar to that of hydraulic lifts and again these must be considered during building design. Twin mast arrangements may be adopted to eliminate the cantilever loads or for even larger lifts. The twin mast arrangement transfers the vertical loading to the pit floor thus minimising any horizontal loading on the structure.

The safety gear will normally be of the type used on construction hoists for over 20 years. Construction hoist applications require regular drop tests to prove the safety gear under loaded and mobile conditions, at least every three months. Therefore, such lifts are designed to enable quick and easy proving of the safety gear, without damage to components

The overspeed safety gear is normally mounted on the car sling and acts directly between the car and rack giving immediate response to an over speed condition. There is neither a governor rope nor any well-mounted equipment. The overspeed governor and arrester gear are usually contained within a sealed enclosure and act as a single system. The overspeed governor is directly driven at car speed by a steel pinion in permanent mesh with the mast rack. The arrester gear applies braking torque to the same pinion and brings the lift to a halt with all the arresting forces being absorbed through the rack. Braking is very

progressive and typical braking distances are about 1 m from the point of tripping.

The brakes themselves are of a centrifugal design and once activated, facilities can be provided to enable the brake to be released manually from within the car to provide a means of self rescue. This might be used on industrial applications such as chimneys, masts or cranes etc where it is not possible to access the lift car from a conventional lift well but should not be provided on lifts used by the public or other untrained operatives.

The lift is usually counterweighted, the weights being guided within the mast, and all vertical forces are transmitted directly to the foundation. The pulleys associated with the counterweight are mounted in the top mast section.

### 5.7.7 Machinery location

There is no requirement for a large machine/pump room and a well is not required to support the vertical loads and forces associated with the lift. All vertical loads from the lift are transferred via the rack to the mast. The drive motors and gearboxes are mounted directly onto the lift car frame. This greatly reduces the need for machinery space and often a small room capable of accommodating the main switchgear, distribution board and the controller cabinet is all that is required. In some cases, it is possible to mount the control cabinet behind an access panel on the lift car producing a machine room less installation although maintenance access and emergency rescue procedures need to be planned carefully in such cases.

## 5.8 Lifts for other purposes

### 5.8.1 Firefighting lifts

Firefighting lifts are described in detail in sections 6.2 to 6.4.

The Building Regulations[28] and BS 5588: Part 5[16] set down when firefighting lifts are required to be installed in a building. The standard indicates that buildings, or parts of buildings, where, either the height of the surface of the floor of the topmost storey (excluding plant rooms) exceeds 18 m, or the depth of the surface of the floor of the lowermost storey exceeds 10 m, should be provided with a firefighting shaft containing firefighting stair, a firefighting lobby with a fire main, and a firefighting lift. The standard recommends one firefighting shaft for every 900 m² of floor area on any given storey. If the building is fitted throughout with an automatic sprinkler system the requirements are less onerous.

The latest version of BS 5588: Part 5 does not define how a firefighting lift should be designed but calls on BS EN 81-72[11] for this detail, which specifies the firefighting lift should have:

— a recall switch located at the fire access level

— been installed to meet the requirements of BS EN 81-1[2], or BS EN 81-2[3], as applicable

— a rated load of at least 630 kg

— internal car dimensions should be a minimum of 1100 mm wide by 1400 mm deep

— run to the furthest floor of the building from the fire service access level (FSAL) in less than 60 seconds.

— automatic power-operated doors

— doors at least 800 mm wide by 2000 mm high with a fire rating of at least one hour

— position indicators provided in the car and at the firefighter's access level (FSAL)

— a two-way intercom between the car, machine room or emergency and inspection panel for machine room less lifts and firefighter's access level (FSAL)

— a notice stating: 'FIREFIGHTING LIFT: DO NOT USE FOR GOODS OR REFUSE'

— a notice stating: 'FIREFIGHTING LIFT: DO NOT OBSTRUCT LIFT DOORS — DO NOT LEAVE GOODS IN LIFT' at every firefighting lift lobby, where the firefighting lift is the only lift in the building

— emergency trap doors in the car roof

— provision for rescue from inside and outside the car

— buttons and controls protected from the effects of dripping water

— all electrical equipment protected against the effects of water

— an audible and visual alarm to alert maintenance personnel of operation of the firefighting switch

— a secondary supply.

The provision of firefighting lifts thus requires substantial expenditure and therefore the need for such a lift must be properly established. Once installed a firefighting lift can be used for normal passenger circulation provided it is not obstructed. Some firefighting lifts may be part of a passenger group, where this can be arranged or where accommodation elsewhere in the building cannot be allocated.

Another firefighting facility found in older buildings and new buildings, where a full firefighting requirement is not required is a 'fireman's lift'. This lift is fitted with a recall switch (behind a break glass) to the main access floor. It should not be confused with a firefighting lift as it is not fire protected and does not incorporate the control features of a modern firefighting lift.

## 5.8.2    Evacuation lifts

It is a requirement of UK building legislation that access provision be linked to egress provision. In response to this BS 5588: Part 8[17] was produced. This standard provides detailed guidance for evacuation procedures and on the types of lift required. The type of building and its use will determine whether disabled people need to be moved by lift. Where there are large numbers of wheelchair users present at, for example, a theatre or a sporting event, those responsible for the building may require that adequate provision be made in terms of the number of lifts installed.

BS 5588: Part 8 recommends that the lift be operated under the direction and control of authorised persons using an agreed evacuation procedure. Only disabled persons should use the lift. It is not intended that the disabled evacuate themselves from the building unaided, even where a lift is provided. Other facilities such as the provision of refuge areas may need to be considered.

Some of the requirements for an evacuation lift are the same as, or similar to, those for a firefighting lift. An evacuation lift should have:

— a recall switch (behind a break glass) at the final evacuation floor labelled 'EVACUATION LIFT'

— been installed to meet the requirements of BS EN 81-1[2], or BS EN 81-2[3], as applicable

— a rated load of at least 630 kg

— internal car dimensions should be 1100 mm wide by1400 mm deep

— run the full travel of the building in less than 60 seconds.

— automatic power-operated doors

— doors at least 800 mm wide by 2000 mm high with a fire rating of at least 30 minutes

— a secondary supply (except for two stop hydraulic lifts)

— a car substantially made of non-combustible materials

— controls at wheelchair height

— a communication system between the main lobby, machine room and all other lobbies for contact with fire marshals on each floor.

Although a firefighting lift can be used for evacuation prior to the arrival of the fire service or with their consent, an evacuation lift cannot be used as a firefighting lift.

## 5.8.3    Passenger lifts for use by persons with disabilities

Transportation systems for people with disabilities is covered in detail in section 11 and for passenger lifts in section 11.7.2.

The Disability Discrimination Act 1995[33] requires building owners and service providers to make reasonable provision to ensure that people with all disabilities can access buildings or services within a building. Passenger lifts designed, manufactured and installed in compliance with the Lifts Regulations 1997[36] are regarded by Approved Document Part M[29] as the best way to do this. The harmonised standard BS EN 81-70[9] provides the detailed requirements to supply or adapt a standard passenger lift to meet the needs of persons with disabilities. A summary of BS EN 81-70 can be found in section 11, Appendix 11.A1.

For adequate disabled access, the internal car sizes of passenger lifts must be suitable for the application. BS EN 81-70 outlines the varying requirements relating to a sole user, accompanied user and the accommodation of different sized wheelchairs defined by BS EN 12183[25] and BS EN 12184[26].

BS EN 81-70 indicates the smallest lift suitable for single wheelchair occupation, with no attendant, as a lift with a rated load of 450 kg (6-person) and internal car dimensions of 1000 mm wide by 1250 mm deep. In private applications, where larger lifts cannot be accommodated, this might provide a compromise solution.

BS EN 81-70 indicates the minimum car size to accommodate a wheelchair and an accompanying person as a lift with a rated load of 630 kg (8-person) car and clear internal dimensions of 1100 mm wide by 1400 mm deep This is the minimum size suitable for use in small offices, residential accommodation and residential care homes. It does not permit the wheelchair to be turned within the car. For new installations in public areas, the 630 kg lift should be considered the minimum suitable size. Lifts of this size meet the minimum requirements of Approved Document Part M.

For larger offices, residential accommodation and residential care homes, a 1000 kg (13-person) lift with an internal car dimensions of 1100 mm wide by 2100 mm deep might be considered as this will accommodate a stretcher. A better choice for all public buildings and offices is a lift with a rated load of 1275 kg (17-person) and clear internal dimensions of 2000 mm wide by 1400 mm deep. This is the minimum size of lift, which will allow access and full manoeuvrability for the largest wheelchairs in a lift car.

It is becoming common practice for designers to include at least one lift of these dimensions in public buildings and residential applications where full compliance with Disability Discrimination Act for the potential needs of wheelchair users is required. Where groups of lifts are installed it is relatively inexpensive to install all lifts compliant to BS EN 81-70.

The varied requirements within a building might require lifts of different dimensions. Since cost is often an issue during the design and construction of a building, it may become necessary to include lifts of different sizes within a single group in order to satisfy the various operational needs of the building. An example of this might be in a residential building where a lift with a rated load of 1275 kg is required, together with a lift capable of accommodating a stretcher or coffin. This would result in the need for a deep 1000 kg car and a square 1275 kg car, which will have varying lift well dimensions and create a non-uniform core arrangement.

## 5.8.4 Lifting platforms for use by persons with disabilities

Transportation systems for people with disabilities is covered in detail in section 11 and for lifting platforms in sections 11.7.3 and 11.7.4.

The Disability Discrimination Act 1995[33] requires building owners and service providers to make reasonable provision to ensure that people with all disabilities can access buildings or services within a building. Whilst passenger lifts are recommended as the preferred lifting device for compliance with Approved Document Part

M[29] lifting platforms may be considered in some circumstances. Lifting platforms fall under the Machinery Directive[30,32] enacted by the Supply of Machinery Regulations[37] (as amended). Recommendations related to the design of lifting platforms are contained in BS 6440[23], BS 5900[22] (domestic buildings only) and a European standard, prEN 81-41[8], is being prepared.

Lifting platforms may be considered suitable in situations where there is insufficient space to accommodate a passenger lift. This can sometimes occur in existing buildings, where there may be no possibility of excavating a pit, or the existing floor heights do not provide the necessary headroom for a passenger lift. Lifting platforms also take up a smaller footprint and can therefore be used in smaller buildings, where it may be impossible to accommodate a passenger lift well.

The travel distance that is required needs to be considered. Lifting platforms are limited to a maximum rise of two stories when supplied to BS 5900 (domestic situations) and to 4.0 m when supplied to BS 6440. In the event a longer travel is required, then a lifting platform type tested, under the Machinery Directive, by a notified body, for that travel can be installed. Generally a travel distance of 9.0 m is considered a practical limit for engineering reasons. Passenger comfort must also be considered. Owing to the maximum permitted rated speed of 0.15 m/s and the need for constant pressure on the control buttons to maintain motion, 9.0 m should also be considered a realistic travel limit. At a speed of 0.15 m/s a trip of nine metres will take one minute.

For low rises, lifting platforms can be arranged without an enclosure and tend to be a platform with a balustrade to two sides and entrance gates on both ends providing a through platform arrangement suitable for bridging a short rise of stairs. For rises above 2.0 m in public, or commercial installations, BS 6440 requires a full enclosure around the platform at the lower level although a balustrade height gate can be used at the top floor. BS 5900 allows a partial enclosure in the domestic environment.

Lifting platforms are mass produced and therefore tend to be available with only a limited range of finishes and enclosure designs. Enclosures are basic in design but can incorporate glazed panels to afford some visual enhancement and transparency to the device.

Although lifting platforms are not within the scope of BS EN 81-70[9], its recommendations should be considered, where appropriate, with regard to the design of pushbuttons, indicators, fixtures and fittings etc. Constant pressure pushbuttons should be located at the top and bottom levels and on the platform for use by the user of the platform. Periodic maintenance and inspections should be carried out at regular intervals.

## 5.8.5 Stairlifts for use by persons with disabilities

Transportation systems for people with disabilities is covered in detail in section 11 and section 11.7.5.

The Disability Discrimination Act 1995[33] requires building owners and service providers to make reasonable provision to ensure that people with all disabilities can access buildings or services within a building. Stairlifts fall under the Machinery Directive[30,32] enacted by the Supply of Machinery Regulations[37] (as amended). Recommendations related to the design of stairlifts are contained in BS 5776[21] and a European standard, prEN 81-40[7], is being prepared.

Stairlifts have a secure chair or platform travelling along a rail running up the length of the stairs and are mainly used in private dwellings. They are suitable for both straight and curved stairs (but not spiral stairs). The use of wheelchair platform stairlifts on curved stairs will require careful planning to ensure adequate width is available to allow the platform to turn within the stair.

Stairlifts are required to operate using a constant pressure button with a maximum permitted rated speed of 0.15 m/s. The travel distance must be considered as some users may suffer from exhaustion if the trip time is too long. Several boarding/alighting points may be necessary for long travel units.

Safety must be considered at all stages of a project, since the people most likely to use such a lift will be old or physically disabled. It should also take into account the future use of the stairlift. Safety belts, handgrips, a safe emergency exit for the user from the unit must all be considered, along with any risks from objects being left or dropped on the stairs. The stairlift installation must not impede the access of able-bodied persons to the stairs, or the fire exit arrangements, for both able-bodied persons, or those with disabilities.

Stairlifts are mass produced and are only available with a limited range of finishes. A certificate of installation, testing and acceptance should be obtained on completion. Periodic inspections and maintenance will be required throughout the life of the installation.

## 5.8.6   Explosion protected lifts

For many decades, specialist lift manufacturers have produced a small quantity of explosion protected lifts specifically for use in hazardous areas where there is a high risk of explosion that could be triggered by loose sparks or excessive heat. The number of such lifts is controlled by the limited demand compared with the numbers of lifts in non-hazardous areas. The volume of related paperwork, the demanding quality controls and the variety of administrative demands imposed by the authorities, result in very few companies being willing to become involved in this market. The manufacturer would need to employ flexible production schedules in order to accommodate an explosion protected unit, therefore suppliers of batch produced or 'packaged' lifts usually cannot contend with such specialist demands.

When a specification is being prepared for an explosion protected lift, the first consideration is whether the lift can be located, where no explosion hazard exists. If an alternative location would involve an increase in cost, this may well be offset by the higher price of a explosion protected lift. There is usually a cost ratio of more than three to one between conventional and explosion protect-

ed lifts of otherwise similar performance, owing to the more expensive equipment required such as motors, switches, enclosures for controls, choice of materials and, above all, the cost of the preparation of supporting documentation.

Explosion protected ('Ex') lifts fall under the Equipment and Systems Intended for Use in Potentially Explosive Atmospheres Directive[31] ('EXAT Directive'), the explosion protected type of electrical apparatus (EEx) to the BS EN 50014-20[27] series of standards and the relevant BS EN 81-1/2[2,3] standard. These requirements are very stringent and owing to the very specialised nature of this lift type a detailed discussion is not appropriate here.

## 5.8.7   Scissor lifts

Scissor lifts provide a simple, robust and low-cost means of lifting loads through short distances. While geometrically inefficient, the lifting mechanism is all contained within the dimensions of the base frame thereby providing a very compact lifting device. Lifting capacities range from a few kilograms to tens of thousands of kilograms and most scissor lifts are bespoke designs manufactured to suit the particular requirements of the specifier. A typical scissor lift is shown in Figure 5.9.

Scissor lifts are generally manufactured in accordance with BS EN 1570[13] although, depending on the application, other standards may be relevant, such as BS 6440[23]. Static or mobile types are available and typical applications include:

— lorry loading/unloading (dock levellers)

— feeding materials to machines

— transferring of materials/equipment

— access lifts for the elderly and people with disabilities (see section 11.7.3).

When positioning, consideration should be given to the configuration of the lift to ensure stability. Scissor lifts are most stable when they are loaded over the platform and

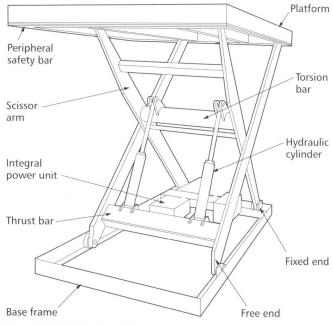

**Figure 5.9** Typical scissor lift

the load being applied is parallel to the plane of the scissor legs.

The load rating depends upon manufacture, but can be as high as 30 000 kg. The rise varies according to the scissor arrangement to a maximum of approximately 3000 mm. For rises in excess of 1500 mm, consideration should be given to providing a vertical guide to maintain stability of the platform when extended. Safety of the load on the platform can be ensured by handrails, interlocking platform and landing gates, wheel stops, loading flaps, or some combination of these or similar restraining devices.

All scissor lifts have a closed height and this may obstruct access onto the lift platform or cause an obstruction. In such cases a pit will be necessary, the depth being determined by the closed height of the lift. External pits should be provided with suitable drainage.

The platform length is dependent upon the vertical travel dimension because the scissor arms are accommodated beneath the platform when in the closed position. For this reason, longer travel units generally require a larger platform or a multiple scissor mechanism resulting in a deeper pit.

The power system usually consists of an electric pump, hydraulic fluid reservoir and control unit. Some units use a screw drive. This is most frequently accommodated beneath the platform, but may need to be remote from the machine. Controls can be fixed or hand-held. The maximum voltage for fixed controls is 240 volts and 110 volts for hand-held controls. The use of electronic valves is not common and therefore the starting and stopping of scissor lifts tends to be abrupt under the control of a simple solenoid valve.

Most scissor lifts will have a safety trip-bar, mounted around the perimeter of the underside of the platform to arrest downward travel in the case of an obstruction. Consideration should be given to guarding the underside of the lift to prevent the trapping of people and objects. In certain locations, e.g. a loading bay, barrier protection must be provided to the underside of the scissor lift to prevent access. BS EN 1570 gives recommendations on guarding requirements.

## 5.8.8    Inclined lifts

Inclined lifts have for many years been installed world-wide to provide access to hill-side apartments, hotels, beaches, churches, etc. Older types of so-called 'incline lifts', such as the cliff lifts at Bournemouth in England, or the lifts of Valparaise in Chile (built 1883–1915) are considered as funicular railways and generally come under tram codes and design specifications. These installations have often been modernised using lift equipment, but are still regarded as funiculars.

Inclined lifts are defined as permanently installed electric lifts, with traction (counterweighted) or positive drive, serving defined landings, with a vehicle designed to convey passengers, or passengers and loads, pulled by ropes, or chains, along guide rails on an inclined path at an angle between 15° and 75° to the vertical, without limitation of the travel. By contrast, conventional lifts move on guide rails inclined between 15° to the vertical and the vertical.

Modern inclined lifts are true lifts and should be designed, installed and operated according to BS EN 81-1[2] supported by the requirements of the proposed prEN 81-22[6] to deal with the range of inclination. This latter standard makes considerable variations on the requirements of BS EN 81-1 in order to deal with the wide range of inclinations possible. Figure 5.10 shows a typical inclined lift, with a counterweight.

Installations of this type should only be considered for speeds of up to 2.5 m/s, although faster speeds up to 4.0 m/s are possible. At all speeds parameters, such as acceleration/deceleration values, especially for emergency braking, need to be taken into account to ensure that horizontal acceleration levels are within acceptable levels to minimise the risk of passengers falling.

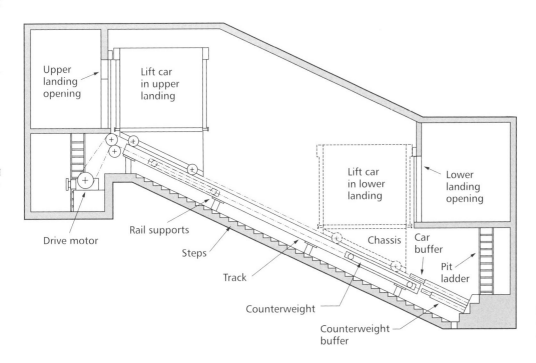

**Figure 5.10** Schematic of a typical inclined lift with counter-weight

Car sizes range from 4 persons to a maximum of 100 persons at rated speeds of 1.0 m/s, or to 40 persons at a rated speed of 4.0 m/s. The cars and running frames travel on tracks, or tensioned wire cables, and use wheels, or rollers.

The introduction of the vector control system has made inclined lifts a viable lift system where smooth acceleration, deceleration and stopping are required. Inclined lifts can operate over a fixed or variable slope or angle.

This type of system may solve the accessibility problems of older underground railways. Inclined lifts have been installed in some applications adjacent to escalators or stairs to provide access for wheelchair users or passengers unable to use escalators. In such schemes, the lift should be arranged to run at a slower speed than the escalators so as to discourage able-bodied people from using it.

## 5.9    Future concepts

There is increasing pressure from within the building industry to reduce costs, time and space requirements while maintaining a high standard of usability. This affects all lift manufacturers and suppliers. It also has a considerable influence on future lift design and installation procedures and new passenger transportation systems are constantly being investigated whilst maintaining the generally high quality of the equipment offered.

The very latest innovation is the application of two separately driven lift cars in a single lift shaft. This offers the additional capacity of a double deck lift without the limitation on service imposed by the cars being located in a common sling. This will create great opportunities for reducing the core space required for lift shafts and enable better lifting performance for slender towers where floor space is limited.

Whilst not exactly a new concept, the recent terrorist atrocities around the globe, have generated a great deal of debate about the use of lifts for general evacuation of tall buildings. If this results in a positive change to adopt lifts for evacuation, there will be additional design considerations for the controls, resilience in power supplies and structural integrity of lifts and wells required to allow the lifts to operate safely in emergency conditions.

Whilst MRL lifts are now firmly entrenched in the current product range of all major lift manufacturers, new systems are being developed including self-propelled cars. Free standing structures, lightly supported from one wall only, will offer a much wider choice of layouts and provide new opportunities for architects.

## References

1    Barney G C, Cooper D A and Inglis J *Elevator and Escalator Micropedia* (Sedbergh: GBA Publications) (2001)

2    BS EN 81-1: 1998: *Safety rules for the construction and installation of lifts. Electric lifts* (London: British Standards Institution) (1998)

3    BS EN 81-2: 1998: *Safety rules for the construction and installation of lifts. Hydraulic lifts* (London: British Standards Institution) (1998)

4    BS EN 81-3: *Safety rules for the construction and installation of lifts. Electric and hydraulic service lifts* (London: British Standards Institution) (1989)

5    prEN 81-7: *Safety rules for the construction and installation of lifts. Rack and pinion lifts* (London: British Standards Institution) (to be published)

6    prEN 81-22: *Safety rules for the construction and installation of lifts. Inclined lifts* (London: British Standards Institution) (to be published)

7    prEN 81-40: 2005: *Powered stairlifts for seated, standing and wheelchair users moving in an inclined plane intended for use by persons with impaired mobility* (London: British Standards Institute) (to be published)

8    prEN 81-41: 2005: *Vertical lifting platforms intended for use by persons with impaired mobility* (London: British Standards Institution) (to be published)

9    BS EN 81-70: 2003: *Safety rules for the construction and installation of lifts. Particular applications for passenger and goods passenger lifts. Accessibility to lifts for persons including persons with disability* (London: British Standards Institution) (2003)

10    BS EN 81-71: *Safety rules for the construction and installation of lifts* (London: British Standards Institution) (2005)

11    BS EN 81-72: 2003: *Safety rules for the construction and installation of lifts. Particular applications for passenger and goods passenger lifts. Firefighters lifts* (London: British Standards Institution) (2003)

12    DD 222: 1996: *Rack and pinion lifts* (London: British Standards Institution) (1996)

13    BS EN 1570: 1999: *Safety requirements for lifting tables* (London: British Standards Institution) (1999)

14    BS ISO 4190-1: 1999: *Lift (US: Elevator) installation. Class I, II, III and VI lifts* (London: British Standards Institution) (1999)

15    BS ISO 4190-2: 2001: *Lift (US: Elevator) installation. Class IV lifts* (London: British Standards Institution) (2001)

16    BS 5588: *Fire precautions in the design, construction and use of buildings*: Part 5: 1991: *Code of practice for firefighting stairs and lifts* (London: British Standards Institution) (1991)

17    BS 5588: *Fire precautions in the design, construction and use of buildings*: Part 8: 1999: *Code of practice for means of escape for disabled people* (London: British Standards Institution) (1999)

18    BS 5655: *Lifts and service lifts*: Part 5: 1981: *Specification for dimensions of standard electric lift arrangements* (London: British Standards Institution) (1981) (withdrawn)

19    BS 5655: *Lifts and service lifts*: Part 6: 2002: *Code of practice for selection and installation* (London: British Standards Institution) (2002)

20    BS 5655: *Lifts and service lifts*: Part 13: 1995: *Recommendations for vandal resistant lifts* (London: British Standards Institution) (1995)

21    BS 5776: 1996: *Powered stairlifts* (London: British Standards Institution) (1996)

22    BS 5900: 1999: *Specification for powered domestic lifts with partially enclosed cars and no lift well enclosures* (London: British Standards Institution) (1999)

23    BS 6440: 1999: *Powered lifting platforms for use by disabled persons. Code of practice* (London, British Standards Institution) (1999)

24    BS 7255: 2001: *Code of practice for safe working on lifts* (London: British Standards Institution) (2001)

25    BS EN 12183: 1999: *Manually propelled wheelchairs, requirements and test methods* (London: British Standard Institution) (1999)

26    BS EN 12184: 1999: *Electrically propelled wheelchairs, scooters and their chargers, requirements and test methods* (London: British Standard Institution) (1999)

27    BS EN 50014: 1998: *Electrical apparatus for potentially explosive atmospheres* (London: British Standards Institution) (1998)

28    The Building Regulations 2000 Statutory Instrument 2000 No. 2531 (London: The Stationery Office) (2000)

29    *Access to and use of buildings* Building Regulations Approved Document M (London: Stationery Office) (2003)

30    Council Directive 89/392/EEC of 14 June 1989 on the approximation of the laws of the Member States relating to machinery ('Machinery Directive') *Official J. of the European Communities* 29.06.1989 L183/9 (Brussels: Commission for the European Communities)

31    Directive 94/9/EC of the European Parliament and the Council of 23 March 1994 on the approximation of the laws of the Member States concerning equipment and protective systems intended for use in potentially explosive atmospheres ('EXAT Directive') *Official J. of the European Communities* 19.04.1994 L100/1 (Brussels: Commission for the European Communities) (1994)

32    Directive 98/37/EC of the European Parliament and of the Council of 22 June 1998 on the approximation of the laws of the Member States relating to machinery ('Machinery Directive') *Official J. of the European Communities* 23.07.1998 L207/1 (Brussels: Commission for the European Communities)

33    Disability Discrimination Act 1995 (London: The Stationary Office) (1995)

34    *Common activity spaces Vol. 4: Circulation areas* Health Building Note HBN 40 (London: Her Majesty's Stationery Office) (1995)

35    *Lifts design considerations* Health Technical Memorandum HTM 2024 (London: Her Majesty's Stationery Office) (1995)

36    The Lifts Regulations 1997. Statutory Instrument 1997 No. 831 (London: The Stationery Office) (1997)

37    The Supply of Machinery (Safety) Regulations 1992 Statutory Instruments 1992 No. 3073 (London: Her Majesty's Stationery Office) (1992)

# Appendix 5.A1: Car, well, headroom, pit and machine room sizes

Tables 5.A1.1 to 5.A1.7 are reproduced from *Elevator & Escalator Micropedia*[15] by G.C. Barney, D.A Cooper and J Inglis by kind permission of Gina Barney Associates. Copies may be obtained from PO Box 7, Sedbergh, LA10 5GE.

The values given in the tables are for guidance only as factors such as door height, door type, internal car height, position of counterweight, provision of counterweight safety gear, multiple lifts in well, equipment in the well (MRLS) etc., would require confirmation from the lift installer.

**Table 5.A1.1** Car, well, headroom and pit sizes: residential and health care lifts

| Speed (m/s) | Dimension | Size for given rated load | | | | | | | |
|---|---|---|---|---|---|---|---|---|---|
| | | Residential class | | | | Health care class | | | |
| | | 320 kg | 450 kg | 630 kg | 1000 kg | 1275 kg | 1600 kg | 2000 kg | 2500 kg |
| N/A | Car: | | | | | | | | |
| | — internal area (m²) | 0.95 | 1.30 | 1.66 | 2.40 | 2.95 | 3.56 | 4.20 | 5.00 |
| | — width (mm) | 900 | 100 | 1100 | 1100 | 1200 | 1400 | 1500 | 1800 |
| | — depth (mm) | 1000 | 1250 | 1400 | 2100 | 2300 | 2400 | 2700 | 2700 |
| N/A | Well: | | | | | | | | |
| | — width (mm) | 1500 (A) | 1600 (B) | 1600 (B) | 1600 (B) | 2100 (D) | 2400 (F) | 2400 (F) | 2700 (F) |
| | — depth (mm) | 1500 (A) | 1700 (B) | 1900 (B) | 2600 (B) | 2900 (D) | 3000 (F) | 3300 (F) | 3300 (F) |
| | — width (mm) | — | 1700 (C) | 1700 (C) | 1700 (C) | — | — | — | 2700 (G) |
| | — depth (mm) | — | 1700 (C) | 1900 (C) | 2600 (C) | — | — | — | 3300 (G) |
| 0.40* | Headroom (mm) | 3600 | 3600 | 3600 | 3600 | N/S | N/S | N/S | N/S |
| | Pit depth (mm) | 1400 | 1400 | 1400 | 1400 | N/S | N/S | N/S | N/S |
| 0.63 | Headroom (mm) | 3600 | 3600 | 3600 | 3600 | 4400 | 4400 | 4400 | 4600 |
| | Pit depth (mm) | 1400 | 1400 | 1400 | 1400 | 1600 | 1600 | 1600 | 1600 |
| 1.00 | Headroom (mm) | 3700 | 3700 | 3700 | 3700 | 4400 | 4400 | 4400 | 4600 |
| | Pit depth (mm) | 1400 | 1400 | 1400 | 1400 | 1700 | 1700 | 1700 | 1900 |
| 1.60 | Headroom (mm) | N/S | 3800 | 3800 | 3800 | 4400 | 4400 | 4400 | 4600 |
| | Pit depth (mm) | N/S | 1600 | 1600 | 1600 | 1900 | 1900 | 1900 | 2100 |
| 2.00 | Headroom (mm) | N/S | N/S | 4300 | 4300 | 4600 | 4600 | 4600 | 4800 |
| | Pit depth (mm) | N/S | N/S | 1750 | 1750 | 2100 | 2100 | 2100 | 2300 |
| 2.50 | Headroom (mm) | N/S | N/S | 5000 | 5000 | 5400 | 5400 | 5400 | 5600 |
| | Pit depth (mm) | N/S | N/S | 2200 | 2200 | 2500 | 2500 | 2500 | 2500 |

\* Hydraulic lifts only

*Source*: BS ISO 4190-1[9]

*Notes*:
(1)   N/S indicates non-standard configuration; N/A indicates that speed of lift is not relevant for car or well dimensions.
(2)   Headroom is top terminal finished floor to well ceiling; pit depth is from bottom terminal finished floor to pit floor.
(3)   Accommodation: 450 kg wheelchair only; 630/800/1000 kg wheelchair and attendant; 1275 kg and larger provides full manoeuvrability.
(4)   Health care lifts accommodate patient trolleys, beds (various sizes), instruments and attendants.
(5)   Door widths: A = 700 mm; B = 800 mm; C = 900 mm; D = 1100 mm; E = 1200 mm; F = 1300 mm; G = 1400 mm.

**Table 5.A1.2** Car, well, headroom and pit sizes: general purpose and intensive traffic lifts

| Speed (m/s) | Dimension | Size for given rated load | | | | | | | |
|---|---|---|---|---|---|---|---|---|---|
| | | General purpose class | | | | Intensive traffic class | | | |
| | | 630 kg | 800 kg | 1000 kg | 1275 kg | 1275 kg | 1600 kg | 1800 kg | 2000 kg |
| N/A | Car: | | | | | | | | |
| | — internal area (m²) | 1.66 | 2.00 | 2.40 | 2.95 | 2.95 | 3.56 | 3.88 | 4.20 |
| | — width (mm) | 1100 | 1350 | 1600 | 2000 | 2000 | 2100 | 2350 | 2350 |
| | — depth (mm) | 1400 | 1400 | 1400 | 1400 | 1400 | 1600 | 1600 | 1700 |
| N/A | Well: | | | | | | | | |
| | — width (mm) | 1800 (B) | 1900 (B) | 2200 (C) | 2500 (D) | 2600 (D) | 2700 (D) | 3000 (E) | 3000 (E) |
| | — depth (mm) | 2100 (B) | 2200 (B) | 2200 (C) | 2200 (D) | 2300 (D) | 2500 (D) | 2500 (E) | 2600 (E) |
| | — width (mm) | 2000 (C) | 2000 (C) | 2400 (D) | — | — | — | — | — |
| | — depth (mm) | 2100 (C) | 2200 (C) | 2200 (D) | — | — | — | — | — |
| 0.63 | Headroom (mm) | 3800 | 3800 | 4200 | 4200 | N/S | N/S | N/S | N/S |
| | Pit depth (mm) | 1400 | 1400 | 1400 | 1400 | N/S | N/S | N/S | N/S |
| 1.00 | Headroom (mm) | 3800 | 3800 | 4200 | 4200 | N/S | N/S | N/S | N/S |
| | Pit depth (mm) | 1400 | 1400 | 1400 | 1400 | N/S | N/S | N/S | N/S |
| 1.60 | Headroom (mm) | 4000 | 4000 | 4200 | 4200 | N/S | N/S | N/S | N/S |
| | Pit depth (mm) | 1600 | 1600 | 1600 | 1600 | N/S | N/S | N/S | N/S |
| 2.00 | Headroom (mm) | N/S | 4400 | 4400 | 4400 | N/S | N/S | N/S | N/S |
| | Pit depth (mm) | N/S | 1750 | 1750 | 1750 | N/S | N/S | N/S | N/S |
| 2.50 | Headroom (mm) | N/S | 5000 | 5200 | 5200 | 5500 | 5500 | 5500 | 5500 |
| | Pit depth (mm) | N/S | 2200 | 2200 | 2200 | 2200 | 2200 | 2200 | 2200 |
| 3.00 | Headroom (mm) | N/S | N/S | N/S | N/S | 5500 | 5500 | 5500 | 5500 |
| | Pit depth (mm) | N/S | N/S | N/S | N/S | 3200 | 3200 | 3200 | 3200 |
| 3.50 | Headroom (mm) | N/S | N/S | N/S | N/S | 5700 | 5700 | 5700 | 5700 |
| | Pit depth (mm) | N/S | N/S | N/S | N/S | 3400 | 3400 | 3400 | 3400 |
| 4.00 | Headroom (mm) | N/S | N/S | N/S | N/S | 5700 | 5700 | 5700 | 5700 |
| | Pit depth (mm) | N/S | N/S | N/S | N/S | 3800 | 3800 | 3800 | 3800 |
| 5.00* | Headroom (mm) | N/S | N/S | N/S | N/S | 5700 | 5700 | 5700 | 5700 |
| | Pit depth (mm) | N/S | N/S | N/S | N/S | 3800 | 3800 | 3800 | 3800 |
| 6.00* | Headroom (mm) | N/S | N/S | N/S | N/S | 6200 | 6200 | 6200 | 6200 |
| | Pit depth (mm) | N/S | N/S | N/S | N/S | 4000 | 4000 | 4000 | 4000 |

\* Using reduced stroke buffering

*Source*: BS ISO 4190-1[9]

*Notes*:

(1) N/S indicates non-standard configuration; N/A indicates that speed of lift is not relevant for car or well dimensions.

(2) Headroom is top terminal finished floor to well ceiling; pit depth is from bottom terminal finished floor to pit floor.

(3) Accommodation: 450 kg wheelchair only; 630/800/1000 kg wheelchair and attendant; 1275 kg and larger provides full manoeuvrability.

(4) Door widths: A = 700 mm; B = 800 mm; C = 900 mm; D = 1100 mm; E = 1200 mm; F = 1300 mm; G = 1400 mm.

**Table 5.A1.3** Car, well, headroom and pit sizes: goods lifts; Series A (Europe)*

| Speed (m/s) | Dimension | Size for given rated load | | | | | | |
|---|---|---|---|---|---|---|---|---|
| | | 630 kg | 1000 kg | 1600 kg | 2000 kg | 2500 kg | 3500 kg | 5000 kg |
| N/A | Car: | | | | | | | |
| | — internal area (m$^2$) | 1.66 | 2.00 | 3.56 | 4.20 | 5.00 | 6.60 | 9.00 |
| | — width† (mm) | 1100 | 1350 | 1400 | 1500 | 1800 | 2100 | 2500 |
| | — depth (mm) | 1400 | 1750 | 2400 | 2700 | 2700 | 3000 | 3500 |
| N/A | Well: | | | | | | | |
| | — width (mm) | 2100 (A) | 2400 (A) | 2500 (A) | 2700 (A) | 3000 (A) | 3500 (A) | 4100 (A) |
| | — depth (mm) | 1900 (A) | 2200 (A) | 2850 (A) | 3150 (A) | 3150 (A) | 3550 (A) | 4050 (A) |
| | — width (mm) | — | 2400 (B) | 2500 (B) | 2700 (B) | 3000 (B) | 3500 (B) | 4100 (B) |
| | — depth (mm) | — | 2300 (B) | 2950 (B) | 3250 (B) | 3250 (B) | 3700 (B) | 4200 (B) |
| | — width (mm)‡ | — | — | 2200 (C) | 2300 (C) | 2600 (C) | 2900 (C) | 3300 (C) |
| | — depth (mm) | — | — | 3050 (C) | 3350 (C) | 3350 (C) | 3650 (C) | 4150 (C) |
| | — width (mm)‡ | — | — | 2200 (D) | 2300 (D) | 2600 (D) | 2900 (D) | 3300 (D) |
| | — depth (mm) | — | — | 3400 (D) | 3700 (D) | 3700 (D) | 4000 (D) | 4500 (D) |
| 0.25 | Headroom (mm) | 3700 | 3700 | 4200 | 4200 | 4600 | 4600 | 4600 |
| | Pit depth (mm) | 1400 | 1400 | 1600 | 1600 | 1600 | 1600 | 1600 |
| 0.40 | Headroom (mm) | 3700 | 3700 | 4200 | 4200 | 4600 | 4600 | 4600 |
| | Pit depth (mm) | 1400 | 1400 | 1600 | 1600 | 1600 | 1600 | 1600 |
| 0.50 | Headroom (mm) | 3700 | 3700 | 4200 | 4200 | 4600 | 4600 | 4600 |
| | Pit depth (mm) | 1400 | 1400 | 1600 | 1600 | 1600 | 1600 | 1600 |
| 0.63 | Headroom (mm) | 3700 | 3700 | 4200 | 4200 | 4600 | 4600 | 4600 |
| | Pit depth (mm) | 1400 | 1400 | 1600 | 1600 | 1600 | 1600 | 1600 |
| 1.00 | Headroom (mm) | 3700 | 3700 | 4200 | 4200 | 4600 | 4600 | 4600 |
| | Pit depth (mm) | 1400 | 1400 | 1600 | 1600 | 1600 | 1600 | 1600 |

* Series B applies for the rest of the world
† Also clear door opening width
‡ Add 150 mm for telescopic vertical sliding doors (type 6)

*Source*: BS ISO 4190-2: 2001[10]

*Notes*:
(1) N/A indicates that speed of lift is not relevant for car or well dimensions.
(2) Headroom is top terminal finished floor to well ceiling; pit depth is from bottom terminal finished floor to pit floor.
(3) Accommodation: 450 kg wheelchair only; 630/800/1000 kg wheelchair and attendant; 1275 kg and larger provides full manoeuvrability.
(4) Door types: A = single entrance, horizontal sliding; B = two opposing entrances, horizontal sliding; C = single entrance, vertical sliding; D = two opposing entrances, vertical sliding.

**Table 5.A1.4** Machine room sizes: passenger lifts

| Speed (m/s) | Dimension | Size for given rated load | | | | | | | | |
|---|---|---|---|---|---|---|---|---|---|---|
| | | 320 kg | 450 kg | 630 kg | 800 kg | 1000 kg | 1275 kg | 1600 kg | 1800 kg | 2000 kg |
| 0.63/1.00/1.60 | Min. width (mm) | 2000* | 2200† | 2500 | 2500† | 3200 | 3200 | 3200 | 3000 | 3000 |
| | Min. depth (mm) | 3000* | 3200† | 3700 | 3700† | 4900 | 4900 | 4900 | 5000 | 5000 |
| 2.00/2.50/3.00 | Min. width (mm) | — | — | 2700* | 2700* | 2700 | 3000 | 3000 | 3300 | 3300 |
| | Min. depth (mm) | — | — | 4700* | 4900* | 5100 | 5300 | 5300 | 5700 | 5700 |
| 3.50/4.00/5.00/6.00 | Min. width (mm) | — | — | — | — | 3000 | 3000 | 3000 | 3300 | 3300 |
| | Min. depth (mm) | — | — | — | — | 5700 | 5700 | 5700 | 5700 | 5700 |

* Estimated value (value not given in BS ISO 4190)
† Value obtained from BS 5655: Part 5[36] (value not given in BS ISO 4190)

*Sources*: BS ISO 4190-1/2[9,10], BS 5655: Part 5[36]

*Notes*:
(1) For multiple lifts (side-by-side or facing), see formulae given in BS ISO 4190.
(2) Machine room clear height to be at least 1.8 m for movement and at least 2.0 m in working areas.

**Table 5.A1.5** Machine room sizes: health care lifts

| Speed (m/s) | Dimension | Size for given rated load | | |
|---|---|---|---|---|
| | | 1275/1600 kg | 2000 kg | 2500 kg |
| 0.63–2.50 | Min. width (mm) | 3200 | 3200 | 3500 |
| | Min. depth (mm) | 5500 | 5800 | 5800 |
| | Area (m²) | 25 | 27 | 29 |

*Sources*: BS ISO 4190-1/2[9,10], BS 5655: Part 5[36]

*Notes*:

(1) For multiple lifts (side-by-side or facing), see formulae given in BS ISO 4190.

(2) Machine room clear height to be at least 1.8 m for movement and at least 2.0 m at working areas.

**Table 5.A1.6** Machine room sizes: goods lifts; Series A (Europe)

| Class (m/s) | Parameter | Size for given rated load | | |
|---|---|---|---|---|
| | | 630 kg | 1000/1600/2000 kg | 2500/3500/5000 |
| 0.25/0.40/0.50 | Min. width (mm) | 2500 | 3200 | 3000 |
| 0.63/1.00 | Min. depth (mm) | 3700 | 4900 | 5000 |

*Notes*:  *Sources*: BS ISO 4190-1/2[9,10]

(1) For multiple lifts (side-by-side or facing), see formulae given in BS ISO 4190.

(2) Machine room clear height to be at least 1.8 m for movement and at least 2.0 m at working areas.

**Table 5.A1.7** Machine room sizes: hydraulic lifts (all)

| Speed (m/s) | Dimension | Size for given rated load |
|---|---|---|
| | | 320/450/630/800/1000/1275/1600/1800/2000/2500/3500/5000 kg |
| 0.25–1.00 | Area (m²) | (Well width or well depth) × 2000 mm |

*Notes*:  *Sources*: BS ISO 4190-1/2[9,10]

(1) For multiple lifts (side-by-side or facing), see formulae given in BS ISO 4190.

(2) Machine room clear height to be at least 1.8 m for movement and at least 2.0 m at working areas.

# 6     Firefighting lifts and escape lifts for people with disabilities

## Principal author

Derek Smith (Otis Ltd.)

## Chapter contents

| | | |
|---|---|---|
| 6.1 | Introduction | 6-3 |
| 6.2 | Need for firefighting lifts | 6-3 |
| | 6.2.1   General | 6-3 |
| | 6.2.2   History and development | 6-3 |
| | 6.2.3   Scope of BS 5588: Part 5 | 6-4 |
| | 6.2.4   General requirements of BS 5588: Part 5 | 6-4 |
| 6.3 | Firefighting lifts: design considerations | 6-6 |
| | 6.3.1   General | 6-6 |
| | 6.3.2   Car entrances | 6-6 |
| | 6.3.3   Machine room location | 6-7 |
| | 6.3.4   Protection of lift shaft from water | 6-7 |
| | 6.3.5   Power supplies | 6-7 |
| | 6.3.6   Firefighter's switch | 6-8 |
| 6.4 | Firefighting lifts: inspection, testing and maintenance | 6-8 |
| | 6.4.1   Operational tests prior to handover | 6-8 |
| | 6.4.2   Routine inspection and maintenance | 6-8 |
| 6.5 | Evacuation lifts for people with disabilities | 6-8 |
| | 6.5.1   General | 6-8 |
| | 6.5.2   Access/egress for disabled persons | 6-9 |
| | 6.5.3   Design considerations | 6-9 |
| | 6.5.4   Communication system | 6-9 |
| References | | 6-10 |

# 6 Firefighting lifts and escape lifts for people with disabilities

## 6.1 Introduction

In event of fire, evacuation routes for occupants of buildings are usually via fire resistant stairways. However, provision may still have to be made for a lift to operate during a fire either to enable firefighters to access upper floors safely or, in some buildings, to assist in the evacuation of disabled people. This chapter explains the basic requirements for lifts that are intended to be used in fire situations.

## 6.2 Need for firefighting lifts

### 6.2.1 General

A standard lift fitted with a fire service switch cannot be considered as a firefighting lift. The provision of firefighting lifts requires substantial expenditure and therefore the need for such a lift must be properly established. This section provides guidance on the design of firefighting lifts. Its aim is to provide a basic understanding of the codes and how they affect lifts. It is not, however, intended to be comprehensive and, where appropriate, reference must be made to the Building Regulations[27] and relevant British Standards[2–26]

### 6.2.2 History and development

As early as 1930, it was recognised that firefighters should be provided with a means of swift access to the upper floors of large buildings. This resulted in conventional passenger lifts being fitted with a break-glass key switch at the firefighter's access floor which, when operated, brought the lift to that floor quickly.

It was determined that such lifts should have power-operated doors 2 ft 9 in (800 mm) wide. Their capacity would be 1200 lb (550 kg) and they would be sufficiently fast to travel the height of the building in less than one minute. Additional requirements, such as fire-tested landing doors, rated at 1 hour, were gradually introduced. Some local authorities imposed further specific requirements such as those contained in Section 20 of the London Building Act 1939[30]. The main requirements were taken into BS 2655: Part 12 which was superseded in 1979 by BS 5655[17–24]. BS 5655 Parts 1 and 2 have subsequently been superseded by BS EN 81[1,2].

Although these standards defined the basic requirements for 'firefighter's lifts', no guidance is given on the circumstances in which such a lift should be provided. This information is contained within the Building Regulations[27] and, since 1988, in BS 5588[8–16].

It is now recognised that modern firefighting techniques involve the use of equipment which needs to be moved by means of the lift. Furthermore, firefighters need a safe and reliable means of access to the upper floors of large buildings. The concept of the firefighting lift was devised to meet these requirements and BS 5588: Part 5 sets down standards for such lifts. This standard has been revised as BS 5588: Part 5: 2004[10]. These lifts are referred to as 'firefighting lifts' and the term 'fireman's lift' is now obsolete.

The 2004 edition of BS 5588: Part 5 represents a major revision of the standard, and introduces the following principal changes:

— new recommendations for vehicle access, water supplies, fire control centre, drawings for fire service use and smoke control

— removal of all recommendations relating to firefighting lifts that are now covered in BS EN 81-72[3]

— detailed recommendations for a fire service communication system

— updating of recommendations to reflect new regulations and changes in practice since the previous edition.

In relation to lifts the major change is the recognition of a new harmonised European standards BS EN 81-72[3]. As a harmonised standard it has been introduced to remove barriers to trade for industry and lifts constructed in accordance with this standard are recognised and accepted across Europe. The standard is a product standard and this means that whilst it defines in detail the requirements for a firefighting lift it does not define when such a lift is required nor does it state requirements for the building. These matters are left to local building codes and legislation.

BS 5588: Part 5 therefore still has a role to play in relation to lifts. It defines when such lifts are required, as well as, the fire resistance requirements for the structure of the lift shaft etc.

The ongoing development of these standards for lifts and buildings is the result of changes in the way that fires are tackled and firefighting techniques need to be understood in order to appreciate fully why the requirements should be met in full.

On arrival at a fire, the fire brigade will establish at the floor where the fire is located. This information can be gained by various means such as fire detection systems, or from persons who have seen the fire. While this information is being obtained, the firefighting lift will be called to the fire access lobby and taken under the control of the fire brigade. When the location of the fire has been established, a team of four firefighters will use the lift to travel to the floor below the floor on which the fire is located. These firefighters will be carrying various items of equipment, including breathing apparatus, and will require all of the space offered by an 8-person lift car, even though they are only four in number.

On reaching the floor below the fire, three firefighters will leave the lift and make their way by the stairs to the floor on which the fire is located. Meanwhile the remaining firefighter will use the lift to return to the fire lobby in order to bring up more firefighters and equipment. In large fires, the floor below the fire will be established as a base where fire crews may rest and recharge breathing equipment, and where casualties may wait for transport to the Fire Service Access (exit) level. In such cases, the importance of the lift will increase, rather than diminish, as the fire develops and therefore it is essential that the fire brigade can maintain good communication with the lift car and retain full control over it.

### 6.2.3    Scope of BS 5588: Part 5

This part of BS 5588 gives recommendations and guidance on access and facilities for fire fighting. It is not applicable to buildings under construction. BS 5588-2: 1985 and BS 5588-3: 1983 have been withdrawn and the requirements for offices and shops are now to be found in BS 5588: Part 11: 1997[15]. This addresses shops and similar places used for retail trades or business, including stores, supermarkets and hypermarkets (but excluding the communal parts of shopping complexes). Part 11 also includes places where goods are traded, cafes, restaurants, public houses, etc. It covers planning for escape, and states that lifts other than firefighting lifts, or those designed specifically for the evacuation of disabled people, should not be used for escape.

The communal areas of shopping complexes are addressed in BS 5588: Part 10[14]. Atria in buildings are covered by BS 5588: Part 7[12]. Residential buildings are addressed in BS 5588: Part 1[8].

These documents define the situation where a firefighting lift is required and state that, where such a lift is required, it shall satisfy BS 5588: Part 5[10]. Where a lift is required for the evacuation of disabled persons, it shall be either a firefighting lift to BS 5588: Part 5 or a lift meeting the requirements of BS 5588: Part 8[13]. Where it is intended to use a firefighting lift for evacuation, agreement should be sought from the fire service.

### 6.2.4    General requirements of
###             BS 5588: Part 5

The requirements are complex and to some extent depend on the building use, size, floors etc. To determine exactly what is required in a given building requires reference to the standard itself, but in essence the following is a general guide.

The standard suggests that buildings, or parts of buildings, where either (a) the height of the surface of the floor of the topmost storey (excluding plant rooms) exceeds 18 m or, (b) the depth of the surface of the floor of the lowermost storey exceeds 10 m, should be provided with a firefighting shaft containing firefighting stair, a firefighting lobby with a fire main, and a firefighting lift.

The number of shafts is determined by the length of a fire hose and the standard recommends that sufficient shafts be provided and positioned to give one firefighting shaft for every 900 m$^2$ of floor area on any given storey. The distance between the shaft and the accommodation to any point on the storey must not exceed 60 m. If the internal layout is not known, a direct route of 40 m may be used for planning purposes.

If the building is fitted throughout with an automatic sprinkler system, and the largest storey is over 18 m above ground level, the number of firefighting lifts should be not less than:

— one lift if the largest floor area over 18 m is less than 900 m$^2$

— two lifts if the largest floor area above 18 m is more than 900 m$^2$ and not more than 2000 m$^2$

— .

Whilst it is desirable for lifts to serve all storeys of a building, it is not essential. In large complexes, several lifts may provide for firefighting some of which may serve upper floors while others serve basements. Figure 6.1 outlines the extent of travel required by a firefighting lift. Note: BS EN 81-72[3] refers to lifts serving all floors. However, a note to clause 7.7.1 in BS 5588: Part 5[10] indicates that fire and rescue services in the UK advise that firefighting lifts serve only the storeys that fire service personnel need to reach.

The location of firefighting shafts should be such that they allow access to every part of every storey that they serve and should, wherever possible, be located against an exterior wall.

If it is not possible to locate the firefighting shaft against an exterior wall, the route from the fire service entrance to the firefighting shaft (protected corridor) should be as short as possible and preferably not more than 18 m in length. It should be protected by fire-resisting construction to ensure that fire does not affect the route or cut off the means of escape for fire service or other personnel within the building.

The layout of the firefighting shaft at fire service access level should be arranged so that such that firefighters and persons escaping down the firefighting stair do not get in each others way.

It should not be necessary for persons escaping down the stair to pass through the firefighting lobby at fire service access level. Where a protected corridor for firefighting access also forms part of the means of escape from the accommodation, it should be 500 mm wider than that required for means of escape purposes (to allow room for fire service personnel to move towards the firefighting shaft), and the firefighting lobby should have a minimum area of 5 m$^2$ clear of any escape routes so that it can act as a fire service mustering point.

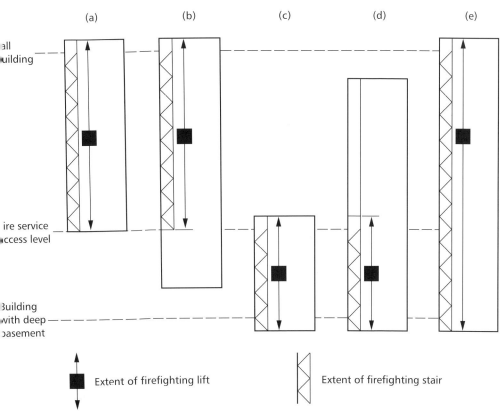

Figure 6.1 Extent of travel of firefighting lift; (a) buildings over 18 m high without basement, (b) buildings over 18 m high with basement less than 10 m deep, (c) buildings with basement only; (d) buildings less than 18 m high with deep basement, (e) buildings over 18 m high with deep basement

The firefighting lobby at fire service access level should be big enough to act as a command post where firefighters and firefighting equipment can be safely assembled.

It should be noted that, although passengers may use the lift during normal operation, its primary function must not be for the transportation of goods, i.e. it must not be a goods lift.

Whichever layout or position is selected, firefighting lifts must be within a firefighting shaft which contains stairs, lobbies, fire main and the lift itself. The entire shaft must be enclosed by a structure which is fire resistant (usually for two hours). Figure 6.2 shows a typical arrangement.

Without the provision of a lobby or stairs, the ability of a lift to operate during a fire is questionable. It is not possible to ensure that the lift can withstand fire and so a

lobby must be provided. In the event of a lift failure, an alternative exit from lobbies must be provided for firefighters, hence the need for stairs.

The firefighting lift may share a common shaft with other lifts, see Figure 6.3. In such cases it must also share a common lobby and all lifts in the shaft will need to be constructed to a similar standard in terms of the fire resistance of the materials used in the cars and all must have fire resistant landing doors.

BS 5588: Part 5 provides detailed guidance on the requirements for fire escape routes, stairs and lifts. While detailed consideration of escape routes and stairs is outside the scope of this Guide, it is important to note that pressurisation of firefighting shafts may be used in certain circumstances. However, the lift supplier should be notified of this intention.

Such pressurisation systems should follow the principles given in BS 5588: Part 4[9] and the system provided should keep both the firefighting lift well and stair enclosure

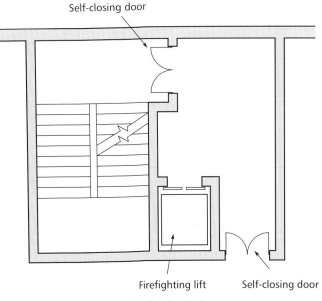

Figure 6.2 Typical layout for firefighting shaft

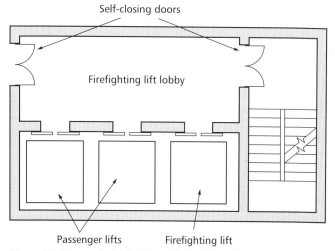

Figure 6.3 Layout of a firefighting cell with shared lift shaft

clear of smoke. In the event of smoke entering the firefighting lobby, the pressure within the stair enclosure should not drive smoke into the lift well or vice versa. Pressure levels and means of calculation are provided in BS 5588: Part 4. These include typical leakage rates through lift doors. It should be noted that it is not practical to seal the lift doors to reduce leakage and the addition of brush or similar seals will generally invalidate the fire certification applicable to the doors. Typical pressure levels for such systems are in the range 30–60 Pa and, while such pressures will not generally disturb operation of the doors, it is advisable to notify the lift supplier of the intention to pressurise the installation and provide details of the likely pressures.

Figure 6 of BS 5588: Part 5: 2004[10] erroneously indicates a requirement for a fire door with 30-minute fire resistance with smoke seal to be provided on lifts. A smoke-sealed door is not required on a lift and, at the time of writing (May 2005), an amendment to the British Standard to this effect is being progressed.

Ventilation of lift wells is not required by BS 5588: Part 5 or by the lift standard BS EN 81-1/2[1,2] as it is not envisaged that smoke will enter the lift well from outside as provisions are required to keep lobbies clear of smoke.

## 6.3    Firefighting lifts: design considerations

### 6.3.1    General

BS 5588: Part 5[10] provides detailed guidance on the design of the building, the location of firefighting shafts and what should be contained within a firefighting shaft. When a firefighting lift is required BS 5588: Part 5 no longer defines how it should be designed but instead it calls on BS EN 81-72[3] for this detail.

BS EN 81-72 specifies the following requirements for the lift. The lift should firstly meet the safety requirements given in BS EN 81-1[1], or BS EN 81-2[2], as applicable. The requirements are:

— Firefighting lifts must be at least 630 kg duty load; the internal dimensions of the car should be 1100 mm wide, 1400 mm deep.

— The speed should be sufficient to enable the lift to run the full travel of the building in less than 60 seconds. (An approximation of the minimum speed required may be obtained by dividing the total travel by 60 seconds minus 8 seconds for the car to accelerate and decelerate.)

— Automatic power-operated doors must be provided, at least 800 mm wide by 2000 mm high. A fire rating of at least one hour is usually required for the doors.

— Lift position indicators should be provided both in the car and at the firefighter's access level to show the car position at all times while power is available.

— A two-way intercommunication system must be provided between the car, machine room, emer-

Illustration in white. Background in red.

Size:

• 20 mm x 20 mm for a symbol on the car operating panel

• a minimum of 100 mm x 100 mm on a landing

• on a dual entry lift the car operating panel used for firefighting operation shall have such a sign 20 mm x 20 mm

**Figure 6.4** Pictogram to identify fire service access level

gency and inspection panel (for machine room-less lifts), and firefighter's access level. It should be switched on automatically when the lift is put to firefighting operation. A handset must not be used for the fire service access level and car. These must use built-in devices. It is important to note that this lift communication system is for the fire service, but is not part of the fire service communication system that is required in firefighting shafts according to BS 5588: Part 5.

— The lift must be clearly marked: 'FIREFIGHTING LIFT: DO NOT USE FOR GOODS OR REFUSE', in accordance with BS 5499: Part 1[7]. Such signs are not considered part of the lift and are therefore not normally provided by the lift manufacturer.

— Every firefighting lift lobby should have a notice stating: 'FIREFIGHTING LIFT LOBBY: DO NOT OBSTRUCT LIFT DOORS: DO NOT USE FOR STORAGE; DO NOT LEAVE GOODS IN LIFT'.

— Provisions for rescue of trapped firefighters from inside and outside the lift car must be provided as follows.

BS EN 81-72 requires that provision be made for the rescue and escape of firefighters who may become trapped in the lift car. To this end firefighting lift cars must be provided with a trap door in the car roof. The trap door varies depending on the lift size. Where an 630 kg, 8-person lift is selected the trap door must be at least 0.4 m × 0.5 m. In the case of larger lifts the door must be 0.5 m × 0.7m.

BS 5588: Part 5, clause 7.2.7, makes it clear that in the UK the method of rescue shall be external. This means provision needs to be made to allow a trapped firefighter to be rescued from outside the lift by colleagues. To do this it must be possible for firefighter to access the roof of the car by way of the landing doors. With the landing doors open it may be a considerable distance down to the roof of the lift car and BS EN 81-72 suggests possible rescue methods. The standard does not specify the method as this is the responsibility of the fire service; instead it gives examples. Fire services in the UK are likely to use a portable ladder when the car is not too far down the lift well. When a ladder cannot be used then a rope climbing system may be employed. This will require the provision of suitable load-tested anchor points on landings adjacent to the lift.

Self-rescue, where the firefighters can open the car trap and escape without assistance, is not favoured by the UK *but* is a requirement to be met in BS EN 81-72 if the supplier wishes to claim compliance with the standard. This provision requires a means of escape such as a ladder to be provided inside the lift car, so that the firefighter can climb onto the roof of the car. Once on the car roof it is likely that the landing entrance is a considerable distance above the car roof and, again, provision must be made to allow persons to ascend to a safe position to open the landing doors. This would normally entail the provision of a ladder attached to the side of the lift car.

— Car buttons and controls should be protected from the effects of dripping water and, in addition to the normal storey markings, should indicate the fire service access level with a pictogram (see Figure 6.4) on or near the controls.

— Electrical equipment on landings, within the lift car and shaft should be protected against the effects of water.

— An audible and visual alarm should be provided within the shaft and machine room to alert maintenance engineers of operation of the firefighting switch while on inspection control.

— The lift should have a secondary supply. In the event of loss of the mains supply and establishment of the secondary supply, the lift must re-establish its position within 10 seconds without returning to the firefighter's access floor.

— Firefighting lifts must meet the requirements of BS EN 81[1,2] in all other respects.

## 6.3.2 Car entrances

Cars for firefighting lifts should preferably be front opening, i.e. entrance to the car is from one side only. If a dual-entry lift with front and rear openings must also serve as the firefighting lift, additional precautions for the rear entrance will be required and it is usually necessary to provide a second fire lobby, as shown in Figure 6.5. However, the additional cost of such arrangements must be carefully considered. The advice of the local building control officer and fire officer should be sought. A dual entry lift should not be used where it is the only firefighting lift serving a particular section of the building. Where specified the number of dual entry firefighting lifts should not exceed half the total number of firefighting lifts.

## 6.3.3 Machine room location

Where provided, a lift machine or pump room (machinery space) should preferably be sited above the lift shaft and access should be via the firefighting stairway adjacent to

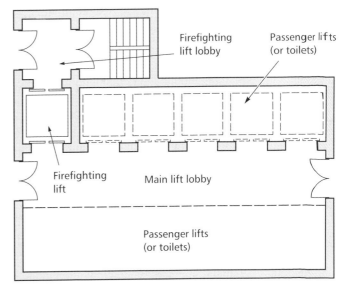

**Figure 6.5** Provision of additional fire lobby for a dual-entry car

the lift. If it is essential to locate the machine or pump room at the bottom of the building, it should be towards the rear or side of the shaft rather than directly below where it is vulnerable to falling water. Access to such machine rooms should still be via a fire protected route, preferably the firefighting stairway. Holes in walls or floors separating machine rooms from lift shafts should always be kept to a minimum. Water must be prevented from entering the machine room.

Machine room less lifts are now common and their use is not precluded by BS 5588: Part 5[10] or BS EN 81-72[3]. With these lifts, the machines, controllers, drives and other equipment that was traditionally placed in the machine room are located in the lift shaft, see section 7.2.5.

For lifts without machine rooms, the equipment should preferably be located away from the pit area to avoid complex water protection of the equipment.

Sprinklers are not required in firefighting lifts and should not be installed in machine rooms or lift wells. Any sprinkler needs to be of a type able to send a signal to the lift before it discharges. The lift should be arranged to remove itself from service at a suitable floor prior to any sprinkler discharge. The power to the lift should be turned off automatically.

## 6.3.4 Protection of lift shaft from water

During a fire, considerable quantities of water will be present on landings. The most likely source of water will be from fire hoses or accidental discharge from risers located in the lift lobby. The flow rate from such sources may be assumed to be about 25 litres per second. Every effort must be made to prevent this water from entering the lift shaft. Floors in the fire lobby should be sloped away from the lift, with drains or scuppers provided to remove water from the immediate area in front of the lift doors. Water should also be directed away from stairways.

Risers should be directed away from lift doors but it is inevitable that there will be at least minor spillages which will find their way into the lift shaft. For this reason it is necessary to provide some degree of water protection to some electrical components in the lift.

BS EN 81-72 requires that protection be provided to electrical lift equipment in the shaft that is located within 1.0 m of the lobby. The protection should cater for splashing water and may be satisfied by either shrouds and covers or by providing IPx3-protected equipment that meets the requirements of BS EN 60529[26]. Attempting to provide a higher degree of protection in the hope of avoiding the need for sloping floors or gullies is not reasonable because, whilst it may be possible to provide complete protection from water, the resulting lift design may no longer comply fully with BS EN 81[1,2].

### 6.3.5 Power supplies

Two independent power supply systems are always required. The primary electrical supply should be from a sub-main circuit exclusive to the lift and independent of any other main or sub-main circuit, see Figure 6.6. Other lifts in the firefighting shaft may be fed from the same primary supply, provided that the supply is adequate for the purpose. Such an arrangement must be designed so that a fault occurring in any other lift in the firefighting shaft, or in the power supplies to any of these lifts, will not affect the operation of the firefighting lift.

The secondary power supply should be independent of the normal power supply to the firefighting shaft, e.g. a standby generator (with automatic start). The lift supplier should not be asked to provide this secondary supply since it serves not only the lifts but also the firefighting shaft and the lift supplier cannot be expected to know what other plant is to be connected to it. The secondary supply should have sufficient capacity to:

— maintain the firefighting lift in operation for at least two hours

— support any auxiliary equipment such as ventilation or pressurisation plant

— be able to recover all other lifts, one at a time if necessary, within the firefighting shaft.

Boundary of fire-fighting shaft

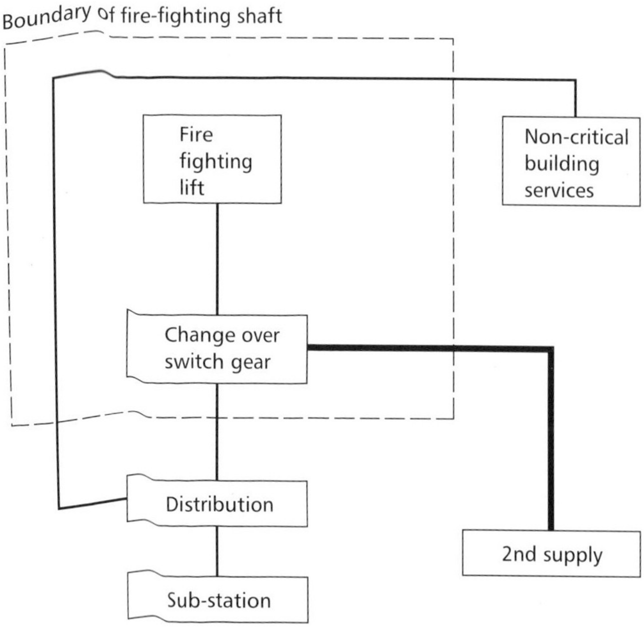

**Figure 6.6** Block diagram for independent power supplies to firefighting lifts

The secondary supply should be available within 30 s of the loss of the normal supply. The supplies must be via fire-protected routes with the same level of protection afforded to the lift by the structure, usually two hours. Cables for these supplies should be terminated in an automatic supply change-over device that may be located in the firefighting shaft (see BS 5588: Part 5[10]) but this does not mean in the lift shaft itself.

### 6.3.6 Firefighter's switch

A switch located within a face plate and marked with a pictogram (see Figure 6.4) should be positioned adjacent to the lift entrance at the fire service access level. Operation of the switch shall be by means of a triangular key with the 'on' and 'off' positions marked by an 'I' and an 'O'. Operation of the switch puts the lift into firefighting service, as follows:

— All special services except inspection are ignored. All lifts within the firefighting shaft must return to the fire access level without stopping (see BS EN 81-73[4].

— When any lift arrives at the fire service access level, it discharges its passengers and then closes its doors unless it is a firefighting lift. Firefighting lifts must remain with their doors open.

— All landing calls are made inoperative but car calls in the firefighting car remain active. On dual-entry cars only the doors on the firefighting lobby side will operate (see section 6.3.2). Passenger detectors or other similar door reversal devices are made inoperative and a communication system is switched on automatically.

— If a call is entered in the firefighting lift car, it responds to that call and no other. While the car is in motion, it should be possible to enter other car calls and thereby stop the car in response to the first call registered.

— When the car stops at a call, this cancels that call and all others. When the lift stops at a floor its doors open only when its door button is pressed and if the button is released while the doors are opening, they immediately re-close.

— Once fully open, the doors close only in response to registration of another car call button. If this button is released before the doors are closed, they re-open. The buttons must illuminate to indicate any call that is registered. Alternatively, a separate indicator light may be provided.

## 6.4 Firefighting lifts: inspection, testing and maintenance

### 6.4.1 Operational tests prior to handover

The testing of firefighting lifts is no longer defined in BS 5588: Part 5 but is given within BS EN 81-72. The lift supplier will need to carry out the tests to satisfy themselves that the lift fully meets the requirements. There is no requirement for the supplier to actually issue to the owner a test certificate, but they are required to state on the lift's Declaration of Conformity those standards to which the lift is designed.

## 6.4.2 Routine inspection and maintenance

Once in service, the lift along with all other firefighting equipment and services should be regularly inspected. For the lift the checks shown in Table 6.1 are recommended.

**Table 6.1** Routine checks

| Frequency | Requirement |
| --- | --- |
| Weekly check | Operation of the firefighting lift switch by the building maintenance staff who should check that the lift returns to the lobby and parks with its doors open. Failure in this simple test should be reported immediately to the lift maintenance company. |
| Monthly check | Simulate failure of the primary power supply. Building maintenance staff should then operate the firefighting lift switch and observe its operation by entering a few calls. The lift maintenance company may be asked to be present at these tests but their presence will probably incur additional charges. |
| Six monthly check | Inspection and testing of the operation sequence of the lift should be made by the lift maintenance company. |
| Annual check | A full operational test of the lift should be performed at least once per year. A record of this test should be retained by the building management. This test is not normally part a regular maintenance contract and this point should be clarified whenever a maintenance/service contract is agreed otherwise additional charges may be imposed. |

## 6.5 Evacuation lifts for people with disabilities

### 6.5.1 General

While planning fire prevention and escape routes for a building, consideration must be given to the evacuation of persons with disabilities, who use the building. In the event of a fire, the occupants will usually evacuate a building by means of stairways, but alternative routes for the evacuation of people with impaired mobility needs to be considered. This section provides guidance for the design of lifts intended to be used for the purposes of escape as given in BS 5588: Part 8[13]. Whilst the type of building and its use will determine whether people with disabilities need to be moved by lift, those responsible for building control may also require that such provision be made.

### 6.5.2 Access/egress for people with disabilities

It is a requirement of UK building legislation that access provision must be linked to egress provision and, since lifts were already being used to provide access for people with disabilities, concern was expressed over the possible use of such lifts for escape. In response to this concern, BS 5588: Part 8[13] was produced. This standard provides detailed guidance for evacuation procedures and on the types of lift required. Although wheelchair and stair lifts fitted to a stairway may be suitable for access, they are not suitable for use as a means of escape and therefore are excluded by the standard. Furthermore, stair lifts may impair evacuation if they reduce the usable width of stairways. Escalators are also excluded as a suitable means of escape, both for able-bodied persons and those with disabilities.

BS 5588: Part 8 recommends that the lift be operated under the direction and control of authorised persons using an agreed evacuation procedure and the successful operation of escape lifts is very dependent upon the competence of the lift operator and the effectiveness of the building management procedure. Only persons with disabilities should use the lift because fixed stairs are still considered as the appropriate means of escape for able-bodied persons. It is not intended that persons with disabilities evacuate themselves from the building unaided, even where a lift is provided, and other means such as the provision of a refuge may need to be considered.

Fire procedures should not include the isolation of electrical circuits that supply the lift or its lighting, communication or ventilation. Any ramps used to allow changes in level or to allow entry into lifts should comply with BS 8300[25] in terms of slope and size.

### 6.5.3 Design considerations

BS 5588: Part 8 makes the following recommendations concerning the design of lifts suitable for the evacuation of disabled people:

—    The lift car must be of at least 8-person capacity, and 1100 mm wide by 1400 mm deep.

—    The lift must be sufficiently fast to run the full travel of the building in less than 60 seconds.

—    Power-operated doors must be fitted, providing an opening of at least 800 mm by 2000 mm. The doors should provide protection from fire for at least half an hour.

—    There must be two separate fire-protected power supplies. However, two-stop hydraulic lifts may not require an alternate means of supply since they can be manually lowered and may not require a special switch to enable the lift to be quickly brought to the main lobby.

—    The car must be made of substantially non-combustible materials.

—    All controls must be at wheelchair height and a handrail must be provided.

— A communications system must be provided between the car and the machine room and the main lobby.

— A break-glass switch, marked 'EVACUATION LIFT', should be located at the final evacuation floor. Operation of this switch should cause the lift to slow down, stop and return to the main evacuation floor without undue delay. While returning it should be prevented from answering any landing calls and, once at the lobby, it should park with its doors open and then respond only to car calls. The lift should be under the sole control of the appointed user (fire warden).

BS 5588: Part 8 allows alternatives to a separate escape lift, as follows:

— A firefighting lift (i.e. a lift to BS 5588: Part 5[10]) which the fire brigade has agreed may be used prior to their arrival as it will already have the main features required.

— In existing buildings, with the prior agreement of the fire authority, a normal passenger lift may be used provided it is of suitable size, has the same structural protection as a protected stairway, a duplicate power supply, a switch enabling authorised persons to take control and an agreed management procedure for its use during a fire.

BS 5588-12: 2004[16] gives excellent advice on managing fire in buildings and evacuating persons, including those with mobility problems. Under certain conditions, e.g. the prior approval of the fire service, it suggests that a firefighting lift may be used for the evacuation of persons with disabilities.

## 6.5.4 Communication system

BS 5588: Part 8 recommends that, except in two-storey buildings, some form of communication system should be provided to enable the rapid and unambiguous identification of those storeys where there are persons with disabilities who require evacuation, and the relaying of this information to the persons operating the evacuation or firefighting lift. Such a system may consist of a control sited at each lift landing linked to the lift car call indicators. Alternatively, requests may be made by the persons requiring assistance to the person controlling the evacuation using visual indicators or by telephone, and these may then be relayed to the lift operator by telephone intercom or radio transceiver.

Communication is a key item during a fire and simple systems generally prove the most reliable. For example, at each landing, adjacent to the lift, there could be a telephone system which connects it to the lift main evacuation lobby. When the lift is required for a particular floor, the person responsible for the evacuation of the disabled from that floor can request the person in charge of the main lobby to despatch the lift who relays the message to the lift driver by an intercom system.

An alternative or addition to this would be the provision of a break-glass switch of the push/pull type at each floor. When pushed it would latch and light an indicator lamp at the main landing. Resetting of the switch would be done manually by the person responsible for entering the call. The provision of complex automatic systems is unnecessary because it is not intended that disabled persons should evacuate themselves from the building.

# References

1    BS EN 81-1: 1998: *Safety rules for the construction and installation of electric lifts. Electric lifts* (London: British Standards Institution) (1998)

2    BS EN 81-2: 1998: *Safety rules for the construction and installation of electric lifts. Hydraulic lifts* (London: British Standards Institution) (1998)

3    BS EN 81-72: *Safety rules for the construction and installation of lifts. Firefighters lifts* (London: The Stationery Office) (2003)

4    BS EN 81-73: 2005: *Safety rules for the construction and installation of lifts. Particular applications for passenger and goods passenger lifts. Behaviour of lifts in the event of fire* (London: British Standards Institution) (2005)

5    BS 476: *Fire tests on building materials and structures*: Part 7: 1987: *Method for classification of the surface spread of flame products* (London: British Standards Institution) (1987)

6    BS 2655: *Specification for lifts, escalators, passenger conveyors and paternosters*: Part 1: 1970 (obsolescent): *General requirements for electric, hydraulic and hand-powered lifts* (London: British Standards Institution) (1970)

7    BS 5499: *Fire safety signs, notices and graphic symbols*: Part 1: 1990 (1995): *Specification for fire safety signs* (London: British Standards Institution) (1995)

8    BS 5588: *Fire precautions in the design, construction and use of buildings*: Part 1: 1990: *Code of practice for residential buildings* (London: British Standards Institution) (1990)

9    BS 5588: *Fire precautions in the design, construction and use of buildings*: Part 4: 1998: *Code of practice for smoke control in protected escape routes using pressure differentials* (London: British Standards Institution) (1998)

10    BS 5588: *Fire precautions in the design, construction and use of buildings*: Part 5: 2004: *Code of practice for firefighting stairways and lifts* (London: British Standards Institution) (2004)

11    BS 5588: *Fire precautions in the design, construction and use of buildings*: Part 6: 1991: *Access and facilities for fire-fighting* (London: British Standards Institution) (1991)

12    BS 5588: *Fire precautions in the design, construction and use of buildings*: Part 7: 1997: *Code of practice for the incorporation of atria in buildings* (London: British Standards Institution) (1997)

13    BS 5588: *Fire precautions in the design, construction and use of buildings*: Part 8: 1999: *Code of practice for means of escape for disabled people* (London: British Standards Institution) (1999)

14    BS 5588: *Fire precautions in the design, construction and use of buildings*: Part 10: 1991: *Code of practice for enclosed shopping complexes* (London: British Standards Institution) (1991)

15    BS 5588: *Fire precautions in the design, construction and use of buildings*: Part 11: 1997: *Code of practice for shops, offices, industrial, storage and other similar buildings* (London: British Standards Institution) (1997)

16    BS 5588: *Fire precautions in the design, construction and use of buildings*: Part 12: 2004: *Managing fire safety* (London: British Standards Institution) (2004)

17    BS 5655: *Lifts and service lifts*: Part 5: 1991: *Specification for dimensions of standard lift arrangements* (London: British Standards Institution) (1991)

18    BS 5655: *Lifts and service lifts*: Part 6: 1990: *Code of practice for selection and installation* (London: British Standards Institution) (1990)

19    BS 5655: *Lifts and service lifts*: Part 7: 1983: *Specification for manual control devices, indicators and additional fittings* (London: British Standards Institution) (1983)

20    BS 5655: *Lifts and service lifts*: Part 10: 1986: *Specification for testing and inspection of electric and hydraulic lifts* (London: British Standards Institution) (1986)

21    BS 5655: *Lifts and service lifts*: Part 10: *Specification for testing and inspection of lifts and service lifts*: Section 10.1: *Electric lifts*: Subsection 10.1.1: 1995: *Commissioning tests for new lifts* (London: British Standards Institution) (1995)

22    BS 5655: *Lifts and service lifts*: Part 10: *Specification for testing and inspection of lifts and service lifts*: Section 10.2: *Hydraulic lifts*: Subsection 10.2.1: 1995: *Commissioning tests for new lifts* (London: British Standards Institution) (1995)

23    BS 5655: *Lifts and service lifts*: Part 11: 1989: *Recommendation for the installation of new, and modernization of, electric lifts in existing buildings* (London: British Standards Institution) (1989)

24    BS 5655: *Lifts and service lifts*: Part 12: 1989: *Recommendation for the installation of new, and modernization of, hydraulic lifts in existing buildings* (London: British Standards Institution) (1989)

25    BS 8300: 2001: *Design of buildings and their approaches to meet the needs of disabled people. Code of practice* (London: British Standards Institution) (1979)

26    BS EN 60529: 1992: *Specification for the degrees of protection provided by enclosures (IP code)* (London: British Standards Institution) (1992)

27    The Building Regulations 2000 Statutory Instrument 2000 No. 2531 (London: The Stationery Office) (2000)

28    Disabled Persons Act 1981 (London: The Stationery Office) (1981)

29    Electromagnetic Compatibility Regulations 1992 Statutory Instrument 1992 No. 2372 (London: The Stationery Office) (1992)

30    London Building Act 1939 (London: The Stationery Office) (1939)

# 7 Lift components and installation

## Principal author

Derek Smith (Otis Ltd.)

## Chapter contents

| | | |
|---|---|---|
| 7.1 | Introduction | 7-3 |
| 7.2 | Electric traction drives | 7-3 |
| | 7.2.1 General | 7-3 |
| | 7.2.2 Gearless machines | 7-4 |
| | 7.2.3 Geared machines | 7-5 |
| | 7.2.4 Planning and layout | 7-7 |
| | 7.2.5 Machine position | 7-7 |
| | 7.2.6 Linear induction drives | 7-9 |
| 7.3 | Hydraulic drives | 7-9 |
| | 7.3.1 General | 7-9 |
| | 7.3.2 Cylinder arrangements | 7-11 |
| | 7.3.3 Power units | 7-12 |
| | 7.3.5 Control valve | 7-12 |
| | 7.3.6 Hydraulic cylinder | 7-12 |
| 7.4 | Controller cabinet | 7-13 |
| 7.5 | Guide rails | 7-13 |
| | 7.5.1 General | 7-13 |
| | 7.5.2 Position of rails | 7-13 |
| | 7.5.3 Size of rails | 7-14 |
| | 7.5.4 Alignment of rails | 7-14 |
| | 7.5.5 Rail fixings | 7-14 |
| | 7.5.6 Length of rails | 7-14 |
| | 7.5.7 Guide shoes | 7-15 |
| 7.6 | Counterweight | 7-15 |
| | 7.6.1 General | 7-15 |
| | 7.6.2 Counterweight sheave | 7-15 |
| | 7.6.3 Counterweight safety gear | 7-15 |
| | 7.6.4 Compensation | 7-16 |
| 7.7 | Lift car | 7-16 |
| | 7.7.1 General | 7-16 |
| | 7.7.2 Car frame (sling) | 7-16 |
| | 7.7.3 Platform/enclosure assembly | 7-16 |
| | 7.7.4 Car safety gear | 7-17 |
| 7.8 | Door operators | 7-17 |
| | 7.8.1 General | 7-17 |
| | 7.8.2 Principles of operation | 7-17 |
| | 7.8.3 Door operator motors | 7-18 |
| | 7.8.4 Door operating times | 7-18 |
| | 7.8.5 Installation | 7-19 |
| | 7.8.6 Passenger safety devices | 7-19 |
| 7.9 | Door configurations | 7-19 |
| | 7.9.1 General | 7-19 |
| | 7.9.2 Single-hinged, manual doors | 7-20 |
| | 7.9.3 Horizontal power-operated sliding doors | 7-20 |
| | 7.9.4 Two-speed, power-operated doors | 7-20 |
| | 7.9.5 Centre-opening, power-operated doors | 7-20 |
| | 7.9.6 Wide entrance doors | 7-21 |

|       | 7.9.7  | Multi-leaf gates | 7-21 |
|       | 7.9.8  | Vertical bi-parting doors | 7-21 |
|       | 7.9.9  | Materials and finishes | 7-21 |
|       | 7.9.10 | Fire rating | 7-21 |
| 7.10  | Overspeed governors | | 7-22 |
|       | 7.10.1 | General | 7-22 |
|       | 7.10.2 | Governor activation | 7-22 |
|       | 7.10.3 | Governor resetting | 7-22 |
| 7.11  | Safety gear | | 7-22 |
|       | 7.11.1 | General | 7-22 |
|       | 7.11.2 | Instantaneous safety gear | 7-23 |
|       | 7.11.3 | Instantaneous safety gear with buffered effect | 7-23 |
|       | 7.11.4 | Progressive safety gear | 7-23 |
|       | 7.11.5 | Resetting the safety gear | 7-23 |
|       | 7.11.6 | Safety gear activating devices | 7-23 |
|       | 7.11.7 | Type-tested safety gear | 7-24 |
| 7.12  | Buffers | | 7-24 |
|       | 7.12.1 | General | 7-24 |
|       | 7.12.2 | Energy accumulation buffers | 7-24 |
|       | 7.12.3 | Energy dissipation buffers | 7-25 |
|       | 7.12.4 | Type-tested buffers | 7-25 |
| 7.13  | Uncontrolled upward movement device | | 7-25 |
| 7.14  | Ropes | | 7-25 |
|       | 7.14.1 | General | 7-25 |
|       | 7.14.2 | Rope construction | 7-25 |
|       | 7.14.3 | Rope sizes | 7-26 |
|       | 7.14.4 | Rope lays | 7-26 |
|       | 7.14.5 | Safety factor for ropes | 7-26 |
|       | 7.14.6 | Terminations | 7-27 |
|       | 7.14.7 | Rope length and rope stretch | 7-27 |
| 7.15  | Roping systems | | 7-27 |
|       | 7.15.1 | General | 7-27 |
|       | 7.15.2 | Compensating ropes | 7-28 |
|       | 7.15.3 | Traction systems | 7-28 |
| 7.16  | Car and landing fixtures | | 7-29 |
|       | 7.16.1 | General | 7-29 |
|       | 7.16.2 | Push buttons | 7-29 |
|       | 7.16.3 | Lift position indicators | 7-29 |
|       | 7.16.4 | Lift direction indicators | 7-30 |
|       | 7.16.5 | Hall lanterns | 7-30 |
|       | 7.16.6 | Passenger communication and alarm devices | 7-30 |
| References | | | 7-30 |

# 7 Lift components and installation

## 7.1 Introduction

This chapter describes the main components used in modern lifts, both electric traction and hydraulic, and their basic installation requirements. The main components of a lift are its prime mover (traction machine or hydraulic pump, depending on the type of drive), the lift car, counterweight (if used), guide rails, entrances, safety gear and governor, buffers, ropes and fixtures (i.e. buttons, indicators and switches).

Typical arrangements and the main components are indicated in Figure 7.1 for electric traction lifts and in Figure 7.12 for hydraulic lifts. Many variations of these basic arrangements are possible but the component parts are fundamentally the same.

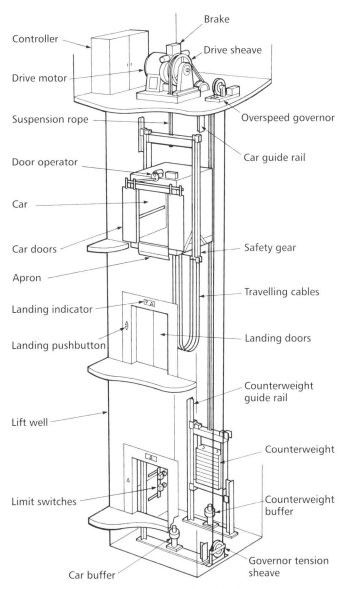

**Figure 7.1** Electric traction passenger lift — principal components

Labels: Controller, Drive motor, Suspension rope, Door operator, Car, Car doors, Apron, Landing indicator, Landing pushbutton, Lift well, Limit switches, Car buffer, Brake, Drive sheave, Overspeed governor, Car guide rail, Safety gear, Travelling cables, Landing doors, Counterweight guide rail, Counterweight, Counterweight buffer, Governor tension sheave

## 7.2 Electric traction drives

### 7.2.1 General

Electric traction drives can be grouped into several categories based on the motor type and its control.

Geared traction drives:

— single-speed AC motor

— two-speed AC motor

— variable voltage AC motor

— variable voltage, variable frequency AC motor

— variable voltage DC motor

Gearless traction drives:

— variable voltage DC motor

— variable voltage, variable frequency AC motor

— permanent magnet synchronous AC motor

To the above types must now be added linear induction drives, see section 7.2.6.

Historically, the required lift speed and ride quality have determined to a large extent which type of drive is used for a particular application. Today, with solid-state control incorporating feedback techniques (see section 8.4), good ride comfort and levelling accuracy can be obtained for most types of electric traction lift without large cost penalties.

In the past, DC motors have provided the best ride quality because the speed of the motor can be easily controlled using a DC generator with a variable output (see section 8.5.1). Consequently, DC motors have been used for the majority of applications requiring a smooth ride and accurate levelling. During the 1980s, static converters were replacing DC generators as the means of supply for large DC motors. Compared with DC generators, static converters are more efficient and provide improved control (see section 8.5.2).

Improvements in the control of AC motors mean that good ride quality may now be achieved using AC motors. Some manufacturers now use AC motors with helical or worm reduction gearboxes to attain speeds of up to 2.5 m/s. Advanced voltage and frequency control techniques have also led to the introduction of AC gearless motor drives. These provide ride quality to match DC gearless machines for any range of speeds.

For guidance on the application of various drive systems refer to BS 5655: Part 6[11].

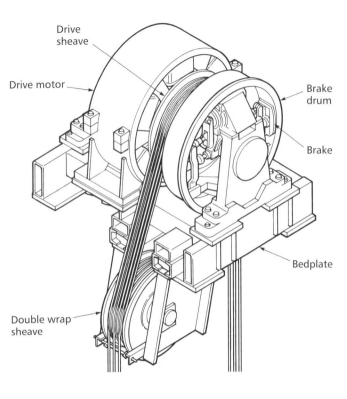

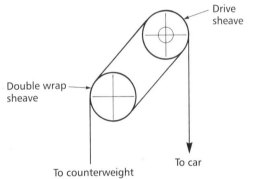

Figure 7.2 Typical gearless machine

## 7.2.2 Gearless machines

The assembly comprises a drive motor, drive sheave, bedplate, brake, direct current armature (or rotor in the case of AC drives), supporting bearings and, possibly, a deflector or double wrap sheave. Gearless machines have generally been used for high-speed lifts, i.e. speeds from 2.5 m/s to 10 m/s. They are, however, now used for all speeds, including low speeds.

Figure 7.2 shows a typical gearless machine. Size, shape and weight may vary considerably between manufacturers but the basic principles and components will be the same.

Until recently, the motor in gearless machines has always been of the DC type but, with the development of high-speed variable frequency drives, AC motors are being introduced. Whichever type of motor is employed, the power developed will be transmitted directly to the driving sheave which is located on the same shaft as the motor. Hence the sheave rotates at the same speed as the motor. The main shaft will be supported on two large bearings that may be of the sleeve, roller or ball race type.

The brake drum is usually formed as an integral part of the driving sheave and this may be one of several types, depending on the type of brake, e.g. external calliper,

internal calliper or disc. Each type has advantages and disadvantages but the main consideration is that the type used must satisfy the relevant code requirements for the country in which it is to be installed. For the UK, the requirement of BS EN 81-1[3] is that it must be capable of stopping the car when carrying 125% load at full speed.

The brake is used only during emergency stopping and when at rest to hold the lift car during loading. Under normal operating conditions, speed controls are employed to bring the car to rest without the use of the brake. This means that the brake is generally little used and the linings will be slow to bed-in if hard materials are selected. For this reason, and because of the low rotational speed of such units, a relatively soft material is used.

### 7.2.2.1 Sheave shaft load

The load lifting capabilities of the machine are not limited by the power of the motor alone. During the design, certain bearings, bolts, steel section and grades of steel will have been selected for the construction of the unit. The materials used and the way in which the components are assembled will place a maximum limit on the load that the main shaft can support safely. This is referred to as the sheave shaft load, the value of which can be obtained from the manufacturer.

The sheave shaft load capability of the machine will vary depending upon the direction in which the load is applied. If the machine is located at the top of the building, with the load acting directly downwards, see Figure 7.3(a), the unit will generally be able to support a higher load than if the ropes are deflected as shown Figure 7.3(b). Locating the machine at the bottom of the building usually results in an upward pull which can drastically reduce the sheave shaft load capability. This may necessitate the use of a

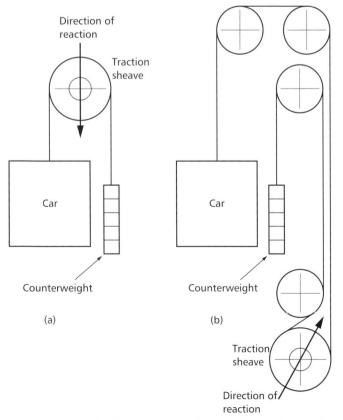

Figure 7.3 Sheve shaft load; (a) machine above with load acting directly downwards, (b) machine below with load acting upwards

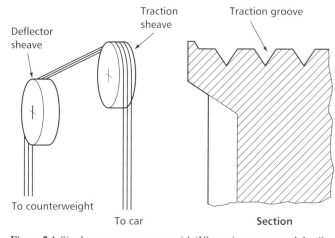

**Figure 7.4** Single wrap arrangement with 'V' traction groove and detail of traction sheave

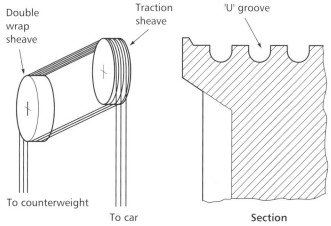

**Figure 7.5** Double wrap arrangement with 'U' groove and detail of traction sheave

much larger machine than was first envisaged. Standard layouts and other arrangements are considered in section 7.2.5.

### 7.2.2.2 Drive sheave

Gearless machines usually employ either a sheave cut with a specially formed traction groove, see Figure 7.4 (see also section 7.15.3, Figure 7.39), or are double wrapped, whereby the lift ropes pass over the drive sheave twice, see Figure 7.5.

Each method has its merits and will provide the required grip to move the car and ensure a long rope life, if properly designed. The main disadvantage of the double wrap method is that it takes up additional space since either a secondary level or pulley room must be provided or the unit must be raised to facilitate servicing of the double wrap sheave. However, with very large loads or speeds greater than 4 m/s, it is often the only method available.

As gear reduction is not employed, the rope speed is equal to the circumference of the drive sheave multiplied by the rotational speed (rpm) of the motor. A sheave diameter of 620 mm requires a motor of only 77 rpm to achieve 2.5 m/s. Gearless units have a slow rotational speed compared with geared machines, therefore sound isolation between the machine and structure is not usually required.

### 7.2.3 Geared machines

These comprise a traction sheave or drum, gearbox, brake, motor and bedplate. It may also include a deflector sheave if mounted as an integral part of the bedplate assembly, see Figure 7.6. Strictly, however, the deflector sheave is not part of the machine assembly.

Geared machines are generally used for speeds between 0.1 m/s and 2.5 m/s and are suitable for loads from 50 kg up to 10 000 kg or more. The size and shape vary considerably with load, speed and manufacturer, but the underlying principles and components are the same.

### 7.2.3.1 Motor

The motor may be of the AC or DC type, either foot- or flange-mounted. Foot-mounted types are available in a wide selection of sizes and makes, while flange mounting provides accurate alignment and, usually, a more compact design. There are no outstanding advantages for either type but for certain applications one particular type may be preferred. For example, for a lift on a ship, a foot-mounted motor would be preferred because of the greater availability of spare parts throughout the world. Whichever arrangement or motor type is employed, the motor transmits its power to the traction sheave or drum via reduction gear.

### 7.2.3.2 Worm shaft

Worm reduction gear, comprising a worm shaft, cut with a coarse helical thread, and a worm wheel, is still the most common worldwide although helical gears have recently started to appear.

The worm shaft has a high running speed compared with that of the worm wheel and therefore is made from either case-hardened or high-grade carbon steel. Both these steels have advantages and disadvantages, but the essential requirement is the smooth running and long-life of the finished assembly. Therefore manufacturers choose materials best suited to the particular application.

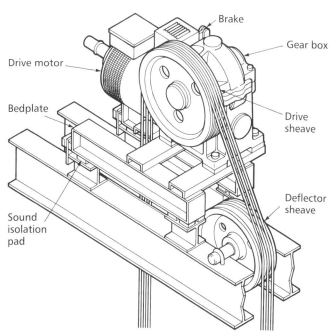

**Figure 7.6** Typical geared machine

The worm wheel can be made from various materials but bronze is by far the most common and has considerable advantages over the alternatives. The performance and reliability of the complete unit is more important than the materials employed for the component parts.

The worm may be cut with one, two, three or more threads or 'starts'. The number of teeth on the worm wheel divided by the number of starts on the worm determines the ratio of the gear. For example, 48 teeth on the wheel and 4 starts on the worm gives a ratio of 12:1.

By selecting different ratios a large combination of speeds and loads can be obtained from a single machine type. Each manufacturer has its own selection of ratios for a particular machine and it is not practical to specify a special ratio as any new design will usually require expensive re-tooling and extensive testing.

The worm may be mounted vertically or horizontally, either above or below the worm wheel. Again each arrangement has its merits but none has any significant disadvantage. The worm shaft will be supported by two bearings of its own or utilise one of the motor bearings. Whichever arrangement is selected, one of the bearings will act as a thrust bearing to prevent the worm from moving laterally. Depending on the design, a thrust movement of one or two thousandths of an inch may be allowed; in other cases no movement is tolerated. The manufacturer's requirements must always be met in this respect.

### 7.2.3.3    Worm wheel

The worm wheel will be supported on bearings, one of which may be either inboard or outboard of the traction sheave which is mounted on the same shaft. There is much argument as to the merits of inboard and outboard bearings. For example, the inboard bearing allows easy replacement of the sheave while the outboard bearing allows easy servicing of the bearing. The maintenance aspect, however, is insignificant since both components, if properly designed, will provide long service and neither arrangement should require frequent dismantling.

One of the main shaft bearings will also serve as a thrust bearing to limit lateral movement of the shaft. Again, the manufacturer's tolerances should be accepted.

### 7.2.3.4    Gear life

As with the gearless units described in section 7.2.2, the load lifting capabilities for geared machines will be limited by the motor size, the load capacity of the main shaft and its bearings (sheave shaft load), and the load and kilowatt capacity of the gearbox. The gears will have been designed to transmit a certain amount of power for a given life. The life will be reduced by the transmission of excessive power or extended if reduced power is transmitted. While worm gears may appear simple their design is complex and there is much debate on the calculation of gear life.

BS 721[8] provides a basis for such calculations, but needs some modification to be realistic for lift gears. To make the calculation of gear life meaningful it is necessary to determine the load carried and the period for which it is carried. In a lift, the load is constantly varying between very light (i.e. empty car) and full load. The gear is not running in the same direction continuously and, for large portions of the day, it is not running at all. Most lifts spend more time at rest, being loaded and unloaded, than running.

It is easy to 'over-engineer', adding unnecessary costs to the installation, by assuming worst-case conditions, such as full load for the life calculation.

At present, gear life is usually expressed in hours, with 15 000 to 20 000 hours being typical. This roughly equates to 15 to 20 years for a lift serving the average office building. It may be tempting to select a higher figure than this, but longer life is achieved by oversizing the gear which results in extra costs. In most commercial buildings, lifts are modernised or replaced after 15 to 20 years (see section 16). At this time, the main components of the gear can also be replaced. If a 25-year gear life is selected, it is likely that the gear will be overhauled at the time of modernisation of the lift even though it will not yet be near the end of its design life.

### 7.2.3.5    Drive sheave

The power transmitted by the gear results in rotation of the worm wheel shaft to which the traction sheave or drum is attached. These items are usually fixed to the main shaft by keys and bolts.

The sheave material is sometimes simple cast iron, but is more usually a complex alloy providing a combination of properties such as 'machine-ability', strength, coefficient of friction and durability. The aim of the traction system should be to provide sufficient traction to hoist the car whilst ensuring good rope life. These criteria are affected by the rope size, number and type, rope pressure, sheave material, sheave groove type (see Figure 7.40), acceleration rate, and the presence of pollutants and abrasives in the atmosphere.

Most manufacturers have, through experience, determined the best combination of these criteria for their particular design and should not be required to use particular materials or rope types that they do not usually employ.

Premature rope or sheave failure is more often due to unequal rope tension than any other single factor and good maintenance is therefore essential. It is not unreasonable to expect the sheave to last the life of the machine provided it is correctly serviced.

### 7.2.3.6    Brake

At some position along the motor or worm shaft a brake drum will be provided. The usual locations are between the motor and gear or on the opposite end of the gear to the motor, see Figure 7.6. The requirements for the brake vary according to the drive system. Figure 7.7 illustrates an electromagnetic brake with spring above.

Simple single-speed and two-speed drives will use the brake for stopping at floors and for emergency stops. With more sophisticated motor controls, the brake may be used only for emergency stopping and parking. Whichever braking system is adopted, it should satisfy the require-

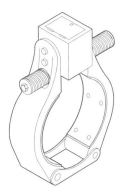

**Figure 7.7** Electromagnetic brake with spring above

ments laid down in BS EN 81-1[3], i.e. it must be capable of stopping the car when carrying 125% load at full speed.

### 7.2.3.7 Bedplate

The gearbox, motor and brake may be assembled on a common bedplate. This fabricated steel structure serves to keep all parts in accurate alignment and allows one-piece shipment. It is important that the bedplate does not deflect under load thereby causing misalignment of the motor and gear. Some machines have the motor and brake as an integral part of the gear case, removing the need for a separate bedplate.

Properly designed and installed machines should be free from perceptible vibration and unusual noises. Worm rub marking on worm wheel teeth should be at or near the centre of the teeth. Any worm shaft float or worm-to-worm wheel backlash (running clearance between meshing teeth) should not be audible in the machine room or felt within the lift car. The complete assembly will usually be mounted onto isolation pads to separate it from the building structure. This may not be necessary in the case of bottom drive machines fixed to a solid foundation.

The unit should be installed with its sheave plumb and located within ±2 mm of its required position. Some manufacturers may employ a roping system (i.e. 'overwrap' or 'longwrap') that requires the sheave to be at an angle to the horizontal to avoid chafing of the rope, see Figure 7.8. In this case the sheave angle should be as recommended by the manufacturer.

### 7.2.4 Planning and layout

Layout dimensions for electric traction lifts are detailed in BS ISO 4190-1/2[9,10]. These dimensions should be used where possible because they are suitable for all lift equipment supplied by reputable manufacturers. The dimensions, however, may be modified provided that careful appraisal of equipment and design is undertaken to ensure that the minimum clearances required by BS EN 81-1[3] are achieved. It should be noted that deviating from the dimensions given in BS ISO 4190 may result in additional costs because non-standard components may have to be fabricated.

The plan dimension of the lift well may increase if bottom drive and/or counterweight safety gear are to be incorporated, see section 7.6.3.

When a new lift is installed in an existing building and structural constraints prevent the provision of the refuge

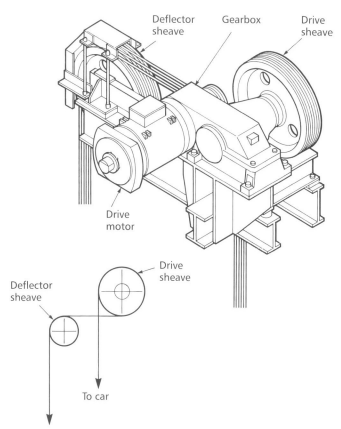

**Figure 7.8** Typical longwrap machine and schematic showing rope path

space required by BS EN 81-1[3], a special derogation against clause 2.2 of the Lifts Regulations 1997[18] is required. This must be obtained from the Department of Trade and Industry (DTI). In addition, and assuming that the derogation has been granted by the DTI, approval must be obtained from a Notified Body. Responsibility for obtaining the derogation and Notified Body approvals rests with the lift installer.

The latest edition of BS 5655: Part 11[14] should be consulted when modernising electric lifts in existing buildings. This standard provides guidance on reduced clearances for situations where structural constraints exist and a lift is being modernised. Where a lift is modernised, see Section 16, a derogation and Notified Body approval are not required since The Lifts Regulations 1997 apply only to new lifts.

### 7.2.5 Machine position

BS ISO 4190/1/2[9,10] gives standardised layouts utilising the traditional preferred top drive arrangement, i.e. where the lift machinery is positioned directly above the lift shaft, see Figure 7.9(a).

Other machine positions can be utilised to minimise headroom requirements. However each of the options may have implications in terms of additional costs, reduction in rope life, increased running noise or a poorer standard of ride quality. Roping systems arrangements are illustrated in Figure 7.39.

#### 7.2.5.1 Top drive: machine adjacent

The machine is positioned adjacent to the shaft at high level, see Figure 7.9(b). A series of pulleys is utilised to

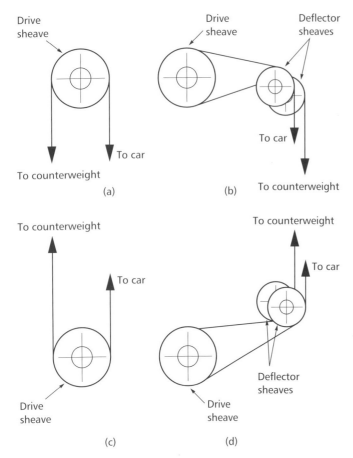

**Figure 7.9** Machine position; (a) top drive, machine above, (b) top drive, machine adjacent, (c) bottom drive, machine below, (d) bottom drive, machine adjacent

achieve the correct rope alignment in the shaft below (see section 7.15).

### 7.2.5.2    Bottom drive: machine below

The machine is positioned directly below the lift shaft, see Figure 7.9(c). The ropes extend the full height of the lift shaft to overhead pulleys which provide the correct rope alignment to the lift car and counterweight below. The overhead pulleys may be positioned in a pulley room directly above the lift shaft. Such pulley rooms require a minimum height of 1500 mm. However, the need for a pulley room may be avoided by using an underslung roping arrangement, see Figure 7.39(h). The top of shaft loadings are approximately double that involved where the machine is positioned overhead. Up thrust loads are also applied to the lift machine.

### 7.2.5.3    Bottom drive: machine adjacent

The machine is positioned adjacent to the shaft at low level, see Figure 7.9(d). The drive sheave can be supported on an extended gear shaft within the lift well or a series of pulleys can be utilised to achieve the correct rope alignment to the overhead pulleys. The pulley room arrangement is as described in section 7.2.5.2. The loadings at the top of the shaft are the same as for bottom drive with machine below.

### 7.2.5.4    Machine room-less lifts

Machine room-less commonly known as 'MRL lifts', see Figure 7.10, are now very common. In these lifts, the

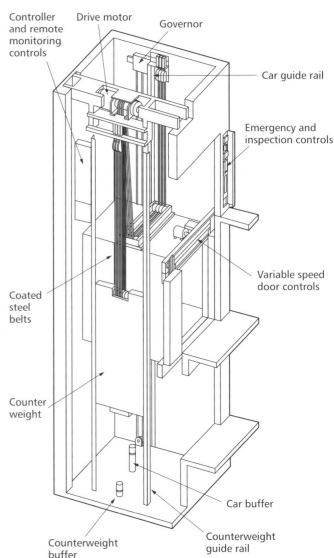

**Figure 7.10** Configuration for a machine room-less (MRL) lift

machine and other equipment that was traditionally placed in the machine room is located in the lift shaft or landing areas, see sections 5.2.5.3 and 5.3.7.3. With the lift machine placed in the lift shaft, special machines and servicing routines have been developed to make inspection of the equipment possible. It is very important for building designers to ascertain at an early stage exactly what will be the required to permit safe servicing and inspection of a given design. Each manufacturer will have their own requirements that must be accommodated within the building design.

The second amendment to the BS EN 81-1[3] standard introduces requirements for machine room-less lifts to the BS EN 81-1: 1998 standard. Until recently it has been necessary for manufacturers to obtain a design examination certificate for each machine room-less lift design because BS EN 81-1 did not recognise these lift types. Providing the manufacturer elects to follows the latest amendment (A2) such a certificate will no longer be required.

The introduction of machine room-less lifts has lead manufacturers to look at other possible changes in design. There are now some products for sales in Europe that have greatly reduced pit and or headroom requirement. It should be noted that putting such products into service in the UK is illegal even if the product has the approval of a recognised Notified Body for lifts. This is because Essential Health and Safety Requirement 2.2 under the UK Lift Regulations[18] enacting the European Lift Directive[17] requires free space to be provided at the extreme positions. A derogation against this requirement is only available from the governments and not from a Notified Bodies. The government will only provide a derogation under very special circumstances and then only on a job by job basis and usually only for an existing building.

### 7.2.6 Linear induction drives

The principle of the linear motor is simple and has been known for many years. It may be regarded as a conventional AC motor 'unrolled' to lie flat. Such machines are sometimes referred to as 'flat-bed motors'. In principle, a linear induction motor could be mounted directly on the lift car but, in practice, this arrangement is ruled out by technical difficulties such as exposing the occupants to intense magnetic fields and, possibly, high noise levels.

Since the system will require a counterweight for reasons of efficiency, it is more logical to attach the motor to the counterweight. Figure 7.11 illustrates a typical modern lift design incorporating a linear induction drive in which the motor primary windings are within the counterweight frame. The secondary is provided by a vertical column for the full height of the lift travel. Note that the secondary is

suspended from the top; the bottom fixing is simply to steady the column.

Such systems are in operation and have been proved to provide excellent service. Control is usually achieved by a variable frequency drive as described in Section 8.4.6.3.

## 7.3 Hydraulic drives

### 7.3.1 General

For certain applications hydraulic drives have many advantages over electric traction. However, when mis-applied, hydraulic drives can cause major problems for the building owner and users.

In its simplest form the hydraulic lift comprises a cylinder and piston located directly below the car. Oil is pumped from a tank by an electric motor. This raises the lift car. To lower the lift a valve is opened that allows the oil in the cylinder to exhaust back into its tank. See Figures 7.12 and 7.13.

Low-traffic passenger and goods, vehicle and bullion lifts are all suitable applications for hydraulic drives. For applications which involve very large loads, hydraulic drives often provide the best solution because the floor of the well carries the load of the lift and its contents. Hydraulic drives, with the cylinder in a borehole (see Figure 7.12), are often specified for observation lifts in commercial buildings, see section 5.3.2.

Hydraulic lifts are often the only type suitable for installation in many older buildings, originally designed without a lift, owing to restricted building height and structural strength.

The practical maximum travel is about 18 m. This is due to the strength and length of the hydraulics piston. As travel increases, larger diameter pistons have to be used to resist the larger buckling forces. This increases equipment costs and makes the use of the hydraulic drive less attractive when an alternative drive is available. Although rated speeds up to 1.0 m/s are permitted the normal limit is 0.63 m/s.

Mechanical anti-creep mechanisms may be used where very heavy loads (i.e. greater than 3200 kg) are carried or fork lift trucks are moving in and out of the lift. Active re-levelling systems may cause problems in these circumstances where small-wheeled trolleys are used.

Caution should be applied in considering hydraulic lifts for commercial buildings where continuous heavy traffic is expected since this may require lift speeds of 1 m/s or greater. Cooling is essential under these circumstances since 0.63 m/s is generally accepted as the maximum for hydraulic lifts without cooling. This cooling requirement is often neglected in the design of the building.

Hydraulic drives are not suitable for intensive use or for groups of lifts. Even duplex lift groups (i.e. two lifts) may exceed the recommended maximum number of motor starts per hour (i.e. 45) without additional cooling. Such cooling may be costly or impracticable. However, a

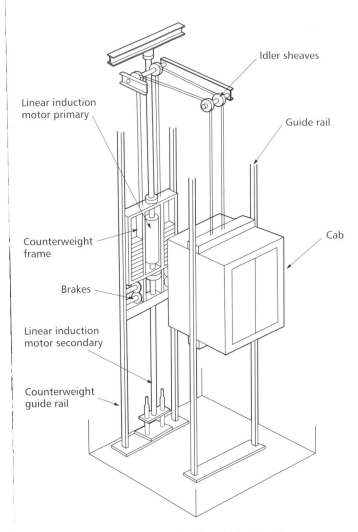

**Figure 7.11** Arrangement for lift using linear induction drive

Labels: Idler sheaves · Linear induction motor primary · Guide rail · Counterweight frame · Cab · Brakes · Linear induction motor secondary · Counterweight guide rail

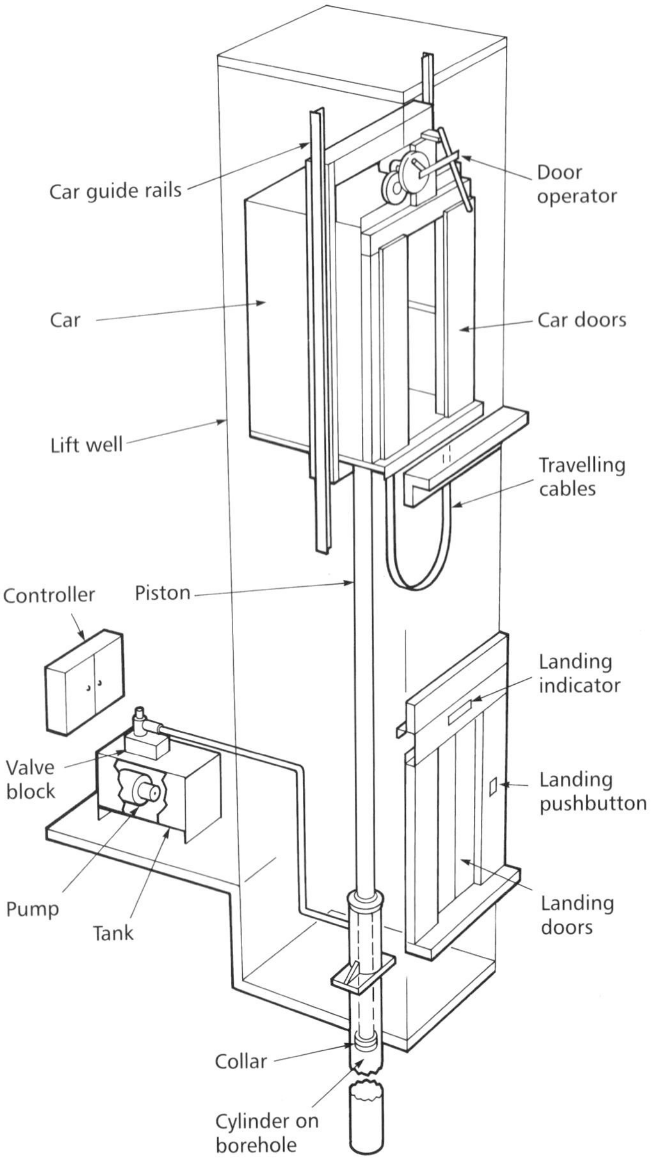
Car guide rails
Door operator
Car
Car doors
Lift well
Travelling cables
Controller
Piston
Landing indicator
Valve block
Landing pushbutton
Pump
Tank
Landing doors
Collar
Cylinder on borehole

**Figure 7.12** Hydraulic passenger lift — principal components

hydraulic drive is sometimes the only solution, even in high traffic situations, due to building structure constraints. In these circumstances, extra cooling for the drive unit and oil must be provided.

Caution should be applied in considering hydraulic lifts for commercial buildings where continuous heavy traffic is expected. Hydraulic drives are not suitable for intensive use or for groups of lifts. Even duplex lift groups (i.e. two lifts) may exceed the recommended maximum number of motor starts per hour (i.e. 45) without additional cooling. Such cooling may be costly or impracticable. However, a hydraulic drive is sometimes the only solution, even in high traffic situations, due to building structure constraints. In these circumstances, extra cooling for the drive unit and oil must be provided. It is also generally accepted that cooling is essential where rated speeds exceed 0.63 m/s. These cooling requirements are often neglected in the design of the building.

For private residential buildings of up to eight storeys, hydraulic lifts may be used due to the low traffic levels in such buildings.

Simple hydraulic drives, which do not use a balance-weight have the following attributes:

— low loads imposed on the building, therefore suitable for large goods lifts

— lift machine room normally positioned in the basement, or other low-cost area of the building

— economic for low-traffic, low rise applications with either single lift or a group of not more than two lifts

— a borehole location for the hydraulic cylinder may provide a visually attractive feature for low-rise observation lifts

— depending on the layout and number of cylinders, the lift well area can be smaller than that for the equivalent electric traction lift.

Hydraulic lifts which use a balance weight save energy but the major advantages of the simple hydraulic lift can be lost due to the increased loads on the building and the cost of fabricating and installing the additional mechanical components.

Pump rooms for hydraulic lifts must have adequate ventilation to prevent extremes of oil temperature (see section 12.9.1). In some cases air conditioning is required. The power dissipation of the drive into the pump room can be obtained from the lift supplier. In the event of a hydraulic fluid leak, the pump room and the lift well must be capable of retaining the hydraulic fluid used in the system by means of an oil-proof floor covering.

With all hydraulic lifts the control equipment and pump unit can be positioned remote from the lift in a more suitable area of the building.

When a new lift is installed in an existing building and structural constraints prevent the provision of the refuge space required by BS EN 81-2[4], a special derogation against clause 2.2 of the Lifts Regulations 1997[18] is required. This must be obtained from the Department of Trade and Industry (DTI). In addition, and assuming that the derogation has been granted by the DTI, approval must be obtained from a Notified Body. Responsibility for obtaining the derogation and Notified Body approvals rests with the lift installer.

Where a lift is modernised, see section 16, a derogation and Notified Body approval are not required since the Lifts Regulations 1997 apply only to new lifts.

The latest edition of BS 5655: Part 12[15] should be consulted when modernising lifts in existing buildings. This standard provides guidance on reduced clearances for situations where structural constraints exist and a lift is being modernised.

## 7.3.2 Cylinder arrangements

### 7.3.2.1 Direct-acting

The cylinder is connected directly below the lift car, see Figure 7.13(a). A lined borehole is required to accommodate the cylinder. A central cylinder is ideal for heavy loads and low rise applications. Effectively there is no limit on the car size or on the rated load capacity. The central cylinder arrangement makes optimum use of shaft

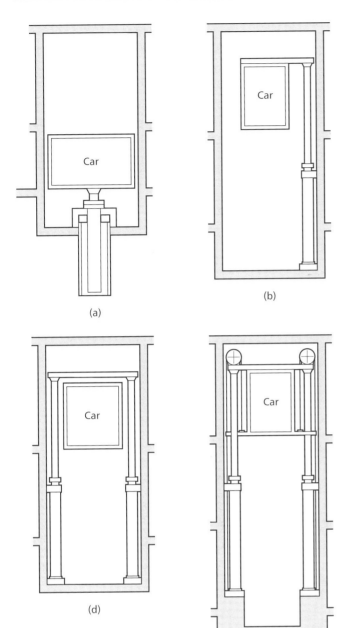

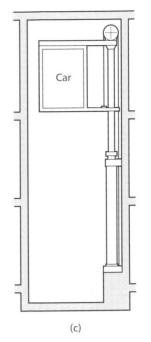

**Figure 7.13** Hydraulic jack arrangements; (a) single, central, (b) single side-acting (direct), (c) single side-acting (indirect), (d) twin side-acting (direct), (e) twin side-acting (indirect)

space because there is no counterweight or hydraulic cylinder alongside the lift car.

The limitations of this arrangement are:

— provision of a lined borehole can prove expensive

— inspection of the cylinders is restricted and, on rare occasions, the unit may have to be lifted out of the borehole for maintenance

— problems may be encountered with underground rock and/or water

— travel is limited to approximately 18 m by the buckling factor for the piston.

### 7.3.2.2 Single side-acting

Side-acting cylinders can be connected either directly or indirectly to the lift car.

With a direct side-acting cylinder, the cylinder is located within the shaft structure alongside the car, see Figure 7.13(b). In this arrangement the car applies a lateral force

to the rails and structure. The cantilever loads imposed on the shaft wall (approximately 1600 kg) restrict the single side-acting arrangement to light loads only. The lift travel is limited by the piston length, usually 3.5 m.

The indirect side-acting cylinder arrangement is similar to the direct side-acting, except that the connection between the piston and lift car is achieved by means of a rope/chain and pulley arrangement, see Figure 7.13(c). This arrangement gives a 2:1 ratio of car travel to piston stroke. Safety gear is required with this arrangement, see section 7.11.

### 7.3.2.3 Twin (tandem) cylinders

As with single side-acting cylinders, the twin cylinder arrangement may be either direct or indirect acting.

The limitations of twin cylinders are:

— increased shaft size

— increased installation and running costs due to the use of two rams

— load limited to approximately 20 000 kg.

In the direct-acting arrangement, a cylinder is positioned at either side of the lift car, see Figure 7.13(d) and this arrangement will accept heavier loads than a single side-acting cylinder.

The indirect-acting arrangement is similar to the direct-acting twin cylinder arrangement, except that the car is connected to the piston by a rope/chain and pulley arrangement, see Figure 7.13(e), giving a 2:1 ratio of car travel to piston stroke. Safety gear is required with this arrangement, see Section 7.11.

### 7.3.3 Power units

There are two basic types; exposed and enclosed. In both cases the components and principles of operation are the same. The main components are as follows:

— tank or oil reservoir

— pump

— pump motor

— flow control valve block.

In exposed types, these items are mounted on a frame for easy installation. However, the enclosed type is now more common in which the pump and motor are submerged in the oil tank, see Figure 7.14. The control valves may sit either inside or on top of the tank unit.

The pump unit should be located as close as possible to the base of the cylinder to avoid an excessive pressure drop between the cylinder and the pump unit.

### 7.3.4 Pump and motor

The most common motor is the single-speed AC induction type. It is usually flange-mounted to the pump on the enclosed versions but may be foot-mounted and belt-driven on exposed types. In enclosed types, open-frame motors are used to ensure that the oil circulates throughout the motor to provide cooling. This has distinct cost advantages because it enables high power outputs to be obtained from relatively small motor frame sizes. However, the heat rejected by the motor heats the oil and thus causes its viscosity to change.

The motor drives the pump, of which the multi-screw type is most common since screw pumps are generally less noisy than other types.

A means must be provided within the lift controller to ensure the pump cannot be run in the wrong direction for any length of time if a fault develops. Submerged pumps use the hydraulic fluid as a lubricant and, if reversed, this lubricant will be pumped away causing the motor to seize. Motor protection in the form of thermistors embedded in the windings is essential and an oil temperature sensor is good practice. This checks oil temperature and ensures the unit is shut down if a certain temperature is exceeded. The tank must be provided with a gauge or dipstick to determine fluid level.

### 7.3.5 Control valve

When upward movement of the lift is required oil is pumped to the flow control valve block at a constant rate. The valve block will allow either all the oil to flow to the cylinder or divert some back into the tank depending on the lift speed required. All valve systems currently available use this system of speed control although construction of the valve blocks vary considerably.

A silencer may be provided, either between the pump and valve block or after the valve block. These devices usually reduce noise by about 2–3 dBA. Most noise occurs when the valve block is bypassing oil to the tank and under such conditions noise levels of 80–85 dBA are common.

A shut-off valve should always be provided on the output of the valve block so that it can be isolated from the cylinder for servicing. A pressure gauge connection point

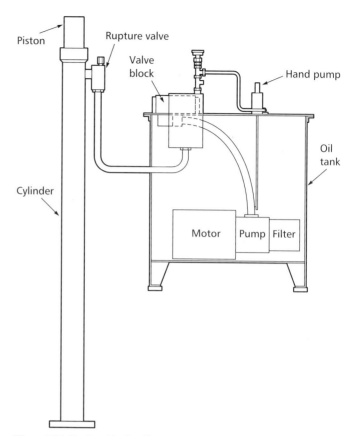

**Figure 7.14** Enclosed hydraulic system

is essential although the gauge itself may not be permanently fitted.

The complete assembly should be mounted on isolating pads. It should be installed plumb and level but absolute accuracy of alignment of the assembly is not essential. The items requiring critical alignment are generally the pump and the motor and this is usually carried out by the manufacturer at the factory.

### 7.3.6 Hydraulic cylinder

In a hydraulic system, power is transmitted to the lift car either directly or indirectly by a hydraulic piston or pistons, see Figure 7.13. Various names are given to this component such as jack, ram, plunger or piston. The main parts of the assembly are the cylinder, piston, seals and collar. Whichever system is provided, the piston and cylinder assembly must stand perfectly plumb and be securely fixed.

The cylinder is made from steel tube and may be in several sections depending on its length. The piston is made from steel ground to fine tolerances. Chromium plating provides a longer seal life and gives protection against certain environmental conditions. However, this is costly and usually not essential.

Like the cylinder, the piston may be made in several sections and various methods of jointing are used. The only criteria for jointing, apart from mechanical strength, should be the accuracy of the joints. Properly made joints should be imperceptible to the touch. At the bottom of the piston, there should be a collar to prevent the lift from striking the building structure in the event of over-travel and to prevent the piston from leaving the cylinder. The top of the cylinder (or the top of each section in the case of telescopic pistons) should have a gland or seal to retain the oil. This gland should seal by the force of the oil acting upon it rather than by being crushed by its retaining plate. When working properly the piston should be covered by a very thin film of oil; anything more than a film indicates a problem. A scraper ring protects the seals from damage by abrasive particles, and the foils guide the piston through the seals.

The piston must satisfy the buckling factor and other requirements stated in BS EN 81-2[4]. Obviously the higher the lift travel, the stronger and heavier the piston will become and this may require solid piston sections. For this and other reasons, hydraulic systems are not normally considered practicable for heights greater than 18 m.

The actual piston length depends on travel distance of the lift and the system employed. For direct-acting systems, the length is approximately equal to the travel plus the top and bottom over-travel, see Figure 7.15(a). For indirect-acting systems, the piston length is approximately equal to half of the sum of the travel and the total (i.e. top and bottom) over-travel, see Figure 7.15(b).

Cylinders and pistons cannot easily be altered in length. Therefore, it is essential to ensure that the cylinder assembly is manufactured accurately and it is vital to ensure that the lift travel is not altered by the builder or architect without first consulting the supplier. Very little tolerance is provided and a variation of travel of as little as 20 mm can have serious consequences. (Note that the tolerances on the building dimensions may be considerably greater than the tolerance on the piston stroke.) With indirect-acting arrangements the travel is still critical, see Figure 7.15(b), as is the pit depth. No variations must be made, however small, without first consulting the supplier.

The most common problem associated with cylinders is premature failure of the seals. This can be caused by long-term storage in a horizontal position, defective scraper ring or impurities in the oil, misalignment of the cylinder, incorrectly installed seals or piston joints of poor quality. Dressing of joints is something that should be done with great care and only if essential.

After manufacture the assembly should be pressure tested to comply with BS EN 81-2[4] or other codes as specified. The assembly is installed to ensure that, when in the fully extended position and against its collar, the car does not strike any part of the structure. When the lift is at the bottom, fully compressing its buffers, the piston should not be touching the bottom of the cylinder. These conditions should be checked as part of the lift testing procedure.

## 7.4 Controller cabinet

The controller cabinet contains the equipment necessary to control and monitor the operation of the lift installation. The drive and control systems are considered in section 8 and traffic control in section 9.

Controller cabinets vary in size according to the complexity of the installation. Typical heights range from 0.5 to 2.5 m. They should be securely fixed, square and plumb, to the machine room wall or floor and in such a position as to ensure easy access for maintenance. Adequate lighting must be provided. Detailed requirements for safety clearances and lighting as given in BS EN 81-1/2[3,4].

Ambient environmental conditions must be maintained as specified by the controls manufacturer, see sections 8 and 12. In some cases it may be necessary to provide coolers on the cabinet to reject the heat generated, see section 12.

## 7.5 Guide rails

### 7.5.1 General

Some form of guide rails are required for the car and counterweight (where provided) to ensure travel in a uniform vertical direction. The position and alignment of the guides is very important and, with the exception of the drive, no other component has such a significant effect on the ride quality. Although round and other sections have been used, T-section rail is now used almost exclusively.

### 7.5.2 Position of rails

The relative position of the guide rails depends upon such factors as location of the entrance, shape of the car and centre of gravity of the car. The actual location will have been determined during the design stage and lift manufacturers will advise on what is and what is not possible.

Guide rails should be kept as near to the centre of gravity of the car as possible. A cantilevered arrangement may be acceptable at speeds up to 1 m/s but ride quality will be difficult to maintain when speed is increased beyond this level. Where possible, the guide rails should be located on either side of the car, see Figure 7.16.

The number of guide rails depends upon the loads to be handled and the sizes available for use. Two rails for the car and two for the counterweight is the most common arrangement but there is no real limit on the number that can be used. The guides are drawn from steel and the running blade is usually machined to a finish, though not in all cases.

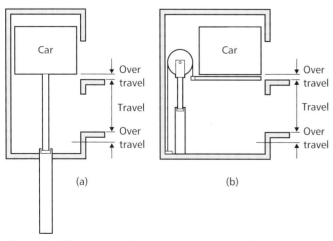

**Figure 7.15** Overtravel; (a) direct-acting arrangement, (b) indirect-acting arrangement

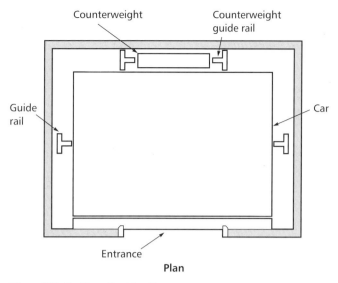

**Figure 7.16** Position of guide rails

### 7.5.3        Size of rails

The size of the rail selected will depend on the forces that it is required to withstand. During lift travel, the forces will be comparatively low, especially if the car is well balanced and the load is well distributed. During loading of the car, however, large loads may be exerted upon the rails. This is especially true of goods lifts being loaded using fork-lift trucks. These loads will produce a twisting moment in the rails. Under extreme conditions, it may be necessary to provide a means of locking the lift to the structure to relieve the rails of some of this load.

The other loads exerted on the rails will be from application of the safety gear under emergency conditions. This will result in a large compressive load being transmitted to the rails as well as a bending stress. The means of calculating these forces, and thereby selecting rail size, is laid down in BS EN 81-1[3] or BS EN 81-2[4], as appropriate.

### 7.5.4        Alignment of rails

The need for accuracy in the installation of the rails cannot be overemphasised, especially for lift speeds of 2.5 m/s and above. At speeds greater than 4 m/s, rail alignment becomes critical. Manufacturers of rails usually offer two grades of finish, first grade being recommended for speeds greater than 2.5 m/s.

It is very difficult, if not impossible, to align rails correctly once the lift car is in the shaft. They should therefore be checked before the car is installed so that any error may be corrected. It is also common practice to use the rails as working centres for all dimensions. Therefore if these are wrongly aligned almost everything else will be wrong. Figure 7.17 provides a guide to installed accuracy. It is often not appreciated that the accuracy of alignment of the rails for the counterweight is as important as the alignment of the car rails.

### 7.5.5        Rail fixings

Guide bracket and clip design is important as these items provide the means of holding the rails in alignment. For low rise installations, forged steel clips may be used to hold the rails rigid. For travels of more than 20 m, spring clips are favoured because they allow for building compression. All buildings expand, contract and move to some degree and rail alignment obtained during initial installation should be maintained while this occurs. Again the taller the building and the faster the lift, the more critical this aspect becomes.

At speeds up to 2.5 m/s, it is good practice to clean the back of rails and face of brackets and to apply a small amount of grease to facilitate movement. At 2.5 m/s and above, most manufacturers provide more sophisticated arrangements to enable movement to occur, e.g. by employing brass shims between the brackets and the back of the rail.

### 7.5.6        Length of rails

While the guides must be long enough to ensure that the car and counterweight never leave the rails during over-travel, clearance must be left between the top of the rails and the structure. This is to ensure that when the building compresses it does not compress the rails. The dimension is approximately 3 mm for every 3.5 m of travel. For travel above 100 m the structural engineer should be consulted regarding the anticipated compression distances. In the absence of specific data, 5 mm per 3.5 m of travel should be allowed.

### 7.5.7        Guide shoes

The lift car, counterweight or balancing weight (as applicable) are provided with guide shoes. There are

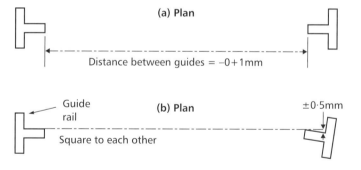

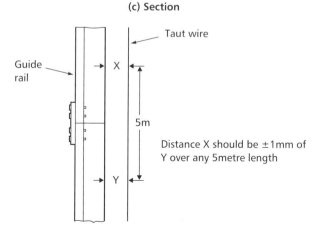

**Figure 7.17** Alignment of rails; (a) tolerance on distance between guides, (b) tolerance on accuracy of angular alignment, (c) tolerance on vertical alignment

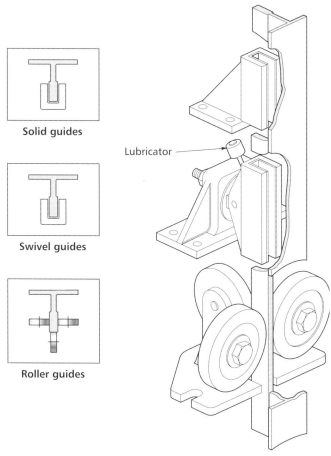

**Figure 7.18** Guide shoes

usually two shoes at the top and two shoes at the bottom. See Figure 7.18.

The shoes, in their simplest form can be solid steel, iron or bronze. These shoes slide on the surface of the rails. Solid shoes are ideal for heavy goods lifts, but for passenger lifts the shoes are normally spring loaded, or resiliently mounted, to reduce noise in the lift car and to absorb small discrepancies in the guide rail alignment. The shoe is often made of steel with a nylon insert to form the running surface. The use of such materials improves noise and minimises the needs for lubrication. Sliding type shoes can be used at speeds up to 2.5 m/s, but are usually limited to 2.0 m/s.

Where the lift is required to operate a higher speeds than 2.5 m/s roller guide shoes are used, as shown in Figure 7.18. These are spring loaded and at speeds of 5 m/s may be provided with shock absorbers to reduce lift car oscillation at speed. Roller shoes provided an excellent ride provided the car is well balanced to avoid high loads on the rollers, when the car is parked. If this is not the case, flat spots will develop on the rollers and these will not only create noise, but also produce a poor lift ride.

# 7.6 Counterweight

## 7.6.1 General

The counterweight provides traction between the ropes and sheave, by balancing the weight of the car and a pro-

portion (normally 40–50%) of the load to be carried. Counterweights usually consist of a steel frame of welded or bolted construction, see Figure 7.19.

The mass of the counterweight is provided by small weights, known as filler weights, made from steel, cast iron or concrete. The material selected is not critical provided its weight stays constant with age and atmospheric changes and does not burn. Some additional weights, known as make weights, may be used for precise balancing. These weights are clamped into place in the frame with clips, rods or plates so that they cannot fall out. Wood or other blocks may be provided underneath the weight to allow for rope stretch. Sliding or roller guide shoes are fitted to the top and bottom of the counterweight to guide it smoothly along the rails.

The frame should be constructed to avoid undue distortion and should hang reasonably central of the rails of its own accord. This ensures that the shoes are subjected to minimum force and therefore minimum wear. This is particularly important for counterweights employing roller guide shoes; if the counterweight is forced into place by undue roller pressure the rollers will develop flats that will result in noise and vibration.

Counterweights with rollers should, therefore, be statically balanced in the same way as the lift cars with roller guide shoes. This involves arranging the filler and make-weights, along with the rope hitch-point, into such a position that the counterweight hangs centrally within the rails without the use of the rollers. The rollers are then adjusted to provide minimal pressure on the guide blade.

In addition to checking the static balance and roller or shoe adjustments, the main considerations during installation of the counterweight are to ensure that it does not strike the building structure when the car is fully buffered and to check that the safety gear, if provided, is operating.

## 7.6.2 Counterweight sheave

A sheave or sheaves may be provided on the counterweight, depending on the rope arrangement employed. When provided, rope 'kick-off' guards should also be included to prevent ropes leaving the sheave during sudden stopping, or if some foreign object should become lodged between the ropes and sheave.

## 7.6.3 Counterweight safety gear

Safety gear (see section 7.11) must be provided if the counterweight is running above an area accessible to persons. This generally means that the size of the guide rail must be increased to take account of the load the gear applies to the rails during application. On a low-speed unit, the safety gear may be operated by the failure of the main ropes (e.g. a broken rope). On units running at 1 m/s or faster, governor actuated gear is required. With speeds of up to 1 m/s the safety gear may be of the instantaneous type, but progressive types should be used above this speed.

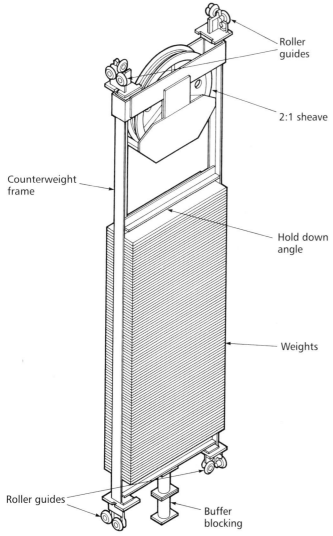

Figure 7.19 Typical counterweight

### 7.6.4 Compensation

The counterweight may also carry compensation ropes, see section 7.15.2. If tied-down compensation is used, the counterweight will be subjected to considerable stress when the car safety gear is applied, over and above the usual stress for which it is designed, such as striking the buffers at full speed.

## 7.7 Lift car

### 7.7.1 General

Most lift cars today consist of two distinct assemblies: the sling or car frame and the car itself. The sling is a steel frame of welded or bolted construction which provides a cradle in which the car can sit. It has to be of sufficient strength to withstand the stresses applied to it when the car is accelerated and the compressive forces resulting from a fully laden car striking the buffers at speed or when the safety gear is actuated.

### 7.7.2 Car frame (sling)

The main parts of the car frame are the crosshead or crown bar, the uprights or side posts, and the bottom

channels or plank channels, see Figure 7.20. Many styles and variations exist and on very large lifts more than one sling may be bolted together to provide the support the car requires. Ropes may be attached directly to the frame or pass around sheaves placed above or below it.

Shoes or rollers are provided at each of the four corners of the frame to guide it along the rails. The construction of the sling is important not just in terms of strength but of alignment It should be assembled free of distortion, especially if roller guide shoes are to be used. Once built, distortions are difficult, but not impossible, to remove.

### 7.7.3 Platform/enclosure assembly

Passenger lifts will usually have an isolation frame attached to the car frame, see Figure 7.20. The purpose of the isolation frame is to separate the passenger compartment from vibrations present in the car frame during running. The platform is supported by rubber pads fixed to the isolation frame. The platform should be levelled front to back and side to side before the walls are attached. The isolation pads compress under load and can therefore be used to provide information on the load in the car.

For passenger lifts, the platform is usually made of steel and may have a timber overlay to reduce noise. If factory-assembled, the walls would then be installed, along with the car front, and finally the roof would be added. If

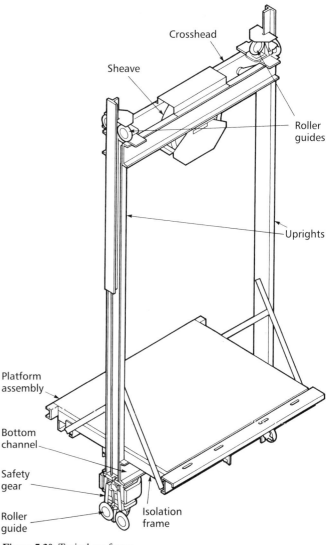

Figure 7.20 Typical car frame

assembly takes place on site, however, it may be necessary to install the roof and hang it temporarily from the crosshead while the walls are installed. The roof is often in one piece and therefore must be installed before the walls are in place. Whichever method is used, the walls must be plumb and square without being forced into position. If not, the car will quickly develop squeaks and rattles. Walls should not deflect beyond the limits indicated in BS EN 81-1/2[3,4].

The roof when installed should be able to support the weight of two persons without permanent deformation. The forces exerted on the platform during passenger transfer are not large and should be based upon the requirements of BS EN 81-1/2. The top of the car is held to the frame by isolated steady devices so that at no point is it mechanically bolted to the car frame. Figure 7.21 shows a typical passenger lift car with the car shell constructed and the door tracks, sill and doors assembled.

For goods lifts, the platform isolation and resilient steady devices are normally omitted because it is important to hold the platform securely to withstand the forces applied during loading. For lifts intended to carry general goods, it is assumed that not more than 25% of the load can be placed in the car in a single operation. If the car is to be loaded using trucks (either hand or power operated), this intention must be made clear to the lift supplier since the combined weight of the truck and its load may exceed the maximum load for which the lift is designed.

Platforms for some passenger lifts will be provided with weights to ensure the finished lift car hangs in the guide rails without imposing large forces on the guide shoes. This features is knows as static balancing and is normally only provided where roller type guide shoes are used as flats will develop on the rollers if they are continuously subjected to large forces.

### 7.7.4 Car safety gear

Safety gear should always be provided if the car is for passenger use, or is of a size that a person can enter for the purpose of unloading even if it is not primarily for passenger use (see also section 7.11). The requirements for the provision of a safety gear are defined in BS EN 81-1[3] for electric traction lifts and BS EN 81-2[4] for hydraulic lifts.

## 7.8 Door operators

### 7.8.1 General

The function of the door operator, or door engine, is to open and close the lift doors in a safe and swift manner. Various methods are used, but the most common is an electric door operator mounted on top of the car, see Figure 7.22. When the lift approaches or arrives at a floor, a mechanical device couples the car doors to the landing doors. As the car doors open they also pull open the landing doors. This method has two distinct advantages. First, only one door operator is required for each car entrance regardless of the number of landing doors on that side of the car. Secondly, the landing doors cannot be opened if the car is not at a floor.

The disadvantage of this arrangement is that the operator may have to open and close doors of different weights. For example, the main lobby may have heavy bronze doors while the doors on all the other floors may be of light panel construction. Under such circumstances the design of the operator must be a compromise; sufficiently powerful to open the lobby doors in a reasonable time but not so powerful that the doors on other floors are opened too fast since this may prevent smooth operation of the doors at all floors.

### 7.8.2 Principles of operation

To open the doors, the operator must accelerate the door from zero to full speed and back to zero in a smooth, quiet manner. This is usually achieved by a mechanical linkage

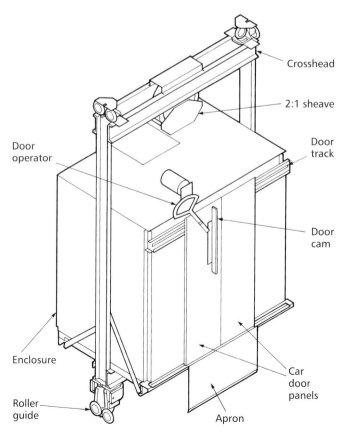

**Figure 7.21** Construction of typical passenger lift car

Crosshead

2:1 sheave

Door track

Door cam

Door operator

Enclosure

Roller guide

Apron

Car door panels

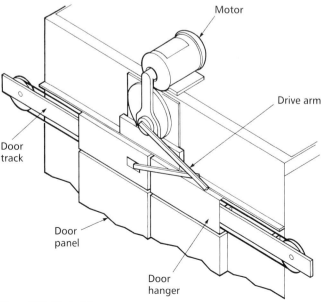

**Figure 7.22** Typical door opener

Motor

Drive arm

Door track

Door panel

Door hanger

which converts the rotational movement of the motor into a sinusoidal or harmonic door movement. The faster this operation the better because it saves time in loading and unloading. To open the doors smoothly at high speed requires good speed control, therefore high-speed door operators are generally more expensive than low-speed types.

Closing the doors raises different problems. While it may be desirable to save time by closing the doors quickly, BS EN 81-1/2[3,4] set limits on the maximum kinetic energy acquired by the closing doors, in order to reduce the risk of injury to passengers. The current figure is 10 J provided that a safety device, such as a passenger detector, is in operation (see section 7.8.6). This limit applies at the average speed of the doors. In addition, the force necessary to prevent the doors closing must not exceed 150 N. If no safety device is provided, or an existing safety device is not operating, the maximum kinetic energy permitted is 4 J.

The most difficult control function, and the most mechanically severe, is the reversal of the direction of motion of the door whilst closing at high speed. Under such conditions the doors must be rapidly decelerated, stopped and then accelerated in the opposite direction. Poor design or incorrect adjustment of the system will result in premature failure of the door drive and its bearings, a common fault with door systems. Bearing and drive failure may also be caused by adding too much weight to the doors, for example by applying a heavy finish to existing doors. The type of door should not be changed unless the capabilities of the door operator are known to be adequate to accommodate the extra weight.

Although initially more expensive than the simple sinusoidal operator, the principle of linear motion, whereby the door movement is linearly proportional to the motor rotation, provides better control of the door movement. With linear door operators, interruption of door closing does not generate such high mechanical forces and this ensures long-term quietness in operation.

## 7.8.3      Door operator motors

The operator itself may use:

—      a DC motor driving through gears or a mechanical linkage system

—      an uncontrolled AC motor driving through a gearbox

—      an AC or DC motor with closed-loop speed control.

Until the 1980s, only DC door operators provided a means of adjusting the door speeds and therefore these were used for lifts with higher door speeds and wider entrances. AC operators, without any speed control, were restricted to smaller lift car entrances and had fixed opening and closing times. Several manufacturers now produce electronically controlled AC and DC door operators suitable for higher door speeds. Some of these use position and velocity control along with sophisticated passenger detection and logic control.

Single-speed AC door operators are most suited for entrances up to 800 mm wide where there is a low density of traffic. In other situations, lift efficiency and passenger

comfort are improved by the use of DC and controlled AC operators.

DC door operators provide good all-round performance for most applications but variable frequency controlled AC operators are now replacing them, due to their excellent performance and low cost. In the case of AC motors, variable frequency control may also be used. Control of door operators is dealt with in section 8.5. The motors are usually designed for the function and, depending on the manufacturer, may be suitable for continuous stalled operation thereby eliminating the need for stall protection.

The operating times can be adjusted to suit user requirements for comfort. It is difficult, however, to modify the speed of the doors in response to varying traffic conditions. Nudging, to close the doors slowly when obstructed or held open unnecessarily, is easily accomplished.

## 7.8.4      Door operating times

The selection of a suitable door operator usually depends upon the application. Generally, high-speed door operators should be used with high-speed lifts. There is little point in having a fast ride if this is followed by slow, noisy door operation.

Table 7.1 shows typical door opening and closing times and likely applications for door operators. The terms low, medium and high speed are not well defined and therefore the figures are given only as a guide. Note that low-speed operators are generally of low cost and usually cannot provide faster opening than closing. For a given width, centre-opening doors will have shorter opening and closing times than side-opening doors. The opening and closing times of the doors have a significant effect on the lift efficiency and cycle time: a one second saving on door operation gives approximately 5% greater traffic handling capability.

**Table 7.1** Door operating times

| Operator | Door type | Opening size† (mm) | Opening time (s) | Closing time (s) |
|---|---|---|---|---|
| Low speed | Two-speed | 800 | 4.8 | 4.8 |
|  |  | 900 | 5.1 | 5.1 |
|  | Centre-opening | 800 | 4.1 | 4.1 |
|  |  | 900 | 4.7 | 4.7 |
| Medium speed | Two-speed | 800 | 2.9 | 3.3 |
|  |  | 900 | 3.1 | 3.5 |
|  |  | 1000 | 3.3 | 3.7 |
|  |  | 1100 | 3.5 | 4.2 |
|  | Centre-opening | 800 | 2.3 | 2.5 |
|  |  | 900 | 2.4 | 2.6 |
|  |  | 1000 | 2.5 | 2.7 |
|  |  | 1100 | 2.7 | 3.3 |
| High speed | Two-speed | 800 | 1.8 | 2.8 |
|  |  | 900 | 1.9 | 3.4 |
|  |  | 1000 | 2.0 | 3.6 |
|  |  | 1100 | 2.2 | 3.4 |
|  | Centre-opening | 800 | 1.5 | 2.0 |
|  |  | 900 | 1.6 | 2.2 |
|  |  | 1000 | 1.7 | 2.5 |
|  |  | 1100 | 1.8 | 2.9 |

† Door height taken as 2100 mm in all cases

### 7.8.5 Installation

With power-operated doors, the operator should be installed to the manufacturer's recommendations. It may bolt directly to the car roof, with or without isolation, or it may be fixed to its own support frame which is, in turn, bolted to the car frame. Following installation of the door operator, it should be checked thoroughly for smooth, quiet operation. Doors and operators often account for some 80% of breakdowns on lift systems. Manufacturers should state opening and closing times, as well as noise levels, and these should be checked after installation. The kinetic energy of the doors when in motion should also be checked, see section 7.8.2.

### 7.8.6 Passenger safety devices

Passenger detection devices are necessary for the safety and comfort of lift users, when moving in and out of lift cars. They also provide controller inputs for the operation of the doors and the lift drive. The time taken to react to an obstruction to door closure varies with the type of detector and several different types may be used. Figure 7.23 shows a typical mechanical safety edge and photocell passenger detector systems and Figure 7.24 shows a typical wide-field electronic safety edge.

A mechanical safety edge can be mounted on the leading edge of the car door. The safety edge moves when it strikes an object and this movement causes the doors to reverse direction. While simple to construct and reassuring to passengers, mechanical safety edges are easily damaged by trolleys etc.

Photocell detectors provide remote sensing across the complete door entrance. They can be a useful addition inside the car, either on the door returns or built into the detector edge, but they should be provided in addition to a safety edge or detector, not as an alternative. For goods lifts, a photocell detector built into the landing architrave is a good way of protecting the landing doors. Despite the claims made by manufacturers, most car door detectors provide only partial protection to the landing doors. A photocell detector can allow more efficient use of the lift, by acting as a 'door open' (dwell time) monitor. These devices modify the dwell time in response to passengers

moving through the entrance. If an obstruction is present, door closure is delayed to prevent unnecessary reopening caused by safety edge operation.

More common are electronic safety edges in which a solid-state detector is located on or beside the leading edge of the car doors. This produces a detection field that may extend for a short distance (say, 100 mm) in front of the door, or it may cover the whole opening width. When the field is interrupted the door reverses direction. This type of system has the advantage of reversing the door before it hits the obstruction. For this reason, electronic safety edges are preferred to mechanical types. Modern electronic edges are robust and stable, and their ability to sense obstructions without contact is more comfortable for passengers and provides better protection for the doors. In the event of failure of the detector, the doors should stay open or be permitted to close only at slow speed (nudging operation) with a warning buzzer sounding.

Optical passenger (obstruction) detectors provide even greater passenger protection in situations where heavy objects have to be moved through the entrance. Again, these detectors should be used in addition to safety edges. Optical passenger detectors use simple video cameras with local image processing to detect passengers and objects approaching the lift entrance. Situated above the car doors, the landing doors or between the car and landing doors, the field of view can be angled to meet the requirements of the application. Typical situations where these devices have proved advantageous are in airport terminals and hospitals. They can, however, interfere with normal service if located above the landing doors by detecting persons passing the lift rather than those waiting to use it. The field of view must be carefully adjusted to avoid false sensing.

## 7.9 Door configurations

### 7.9.1 General

While various types of door exist, all serve the same prime function: to prevent persons or objects from entering the path of the lift. Each type, however, offers certain features

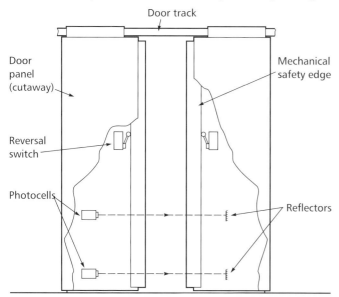

**Figure 7.23** Schematic of typical mechanical safety edge

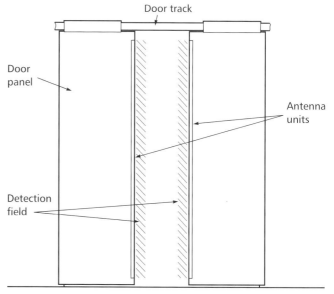

**Figure 7.24** Schematic of typical electronic passenger detector

or advantages. The mechanical strength required for doors and their locking mechanism is laid down in BS EN 81-1/2[3,4]. The completed panel assembly should be designed to be as free running as possible, with all clearances within the limits laid down by BS EN 81-1/2. The face of sliding doors should always be kept as flush as possible. While the standard permits recesses and projections up to 3 mm in the face of the door, these should be avoided if possible. Safety must always be the prime consideration.

### 7.9.2    Single-hinged, manual doors

The simplest, and generally the least expensive, type of landing door is the single-hinged, see Figure 7.25. In the past, these were frequently made from wood but, because of its flammability and its tendency to warp, steel doors are now more common. Single-hinged doors require very little space in terms of width since they consist of only the door and a simple frame. The disadvantage is that they usually open out to a right angle with the wall and therefore obstruct corridors. They are difficult to open for persons in wheelchairs or elderly or disabled people. They are, however, acceptable for simple, low-cost passenger lifts serving a small number of floors. Typical opening widths for these doors are 700, 800 and 900 mm.

### 7.9.3    Horizontal power-operated sliding doors

The most frequently used power-operated door for passenger lifts are horizontal sliding doors, see Figure 7.26. The simplest of these is the single-slide (single-panel) version, see Figure 7.26(a). The single panel is pulled open or shut by the car door operator. As only one panel is used the construction is simple and reliable but requires a greater shaft width in many instances for a given opening, i.e. approximately twice the opening width plus 300 mm. The typical opening width is 840 mm. These types of doors were commonly used for lifts in local authority

housing during the 1960s and 1970s. They are still used for some applications but less frequently so.

### 7.9.4    Two-speed, power-operated doors

Two-speed side-opening (two-panel side opening) door may be used where space is at a premium but powered doors are required, see Figure 7.26(b). These doors are sometimes referred to as two-speed because while both panels close simultaneously, the leading panel travels at twice the speed of the trailing panel. This means that, although the leading panel has twice the distance to travel of the trailing panel, they cover the distance in the same time. The space required by these doors is approximately 1.5 times the opening width plus 400 mm. Opening sizes for these doors are generally between 600 and 1300 mm, the most common sizes being 700, 800, 900, 1100 and 1300 mm.

### 7.9.5    Centre-opening, power-operated doors

The most common entrance for passenger lifts is the single-speed centre-opening door (two-panel centre opening), see Figure 7.26(c). This arrangement is mechanically relatively simple, visually attractive and fast in operation because both panels move simultaneously, either away from or toward each other. For a panel speed during opening of 0.3 m/s, an opening of 900 mm may be created in approximately 1.6 s, whereas a two-speed door would require approximately 3.0 s. This time saving can be critical on large installations and groups of lifts. The space required by the doors is more than other types being approximately twice the opening width plus 200 mm. However, centre-opening doors are preferred to side-opening where the depth of the shaft is limited.

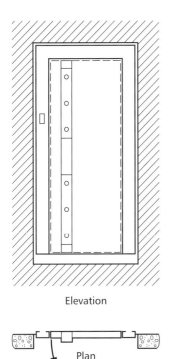

Figure 7.25 Single hinged door

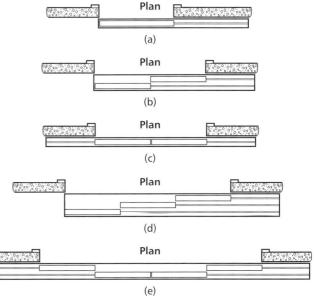

Figure 7.26 Horizontal power-operated sliding doors; (a) single slide, (b) two-speed side-opening, (c) single-speed centre-opening, (d) three-speed side-opening, (e) two-speed centre-opening

Opening sizes for these doors are usually between 800 and 1300 mm; larger sizes are possible but generally unacceptable because of the space required. The most common door opening widths are 800, 900, 1100 and 1300 mm.

### 7.9.6    Wide entrance doors

For special applications, such as very large passenger or goods lifts, other horizontal doors are available. For example, two-speed centre-opening (four-panel centre opening) or three-speed side-opening (three-panel side opening) doors are suitable for opening widths from 1200 to 2500 mm or greater, see Figure 7.26(d) and (e). However, these arrangements are generally costly and noisy because of the complexity of mechanical linkages.

### 7.9.7    Multi-leaf gates

For goods lifts, the requirements are generally different. Adequate space to enter the lift and within the shaft, combined with rugged, reliable operation are more important than speed of operation. Where cost and space are at a premium, manually operated shutter gates may be used, see Figure 7.27. These are simple and rugged. The space required is the opening width plus the bunching width. The space required for bunching will vary according to the widths of opening and leaf size used.

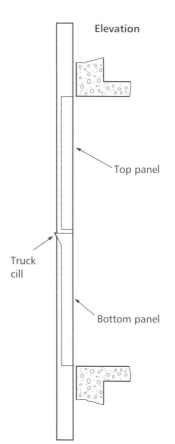

Figure 7.28 Vertical bi-parting door

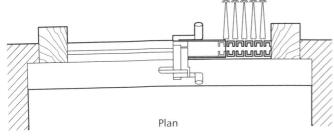

Plan

Figure 7.27 Multi-leaf gate

### 7.9.8    Vertical bi-parting doors

For very large goods lifts, where loading will be by powered truck, vertical bi-parting doors may be used, see Figure 7.28. These may be either manual or power operated. Space requirements vary between different manufacturers. The powered versions usually have an operator motor per entrance (i.e. on each floor served). This enables each entrance to be individually operated.

The two panels that form the door counterbalance each other. As the bottom panel moves down the upper panel moves up. When fully open, the top edge of the bottom panel forms a trucking sill. The doors are designed to accept different trucking loads and the intended load should be specified.

Although opening may be fully automatic, closing is usually performed by constant-pressure button operation. The door closing sequence may be interrupted if necessary by releasing the door close button. Fully automatic power closing of these types of doors is not permitted under BS EN 81-1/2.

### 7.9.9    Materials and finishes

BS EN 81-1/2[3,4] set limits on the closing force and kinetic energy of moving doors (see section 7.8.2), and these may have a bearing on the materials selected for the door. Most doors are made from steel with either a painted or applied skin finish. While the finish is a matter of design choice, certain factors should be considered. For example, if heavy materials are used, door closing speed will have to be reduced to keep within the requirements of BS EN 81-1/2. Some materials, especially those with heavy embossed patterns, may be difficult to form and will therefore increase costs. Finally, heavy materials may require that the door tracks, rollers, bearings and driving operators are all increased in size to handle the extra weight.

### 7.9.10    Fire rating

Lift doors are often required to be fire rated. In the UK, testing of this property is laid down in BS 476: Part 22[7]. Unlike other fire doors, lift doors are tested from the outside only, i.e. the landing side, and the ability to stop fire from the lift shaft side is not a requirement. Doors are tested within their frames built into a typical structure in a test furnace. The test report obtained will be for a given duration, typically 30, 60, 90 or 120 minutes, and will cover both integrity and stability. Insulation properties are not required or tested nor smoke control.

A new fire testing method has recently been published by the British Standards Institute. This is a harmonised European standard BS EN 81-58[6] and is published in support of the Lift Directive (Lift Regulations). The BS EN 81-58 uses a test commonly known as the 'tracer gas test' because carbon dioxide is introduced into the test furnace as a tracer gas and its rate of leakage through the doors is measured. Manufacturers of lift doors will increasingly adopt this test method as it enables a door design to be recognised as acceptable in all European member states with only a single fire test.

It should be noted that modifying doors by removing entrance upright sections, changing the locking system, closing system or the addition of finish materials such a woods, plastics etc. would invalidate the report. The addition of a skin may also render the report invalid if flammable materials are used and this should be borne in mind during the selection of finishes and adhesives for fixing skins. Where it is planned to make such changes a professional opinion should be sought from any appropriate fire testing laboratory.

## 7.10 Overspeed governors

### 7.10.1 General

Overspeed governors have been used on lifts almost since the first lifts were installed. The purpose of the overspeed governor is to stop and hold the governor rope with a predetermined force in the event of the descending car or counterweight exceeding a specified speed. The rope may be held by traction forces developed between the governor sheave and its groove or by a special rope-clamping device designed to hold the rope without damaging it. The force exerted on the rope must be at least 300 N or twice the force necessary to engage the safety gear, whichever is greater. For governors using rope traction to obtain this force, the force must be calculated in accordance with BS EN 81-1/2.

Governors for use in new lifts are type tested and British Standard specification PAS 32-1[1] sets down the requirement for on-site testing at completion of a new lift installation. The general requirements for governors are laid down in BS EN 81-1/2.

In the past, vertical shaft fly-ball governors were common but, although many still exist, their use is becoming less frequent. Horizontal shaft, centrifugal governors are now preferred, see Figure 7.29. The centrifugal governor consists of a sheave, flyweights and a rope clamping

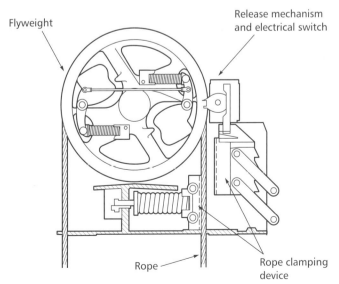

Figure 7.29 Centrifugal governor

device. As the sheave rotates, the pivoted flyweights move outwards due to centrifugal force. At a predetermined speed, the weights strike a release mechanism that causes the rope-clamping device to grip the governor rope. The rope-clamping device is designed to allow the rope to slip through its jaws if the load on the rope is too great. This ensures that the safety gear stops and holds the car rather than the governor.

### 7.10.2 Governor activation

BS EN 81-1/2 requires that tripping of the overspeed governor for the car safety gear shall occur at a speed at least equal to 115% of the rated speed and less than:

— 0.8 m/s for instantaneous safety gears except for the captive roller type

— 1 m/s for safety gears of the captive roller type

— 1.5 m/s for instantaneous safety gears with buffered effect and for progressive safety gear used for rated speeds not exceeding 1 m/s

— $(1.25v + 0.25/v)$ for progressive safety gear for rated speeds not exceeding 1.0 m/s (where $v$ is the rated speed).

A governor used to operate counterweight safety gear shall be set to activate the safety gear at a speed not more than 10% greater than the speed at which the car safety gear is activated.

Governors are provided with an electrical switch which removes power from the lift motor and applies the brake before the safety gear is activated. However, if the rated speed of the lift is 1.0 m/s or less, this switch may trip simultaneously with the safety gear. For speeds above 1.0 m/s the switch is set to operate at approximately 115% of rated speed.

### 7.10.3 Governor resetting

After operation, the governor will either be reset by raising the car or it may require to be reset manually. The rope-gripping device should always be inspected for signs of wear after an application.

## 7.11 Safety gear

### 7.11.1 General

Safety gear is the term given to a mechanical clamping device located on the car, the prime function of which is to grip the guide rails to prevent the uncontrolled descent of the car if the lifting ropes were to part. Any lift car designed for transporting passengers, or into which persons may enter to load or unload goods, and that is suspended by ropes requires the provision of safety gear. The safety gear will usually be located under the car frame but may be at the top or halfway up. The position is not important provided that the gear is fixed securely to the frame. Figure 7.30 shows a typical car frame with progressive gear located at the base of the uprights. All types of safety gear should be applied mechanically and not rely on

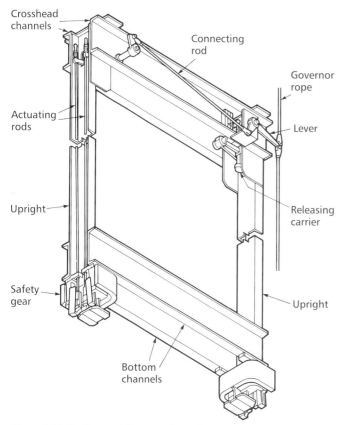

**Figure 7.30** Car frame with progressive safety gear

the operation of electrical circuits. Activating devices for safety gear are considered in section 7.11.6.

Safety gear may also be fitted to the counterweight, see section 7.6.3.

## 7.11.2 Instantaneous safety gear

This is the simplest type of safety gear, see Figure 7.31. It is almost instantaneous in operation but limited to lifts with speeds of not more than 0.63 m/s. This is because the small stopping distance results in heavy shock and strain, not only to the lift equipment but also to the passengers.

When fitted to a counterweight frame, the device may be used at speeds up to 1 m/s. Although the counterweight may be stopped instantly, the car will come to rest under the action of gravity.

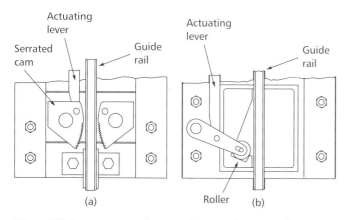

**Figure 7.31** Instantaneous safety gear; (a) serrated cam, (b) roller type

## 7.11.3 Instantaneous safety gear with buffered effect

Instantaneous safety gear with buffered effect may be used on cars with speeds up to 1.0 m/s. The safety gear again applies a rapidly increasing pressure on the guide rails but oil-filled buffers, interposed between the lower members of the car frame and the safety plank, dissipate the energy and reduce the shock to passengers.

## 7.11.4 Progressive safety gear

For speeds in excess of 1 m/s, progressive safety gear must be used. This device clamps the guide rails by applying a limited pressure which brings the car progressively to a standstill, see Figure 7.32. These devices are also used where several safety gears are fitted to the car as is the case with some large goods lifts. Progressive safety gear may be used at speeds below 1.0 m/s, if required.

The gear is designed so that under free fall conditions the average retardation of a fully loaded car lies between 0.2 g and 1.0 g. The actual distance taken to stop the lift depends upon its speed. Requirements for stopping distances and methods of testing are given in BS 5655: Part 10.1.1[12] for existing electric traction lifts and BS 5655: Part 10.2.1[13] for existing hydraulic lifts and PAS 32-1[1] for new electric traction lifts and PAS 32-2[2] for new hydraulic lifts.

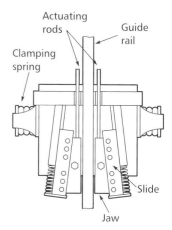

**Figure 7.32** Progressive safety gear

## 7.11.5 Resetting the safety gear

All modern types of safety gear are reset after application by upward movement of the car. This requires the intervention of a competent person not only to release the safety gear and check its condition after operation but also to determine the reason for its operation.

## 7.11.6 Safety gear activating devices

The most common arrangement for activation of a safety gear is by way of an overspeed governor, see section 7.10. The linkage mechanism that operates the safety gear is connected to a steel rope of at least 6 mm diameter (the 'governor rope') which passes from the safety gear linkage up the lift shaft, over a governor sheave, back down the shaft to the pit, around a tension sheave and back to the lift car, see Figure 7.33. In the event of the car exceeding a

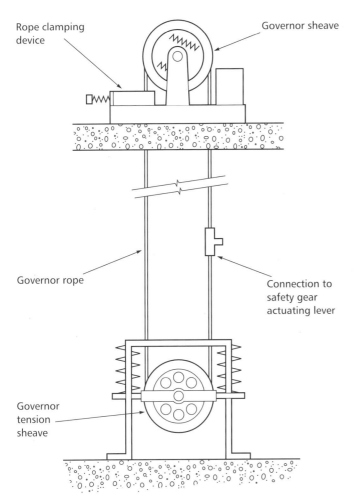

**Figure 7.33** Governor rope — general arrangement

predetermined speed, the governor operates a device which grips and holds the governor rope, causing the safety gear to be applied. The downward motion of the car, or counterweight, is then arrested by friction between the wedges, rollers or jaws of the safety gear and the guide rails. The safety gear should also operate an electrical switch which disconnects the motor at, or before, the instant of application of the safety gear, see section 7.10.2.

With progressive safety gear, the car may slide some distance before stopping so the governor must allow the rope to move under force. This ensures that while the safety gear is properly engaged the weight of the lift is not directly placed on the governor or governor rope. The governor must grip and hold the governor rope with a force of 300 N or twice the force required to engage the safety gear, whichever is greater. Typically, the force required to engage the safety gear is 250 N whereas the force in the governor rope is 500–600 N.

### 7.11.7     Type-tested safety gear

Safety gear are now available 'type-tested'. This means they have been laboratory tested in accordance with BS EN 81-1[3] or BS EN 81-2[4] as appropriate. The tests required on-site after installation are described in British Standards specifications PAS 32-1[1] and PAS 32-2[2] and differ from those required for non-type tested safety gear as described in BS 5655: Parts 10.1.1[12] and 10.2.1[13], as appropriate.

## 7.12     Buffers

### 7.12.1     General

Buffers are placed below the car and counterweight to arrest them should they over travel into the lift pit. In the case of positive drive lifts buffers are also required at the top of the shaft or on top of the car. The number of buffers will vary according to the design capacity of the buffers and the load to be stopped, but the stroke is dependent on the speed of the car or counter-weight. There are two basic types of buffers: energy accumulation types using springs or rubber, and energy dissipation types such as hydraulic buffers. These are illustrated in Figure 7.34.

### 7.12.2     Energy accumulation buffers

The kinetic energy is stored in the gradual compression of springs or rubber blocks, which provides a progressive retarding force, see Figure 7.34(a). The range of speeds for which they can be used is normally limited to 1.0 m/s. For buffers with linear characteristics, the distance the contact end of the buffer can move (i.e. the stroke) must be at least equal to twice the gravity stopping distance corresponding to 115% of the rated speed, i.e:

$$s = 2 \times 0.0674\, v^2 = 0.135\, v^2 \qquad (7.1)$$

where $s$ is the stroke (m) and $v$ is the rated speed (m/s).

However, the stroke must not be less than 65 mm. The buffer must be able to cover this stroke under a static load of between 2.5 and 4 times the sum of the mass of the car and its load.

Energy accumulation buffers with non-linear character-istics are required to be type-tested. The test requires that when the car impacts the buffer at 115% of rated speed, its retardation does not exceed 2.5 $g_n$ for more than 0.04 $s$, and that the average retardation does not exceed 1.0 $g_n$ ($1.0\, g_n = 9.81$ m/s$^2$).

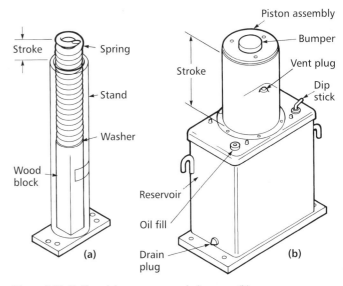

**Figure 7.34** Buffers; (a) energy accumulation type, (b) energy dissipation type

### 7.12.3 Energy dissipation buffers

The kinetic energy is dissipated by forcing oil through a series of holes, see Figure 7.34(b). Energy dissipation buffers provide a near constant rate of deceleration and are therefore suitable for all speeds.

The stroke (i.e. the distance moved by the buffer piston or plunger) required shall be at least equal to the gravity stopping distance corresponding to 115% of the rated speed, see BS EN 81-1/2[3,4], i.e:

$$s = 0.0674 \, v^2 \qquad (7.2)$$

It is permissible to reduce the stroke so as to avoid excessive pit depth, provided that additional speed monitoring equipment is installed to ensure that the car speed is reduced even under fault conditions at terminal floors. If such equipment is provided, the speed at which the car strikes the buffer may be used in the calculation instead of the rated speed. However, the stroke cannot be less than 50% of that resulting from equation 7.2 for lift speeds up to 4.0 m/s and not less than 33.3% for speeds above 4.0 m/s. In no circumstances should the stroke be less than 420 mm.

### 7.12.4 Type-tested buffers

Buffers for new lift installations are required to be type-tested and final testing at site should therefore be carried out in accordance with PAS 32-1[1] or PAS 32-2[2], as appropriate. These tests differ from those required for non-type tested buffers as described in BS 5655: Parts 10.1.1[12] and 10.2.1[13]. Testing at full speed will not damage the buffers or the lift but the tests are severe and should not be repeated unnecessarily. Energy dissipation buffers should be inspected after testing to check that they have not lost oil and have returned to their fully extended position. BS EN 81-1/2[3,4] requires an electrical switch to be fitted to ensure the car cannot run if the buffer is not fully extended.

## 7.13 Uncontrolled upward movement device

New lifts are now required by the UK Lift Regulations[18] enacting the European Lift Directive[17] to apply Essential Health and Safety Requirement 3.2 by providing a means to prevent uncontrolled upward movement where such a risk exists. The risk does not exist in all lift designs but where failure of a component, either electrical, mechanical or electronic would result in the lift travelling up at a speed greater than the designer intended a device to stop the condition must be provided.

In a electric traction lift a counterweight is normally employed. The lift motor may drive the car and its counterweight via a gear box with the traction sheave attached to the low speed output shaft (see Figure 7.8). In such a design the main brake is acting on the gearbox high-speed input shaft and a failure in the gear box would in effect separate the motor and brake from the load (lift car and counterweight). In this condition gravity acting on the counterweight would result in the counterweight weight descending and the car moving upwards. This movement could not be stopped by the brake or lift motor and so it would be uncontrolled upward movement.

In a conventional hydraulic lift without a counterweight, see Figure 7.13 the upward speed of the lift is controlled by the delivery of the pump unit. Over-speeding in the up direction is not possible and such designs do not therefore require a device to prevent the condition.

Various means can be employed to stop uncontrolled movement but they should act directly on the car, counterweight, main ropes or driving sheave. It is also permissible for the device to act on the same shaft as the traction sheave if it acts in the immediate vicinity of the sheave. A conventional safety gear fitted to the counterweight and activated by an overspeed governor is one simple solution. This can be economical if a counterweight safety gear is already required to address the risk resulting from it running above an accessible space. A car safety gear capable of operating in either the up or down direction is another possibility as is a brake acting directly on the traction sheave. A further possibility is a rope brake. This device will clamp the main ropes under the required conditions to arrest the car.

Whatever device is used it is required to operate at not less than 115% of rated speed and not more than 125% of rated speed. When activated it must bring the car to a stop with a rate of retardation not greater than 1.0 $g_n$ (9.81 m/s$^2$). Once activated it should be possible for a competent person to release the device without having to gain access to the car or counterweight.

Devices used for uncontrolled upward movement are classed as Safety Components under Annex IV of the Lift Directive (UK Lift Regulations) and as such must be type tested, CE-marking applied and issued with a Declaration of Conformity. BS EN 81-1[3] Annex F defines the type test requirements for such devices.

## 7.14 Ropes

### 7.14.1 General

Steel ropes used for hoisting lift cars are of standard construction, each strand consisting of a number of wires. Strength and flexibility are the most important properties. The strength is obtained by the use of a steel with a high carbon content while flexibility is provided by the stranded construction.

### 7.14.2 Rope construction

Various rope constructions are used, and the size and tensile strength of the wires vary according to the construction. BS EN 81-1/2[3,4] states that the strength of wires for single tensile strength ropes should be 1570 N/mm or 1770 N/mm; and for dual tensile strength ropes 1370 N/mm for the outer wires and 1770 N/mm for the inner wires. The wires are formed around a fibre core. This core is impregnated with a lubricant to reduce friction of the internal parts when in use and prevent corrosion when not in use.

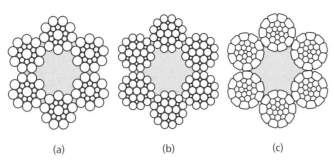

**Figure 7.35** Types of rope construction; (a) 6×19(9/9/1),
(b) 6×19(12/6+6F1), (c) 6×26 Dyform rope with fibre core

Rope construction is referred to by numbers such as 6 × 19(9/9/1), see Figure 7.35(a). The first number '6' indicates the number of strands used to form the rope whilst the second number '19' indicates the number of wires used per strand. The way the strand is constructed is indicated by '(9/9/1)'; nine outer wires around nine inner wires around a single central wire. A rope designated as 6 × 19(12/6+6F1), see Figure 7.35(b), indicates six strands each made up of 19 wires. The 19 wires are arranged with 12 on the outside, within which is a ring of six wires, plus six smaller 'filler' wires (i.e. 'F') around a single central wire.

Conventional lift ropes use wires of round sections, see Figure 7.35(a) and (b). In the dyform rope, the outer wires are not of simple circular section but are shaped to provide a larger exposed area, see Figure 7.35(c). This results in an increased breaking load, reduced stretch, and maintains fatigue resistance. Dyform ropes have been developed for high-speed high-rise applications but may also be used for other applications.

New developments in ropes include flat construction and non-metallic ropes. These ropes are lighter and much more flexible than traditional ropes, enabling them to be used with smaller sheaves. They produce less noise when passing over the sheaves, and are claimed to have less stretch and a longer life expectancy than conventional ropes. Figure 7.36 shows a flat construction rope with a non-metallic covering.

### 7.14.3 Rope sizes

The size of a rope is its nominal diameter which, for lifts, is usually between 8 and 22 mm, according to the strength required. The most common sizes are 11, 13, 16 and 19 mm. The diameter is that of the circumscribed circle and is measured over each pair of opposite strands. BS EN 12385-5[16] specifies that the actual diameter when supplied is that measured with the rope under a tension of 10% of the minimum breaking load. The size must be within +3% and –0% of the nominal diameter. Some

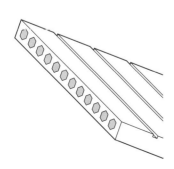

**Figure 7.36** Section through a flat construction rope with non-metallic covering

special ropes may be manufactured to even tighter tolerances.

### 7.14.4 Rope lays

Generally, two types of lay are employed in lift ropes: Lang's lay and the 'ordinary' lay, see Figure 7.37.

In the Lang's lay, the direction of the twisting of wires in the strand is the same as the direction of the twisting of the strands that form the rope, see Figure 7.37(a). The advantages of this arrangement over the ordinary lay are that it offers a greater wearing surface when in use and therefore a longer life. It is also more flexible but the rope is easy to kink if mishandled during installation and any benefits are then lost. A disadvantage with Lang's lay is that it does not exhibit the same surface strand breakage as ordinary lay, thus making their detection more difficult.

In the ordinary lay, see Figure 7.37(b), the wires in the strand are twisted in the opposite direction to the strands in the rope. Ordinary lay ropes are now used more frequently because they are more tolerant of mishandling and, provided the rope and sheave system is properly designed, give adequate life.

For both Lang's and ordinary lays, the length of lay of a rope is the distance, measured parallel to the axis of the rope, in which a strand makes one complete turn about the axis of the rope. The length of lay of a strand,

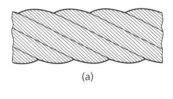

(a)

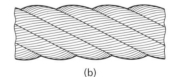

(b)

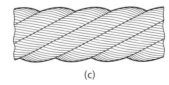

(c)

**Figure 7.37** Rope lays; (a) Lang's lay, (b) ordinary lay, right hand, (c) ordinary lay, left hand

similarly, is the distance in which a wire makes one complete turn about the axis of the strand. The rope strands can rotate either clockwise (right hand) or anti-clockwise (left hand) for both types of lay.

### 7.14.5 Safety factor for ropes

The rope safety factor is the ratio between the minimum breaking load of rope and the maximum force in the rope when the car is stationary at the lowest landing.

$$S_r = n F K / w \qquad (7.3)$$

where $S_r$ is the safety factor for the rope, $n$ is the number of separate suspension ropes, $F$ is the nominal breaking strength (N) of one rope, $K$ is the roping factor (1 for 1:1, 2 for 2:1, etc.) and $w$ is the load (N) suspended on the ropes with the car at rest at the lowest floor (N).

The load suspended includes the weight of the rope, the car and its rated load, a percentage of the suspension ropes plus a percentage of the compensation, if provided. BS EN 81-1[3] states that a safety factor of 12 shall be used for traction lifts with three or more ropes; 16 in the case of traction drive with two ropes, and 12 for drum drive arrangements.

## 7.14.6 Terminations

Various methods of terminating the rope are available, the most common being bulldog grips, swaged and socketed, see Figure 7.38. Whichever form of termination is used, its

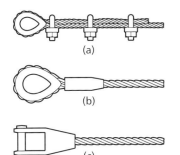

(a)

(b)

(c)

**Figure 7.38** Rope terminations; (a) bulldog grip, (b) swaged end, (c) socket end

strength should equal at least 80% of the minimum breaking load of the rope. With bulldog grips, see Figure 7.38(a), it is important to use the correct number, tightened to the correct torque. Where socket terminations are used, the ends of the rope are bent over and tucked into the socket, see Figure 7.38(c). The socket is then filled with white metal (also known as babbitt) or resin.

## 7.14.7 Rope length and rope stretch

When installed on a traction lift, the rope length should be such that when the car is on its buffers, and the buffers are fully compressed, the counterweight is clear of the underside of top of the lift shaft or any other obstruction. When the counterweight rests on its fully compressed buffers, no part of the car may touch the top of the shaft or any obstruction in it. The actual clearance depends upon car speed. BS EN 81-1[3] stipulates requirements for these dimensions.

When a load enters a car elongation of the rope will occur. The amount will depend on the type of rope, its length and the load applied. On high rise installations this elongation can cause the car to rise or move down below the floor by a small amount. To compensate for this the lift can be provided with a re-levelling feature to maintain the lift at floor level.

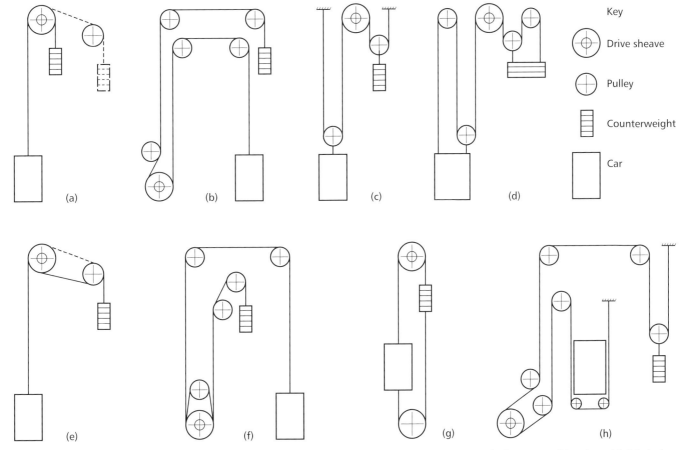

Key

Drive sheave

Pulley

Counterweight

Car

(a)    (b)    (c)    (d)

(e)    (f)    (g)    (h)

**Figure 7.39** Roping systems; (a) 1:1 single wrap, machine above, (b) 1:1 single wrap, machine below, (c) 2:1 single wrap, machine above, (d) 3:1 single wrap, machine above, (e) 1:1 double wrap, machine above, (f) 1:1 double wrap, machine below, (g) 1:1 machine above with compensation, (h) 2:1 single wrap, machine below, underslung car

# 7.15 Roping systems

## 7.15.1 General

There are many different roping systems, some of which are shown in Figure 7.39. The best method to employ will depend upon the particular situation, e.g. machine position, available headroom, rated load and speed. However, whatever the requirements, the simpler the roping system the better.

The lift machine is usually situated either at (or near) the top or bottom of the shaft. All types of electric traction drive are suitable for either top or bottom drive, but the best, and simplest, roping system is with the machine at the top. This usually provides the best rope life, lowest capital cost, least power consumption and minimum structural loads. Bottom drive is generally mechanically more complex in its roping arrangement and hence more expensive than top drive.

Typically, the structural load applied to a building with the machine above is the total weight of the lift machine, control gear, car, car load and counterweight. With the machine below, the structural load is approximately twice the sum of the weight of car, car load and counterweight. If the weight of the machine and control gear is considerably greater than the combined weights of the car, car load and counterweight, the structural load may be less with the machine below, but this is unusual.

For a machine located at the top of the building, the simplest rope arrangement is that of the single wrap 1:1 system in which the ropes pass over the traction sheave once and the rope ends are terminated at the car and counterweight, see Figure 7.39(a). With this system, the car travels 1.0 m for every metre of rope moved over the traction sheave.

Figure 7.39(b) shows a single wrap 1:1 arrangement with the machine located below. This arrangement removes the need for a full height machine room at the top of the building, but space for the overhead sheave will still be required. The saving is generally about 900 mm in height but extra costs may result due to the additional rope and sheaves. Figure 7.39 (g) is also a single wrap 1:1 arrangements but with the drive sheave in a different locations.

With a 2:1 roping system, the car travels 0.5 m for every metre of rope moved over the traction sheave. This means that the speed of the car is half that of the driving machine. Either top- or bottom-located machines may be used with a 2:1 roping system. An advantage of this arrangement is that it enables a small number of machines to cover a wider range of speeds and loads since, by halving the speed, the load may be doubled. In addition, the load imposed on the machine sheave shaft is effectively halved as half the mass of the car and half the mass of the counterweight is supported by the building structure, see Figure 7.39(c). The reduction in the load carried by the ropes passing over the traction sheave reduces rope pressure and may enable fewer ropes to be used. The system does, however, require longer ropes and rope life may be reduced by the additional bending stress caused by the number of sheaves that the ropes must pass over. Figure 7.39(h) is also a 2:1 arrangement but with sheaves located below the lift car.

Where bottom drive is employed, a reduction in headroom may be obtained using an underslung arrangement for the lift car. This involves mounting pulleys on the underside of the car and positioning high-level pulleys and rope anchorages (outside the line of the car roof) at the top of the lift shaft, see Figure 7.39(h). No pulley room is required with this arrangement. It should be noted that increased running noise may be apparent with the underslung arrangement, therefore speeds are usually limited to 1.6 m/s.

Many other rope systems have been used, such as 3:1 (see Figure 7.39(d)) but these are not commonly used except for very large goods lifts or other special applications.

Figure 37(e) and (f) show double wrap arrangements. The ropes pass twice over the drive sheave and as a result the traction is increased dramatically.

## 7.15.2 Compensating ropes

Ropes may be hung under the car to the counterweight in order to compensate for the weight of main ropes, see Figure 7.39(g). Compensation is used to ensure that adequate traction is available, wherever the car is in the shaft, and/or to reduce the power requirement for the drive motor. For lifts up to 2.5 m/s, chains or free ropes may be used, tensioned by gravity. For speeds above 2.5 m/s, a tensioning device is required. This usually takes the form of a weighted sheave fixed between two guides. For speeds above 3.5 m/s, an anti-rebound device is required. This prevents the counterweight from rising through its own inertia if the car should be stopped abruptly, and prevents the car from continuing upwards if the counterweight should be stopped suddenly. This is sometimes referred to as 'tied-down' compensation, see section 7.6.4.

## 7.15.3 Traction systems

In all rope systems, the power developed by the machine is transmitted to the ropes either by a single-wrap or double-wrap traction system. In the single-wrap system the ropes pass once over the sheave, into which specially shaped grooves are cut. These are known as traction grooves. The traction force depends on the specific pressure between the ropes and the sheave, the frictional properties of the rope and sheave materials, the groove angle and the amount by which the ropes wrap around the sheave.

These factors govern the ratio which can exist between the rope tensions on the two sides of the sheave before slipping occurs. The traction developed must be sufficient to enable the car plus 125% load to be safely supported but must be low enough to ensure that, if the tension in either the car or counterweight side of the rope is reduced to zero, the traction will be insufficient to permit the car or counterweight to be hoisted. Excessive traction will also result in excessive sheave and rope wear. BS EN 81-1[3] provides formulae for the calculation of traction.

The shape of the groove has a considerable influence on the tractive force. Figure 7.40 shows typical grooves that may be employed. The straight V-shape provides the greatest traction, the least support to the rope and,

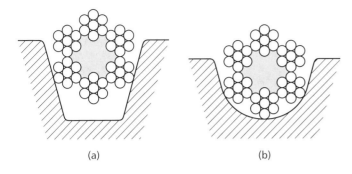 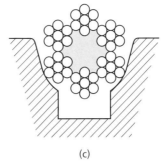

**Figure 7.40** Common types of groove; (a) 'V' groove, (b) round seat ('U' groove), (c) progressive or undercut groove

therefore, the greatest wear. The round-seat type provides the most support and the least traction and wear.

Flat construction ropes do not use shaped grooves to develop the required traction. Traction is achieved by means of the large surface area of material in contact with the sheave, the surface of which is also virtually flat. The absence of a groove avoids pinching the rope which greatly extends the life of the rope.

The number of variables involved in the traction and rope life means that it is unreasonable to request a particular groove or material and the manufacturer should be allowed to provide the combination that they feel to be the most appropriate. Ropes may be expected to last seven to ten years for the lifts in a typical office building. However, this may not be achievable in environments such as large hotels, where lifts may operate for up to 20 hours per day.

## 7.16        Car and landing fixtures

### 7.16.1        General

The term fixtures embraces car operating panels, indicators, push buttons, hall lanterns and any signs, magnetic card readers or key-pads. If properly designed, they can help to make a lift more 'user friendly' and will improve service. While these items will contribute greatly to the appearance of the lift, their prime function is to inform users of what is happening and/or to enable instructions to be given to the lift control system. Essential fixtures such as buttons, indicators and hall lanterns should be large, conspicuous and easy to see against the surrounding walls.

### 7.16.2        Push buttons

Buttons may be square, round or any other shape but should not be small. Ideally, the area pressed should be at least 400 mm$^2$ and no side should be less than 20 mm. Some means of informing users that their call has been registered is good practice and this may be by illumination of the button or a surrounding halo or by a separate indicator. In addition to this visual feedback, audible feedback may also be provided. Illumination is best provided by light emitting diodes (LEDs), which give long trouble-free life. Face plates should be of sufficient size to make the buttons easily noticed. Buttons without face plates are difficult to see and therefore should never be installed on landings without a face plate. The face plate should contrast both with the button and the surrounding wall to ensure that it is easily noticed.

Markings on buttons should be in a clearly, easily read typeface such as Helvetica and by some form of tactile indicator, if possible. Braille markings are sometimes provided, to assist those persons with impaired vision who can read Braille. Simple tactile markings are preferred since these are discernible by all. Any such markings should be on the button itself or adjacent to it. The size of the markings should be of the order of 15 mm in height and located at between 10 and 15 mm from the button.

The height of the buttons above floor level in the car should be between 900 mm and 1200 mm. Where it is intended that the lift should be accessible to wheelchair users, buttons inside cars and on landings should be not less that 400 mm from any wall at right angles to the buttons.

### 7.16.3        Lift position indicators

Preferably indicators should be provided within the car and on the main landing. On single units, an indicator at all floors is a useful addition which provides users with a visible indication of the progress of the lift. It may be desirable to indicate when lift cars are unavailable for passenger use, although this is not required by BS EN 81-1/2[3,4]. On non-collective lifts, a 'lift busy' indicator is necessary so that users know that the lift cannot accept calls.

Some lift systems deliberately order a car to bypass a landing call in order to optimise overall response times. Passengers observing this operating sequence are likely to interpret it as a fault. Thus, when two or more lifts are operating together, it is better not to provide indicators on every landing but only at the main entrance floor for the building. Figure 7.41 illustrates three types of indicators; multi-light, dial and digital.

Incandescent bulbs are not a good choice for position indication since they consume more energy and have a shorter life than other forms of illumination. On large groups, indicator bulb replacement can become a frequent

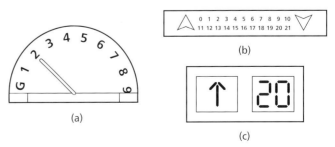

**Figure 7.41** Lift position indicators; (a) multilight, (b) dial type, (c) combined hall lantern and digital indicator

maintenance task. The power requirements are illustrated by the fact that the car lighting and indication can consume half the total energy required to run the lift.

Digital-type indicators are by far the most popular and many versions exist. Illumination may be by vacuum fluorescent display or solid-state indication using LEDs. LED displays provide a compact, energy efficient solution. Dot matrix displays allow great flexibility in floor identification. Large dot matrix displays can be used to display messages which can be read easily from anywhere in the car.

Whichever type is chosen, the display should be clear to all users including the partially sighted. This requires that any symbols should preferably be between 30 and 60 mm in size and located between 1600 and 1800 mm from floor level. It is also good practice to provide audible feedback with any such signals. Voice annunciators are useful in situations where the lifts are regularly used by the general public or by blind or partially sighted people. However, the announcements can become a source of irritation to lift users. This can be avoided in part by enabling the volume to be adjusted between 35 and 55 dBA.

Fixtures should be displayed against a dark background to provide a sharp contrast in colour and should be visible from acute angles, especially where there is only one indicator, placed to one side of the car entrance. In large cars (i.e. 1600 kg and above), two operating panels, each with an indicator, should be considered.

## 7.16.4 Lift direction indicators

On any simplex collective lift, passengers should be provided with a means of determining the direction of travel of the car before they enter. This can be achieved by providing a hall lantern or direction indicator at each landing or a single direction indicator within the car, positioned so as to be visible when the doors open. Again illuminations by LEDs or vacuum display is preferable because of their high reliability. The sizes and sound levels should follow the guidelines for lift position indicators given in section 7.16.3.

## 7.16.5 Hall lanterns

Hall lanterns should always be provided at each landing for groups of two or more cars and may be provided on single lifts, if desired. The lantern should illuminate and chime before the car arrives at the floor to alert waiting passengers. This enables the passengers to start moving toward the arriving lift so that door dwell times can be kept to a minimum. To assist the partially sighted, the chime should emit notes of different tones or sound once for up and twice for down. Numerous designs are available but again the essential points are reliability and practicality. It must be borne in mind that the principal function of lanterns is to provide the passengers with information. The sizes and sound levels should follow the guidelines for lift position indicators given in section 7.16.3.

## 7.16.6 Passenger communication and alarm devices

All lifts require an alarm device for use in an emergency. In the past, this has taken the form of a simple bell to summon help. However, the Lift Regulations 1997[18] now require new lifts to be connected to a device that allows entrapped passengers both to summon help and to communicate directly with those who will arrange for their rescue. BS EN 81-28[5] is a harmonised standard that defines requirements for such devices. Other designs are still possible but as a harmonised standard it will be increasingly used by lift suppliers as it offers a presumption of conformity with the Lifts Directive[17], thus avoiding the need for an approval from a Notified Body for lifts.

The button or other device used to activate the alarm shall be provided in the car operating panel, shall be yellow and marked with a bell shape symbol. When operated it shall provide both audible and visual information to the user. A yellow pictogram shall indicate that the alarm has been sent. A green illuminated pictogram in addition to any audible signal shall indicate when the alarm call has been registered by the rescue organisation.

The design of the system shall be such that once the alarm has been raised there should be no need for further action or speech by the trapped passenger. The system should inform the rescue service of the location of the lift. This ensures that in the event of the person being unable to communicate for any reason their predicament and location will be known. A conventional telephone does not therefore satisfy this requirement.

Note that the requirements for the pictogram are not defined in BS EN 81-28, but will be defined in a future standard.

# References

1     PAS 32-1: 1999: *Specification for the examination and test of new lifts before putting into service. Electric traction lifts* (London: British Standards Institution) (1999)

2     PAS32-2: 1999: *Specification for the examination and test of new lifts before putting into service. Hydraulic lifts* (London: British Standards Institution) (1999)

3     BS EN 81-1: 1998: *Safety rules for the construction and installation of lifts. Electric lifts* (London: British Standards Institution) (1998)

4     BS EN 81-2: 1998: *Safety rules for the construction and installation of lifts. Hydraulic lifts* (London: British Standards Institution) (1998)

5     BS EN 81-28: 2003: *Safety rules for the construction and installation of lifts. Remote alarm on passenger and goods passenger lifts* (London: British Standards Institution) (2003)

6     BS EN 81-58: 2003: *Safety rules for the construction and installation of lifts. Examination and tests. Landing doors fire resistance test* (London: British Standards Institution) (2003)

7     BS 476: *Fire tests on building materials and structures*: Part 22: 1987: *Methods for determination of the fire resistance of load bearing elements of construction* (London: British Standards Institution) (1987)

8  BS 721: *Specification for worm gearing*: Part 1: 1963 (1984): *Imperial units*: Part 2: 1983: *Metric units* (London: British Standards Institution) (dates as indicated)

9  BS ISO 4190-1:1999: Lift (US: Elevator) installation. Class I, II, III and VI lifts (London: British Standards Institution) (1999)

10  BS ISO 4190-2:2001: Lift (US: Elevator) installation. Class IV lifts (London: British Standards Institution) (2001)

11  BS 5655: *Lifts and service lifts*: Part 6: 2002: *Code of practice for selection and installations* (London: British Standards Institution) (2002)

12  BS 5655: *Lifts and service lifts*: Part 10: *Specification for testing and inspection of lifts and service lifts*: Section 10.1: *Electric lifts*: Subsection 10.1.1: 1995: *Commissioning tests for new lifts* (London: British Standards Institution) (1995)

13  BS 5655: *Lifts and service lifts*: Part 10: *Specification for testing and inspection of lifts and service lifts*: Section 10.2: *Hydraulic lifts*: Subsection 10.2.1: 1995: *Commissioning tests for new lifts* (London: British Standards Institution) (1995)

14  BS 5655: *Lifts and service lifts*: Part 11: 1989: *Recommendations for the installation of new, and the modernization of, electric lifts in existing buildings* (London: British Standards Institution) (1989)

15  BS 5655: *Lifts and service lifts*: Part 12: 1989: *Recommendations for the installation of new, and the modernization of, hydraulic lifts in existing buildings* (London: British Standards Institution) (1989)

16  BS EN 12385-5: 2002: *Steel wire ropes. Safety. Stranded ropes for lifts* (London: British Standards Institution) (2002)

17  Directive 95/16/EC of the European Parliament and of the Council of 29 June 1995 on the approximation of the laws of the Member States relating to lifts ('The Lifts Directive') *Official J. of the European Communities* 9.7.1995 L213/1 (Brussels: Commission for the European Communities) (1995)

18  The Lifts Regulations 1997 Statutory Instruments 1997 No. 831 (London: The Stationery Office) (1997)

# 8 Lift drives and controls

## Principal author

Adrian J Shiner (KONE plc)

## Chapter contents

| | | |
|---|---|---|
| 8.1 | Introduction | 8-3 |
| | 8.1.1 Performance parameters | 8-3 |
| | 8.1.2 Operation monitoring | 8-3 |
| 8.2 | Lift controllers | 8-4 |
| | 8.2.1 General | 8-4 |
| | 8.2.2 Lift control options | 8-4 |
| | 8.2.3 Fail-safe operation | 8-4 |
| | 8.2.4 Controller cabinet and its location | 8-4 |
| 8.3 | Controller technology | 8-5 |
| | 8.3.1 General | 8-5 |
| | 8.3.2 Electromechanical switching | 8-5 |
| | 8.3.3 Solid-state logic technology | 8-5 |
| | 8.3.4 Computer-based technology | 8-6 |
| 8.4 | Control of lift drives | 8-6 |
| | 8.4.1 General | 8-6 |
| | 8.4.2 Motor speed reference | 8-7 |
| | 8.4.3 Protection against failure of feedback systems | 8-8 |
| | 8.4.4 Traction lift hoisting motor rating | 8-8 |
| 8.5 | DC motor control techniques | 8-8 |
| | 8.5.1 Ward Leonard set | 8-8 |
| | 8.5.2 Static converter drives | 8-9 |
| | 8.5.3 Single bridge static converter with motor field control | 8-10 |
| | 8.5.4 Two-bridge static converter with fixed motor field | 8-11 |
| 8.6 | AC motor control techniques | 8-11 |
| | 8.6.1 Variable voltage drive with single-speed motor | 8-11 |
| | 8.6.2 Variable voltage drive with two-speed motor | 8-12 |
| | 8.6.3 Variable voltage, variable frequency drives | 8-12 |
| | 8.6.4 Variable voltage, variable frequency drives with permanent magnet synchronous motors (PMSM) | 8-13 |
| | 8.6.5 Linear induction drives | 8-13 |
| 8.7 | Control of hydraulic drives | 8-13 |
| | 8.7.1 Control valves | 8-13 |
| | 8.7.2 Speed control | 8-13 |
| | 8.7.3 Anti-creep devices | 8-13 |
| | 8.7.4 Hydraulic drives with energy accumulators | 8-14 |
| | 8.7.5 Variable frequency pump motor drive | 8-14 |
| 8.8 | Control of door operators | 8-14 |
| | 8.8.1 General | 8-14 |
| | 8.8.2 Control of DC door operators | 8-14 |
| | 8.8.3 Control of AC door operators | 8-15 |
| | 8.8.4 Electronic control of AC door operators | 8-15 |
| | References | 8-15 |

# 8 Lift drives and controls

## 8.1 Introduction

The objective of this section is to provide an unbiased guide to lift controls so that users and specifiers may compare manufacturers' products and have confidence that they are specifying the correct control equipment for each application. It is intended to help the reader to look for good and bad features and to be in a position to ask the right questions about manufacturers' products. Documentary proof of performance, reliability and control characteristics should always be requested from the manufacturer in case of uncertainty.

Until the 1980s, buildings and users have often suffered because of the incorrect application of lift products to the building. In many cases, this was due to speculative building decisions, providing less than the optimum number of lifts for the building. In other cases, the specifier has failed to take advice, or taken incorrect advice, from a lift sales person. Changes in office working practices and the cost of office accommodation have also resulted in problems. Both can lead to the building population increasing far beyond the capabilities of the existing lift control systems. In these cases, installing new computer-based equipment will normally improve the passenger-handling capacity of existing groups of lift cars.

### 8.1.1 Performance parameters

The controller influences the efficiency of a given group of lifts to move people. Parameters such as flight times, round trip times and interval (see section 3.4) provide a guide to the relative efficiency and these parameters can be either measured or obtained from the lift supplier. As an example, one second saved on single floor transit time (see section 3.4.2) improves the traffic handling capacity of the lift by approximately 5%.

To maximise the transportation capacity for a given size and speed of lift car, the cycle time must be as short as possible. In practical terms this means that:

— the lift should drive straight to floor level without the need for a slower levelling speed to ensure accurate stopping at floor level and a short single-floor flight time

— the opening time for the doors must be short; this time may overlap with levelling

— the door open time must be optimised to the building type, size of the lift car and passenger movement; non-contact passenger detectors (see section 7.8.6) can be used to shorten the door open time.

— the door closing time should be as short as possible, commensurate with the kinetic energy

limitations imposed by BS EN 81[1,2] (see section 7.8.2).

These factors have important consequences for the design of lift components and control devices.

### 8.1.2 Operation monitoring

In the past, lift controllers have provided little information on the operational state of the lifts. This information has been typically confined to:

— lift position indication on landings and in the car

— actual and intended travel direction

— 'lift in use' indication for simpler lifts using automatic push button control.

The Lifts Regulations 1997[3] require that a new lift has a means of generating an alarm and two-way communication system that provides direct communication to an organisation capable of releasing the passengers safely. This organisation and communication must be permanently available. The organisation is typically the lift maintenance company. However, it may be a 24-hour security organisation on a large industrial site. BS EN 81-28[11] is the harmonised standard that defines the requirements for the alarm equipment and management of the alarm.

Computer-based control systems have resulted in the development of more sophisticated monitoring of the state of the lift and its traffic handling efficiency. Features typically available include:

— add-on or built-in fault detection and diagnosis

— statistics on call handling and lift usage

— communications capability for transmission of information to a remote point

— video monitor displays of the real-time operation of the lift group(s)

— voice annunciation of lift position and other messages.

Groups of lifts in busy public use, e.g. those in airports and hospitals, should always have some form of lift monitoring, either local to or remote from the building. If monitoring of small groups or individual lifts is installed for maintenance purposes, the equipment local to the lift should not be over-complex. The monitored information must be checked for accuracy and relevance. False or irrelevant information can be worse than no information at all. Current alarm systems can have integrated remote equipment monitoring capability. This allows reporting of faults and equipment condition to the maintenance organisation.

Most manufacturers have their own solutions to lift monitoring which, in the main, rely on special computer software and it is essential to consult with the potential suppliers before specifying non-standard monitoring equipment (see section 14). It is rarely cost-effective for manufacturers to design one-off software for individual customers. Furthermore, it may prove difficult to locate a maintenance company willing to accept responsibility for such software.

## 8.2 Lift controllers

### 8.2.1 General

The function of a lift controller is to respond to inputs and produce outputs in order to control and monitor all the operations of an individual lift car. The controller may be considered to comprise power control (i.e. motion control, door control) and traffic control (passenger demands).

The power controller must control the lift drive motion so that the lift always achieves the optimum speed for any travel distance. Uneven floor heights must not result in long periods of low speed travel when slowing to some floors. The power controller must also operate the doors and may modify the opening time and speed of the doors in response to signals from the passenger detectors.

In general, the controller inputs are:

— car calls

— landing calls (direct or from a group controller)

— door safety device signals

— lift well safety signals

— signals from passenger detection devices on car, doors and landings.

The controller outputs are:

— door control signals

— lift drive control signals

— passenger signalling (call acceptance, lift position, direction of travel indication).

The basic traffic control task of moving a lift car in response to calls is trivial. However, two factors combine to make the lift controller one of the most complex logic controllers to be found in any control situation. These are:

— control options

— fail-safe operation if faults occur.

### 8.2.2 Lift control options

Lift control options are customer-defined modes of operation of the lift. Many options are standard and defined in the operation sequence of the lift, and are offered by all major lift manufacturers. In some circumstances, the complexity or combination of options makes the use of computer-based controllers essential. Among the most common options are:

— car preference or independent operation of one lift car

— rapid closing of doors, when a car call is registered

— reduction in door open time, when passengers are detected by interruption of the light ray or other passenger detection device

— differential door timing so that doors stay open longer at the main floor and/or vary according to the lift traffic

— 'door open' button

— 'door close' button

— attendant operation (becoming less common)

— recall of all or some lifts to specified floor(s) in the event of fire

— emergency power operation (the exact operational sequence is usually defined by the customer)

— bed service (for hospital lifts).

A detailed description of the operation of the particular lift manufacturers' version of these options should always be provided by the manufacturer when discussing the specification with the customer. This can avoid ambiguity and misunderstandings leading to excessive costs.

Other modes of operation may be specified by the customer. Where these modes are unique, it is important to note that they may require special computer software and/or controller hardware. The commissioning and maintenance of such special modes is not always as straightforward as that for conventional lifts.

### 8.2.3 Fail-safe operation

Safety requirements are laid down in BS EN 81-1[1] for electric traction lifts, BS EN 81-2[2] for hydraulic lifts (other than home lifts) and BS 5900[4] for powered domestic home lifts. These standards require that both the lift controller and the lift must be designed so that a single fault in the lift or the controller shall not cause a dangerous situation to arise for the lift user.

Note that the safety requirements and standards for lifts in the home (i.e. private dwellings) are less rigorous than those for lifts in public areas and work places.

### 8.2.4 Controller cabinet and its location

The introduction of machine room-less lifts and the associated amendment A2 to BS EN 81-1[1] and BS EN 81-2[2] has fundamentally changed the design of the lift. Now it is possible for the controller to be split into several distributed components located 'somewhere' in the lift installation. The major part of the controller (e.g. hoist motor drive) may be mounted in the top of the well, the pit, in an enclosure on a landing or to the side of the well. Other parts may be located on top of the car, call buttons, indicators and door operator may be intelligent and communication between all parts of the control system carried out using serial data transmission or even by radio or laser in some applications. Large, high speed lifts may still use machine rooms due to the size of the hoisting machine and its drive.

The size of controller cabinets varies with complexity of the controls. Most cabinets are between 0.8 and 2.5 m high. They should be installed plumb, square and securely fixed in place. They should not be located in awkward corners or restricted spaces that may cause servicing or safe-working problems. Control cabinets should be positioned such that they are not subjected to the heat resulting from machine ventilation fans or any other direct source of heat. Lighting with an illumination of 200 lux (BS EN 81) must be provided where work needs to be carried out on control systems and machinery should be provided and the environmental conditions required by the manufacturer must be observed.

The physical arrangement of the components within the cabinet may cause the local temperature for some components to rise above the ambient temperature in the machine room by up to 10 °C. All power resistors and high-temperature components should be mounted so as to avoid undue heating of other components. The cabinet should be designed to allow a free flow of air from bottom to top of the controller without any fan assistance in order to limit the internal temperature rise to 10 °C.

High humidity and rapid changes in temperature may cause condensation and these conditions should be avoided in the machine room or the machinery space. This is not a problem in most applications. However, where the environment is severe and condensation cannot be avoided, the following precautions should be considered:

— all equipment should be 'passivated' or galvanised and extra coats of paint applied

— all components and printed circuit boards should be 'tropicalised'

— forced ventilation and temperature control of the cabinet should be considered.

## 8.3 Controller technology

### 8.3.1 General

The size of the building (i.e. number of floors) and the complexity of the lift operations required determine the technology used for the controller. Three basic controller technologies have been used:

— electromagnetic relays

— solid-state logic

— computer-based ('intelligent') systems.

Computer-based systems offer the greatest flexibility to accommodate changes in the use of the building and the requirements of the user. For this reason, it is now, by far, the most commonly-used technology. Electromagnetic relays offer the least flexibility. Electromagnetic relays and contactors are used in computer-based and solid-state logic controllers in order to satisfy the requirements of the relevant British and European safety standards[1,2,4].

### 8.3.2 Electromechanical switching

Electromechanical switching devices include electromagnetic relays and mechanically driven selectors. Relays are designed for low power switching operations and contactors for higher powers. Lift selectors, mechanically driven from the motion of the lift by a tape or rope drive, may be used for low-power logic operations in lift control. Some manufacturers use tape drives for lift position indicators, even in computer-based controllers.

To maximise the reliability of the lift controller, the number of electromechanical components should be kept to a minimum. When a relay controller is 8–10 years old, the breakdown rate of the lift rapidly increases as the relays wear out. O'Connor[5] gives intermittent faults as 70% of relay failures during the wear-out phase.

Relay-based controllers have often presented maintenance problems when fitted to larger lifts and group systems (see section 9). Often, manufacturers do not include sufficient indicator lights to show the operational state of the relays. In cases of intermittent faults, this lack of indicators can increase repair times unnecessarily. Although the controller drawings are on site, they often do not show the actual circuits, because modifications may have been made, without the appropriate changes being made to the circuit diagrams.

### 8.3.3 Solid-state logic technology

Solid-state logic technology includes both discrete transistor circuits and integrated circuit boards. With integrated circuits based on complementary metal oxide silicon (CMOS), 12–15 V power supplies may be used, which provide high immunity to electrical noise interference.

Call signals and other direct current input signals are usually interfaced via passive filter circuits. Light-emitting diodes (LEDs) may be easily incorporated into the design to aid maintainability. It is still normal practice to use some contactors and relays to satisfy requirements of BS EN 81-1[1] and BS EN 81-2[2] and BS 5900[4]. Small cased relays may be used to interface between logic circuits and the high voltage parts of the controller and lift. Figure 8.1 illustrates the basic features.

The reliability of solid-state logic devices is dependent upon the ambient temperature, the operating point of the device (in relation to its maximum rating) and the complexity of the device. The following points should be considered to ensure maximum life:

— Increasing the ambient temperature by 25 °C increases the failure rate of a device by a factor of ten. Therefore, the lift motor room should be kept as cool as possible while staying within the minimum set by BS EN 81-1[1] and BS EN 81-2[2] of 5 °C (see section 12).

— Running a solid-state device at 70–80% of its maximum rating doubles its reliability compared with running at maximum rating.

Integrated circuits allow lift controllers to incorporate many lift options and are suitable for single and duplex lifts, where there is a low density of traffic.

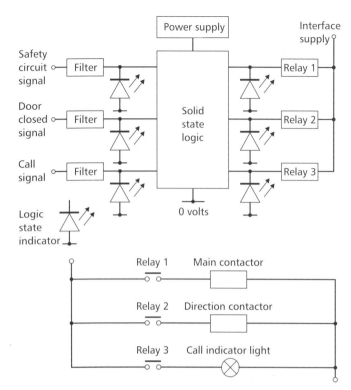

**Figure 8.1** Schematic of typical solid-state logic controller

### 8.3.4        Computer-based technology

Computer-based technology enables complex and adaptable functions to be performed. However, non-standard features should be avoided because of the expense involved in developing and testing special computer software. Computer-based controllers offer flexibility in the options provided and permit fine-tuning to match the building requirements. They are at present the preferred choice for lift groups of any size and for all lift traffic situations. The following features should be provided to ensure adaptability and trouble-free operation:

—       isolated floating power supply for the computer (i.e. not connected to the electrical safety earth or supply common)

—       power supply regulator with a high input/output voltage differential to ensure immunity from fluctuations in the mains supply

—       galvanic isolation (also known as opto-isolation) of all inputs and outputs to the computer to reduce pick-up of electrical noise and possible destruction of low-voltage components

—       program written in a high-level language for ease of program maintenance

—       real-time operating system to control lift program execution

—       diagnostic capability to monitor performance and record basic information to aid fault diagnosis

—       visual indicators on key input and output signals to aid maintenance

—       means of altering lift parameters (e.g. door times, parking floor) on site, without the use of special programming equipment or replacement programs.

The basic reliability of computer-based devices is the same as for solid-state devices. However, considerably improved reliability is achievable if the hardware and software are engineered carefully. The construction of the computer, programming and its interface to the rest of the lift controller profoundly affects the reliability of the controller. Software also affects reliability. The use of a high-level language is essential for all but the simplest programs. It is necessary to test thoroughly new software and software modifications to ensure that any programming errors cannot cause lift malfunctions.

Computer-based controllers are suitable for:

—       all types of lifts

—       all drive speeds (i.e. 0.5 to 15 m/s)

—       lift groups of all sizes (see also section 8.6). The group control function should have at least one level of backup to ensure continued landing call service if the main group control fails.

## 8.4        Control of lift drives

### 8.4.1        General

Drives for lifts are separated into two main categories; electric traction (see section 7.2) and hydraulic drive (see section 7.3). Electric traction drives are further divided into geared and gearless drives. It should also be noted that hydraulic lifts also use electric motors for driving the hydraulic pump. The characteristics and applications of each type of drive vary considerably and an inappropriate drive can have disastrous effects on the reliability and efficiency of the lift installation. It may also lead to increased capital and recurrent costs for the building.

Irrespective of space considerations, the key parameters in choosing between hydraulic or electric traction lifts are as follows:

—       height of travel

—       projected number of starts per hour

—       required ride quality

—       nominal lift speed to provide an acceptable transit time between terminal floors of the building (e.g. 20–40 s)

—       number of lifts required to move the projected building population.

As a general guide, hydraulic lifts should not be specified if the number of motor starts per hour is likely to exceed 45 (or up to 120 starts per hour, if additional oil cooling is provided, see section 12.9.1, or if more than two lifts are necessary to move the population efficiently. This is because the temperature of the oil is very important for reliable operation and most of the energy from the motor is dissipated in the oil, causing its temperature to rise. However, it should be noted that for hydraulic lifts, which do not use a counterweight, the number of motor starts is not equal to the number of lift starts since, for travel in the down direction, only the fluid control valve is opened.

The ride quality of hydraulic lifts at high speeds is generally inferior to that of controlled electric traction drives. For goods and service lifts, however, this is of minor importance provided that levelling accuracy is not compromised.

Guidance on the selection and application of various drive systems is given in BS 5655: Part 6[6]. Unlike many industrial or plant applications of motors and their solid state drives, lift applications impose heavy stresses on the equipment. Lift motors and their drives have to be capable of starting at up to 240 starts per hour under widely varying load conditions. Thus the motor and its drive can spend a large proportion of time under accelerating and decelerating load conditions. Whilst the drive's nominal rating may be the same as that for a comparable non lift application, its overload capacity should be larger to cater for these repeated excursions of acceleration and deceleration. In addition, there is a need to be able to reverse the hoist motor torque linearly at any speed without causing jerk to the lift car. In particular, standard industrial DC and variable frequency AC drives are unsuitable for direct application to lift hoisting applications.

## 8.4.2        Motor speed reference

The motor speed reference is a control signal generated by some device, which indicates the speed and direction of movement of the lift. Some motor speed reference generators also provide information on the present position of the car. These signals are used to control the speed and direction of the motor to enable the lift to respond to instructions received from the controller.

Motor speed references may be divided into two categories: time-based and distance-based[7]. In general, provided that the motor speed is accurately controlled and stable under all likely environmental and load conditions, the choice is not critical. However, the distance-based speed reference provides better control, maximum handling capacity and in most cases superior ride comfort.

### 8.4.2.1        Time-based speed reference

Figure 8.2 shows a typical velocity/time graph for a time-based speed reference. The speed reference may be generated by simple analogue or precision digital computer methods in response to a lift call. It has preset acceleration and deceleration values but, often, may not have a predefined value of jerk. At the start of a run

between floors the speed reference increases to the maximum speed for multi-floor runs. For one-floor runs, the speed is limited to an intermediate value determined by the shortest interfloor distance. For lifts with speeds greater than 1.5 m/s, two or more intermediate speeds may be used for two- and three-floor runs, where the lift does not reach its maximum speed.

For simple time-based speed generators, there is no feedback of lift position to the reference generator. Furthermore, since the lift position during deceleration is dependent upon the load, it is not possible for the controller to bring the lift to rest at floor level by means of constant deceleration. This difficulty can be overcome by ensuring that, as the car nears the required floor, its speed is reduced to a constant 'approach speed', typically 0.4 to 0.5 m/s, and then further reduced to a 'levelling speed' of about 0.06 m/s, just before the car reaches floor level.

The multi-step deceleration is initiated at one or more fixed points in the shaft. The speed reference causes the lift to decelerate at a constant rate, until it reaches a second point at which the approach speed is set. The lift then runs at constant speed until a third point is reached at which the speed reference causes further deceleration to the levelling speed. The lift is finally brought to a standstill, either by the brake or by electrical regeneration in response to a signal from a position sensor. Lifts using a digital time based speed reference, with a well tuned velocity control, can reduce the levelling time to less than one second. It is not uncommon for poorly adjusted lifts to run at approach and levelling speeds for four or five seconds.

### 8.4.2.2        Distance-based speed reference

Figure 8.3 shows a typical velocity/time graph for a distance-based speed reference, also known as optimal speed reference. The acceleration and deceleration values are preset with a predefined value of jerk.

There are no intermediate speeds used for short distance travel, where the lift cannot attain rated speed. The speed reference generator has inputs, which are dependent on lift position and velocity. These allow the reference to generate the maximum possible speed for the distance to be travelled.

For speeds of up to approximately 1.6 m/s, signals from devices mounted on the car or in the lift well are used to initiate deceleration. Because the speed of the lift is known

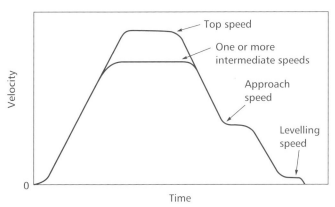

**Figure 8.2** Velocity/time graph for time-based speed reference

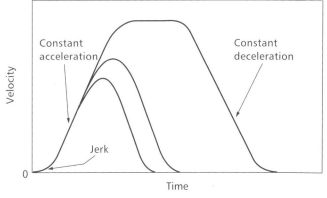

**Figure 8.3** Velocity/time graph for distance-based speed reference

at the signal point, the deceleration distance can be calculated by the speed reference generator. The start of deceleration can be immediate or delayed corresponding to the actual lift speed. During deceleration, the distance from floor level is calculated continuously and the braking torque applied to the motor is varied to maintain the lift on the required velocity distance curve.

For high lift speeds and buildings with several uneven interfloor distances, it is common to use a digital counter-based lift position and deceleration system. This technique can resolve the lift position in the shaft to an accuracy of 3 mm per count or better. The counter input is usually derived directly from a pulse generator connected to the lift or from a motor speed transducer. Typically, to correct for possible counting errors, a spatial image of the lift well is stored in computer memory and used for error correction, whenever the lift is running. Other techniques use directly coupled digital pulse encoders or resolvers. These are commonly used to determine position and for control of motor speed and load angle for variable frequency drives used with induction and permanent magnet synchronous motors.

Using the stored image of the well and information derived from it, the speed reference is continuously provided with information on the distance the lift needs to travel to the next possible stopping point. Using this information, the speed reference determines the maximum possible speed for the distance the lift has to travel. The lift is decelerated in the same way, as described above for lower speed lifts.

### 8.4.3 Protection against failure of feedback systems

Closed-loop drive systems operate by attempting to reduce to zero the difference between the speed reference signal and the feedback signal. Thus if a feedback device fails or becomes disconnected, the output of the drive becomes large and uncontrolled. The most vulnerable of feedback devices is usually the speed sensing device, which is often duplicated for additional security. Monitoring circuits built into the drive compare the difference signals between the outputs of the two sensors and the speed reference. Figure 8.4 shows such a system applied to a static converter drive. The motor armature current feedback is monitored separately.

Protection against failure of feedback systems must be built into all closed loop drive systems. The protection must be fast acting and stop the lift immediately.

### 8.4.4 Traction lift hoisting motor rating

For a given lift capacity and speed, the hoisting motor power can vary substantially dependant on:

—   whether a gear box is used or not

—   the roping arrangement of the lift, e.g. 1:1, 2:1

—   the percentage of rated load counterbalanced by the counterweight

—   the type of guide shoes: e.g. sliding, roller

—   the type of motor: e.g. DC, AC induction, AC permanent magnet synchronous (AC PMS)

—   design values of acceleration, deceleration and jerk.

To minimise the energy used by the hoisting machine, it is preferable to avoid the use of a gearbox, minimise the roping ratio, use the highest efficiency motor type (AC PMS) and use roller guide shoes. Other engineering and cost factors will affect the combination of these parameters for a particular lift design.

Modern traction lifts minimise the torque (and ampere) requirements of the motor to lift the payload by counter-balancing the mass of the moving equipment at mid-range payload. However, with a high speed lifts a significant amount of energy is still necessary to accelerate the inertia of the moving equipment and load (see section 13.3.2). When stopping the lift, the kinetic energy stored in the moving mass must be removed in order to cause deceleration. This phenomenon occurs during every start–stop cycle of the lift. What happens to the inertial energy (wasted by machine friction, or as heat in the motor, or electrical resistor bank, or reclaimed by regeneration back into utility mains) is an important factor to determine overall energy consumption (kW·h) over the course of a year and for the entire life-time span of the equipment. This becomes an increasingly important consideration with higher lift speeds as the inertial energy is proportional to the square of lift speed.

## 8.5 DC motor control techniques

DC gearless machines are still the most common type of drive for lift speeds greater than 2 m/s. There are two basic methods of controlling DC motors: the Ward Leonard set and the static converter drive. Static converter drives are the most economical in operation with energy costs up to 60% less than those for equivalent Ward Leonard drives.

### 8.5.1 Ward Leonard set

A Ward Leonard set[8] is an AC motor driving a DC generator using a mechanical coupling, see Figure 8.5. Open loop control, i.e. no feedback of the motor speed to the control device, or simple armature voltage control allows tolerable performance over a 30:1 speed range. Speed control is obtained by switching resistances in series with the generator field. Careful adjustment of series field windings in the machines is necessary to equalise the up and down direction speeds. The dynamic characteristics of

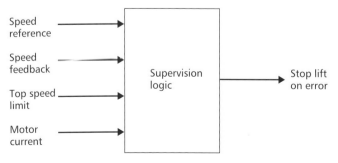

**Figure 8.4** Supervision logic for closed-loop drive

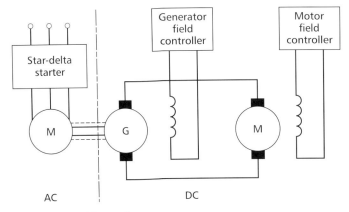

Figure 8.5 Ward Leonard set

circuits of this type are not stable, both over time or temperature, which generally appears as variations in the slow speed approach to floor level.

Surveys carried out prior to modernisation show that many generators are too small for the rated load and speed. Consequently, to prevent overheating of the equipment, such lifts usually run slower than specified and therefore the transportation capacity is restricted. The solution is either to install a larger generator or to fit a static converter, see section 8.4.4.2.

The best control for generators is achieved by using feedback techniques to regulate the motor speed, armature current and the generator field current, see Figure 8.6. This reduces the energy losses in the generator by at least 20%, and reduces the current peaks in the machines. The control of armature current ensures a stable drive, which does not drift with time and temperature. Within the limits of the generator capacity, the ride performance of the lift can be as good as that using static converter drive. Another consideration in favour of the motor-generator is that the system is inherently regenerative. In spite of the somewhat lower efficiencies, a significant amount of energy is returned to the mains supply on each deceleration, or with overhauling loads, without creating unwanted current harmonics.

However, the generator requires regular maintenance to maintain it in good condition. The accumulation of carbon dust from the brushes can cause earth leakage currents. Incorrect brush pressure, material and brush gear settings cause scoring of the commutator and consequent sparking leading to rapid deterioration of the machine. Undersized generators and poor control cause overheating of the machine, thus shortening the life of the insulation.

## 8.5.2    Static converter drives

A static converter is an electronically controlled power converter which converts AC to DC and inverts DC to AC. Used with a DC motor, static converters provide high efficiency and accurate speed control without the use of a DC generator. The power losses are very low, typically less than 5%.

Lifts require a smooth, linear reversal of motor torque to obtain a good ride. The majority of drives designed for industrial use cannot reverse motor torque with the smoothness required for lifts. Hence, purpose-designed drives are preferred.

Power conversion is accomplished using bridges of thyristors or silicon controlled rectifiers (see Figure 8.7). Using phase control, the DC output of the bridge can be varied from zero to full power, in order to drive the motor.

Dual-way static converters enable the kinetic energy of the lift to be returned to the mains supply by the process of inversion. When the motor voltage is higher than the supply, energy can be returned to the mains at high efficiency by suitably controlling the conduction angle of the bridge thyristors.

A detailed description of the characteristics of the basic types of thyristor bridges is given in Davis[9]. The waveform of the current drawn from the supply to a static converter is substantially a square wave. This produces harmonic currents in the supply which interact with the supply impedance to produce voltage distortion. The Electricity Association's Engineering Recommendation G5/4: *Limits for harmonics in the UK electricity supply*[10] sets down limits for harmonic distortion. Note that AC drives also produce harmonic currents.

The harmonic current levels generated by the basic three-phase bridge (6-pulse bridge) can be reduced by using two bridges in series or parallel (12-pulse bridge). The 12-pulse bridge construction is more expensive and has latterly not been economically viable for lift control.

All controlled drives using switching devices produce short duration voltage disturbances to the supply. Input filters must be used both to protect the thyristors from

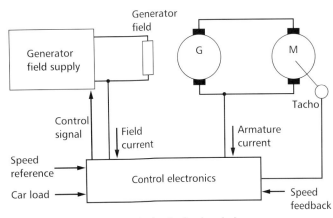

Figure 8.6 Generator control using feedback techniques

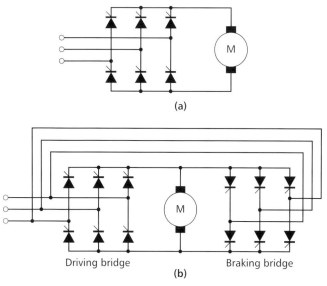

Figure 8.7 Static converter drives; (a) non-regenerative, (b) regenerative

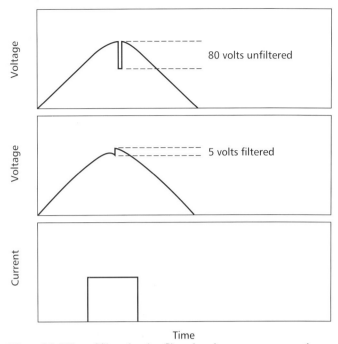

**Figure 8.8** Effect of filtered and unfiltered static converters on supply voltage

damage during switching and to function as voltage disturbance and harmonic attenuators.

The input impedance of the static converter should be at least 10 times the supply impedance to the lift installation. The input filter inductors should ideally be air cored to maintain the inductance value under all possible operating conditions of the drive. In contrast, iron cored inductors suffer from loss of inductance under high and fault current conditions. Figure 8.8 shows the typical effect on the supply voltage of filtered and unfiltered static converters. Motor drives using thyristors will often use a power transformer to adjust utility voltage level to better suit the voltage rating of the lift motor. A second function is that the impedance of the power transformer is part of the filter. Other special filters may also be required to reduce current harmonics or high frequency electromagnetic interference (EMI).

Filters should also be used on the output. Three phase six-pulse DC bridges produce a 300 Hz AC voltage ripple on the DC output when supplied from a 50 Hz mains. Without filtering, the amplitude of the voltage ripple can be as great as 50% of the rated DC output voltage. This can cause

the lift motor to produce substantial audible noise at the ripple frequency, if there are no output filters. This noise is obtrusive and easily transmitted into the building via the structure and the lift well. Output filters can reduce the ripple by a factor of ten.

All static converters should have built-in protection for current overload and supply failure. Ideally, this should not rely on high speed semiconductor fuses or circuit breakers for the first line of protection. Semiconductor fuses deteriorate with age and can often be the source of unnecessary lift breakdowns. For maximum reliability, the first line of overload protection should be electronic.

The drive, in conjunction with the lift controller, should be capable of automatic return to operation after a mains supply failure. It should be able to tolerate repeated mains supply disconnection, when the lift is running at contract speed.

There are two basic types of static converter drive suitable for use with lift motors. These are classified by the number of bridges used to supply the motor armature, i.e:

— single bridge with motor field control

— two bridge with fixed motor field.

Both types should use a distance-based speed reference to obtain maximum electrical efficiency and lift transportation capacity.

### 8.5.3    Single bridge static converter with motor field control

This system is used in an attempt to save the high costs associated with the large thyristors used to supply the motor armature. Figure 8.9 shows a schematic diagram of the system.

A single thyristor bridge is used for the conversion of power to supply the motor armature. The motor field is controlled to reverse the power flow, motor torque and direction of rotation. Two low-power thyristor bridges are used to supply a variable polarity and current magnitude current to the motor field.

Although cheaper to build than two-bridge drives, there are some significant disadvantages with the single bridge

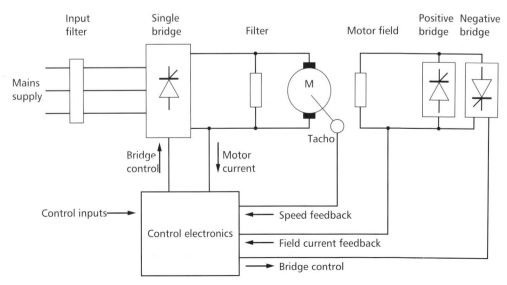

**Figure 8.9** Schematic of single bridge static converter with motor field control

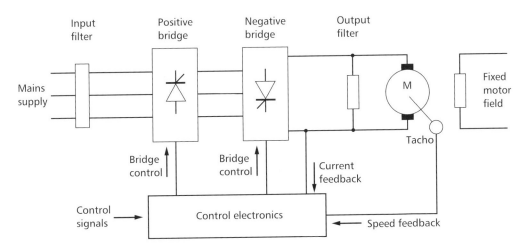

**Figure 8.10** Schematic of two-bridge static converter with fixed motor field

approach. First, the control circuit is complex since it is required to control three thyristor bridges. Secondly, field control depends on the motor characteristics, which vary with type and manufacturer. Consequently, it is difficult to design the control circuits to compensate accurately for all motor types. The control of the motor, therefore, may not be sufficiently stable with time and car load over the speed range of the motor.

### 8.5.4 Two-bridge static converter with fixed motor field

Figure 8.10 shows a block diagram of the most common type of two-bridge static converter. The motor field is supplied from a constant voltage, or constant current, supply, set at the nominal value for the motor. Some types of gearless motor require a reduced field current to achieve rated speed, the field current being higher during acceleration and deceleration. This is the only variation of the motor field, which may occur while the lift is running.

This system does not depend on motor field current or armature characteristics and a standard design can be used for all types of motor. Using current control for both armature and field, the drive is stable with time, temperature and mains fluctuations.

## 8.6 AC motor control techniques

The AC variable voltage drive is suitable for lift speeds up to 2 m/s. For speeds of 1 m/s or less, and small lift cars (i.e. less than 8-person), a simple AC drive without re-levelling may be satisfactory. A drive with re-levelling should always be specified for larger lift cars and higher speed applications or where small wheeled trolleys etc. may be used.

Compared to variable voltage control only, variable voltage, variable frequency drives provide better all-round drive performance for lift speeds from 0.4 m/s to 10 m/s. They give near unity power factor operation and draw lower acceleration currents (e.g. twice the full load current) requiring smaller mains feeders. Provided that it is correctly designed and filtered, the variable voltage, variable frequency drive produces the lowest harmonic current and voltage values in the supply of all the various types of solid-state drive.

### 8.6.1 Variable voltage drive with single-speed motor

There are several variations using the variable voltage technique, depending on whether the speed of the motor is controlled during all phases of the lift movement.

For low-speed, low-grade lifts (e.g. car park lifts and goods lifts) it is possible to obtain accurate and consistent stopping at floor level by controlling only the deceleration of the lift. This technique is suitable for lift speeds up to 1 m/s. Some drives of this type do not allow re-levelling.

Thyristors can be used to control the acceleration of the lift. They also reduce the voltage on the motor during deceleration and can be controlled to produce DC to obtain more braking torque if necessary. This technique is also suitable for lift speeds up to 1 m/s.

Both the acceleration and deceleration of the lift can be controlled using thyristors by reversing the phase rotation of the supply, see Figure 8.11. Due to the lower efficiency of AC phase rotation reversal for braking, the design of the control for the thyristors is critical to obtain good jerk-free torque reversal of the motor. This technique also increases motor and machine room heating compared with DC braking. This technique is suitable for lift speeds up to 1.6 m/s. However, using variable voltage to control the torque and speed of an AC motor causes a great deal of internal motor heating. In all but low traffic situations a special motor design must be employed for a successful installation.

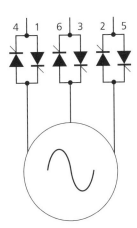

**Figure 8.11** Variable voltage drive with single speed motor

## 8.6.2 Variable voltage drive with two-speed motor

In general, the low-speed windings of the motor are used as braking torque windings. The AC supply voltage to the high-speed windings is controlled using phase control by means of thyristors, see Figure 8.12. The speed of the motor is under control at all times during movement of the lift. With variable voltage control, the starting current of the motor is reduced to approximately 50% of the current drawn by the same motor running as a an uncontrolled two-speed motor. During deceleration, the AC voltage is reduced and a variable DC voltage is applied to the low-speed winding to produce additional braking torque if required.

Some drives of this type limit the maximum speed of the motor to approximately 90–95% of its full load maximum speed. This is because the speed reference and deceleration control cannot deal with variations in the rated speed of the motor due to the load and bring the lift to a halt accordingly at floor level under such circumstances. The electrical efficiency of these drives is considerably reduced and heat losses are increased by limiting the top speed. The motor is working with large slip and DC power has to be applied to the low-speed winding to maintain motor control. Additionally the traffic handling capacity of the lift is unnecessarily reduced.

All drives of this type should have relevelling and levelling accuracy of at least ±5mm under all load conditions and are suitable for lift speeds from 1.0 to 2.0 m/s.

The ride comfort, levelling accuracy and traffic handling achieved using two-speed motors can be easily improved by using an electronic drive. Electronic drives are used for speeds up to 1 m/s. The peak starting currents are higher for two-speed drives. However, in low traffic situations and for some goods lifts, the extra costs of electronic drives may not be warranted.

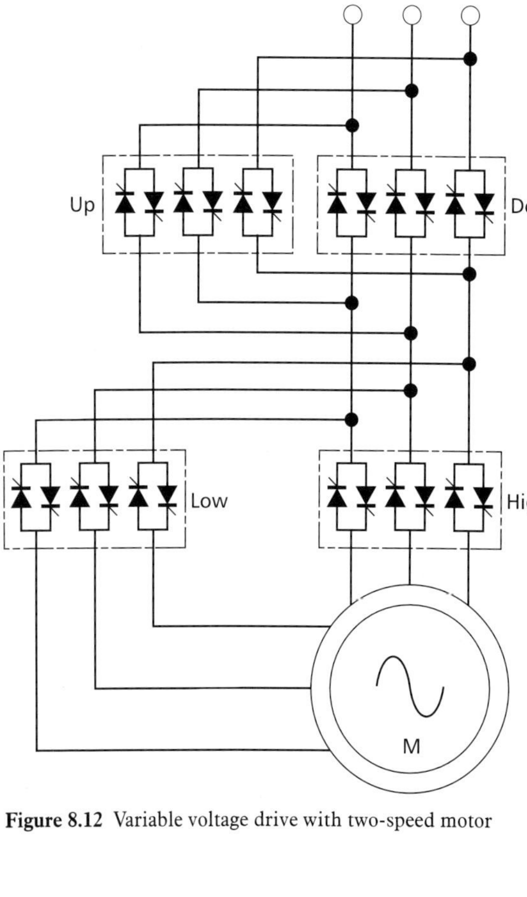

## 8.6.3 Variable voltage, variable frequency drives

Variable voltage, variable frequency drives use the fundamental characteristic of the AC induction motor, i.e. that its synchronous top speed is proportional to the supply frequency. By varying the supply frequency the motor can be made to function at its most efficient operating point over a wide speed range. However, the conversion of power at a frequency of 50 Hz to power at a variable frequency suitable for the motor is a complex process, see Figure 8.13.

These drives provide a high power factor (i.e. >0.9) at all lift speeds and with low electricity and machine room cooling costs.

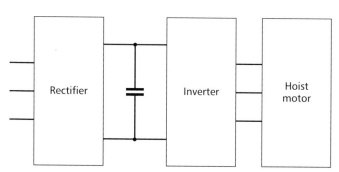

**Figure 8.13** Schematic of a variable voltage, variable frequency drive

Variable voltage, variable frequency drives need only a single speed motor. Where existing lifts are being modernised, the drive may be fitted to an existing single or 2-speed motor. In such cases, the lift manufacturer must always be consulted to determine the suitability of retaining the existing motor for use with a variable voltage, variable frequency drive.

Also variable voltage, variable frequency drives are used with permanent magnet synchronous motors. These motors are more efficient than induction motors and are physically more compact. This reduces the required space and floor loading in machine rooms.

For lift speeds up to 2 m/s, using gearboxes, the energy regenerated by the lift is relatively small and can normally be dissipated by a resistor. The cost of a 4-quadrant drive to regenerate power to the mains is usually not warranted.

Lifts capable of speeds up to 10 m/s can be installed using AC gearless motors, and still higher speeds are possible. In these circumstances a 4-quadrant drive is usual, regenerating energy to the mains supply, rather than dissipating it by means of a dynamic braking resistor.

'Flux vector control' is a type of variable voltage, variable frequency control system that operates in the following

**Figure 8.12** Variable voltage drive with two-speed motor

manner. In mathematics, vector quantities (such as force) have both magnitude and direction and may be resolved into components. In AC motors, the torque generated by the motor depends on the magnetic flux produced between the rotor and the stator. This flux is a variable quantity, the value of which may be determined using a vector diagram. Two vector quantities are controlled: the flux and the torque. The input currents representing these vectors are the magnetising current and the rotor current, respectively. Drives that control the flux are referred to as 'flux vector' drives. Digital encoders are typically used as a motor speed sensor for medium and high speed induction motor drives. Resolvers or digital encoders are generally required to measure rotor position and speed with permanent magnet synchronous motors (PMSM).

There are variations on this principle. In so-called 'sensorless' flux vector drives, computer processing is used to determine the torque and magnetising currents from the motor current, and to determine slip. Hence, the vector is calculated. This enables the motor speed sensor to be eliminated on low speed systems. (Usually, however, it is still required on medium and high speed systems in order to obtain the required accuracy of control.)

In order to provide optimum performance, the motor and drive systems need to be matched. Sensorless flux vector systems can be easily retro-fitted because the characteristics of the existing motor can be programmed into the drive and the motor does not need to be physically adapted to the encoder in every case. In effect the motor also acts as the speed sensor in this case. Furthermore, sensorless drives do not usually provide the level of performance that may be obtained from speed regulated drives with encoder feedback, or from the more sophisticated flux vector control systems.

### 8.6.4 Variable voltage, variable frequency drives with permanent magnet synchronous motors (PMSM)

Permanent magnet synchronous motors have a significant energy saving advantages over the use of induction motors. This is due to the absence of losses due to the rotor running at less or faster than synchronous speed in most situations for an induction machine. It also does not have magnet excitation losses that are also present in the induction machine. PMSM can easily be designed in pancake or axial forms providing a wide range of low torque, high rotational speed or high torque, low rotational speed. They cannot be run direct from a mains supply with its fixed 50 or 60 Hz frequency. A variable voltage, variable frequency drive is thus necessary and its control must be designed to ensure that the maximum safe load angle of the motor is not exceeded under all conditions.

### 8.6.5 Linear induction drives

A linear motor may be regarded as a conventional AC motor 'unrolled' to lie flat (see section 7.2.6). Such machines are sometimes referred to as 'flat-bed motors'. Control is usually achieved by a variable voltage, variable frequency drive as described in section 8.4.5.3

## 8.7 Control of hydraulic drives

A schematic of a typical hydraulic installation is shown in Figure 8.14.

### 8.7.1 Control valves

Hydraulic valves produced in the early 1970s were generally not very well compensated for control variations with car load, oil viscosity and temperature. Consequently the levelling accuracy and lift speed varied according to the load. Many modern control valve designs are fully compensated for pressure and viscosity variations and therefore provide stable characteristics over long periods. This allows higher lift speeds (i.e. up to 1.0 m/s) with accurate levelling and short levelling times.

The flow of oil is controlled either by internal hydraulic feedback (pilot valve) or by electronic sensing of the oil flow. Electronically controlled valves use proportional solenoids to control the oil flow. Electronically controlled valves are more efficient than hydraulic feedback types when operating at extremes of oil temperature.

### 8.7.2 Speed control

The pump motor runs only when the lift travels upwards and the pump has to lift the entire load when a counterweight is not used. The motor power is therefore approximately twice that of an equivalent electric traction lift. Star-delta starting is generally employed to prevent large acceleration currents. Usually, the motor runs at a constant speed. The oil pressure and flow to the hydraulic ram is controlled by returning oil direct to the tank, bypassing the jack.

When the lift runs downwards, the control valve is opened and the lift car makes a controlled descent under the effect of gravity. The up and down speeds are generally independently adjustable on the valve block. The down speed can be higher than the up speed. This allows the average lift velocity to be higher than that provided by the pump. This reduces the round trip time of the lift and increases the traffic handling capability, see section 3.

Valves are rated by oil flow rate (litre/minute) and maximum top speed. Electronically controlled valves are suitable for speeds up to 1 m/s. Hydraulic feedback valves are more suited to lower speed applications, i.e. up to 0.75 m/s.

### 8.7.3 Anti-creep devices

BS EN 81-2[2] specifies the use of some form of anti-creep device on all hydraulic lifts. This is a safety measure to prevent the lift sinking down from floor level due to oil leakage. The anti-creep action may be 'active' whereby the lift is driven up if the lift sinks below floor level due to leakage or oil compression when a heavy load is placed in the car.

For large goods and vehicle lifts, the lift can be physically held at floor level using mechanical stops in the lift well. This is complicated, both mechanically and electrically,

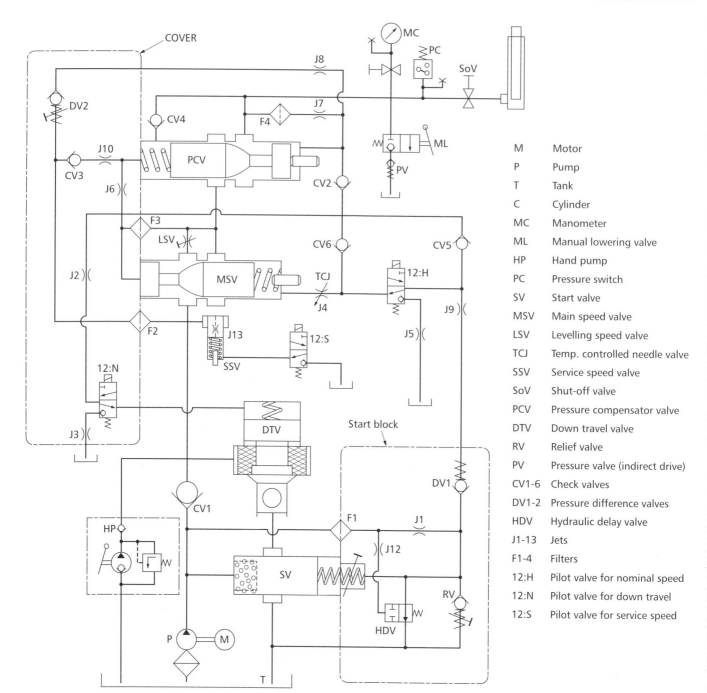

**Figure 8.14** Typical hydraulic installation

| | |
|---|---|
| M | Motor |
| P | Pump |
| T | Tank |
| C | Cylinder |
| MC | Manometer |
| ML | Manual lowering valve |
| HP | Hand pump |
| PC | Pressure switch |
| SV | Start valve |
| MSV | Main speed valve |
| LSV | Levelling speed valve |
| TCJ | Temp. controlled needle valve |
| SSV | Service speed valve |
| SoV | Shut-off valve |
| PCV | Pressure compensator valve |
| DTV | Down travel valve |
| RV | Relief valve |
| PV | Pressure valve (indirect drive) |
| CV1-6 | Check valves |
| DV1-2 | Pressure difference valves |
| HDV | Hydraulic delay valve |
| J1-13 | Jets |
| F1-4 | Filters |
| 12:H | Pilot valve for nominal speed |
| 12:N | Pilot valve for down travel |
| 12:S | Pilot valve for service speed |

but provides a better solution for these applications than active relevelling.

### 8.7.4 Hydraulic drives with energy accumulators

Products are now available which use gas filled energy accumulators as a means to reduce the energy consumption of the lift. During the down travel of the lift car, the potential energy of the lift car and ram are used to increase the pressure of the gas in the accumulator. This stored energy is used to reduce the energy demand on the electricity supply.

It should be noted that gas accumulators are pressure vessels and as such are subject to the Pressure Equipment Directive[12]. Lifts using pressure vessels require safety examinations of the vessels in addition to the usual examinations required for lifts.

### 8.7.5 Variable frequency pump motor drive

Products are now available which use a variable frequency drive to power a variable flow hydraulic pump. This decreases starting currents and reduces energy consumption compared to lifts using flow control valves. These drives may be used in combination with energy accumulators, see section 8.4.6.4.

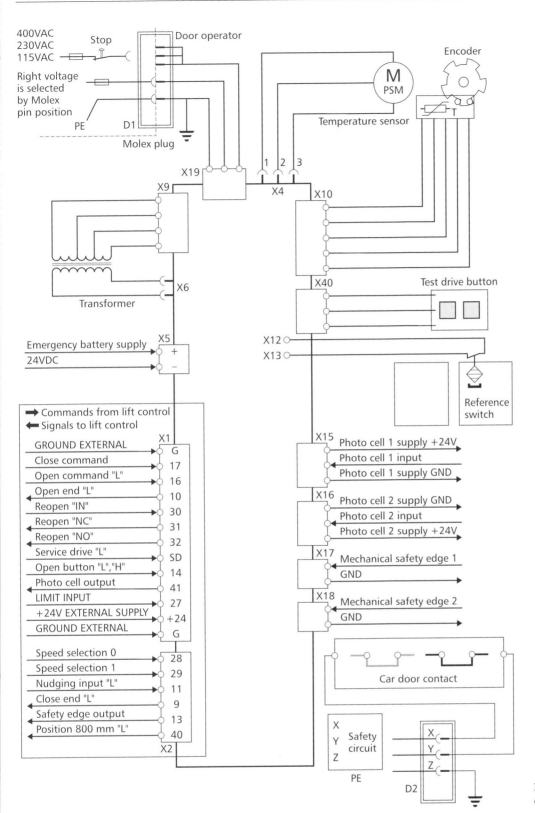

**Figure 8.15** Door operator and control system

# 8.8    Control of door operators

## 8.8.1    General

The door operator (see section 7.8) and its control system (see Figure 8.15) must meet the following requirements:

—  the opening and closing speeds must be independently adjustable

—  for high-performance lifts, the opening and closing speeds must be automatically adjustable according to the prevailing traffic conditions at the floor

—  safety edges must be fast acting and tolerant of mechanical impact; remote sensing edges (i.e. electronic) are inherently better than mechanical edges in these respects.

Optical (i.e. photocell) or other passenger/object detection devices may be used to modify door control. Additionally, they can be used in conjunction with a load sensor to prevent nuisance car calls.

Advanced opening is a time-saving feature widely used in office buildings to improve performance, see section 3.5.3.2. This allows the doors to commence opening once the car speed is below 0.3 m/s and the lift is within the door zone (typically ±100 mm, maximum ±200 mm). However, it can be disturbing to elderly users and may not be suitable in some buildings.

## 8.8.2 Control of DC door operators

Two methods have been in use for many years:

— resistance control of motor field and armature

— saturable reactor control.

These methods control the door velocity depending on the position of the doors in relation to the open and closed positions. DC motors are often provided with additional velocity control to provide a smooth stop at the extremes of travel of the doors.

Position sensing is normally by limit switches. It is difficult, and almost impossible economically, to vary the door speeds in response to prevailing lift traffic conditions using commands from the controller. This is a major limitation to obtaining maximum handling efficiency in large lift groups with heavy traffic.

Some manufacturers have introduced electronic speed control of the motor. Control of deceleration is by limit switches. The speed reference is usually time-based. This removes the need for banks of resistors and makes the door operator easier to set up, the electronics merely replacing the resistors. Unfortunately many of these operators still retain sinusoidal mechanical linkages. The bearings in these mechanisms are subject to very high peak loading if the doors are reversed during closing or stopped by the safety devices. It is important to ensure that the operator mechanism is suitable if a drive of this type is offered.

The motors typically used for modern door operators are low voltage (e.g. 24 volt) using electronic control of speed, torque and door position. This provides good performance with a compact door operator design.

## 8.8.3 Control of AC door operators

Simple AC door operators do not have speed control, and the motor runs at a constant speed. The door motor may be designed to run safely, when stalled with the full supply voltage applied. Constant speed door operation is suitable for narrow doors and where traffic is low so that the limited speed does not restrict lift performance.

## 8.8.4 Electronic control of AC door operators

AC variable voltage door operators typically use a single speed motor. Braking torque and direction is controlled by reversing the phase rotation of the supply. This technique is satisfactory with low-power motors. The speed, position of the doors and motor torque can be controlled using closed-loop feedback. The feedback signals are monitored and compared with reference signals. If there is loss of, or large errors in, the feedback signal the door drive is stopped.

Logic circuits built into the door operator control the speed reference so that the doors always follow a distance-based velocity curve. This safely minimises opening and closing times and prevents high acceleration forces on the doors. Logic circuits can also control the reopening of the door in response to safety signals. For example on a 1200 mm entrance, the doors open only to 800 mm in response to the first reopen signal. This minimises the door operation time to maintain the maximum possible traffic handling capability. Additionally, the lift controller can, as an option, modify the door speeds and open times in response to changes in the level of traffic.

Good electronic controlled operators, using velocity and position closed-loop control, are suitable for both general use and for demanding applications. In modernising a lift system, electronic operators, used in conjunction with good group control and lift motor control, can produce dramatic increases in the traffic handling capacity of the lift group (typically 30–40% improvement).

## 8.8.5 Electromagnetic compatibility, environment and reliability

The use of solid state drives and computers in lifts requires more attention to these aspects than was necessary previously. The Electromagnetic Compatibility Directive[13] requires, in general terms that equipment shall not generate interference which can damage or cause malfunctions in other equipment and shall be immune or respond to interference in a way which is not hazardous. The harmonised product standards for lifts and escalators are BS EN 12015[14] (emission) and BS EN 12016[15] (immunity), see section 12. All (new) equipment should be compliant with these standards. Note that due to the distributed layout the lift and escalator equipment in the building (parts of a lift are on each floor) it is not meaningful to make compliance tests on site.

Of particular importance in the construction of the equipment is the design and installation of the electrical earthing both internal to control cabinets and external, including the coaxial termination of screened signal and power conductors.

The environment must be controlled to ensure that the storage and operating temperature and humidity limits are not exceeded. The performance and reliability of the equipment is adversely affected by operation outside of its design parameters. Such operation may cause breakdowns and adversely affect warranties.

# References

1    BS EN 81-1: 1998: *Safety rules for the construction and installation of electric lifts. Electric lifts* (London: British Standards Institution) (1998)

2    BS EN 81-2: 1998: *Safety rules for the construction and installation of electric lifts. Hydraulic lifts* (London: British Standards Institution) (1998)

3    The Lifts Regulations 1997 Statutory Instrument 1997 No. 831 (London: The Stationery Office) (1998)

4    BS 5900: 1999: *Specification for powered domestic lifts with partially enclosed cars and no lift well* (London: British Standards Institution) (1999)

5    O'Connor P D T *Practical Reliability Engineering* (Chichester: John Wiley and Sons) (1991)

6    BS 5655: *Lifts and service lifts*: Part 6: 2002: *Code of practice for selection and installation* (London: British Standards Institution) (1990)

7    Barney G C and Loher A G *Elevator Electric Drives* (Chichester: Ellis Horwood) (1990)

8    Hindmarsh J *Electrical Machines and their Applications* (Oxford: Pergamon Press) (1984)

9    Davis R M *Power diode and thyristor circuits* (London: Peter Peregrinus) (1979)

10   *Planning levels for harmonic voltage distortion and the connection of non-linear equipment to transmission systems and distribution networks in the United Kingdom* Electricity Association Engineering Recommendation G5/4 (London: The Electricity Association) (2001)

11   BS EN 81-28: 2003: *Safety rules for the construction and installation of lifts. Lifts for the transport of persons and goods. Remote alarm on passenger and goods passenger lifts* (London: British Standards Institution) (2003)

12   Directive 97/23/EC of the European Parliament and of the Council of 29 May 1997 on the approximation of the laws of the Member States concerning pressure equipment ('Pressure Equipment Directive') *Official J. of the European Communities* 9.07.1997 L181 (Brussels: Commission for the European Communities) (1997)

13   Council Directive of 3 May 1989 on the approximation of the laws of the Member States relating to Electromagnetic Compatibility EC Directive 89/339/EEC ('Electromagnetic Compatibility Directive') *Official J. of the European Communities* 23.05.1989 L139/19 (Brussels: Commission for the European Communities) (1997)

14   BS EN 12015: 1998: *Electromagnetic compatibility. Product family standard for lifts, escalators and passenger conveyors. Emission* (London: British Standards Institution) (1998)

15   BS EN 12016: 1998: *Electromagnetic compatibility. Product family standard for lifts, escalators and passenger conveyors. Immunity* (London: British Standards Institution) (1998)

# 9 Lift traffic control

## Principal authors

Simon Russett (Hoare Lea)
Dr Gina Barney (Gina Barney Associates)

## Chapter contents

| | | |
|---|---|---|
| 9.1 | The need for lift traffic control | 9-3 |
| 9.2 | Single lift traffic control | 9-3 |
| | 9.2.1 Single call automatic control | 9-3 |
| | 9.2.2 Collective control | 9-3 |
| 9.3 | Purpose of group traffic control | 9-4 |
| 9.4 | Types of traffic control algorithms | 9-5 |
| | 9.4.1 Legacy traffic control systems | 9-5 |
| | 9.4.2 Modern traffic control systems | 9-7 |
| 9.5 | Advanced group traffic control features | 9-8 |
| | 9.5.1 Use of artificial intelligence (AI) in group traffic control | 9-8 |
| | 9.5.2 Methods of detecting traffic patterns and the incidence of peak traffic | 9-9 |
| | 9.5.3 Data logging | 9-9 |
| | 9.5.4 Centralised and distributed control and back-up | 9-9 |
| 9.6 | Other group traffic controller features | 9-10 |
| | 9.6.1 Load bypass | 9-10 |
| | 9.6.2 Up-peak service | 9-10 |
| | 9.6.3 Down-peak service | 9-10 |
| | 9.6.4 Heavy demand floors | 9-11 |
| | 9.6.5 Lobby and preferential floor service | 9-11 |
| | 9.6.6 Parking policy | 9-11 |
| | 9.6.7 Car preference | 9-11 |
| | 9.6.8 Fire service | 9-11 |
| | 9.6.9 Other facilities | 9-11 |
| 9.7 | Effect of the traffic control algorithm on traffic design | 9-12 |
| 9.8 | Case studies | 9-13 |
| | 9.8.1 Design case study | 9-13 |
| | 9.8.2 Installation case study | 9-13 |
| References | | 9-15 |

# 9     Lift traffic control

## 9.1     The need for lift traffic control

Individual lift control is a basic necessity and, as such, was present from the very beginnings of lift usage. Early systems used 'car switch' controls, in the car operated by an attendant, to move and stop the lift at the various landings. The introduction of automatic motion control eliminated the car switch, but the attendant remained to collect and transport intending passengers. The early group traffic control systems were human dispatchers who directed the movement of cars during the morning up-peak at the main terminal landing.

After the second world war automatic systems utilising relay logic were designed which dispatched individual lift calls in a group from terminal landings separated by a time headway. They picked up any landing cars encountered in their path. These relay based systems were eventually developed to operate 'on-demand' and only react to the registration of landing calls. As time passed these relay based systems gave way to hybrid relay/electronic controllers and eventually to programmable logic controllers (PLCs) and microprocessor based systems.

Thus the development of fully automatic push button (FAPB) controls has almost completely eliminated the use of an attendant in the car and a dispatcher on the main landing and passengers to 'drive' the lifts themselves. The attendant is only retained in exceptional cases, e.g. where there is a security issue, customers or builders beneficial use prior to handover, or to provide a special service to VIPs.

The overall control of lift systems presents two different engineering challenges:

—     First, some means of commanding a lift car to move in both up and down directions and to stop at a specified landing must be provided.

—     Second, to serve passenger demands (landing and car calls) and for a group of lifts to work together in order to make efficient use of the individual lifts in the group.

The first challenge is concerned with drive systems and drive control, which was discussed in Chapter 8 of this Guide. The second challenge is concerned with (passenger) traffic control and is the subject of this chapter.

Both control systems are often found in the same cabinet and thus have become known collectively as the 'controller'. Another term sometimes used today to describe the traffic controller is 'dispatcher' — an echo from history. Guidance on the selection and installation of new lifts, including traffic control, can be found in BS 5655: Part 6[7].

Appropriate automatic traffic control systems can enable a single lift, or a group of lifts to operate at high efficiency, provided the equipment is well designed, properly installed, adequately maintained and reliable. This chapter provides guidance on the traffic control of single lifts, and for lift groups through legacy systems, based on relay logic, to modern day systems, utilising microcomputers.

In the discussions, the various types of passenger demand (up-peak, down-peak, mid day and interfloor traffic) will be mentioned. These terms are fully discussed in Chapter 3.

## 9.2     Single lift traffic control

There are many lifts installed as single units in buildings, such as hotels, small offices, car parks, museums, railway stations, schools etc. They must respond to the registration of landing calls and the resulting registration of car calls. Where a single lift is proposed, purchasers should consider which control system will suit their purpose from those described below.

### 9.2.1     Single call automatic control

The simplest form of automatic lift control is single call automatic control. Single push buttons are provided on the landings. This form of control is also termed non-collective or automatic push button (APB) control.

The passengers operate the lift by pressing landing and car buttons. Car calls are given absolute preference over landing calls. Once a passenger in the car presses a car call push button corresponding to the required destination floor, the lift moves directly to this floor bypassing any intermediate floors. When a landing call push button is pressed and the lift is free, the call is immediately answered. If the lift is in use, a landing signal indicates a 'lift busy' and the landing call must be re-registered.

This type of control is only suitable for short travel passenger lifts serving up to four floors, for example, in small residential buildings with a light traffic demand. It provides a very low carrying capability, as most of the time the lift carries a single passenger. It can also produce long passenger waiting times, owing to the many trips that bypass passengers on the intermediate landings. This type of automatic push button control is, however, suitable for goods lifts, particularly when a single item of goods can fit in the lift at one time.

### 9.2.2     Collective control

The most common form of automatic control used today for a single lift is collective control. This is a generic designation for those types of control where all landing and car calls made by pressing push buttons are registered and answered in strict floor sequence. The lift automatically stops at landings for which calls have been registered, following the floor order rather than the order in which the push buttons were pressed. Collective control can either be of the single button, or of the two push button types.

### 9.2.2.1 Non-directional collective

Single push button collective control provides a single push button at each landing. This push button is pressed by passengers to register a landing call irrespective of the desired direction of travel. For example, a lift travelling upwards, detecting a landing call in its path will stop to answer the call, although it may happen that the person waiting at the landing wishes to go down. The person is then left either to step into the car and travel upwards before going down to the required floor, or to let the lift depart and re-register the landing call. Owing to this inconvenience, this type of control is only acceptable for short travel lifts.

### 9.2.2.2 Down collective (up-distributive, down-collective)

Despite the disadvantages expressed in 9.2.2.1, single push button call registration systems may be adequate in buildings where there is traffic between the ground floor and the upper floors only and no interfloor traffic is expected, e.g. car parks, public high-rise housing, flats etc. While retaining the single push button on the landing, a suitable control system is the down collective control (sometimes called up-distributive, down-collective) where all landing calls above the ground are understood to be down calls. A lift moving upwards will only stop in response to car calls. When no further car calls are registered, the lift travels up to the highest landing call registered, reverses its direction and travels downwards, answering both car and landing calls in floor sequence.

### 9.2.2.3 Full collective (directional collective)

The two push button full collective control (also designated 'directional collective control') provides each landing with one 'up' and one 'down' push button. Passengers are requested to press only the push button for the intended direction of travel. The lift stops to answer both landing and car calls in the direction of travel, and in floor sequence. When no more calls are registered in the direction ahead of the lift, the lift moves to the furthest landing call in the opposite direction, if any, and reverses its direction of travel and answers the calls in the new direction. This control system is suitable for single lifts or duplexes (two lifts) serving a few floors with some interfloor traffic. Typical examples are small, low rise office buildings, hotels and apartment blocks.

Directional collective control applied to a single lift car is also known as simplex control. This system can be applied to two or three interconnected lifts to provide control, where fully configured group control is not appropriate. Two lifts are termed a duplex and three lifts a triplex. This is the simplest form of group control.

## 9.3 Purpose of group traffic control

A single lift will not always be able to cope with all the passenger traffic in a building. Where a number of lifts are installed together, the individual lift control mechanisms should be interconnected and also there should be some form of automatic supervisory control provided. In such a system the landing call push buttons are common to all the lifts which are interconnected, and the traffic supervisory controller decides which landing calls are to be answered by each of the individual lifts in the group.

The function of efficiently distributing landing calls to individual lift cars in a group is basically the same for both large and small groups. Therefore, a 2-car duplex can benefit from the use of group control as much as an 8-car group. This is called group traffic control, which can be defined (see Appendix A1: Glossary) as:

> a number of lifts placed physically together, using a common signalling system and under the command of a group traffic control system

The purpose of group control is to allocate (or assign) the landing calls in an optimum way to the various individual lifts in the group. The term 'optimum' is difficult to define. Equally difficult is 'What to optimise?'. A number of possibilities have been suggested, for example:

— minimises passenger waiting time

— minimises system response time (i.e. the time between the registration of the call until it is answered; this will be equal to the waiting time of the passenger who registered the call)

— minimises passenger journey time

— minimises the variance (in statistical terms) in passenger waiting time (or system response time)

— maximises the handling capacity

— minimises the energy consumption

— reduces 'bunching' (see Appendix A1: Glossary)

Various traffic control algorithms have been developed to achieve some of the above goals and if there is a specific requirement for one of these this should be written into any specification and discussed with the potential suppliers at the design stage.

The definition of a traffic algorithm is:

> a set of rules defining the traffic control policy, which is to be obeyed by the lift system, when a particular traffic condition applies

Modern group traffic control systems are expected to provide more than one control algorithm or program in the traffic control system to allocate lifts to landing calls. The appropriate operating program is determined by the pattern and intensity of the traffic flow encountered by the lift system. The ability of a traffic controller is defined by the number and type of input data it can accept. A supplier will be able to indicate the category in which their equipment falls. A simple triplex controller would not be suitable for a busy office building. The issue can be complicated by the fact that some algorithms are more suitable than others under differing types of traffic. At an early stage the expected or predicted type of traffic demand should be established in order to match a suitable traffic controller to the demand.

For any control algorithms to be effective, certain input information about the lift system and the traffic to which it is subjected, needs to be provided to the controller, see Figure 9.1. The basic data are:

— all the landing calls

— position of all lift cars

— status of each lift car (i.e. moving up/down, door status, car load, in/out of service etc.).

Further improvement to the performance of the system is achieved if variables such as the following are also provided to the group controller:

— all the car calls registered in the lifts

— type of prevailing traffic (i.e. up-peak, down-peak, interfloor traffic etc.)

— the destination of each passenger prior to boarding the lift (as in hall call allocation systems (see section 9.4.2.3).

As a general rule, the more information about the lift system that the group controller has access to, the better the performance of the group controller in allocating the landing calls and optimising the relevant parameter (e.g. passenger waiting time).

Figure 9.1 shows the basic schematic for signal flows in a group traffic controller.

# 9.4 Types of traffic control algorithms

The traffic control system complexity depends not only on the number of available control programs, but also on the complexity of the algorithms themselves. A lift system with a large variety of control algorithms is not necessarily the best system. Problems may arise in the transfer of control from one algorithm to another, as an effective redistribution of lifts takes some time, making response to transient changes in traffic requirements very difficult to achieve consistently.

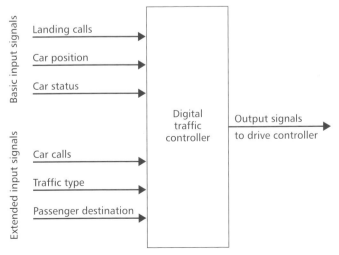

**Figure 9.1** Basic schematic of signal flow in a lift group traffic controller

Lift group control systems respond to the necessity of providing efficient control of a group of automatic lifts servicing a common set of landing calls. The main goals are to provide the maximum handling capacity and the minimum waiting and travelling time of passengers, whilst using the most economical installation. The criterion is to determine the best arrangement of landing calls and to allocate the best lift car to serve the particular landing call. Various algorithms have been developed throughout the decades.

## 9.4.1 Legacy traffic control systems

When modernising a lift installation the existing traffic controller may be considered for replacement, often due to reliability or maintainability issues. It is important that the replacement traffic controller, which will almost certainly be microcomputer based, will perform as well, or better, than the system it replaces. The systems developed and installed a quarter of a century ago were all based on relay logic or primitive programmable logic controllers (PLCs). This does not mean the control algorithms provided were significantly inferior to those available today. In general, these legacy traffic controllers concentrated on dealing with the most significant traffic pattern of the day, namely up-peak. The exception to this philosophy was the dynamic sectoring system (see section 9.4.1.4). It is important to understand these legacy controllers when choosing a replacement.

There were four basic (generic) types of traffic controller developed by the proprietary and independent manufacturers. These are briefly described below. A fuller description can be found elsewhere[1,3].

### 9.4.1.1 Nearest car

The simplest type of group control is the directional collective control described in section 9.2.2.3. It is suitable for a group of two, or three lifts, each operating on the directional collective principles, serving around seven floor levels. The assignment of lifts to landing calls is achieved by the 'nearest car' control policy.

A single landing call system with one 'up' and one 'down' push button at each landing, except for the terminal landings is required. The nearest car traffic control system is expected to space the lifts effectively around the building, in order to provide even service, and also to park one or more lifts at a specified parking floor, usually the entrance lobby floor (main terminal). Other features, which might be included, are the bypassing of landing calls when a lift is fully loaded.

Car calls are dealt with according to directional distributive control principles. Landing calls are dealt with by reversal at highest down and lowest up calls. Thus the lift answers its car and landing calls in floor sequence from its current position and in the direction of travel to which it is committed.

The only group traffic control feature contained in this simple algorithm is the allocation of each landing call to the lift that is considered to be the best placed to answer this particular call. The search for the 'nearest car' is continuously performed until the call is cancelled after being serviced.

### 9.4.1.2 Fixed sectoring — common sector system

A fixed sectoring, common sector control system can be devised for dealing with off-peak traffic and can be complemented with special features to cater for heavy unbalanced traffic. The system divides a building zone into a number of static demand sectors (Figure 9.2) equal to the number of lifts. Note that a building zone is a number of floors served by a group of lifts. Zones can be adjacent to the main terminal (low zone) or above the low zone (high zones). A sector includes both the up and down landing calls at the floors within its limits. A lift is allocated to a sector if it is present in that sector and the sector is not committed to another lift. Fully loaded lifts are not considered for allocation.

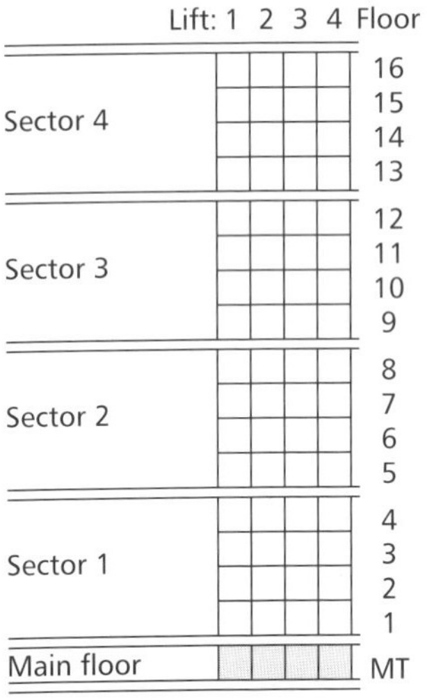

**Figure 9.2** Illustration of the fixed sectoring of a building zone

An assigned lift operates on the directional collective principle within the limits of its range of activity. The de-assignment of a lift from its sector takes place when the lift leaves the sector. A lift picks up calls ahead when travelling in either direction, even if it is not assigned to the sector.

The system, by distributing the lifts equally around the building, presents a good performance under balanced interfloor traffic. It also performs well for up-peak and unbalanced interfloor traffic conditions. It lacks a proper procedure to cater for sudden heavy demands at a particular floor. Under heavy down-peak traffic conditions, a poor service may be provided to the lower floors of the building owing to problems in recycling the lifts to unoccupied sectors.

### 9.4.1.3 Fixed sectoring — priority timed system

Static directional sectoring systems can also allocate the lifts on a priority timed basis. The landings in the building zone served by the group of lifts are grouped into up and down sectors. Each sector is timed as soon as a landing call is registered within its limits. The timing is measured in predefined periods of time, designated the priority levels. The system is unique among the classical traffic control systems as it considers time when making an assignment. The other algorithms only consider position.

The assignment of lifts to the sectors takes into account the number and positions of the available lifts and the sector priority levels. A lift is available for allocation when it has completed its previous assignment and has dealt with all the car calls that have been registered. The sector with the highest priority is the first to be allocated a lift.

The control system provides a good up-peak performance. Its down-peak performance is very good, especially under very heavy traffic conditions. The interfloor traffic performance is fair, but not as good as can be obtained from dynamic sectoring.

### 9.4.1.4 Dynamic sectoring system

The dynamic sectoring group supervisory control system provides a basic algorithm and is suitable to deal with light to heavy balanced interfloor traffic. It is complemented by a number of other control algorithms to cater for unbalanced traffic conditions.

The basic dynamic sectoring algorithm groups landing calls into dynamic sectors. The position and direction of each lift defines the sector, see Figure 9.3. Each lift answers the landing calls in the sector 'ahead' of it. In parallel with the basic traffic algorithm, another dynamic sectoring algorithm is provided to insert free lifts ahead of lifts serving a large number of floors (e.g. sector 3 in Figure 9.3) or a large number of calls registered in their dynamic sector.

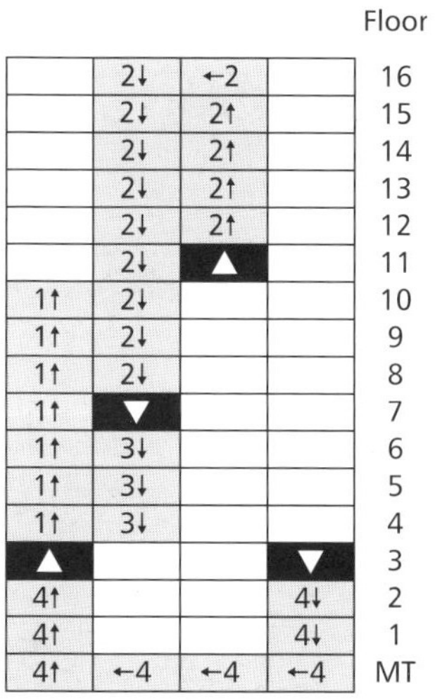

|  |  |  |  | Floor |
|---|---|---|---|---|
|  | 2↓ | ←2 |  | 16 |
|  | 2↓ | 2↑ |  | 15 |
|  | 2↓ | 2↑ |  | 14 |
|  | 2↓ | 2↑ |  | 13 |
|  | 2↓ | 2↑ |  | 12 |
|  | 2↓ | ▲ |  | 11 |
| 1↑ | 2↓ |  |  | 10 |
| 1↑ | 2↓ |  |  | 9 |
| 1↑ | 2↓ |  |  | 8 |
| 1↑ | ▼ |  |  | 7 |
| 1↑ | 3↓ |  |  | 6 |
| 1↑ | 3↓ |  |  | 5 |
| 1↑ | 3↓ |  |  | 4 |
| ▲ |  |  | ▼ | 3 |
| 4↑ |  |  | 4↓ | 2 |
| 4↑ |  |  | 4↓ | 1 |
| 4↑ | ←4 | ←4 | ←4 | MT |

DS1: floors 4–10
DS2: floors 12–16–8
DS3: floors 6–4
DS4: floors 2–MT–2

**Figure 9.3** Illustration of the dynamic sectoring of a building zone

The dynamic sectoring system provides a very good performance for up-peak and interfloor traffic conditions, but a poor performance for down-peak.

## 9.4.2 Modern traffic control systems

The concept of centralised supervisory control systems for buildings, known as building management systems (BMS) using computers, is already well established. As part of the comprehensive information system for a whole building it includes facilities such as employee identification, security control, fire control, environmental control, water treatment, data logging, etc. It is not sensible to include the task of lift traffic control in any centralised building control system. Thus, a lift should have all aspects of its traffic and drive control managed independently of other building systems.

The opportunity exists with a computer to program complex tasks to assist the call allocation process, which are impossible to achieve with fixed program systems. This might be considered to lead to truly optimal traffic control. Unfortunately humans (passengers) are involved and they expect certain rules to be obeyed. In summary these are:

— *Rule 1*: car calls always take precedence over landing calls.

— *Rule 2*: a lift should not reverse its direction of travel with passengers in the car.

— *Rule 3*: a lift should stop at a passenger destination floor (it must not pass it).

— *Rule 4*: passengers wishing to travel in one direction should not to enter a lift committed to travel in the opposite direction.

— *Rule 5*: a lift with passengers in the car should not stop at a floor where no passengers wish to enter or leave the car.

Absent-minded passengers could infringe rule 4, but its likely violation can be reduced by effective signalling (indicators, lanterns and gongs). Rule 5 could be violated by the passengers, either in the car or, on the landing, accidentally, or deliberately, registering incorrect calls.

There are three basic (generic) types of traffic controller developed by both proprietary and independent manufacturers. These are described below. A comprehensive description can be found in reference texts[1,3]. Incorrect selection of the traffic control system will have significant consequences and independent advice may be needed for complex projects.

### 9.4.2.1 Estimated time of arrival (ETA)

An estimated time of arrival (ETA) computer based traffic control system allocates lifts to landing calls, based upon computed car journey times, i.e. how long it will take a lift to arrive. Early systems of this type, developed in the 1970s, substituted relay or solid state fixed logic by a truly programmable computer. This technique was an obvious one to use once programming facilities were available. The ETA technique remains the underlying basis of many computer based systems on the market. The quality of the estimation can be improved by use of artificial intelligence (AI) techniques (see section 9.5.1).

The ETA control system can be expected to provide a good up-peak performance. By declaring the main terminal floor as a parking and priority floor, cars will be sent down to deal with the incoming traffic. The system is not, however, particularly suitable for down-peak traffic. Under light to medium balanced interfloor traffic conditions, the system behaviour is very similar to a dynamic sectoring system, and good performance is to be expected. For heavier traffic conditions the ETA system can only be said to be reasonably good, presenting a performance lying between the dynamic sectoring and the fixed sectoring system performances.

A variation[17] of ETA is estimated time to destination (ETD). This system not only estimates the time to arrive and pick up the intending passenger(s), but also the time it will take to their destination. The system takes into account the commitments an arriving car has in terms of landing calls already allocated and the current car calls it must honour. AI techniques can be used to improve the estimations.

### 9.4.2.2 Stochastic control

The stochastic control algorithm provides an even service to all floors, where every landing call is given fair consideration. This means that the landing call that has been waiting the longest should be given the first consideration for service. The normal distribution curve of how the landing calls are answered shows some answered in zero time whilst there is a long tail to the distribution with some calls waiting very long periods of time, see Figure 9.4(a). The underlying premise of the stochastic algorithm[8] is to bring the tail closer to the average and to sacrifice the 'instant' collection of some calls. The effect is to give a more even and more consistent service to passengers, by trading the instant response calls for the long tail calls, see Figure 9.4(b).

The system is designed to serve the balanced interfloor traffic condition, with considerations of the other traffic conditions.

### 9.4.2.3 Hall call allocation (HCA) control

It would be much more useful if the traffic controller knew the intended destination of each landing call. This information can be obtained by replacing the conventional up/down buttons (Figure 9.5(a)) by a panel of passenger destination buttons at each landing similar to the keypad on telephones (Figure 9.5(b)). Hall call allocation[10] gives the opportunity to track every passenger from landing call registration through to their destination.

The basic system works[3,15] by the computer allocating each new passenger call, as it is registered, to each car in

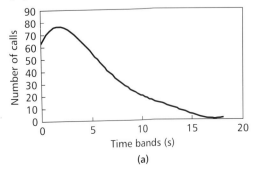

(a)

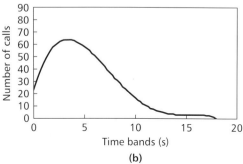

(b)

**Figure 9.4** Illustration of the stochastic process; (a) normal landing call service, (b) stochastic landing call service

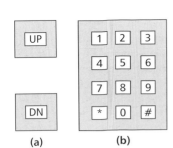

**Figure 9.5** Illustration of hall call allocation landing registration panel; (a) conventional, (b) key pad

turn and evaluating the cost of each allocation. The allocation giving the lowest cost is then adopted. Suitable cost functions are passenger average waiting time, passenger average journey time or a combination of both.

During up-peak, passengers can be grouped to common destinations as there are large numbers of them. The individual waiting time may increase, the travel time may decrease, and there would be an overall reduction in journey time. During down-peak there is no advantage as the destination floor is known. During reasonable levels of balanced interfloor traffic there is little advantage as most landing calls and car calls are not coincident. However, during an up-peak with some down travelling traffic, or a down-peak with some up travelling traffic, or during mid day traffic, there are benefits. An optimum cost (money) system would have a full call registration station at the lobby and other principal floors and two button stations at all other floors.

The advantages of the system are:

— Passengers do not need to translate their intention to travel to a specific floor into a request for an up or down command.

— Passengers do not need to rush to the lift whose hall lantern is on as they stand by the pre-assigned lift.

— The supervisory system receives full information regarding the destinations of all passengers and thus it can make more intelligent decisions.

— Handling capacity is increased.

— Reductions in the passenger time to destination are possible.

The disadvantages of the system are:

— The passenger waiting time may increase.

— Each passenger must register a call.

— Passengers cannot register destination calls in the car.

— Increased cost of call station fixtures.

— Possible passenger misunderstanding of the system.

— Possible abuse.

The 'positive' concept of using a cost function as a performance index can be transposed into a 'negative' concept of penalty functions in order to promote higher efficiency. An example of a penalty function is the rejection of an allocation which introduces an additional stop.

The HCA system is often used to boost[13] an under-provided building during the up-peak period. Unfortunately it does not significantly change the performance during other traffic conditions, see section 3.10.4.

## 9.5 Advanced group traffic controller features

### 9.5.1 Use of artificial intelligence (AI) in group traffic control

The engineering goal of artificial intelligence is to solve real-world problems using ideas representing knowledge, using knowledge, and assembling knowledge-based systems. Generally, the application of AI techniques to lift systems has not been shown to bring significant advantages to the 5-minute peak traffic situations. This is because the demand varies from moment to moment and is not consistent day-by-day. Thus the AI technique is unable to respond fast enough to produce an advantageous result. However, where the traffic demand is less than the capacity of the lift installation AI techniques do improve overall performance.

A number of AI techniques have been applied to lift traffic control, and some manufacturers claim they are advantageous. These claims should be checked with the supplier, in particular whether the improvements are for the peak periods, or are averaged over long periods of time. A summary of the most common systems is given below.

(a) *Expert system control*: the philosophy of supervisory control based on traffic sensing and rule-based expert systems was developed in the 1990s. The system was implemented using standard packages, built on a spreadsheet in the first instance. Simulated input traffic was generated and dynamically linked to the simulator, showing car movements. An expert system linked to the traffic sensing system continuously calculated optimal car movements.

(b) *Fuzzy control*: the application of 'fuzzy logic'[12,16] on elevator systems was first achieved in Japan where the appropriate rule was selected immediately after any hall call button was pressed. A fuzzy logic dispatching system reduces waiting time by operating in an active mode. The dispatcher uses fuzzy rules based on past experience to predict how many people will be waiting for elevators at various times of the day, rather than simply reacting to calls. When several fuzzy features are included in the dispatching decision process, the result is a more effective approach to elevator dispatching than systems based on conventional digital logic.

(c) *Artificial neural network control*: such networks[9] have been used to select the appropriate traffic patterns so that the traffic control module could choose the best hall call assignment algorithm. A destination-oriented car allocation service has also been developed to improve services during rush hours.

(d) *Optimal variance method*: a statistical approach involving variance analysis has been adopted where the variance of hall call response time could be decreased by computerised elevator dispatch systems utilising cost function minimisation. The idea is to improve the variance performance by sacrificing the mean response time to a small extent.

(e) *Genetic algorithms*: emulating animal genetics and based on the concept that the fittest individuals survive, genetic algorithms[18] can be used to search for a global optimisation of lift service times.

## 9.5.2 Methods of detecting traffic patterns and the incidence of peak traffic

Until the 1980s, office working hours were relatively stable. Incoming and outgoing traffic peaks could be predicted and simple time clocks used to switch the mode of operation of the group control. The installation of analogue computer circuits to measure the number and direction of landing calls provided additional discrimination. Changes in working practices to more flexible and staggered office hours defeat these simple strategies for handling peak traffic. Also building population densities have often increased beyond the original designed capacity of the lifts using non-computer-based systems. For these reasons, it has become necessary to enable the controller to detect the type of traffic prevailing. The techniques described below should be discussed with any prospective supplier.

— *Load weighing devices*: in most cases these devices give the estimated weight in discrete steps of full load, and give a rough estimate of the number of passengers. The conversion process from measured weights to passenger numbers assumes a fixed weight figure per passenger, which could vary widely owing to the differing weights of passenger groups (adults, children etc.) and other disturbances (e.g. passengers carrying objects, or pushing trolleys etc.).

— *Photocell signals*: this method is used to identify the number of passengers leaving or entering the car. In cases where the lift responds to both a landing call and a car call, it is difficult to distinguish between in-going and out-going passengers.

— *Pressure sensitive device*: this can be a platform switch or pressure sensitive pad on the floor of the car, which determines the number of passengers.

— *Imaging systems*: these use artificial intelligence techniques to identify the number of passengers.

## 9.5.3 Data logging

Data logging is essential in facilitating routine maintenance (see Chapter 14). Before any traffic control algorithm is performed, information reflecting the current status of every car within the system must also be retrieved. This relies on an advanced digital monitoring system.

All modern controllers provide various degrees of data logging. The owner should have access to all operational data in a form which allows its analysis and presentation. At the very least all data concerned with failures and faults should be available. Additional performance data, dependent on the size of the installation, should be accessible to the owner. This should comprise performance data such as door times, dwell times, system response times, out of service times etc. A prospective supplier should be asked exactly what will be available to the owner.

In addition to remote status monitoring, a diagnostic system should be provided on intensive traffic installations to allow pro-active preventive maintenance procedures to be put in place by the installation maintainer. The system should detect failure symptoms, which would not be noticed by even a skilled maintenance technician. It has been found that small abnormalities in some equipment can cause serious problems when amplified by factors such as component wear and system deterioration.

## 9.5.4 Centralised and distributed control and back-up

There is a vast amount of data to collect and process with modern lift installations. As there are a number of lifts in the group, there are a number of methods by which the data, including landing calls, are collected and processed.

A dedicated group controller can be employed which collects the data and allocates landing calls to a lift according to a certain algorithm (see Figure 9.6). The disadvantage of this method is that the group controller may need extra space, and if it fails, it jeopardises the whole system.

An alternative favoured by most controller suppliers is the master–slave configuration, see Figure 9.7. In this configuration all individual lift controllers receive the data, including the landing calls. Redundancy is built in as all the lifts in the group communicate with each other via high speed serial and parallel data links. For example, on a 4-car group this means that there are four computers able to operate as the group controller. If the computer currently running the group control fails, one of the other computers automatically takes over. Even if all the group control programs were out of action the lift control can still perform a basic collective operation in response to the calls, because all landing calls are registered in each lift

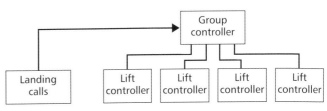

**Figure 9.6** Dedicated group controller

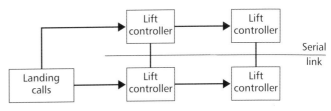

**Figure 9.7** Master–slave configuration

computer. In practice, this means that group control reliability is very close to 100%.

With computer-based systems it is relatively simple to provide back-up to normal operation to accommodate failures in the controller which would otherwise cause complete loss of lift service. The first level of group control back-up, however, should never be a 'bus service' where landing calls are ignored and lifts move continuously between floors, stopping at each floor to pick up any waiting passengers. Back-up service of this kind is inefficient and gives very poor lift service to the building.

It is advisable for a prospective purchaser to determine with their supplier the type of data and control configuration to be supplied.

# 9.6 Other features of group traffic control systems

There are a number of other features that lift group control systems might provide such as, up-peak service, down-peak service, load bypass, heavy demand floors, lobby floor preference service, parking policy, car preference, fire service.

These features are not always necessary or appropriate in many cases. They should be decided at the time of specifying the system to be installed and then discussed with prospective suppliers. Additional costs may be incurred for some of the advanced features.

## 9.6.1 Load bypass

When a lift fills to its capacity it should not stop in response to further landing calls, as such stops would be useless and particularly annoying to the passengers already in the lift. A load weighing system is usually available to prevent this. As indicated in section 3.5.1 larger lifts cannot accommodate the rated capacity as indicated in the standards. For example, if the load detection for a 2500 kg lift were to be set to 60% this would equate to 1500 kg. However, from Table 3.3 a 2500 kg can only accommodate 23.8 passengers. The real 60% value would be equivalent to 60% of 23.8 persons, i.e. 1071 kg. It is important that the load bypass detection is set correctly. (See section 9.8 for an example.)

## 9.6.2 Up-peak service

Most lift group control systems detect and take special action for up-peak traffic conditions. Whilst the up-peak condition applies, the lifts may only answer car calls, bypassing the landing calls. As soon as a lift discharges its last passenger on its way upwards, it reverses direction and travels non stop to the main terminal. Some systems permit service to landing calls on a timed basis.

There are several up-peak detection mechanisms. A common method is based on weighing devices installed in the car floor or by measuring the motor load current as an indicator of loading. When heavily or fully loaded lifts leaving the main terminal floor are detected, the up-peak

control algorithm is selected for a specific time period. A variation of this method, which is able to cater for slight up-peak situations, detects a lift car load at the main terminal in excess of a predefined level, say 50% or 60%. (*Warning*: see section 9.6.1 above.) For a certain period of time a dummy call is set up at the main terminal to ensure that a lift is available there as soon as possible. Another method counts the car calls registered and when a predetermined number are registered, initiates the up-peak algorithm.

A more sophisticated approach employs an up/down logic counter which increments, when loads are above a predefined level, and decrements for loads below this level. Additionally, the counter decrements on a timed basis, say every 60 s or so, to ensure that the up-peak algorithm is switched off quickly as the up-peak traffic diminishes.

During up-peak any passenger wishing to travel up from floors other than the main terminal floor should have little difficulty, as the lifts are frequently stopping at the floors, whilst travelling upwards, to discharge passengers. However, passengers wishing to travel down may find a restricted service or no service at all during the 10 to 15 minutes of heavy up-peak demand. With restricted service, down landing calls can be served by a single lift at fixed time intervals (say from 30 seconds to 3 minutes) or, alternatively, when they reach the highest priority level.

## 9.6.3 Down-peak service

Group control systems frequently include a means to detect down-peak traffic situations, employing similar methods as those used for up-peak detection, but considering heavy loaded lift arrivals at the main terminal floor. Whilst the down-peak condition applies, these systems will restrict the service provided to any up traffic and cancel the allocation of lifts to the main terminal, whilst the traffic condition lasts.

Unlike up-peak where the lifts start and finish their round trips at the main terminal, during down-peak, lifts can start their journey anywhere in the building before travelling to the main terminal. If the lifts are commanded to travel to a high call reversal floor the lower floors will be starved of service as cars will arrive (or pass by) fully loaded. One system which avoids this groups the down landing calls into sectors and assigns lifts to serve call groups in the sectors in a 'round robin' fashion.

## 9.6.4 Heavy demand floors

Heavy floor demands can occur, for example, at the closing of a meeting or lecture. It is then justifiable to bring extra lifts to the floor to deal with such peaks of demand.

A simple method is to detect at individual floors that a fully loaded lift has left that floor and a new landing call has been registered within 2.0 s (say) for the same direction of travel. The traffic controller can then send free lifts to this floor.

Where controllers use sectors based algorithms the number of landing calls in each sector can be evaluated by the traffic analyser and compared with the average number of landing calls per sector. A particular sector exceeding the average value by more than a predefined quantity can be set up as a heavy traffic sector. Extra lifts can then be brought to this sector, bypassing the landing calls at other sectors.

### 9.6.5 Lobby and preferential floor service

The lobby or main terminal floor in a building is normally of great importance, owing to the steady flow of incoming passengers. Preferential service is usually provided for these passengers by parking a lift at the main terminal prior to any other sector. The lobby floor preferential service implies that a slightly poorer service is provided to the remaining floors in the building. The feature is highly undesirable under certain traffic conditions, such as down-peak.

A feature called 'director' or VIP service gives special service to floors, where senior executives or directors are located. The lift system can be made to recognise landing calls at such floors and to deal with them with higher priority. Key operated switches may be available at these preferred landings, which cause a lift to travel direct to the executive floor bypassing all other landing calls, or a lift may be completely segregated out of the bank of lifts for director's service. It is obvious that this sort of preferential treatment can seriously affect the efficiency of the service as a whole and it should be avoided where possible unless system capacity is designed to cater for this feature.

### 9.6.6 Parking policy

Under light-to-medium traffic conditions, a lift frequently has no calls to answer. The lift is then free for allocation, and if no further demand exists it might be parked at its current position, at a convenient floor, or in a sector in the building zone. The parking procedure is mainly intended to distribute the lifts evenly around the building. A proper parking policy is essential for good lift system performance. At the design stage a suitable number of floors, in addition to the main terminal floor, should be identified where the lifts may be parked. These could include, for example, basement areas, leisure, restaurant and facility floors.

### 9.6.7 Car preference

When a lift is taken out of normal passenger control to be exclusively operated from the inside of the lift, it is said to be in car preference. Also referred to as 'independent service', 'emergency service' or 'hospital service'. The transfer is made by a key operated switch in the lift, which causes the doors to remain open until a car call is registered for floor destination. All landing calls are bypassed and car position indicators on the landings for the lift are not illuminated. The removal of the key, when the special operation is complete, returns the lift to normal control.

Car preference may be useful to give a special personal service, or for an attendant to have complete control of the lift, whenever it is required. A typical example is in hospital buildings, where lifts for carrying beds and stretchers require the provision of a car preference switch.

### 9.6.8 Fire and evacuation service

Some lifts may be designed as firefighters' lifts (to BS EN 81-72[6]) or the older (now obsolete) 'firemans' lifts and special recall features are provided. Some lifts may be designated as evacuation lifts provided to allow the safe egress of persons with mobility problems. The behaviour of lifts in the event of a fire is the subject of a CEN working group. These are complex areas (see Chapter 6) and expert assistance should be sought.

### 9.6.9 Other facilities

Some lifts may be designated to provide service to persons with disabilities to BS EN 81-70[5] (see Chapters 6 and 11). This is also a complex area and expert assistance should be sought.

The provision of suitable indicators, lanterns and gongs to indicate lift arrivals and direction at landings, their direction and floor indication in the car and other landing and in-car announcements are important to ensure improved passenger communication. These will require special interfacing to the group control system.

Another useful feature is the provision of anti-nuisance devices to ensure that a lift does not answer car calls, if it is empty. This avoids unnecessary car trips and stops due to a practical joker who registers car calls sometimes pressing or touching all the car push buttons and then leaving the lift.

Other features which improve the efficiency of people movement which should be considered are:

— Adjustable car and landing door dwell times

— Differential door timing

— Only one door re-opening sequence on the re-registering of a landing call at a floor where a lift is about to depart.

— Adjustable sound levels on gongs at all floors and in-car voice announcements.

— Easily seen and brightly illuminated position indicators on landings and in the back and the front of the car.

— Advanced door opening at landings.

## 9.7 Effect of the traffic control algorithm on traffic design

Chapters 3 and 4 indicate traffic design methods to size an installation to meet the expected passenger demand. Chapter 3 dealt with methods, which were independent of the traffic control system used. The simulation methods outlined in Chapter 4, however, allow an actual traffic control system to be simulated against a defined passenger demand.

Owing to the fact that the up-peak traffic has, in the past, usually been the most demanding type of traffic for lift systems, most traditional algorithms are built around that type of traffic. Moreover, much of the terminology and the methodology used in lift design still relies on the concept of meeting a heavy up-peak influx over a period of five minutes by circulating lifts at the main terminal, delivering the passengers and returning the lift to the main terminal. Nowadays the mid day period can often be the most severe traffic condition.

Sometimes the traffic designer specifies too few lifts, or the architect is unable to provide sufficient space for the number of lifts required, or the building population increases and the installed lift system cannot handle the up-peak traffic demand. Several techniques[2] are available to improve the up-peak handling capacity of an installation sometimes called up-peak 'boosters'. The main techniques available are up-peak subzoning, up-peak sectoring and hall call allocation and these are available from many manufacturers. Discussions should be carried out with the manufacturers at the design stage in order to determine the most suitable type for a particular installation.

In subzoning systems, the building zone is divided into two subzones and the lift group is divided into two subgroups for the duration of the up-peak period. The cars are permanently allocated to a subzone and passengers are directed to the subgroup which serves their floor by illuminated signs. The subzones may not contain equal numbers of floors, nor may equal numbers of lifts serve each subzone, see Figure 9.8. The technique works well with at least six lifts in the group and is available from a number of lift manufacturers.

Up-peak subzoning can be extended by dividing the building into more than two sectors to provide an up-peak sectoring traffic control system[11]. The number of sectors can be made equal to (or slightly less than) the number of lifts. Each sector generally contains the same number of floors, except the highest may have less floors and the lowest may have more floors. The number of floors in each sector is small, e.g. 3/4/5, and consequently the round trip time is reduced and the handling capacity increased. An illustration of the up-peak sectoring system is shown in Figure 9.9.

Lifts controlled under an up-peak sectoring traffic algorithm are not permanently assigned to a specific sector. As lifts arrive at the main terminal floor they serve the sectors in a strict 'round robin' fashion. Passengers will have to wait longer for service, but the group interval is smaller. Passengers are directed to lifts serving their floors by destination signs above the lifts. These have to be continually scanned by the passengers until they find a lift serving their desired destination. Where there are more lifts than sectors, it allows some lifts to be travelling back to the main terminal as the others travel up the building. One lift manufacturer has proposed this system.

Basic hall call allocation traffic control, available from a number of manufacturers[13], has been discussed in section 9.4.2.3. A further technique with hall call allocation is to use dynamic subzoning. Here the building is divided into two subzones similar to subzoning described above. The boundary of the subzones can change according to the demand to each of the subzones, determined by the individual car loadings. The intending passengers will be unaware of the changing boundary, as they are always told at call registration which lift they are to travel in.

Up-peak boosters can increase[2] the up-peak handling capacity by approximately:

— 15% using up-peak subzoning;

— 40% using up-peak sectoring;

— 15% using basic hall call allocation;

— 50% using hall call allocation with dynamic subzoning.

However, it is not possible to obtain something for nothing and the increase in handling capacity usually results in longer passenger waiting times, but can reduce time to destination.

Boosters improve the overall performance of a installation for up-peak, either by increasing the handling capacity with longer passenger waiting times, or by improving the passenger waiting times for the same number of passenger arrivals. However, such techniques do not generally improve the performance of the other major traffic conditions. Their performance may stay the same. Up-

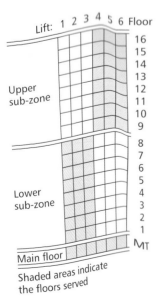

Main floor

Shaded areas indicate the floors served

**Figure 9.8** Illustration of up-peak subzoning

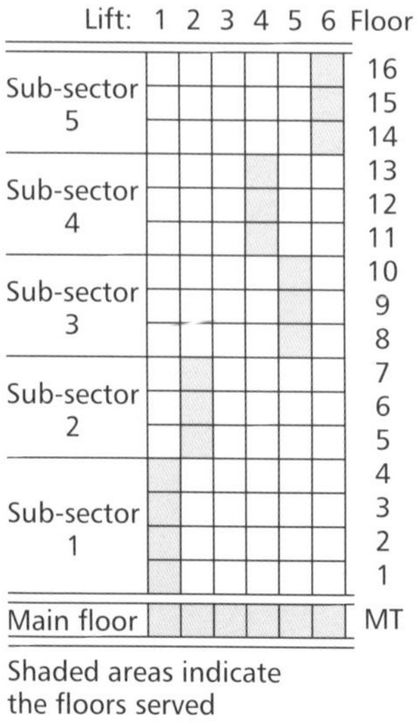

Shaded areas indicate the floors served

**Figure 9.9** Illustration of up-peak sectoring

peak 'boosters' have to be used carefully and independent expert advice should be sought if such a system is considered.

Calculation methods are available[3] to analyse the four up-peak booster techniques described above and the other traffic conditions[1]. These are, however, only indicative and a better evaluation of the performance of an installation can only be obtained by the use of simulation techniques (see Chapter 4). Many manufacturers claim the application of the AI techniques described in section 9.5.1 enhance installation performance for the other traffic conditions. These claims should always be checked by simulation at the design stage. This is a complex area and independent advice may need to be sought.

# 9.8    Case studies

## 9.8.1    Design case study

This case study illustrates how the handling capacity of a lift installation can be increased to meet the changed specification of the occupier.

### 9.8.1.1    Background

A developer speculatively built an office block on the assumption that a cellular office layout would be fitted. The building comprised 16 floors above the ground floor with a total net internal area of 14 000 m².

The original lift system was to be designed to the 'one size fits all' BCO criteria[4] of a 15% percentage arrival rate, a 30 second average interval and an occupational density of 14 m² net internal area per person. The design population was 1000 persons (14 000 / 14) and the 5-minute peak arrival rate was 150 persons (1000 × 0.15). The lift system specified comprised six lifts, 1275 kg rated load, 2.5 m/s rated speed and provided a handling capacity of 147 persons/5-minutes at an interval of 22 seconds. Although the handling capacity is just short of that required the interval is considerably better than that required by BCO criteria. The building was to be constructed to accommodate this lift installation.

During construction a tenant became interested in the building, but only if an open plan office arrangement could be accommodated. The tenant measured the net usable area (NUA), i.e. the rentable space as 12 000 m² and intended an occupation density of 9 m² NUA per person. This implied a design population of 1333 persons (12 000 / 9). However, a more likely peak arrival rate of 13% was proposed. This requires a lift system handling capacity of 173 persons/5-minutes (1333 × 0.13). Would the lifts cope with the increased demand? The answer is 'no' as the new demand is approximately 16% larger than the core being developed.

### 9.8.1.2    Boosting the lift capacity

It was not possible to add an extra lift and so another solution must be sought. The extra handling capacity during the morning peak can only be obtained if an up-peak booster is applied. Section 9.7 suggested that up-peak boosters can increase the up-peak handling capacity by between approximately 15% and 50%.

Either the up-peak subzoning or the basic hall call allocation boosters can provide a 15% increase and of these two the up-peak subzoning system is the simplest to adopt. The next decision is should the subzones contain equal numbers of floors, or equal numbers of lifts. The six lifts are arranged as three opposite three leading to the consideration that during subzoning operation they can be easily presented to intending passengers by indicators placed over each sub group of three lifts. In any case a two lift group would provide a very poor interval and in the event of the failure of one would only leave one lift to serve that subzone. Changing the number of floors per subzone also provides a finer adjustment. The next decision is how many floors should be contained in each subzone.

The logical split would be 8 floors by 8 floors, but it must be remembered that the upper subzone lifts have further to travel before reaching their first served floor than the lower subzone lifts, thus increasing their round trip time and reducing their handling capacity. Table 9.1 summarises three subzone schemes and compares them to the original design.

The 8/8 split provides the required handling capacity (173) precisely, but there is a considerable mismatch of percentage population served (15.1%/10.7%). The split 9/7 nearly provides the 13% percentage arrival rate value and only just misses the handling capacity target (167). The final 10/6 split shows a deterioration in all criteria. The 9/7

**Table 9.1** Comparison of three subzone schemes with underlying installation

| Number of floors served | Floor number | Number of lifts | Population served (person) | Handling capacity | Population served (person/5-min) | Interval (s) |
|---|---|---|---|---|---|---|
| 16 | 1–16 | 3 | 1000 | 147 | 14.7% | 22 |
| 8 | 1–8 | 3 | 667 | 101 | 15.1% | 32 |
| 8 | 9–16 | 3 | 667 | 72 | 10.7% | 46 |
| Scheme 1: 8/8 split | | | | Total: 173 | | |
| 9 | 1–9 | 3 | 750 | 95 | 12.7% | 35 |
| 7 | 10–16 | 3 | 583 | 72 | 12.3% | 46 |
| Scheme 2: 9/7 split | | | | Total: 167 | | |
| 10 | 1–10 | 3 | 833 | 91 | 10.9% | 36 |
| 6 | 11–16 | 3 | 500 | 72 | 8.6% | 46 |
| Scheme 3: 10/6 split | | | | Total: 163 | | |

split is preferred even if the intervals (35 s/46 s), as would be expected with only three lifts, are poor. The subzoning solution with a 9/7 split is not ideal, but does provide nearly the handling capacity required.

To implement this solution the traffic controller must detect the onset of the up-peak condition and then split the control system into two groups of three lifts serving the designated floors. Passenger information displays would need to be illuminated to inform passengers which side of the lift lobby to stand, in order to travel to their destination. The service will not be ideal, but the tenant's requirements are almost achieved. Note, however, that the ability to serve mid-day and down-peak traffic has not been enhanced.

## 9.8.2 Installation case study

This case study illustrates how a traffic controller can be designed correctly but so badly set up that the installation performs badly.

### 9.8.2.1 Background

The building was occupied by a single tenant with a daily population of 1800–1900 persons attending on a flexitime regime. There are 17 floors designated 'Basement', 'Ground' and floors 1–15. There is a restaurant at floor 1 and office services in the basement.

The lift installation was provided by a reputable, major manufacturer with extensive experience of traffic control algorithms. The lift installation comprised eight, 1250 kg (16 person) lifts with a rated speed of 2.5 m/s and good dynamic performance.

The building tenant complained that the lift installation was performing badly in the building they occupied. Complaints presented included:

During the morning arrivals:

(a)   the lobby 'backed-up' with waiting passengers

(b)   some cars could only load 10 persons before the overload operated

(c)   loaded cars did not immediately leave the lobby but continually opened and shut their doors

(d)   some lifts stopped on the way up for landing calls despite being full

(e)   when lifts stopped at a floor and no one entered, or left, the lift did not close its doors for eight seconds

(f)   when lifts stopped at a floor and a person entered, or left, the lift did not close its doors for eight seconds

(g)   up-travelling passengers entered cars which did not travel up, but down to the basement.

During the evening departures:

(h)   lifts arrived at the ground floor with only 5-6 persons exiting

(i)   long waits were reported at lower floors (Floor 4 reported 10 minutes)

During mid-day period

(j)   Lifts rarely called at floor 1

Generally:

(j)   passengers hesitated when entering and leaving a car delaying the journey.

### 9.8.2.2 Complaint resolution

On investigation it was found that many of the traffic controller features were incorrectly set. The installation maintainer was asked to attend to the following items:

—   The load weighing system for each lift should be calibrated. The lifts are 1250 kg so the overload setting would be 1375 kg. This would deal with complaint (b).

—   The load by-pass should be set to 750 kg (60%). This means that when more than 10 (average) weight persons are in the car then the lift will not stop for any further landing calls. This would deal with complaints (d) and (h).

—   The current door dwell times should be reduced and all lifts should present the same times. Car call dwell times should be set to 2.0 s and the landing call dwell times to 5.0 s. This would deal with complaint (e).

—   The differential door times should be set to 0.5 s. This would deal with complaint (f).

—   The lift doors should re-cycle only once, in order to allow additional passengers to enter, after the first closure of the doors prior to departure. This will deal with complaint (c).

—   The lifts should be parked whenever they become idle in an even distribution around the building. Two lifts should always be directed to be present at Ground. One lift should be parked at floor 1. The remaining lifts should be parked at floors 3, 6, 9, 12 and 15. This would improve the situation with complaints (i) and (j).

Further actions to deal with complaint (a), i.e. to increase the handling capacity would be:

—   Each door operator should be individually adjusted to the contract values of door operating times.

—   Each drive system should be individually 'tuned' to achieve the contract flight times.

—   The up-peak and down-peak thresholds (complaint (i)) should be set at three cars leaving/arriving at the ground floor 60% full.

—   The traffic controller should not accept any calls registered on the car operating panel 'behind the car' (car calls for floors already passed). Alternatively at the reversal floor any outstanding car calls remaining should be cancelled.

Complaint (g) can be dealt with by providing large, high illumination direction lanterns and loud gongs on the landing and direction arrows in the back of the car visible from the landing.

Complaint $(k)$ can be dealt with by providing large floor indicators in the cars, audible floor announcements and large visible floor identification signs on the landings visible for the cars.

# References

1    Barney G C and Dos Santos S M *Elevator traffic analysis, design and control* (London: Peter Peregrinus) (1985)

2    Barney G C Uppeak revisited *Elevator Technology 4* (Stockport: International Association of Elevator Engineers) (1992)

3    Barney G C *Elevator traffic handbook* (Spon Press: London) (2003)

4    *British Council for Offices: Best practice in the specification for offices* (London: British Council for Offices) (2000)

5    BS EN 81-70: 2003: *Safety rules for the construction and installation of lifts. Particular applications for passenger and goods passenger lifts. Accessibility to lifts for persons including persons with disability* (London: British Standards Institution) (2003)

6    BS EN 81-72: 2003: *Safety rules for the construction and installation of lifts. Particular applications for passenger and goods passenger lifts. Firefighters lifts* (London: British Standards Institution) (2003)

7    BS 5655: Part 6: 2002: *Selection and installation of new lifts* (London: British Standards Institution) (2002)

8    Halpern J B Variance analysis of hall call response time: trading mean hall call response time for increased variance performance *Elevator Technology 5* (Stockport: International Association of Elevator Engineers) (1993)

9    Kubo S, Nakai S, Imasaki N and Yoshitsugu T Elevator group control system with a fuzzy neural network model *Elevator Technology 6* (Stockport: International Association of Elevator Engineers) (1995)

10    Port L W Australian patent specification 255218 1961 (Woden, Australian Capital Territory: Commonwealth of Australia Patent Office) (1961)

11    Powell B A Important issues in up-peak traffic handling, *Elevator Technology 4* (Stockport: International Association of Elevator Engineers) (1992)

12    Powell B A and Sirag D J Fuzzy logic *Elevator World* (September 1993)

13    Russett S An open and shut case *RIBA J.* (August 2002)

14    Russett S Theme: lifts and escalators *Architects J.* (April 2003)

15    Schroeder J Elevatoring for modern supervisory techniques, *Elevator Technology 3* (Stockport: International Association of Elevator Engineers) (1990)

16    Siikonen M-L and Leppala J Elevator traffic pattern recognition *Proc. Int. Congress of Fuzzy Systems Assoc., Brussels, July 1991* (1991)

17    Smith R and Peters R *Enhancements to the ETD dispatcher algorithm* (Tel Aviv: International Association of Elevator Engineers) (2004)

18    Xiaoliang B, Changming Z and Qingtai Y A GA-based approach to the multi-object optimisation problem in elevator group control systems *Elevator World* (June 2004)

# 10 Escalators and moving walks

## Principal authors

Dr Lutfi Al-Sharif (Al-Sharif-VTC)
Dr Gina Barney (Gina Barney Associates)

## Chapter contents

10.1 Introduction                                                                10-3

10.2 Definitions, commonly available equipment and duty                           10-4
    10.2.1 Definitions                                        10-4
    10.2.2 Commonly available equipment                       10-4
    10.2.3 Duty                                               10-4

10.3 Principal components                                                         10-4

10.4 Installation planning                                                        10-6
    10.4.1 Specifying the equipment                           10-6
    10.4.2 Traffic sizing                                     10-6
    10.4.3 Location                                           10-6
    10.4.4 Aesthetic design                                   10-6
    10.4.5 Safe use of escalators and moving walks           10-6
    10.4.6 Machine rooms                                      10-7
    10.4.7 Electrical supply and electromagnetic compatibility 10-7
    10.4.8 Noise                                              10-7
    10.4.9 Fire protection                                    10-8
    10.4.10 Installing equipment                              10-8

10.5 Drive systems, energy usage and safety devices                              10-8
    10.5.1 Motor sizing and selection                         10-8
    10.5.2 Methods of starting                                10-8
    10.5.3 Modular escalator drives                           10-9
    10.5.4 Energy usage                                       10-9
    10.5.5 Safety devices                                     10-10

References

# 10    Escalators and moving walks

## 10.1    Introduction

Escalators have been in public use since the turn of the century and their derivative the pallet-based moving walk (previously known as 'passenger conveyors') since the 1950s. Escalator applications range from low rise installations to accommodate a small change in level within a storey of a building to high rise installations found in deep underground railways. Inclined moving walks are found in retail premises and transportation facilities, where trolleys need to be accommodated. These two items are installed into a structural opening provided in the building. Horizontal moving walks are typically found in transportation facilities such as airports. Horizontal moving walks are installed along wide corridors generally with a fixed walkway alongside. A general arrangement of a typical escalator is shown in Figure 10.1.

With few exceptions, escalators and moving walks are installed for use by the general public of all ages. Therefore, great care must be taken to ensure compliance with all the safety and operating requirements. These are covered in BS EN 115: 1995[1] and BS 7801: 2005[5]. Escalators and moving walks are unsuitable for the conveyance of a means of transportation, e.g. wheelchair, pram, pushchair, etc., as the risks are considered to be too high  The transportation of shopping/baggage trolleys can be accommodated provided various safety measures are put in place, see section 10.4.5

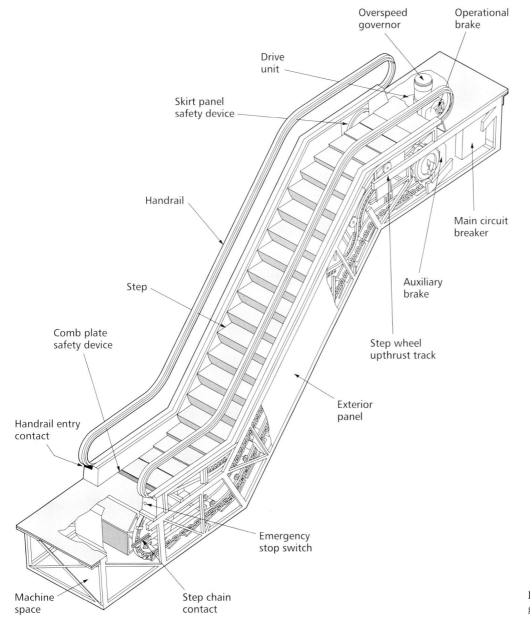

**Figure 10.1** Typical escalator; general arrangement

## 10.2 Definitions, commonly available equipment and duty

### 10.2.1 Definitions

BS EN 115: 1995[1] defines these devices as follows:

— *Escalator*: power driven installation with endless moving stairway for the conveyance of passengers in the upward or downward direction

— *Moving walk*: power driven installation with endless moving walkway (e.g. pallets, belts etc.) for the conveyance of passengers either on the same or between different traffic levels. *Note 1*: a traffic level is the boarding/alighting landing area. *Note 2*: the term 'passenger conveyor' is to be discontinued in the next issue of BS EN 115 in favour of the US term 'moving walk'.

Escalator and moving walks are machines under the Machinery Directive enacted as the Supply of Machinery Regulations 1992[9] and as such the CE-marking is carried out by the supplier by compliance to a harmonised standard or to an EC type examination certificate obtained for a model equipment from a notified body. However, before first use an escalator or moving walk should be tested using BS 5656-1: 1997[2].

### 10.2.2 Commonly available equipment

There are two types of escalator equipment available. The compact escalator is the most common, where all the drive machinery is located within the truss (structural framework). The remote drive escalator is less common and is typical of underground railway systems. Here the drive machinery is located external to the truss in a separate machine room

Escalators and moving walks are factory built equipment and their characteristics can be closely defined. The most commonly available equipment is as follows.

(*a*)  Escalator:

— *Speeds*: 0.5 m/s (also 0.65, 0.75 m/s)

— *Inclination*: 30°; an inclination of 35° is permitted for rises <6 m and rated speeds <0.5 m/s.

— *Step sizes*: 600, 800, 1000 mm

(*b*)  Moving walk:

— *Speeds*: 0.5, 0.65, 0.75 m/s

— *Inclination*: 0°, 6°, 10°, 12°

— *Pallet sizes*: 800, 1000, 1400 mm (for inclination ≤ 6°); 800, 1000 mm (for inclination >6°). *Note 1*: the maximum inclination of 12° for inclined moving walks was established as the largest safe inclination that most persons could stand on and walk on without overbalancing. *Note 2*: Some moving walks up to an inclination of 6°

may be adapted to permit the safe transportation of shopping and baggage trolleys.

### 10.2.3 Duty

According to BS 5656-2[3]. The design of escalators and moving walks falls into four distinct duty categories, as shown in Table 10.1.

The differences in cost between the categories are significant and care must be taken in assessing the demand, in order to make an appropriate selection to meet the needs of a specific location. When deciding the duty category, account should be taken of:

— the peak demands that might be made on the equipment

— the number of passengers using the escalator or moving walk per day.

BS EN 115[1] defined a public service escalator/moving walk. The definition was based on hours of service per day, periods of 100% brake loading etc. This type of equipment would fall into duty categories 3 or 4 in Table 10.1.

## 10.3 Principal components

Figure 10.1 (page 10-3) shows a cutaway view of a typical escalator, showing the passenger and machine sides of the equipment. The machine side is completely enclosed and is commonly known as the truss.

On the passenger side the machine covers are fitted over the machine spaces at the top and bottom of the escalator. The upper machine space, called the drive station, contains the drive machinery and the lower machine space is the return station. As a boarding passenger passes over the machine covers onto the first escalator step the handrails become available running above skirt panels and balustrades. The interface between the stationary machine covers and the moving steps is protected by a comb plate, which is intended to prevent any entrapment by deflecting any intruding material, object, or passenger body part. Several flat steps then present themselves to the boarding passenger before the escalator rises, or falls, depending whether it is an up escalator or down escalator.

**Table 10.1** Duty categories of escalators and moving walks

| Duty category | Typical usage (passengers per day) | Typical locations |
|---|---|---|
| Light | Up to 3000 | Shops, museums, libraries and leisure facilities |
| Medium | Up to 10 000 | Department stores, shopping centres, regional airports and regional railway stations |
| Heavy | Up to 20 000 | Major railway and metro stations, major international airports and critical locations such as underground railway systems |
| Intensive | Over 20 000 | Ditto |

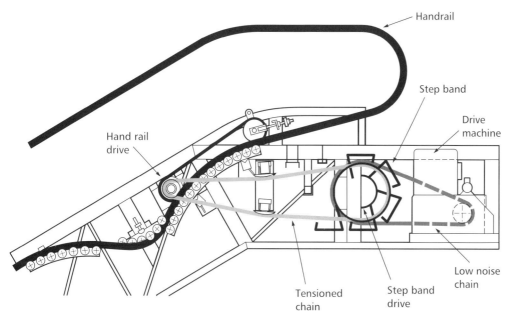

**Figure 10.2** Principal components of an escalator drive system

In general, the more flat steps that there are available the easier and safer it is for passengers to adjust their balance from a walking movement to a transported movement. Five flat steps are considered adequate in most locations – space and cost can be a consideration. At the bottom of the skirt panels, deflector devices are fitted to deflect any material, object or passenger body parts. These devices are mandatory under Amendment 2 (dated 2003) to BS EN 115: 1995. Another safety device protects the entry and exit points of the handrail as it disappears into the truss. Emergency stop switches are provided at suitable positions along the length of the escalator.

Some of the machine side components, such as the drive unit, operational and auxiliary brakes, together with other safety devices, are also indicated in Figure 10.1. The principal components of machine side are shown in Figure 10.2. In this example, the drive machine is situated outside of the step band to allow ease of maintenance. Power transmission from the machine to the main drive of the step band is via a shock absorbing low-noise duplex chain. The handrail is driven from the main drive via an automatically tensioned chain. The handrail drive is designed to ensure synchronous handrail and step band speeds. Figure 10.3 provides a balustrade section view, illustrating the relationship of all the components.

The main components of the step and step chain are illustrated in Figure 10.4. Each step is located by an axle. The intermediate wheels ensure that the load is distributed evenly around the track system.

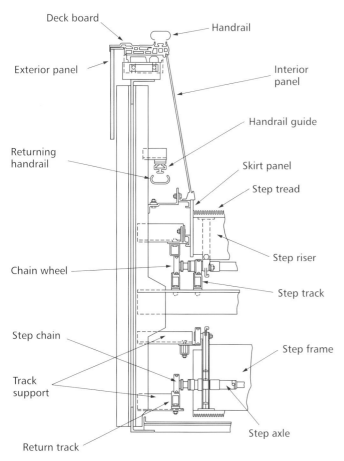

**Figure 10.3** Detail of balustrade

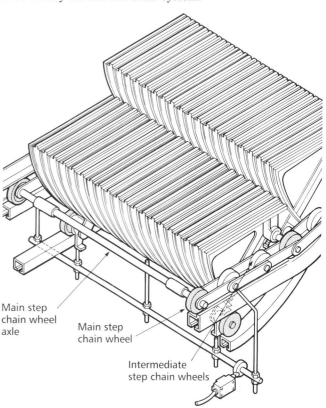

**Figure 10.4** Detail of escalator step and step chain

# 10.4      Installation planning

## 10.4.1      Specifying the equipment

Although an escalator or moving walk is factory-built equipment, there is a large amount of information that needs to be exchanged. General guidance is given in BS 5656-2[3] on the procedure and overall chronological sequence to be adopted in obtaining an installation that is satisfactory from the aspects of operation, safety and maintenance. This code of practice also provides guidance on the exchange of information between the purchaser and the escalator/moving walk supplier. A series of checklists for the various tender documents is given in Annex B to BS 5656-2 detailing the initial exchange of information prior to and at the time of the tender, and the contract inclusions and exclusions.

Specialist advice should be sought at the design stage, where unusual environments are likely to be encountered, for example:

— potential exposure to weather

— low/high temperatures and or high humidity

— hosing-down for hygiene or decontamination

— corrosive/dusty atmospheres

— the need for quiet operation

— vandal-prone installations

— the transportation of shopping/baggage trolleys.

The installation of equipment in these environments will increase the cost owing to the complications involved.

It should be borne in mind that the design, installation and maintenance of escalators and moving walks is always subject to risk assessments being carried out and their installation will be subject to the CDM Regulations[8].

## 10.4.2      Traffic sizing

The number, speed, step/pallet width can be determined using the procedures and information in sections 2.4.4, 2.4.5 and 2.5.3(d) to meet the expected traffic demand.

## 10.4.3      Location

The location of escalators and moving walks is fully discussed in section 2.7. Care must be taken to ensure that the alighting areas are not obstructed either by fixed furnishings or by alighted passengers, whose departure from the alighting area is also obstructed or the succeeding area is too small. The full traffic function must be considered particularly in intensive traffic locations. Particular care should be taken not to obstruct the unrestricted area according to Clause 5.2.1 of BS EN 115[1], where successive escalators and moving walks are installed.

## 10.4.4      Aesthetic design

Escalators and moving walks are not enclosed like lifts and most of the equipment is in the view of the public.

They offer considerable scope to the designer by the imaginative use of glass, cladding and polished metal finishes. Careful design of the lighting may also enhance the appearance. However, consideration must also be given to the following:

— Coloured handrails require regular cleaning, using special materials, at least every two weeks if the appearance is to be preserved. Black handrails are less attractive but more practicable for public usage.

— Where glass balustrades are installed close to a wall, rubbish will collect in the space between the wall and the balustrade. This will be difficult and expensive to remove.

— Stainless steel does not suffer damage by scratching from shoes, luggage etc. and is therefore an appropriate material for intensive duty applications.

— In some recent designs, the moving equipment is observable through glass cladding. This is very effective when the escalator is lit internally, but the difficulties of cleaning the glass (externally and internally) and the equipment must be considered.

— Some manufacturers have developed curved escalators (see Figure 10.5)

— Designs which create voids at the sides of the equipment or gaps between equipment should be avoided as these present a risk of falling or entrapment to users.

## 10.4.5      Safe use of escalators and moving walks

The following features are some of the safety features which should be included to assist passengers in their safe use of modern escalators and moving walks:

— *Yellow lines on steps*: the border of the step is painted with a yellow line. This enables visually impaired passengers to see the step border and encourages passengers to keep their feet away from the step sides.

— *Brush guards*: installed above the edges at the sides of the step, and fixed to the skirting. They are effective in reducing passenger entrapments. *Note*: this is a mandatory requirement under Amendment 2 to BS EN 115[1].

— *Yellow spots on handrails and coloured handrails*: this helps visually impaired passengers see the moving handrail.

— *Adequate permanent lighting*: at the landings of at least 100 lux.

— *Safety signs and warning notices*: to Annex C of BS 5656-2[3].

— *Guards*: end barrier, intersection, outer decking etc.

— The angle of inclination of balustrade panels should be greater than 25° and preferably greater than 27° to discourage children from climbing on the panels.

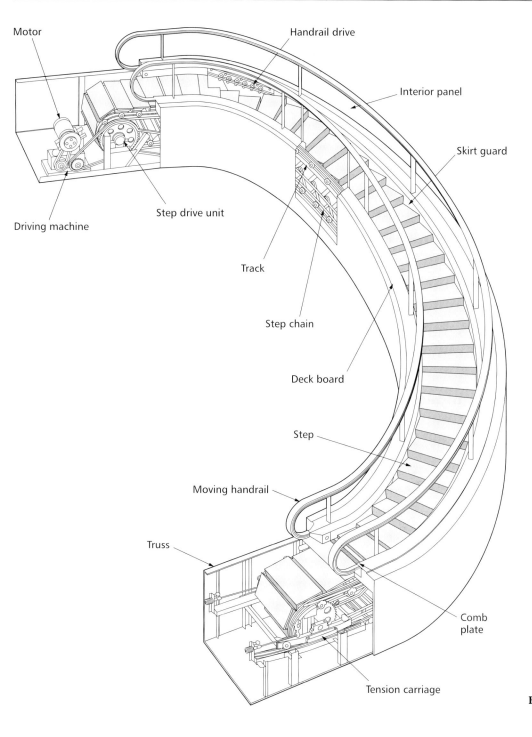

Motor

Handrail drive

Interior panel

Skirt guard

Driving machine

Step drive unit

Track

Step chain

Deck board

Step

Moving handrail

Truss

Comb plate

Tension carriage

**Figure 10.5** Curved escalator

— The guard rails connecting to the escalator/moving walk should be a similar height to the handrail height of the equipment.

— Escalators are unsuitable for use as fixed stairs and should not form part of an emergency exit route.

An assumption has been made that persons using escalators and moving walks are able to do so unaided. However, they are also likely to be used by persons with a range of disabilities. Factors to be considered are:

— speed

— step/pallet width

— inclination

— number of horizontal steps at landings

— handrails

— surface finishes

— controls

— lighting

— signs and information

— landings clear space

— guarding.

Chapter 10 of BS 5656-2 gives specific recommendations and guidance intended to assist persons with disabilities. These recommendations can also improve the level of safety of other users and improve circulation efficiency.

Where shopping/baggage trolleys are to be transported special measures should be put in place. The escalator/moving walk should be designed to accept the shopping/baggage trolleys to be used, such that they can be locked into a safe position. The unrestricted area should be extended to 5.0 metres and additional emergency stop switches placed approximately two metres before each comb intersection.

For escalators the rated speed should not exceed 0.4 m/s, the inclination should be no more than 30° and the transition radius should be at least 2.9 metres.

For moving walks the rated speed for inclinations greater than 6° should not exceed 0.5 m/s and be fitted with an upper and lower transition curve.

At the time of writing (April 2005) BS EN 115: 1995 is under review and should be consulted for further details of requirements.

### 10.4.6    Machine rooms

Machine rooms are required for remote drive escalators. Many of the requirements are similar to those for lift machine rooms. Section 5.4 of BS 5656-2 provides guidance.

### 10.4.7    Electrical supply and electromagnetic compatibility

The supplier should provide details of the full load current, the starting current and its duration, the maximum permissible voltage drop etc. in order to enable the size of the main supply cable to be determined. The electrical installation should conform in all respects to BS 7671[4] (the IEE Wiring Regulations). The main supply from the intake room should be separate from other building services. A temporary electricity supply may be required during the installation and its characteristics should be the same as the permanent supply. BS 5656-2[3] gives further details. The electrical installations should be in accordance with BS EN 12015[6] and BS EN 12016[7] to ensure electromagnetic compatibility.

### 10.4.8    Noise

The location of escalators or moving walks should be such as to cause minimum noise disturbance, although no equipment can be totally silent or vibration-free in operation. The design of the building is significant in noise and vibration reduction. The walls, floor and ceilings of machinery spaces and machine rooms should be designed to substantially absorb the sound. Beams and structural members should not penetrate into occupied areas. If there is any doubt about the equipment then a similar installation should be checked. If the escalator or moving walk is required to operate to specific requirements this should be agreed at the contract stage. Specialist advice may need to be sought.

### 10.4.9    Fire protection

When fire protection systems, such as smoke detectors, sprinklers and shutters are required by the relevant fire authority the owner should provide such equipment and any necessary interfaces and arrange for the system to be tested. Fire shutters are provided by specialist subcontractors. When such devices are installed it is necessary for the escalator or moving walk supplier to include control interfaces to ensure their correct and safe operation.

### 10.4.10    Installing equipment

Generally an escalator or moving walk is delivered and installed as a single unit. This allows for maximum pre-assembly and testing at the factory, including running-in, and will ensure rapid and efficient installation on site. A typical one-piece escalator unit may be more than 16 m long, 1.6 m wide and 3 m high, and weigh up to 9000 kg. Thus careful planning is essential, if costly installation difficulties are to be avoided. Therefore consideration must be given to the following:

— A clear, straight access route onto and across the site must be provided. Normally this should be at least 3 m wide, with a minimum vertical clearance of 3.5 m. *Note*: the 3.5 m dimension can be reduced for the installation of moving walks.

— Police approval will be needed if unloading is to be carried out on a public highway.

— Consideration must be given to permitted floor loadings along access route.

— Suitable hoisting points must be provided.

Early planning is essential, particularly in the case of installations in existing buildings.

## 10.5    Drive systems, energy usage and safety devices

### 10.5.1    Motor sizing and selection

The sizing of the drive motor depends on a number of factors:

— vertical rise of escalator or travel distance of a moving walk

— escalator or moving walk equipment efficiency;

— efficiency of gearbox

— running speed

— angle of inclination of escalator or moving walk

— number of passengers assumed to occupy a step/pallet

— rise of each escalator step.

For an escalator, the output power ($P$) in kW required for the motor is given by:

$$P = \frac{\left(smgn\left(R_e / R_s\right)\sin\theta\right) + p_h}{\eta_s\,\eta_g \times 1000} \tag{10.1}$$

where $P$ is the motor output power (kW), $s$ is the speed (m/s), $m$ is the passenger mass (kg), $g$ is the gravitational force (9.81 m/s²), $n$ is the number of passengers, $R_e$ is the rise (m), $R_s$ is the step riser (m), $\theta$ is the inclination (degrees), $p_h$ is the handrail power (W), $\eta_s$ is the escalator efficiency (%) and $\eta_g$ is the gearbox efficiency (%).

## 10.5.2 Methods of starting

The majority of systems currently employ induction motors in the drive systems of escalators and moving walks. The drive motors are controlled and started by one of the following systems.

### 10.5.2.1 Direct-on-line start (or star-delta)

A star-delta starter is used to start the system and the motor is then directly connected to the supply during service. For maintenance speed, a second slow speed winding in the motor is used, which usually achieves one quarter (25%) of the normal running speed. The motor has two sets of windings, each with a different number of poles (in the ratio of 4:1). Some controllers allow the system to revert to a star connection during periods of inactivity for energy-saving purposes. The main disadvantage of direct-on-line, or star-delta, systems is the large in-rush current during start up (up to seven times the full load current for direct-on-line and up to 3.5 times the full load current for star-delta), the mechanical shock to the equipment components, the very poor power factor at light loads and poor speed control. These systems are less used nowadays, having been replaced by solid state electronic drives, but are inexpensive and appropriate where equipment is switched on/off infrequently.

### 10.5.2.2 Inverter (VVVF) drives

A VVVF drive uses a fully rated inverter system to start the system and then drive it up to full speed. Then either the inverter carries on driving the motor, or a contactor is used to bypass the inverter. The disadvantage with the former method is the heat loss in the inverter, while the disadvantage with the latter is the high changeover current and the resulting jerk in the motor at the moment of changeover.

A feature of VVVF drives is that the speed can be varied to suit a number of different applications, such as a low speed for inspection and maintenance, very low speed for releasing trapped objects from the comb, reduced speed during periods of low or no usage. This has the advantage of reducing the power consumption as well as reducing the wear. The use of an inverter allows imperceptible acceleration and deceleration between the low speed and the running speed.

The advantages of a VVVF drives are that they give a very smooth start (reducing the mechanical shock to the equipment components), they run at a very good power factor (even under no load) and they reduce the starting current to around 1.5 times the full load current. Another advantage is that a standard motor can be used and there is no need to use a pole changing two speed motor to achieve maintenance speed, as this can be done via the inverter. The main disadvantages of VVVF drives is are that they occupy more space, need extra maintenance (the capacitors in VVVF drives have a limited lifetime), and generate extra heat that needs to be removed from the machinery space.

### 10.5.2.3 Soft starters

Soft starters employ power electronics (usually three pairs of back-to-back thyristors) to bring the system up to full speed, after which the thyristors are bypassed by a contactor that puts the motor direct-on-line. The in-rush current is about 1.5–2.5 times the full load current. However, for maintenance speed, there still is a need for a pole changing, two-speed motor. These systems are simple and provide a smooth start, but have a very limited functional capability compared to VVVF drives.

## 10.5.3 Modular escalator drives

A problem with escalator traffic is that it varies widely during the day. There are periods in the day when no one uses the escalator at all, although the escalator has to be kept running. At other times of the day, during peak periods, the escalator is heavily loaded. The motor has to be sized to cope with the maximum demand. This results in the fact that during low usage periods, the motor will running very lightly loaded. This is undesirable, as the efficiency of the system is very low under these conditions. As an answer to this problem, some companies have developed a modular drive system, which employs two or three motors coupled to the same gear box. This type of drive system is particularly appropriate for intensive duty underground railway and other transport system. The control system detects the level of loading and operates as many motors as is needed. In this way the efficiency of the system is kept high enough and the power factor does not drop to unacceptable levels. It also allows energy reduction, improved efficiency and extended life for the motors.

## 10.5.4 Energy usage

Manufacturers can provide figures for the energy consumed by an escalator or moving walk. Section 13 gives information regarding escalator and moving walk energy consumption. The type of operating control employed has an effect on energy usage. There are three types of control option: continuous, variable speed and on demand.

### 10.5.4.1 Continuous operation

The escalator or moving walk operates continuously at a single speed with the starting and stopping carried out manually.

This type of operation would be suitable for locations where there are continuous traffic flows.

### 10.5.4.2 Variable speed operation

A common method used to reduce losses is the reduction in the speed of the escalator or moving walk during periods of inactivity. The change of speed is initiated by the use of a passenger detection system such as pressure mats, photocells or passive infra red beams. The equipment reverts to its highest speed when sensors (switches under mats at landings, photo-sensors on newels etc.) are activated by passengers on the approaches. The advantage of a system that the equipment slows the speed down in contrast to stopping is that passengers are aware of the direction of travel of the equipment, when approaching, and there is no risk that they would think that the equipment is out of service.

**Table 10.2** Items causing automatic stopping of the escalator

| Description | Safety device (clause 14.2.2.4.2) | Self-resetting (clause 14.2.4) | BS EN 115 clause number |
|---|---|---|---|
| No control voltage | | ● | 14.2.2.4.1(a) |
| Earth fault in electrical safety device circuit | | ● | 14.2.2.4.1(b) |
| Motor overload | | ● | 14.2.2.4.1(c) |
| Motor windings over temperature | | ● | 14.2.2.4.1(d) |
| Overspeed | ● | | 14.2.2.4.1(e) |
| Unintentional reversal of direction | ● | | 14.2.2.4.1(e) |
| Operation of auxiliary brake | ● | | 14.2.2.4.1 (f) |
| Breakage or elongation of step, etc. | ● | | 14.2.2.4.1(g) |
| Reduction of distance between stations | ● | ● | 14.2.2.4.1(h) |
| Entrapment of foreign bodies at comb | ● | ● | 14.2.2.4.1(i) |
| Stopping of succeeding escalator | ● | ● | 14.2.2.4.1(j) |
| Operation of handrail entry guard | ● | ● | 14.2.2.4.1(k) |
| Operation of sagging step detector | ● | | 14.2.2.4.1(l) |
| Broken handrail | ● | | 14.2.2.4.1(m) |

When the equipment changes speed after periods of low passenger activity, it is important that the transition be smooth in order to prevent passenger falls. An advantage of VVVF drives is as they provide a very smooth transition between speeds.

This type of operation would be suitable for locations where there are periods of time when there is no passenger demand.

### 10.5.4.3    On-demand start

The escalator or moving walk is available for use in either direction of travel and automatically starts operating as a result of passenger demand. After a period of no passenger flow the equipment stops automatically. The starting is initiated by the use of a passenger detection system such as pressure mats, photocells or passive infra red beams. A system has to be provided to manage the direction of operation.

This type of operation would be suitable for locations where there are long periods of time when there is no passenger demand and can cater for either direction of travel.

### 10.5.5    Safety devices

Although modern escalators and moving walks employ electronic control, the safety line is still retained. All electrical safety devices are wired in series, forming the so-called 'safety line' or 'safety chain'. All safety devices should act directly on the final contactors, as stipulated by the following clause in BS EN 115[1]:

> 14.1.2.4. When operated, a safety device shall prevent the setting in motion of the driving machine or immediately initiate its stopping. The operational brake shall be applied. Electrical safety devices shall act directly on the equipment controlling the supply to the driving machine.

The concept of a separate safety line is quite important in escalators because it removes the safety critical elements from the electronic programmable systems and puts it in a separate hard-wired configuration.

Each component monitoring a safety function is called a safety device. Table 10.2 shows all functions causing automatic stopping of the escalator. Some of them are not safety devices. Moreover, some of them need to be reset before the escalator can be re-started. At the time of writing (April 2005) BS EN 115[1] is being revised and may include further safety checks, for example, handrail speed monitoring and missing step devices.

Today, escalators and moving walks are generally controlled by microprocessor and solid state devices, replacing the relay controllers used in the past. These programmable electronic devices should provide the same level of safety and in the case of failure, the system should always revert to a safe state.

# References

1    BS EN 115: 1995 (amd. 1998, 2003): *Safety rules for the construction and installation of escalators and passenger conveyors* (London: British Standards Institution) (dates as indicated)

2    BS 5656-1: 1997 (amd1998): *Safety rules for the construction and installation of escalators and passenger conveyors. Specification and proformas for test and examination of new installations* (London: British Standards Institution) (1997/1998)

3    BS 5656-2: 2005: *Selection, installation and location of escalators and passenger conveyors* (London: British Standards Institution) (2005)

4    BS 7671: 2001: *Requirements for electrical installations. IEE Wiring Regulations. Sixteenth Edition* (London: British Standards Institution) (2001)

5    BS 7801: 2005: *Safe working on escalators and passenger conveyors* (London: British Standards Institution) (2005)

6        BS EN 12015: 2001: *Electromagnetic compatibility. Product family for escalator or moving walks, escalators and passenger conveyors. Emission* (London: British Standards Institution) (2001)

7        BS EN 12016: 2001: *Electromagnetic compatibility. Product family for escalator or moving walks, escalators and passenger conveyors. Immunity* (London: British Standards Institution) (2001)

8        Construction (Design and Management) Regulations 1994 Statutory Instruments 1994 3140 London: The Stationery Office) (1994)

9        Supply of Machinery (Safety) Regulations 1992 Statutory Instruments 1992 3073 and the Supply of Machinery (Safety) (Amendment) Regulations 1994 Statutory Instruments 1994 2063 (London: The Stationery Office) (1992/1994)

# 11 Transportation facilities for persons and persons with disabilities

## Principal authors

Jerry Brace (Axes4All)
Dr Gina Barney (Gina Barney Associates)

## Chapter contents

| | | |
|---|---|---|
| 11.1 | Access for everyone | 11-3 |
| 11.2 | Disability or impairment? | 11-3 |
| 11.3 | Disability Discrimination Act 1995 | 11-3 |
| 11.4 | Building Regulations Approved Document M | 11-4 |
| 11.5 | Equipment selection to meet user needs | 11-4 |
| | 11.5.1 Existing and future user needs | 11-4 |
| | 11.5.2 Foreseeable rated load | 11-4 |
| | 11.5.3 User position | 11-4 |
| | 11.5.4 Entrance facilities | 11-4 |
| | 11.5.5 Control devices | 11-5 |
| | 11.5.6 Location | 11-5 |
| | 11.5.7 Duty cycle | 11-5 |
| | 11.5.8 Alarm system | 11-5 |
| | 11.5.9 Type of wheelchair | 11-5 |
| 11.6 | Environmental considerations | 11-5 |
| 11.7 | Equipment provision | 11-6 |
| | 11.7.1 Provision to the Machinery Directive or the Lift Directive | 11-6 |
| | 11.7.2 Passenger lifts | 11-6 |
| | 11.7.3 Lifting platforms | 11-7 |
| | 11.7.4 Domestic lifting platforms | 11-8 |
| | 11.7.5 Stairlifts | 11-8 |
| 11.8 | Escalators and moving walks | 11-9 |
| 11.9 | Egress for disabled persons | 11-9 |
| 11.10 | Selection of lifting device | 11-10 |
| References | | 11-11 |
| Appendix 11.A1: Principal requirements of BS EN 81-70 | | 11-12 |

# 11 Transportation facilities for persons and persons with disabilities

## 11.1 Access for everyone

Accessibility enables people , including persons with disability, to participate in the social and economic activities for which the built environment is intended — Annex A, BS EN 81-70[9]

Transportation systems in buildings should provide independent and equal access for everyone. This chapter provides general guidance. It cannot be specific and attention is drawn to the references for further information. Expert assistance may be needed to deal with particular situations.

In general, facilities designed to permit their use by people with disabilities will assist in their use by able-bodied people. BS 8300: 2001[18] gives valuable general guidance. It provides little information for vertical transportation and unfortunately gives some conflicting information in respect to lifting platform standards and to some of the recommendations of Approved Document M: *Access to and use of buildings*[21] (2004). This latter document recommends that planning applications include an 'access statement'[26] to indicate how people will access any new building, or extension to an existing building and this should indicate any provision of building transportation systems.

Appendix 3.A2 to section 3 of this Guide provides a list of relevant standards.

## 11.2 Disability or impairment?

Many people suffer from a disability (see BS EN 81-70[9], Annex B), or impairment. Examples include:

(a) *Physical disability*: people who are unable to use stairs, or negotiate a (step) change in level due to:

   — a temporary mobility impairment, e.g. a broken leg

   — a permanent mobility impairment, e.g. loss of the use of a lower limb

   — limited range of movement and weight-bearing ability, e.g. arthritis

   — reduced strength and endurance, e.g. as a result of a heart or lung complaint.

(b) *Sensory disability*: people who have sensory limitations due to:

   — poor vision;

   — impaired balance;

   — impaired hearing.

(c) *Intellectual disability*: people who have cognitive impairments due to:

   — learning difficulties

   — intellectual deterioration.

The motor and sensory abilities in a population can vary over a wide range. Transportation facilities in buildings are likely to be used by persons with a range of disabilities. Some individuals, in particular older people, may have more than one impairment. Some individuals are not able to use transportation facilities unaided and rely on assistance/support being provided by a companion. Some individuals can be handicapped by objects they are carrying, or be responsible for other persons, which can also affect their mobility. The extent to which an individual is incapacitated by impairments and encumbrances often depends on the usability of the equipment provided. The most important issue to take into account during the selection and installation of transportation equipment is their safe use by all persons.

## 11.3 Disability Discrimination Act 1995

The Disability Discrimination Act 1995[24] (DDA) gave disabled people new rights in such areas as access to goods, facilities and services. The Act requires goods and services to be accessible to disabled people. This is mainly concerned with the removal of physical barriers to the free circulation of all people.

From 1 October 2004, businesses and service providers have a duty to make 'reasonable adjustments' to the physical features of their premises in order to overcome barriers to access. Service providers have a duty to consider the use of premises by people with mobility, visual, hearing, speech and dexterity impairments as well as those with learning difficulties and mental health disabilities. 'Reasonable adjustments' may take account of:

   — practicality

   — financial and other costs

   — disruption

   — resources available

   — availability of financial assistance.

Lifts, lifting platforms, stairlifts, escalators and moving walks are examples of 'physical features'. The Disability Rights Commission has published a number of codes of practice relating to duties applicable under the Disability Discrimination Act 1995.

'Barriers to access' are also physical features to the building, which reduce its accessibility to all people. Examples include:

—    small changes in level from one stair step to part of
     the height of a storey

—    large changes in level of one or more storeys

—    inadequate width of doors

—    insufficient manoeuvring space.

In new buildings such 'barriers' should be designed out.
In existing buildings an access statement[26] should
indicate that a reasonable provision is being made and if
not, why not.

In 2003, the Disability Discrimination Act 1995
(Amendment) Regulations 2003[25] were enacted, virtually
bringing most non-domestic environments within its
remit. For example, small businesses with less than 20
employees ceased to be exempt.

## 11.4    Building Regulations Approved Document M

The Office of the Deputy Prime Minister (ODPM)
publishes Approved Documents to provide practical
guidance to the requirements of the Building Regulations
2000. There is no obligation to apply the guidance if the
relevant requirements can be met in some other way.
Approved Document M: *Access to and use of buildings*[21],
(known as 'Part M'), came into effect on 1 May 2004. It is
in the hands of many professionals (architects, developers,
designers, surveyors, chartered engineers etc.), who
faithfully follow its guidance. Amongst its guidance (on
steps, ramps, stairs, handrails, lobbies, sanitary accommodation etc.) vertical circulation is discussed in Clauses
3.17–3.49 for 'buildings other than dwellings' and in
Clauses 9.6–9.7 for dwellings (which includes buildings
containing flats).

Part M states 'the objective is for people to travel vertically
and horizontally within buildings conveniently and
without discomfort in order to make use of the facilities'.
The services provided should accommodate all people
with disabilities, not simply those with a mobility
problem. Part M ranks the equipment provision in public
buildings with the order of preference: passenger lifts,
lifting platforms, wheelchair platform stairlifts, as follows:

—    For all public buildings, a passenger lift is the
     most suitable form of access.

—    For public buildings, where space is restricted, a
     vertical lifting platform, although it is not equiv-
     alent to a passenger lift, may be considered as an
     option.

—    In exceptional circumstances in an existing public
     building, a wheelchair platform stairlift may be
     considered.

A passenger lift is thus the most suitable means of vertical
access and should be provided wherever possible.
However, given the space constraints in some buildings, it
may not always be possible to install the type and size of
passenger lift that would be suitable for use by all
mobility-impaired users and other options may need to be
provided. The case for using each lifting device should be
argued in the access statement[26].

For buildings containing flats, Part M recommends that
passenger lift access be provided.

## 11.5    Equipment selection to meet user needs

The selection of the equipment to meet the needs of
disabled people must be carefully considered to ensure it
is appropriate and meets the needs of the user(s). Below
are some important considerations.

### 11.5.1    Existing and future user needs

When selecting a lift, lifting platform or stairlift, both the
existing and the future needs of the user(s) should be
considered. This is important in a domestic environment,
as people age and become less capable or where a disability
becomes more severe. Therefore, the installation of a
seated stairlift might be unsuitable, should the user later
become dependent on a wheelchair. In non domestic
environments, the use of the building can change significantly over its life affecting the facilities to be provided.

### 11.5.2    Foreseeable rated load

If a lifting device is not dedicated to a particular user the
foreseeable load may difficult to predict. The smallest
suitable passenger lift has a rated load of 450 kg and this is
likely to meet many of the needs of most people with
disabilities. An exception could be where the person needs
to be accompanied by a companion and medical equipment. Lifting platforms and stairlifts should be selected
that are capable of carrying the maximum foreseeable
load. The largest lifting platforms have a maximum rated
load of 500 kg, sufficient for a wheelchair user
accompanied by a companion and some equipment. A
stairlift should be selected with a rated load that is capable
of carrying the maximum foreseeable load. For example a
larger rated wheelchair platform stairlift will be required if
an electrically powered wheelchair is to be transported.

### 11.5.3    User position

An ambulant disabled person may stand or sit and may be
using a walking aid. It should be noted that some users
with walking aids cannot easily turn through 180°. Other
users will be seated in a wheelchair. It is important to
ensure that the user(s) can be safely transferred on and off
as well as safely transported on a lift, or on a lifting
platform, or on a platform stairlift, whether sitting, or
standing, or seated in a wheelchair. Note that standing
platform stairlifts are not suitable for use in public
situations.

### 11.5.4    Entrance facilities

The limits to the ability of the users to enter and exit the
lifting device must be considered. Manual or automatic
operation may need to be available for doors, barriers or
hinged platforms. The orientation of the floor of the
lifting device with respect to the entrance should be

considered and whether there is sufficient manoeuvring space.

### 11.5.5 Control devices

Consideration should be given to the position, type and number of controls that would suit users with differing disabilities. Stairlifts will have to be provided with operating controls to suit a number of users with differing mobility impairments. Specially adapted operating devices, switches and sensors may be required to suit individual users. A key switch, electronic card or similar means may be necessary to restrict the use of the lifting device to authorised users in some environments. The provision of attendant controls should be considered.

### 11.5.6 Location

The suitability of the proposed location of the equipment should be checked. For example:

— Will the installation of a stairlift obstruct normal activities in and about the building?

— Will the location and proposed supporting structure be strong enough to support a lifting platform or stairlift?

— Is there is an unobstructed manoeuvring space of 1500 mm × 1500 mm (public access) or 1200 mm × 1200 mm (private domestic use), or a straight access route at least 900 mm wide?

### 11.5.7 Duty cycle

The anticipated maximum number of journeys per hour for a passenger lift is unlikely to be a problem as most passenger lifts are capable of 90 starts per hour. Lifting platforms and stairlifts are designed to provide a minimum of 10 starts per hour, although many manufacturers design for 30 starts per hour. Lifting platforms are designed for 500 000 load cycles and stairlifts for 100 000 load cycles. Care must be taken to ensure the equipment is fit for its purpose with respect to the anticipated duty cycle.

### 11.5.8 Alarm system

New passenger lifts will be fitted with an alarm system which will connect to a rescue service. Existing passenger lifts without a remote alarm system should be considered for upgrading. Consideration should be given to the desirability of providing an alarm system that would alert a dependable assistant or summon help from beyond the immediate location of any lifting platform or stairlift.

### 11.5.9 Type of wheelchair

Consideration should be made of the type of wheelchair that is likely to require transportation, i.e: whether it is a manual wheelchair to BS EN 12183: 1999[19], or a Class A, B or C electric wheelchair to BS EN 12184: 1999[20].

Manual wheelchairs to BS EN 12183 can be accommodated in all the lifts with a rated load of at least 450 kg, and in lifting platforms with platform dimensions of at least 800 mm by 1250 mm.

Electric wheelchairs of Classes A, B, C to BS EN 12184 are larger and less manoeuvrable:

— Class A wheelchairs are intended for indoor use

— Class B for some indoor environments and can navigate some outdoor obstacles

— Class C are generally not intended for indoor use and can navigate many outdoor obstacles.

The minimum sizes of lifting devices required to meet these requirements are given in section 11.7.

In some locations, such as shopping centres, specially adapted electric wheelchairs are available, which have baskets at the front and rear, which can have a combined length of over 1700 mm. These are larger than the standard sizes indicated above and appropriately sized lifting devices should be provided.

## 11.6 Environmental considerations

The environment in which a lifting device is installed should be carefully planned. Below are some considerations:

— signs indicating the location of a lifting device should be clearly visible in all buildings

— signs should identify each floor, which can be easily seen from the lifting device and which are designed to contrast visually with the surroundings

— stairs should always be provided as an alternative means of vertical access designed to suit ambulant disabled people and those with impaired sight

— ramps of suitable gradient may be appropriate on an internal circulation route if a change of level is unavoidable

— the location of lifting platforms and stairlifts should not restrict the means of emergency access or egress in public buildings

— equipment should be easily accessible for maintenance of lifting platforms and stairlifts

— lifts should be provided with audible and visual indication of their arrival at a landing, both in the car and on the landing

— materials should not be used in the surroundings or in the equipment which are likely to cause allergic reactions, e.g. metals (nickel, chromium, cobalt), materials (plastic wall papers, thick carpets) etc.

— adequate lighting (>100 lux) should be provided on all routes accessing lifting devices

— adequate lighting (>100 lux)should be provided for all lifting devices

— reflective surfaces should be avoided

— colour/tone contrasting surfaces should be employed, for example, to distinguish landing and lifting device floors and entrances

— landing and lifting device floors should have similar surface characteristics, e.g. texture, frictional (non-slip) characteristics.

# 11.7    Equipment provision

It is not intended in this section to repeat the provisions of Part M or to recite parts of the applicable standards. This section will concentrate on the selection, location and installation of the equipment to provide transportation facilities for disabled people.

## 11.7.1    Provision to the Machinery Directive or the Lift Directive

New passenger lifts must be in compliance with the Essential Heath and Safety Requirements (EHSRs) of the Lifts Regulations 1997[27] enacting the European Lift Directive[23]. Because lifts are classed as special machinery the EHSRs of the Supply of Machinery Regulations 1992[28] also apply, where appropriate. The usual route to achieve conformity is for the installer to provide a lift, which is suitable for use by disabled people, by compliance to the relevant harmonised standards. Alternatively, an EC-type examination certificate can be obtained for a model lift from a notified body.

Lifting platforms and stairlifts are classed as machines and must comply with the Supply of Machinery Regulations 1992 under the European Machinery Directive[22]. As these lifting devices transport people, there are particular essential health and safety requirements (EHSRs) indicated in Chapter 6 of the Machinery Directive. There are also other two main characteristics of lifting platforms and stairlifts:

— the rated speed is not to exceed 0.15 m/s

— provision of hold to run controls.

These two characteristics distinguish a lift under the Lift Directive from other lifting devices, which fall under the Machinery Directive. The usual route to achieve conformity is for the manufacturer to supply a lifting device, which is suitable for use by disabled people, by compliance to the relevant harmonised standards. Annex 4 of the Machinery Directive states that any passenger carrying device having a travel over 3.0 metres must be type tested by a notified body.

There is no limit to the travel distance, but travel over large distances could be uncomfortable for the disabled passengers, particularly those who fatigue easily. With a maximum permitted speed for lifting platforms and stairlifts of 0.15 m/s, a travel of 9.0 m will take 60 seconds. Where travel times exceed 60 seconds another means to travel between storeys should be considered.

## 11.7.2    Passenger lifts

Passenger lifts are the preferred lifting device under Approved Document M. The applicable standards for passenger lifts are:

— BS EN 81-1: 1998 for electric traction lifts[4]

— BS EN 81-2: 1998 for hydraulic lifts[5]

plus:

BS EN 81-28: 2003: *Remote alarms on passenger and goods passenger lifts*[6]

BS EN 81-70: 2003: *Accessibility to lifts for persons including persons with disabilities*[9]

Passenger lifts can be provided with rated loads from 320 kg to 2500 kg and larger, and rated speeds from 0.4 m/s to 6 m/s and higher. The passenger carrying unit is a car completely enclosed by walls, floor and roof running in a well enclosure which may be totally or partially enclosed. The entrance doors may be manually or automatically operated, although the latter are more suitable for use by persons with disabilities. The passengers can select their destination on the car operating panel after which no further passenger actions are required.

Where a single lift is installed, it would be wise to ensure it complies with all the relevant standards for disabled use. Where more than one lift is installed, reasonable provision should be made. This means that not all the lifts need be suitable for disabled use. However, the cost of all lifts being in compliance is small and becoming smaller.

The dimensions of passenger lifts are defined in BS ISO 4190-1: 1999[12]. The smallest suitable size is 450 kg, which will accommodate a single wheelchair, without a companion. Lift cars with rated loads 630/800/1000 kg can accommodate a single wheelchair and companion(s). Lift cars with rated loads 1275 kg, and larger, provide sufficient space for a wheelchair to turn through 180° and allow persons using walking aids to position themselves. Lifts of this latter size range are typical of those installed in commercial buildings. A summary is given in Table 11.1.

Figure 11.1 illustrates the main dimensions and features of a passenger lift to meet the requirements of BS EN 81-70. Suppliers in compliance with BS EN 81-70 will meet this requirements. Although the clear opening width of the entrance doors is shown as 800 mm, this is a minimum and larger openings, e.g. 900 mm should be considered, particularly where public use is anticipated.

Existing lifts may have been installed to earlier versions of EN 81, or even BS 2655 and BS 5655. To comply with the requirements of the DDA, some, or all lifts, in a building may need to be upgraded. Full compliance with BS EN 81-70 may be impossible. For example, it may not be possible to position the car operating panel 400 mm from a return wall. In such cases 'reasonable provision' should be made to comply as closely as possible. To show due diligence, the reasons for any deviations should be recorded.

It should be noted here that existing lifts do not have to be retrospectively upgraded to the latest lift standards.

**Table 11.1** Lift car dimensions

| Principal use | Minimum rated load and minimum platform sizes (width × depth) |
|---|---|
| Manual and Class A, B and C electric wheelchairs with companion(s) (Manual and Class A and B electric wheelchairs can turn through 180°; Class C electric wheelchairs require opposite entrances) | 1275 kg; 2000 mm × 1400 mm |
| Manual and Class A and B electric wheelchairs with a companion (Wheelchairs cannot turn through 180° and must reverse in/out; opposite entrances should be considered) | 630 kg; 1100 mm × 1400 mm |
| Manual and Class A electric wheelchairs with a lone user or a standing lone user and companion (Wheelchairs cannot turn through 180° and must reverse in/out. Opposite entrances should be considered) | 450 kg; 1000 mm × 1250 mm |

However, BS EN 81-80: *Rules for the improvement of safety of existing passenger and goods passenger lifts*[11], which is not a harmonised standard, draws owners attention to the importance of reviewing the safety of existing lifts.

All new passenger lifts have the CE-marking applied by the installer before they are placed in service. At the same time a test document is completed and a copy should be provided to the owner/operator. Suitable documents are PAS 32-1/2: 1999: *Specification for examination and test of new lifts before putting into service*[2,3].

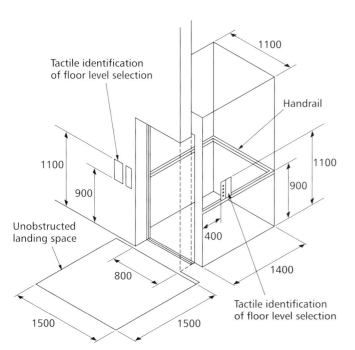

**Figure 11.1** Principal features of a passenger lift for use by people with disabilities

## 11.7.3 Lifting platforms

Lifting platforms are the second choice lifting device under Approved Document M. The applicable standard for totally enclosed or partially enclosed vertical lifting platforms is prEN 81-41: *Vertical lifting platforms intended for use by persons with impaired mobility*[8] (under development and yet to be published).

Some existing lifting platforms will have been installed to an older British Standard, viz: BS 6440: 1999 (amd. 2000): *Powered lifting platforms for use by disabled persons — code of practice*[17].

Lifting platforms are designed particularly to transport wheelchairs. This determines the minimum platform sizes to those given in prEN 81-41 shown in Table 11.2.

The maximum platform area that is permitted is 2.0 $m^2$, excluding hand rails. All lifting platforms require wheelchair users to reverse in/out, unless two entrances opposite/adjacent to each other are provided. The clear entrance and platform widths should be at least 800 mm and where public use is anticipated they should be 900 mm.

To accommodate the anticipated loads the minimum rated load for a lifting platform occupied by a lone user, either standing, or sitting in either a manual or Class A electric wheelchair, is 250 kg. If occupied by a user, either in a manual, or Class A or Class B electric wheelchair, with a companion, then the minimum rated load is 360 kg. These rated loads are based on minimum loading of 250 $kg/m^2$ of the clear loading area.

The passenger carrying unit is a platform with as a minimum one wall and floor (no roof) running in a well enclosure, which may be totally, or partially, enclosed. Some manufacturers provide a car with floor, ceiling and four walls. The entrance doors may be manually or automatically operated. The passengers can select their destination on the car operating panel, but must maintain pressure on the run control, in order to cause the platform to move.

Six types of drive system are permitted under prEN 81-41: rack and pinion, rope/chain, screw and nut, friction/traction, guided chain and hydraulic. The most commonly types used are screw and nut, and hydraulic. The practical (engineering) limit to the travel distance for a screw type drive system is nine metres. Hydraulic drives can travel up to 18 metres, but at a rated speed of 0.15 m/s; this is not recommended. These factors limit the provision of lifting platforms to distances less than nine metres, i.e.

**Table 11.2** Minimum dimensions of lifting platforms

| Principal use | Minimum platform size (width × depth) |
|---|---|
| Manual and Class A and B electric wheelchairs with a companion and opposite/adjacent entrances | 1100 mm × 1400 mm |
| Manual and Class A and B electric wheelchairs with a companion | 900 mm × 1400 mm |
| Manual and Class A and B electric wheelchairs with a lone user or a standing lone user and a companion | 800 mm × 1250 mm |

two to three commercial storeys, or three to four domestic stories.

Lifting platforms can be installed with a minimal loading demand and structural alterations on a building. This is an advantage for installations into existing buildings. The amount of work involved depends on the type of enclosure chosen. Figure 11.2 illustrates a lifting platform, where there is a total enclosure at the lower level and a partial enclosure at the upper level. The height of the upper enclosure is dependent on the travel. For up to two metres travel, the height of the enclosure must be at least 1.1 m, and over two metres travel, the height of the enclosure must be at least 2.0 m. In the UK it is recommended that all enclosures at an upper landing extend to the ceiling of that storey as this provides better protection for passers-by and passengers. It is also more aesthetically pleasing.

Short travel lifting platforms of the scissor type (see section 5.8.7) are often installed within stories (without floor penetration) to overcome small changes in level, up to two metres. In the UK it is recommended that the platform is fully enclosed in order to prevent any unauthorised access onto the platform and under the platform when it is at its highest level. BS 6440: 1999[17] provides guidance for entrance protection and safety curtains under the platform.

The CE-marking is applied by the manufacturer against a model approval certificate issued by a notified body. prEN 81-41 requires a test and examination document to be completed by the supplier immediately on completion of the installation and before first use. It is recommended that a copy of this document is given to the owner/end user together with the operating instructions.

### 11.7.4    Domestic lifting platforms

The applicable standard for vertical lifting platforms for domestic use is BS 5900: 1999: *Specification for powered domestic lifts with partially enclosed cars and no lift well enclosures*[16].

Domestic lifting platforms to this standard restrict the travel between two storeys in private dwellings (no travel

distance limitation is indicated). This type of lifting platform should only be installed in a domestic environment. The lifting platform can have a rated speed up to 0.15 m/s and a rated load between 150 kg and 400 kg, depending whether the user is standing, sitting or in a wheelchair. The size of the lifting platform is not defined, except its width shall not be less than the clear entrance width. The clear entrance width is either 500 mm to accommodate a standing or sitting person, or 650 mm to accommodate a wheelchair. Two types of drive are permitted: rope/chain and hydraulic.

The passenger carrying unit is a partially enclosed car, which runs in a totally open space (see Figure 11.3). Sensitive edges are employed to prevent crushing. This type of lifting device has limited applicability, being suitable for use by an individual rather than any general use. It has the advantages of being simple to install and being inexpensive.

The CE-marking is applied by the manufacturer against a model approval certificate issued by a notified body. Under BS 5900, after the installation is complete and before the installation is put into service, a test and examination certificate is required to be given to the owner/end user, together with the operating instructions.

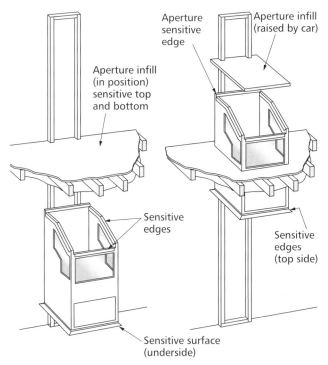

**Figure 11.3** Illustration of a domestic lifting platform

### 11.7.5    Stairlifts

There are three types of stairlifts: wheelchair platform, chair stairlifts and standing (perch) stairlifts.

The applicable standard for stairlifts is prEN 81-40: *Powered stairlifts for seated, standing and wheelchair users moving in an inclined plane intended for use by persons with impaired mobility*[7] (under development and yet to be published).

Some existing stairlifts will have been installed to an older British Standard, viz: BS 5776: 1996 (amd. 2001): Powered

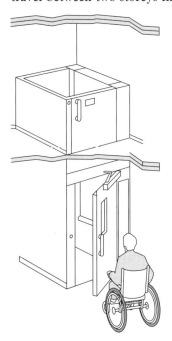

**Figure 11.2** Illustration of lifting platform

stairlifts[15]. This standard was developed for use in private dwellings and is not recommended for use in public buildings.

A stairlift runs up the side of a stairway and care must be taken neither to obstruct normal circulation on the stair for other users nor to obstruct the means of escape in an emergency. Stairlifts can follow the contour of the stairwell and can be provided with extended travel at the ends of the stair to enable easy boarding/alighting and parking. Alternatively a swivel seat can assist the safe transfer of the user on and off the stairlift. Most stairlifts provide travel across one flight of stairs, but some stairlifts, particularly in private dwellings, cover several flights with travels up to 30 metres. Boarding/alighting points are usually provided at each landing.

These lifting devices place only a small load on the building structure and can be installed relatively inexpensively. The maximum rated speed of all stairlifts is 0.15 m/s and are equipped with hold to run controls, suitable for each potential user.

Six types of drive systems are available: rope suspension, rack and pinion, chain, screw and nut, friction/traction, and ball and rope.

The CE-marking is applied by the manufacturer against an model approval certificate issued by a notified body. Under prEN 81-40, after the installation is complete and before the installation is put into service, a test and examination certificate is required to be given to the owner/end user, together with the operating instructions.

### 11.7.5.1 Wheelchair platform stairlifts

Wheelchair platform lifts are the final choice lifting device under Approved Document M, see Figure 11.4(a).

The platform size when installed in buildings with public access is required to be 900 mm wide by 1250 mm long. For installations in private dwellings the width can be reduced to 800 mm. Their location must be chosen carefully (see 11.5.6).

Wheelchair platform stairlifts are designed for a minimum rated load of 250 kg/m² of the clear loading area. The maximum rated load is 350 kg. The rated load for a wheelchair platform lift occupied by a lone user in a manual wheelchair to BS EN 12183 is 210 kg and for a lone use in an Class A electric wheelchair to BS EN 12184 is 300 kg.

### 11.7.5.2 Stairlifts for seated persons

Stairlifts for seated persons have a rated capacity for one person, i.e. a rated load not less than 115 kg. A chair to closely defined dimensions is fitted on which the user travels, see Figure 11.4(b). These lifting devices are only suitable for private dwellings.

### 11.7.5.3 Stairlifts for standing persons

Stairlifts for standing persons have a rated capacity for one person, i.e. a rated load not less than 115 kg. The dimension of the platform area is 325 mm by 350 mm, see Figure 11.4 (c). These lifting devices are only suitable for private dwellings.

## 11.8 Escalators and moving walks

Lifts are the preferred method of vertical travel for wheelchair users and persons with assistance dogs, but wheelchair users can generally use horizontal moving walks and inclined moving walks with an inclination of up to 6°, either unaided, or with a companion. Moving walks with inclinations greater than 6° and escalators, are not suitable for use by persons with assistance dogs (unless the dogs are carried), or by wheelchair users. Their use in this way is unsafe for the disabled user and is a risk to able bodied users travelling with them. Signs should be provided to indicate the location of alternative facilities, which should be situated nearby.

Escalators can be used safely by many persons with disabilities. Some guidance is given in BS 5656-2[14].

## 11.9 Egress for persons with disabilities

A great deal of attention has been paid to making buildings accessible to everyone and enable circulation around the building (see Chapter 2), but little attention has been given to how to enable people to escape in an

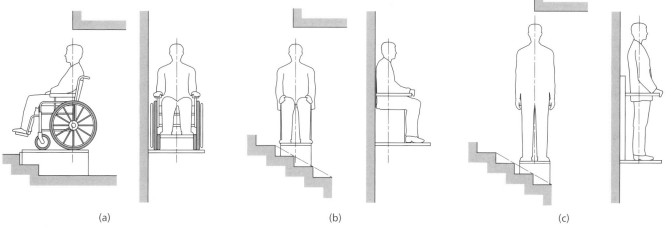

(a)                                    (b)                                    (c)

**Figure 11.4** Types of stairlift; (a) wheelchair, (b) seated, (c) standing emergency. In the UK, lifts must not be used regardless of building height. The able bodied use the escape stairs provided. Disabled people, in well managed buildings, are recommended to assemble in 'refuge spaces' placed on or close to each floor and await rescue. Rescue may then be manually using an evacuation chair.

At the present time the only lifts in a building that can be used during a fire are the specially designed firefighting lifts to BS EN 81-72: 2003: *Firefighters lifts*[10]. These lifts are reserved strictly for fire service use, under their control. Such a lift is designed to operate for a period of two hours, see Chapter 5.

In the UK, evacuation lifts can be provided under BS 5588-8: 1999: *Fire precautions in the design, construction and use of buildings. Code of practice for means of escape for disabled people*[13]. This standard deals with such elements as refuges, stairways, ramps, lifts, signs, etc. Section 11 of the standard deals with the use of lifts to evacuate disabled people. A firefighting lift can be used, under the supervision of the building management, to evacuate disabled people until the arrival of the fire service, who then assume responsibility for the evacuation of any remaining persons.

Evacuation lifts are being provided to BS 5588-8 in many public facilities such as sports stadia, entertainment centres, public halls etc., where large numbers of disabled people are expected. The lift should be used routinely as a passenger lift (not for goods) and should always be available. The specification for an evacuation lift is similar to, but not the same as, a firefighting lift, see Chapter 5. For example, an evacuation lift cannot be used as a firefighting lift.

In time it may be necessary to improve the ability of other lifts in a building to survive a fire and therefore provide an evacuation facility (see Barney (2002)[1]).

# 11.10    Selection of lifting device

Table 11.3 provides a summary of the different type of lifting devices available for the transportation of disabled people. It is recommended that the detailed text in this chapter be consulted and that the appropriate standard(s) be obtained when considering a specific design. Specialist assistance may be necessary.

**Table 11.3** Summary of lifting devices suitable for the transportation of people with disabilities

| Lifting device | Travel | Rated speed (m/s) | Rated load (kg) | Platform size (mm) (width × depth) | Applicable standards | Relative cost |
|---|---|---|---|---|---|---|
| *Buildings other than dwellings* | | | | | | |
| Lift | Unlimited (typical = full travel) | 0.4–6.0 and higher | 450 | 1000 × 1250 | BS EN 81-1: 1998 BS EN 81-2: 1998 BS EN 81-28: 2003 BS EN 81-70: 2003 | High |
| | | | 630 | 1100 × 1400 | | |
| | | | 1275 | 2000 × 1400 | | |
| | | | 1600 | 2100 × 1600 and larger | | |
| Lifting platform | Unlimited (typical = 6.0 m) | 0.15 | 250 (min.) 500 (max.) | 800 × 1250 900 × 1400 1100 × 1400 | BS EN 81-41: 2005 BS6440: 1999 (amd. 2000) | Medium |
| Wheelchair stairlift | Unlimited (typical = flight of stairs) | 0.15 | 210 (manual) 300 (electric) 350 (max.) | 900 × 1250 | BS EN 81-40: 2005 | Low |
| *Dwellings* | | | | | | |
| Lift | As above | As above | As above | As above | As above | As above |
| Lifting platform | As above | As above | As above | As above | As above | As above |
| Lifting platform | Two storeys (typical = 3.0 m) | 0.15 | 150 (min.) 400 (max.) | Depth not defined Min. width = 500–650 | BS 5900: 1999 | Medium |
| Wheelchair stairlift | Unlimited (typical = flight of stairs) | 0.15 m/s | 210 (manual) 300 (electric) 350 (max.) | 800 × 1250 | BS EN 81-40: 2005 | Low |
| Seated stairlift | Unlimited (typical = flight of stairs) | 0.15 | 115 (min.) | N/A | BS EN 81-40: 2005 BS 5776: 1996 (amd. 2001) | Lowest |
| Standing stairlift | Unlimited (typical = flight of stairs | 0.15 m/s | 115 (min.) | 325 × 350 | BS EN 81-40: 2005 BS 5776: 1996 (amd. 2001) | Lowest |

*Note*: any variation from a harmonised standard, e.g. rated load, requires notified body approval

# References

1    Barney, G C Behaviour of lifts and their use for evacuation *Elevation* 33 (2002)

2    PAS 32-1: 1999: *Specification for examination and test of new lifts before putting into service. Electric traction lifts* (London: British Standards Institution) (1999)

3    PAS 32-2: 1999: *Specification for examination and test of new lifts before putting into service. Hydraulic lifts* (London: British Standards Institution) (1999)

4    BS EN 81-1: 1998: *Safety rules for the construction and installation of lifts. Electric lifts* (London: British Standards Institution) (1998)

5    BS EN 81-2: 1998: *Safety rules for the construction and installation of lifts. Hydraulic lifts* (London: British Standards Institution) (2001)

6    BS EN 81-28: 2003 *Remote alarms on passenger and goods passenger lifts* (London: British Standards Institution) (2003)

7    prEN 81-40: 2005: *Powered stairlifts for seated, standing and wheelchair users moving in an inclined plane intended for use by persons with impaired mobility* (London: British Standards Institution) (2005)

8    prEN 81-41: 2005: Vertical lifting platforms intended for use by persons with impaired mobility (London: British Standards Institution) (2005)

9    BS EN 81-70: 2003: *Accessibility to lifts for persons including persons with disabilities* (London: British Standards Institution) (2003)

10   BS EN 81-72: 2003: *Firefighters lifts* (London: British Standards Institution) (2003)

11   BS EN 81-80: 2003: *Rules for the improvement of safety of existing passenger and goods passenger lifts* (London: British Standards Institution) (2003)

12   BS ISO 4190-1: 1999: *Lift installation — Part 1: Class I, II, III and VI lifts* (London: British Standards Institution) (1999)

13   BS 5588-8: 1999: *Fire precautions in the design, construction and use of buildings. Code of practice for means of escape for disabled people* (London: British Standards Institution) (1999)

14   BS 5656-2: 2004: *Selection, installation and location of escalators and moving walks* (London: British Standards Institution) (2001)

15   BS 5776: 1996 (amd. 2001): *Powered stairlifts* (London: British Standards Institution) (1996/2001)

16   BS 5900: 1999: *Specification for powered domestic lifts with partially enclosed cars and no lift well enclosures* (London: British Standards Institution) (1999)

17   BS 6440: 1999 (amd. 2000): *Powered lifting platforms for use by disabled persons. Code of practice* (London: British Standards Institution) (1999/2000)

18   BS 8300: 2001: *Design of buildings and their approaches to meet the needs of disabled people. Code of practice* (London: British Standards Institution) (2001)

19   BS EN 12183: 1999: *Manually propelled wheelchairs. Requirements and test methods* (London: British Standards Institution) (1999)

20   BS EN 12184: 1999: Electrically powered wheelchairs, scooters and their chargers. Requirements and test methods (London: British Standards Institution) (1999)

21   Building Regulations Approved Document M: *Access to and use of buildings* (London: The Stationery Office)

22   Council Directive 89/392/EEC of 14 June 1989 on the approximation of the laws of the Member States relating to machinery ('Machinery Directive') *Official J. of the European Communities* 29.06.1989 L183/9 (Brussels: Commission for the European Communities)

23   Directive 95/16/EC of the European Parliament and of the Council of 29 June 1995 on the approximation of the laws of the Member States relating to lifts ('The Lifts Directive') *Official J. of the European Communities* 9.7.1995 L213/1 (Brussels: Commission for the European Communities) (1995)

24   Disability Discrimination Act 1995 (London: Her Majesty's Stationery Office) (1995)

25   Disability Discrimination Act 1995 (Amendment) Regulations 2003 Statutory instruments 2003 No. 1673 (London: The Stationary Office)

26   Disability Rights Commission *Access Statements: Achieving an inclusive environment by ensuring continuity throughout the planning, design and management of buildings and spaces* (London: Disability Rights Commission) (undated) (available from DRC website: www.drc-gb.org)

27   The Lifts Regulations 1997 Statutory instruments 1997 No. 831 (London: The Stationary Office)

28   The Supply of Machinery (Safety) Regulations 1992 Statutory instruments 1992 No. 3073 (London: The Stationary Office)

# Appendix 11.A1: Principal requirements of BS EN 81-70

*Note*: This appendix provides a descriptive summary of the principal requirements of BS EN 81-70[9], which should be referred to for specific details.

BS EN 81-70 provides recommendations for lifts, constructed to BS EN 81 series of standards, relating to the design and positioning of fittings, controls and indicating equipment as well as the use of materials to maximise contrasts between controls and doors and the surrounds. The primary aim is to ensure that the design does not obstruct or impede the use of the lift by disabled people and to enable the unassisted use of lifts by all people including those with disabilities.

The landing area should be free of obstacles and sufficiently large to allow the free movement of persons, wheelchairs and accompanying persons, when entering or leaving the lift car with landing call buttons positioned 900 mm to 1100 mm above the floor level.

The lift should be able to provide a stopping accuracy of ±10 mm and a levelling accuracy of ±20 mm.

Automatic doors should be at least 800 mm clear width and protected with full height non-contact, infra-red (or similar) safety edges (see section 7.8.6).

It is important, particularly on groups of lifts, that the door operation allows suitable dwell times for passengers, who may have restricted mobility, to reach and enter the lift. An adjustable dwell time between 2 and 20 seconds should be provided accordingly. Typically this is set to 5 seconds. (It should be noted that extended dwell times will have a significant effect on the traffic handling capacity of a lift system, see section 3.7.1. This can result in increased costs to install extra equipment or the need to provide special signalling to enable anyone to call a lift with extended door dwell times.)

Control features such as advanced door opening should be avoided in hospitals and nursing homes or other environments where wheelchairs or trolleys etc. could be inconvenienced by the momentary presentation of a ledge as the doors open approaching floor level.

The lift car platform area should be large enough to meet the requirements of all persons. Special considerations may need to be made to accommodate some types of electrically driven wheelchairs.

Light colours are recommended inside the car to reduce the claustrophobic effects of small lifts and to optimise light levels within the car. Colour should be used to provide clear demarcation between the floor of the car and the landing entrance for users with visual impairment.

Functional, easily cleaned surface finishes are recommended, together with a half-height mirror which creates an impression of increased car size. *Note*: full height mirrors can be confusing for visually impaired passengers and therefore there should be a clear band of at least 300 mm between the bottom of a mirror and the floor.

A handrail along one side of the lift is essential together with large, easily operated push buttons. All control buttons in the lift car should be placed at between 900 and 1200 mm (1100 mm preferred) above the lift car floor level, and not less than 400 mm from the front or rear wall. The provision of a tip-up seat improves comfort for the elderly and infirm.

All push buttons should be provided with tactile, and possibly also Braille markings, either on or adjacent to the buttons. Since many visually impaired people are unable to read Braille it is recommended that Braille markings should only be used in addition to tactile markings and not on their own.

In addition to the visual enhancements, voice synthesised announcements, of sufficient sound level to overcome background noise, should be included to announce door actions (opening and closing) as well as the floor level and direction of travel as the lift arrives at a landing. Emergency signals received from a fire alarm or building management system can also be announced by the voice synthesiser.

The inclusion of inductive loops is required in conjunction with the voice synthesiser and emergency communication unit to assist passengers who use hearing aids.

Provision of a 24-hour communication link is required in accordance with The Lifts Regulations 1997[27]. This is normally satisfied by utilising an auto-dial telephone unit although a new standard, BS EN 81-28[6] now provides additional recommendations on the design and minimum performance requirements of suitable systems. In premises that are attended 24 hours a day, consideration should be given to programming the auto-dial telephone system to call an attended telephone on the premises. This will minimise the possibility of false alarms being registered with the lift maintenance company, and also improve the response time to make a direct contact with any trapped passengers, enabling reassurance to be provided until release can be effected.

In environments where the lifts may be used by elderly or infirm passengers such as nursing homes, the use of an additional alarm push button mounted at low level should be considered. This will enable access to the alarm facility for passengers that may have fallen or collapsed in the lift car.

When designing lifts to provide access for persons with disabilities, reference should be made to Building Regulations Approved Document M[21].

# 12 Electrical systems and environmental conditions

## Principal author

Adrian J Shiner (KONE plc)

## Section contents

| | | |
|---|---|---|
| 12.1 | Introduction | 12-3 |
| 12.2 | Lift power supplies | 12-3 |
| 12.3 | Protection of supplies | 12-4 |
| 12.4 | Standby power | 12-4 |
| 12.5 | Isolating switches, lighting and socket outlets | 12-5 |
| 12.6 | Harmonic distortion | 12-5 |
| 12.7 | Harmonic interference | 12-6 |
| 12.8 | Cabling and wiring | 12-6 |
| | 12.8.1  Cable sizing | 12-6 |
| | 12.8.2  Cable routes and protection | 12-6 |
| | 12.8.3  Wiring interfaces | 12-7 |
| | 12.8.4  Maintenance safety and records | 12-7 |
| 12.9 | Machine room environment | 12-8 |
| | 12.9.1  Temperature considerations | 12-8 |
| | 12.9.2  Ventilation | 12-8 |
| | 12.9.3  Heating | 12-9 |
| | 12.9.4  Cooling | 12-9 |
| | 12.9.5  Lighting | 12-10 |
| 12.10 | Lift well environment | 12-10 |
| 12.11 | Lift car environment | 12-11 |
| 12.12 | Human comfort considerations | 12-11 |
| | 12.12.1 Noise | 12-11 |
| | 12.12.2 Vibration | 12-11 |
| | 12.12.3 Acceleration and deceleration | 12-12 |
| | 12.12.4 Jerk | 12-12 |
| | 12.12.5 Communication with trapped passengers | 12-12 |
| | 12.12.6 Lighting at landings | 12-12 |
| 12.13 | Environment for maintenance | 12-12 |
| | 12.13.1 General | 12-12 |
| | 12.13.2 Lift well | 12-12 |
| | 12.13.3 Machine room | 12-13 |
| | 12.13.4 Machine room-less installations | 12-13 |
| | 12.13.5 Physical requirements | 12-13 |
| | 12.13.6 Maintenance of third party equipment | 12-13 |
| References | | 12-13 |
| Appendix 12.A1: Schedules for electrical systems requirements | | 12-15 |

# 12 Electrical systems and environmental conditions

## 12.1 Introduction

In designing a new lift system for a given building, the designer must consider not only the interface of the lift system with the building and its users, but also the more particular requirements of the lift system itself in terms of its environment, its dependence upon other services and future maintenance needs. It is important that the designer also considers the environment of those involved in installing, maintaining and inspecting the lift system, and builds into the design appropriate features to minimise hazards to such persons.

This section provides guidance on the key environmental factors which must be considered during the design process. It should be remembered, however, that the recommendations contained in various regulations and standards covering lift systems, e.g. British Standards, The Lifts Regulations 1997[27] and the Building Regulations[19], often differ. Therefore, careful reference must be made to all the applicable regulations and standards.

The upgrading and modernisation of lifts installed before 1 July 1999 do not fall under the Lifts Regulations and are still subject to BS 5655-1[18] (electric) and BS 5655-12[9] (hydraulic) standards and the upgrading of safety is covered by BS EN 81-80[5]. However, the guidance given in this chapter can be taken as a basis for design.

## 12.2 Lift power supplies

The provision of power supplies and electrical systems for lifts must be considered in relation not only to the power supplies for the whole building but also to other electrical systems which may interact with the lift installation. In all buildings, the power supply and electrical systems should be fully integrated so as to serve the demands of the building as a whole. Failure to consider the complete lift installation as an integral part of this system can result in an unsatisfactory lift service for the entire life of the building.

A series of questions needs to be considered to determine how and why power supplies are required to meet the lift demands, followed by further questions to clarify how these requirements will be met in terms of power distribution hardware and its installation. The lift power supplies form part of a more extensive power distribution system and the power requirements of the lifts must be considered in relation to the other users of the system. In addition, the potential operating modes of the power distribution system and the building usage patterns should be investigated to determine how the services in the building are expected to perform when:

— the building is normally occupied
— the building is partially occupied
— the mains power fails
— systems fail or system faults are experienced.

Typical schedules for the electrical system requirements can be drawn up for the lift installation with cross-references to associated services (see Table 12.A1.1 for the machine room, Table 12.A1.2 for the lift car and Table 12.A1.3 for the lift well). This information should be given to all parties involved in specifying and designing the finishes and services for the building. At each interface it should be made clear who is responsible for designing and supplying the relevant equipment and systems. It must also be agreed what facilities are considered essential.

The type of lift drive and associated control equipment will influence the design of the power supply system in terms of the cable distribution requirements, back-up supplies and with respect to the problems of harmonic currents drawn by the lift equipment, see sections 12.6 and 12.7. The design must result in adequately rated supplies to meet all operational demands, including meeting maximum power demands for simultaneous starting and stopping of lift cars.

Firefighting and evacuation lifts are provided with alternative supplies. Such supplies must, wherever possible, be physically protected by being installed along a different route to that of the normal mains supply. Where it is not physically possible to provide an alternative route, mineral insulated cable systems (MICS) cables with a low smoke and fume (LSF) sheath should be used. Recommendations for compliance are provided in BS 7671[14] and BS 5588: Part 5[6]: Section 44. Firefighting lifts must also comply with the harmonised standard BS EN 81-72[4] which replaces parts of BS 5588: Part 5.

Specifically, the lift contractor should declare, on a schedule, values of full load current, starting current and its duration, maximum permissible volt drop and any other relevant details to enable the electrical contractor to determine the size of the mains isolating switch. Where an installation has more than one lift supplied from a common feeder, a diversity factor may be applied to the cable size. (see section 12.8.1).

Installation methods for lifts may require temporary supplies at both a standard 110 volt (550-55 centre tapped to earth) safety supply in accordance with BS 7375[13] and a 400 (−6%+10%) volt, three-phase supply to be available. The power capacity of the three-phase supply should be such as to allow the lifts to be commissioned and tested. Low capacity can cause delays and may require re-tests when the correct supply is available.

## 12.3    Protection of supplies

Lifts must be protected against malfunctions in the power supply feeding the lift installation as shown in Table 12.1. Table 12.2 provides a checklist to help determine the cause of voltage drops.

## 12.4    Standby power

In many buildings, particularly large ones, standby power supplies are installed to allow some or all of the normal activities of the building to continue and to ensure that the building can be evacuated safely[21]. The cost of providing a standby supply is usually high in relation to its expected operating life. The tendency, therefore, is to keep the standby capacity to a minimum to meet only essential loads.

Essential loads may include firefighting plant, partial or full lighting, consumer power supplies, computer power supplies, lifts, HVAC plant etc. The requirements for standby power will depend, therefore, on which of the services are to remain partially or fully operational during a mains failure.

The load to be imposed on the standby power plant will also vary, depending on when it is called upon to operate,

i.e. night or day, winter or summer. It will also vary with any changes of building use. The standby supply must be able to meet all the demands of the dynamic loads (electrical) of the complete distribution system. The general design considerations noted in the previous sections. In addition the following must be provided:

— controlled sequential starting systems for other loads, if necessary

— a limited or special-purpose mode of operation of the lifts (if a full service is not required)

— controls for sequential starting of the lifts to limit power demand surges

— effect of lift braking on power demands

— sufficient capacity to absorb regenerative braking or prevent overspeed of the lifts when fully loaded.

— Where there are several lifts or groups of lifts, the lift supplier should specify the type and number of control cables to be run between lifts for stand-by supply control purposes.

Any operational restrictions imposed on the lift installation when operating under standby power must be clearly identified and agreed between the lift supplier and the purchaser. The lift supplier should indicate the capacity of the supply necessary to achieve an agreed level of performance. The characteristic of the lift load also

**Table 12.1** Protection of mains power supplies

| Fault | Cause |
| --- | --- |
| Absence of voltage operation of a protective device | Loss of voltage may be due to a system fault where power has been cut off by the operation of a protective device or due to loss of mains supply. |
| | On restoring power, the lift should be returned to service automatically. The lift controller must ensure that normal controls and safety devices function correctly when power is restored. |
| Voltage drop | A drop in voltage may be caused by a weak supply (i.e. high impedance source) and/or a particular mode of operation of plant and equipment in the building. Such conditions may exist when many independent loads are switched at the same time. Table 12.2 provides a checklist to help determine the cause. If the power distribution system for the building is incorrectly designed, the problem may occur every time there is a multiple switching of loads. When correctly designed, the power supply to the lift installation should not suffer a drop in voltage outside the limits agreed with the lift contractor for all modes of operation of all of the services in the building. |
| Loss of a phase | Loss of continuity of a conductor or loss of a phase can be the result of a broken conductor, or the operation of a fuse. The lift control equipment should detect this condition and shut down. Normal operation can be resumed when the three-phase supply is restored and any lift control and/or motor protection has been reset. |
| Phase reversal | This can occur when alterations are made to the main electrical distribution system in a building. Means should be provided to detect an accidental phase reversal where traction motors derive their supply directly from the mains, i.e. not through an inverter. |

**Table 12.2** Typical schedule of voltage drop checks

| Item | Check required | Comments |
| --- | --- | --- |
| 1 | Reliability of external supply | If the supply is subject to voltage fluctuations consider the installation of a voltage stabiliser to feed the lift |
| 2 | Operation of other loads on the power distribution system* | Carry out load flow study |
| 3 | Operation of other independent loads* | Consider interlocked or sequential starting controls |
| 4 | Volt drop on lift feeder cables* | Size cables to ensure that under the worst operating conditions the voltage drop is always within limits agreed with the lift designer |

* May require dynamic load flow study of the power distribution system

affect the type of alternator and its control. Electronic drives can produce levels of harmonic currents which are not compatible with alternators designed to supply lighting loads. The amount of regenerated energy which the lift installation may require the supply to absorb must be clearly identified. It is often necessary to provide additional load on the supply just to absorb this energy because the engine driving the alternator cannot absorb the regenerated energy.

## 12.5 Isolating switches, lighting and socket outlets

Harmonised standards require that each lift shall have a main switch capable of breaking the supply to the lift on all live conductors at the highest normal load current. Mains isolating switches should be provided at the intake point and in the machine room. They should be lockable in the off position, and readily identified and accessible from the machine room entrance(s). It is common to identify the main switch in multi-lift machine rooms and major lift equipment components by large, clearly visible numbers or letters. It should be possible on groups of interconnected lifts, to isolate an individual lift without affecting the supervisory control of the remainder.

The isolating switch should accept either high rupture capacity (HRC) fuses or an equivalent circuit breaker. The lift manufacturer must provide suitable protection for the lift controller. All such protection devices must be carefully coordinated with the electrical contractor to ensure proper fault clearance discrimination (see BS 5655-6[7], Chapter 8). No form of no-volt trip mechanism should be included anywhere in a lift power supply.

The lifts main switch is dedicated to the lift and it should not isolate:

— the lift car lighting or ventilation

— the lift car roof socket outlet

— the machine or pulley room lighting

— the lift well lighting

— the alarm device (often a dialler powered from a separate supply to that of the lift)

— pit, pulley room or machine room socket outlets.

The lighting supply to the car, machinery space/pulley space, machine room/pulley room and well should be from a circuit separate from the lift power supply or taken from a point on the supply side of the mains isolating switch and controlled by a fused switch in the machine room. For multiple lifts with a common machine room, a separate fused switch should be provided to the lighting supply for each car. It is convenient to have two-way or three-way switching on the well lighting with operation points in the machine room and well.

The socket outlet supply to the machinery space/pulley space, machine room/pulley room and well should be from a circuit separate from the lift power supply or taken from a point on the supply side of the mains isolating switch and controlled by a fused switch in the machine room. At least one socket outlet should be provided in each of the following locations:

— machine room

— pulley room

— pit

— car top.

Large machine rooms may warrant several outlets to enable effective maintenance. These may be 230 V mains outlets, preferably fitted with RCD protection, or provide separated extra low voltage (SELV).

It is recommended that a consumer unit be fitted, dedicated to the lift installation's small power and lighting circuits. All isolators and switches must be clearly and indelibly marked and identifiable when viewed from the entrance to the machine space (if directly visible from that point).

## 12.6 Harmonic distortion

Lifts are non-linear loads. All lift controllers and their associated motor drives draw non-sinusoidal currents. These include harmonic currents which will generate harmonic voltages on the power distribution system. The magnitude of the harmonic voltages will be dependent on the impedances of the distribution system and of the power source. These harmonic voltages can cause damage to other equipment if they exceed the limits specified by the electricity supply authority or the power system designer.

Lift installations which incorporate solid-state controllers (see sections 8.3.3 and 8.3.4) will draw significant harmonic currents, which must not exceed those permitted by the electricity supply authority. These limits relate to the maximum kV·A rating of the device drawing the harmonic current. Electricity Association Engineering Recommendation G5/4[24] sets down limits for the magnitude of the individual current harmonics and the voltage distortion. Lifts are also required to comply with the harmonised standard BS EN 12015: 2004[15].

Where multiple controllers are provided to control multiple lifts, and they are fed from the same supply, an assessment should be made of how the individual harmonic currents for each individual load will add up. However, in determining the total it should be noted that the arithmetic sum of the individual harmonic load currents is modified by a 'coincidence factor'.

In many large installations, filtering equipment will be needed for the lift controllers to ensure that the harmonic currents drawn do not exceed the supply authority's specified limits. However, filters should not be introduced without considering their adverse effects. For example, under certain load conditions they may cause damage to, or malfunctioning of other equipment connected to the power distribution system, particularly power factor correction capacitors.

Information on the magnitude of the harmonic currents drawn by the lift controllers must be conveyed to the manufacturers of any standby power plant. Failure to do so could cause damage to, and/or malfunctioning of the standby power system.

## 12.7 Harmonic interference

The lift installation will be subject to varying degrees of interference caused by voltage disturbances on the mains power supply (i.e. switching surges), induced voltages in control cabling and radio-frequency interference. The lift installation must not malfunction in an unsafe manner as a result of such interference, no matter how caused.

The system designer has a duty to minimise the possibility of interference being caused to the lift installation while the lift manufacturer is responsible for ensuring that the equipment is properly designed and protected to prevent malfunctioning should any interference occur.

The complete lift installation must comply with the EMC Directive[22] and product specific requirements relating to the emission of, and immunity from, electromagnetic interference are given in harmonised standards BS EN 12015[15] and BS EN 12016[16], respectively. Both the system designer and the lift manufacturer must comply with these requirements.

The components used to make up the lift installation need to satisfy all of the requirements of the various standards concerning interference. In some instances, this may be enough to satisfy the demands for the installation to comply. However, where lifts may be installed close to sensitive electronic equipment such as that found in laboratories, hospitals, operating theatres, computer rooms, communications facilities etc, extra design measures may need to be taken over and above compliance with the harmonised standards. The BS EN 81-72[4] Clause 6, Table 3 sets out the tests required to be carried out in a completed firefighting lift installation.

Notwithstanding any such tests and individual component compliance, the lift manufacturer should confirm in writing any limitations on the use of radio equipment in the vicinity of the lift installation. In particular, whether hand-held radio transmitters may be used adjacent to the lift controllers during maintenance work when covers are removed or panel doors are open. Similar assurances are also required for the use of hand-held radio transmitters either inside or on top of the lift car. Consideration must also be given to the effect of fixed radio or microwave transmitters mounted on the roof near to the lift machine room.

## 12.8 Cabling and wiring

### 12.8.1 Cable sizing

The requirements of sizing cables for voltage drop, current carrying capacity and the ability to withstand bursting and heating effects of short circuit currents are covered in BS 7671[14] (IEE Wiring Regulations, 16th edition). However, the regulations assume that the designer has knowledge of the system being designed; the requirements must be used with judgement.

When determining what is an acceptable voltage drop, it is essential to take account of conditions of the power distribution system for its worst operating conditions at:

(a)     start up

(b)     abnormal or emergency conditions.

The power distribution system may be particularly heavily loaded under these conditions and normal voltage limits may be exceeded. The maximum variation allowed for the equipment connected to the system must not exceed the calculation for the worst case situation.

Motor starting currents can be high. The maximum voltage drop during starting must not allow the voltage across the motor terminals to fall below that required for the pull-out torque needed to get the connected mechanical load up to speed. It is most important that the minimum and maximum allowable voltage limits are provided by the lift manufacturer for both the power supply to the controller and to the lift motor.

*Warning*: some computer programs for cable sizing do not take account of the increase in fault current that synchronous or induction motors contribute to faults. There is no allowance that can be included in these programs. The calculated results will therefore be lower than measured (e.g. a roof top plant room with large fans and pumps fed from a switchboard in the roof top plant room will experience higher short circuit currents than those calculated taking into account its supply feeders from the ground or basement transformers).

Diversity factors may be applied to cables which supply more than one lift. Examples are given in Table 12.3. Where there are more than four lifts, the lift installer should be consulted.

**Table 12.3** Diversity factor for lifts

| Number of lifts | Diversity factor |
| --- | --- |
| 1–2 | 1.0 |
| 3 | 0.9 |
| 4 | 0.8 |

Supply cables for lift installations and their ancillary services, lighting and socket outlets must be segregated from other building services (see BS 5655-6[7]). Supplies for fire fighting and evacuation lifts must be segregated so that the rest of the building supply can be isolated in the event of fire in all or part of the building.

### 12.8.2 Cable routes and protection

Where lifts are essential for emergency evacuation or are used for firefighting (see section 6), the cable routes for both the control wiring and the power supplies should be assessed and additional design precautions may be necessary to ensure that essential cables are protected from fire hazards. Where multiple lifts are used for these essential duties, the cable routes should be physically separate for each lift or subgroup of lifts.

Consideration should also be given as to how the integrity of the fire protection is to be maintained throughout the life of the building. For firefighting lifts, cables must be selected and protected in accordance with BS 5588: Part 5[6] and BS EN 81-72[4]

The basic requirements for electrical installations are identified in the Electricity at Work Regulations[23], BS EN 81-1[2] and BS EN 81-2[3], and BS 7671[14]. It should be noted that the lift installation on the lift side of the mains isolator which is covered by BS EN 81-1/2 is excluded from the scope of BS 7671. However, in addition, the initial specification given to the lift manufacturer should state the type of mechanical protection to be provided for fixed wiring in the lift well, machine room and car.

The options available are:

— rigid wiring clipped to surfaces where other mechanical protection is not essential

— proprietary multicore cable systems with special cleating tap-off and terminating components

— PVC conduit and trunking

— steel conduit and trunking.

## 12.8.3　Wiring interfaces

The initial specification must identify clearly the interfaces between wiring directly associated with the lift installation and wiring for other services. These are likely to include:

— intercom systems

— telephone handsets in lift cars

— warden alarm systems (in sheltered accommodation)

— remote emergency bells

— connections required for earthing and equipotential bonding

— remote monitoring and signalling to building management systems

— heating and ventilation of the machine room and lift well (see sections 12.9 and 12.10)

— lift well lighting

— lift well socket outlets

— fire alarms and detection equipment

— security systems.

Precise information must be provided wherever such interfaces occur to ensure that the correct signals will be transferred. A schedule of interfaces (see Table 12.4) is recommended so that all the relevant parties can comment on the proposed system and confirm that the required signals are compatible.

## 12.8.4　Maintenance safety and records

A rubber safety mat should be placed in front of the lift controller and also behind where rear access is provided. A card or poster giving guidance on treatment following electric shock should be provided in the machine room.

The designer should consider risks that maintenance staff may encounter during the routine maintenance of the lift installation; in particular, work in the lift well and on the car top. This is of particular importance when the lift control equipment or machine is located within the well or some other machine space. The designer should identify what provision is to be made for safety in the event of mains failure while working on the lift installation.

The technical dossier provided with each lift installation should comply with BS EN 13015[17].

Maintenance and operating personnel should be given essential information about the system. It is recommended that lift motor rooms have the same basic information as electrical plant rooms. This should include the following:

— wall mounted schematics and single-line diagrams of the associated power distribution system feeding the lift showing power source(s), points of isolation and device ratings.

— schedules for all distribution boards associated with the lift installation .

**Table 12.4** Example of an interface schedule for lifts

| Data transferred | Transfer from | Transfer to | Comments |
|---|---|---|---|
| Power supply (voltage, phases, frequency) | Local isolator (rating) | Lift controller | Interface at isolator (load current) |
| Lift car lighting (voltage, phases, frequency) | Local isolator at controller | Lift controller (load current) | Fused before isolator; interface at isolator |
| Lift car power (voltage, phases, frequency) | Local isolator at controller | Lift controller (load current) | Fused before isolator; interface at isolator |
| Earthing and bonding (cross sectional area of cable) | Earth bar in machine room | All metalwork | Interface at earth bar bonded to earth |
| Standby power in operation (contacts close when generator is supplying load) | Standby generator controls (volt-free contracts) | Lift controller | Interface at lift controller |
| Emergency bell (sound output level of bell) | Lift controller via terminal in lift well at ground floor (24 V DC supply) | Remote bell in entrance hall (24 V DC, 5 A load) | Interface for wiring at terminal box in lift well |

*Note*: The schedule should be extended to cover all interconnections between the lift installation and other services and/or plant in the building

## 12.9 Machine room environment

### 12.9.1 Temperature considerations

At the planning stage for a building, the designer should be aware of the likely need for the heating, ventilation and cooling of the machine room. Adjustments may be necessary when the precise operating conditions for the building are later established. For example, solar heat gain through windows, or waste heat from other parts of the building rising up the lift well to the machine room, can considerably affect temperatures.

The motor and control equipment of a lift can generate significant quantities of heat such that special ventilation and cooling facilities are needed in the machine room. This is not only to maintain the ambient temperature within reasonable limits for consistent operation of the equipment, but also to make conditions tolerable for service personnel. In a large installation the amount of heat generated may be such that the building services designer should consider the recovery of surplus heat, for example to preheat the domestic hot water supply.

Equipment supplied by different manufacturers will vary in terms of the amount of heat generated and the exact value should be obtained from the motor supplier or the lift installer. Some guidance is given in Table 12.5, which indicates that lifts with a large rated load are more efficient.

To a first approximation[1] the rating $(R)$ in kW of the electric motor for an electric traction lift can be estimated from:

$$R = \beta v / \eta \qquad (12.1)$$

where $R$ is the motor rating (kW), $\beta$ is the out of balance load (kg), $v$ is the rated speed (m/s) and $\eta$ is the gear box (if any) efficiency (%).

For example, for a gearless lift having a rated speed of 1.0 m/s and a rated load of 800 kg the motor rating would be 4.0 kW and the heat losses would be about 1.5 kW. A PMSM lift with a rated speed of 5.0 m/s and a rated load of 1600 kg would have a motor rated at 40 kW and heat losses of approximately 8 kW.

BS EN 81-1[2] and BS EN 81-2[3] require the ambient temperature of machine rooms to be maintained between 5 °C and 40 °C. Except for single-unit installations, it will probably be necessary to provide some means of heating and/or cooling in the machine room to keep the temperature within these limits. In cases where the machine room temperatures are controlled within closer limits, the

reliability of the lift machinery may improve. For new lifts, The Lifts Regulations[27] require the lift to be removed from service should the ambient temperature in the machine room fall outside the limits. Although the maximum temperature value varies between lift equipment manufacturers, 40 °C is a reasonable initial assumption for an upper limit. The actual value must be checked with the lift installer prior to finalising the machine room cooling and ventilation systems.

Most geared electric traction drives employ an oil-bath worm reduction gear driven by an electric motor. However, the use of gearless drives is increasing, not just the traditional 'high speed, high rise' situations but across all applications. All such electric motors produce heat which is dissipated directly into the machine room. The exception is 'machine room-less' lifts, where the motor is situated within the lift well.

The majority of hydraulic equipment presently available utilises an electric motor and screw driven pump, submerged in the oil reservoir tank (see section 7.3.4) The waste heat generated by hydraulic lifts is considerably more than that from a comparable electric traction lift, and the problem of heat disposal is often made greater because the machine room is sited within the building rather than on the roof. Unlike electric traction lifts, this heat is not dissipated directly into the machine room, but into the oil reservoir itself. This has the effect of reducing the oil viscosity. The opposite effect can be observed during periods of infrequent use. It is thus necessary to maintain the oil viscosity within acceptable limits for optimum performance of the equipment. To achieve these levels, direct oil heating or cooling may be required in many applications (see sections 12.9.3 and 12.9.4). This must be provided by the lift supplier.

Building designers should take into also take account of the possible need for standby heating and ventilating equipment. If the building has an integrated heating and ventilating system, they should make suitable arrangements to cope with lift operations when other building services are shut down, e.g. at weekends. Precautions against failure of air conditioning or cooling plant may also be necessary in busy buildings.

### 12.9.2 Ventilation

Under the section dealing with machine room construction, the harmonised standards requires that stale air from other parts of the building should not be exhausted into the machine room. Suitable ventilation should be provided such that, as far as reasonably practicable, the equipment is protected from dust, harmful fumes and humidity. Although not prescribed by the standards, it is recommended that the free area of ventilation should be not less than 0.1 m² per lift.

For lifts installed in low- to medium-rise buildings where the winding machine is installed within the lift well, i.e. the 'machine room-less' (MRL) configuration now offered by some manufacturers, the provision of ventilation to the lift well will be sufficient for all ventilation requirements.

Machine rooms for some lifts in high rise buildings may not have (adequate) access to natural ventilation from outside the building. For these cases, it is essential to

Table 12.5 Estimation of heat losses dissipated in the machine space

| System type | Range of motor rating / kW | Range of heat losses (% of motor rating) |
|---|---|---|
| Geared VVVF | 7.5–30 | 40–28 |
| Gearless VVVF | 7.5–40 | 38–26 |
| Gearless permanent magnet synchronous motor | 3–90 | 28–13 |
| Hydraulic | 4–20 | 70–30 |

provide adequate forced air cooling or air conditioning. This must be dimensioned in order to maintain the equipment operating and storage ambient temperature range defined by the lift installer. If forced ventilation or cooling is provided, it must be arranged so as not to leave undisturbed 'hot spots', such as the regions near a lift motor or a bank of resistors adjacent to a control panel. The air handling equipment should be integrated into the building requirement and not designed as a stand alone system specific to the lift machine rooms. This will allow a more energy efficient design and minimise building design coordination issues. Maintenance of the air handling equipment located in the machine room must be carried out under the supervision of the lift maintenance company or by competent persons trained in working around lift equipment.

Exposed locations such as public multi-story car parks and lift entrances to the outside of a building provide environmental conditions which can fall outside the storage and operational conditions for the lift equipment. In particular, hydraulic lifts are susceptible to extreme oil temperature variations which may cause breakdowns in low temperature conditions when the lift has not been used for some time. It is essential to provide adequate heating and cooling for the equipment both in the machine room and in other areas of the installation which may be affected in this manner. Incident solar radiation on to landing doors and entrances through south facing windows has been known to cause unsafe high surface temperatures and door distortion. Such locations may need the use of reflective window surfaces and other means to control the incident level of radiation.

## 12.9.3    Heating

Heating to lift machine rooms should be available at all times and, for this reason, local electric heating is widely used, often in the form of thermostatically-controlled tubular heaters. Where cooling is required, packaged heat pumps may offer a cost-effective solution.

Harmonised standards require the control of condensation or/and frost protection in pulley rooms. If electrical equipment is also contained within the pulley room the temperature should be similar to that of a machine room.

Hydraulic lift machine rooms are often placed in architecturally convenient locations, such as basement areas or stair cores. In such locations, the ambient temperature may drop considerably, which has a thickening effect upon the oil. Light duty hydraulic lifts and those with machine rooms in convenient locations may require oil heaters to ensure that the oil viscosity is at the correct level after, for example, overnight shut-down. This may be readily achieved by an immersed heating element in the oil reservoir, controlled by a thermostat. Such devices must be provided by the lift supplier. The provision of a separate oil heater, however, does not affect the need to maintain the machine room ambient temperature between 5 °C and 40 °C.

## 12.9.4    Cooling

All machine rooms should be provided with adequate means of removing the heat generated by the lift equip-

ment. The upper limit of 40 °C sometimes enables outside air to be used as the cooling medium, where ambient temperatures are not high. For some low usage single and double lift installations, natural ventilation by convection, using a high- and low-level louvered ventilator arrangement, may be adequate. For high usage lifts, where the heat generated is likely to be significant, and also for groups of lifts, mechanical ventilation will probably be required. This may range from a simple thermostatically controlled fan on the roof which takes in outside air through external louvers, up to sophisticated ducted systems. Care should be taken in all cases to prevent local 'hot spots'.

The main sources of heat gain within the machine room with electric traction lifts are the motors and, in the case of variable frequency drives, the banks of resistors. In some older installations, where the motors may be fan cooled, rather than allow the hot air generated in the motor to discharge directly into the machine room, it can be ducted to outside. With some types of motor, a secondary fan may be necessary but many motors are fitted with centrifugal blowers which develop sufficient pressure to deal with such discharge by themselves. Where all of the motor air is ducted to the outside, the reduction in room heat gain from the motor can be as much as 75%. This substantially reduces the cooling load and may remove the need to provide machine room air conditioning.

Where cooling air from the motor is ducted directly to the outside, replacement air will have to be drawn in. However, the replacement air will be warm during the summer and, in order to reduce running costs, the setpoint of any supplementary cooling system should not be less than the temperature of the incoming air.

With large multiple lifts and intensive duty hydraulic lifts, vast quantities of ventilation air may be necessary to provide the cooling required. In many instances this is not practicable within the overall building constraints and air conditioning may prove to be a more acceptable means of cooling. Ideally, the cooling plant should be located in a separate room so that it can be maintained without entry to the machine room. Where this is not possible and building services personnel are required to work within lift machine rooms, precautions must be taken to ensure compliance with the requirements of the Health and Safety at Work etc. Act 1974[26].

Machine rooms which rely on cooling equipment to control the temperature should be provided with a remote alarm to draw immediate attention to system failures.

In rare instances, lift control panels may require their environment to be more closely controlled than is usually the case, and may require temperatures lower than those specified in harmonised standards. In some cases this may be limited to the control panel itself and panel coolers would be provided. These usually take the form of small proprietary direct expansion air conditioners mounted on top of each panel blowing cooled air downwards through the cabinets, see Figure 12.1.

Oil cooling should be considered, where the duty of a hydraulic lift is likely to result in the dissipation of considerable amounts of heat into the hydraulic oil. This is best provided by the lift supplier as an integral part of the hydraulic pump and power unit. Oil cooling is usually

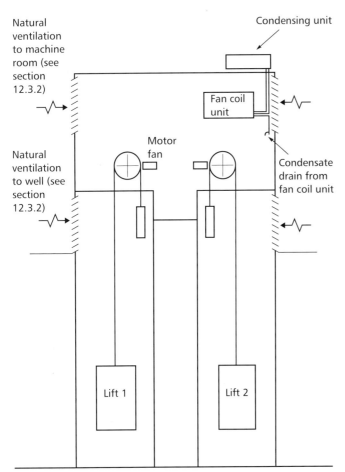

**Figure 12.1** Schematic of typical combination heating, ventilation and air conditioning system applied to a rooftop machine room

achieved by passing the oil through a radiant fin cooler on its return to the reservoir. The radiator should be mounted outside the machine room otherwise it has no effect on the machine room and oil temperature unless there is a large volume of cooling air to remove the energy.

Nowadays many building operators consider that the lift machinery will have a longer and more reliable working life if the temperature is maintained well below the upper limit, and therefore require air conditioning to be provided. An additional benefit is improved working conditions for maintenance personnel.

### 12.9.5     Lighting

Machine room electric lighting, with good colour rendering, should provide at least 200 lux at floor level in working areas, should be permanently installed and controlled from switches (two-way or intermediate, if appropriate) adjacent to all of the access doors. A pulley room can be fitted with similar lighting providing 100 lux at the pulleys unless the pulley room contains control panels, when it is considered a machine room in terms of lighting. Access to machine and pulley rooms is required to be permanently lit.

## 12.10     Lift well environment

Harmonised standards require that the well be suitably ventilated and not used to provide the ventilation of rooms other than those for the service of the lifts. Clause

5.2.3 of BS EN 81-1[2] and BS EN 81-2[3] has a note stating that provision be made at the top of the well for ventilation openings to the outside, either directly or via the machine or pulley room. The minimum ventilation area is 1% of the horizontal cross section of the well. This note is not part of the harmonised standard. Consequently, compliance with the note is not necessary. Generally there is sufficient ventilation of the well via clearance gaps in the door entrances. If ventilation air is provided via the machine or pulley room, through-ductwork should be used.

Lift buffers, other than spring buffers, usually found in the lift well pit may require a declaration of conformity as a safety component identified in The Lifts Regulations[27]. The testing of these CE-marked buffers requires ambient temperatures between 15 °C and 25 °C. Although many manufacturers will test and certify their buffers beyond this temperature band, if the ambient well temperature is likely to fall outside these temperatures the actual test parameters defined on the type-examination certificate for the buffer should be ascertained. The same principle applies to rupture and restrictor valves fitted to hydraulic lifts where the range of ambient temperatures applicable is stated on the type-examination certificate.

For lifts with speeds in excess of 2.5 m/s, wind noise and transient changes in lift well air pressure may occur due to lift car movement if pressure relief vents are not provided in the lift well walls. This can cause landing door rattle, wind whistle in lobbies and poor ride comfort. It is recommended that ventilation vents should be not less than 0.3 m² in free area for each lift well. A common lift well for two or three lifts having speeds in excess of 2.5 m/s requires a minimum vent area of 0.30 m². Where the common well accommodates four, five or six lifts, minimum vent areas of 0.40 m², 0.50 m² or 0.60 m² respectively should be used. The vents should be positioned at suitable intervals in the well walls. Vents in outside walls of the building should be louvered or otherwise protected to prevent rain, snow or vermin from entering the lift well. Local building regulations should also be consulted since these may require larger vent areas under certain circumstances.

For compliance with BS EN 81-1[2] and BS EN 81-2[3], lift well lighting should be installed so as to provide a minimum light intensity of 50 lux on the car top and in the pit. When control equipment and machinery is located in the well then the lighting level at the working location for those devices must be 200 lux. Where there is a machine room, these should be controlled from the lift machine room by a switch with a warning pilot light and by a switch within the lift well, either at the bottom entrance or at pit level. In any case the well lighting switch should be accessible from the entrance to the well.

## 12.11     Lift car environment

Under normal operation, the environmental conditions within lift cars present few problems. However, consideration must be given to the effects of breakdowns, especially if people are trapped inside a car. Sufficient ventilation within a lift car is deemed an Essential Health and Safety Requirement under The Lifts Regulations. Minimum ventilation apertures in the upper and lower parts of the car should be provided, as described in harmonised standards at least 1% of the available car area.

For internal lift wells, a small fan extracting air from the car into the lift well may also be provided. It is prudent to ensure that the fan is able to operate on a back-up battery supply in case passengers are trapped as a result of mains supply failure.

Heat gains from light fittings should be considered, especially spotlights which can dissipate substantial amounts of heat. If spotlights are used, an emergency 'off' switch should be provided to reduce the lighting to an emergency level.

For external observation lifts, the effects of solar heat gains must also be considered. These may be sufficient to require the provision of comfort cooling during normal operation. During winter periods lift car heating may need to be provided. In the event of a breakdown, the loss of comfort heating/cooling could be dangerous to the occupants and the provision of a maintained electrical supplies or even duplicate plant should be considered. Where comfort cooling is provided to the lift car, consideration should be given to the disposal of the condensate. This could provide a hazard to health if allowed to collect in the base of the lift well. For installations in tropical climates, where lift car cooling is commonplace, small packaged electric boilers may be employed to evaporate the condensate. However, these may not be commercially available in the UK.

# 12.12 Human comfort considerations

## 12.12.1 Noise

Criteria for in-car noise levels must take into account lift speed, as high-speed lifts are subject to wind noise. In-car noise criteria must also cover noise resulting from door operations. In hydraulic lifts, the oil flow can generate wide-band high frequency noise which is coupled to the lift car via the cylinder. The addition of a silencer on the valve output can reduce this noise level in the car by up to 8 dBA.

Door noise, when measured at 1.5 m from the centre of the floor and 1.0 m from the door face with a precision grade sound level meter set to 'fast' response, should not exceed 65 dBA. Noise levels in the car at the rated in the cycle, when measured as above, should not exceed 55 dBA for lift speeds of 0.5–2.0 m/s and should not exceed 60 dBA for lift speeds of 2.0–7.0 m/s.

The acceptable level of noise in lobbies will vary according to the function of the building. Noise Ratings (NR values) for various areas within buildings are given in CIBSE Guide A[20]. NR values are dependent on the frequency spectrum of the noise and there is no constant relationship between NR value and dBA. However, for practical purposes, the NR is approximately equal to dBA value minus 6.0. The recommended NR for reception areas in offices and hotel lobbies is NR35–40. For public areas in banks, building societies etc., NR35–45 is recommended.

For circulation spaces between wards in hospitals, NR35 is recommended.

Noise limits in the lift machine room should be specified in accordance with the Noise at Work Regulations 1989[28]. It is therefore essential that levels of machine noise are obtained from the lift supplier.

Lift noise, when measured at 1.5 m from the floor and 1.0 m from the door face using a precision grade sound level meter set to 'fast' response, should generally not exceed 55 dBA at any time during the lift cycle. Where lifts open directly into office spaces (i.e. where there is no lift lobby), this limit should be reduced to 50 dBA. However, there may be situations where levels up to 65 dBA may be acceptable and this should be checked with the client on each particular project.

It is also necessary to ensure that the sound reduction properties of the lift machine room construction, including doors, hatches, ventilation openings etc, are adequate to prevent the escape of noise at values which exceed the acoustic design criteria for the surrounding areas. Noise level information shall be made available as follows:

— maximum and average (L50) dBA level over a complete cycle of lift operation

— maximum levels in each of the eight octave bands centred at 63, 125, 250, 500, 1000, 2000, 4000 and 8000 Hz.

The measurements shall be made with a precision grade sound level meter fitted with an octave band filter set. The positions at which measurements are made should be noted on a drawing showing the principal noise-producing elements of the lift machinery. No measurements should be closer than one metre from any wall or floor surface. All measurements should be made using the 'fast' meter response.

## 12.12.2 Vibration

Human response to vibration is greatest at low frequencies. Therefore vibration limits in the range 1 to 80 Hz should be specified. Furthermore, human susceptibility to vibration differs between horizontal and vertical vibration and this should be taken into account when specifying acceptable limits of vibration.

Vibration measurements should be made at the centre of the car, at floor level, in three mutually perpendicular axes corresponding to vertical, front-to-back and side-to-side. Measurements should be made of the acceleration level in each direction over two complete cycles, one from the bottom of the building to the top, and one from the top of the building to the bottom. The measurement method is critical to the repeatability of results. It is, therefore, preferable to use an automatic recorder covering all frequency bands, as opposed to taking individual frequency band measurements over repeated lift runs. A cycle is defined as the period from just before the doors start to close at one level, to just after the doors open at the final level.

Measurements and analysis should be carried out in accordance with BS ISO 18738: 2003[18], which defines methods for the measurement of lift ride quality that have been adopted as standard by the lift industry. Acceleration levels should be measured as root mean square (RMS) values using a time constant of 0.125 s ('fast'), and the maximum values recorded in each $1/3$rd-octave band from 1–80 Hz inclusive over each complete cycle. The following limits will apply:

(a)    Horizontal vibration frequency range 1–80 Hz inclusive: maximum (RMS) acceleration level should not exceed 0.08 $m/s^2$.

The above limit applies to any time during a complete cycle, in any $1/3$rd-octave band in the frequency range specified.

(b)    Vertical vibration:

—    at maximum speed: maximum (RMS) acceleration level in any $1/3$rd-octave band should not exceed 0.08 $m/s^2$ in the frequency range 1–80 Hz.

—    during acceleration/deceleration and start/stop periods: the maximum (RMS) acceleration level in any $1/3$rd-octave band should not exceed 0.1 $m/s^2$ in the frequency range 1–80 Hz.

The above limits apply to lifts with speeds up to 4 m/s. Lifts having speeds above this will be subject to increased vibration limits. For lift speeds in the range 4–7 m/s, a multiplier of 1.5 may be used for all acceleration level limits.

These measurements are taken using computer controlled measuring equipment that allow direct comparison of ride quality from installation to installation. The use of Fourier analysis techniques also allows the fine resolution in the frequency domain not given by $1/3$rd-octave filters as given in BS 6472[10]. This is essential for the identification of any troublesome sources of vibration in the lift. The use of special filter systems such as those described in BS 6841[11] are not recommended.

### 12.12.3    Acceleration and deceleration

'Ride quality' is also a function of the acceleration and deceleration and it may be considered necessary to specify criteria for these characteristics. To avoid excessive discomfort for persons with disabilities, pregnant women and older people it is suggested that lift acceleration and deceleration values should not exceed 1.2 $m/s^2$ and this figure should only be considered where a high degree of control is provided. Acceleration and deceleration values are obviously linked to optimum lift response times and, to some extent, it may be necessary to compromise between comfort and travel times. The highest values that should be considered are 1.5 $m/s^2$.

### 12.12.4    Jerk

Passenger and ride comfort will also be affected by the jerk, i.e. the rate of change of acceleration and/or deceleration. Acceptable jerk values for lift performance are dependent on the lift speed. Their values are linked to optimum lift response times and it may again be necessary to compromise between comfort and travel times. It is

suggested that jerk values 50% numerically larger than the numerical for acceleration/deceleration values should be used with a maximum value of 2.2 $m/s^3$.

### 12.12.5    Communication with trapped passengers

The Lifts Regulations[27] require that passengers trapped in a lift car have the means of two-way voice communication with a 24-hour attended rescue service (see section 14).

### 12.12.6    Lighting at landings

Harmonised standards require the luminance of electric or natural lighting to be at least 50 lux at floor level at each landing served. This requirement needs to be satisfied when a new lift is being installed.

## 12.13    Environment for maintenance

### 12.13.1    General

In designing the transportation system, it is not only necessary to include those provisions required to ensure that the environment is suitable for the satisfactory operation of the lift. Consideration must also be given to those provisions necessary to ensure a safe and suitable environment for those persons involved in maintaining and inspecting the installation.

Many of these considerations are identified in the Health and Safety at Work etc. Act[26], the Workplace (Health Safety and Welfare) Regulations 1992[30], the Provision and Use of Work Equipment Regulations 1998[29], BS EN 13015[17] and/or BS 7255[12]. For new lifts installed to harmonised standards, the building fabric and building services requirements for the lift installation, including the machine rooms, wells and pulley rooms, is defined.

### 12.13.2    Lift well

Harmonised standards require that the lift well is used exclusively for lift equipment. Cables, ducts, pipes or devices other than for the lift installation are not permitted. Heating equipment for the lift well (not steam or high pressure water systems) are permitted as long as the controls remain outside of the well.

Harmonised standards require and define the provision of permanent electric well lighting to ensure an intensity of illumination of at least 50 lux one metre above the car roof and pit floor. This should preferably be installed by the lift supplier but is often installed by the electrical contractor who, if working from the lift car roof, should be under the supervision of the lift installer. The lift well lighting should incorporate emergency lighting to provide illumination in the event of power failure. Responsibility for subsequent maintenance of the well lighting is unclear because, generally, only the person maintaining the lift is likely to notice the failure of lamps. It should be noted that decorative lighting which is not part of the lift installation should not be designed to be located in the lift well. It is not certain that a Notified Body under the Lifts Regulations[27] will provide a design examination certificate for such an installation.

A supply of replacement lamps should be kept on site to reduce the delay in replacing failed lamps. In modern buildings, fluorescent lamps are the most common and maintenance will be simplified if lamps of the same type are used for both the lift well and machine room.

For wells that are partially enclosed, such as observation lifts, well lighting may be omitted provided that the prescribed luminance can be achieved by surrounding ambient lighting at all positions of the lift car, and at all times when access to the lift well may be necessary.

Attention should be given to the internal wall surfaces of the well. The walls of the well may be constructed of brick, concrete or blockwork, and dry-lined internal facings may also be employed. Each of these can give rise to dust. This should be limited by painting the walls with a suitable proprietary surface treatment. Painting the internal surface of the well will not only inhibit the spread of dust but will also provide a clean and safe working environment. For maximum visibility white paint should be used.

### 12.13.3 Machine room

Harmonised standards prescribe the construction, dimensions, lifting equipment, means of access and the provision of building services in machine and pulley rooms. The standards also limit the use of machine and pulley rooms to:

— lift equipment

— machines for service lifts or escalators

— cooling and heating equipment for machine and pulley rooms (except steam and high pressure water heating systems)

— defined fire extinguishers and detectors.

Fire extinguishers should be suitable for electrical fires and be stable over a period of time, and should be mounted so as to be suitably protected against accidental impact. The room should be accessible only to authorised persons and should not contain ducts, cables, pipes or other devices not associated with the lift installation, e.g. television signal amplifiers etc.

Emergency lighting should be provided in machine and pulley rooms not only to permit escape but also to enable the undertaking of emergency procedures such as hand-winding to effect passenger release during a power failure.

Should certain control circuits in a lift controller remain live after the particular lift is isolated, as is common where groups of lifts are interconnected, means of total isolation should be provided in the machine room. This is usually achieved by isolating all of the other lifts in the group.

Additional means of lift movement prevention, in the form of a stay-put 'stop' button, must be provided in the following locations:

— adjacent to the lift motor and pulleys in pulley rooms

— on the top of the lift car (part of the car top controls), within 1 metre of car door entrances.

— 1 metre above the sill at the lowest lift entrance

— at the bottom of the lift well.

### 12.13.4 Machine room-less installations

Maintenance of control equipment and machinery in a machine room-less installation is undertaken will be undertaken in the machinery spaces and on a landing for emergency access and movement control panels. All such locations should be illuminated to a level of at least 200 lux for safe working. Sufficient working area should be allowed for maintenance and the safe passage of building occupants. The winding of the lifting machine also occurs at the top landing and lighting in the lift lobby should be sufficient to undertake maintenance and emergency procedures. All intervention cabinets should be clearly marked and any emergency instructions displayed inside the cabinet. Consideration should be given to the location and safe storage of the landing door emergency unlocking key and its ready access to authorised persons.

### 12.13.5 Physical requirements

Harmonised standards define key dimensions of the machine room, machine room door and trap requirements as well as the requirement for the lifting beams. Where machine rooms are built on different levels, permanent ladders and removable guard rails should be fitted if there is a change of level greater than 500 mm. It is recommended that the floors and walls of the machine room are treated with dust inhibiting paint.

### 12.13.6 Maintenance of third party equipment

Equipment associated with the lift installation such as fire and smoke detectors, fire extinguishers, air conditioning plant, communications systems, etc. require maintenance by persons not normally authorised to work in lift environments. Arrangements must be made to accompany these persons. However, wherever possible, arrangements should be made to allow these activities to be carried out safely by, for example, locating plant outside lift areas, or in the case of fire and smoke detectors, providing a means of withdrawing them from the well for testing.

## References

1    Barney G C, Cooper D A and Inglis J *Elevator and escalator micropedia* (Sedbergh: GBA Publications) (2001)

2    BS EN 81-1: 1998: *Safety rules for the construction and installation of lifts. Electric lifts* (London: British Standards Institution) (1998)

3       BS EN 81-2: 1998: *Safety rules for the construction and installation of lifts. Hydraulic lifts* (London: British Standards Institution) (1998)

4       BS EN 81-72: 2003: *Safety rules for the construction and installation of lifts. Particular applications for passenger and goods passenger lifts. Firefighters lifts* (London: British Standards Institution) (2003)

5       BS EN 81-80: 2003: *Safety rules for the construction and installation of lifts. Rules for the improvement of safety of existing passenger and goods passenger lifts* (London: British Standards Institution) (2003)

6       BS 5588: *Fire precautions in the design, construction and use of buildings*: Part 5: 1991: *Code of practice for firefighting stairs and lifts* (London: British Standards Institution) (1991)

7       BS 5655: *Lifts and service lifts*: Part 6: 2002: *Code of practice for selection and installation* (London: British Standards Institution) (2002)

8       BS 5655: *Lifts and safety lifts*: Part 11: 1989: *Recommendations for the installation of new, and modernization of, electric lifts in existing buildings* (London: British Standards Institution) (1989)

9       BS 5655: *Lifts and safety lifts*: Part 12 : 1989: *Recommendations for the installation of new, and modernization of, hydraulic lifts in existing buildings* (London: British Standards Institution) (1989)

10      BS 6472: 1992: *Guide to evaluation of human exposure to vibration in buildings (1 Hz to 80 Hz)* (London: British Standards Institution) (1992)

11      BS 6841: 1992: *Guide to measurement and evaluation of human exposure to whole-body mechanical vibration and repeated shock* (London: British Standards Institution) (1992)

12      BS 7255: 1989: *Code of practice for safe working on lifts* (London: British Standards Institution) (1989)

13      BS 7375: 1996: *Code of practice for distribution of electricity on construction and building sites* (London: British Standards Institution) (1996)

14      BS 7671: 2001: *Requirements for electrical installations. IEE Wiring Regulations. 16th Edition* (London: Institution of Electrical Engineers) (2001)

15      BS EN 12015: 1998: *Electromagnetic compatibility. Product family standard for lifts, escalators and passenger conveyors. Emission* (London: British Standards Institution) (2004)

16      BS EN 12016: 2004: *Electromagnetic compatibility. Product family standard for lifts, escalators and moving walks. Immunity* (London: British Standards Institution) (2004)

17      BS EN 13015: 2001: *Maintenance for lifts and escalators – Rules for maintenance instructions* (London: British Standards Institution) (2001)

18      BS ISO 18738: 2003: *Lifts (elevators). Measurement of lift ride quality* (London: British Standards Institution) (2003)

19      Building Regulations 1991 Statutory Instrument 1991 No. 2768 (London: The Stationery Office) (1991)

20      CIBSE Guide A: *Environmental design* (London: Chartered Institution of Building Services Engineers) (1999)

21      CIBSE Guide K: *Electricity in buildings* (London: Chartered Institution of Building Services Engineers) (2005)

22      Council Directive of 3 May 1989 on the approximation of the laws of the Member States relating to Electromagnetic Compatibility EC Directive 89/339/EEC ('Electromagnetic Compatibility Directive') *Official J. of the European Communities* 23.05.1989 L139/19 (Brussels: Commission for the European Communities) (1997)

23      Electricity at Work Regulations 1989 Statutory Instrument 1989 No. 635 (London: Her Majesty's Stationery Office) (1989)

24      Electricity Council Engineering Recommendation G5/4: *Limits for harmonics in the UK electricity supply* (London: The Electricity Association) (2001)

25      European Parliament and Council Directive 95/16/EC of 29 June 1995 on the approximation of the laws of the Member States relating to lifts ('The Lifts Directive') *Official J. of the European Communities* L213/1 07/09/1995 (1995)

26      Health and Safety at Work etc. Act 1974 (London: Her Majesty's Stationery Office) (1974)

27      Lifts Regulations 1997 Statutory Instrument 1997 No. 831 (London: The Stationery Office) (1997)

28      Noise at Work Regulations 1989 Statutory Instrument 1989 No. 1790 (London: Her Majesty's Stationery Office) (1989)

29      Provision and Use of Work Equipment Regulations Statutory Instrument 1992 No. 2932 (London: The Stationery Office) (1992)

30      Workplace (Health, Safety and Welfare) Regulations Statutory Instrument 1992 No. 3004 (London: The Stationery Office) (1992)

# Appendix 12.A1: Schedules for electrical systems requirements

**Table 12.A1.1** Typical schedule for electrical system requirements — machine room

| Requirements | Interface and notes |
| --- | --- |
| Power supply for lifts: | |
| — single main for firefighting lift | Supply monitored by building management system (BMS). |
| — single main for each lift or a single supply to feed each group of lifts | Supply monitored by BMS. |
| — single main for lift well and machine room power and lighting | Supply monitored by BMS. |
| Power for lift machine room: | |
| — small power socket outlets | See BS 5655[5]. |
| Lighting: | |
| — lift well lights | |
| — lift car lights | Prominent means of isolation. |
| — lift car (top) maintenance socket outlet | Prominent means of isolation. |
| — emergency lighting | Emergency lighting to enable safe hand-winding operations during a power failure. |
| Environmental control: | |
| — heating | May be linked to central controls. |
| — ventilation | May be linked to central controls. |
| — cooling | Check if required for internal motor rooms or those subject to high solar gains. |
| Earthing and bonding: | |
| — all metal work to be bonded and connected to machine room earth bar | Separate machine room earth bar cabled to main building earth. |
| Fire detection and alarm: | |
| — smoke, rate of rise detectors, manual break-glass stations and sounders | Integrated with main building fire alarm system. |
| Communications: | |
| — car intercom | Linked to internal building intercom system. |
| — external communications (telephone) | Emergency dial-out feature through public network. Where this may be abused the dial-out may be barred to a single number or routed through the main reception or security desk serving the building. |
| — automatic dial-out | Where remote monitoring of the lift installation for performance and/or alarms is required, an automatic dial-out facility will be necessary using the public network |
| Fire service | Separate communication between lift motor room, lift car, firefighting lobbies and control rooms. |
| Monitoring and controls: | |
| — control for reduced lift service (i.e. reduced speed and acceleration when power is limited) | Signal from standby power supply to prevent simultaneous starting and overload, reduce speed and acceleration or other means to limit the lift load current |
| Status indication and alarms | Interface to BMS and automatic call-out for maintenance |

**Table 12.A1.2** Typical schedule for electrical system requirements — lift well

| Requirements | Interface and notes |
|---|---|
| Lighting†: | |
| — normal and emergency lighting | Emergency standby battery system (specify minimum lighting levels required). |
| — car top | Consider emergency lighting. |
| Controls†: | |
| — car destination controls | Operation through the lift controller. Is 'key holder' override required? |
| — door hold controls | |
| — alarm control | |
| — maintenance controls (on car top) | Maintenance switch and push. |
| Indication†: | |
| — position | Operation through lift controller. |
| — selected floor | Operation through lift controller. |
| — overload/car out of service | Operation through lift controller. |
| Communication: | |
| — emergency bell | Remote sounder — off-site. |
| — intercom | Machine room and building system. |
| — telephone | Connected to external telephone line — single number auto-dial. |
| — audio system | Building or lift PA system. |
| Firefighting communications | Linked to landing and control room. |
| Ventilation | Forced ventilation if required. |
| Power | Maintenance power outlet on car top. |

† These items interface with requirements for special finishes and decor

**Table 12.A1.3** Typical schedule for electrical system requirements — lift car

| Requirements | Interface and notes |
|---|---|
| Lighting: | |
| — permanent well lighting | Controlled from machine room and/or pit with warning pilot light |
| Power: | |
| — socket outlet in lift pit | See BS 5655[5] |
| Earthing and bonding: | |
| — guide rails and metal landing door surrounds bonded to earth | Connect to building earth system |
| Heating: | |
| — provided if necessary where there is a risk of condensation | Automatic controls or connection to central system |
| Monitors: | |
| — pit water flood detector if necessary | Remote alarm |
| Fire detection: | |
| — smoke detector | Linked to fire alarm system; detector located at top of the well |

# 13 Energy consumption of lifts, escalators and moving walks

## Lead authors

Dr Lutfi Al-Sharif (Al-Sharif VTC)
Dr Gina Barney (Gina Barney Associates)

## Chapter contents

| | | |
|---|---|---|
| 13.1 | Energy consumption and energy efficiency | 13-3 |
| 13.2 | Energy consumption of lifts | 13-4 |
| 13.3 | Factors affecting lift energy consumption | 13-4 |
| | 13.3.1 Mechanical system | 13-4 |
| | 13.3.2 Drive system | 13-5 |
| | 13.3.3 Control system | 13-5 |
| | 13.3.4 Electrical system | 13-5 |
| | 13.3.5 Duty | 13-5 |
| | 13.3.6 Regenerating energy back into the supply | 13-6 |
| 13.4 | Estimating the energy consumption of lifts by calculation | 13-6 |
| 13.5 | Estimating the energy consumption of lifts by measurement | 13-7 |
| 13.6 | Estimating the energy consumption of lifts by modelling | 13-8 |
| 13.7 | Estimating the energy consumption of escalators | 13-8 |
| 13.8 | Measuring the energy consumption of escalators and moving walks | 13-9 |
| 13.9 | Measures to conserve energy | 13-9 |
| | 13.9.1 Lifts | 13-10 |
| | 13.9.2 Escalators and moving walks | 13-10 |
| References | | 13-10 |

# 13 Energy consumption of lifts, escalators and moving walks

## 13.1 Energy consumption and energy efficiency

The European community is increasingly dependent on external energy sources, but has little influence on the energy supply (oil etc.). A possible solution is to reduce energy consumption by improving energy efficiency. There has already been a directive on the energy certification of buildings (Directive 93/76/EEC[5]) adopted before the Kyoto agreement. A proposal for a new directive on the energy performance of buildings was published in the Official Journal of the European Union on 31 July 2001[10]. The objective is to create a common framework to promote the improvement of the energy performance of buildings in the context of climate change. The proposal concerns the residential sector and the tertiary sector (offices, public buildings etc.). It covers all aspects of energy efficiency in buildings in an attempt to establish a truly integrated approach.

The UK Government published an Energy White Paper in February 2003 and started on a revision of the Building Regulations energy efficiency provisions (Building Regulations Part L). These are to come into effect in 2005. The Office of the Deputy Prime Minister developed the proposals for the changes in consultation with experts from a broad spectrum of interests in the energy efficiency of buildings. The minutes of an Industry Advisory Group meeting, as reported on the ODPM website, state that: 'Lifts and other people transportation systems are to be looked at to identify if these are worthy of bringing into the regulations.' However, the draft Part L published in July 2004 states 'vertical transportation systems are not currently subject to the requirements of Part L' and '... should be excluded from the notional building calculation'.

The total power consumption over the entire life cycle of any equipment consists of the power consumed to manufacture, install, operate, dismantle and for disposal. Of these phases the operational phase is probably the most significant. CIBSE Guide F: *Energy efficiency in buildings*[6] suggests that lifts and escalators can consume between 5% and 15% of the energy of a building depending on the type of the building and its equipment provision. Figure 13.1 illustrates for lifts the relationship of their energy consumption in comparison to other energy users in an office building.

Where possible, designers should aim to minimise transportation requirements through good building layout during the design stage (see Chapter 2). The amount and types of transportation equipment installed in a building are determined by the traffic requirements of the building occupants. Energy cannot be sensibly saved by reducing the number of units installed. However, energy consumption can be minimised through good equipment design, appropriate selection to meet the traffic demands and efficient operational control of the transportation equipment (see Chapter 3).

Although increased energy efficiency can sometimes involve higher initial capital costs, this may be recovered through energy savings over the life time of the equipment and thus each application warrants a full cost analysis.

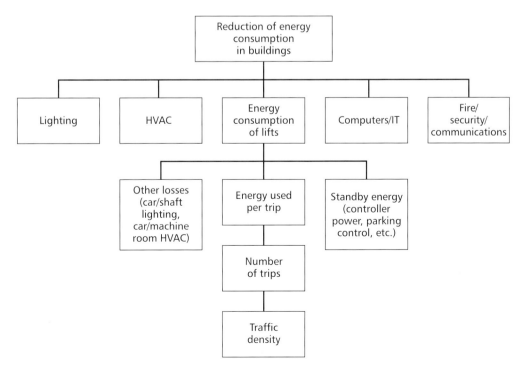

**Figure 13.1** Relationship of lifts to other energy consumers in an office building

Importantly, capital and recurrent costs have been reducing as variable speed drives become cheaper. Obviously, the utility supply company's tariff structure will affect the final cost of the electricity consumption.

## 13.2    Energy consumption of lifts

Different estimates for the energy dissipation of lifts as a percentage of the energy consumption of the whole building have been suggested. KONE[13] estimates it at 5–10%, whereas Schroeder (1986)[11] estimates it at 15% of the total building electric energy consumption (assuming no air conditioning or oil heating). Schroeder also estimates lift energy costs at 1% of the total cost of the rental of the office space, as a useful comparative cost. All these estimates are dependent on any other services running in the building and their efficiency.

There are different motivations for carrying out energy consumption estimation and energy measurement of lift systems, which arise from different needs. The four main motivations suggested by Al-Sharif[3] for examining the energy consumption of lift systems are outlined below (and each is used to answer a different question):

(1)     Understanding the energy consumption of one specific installation.

        This answers the question: 'How much energy does the installation consume?'

(2)     Comparing the energy consumption of two different types of lift (e.g. different drives).

        This answers the question: 'How much energy will be saved by replacing drive A with drive B?'

(3)     Minimising the energy consumption of the lift on a journey by journey basis.

        This attempts to answer the question: 'What is the optimum speed profile for the next journey that would minimise the energy consumption based on the load, direction and travel distance ?'

(4)     Predicting the energy consumption of a lift system based on its various parameters (e.g. type of drive, gearing, capacity, speed, travel distance etc.).

        This answers the question: 'What would the energy consumption of a new design of lift system be with a certain configuration and a specified set of components?'

These motivations have important applications in terms of design of new lift configurations and predicting changes of energy consumption following modernisations. The last method aims to predict the energy consumed by a lift system, based on the various parameters of the lift system, its speed and loading.

## 13.3    Factors affecting lift energy consumption

Many factors affect the energy consumption of lift systems. An International Standards Organisation (ISO) working group has identified 18 factors affecting the energy consumption of the equipment. These are summarised below:

—     mechanical system
—     drive sheave efficiency (traction, etc.)
—     idler sheave efficiency
—     roping (reeving) ratio (1:1, 2:1 etc)
—     guidance system (rails/slider/rollers)
—     counterbalancing ratio
—     compensation system
—     drive system
—     motor efficiency including any cooling fans
—     gear efficiency (if any)
—     drive regeneration
—     acceleration/deceleration profile
—     creeping/levelling time
—     brake consumption
—     control system
—     controller (traffic and drive) consumption
—     door system (drive, passenger detection, etc.)
—     traffic (dispatcher) efficiency
—     electrical system
—     power factor
—     heating and cooling
—     well/machine room/car lighting

In addition to the lift equipment aspects an important factor in energy consumption is the way the lift is operated. Operational aspects include:

—     number of starts
—     travel distance
—     speed
—     load
—     duty etc.

Some factors are fundamental to providing the transportation service such as travel distance, car capacity (rated capacity), speed (rated speed) and the number of landings served (number of possible stops), and cannot be changed. There are several other factors which should be considered at the design and specification stage, which affect energy consumption.

### 13.3.1    Mechanical system

The type of gearing (if applicable) used will affect the consumption, for example worm gearboxes are less efficient that helical gearboxes (Stawinoga)[12]. Worm type gears have an efficiency significantly lower in the reverse direction compared to the forward direction. Gear box efficiencies can be as low as 30% for low torque systems approaching 70% for high torque systems. Modern gearbox efficiencies can be higher, typically 70–90%.

Lift systems employ a number of roping systems, such as 1:1, 2:1, etc. and single and double wrap. Generally the simpler the roping system, i.e. 1:1 the more efficient is the lift system.

Sometimes a flywheel is used on two-speed systems to smooth out the sudden changes in torque. The use of a flywheel reduces the efficiency of the system. The inertia of other moving masses should be minimised.

All lift systems need to overcome friction in the guide rails, guide shoes, etc. and air resistance to the car moving in the well. The weight of the empty car has an important effect and should be kept as small as possible. In general (Al-Sharif; 2002)[2], the weight of the empty car can be twice that of the rated load for the larger car sizes. Reducing the weight of the empty car has the advantage of also reducing the weight of the counterweight and hence the energy consumption.

### 13.3.2    Drive system

Drive systems are fully discussed in Chapter 8. The main types of drive systems available today are hydraulic, single/two speed AC variable voltage (ACVV) with DC injection braking and variable-voltage, variable-frequency (VVVF). Older drive systems include Ward-Leonard, thyristor-Leonard and AC-thyristor. Doolard (1992)[7] compared the energy consumed for various drives, when undertaking a simple round trip of a journey of three floors up and three floors back. The results obtained offer a simple comparison between the drive types and are shown in Figure 13.2.

Figure 13.2 shows the hydraulic drive to be the least efficient and the VVVF drive to be the most efficient. The conventional hydraulic drive is unable to recover any of the energy consumed to drive the lift up on the return journey down. New systems are appearing in the market place, which overcome this problem, They use a pressurised accumulator to collect some of the energy back during the down trip.

### 13.3.3    Control system

The drive control system can allow the drive to operate efficiently by profiling the movement between stops in an optimal manner. The values selected for speed, acceleration and jerk (often dictated by the traffic design and ride comfort requirements) will affect the energy consumption. Some drive systems can optimise the energy used for the next journey dependent on the car load, direction of travel, distance to be travelled.

Some traffic control systems move lifts to parking floors when they become idle. This feature may be useful during peak periods, but is wasteful out of hours or in light duty environments.

### 13.3.4    Electrical system

The efficiency of various components is important. The motor and any generators will incur iron and copper losses and suffer internal windage losses. There will be losses due to the system running at power factors less than unity. Table 12.5 gives estimates of energy dissipation. Losses will also occur in the connecting wiring.

The drive and traffic controller will use energy (standby power) even when the lift is not moving. A system of powering off a controller during low traffic conditions should be considered similar to the motor–generator (MG) set shut-down sequence used on the older Ward-Leonard systems. Energy is also used for car and machine room lighting, heating, cooling etc. If the car lighting can be reduced (not switched off) this can make save significant energy savings.

The Hong Kong Government has proposed limiting the size of the hoist motor as a means of limiting energy consumption and has published a Guide[8] and a Code of Practice[9]. This proposal will have a considerable effect on the handling capacity, passenger waiting and passenger waiting times and would not be acceptable in most situations.

### 13.3.5    Duty

The level of usage, that is the numbers of passengers demanding service, the number of journeys the passengers make and their destinations, the variation of the load in the car, the direction of travel, idle time, the weight of the car, have a significant effect on energy consumption. Figure 13.3 shows the energy consumption graph for different car loads. The shaded area shows the opportunity to recover energy back into the power supply for a 75% loaded down trip

Lifts are generally designed to be counterbalanced at 40–50% of rated load. This is arranged by making the mass of the counterweight equal to the mass of the empty car plus 40–50% of the rated load in the car. Figure 13.3 assumes that the installation has a 42% counterbalancing. Thus the most efficient use, in this case, is when the car is 42% loaded. Unfortunately this is a rare occurrence.

The traffic control algorithm (see Chapter 9) can have an influence on how the traffic demand is handled. For example, under heavy demand conditions, a hall call allocation system can be inherently more energy efficient as it groups passengers travelling to the same floors together. It is also possible for the traffic controller to operate an energy saving algorithm.

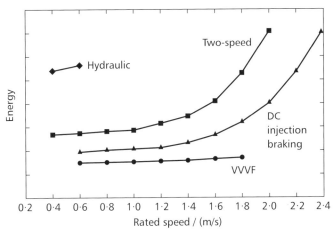

**Figure 13.2** Energy consumptions of various types of drive

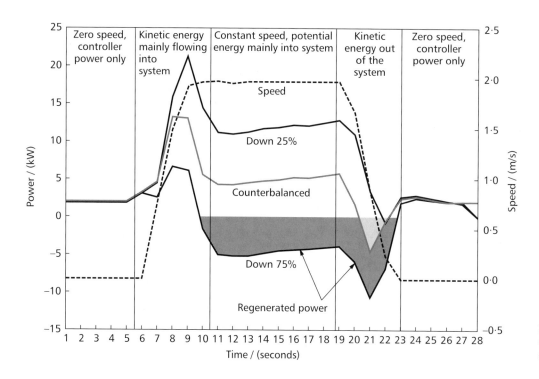

**Figure 13.3** Speed and energy consumption of an elevator carrying different loads

### 13.3.6 Regenerating energy back into the supply

In any hoisting application, potential energy is transferred back and forth from the power supply to the load and vice versa. When a lift system is running up empty (or down full), it will be overhauling. The motor is effectively driven by the load, under the influence of gravity thus braking the lift system and preventing freefall. Lifts always need to dissipate excessive energy from the system, either as waste heat into banks of resistors, or by regeneration. Whether the energy can be regenerated and the mechanism for achieving it depends on the type of drive.

Regenerating lift systems return the excessive energy back to the supply through the meter. However, not every meter will record this reverse power and deduct units from the total. A special meter has to be fitted by agreement with the utility company. Where this is not possible arrangements should be made for the regenerated power to be used by other building services, such as lighting, HVAC etc. (see Figure 13.1). It is important to remember that regeneration can cause the supply voltage to rise at the lift input terminals, unless it is connected to a low impedance supply.

Table 13.1 gives a summary of the drive systems available and indicates the regeneration capability of each drive type.

If the lift system had been an ideal system, with no friction and 100% efficiency, the regenerated energy would be equal to the consumed energy.

### 13.4 Estimating the energy consumption of lifts by calculation

Doolard's data shown in Figure 13.2 is a useful guide and allows a comparison of the energy consumption for different lift drive systems travelling three floors (see section 13.3.1). However, it is of limited value as it represents only a small number of installations.

Schroeder (1986)[11] carried out a large number of measurements assuming an average trip distance of 1.1 floors. He developed a generalised formula for calculating the daily energy consumption ($E_d$) of a lift installation.

$$E_d = \frac{R \times \text{ST} \times \text{TP}}{3600} \tag{13.1}$$

**Table 13.1** Regeneration capability of various drives

| Type of drive | Regeneration? | Description |
|---|---|---|
| Ward-Leonard | Yes | Regeneration takes place naturally, via the direct connection to the main supply. Hoist motor becomes a DC generator, the DC generator of the MG set becomes a motor and the AC prime mover becomes an AC generator. |
| AC single speed and AC two-speed | Yes | Regeneration takes place naturally, via the direct connection to the main supply. |
| ACVV (DC injection braking) | No | Energy usually dissipated as heat in the low speed windings and rotor. |
| DC thyristor | Yes | Regeneration is possible in 4 quadrant drives. |
| VVVF | Yes | Regeneration possible if special unit fitted. |
|  | No | Heat dissipated in chopper resistor/transistor combination. |

**Table 13.2** Values of typical trip time, TP, for various types of drives and installations[2]

| Drive | Floors above ground | Typical trip time, TP (s) | |
|---|---|---|---|
| | | Range | Mean |
| Hydraulic (without counterweight) | <6 | 5–7 | 6 |
| Geared: | | | |
| — AC 2-speed | 6 | 9–12 | 10.5 |
| — ACVV (high mass) | 12 | 7–10 | 8.5 |
| — ACVV (low mass) | 12 | 5–8 | 6.5 |
| Gearless: | | | |
| — motor-generator | 18 | 4–6 | 5 |
| — thyristor | 18 | 3–5 | 4 |
| — VVVF* | 18 | 2–4 | 3 |

* Estimated

where $E_d$ is the daily energy consumed ((kW·h)/day), $R$ is the motor rating (kW), ST is the daily number of starts (day$^{-1}$) and TP is the trip time factor.

The parameter TP was obtained by measurement and depends on the number of floors, the type of drive and the rated speed. Table 13.2 shows the values calculated by Schroeder for various installations and drives. The VVVF figure is estimated, as Schroeder did not have the opportunity to measure a VVVF system.

The main difficulty with this method is that the number of starts parameter (ST) has to be estimated, or measured, thus affecting the final accuracy of the calculation. The mean value of TP for the relevant installation can be found from Table 13.2. For more accuracy Schroeder suggests the lower end of the range is used for 1:1 roping and a relatively large motor and the upper end of the range is used for 2:1 roping and a relatively small motor.

This rule of thumb in practice has been found to significantly underestimate the energy consumed in a building. This is due to the fact that Schroeder based his calculations on an average trip of 1.1 floors per journey, which is representative of up-peak traffic, but not of the average daily traffic. The method thus does not return very accurate results and should be used with caution.

The annual energy consumption per year can be estimated based on the usage pattern of a building during each week of activity. The ISO working group suggests the usage pattern shown in Table 13.3. This table indicates, for seven different building types, the assumed number of operating hours per day. Using an intensity index of unity for the weekdays the relative intensity is given of the weekend days.

**Table 13.3** Usage patterns for different building types

| Building type | Operating hours | Intensity index | | |
|---|---|---|---|---|
| | | Weekdays | Saturday | Sunday |
| Residential | 16 | 1.0 | 1.0 | 1.1 |
| Commercial | 12 | 1.0 | 0.5 | 0.1 |
| Service utility | 10 | 1.0 | 0.9 | 1.3 |
| Retail | 10 | 1.0 | 1.4 | 1.5 |
| Hotel, accommodation | 10 | 1.0 | 1.1 | 1.3 |
| Medical | 12 | 1.0 | 1.0 | 1.0 |
| School, educational | 10 | 1.0 | 0.5 | 0.1 |

*Example 13.1*

Calculate the weekday and annual energy consumption for a very active (intensive duty) commercial building served by six, 1600 kg, gearless lifts, with a rated speed of 4 m/s controlled by a thyristor drive. The motor size is 33 kW.

From Table 13.2, TP is 4 seconds (the mean value).

It is necessary to estimate the number of starts per day. From Table 13.3, assume a 12 hour day.

For each lift assume a morning up-peak of one hour with 240 starts, a two hour period of 240 starts per hour during the mid-day period, and an evening down-peak of one hour with 240 starts. During the eight hours of low (interfloor) activity assume 40 starts per hour This gives the total number of starts per day as:

$$ST = 240 + (2 \times 240) + 240 + (8 \times 40)$$

$$= 1280 \text{ starts per day}$$

Then the total consumption per weekday per lift will be:

$$E_d = \frac{33 \times 1280 \times 4}{3600} = 47 \text{ kW·h/weekday/lift}$$

For all six lifts in the group:

$$E_d = 6 \times 47 = 282 \text{ kW·h/weekday}$$

In a year there will be 260 weekdays, 52 Saturdays and 52 Sundays. Thus the annual consumption ($E_a$) using the usage factors from Table 13.3 will be:

$$E_a = [(260 \times 1.0) + (52 \times 0.5) + (52 \times 0.1)] \times 282$$

$$= 79.3 \text{ MW·h/year}$$

The cost of this energy will depend on the tariff offered by the utility company.

# 13.5 Estimating the energy consumption of lifts by measurement

Measuring the actual energy consumption of an installation is often a prelude to a modernisation, where energy consumption is a concern. The measurements are usually taken under the prevailing traffic conditions. Measures can then be taken by the building owner to reduce energy consumption. After a modernisation so many factors may have changed, e.g. traffic control algorithm, drive system, etc., that a direct comparison cannot be made.

It would be helpful to determine the energy efficiency of a lift system prior to installation, modernisation and after installation for a specified traffic demand. Measurements should be taken in a controlled fashion. The ISO working group approach is to measure the energy consumed for a test cycle. Their test cycle is defined for a lift running between terminal floors for one hour of activity. The automatic door operation is disabled and the lift remains

**Table 13.4** One hour test parameters

| Building type | Number of starts per hour | Average number of stops travelled |
|---|---|---|
| Residential | 100 | 1.51 |
| Commercial | 150 | 2.00 |
| Service utility | 180 | 2.10 |
| Retail | 150 | 2.00 |
| Hotel, accommodation | 100 | 2.00 |
| Medical | 180 | 2.10 |
| School, educational | 100 | 2.46 |

idle at the upper terminal floor for 5-minutes. This approach measures the actual installation under contrived operational conditions. These test conditions are unrealistic for a commercial building as the lift will only make 12 trips per hour and the travel distance will always be the total travel possible.

A more realistic approach is to require the one hour test cycle to cause the lift to make a likely number of stops in the hour of activity, when making journeys equal to the average trip distance. The ISO working group have suggested a likely number of starts and average distance travelled as shown in Table 13.4.

During any test the following data should be recorded:

— peak (starting) and running current

— standby current

— energy used at the end of test

— number of starts

— total travel distance after 1 hour test

— installation parameters, e.g. motor rating, rated load, compensation, balance etc.

— details of any significant factors that affect the energy consumption, e.g. car mass, counter-balancing ratio, etc.

— environmental conditions (ambient temperature in the well, machine room, etc.)

— other standby power requirements

— peak demand requirement (connection costs)

— power factor (average and at rated speed).

From this data a Schroeder TP parameter can be obtained from the energy used, the number of starts and the hoist motor rating. This can then be used for future calculations.

# 13.6    Estimating the energy consumption of lifts by modelling

The methods described in sections 13.4 and 13.5 suffer from the disadvantages that they cannot predict the energy consumption for a lift system in increments of time (e.g. journey by journey, or second by second) or predict the energy consumption of various electrical and mechanical designs and installation configurations. Modelling

offers the advantage of allowing the user to predict the energy on a time basis and with different configurations.

The main difference between modelling methods and conventional methods is that the former are analytical in their approach while the latter are empirical. In the empirical approach the energy for a specific lift system is calculated based on preliminary measurements carried out on that site or from rules of thumb and tables. As it is not an analytical tool, it cannot predict energy on a time basis or for different configurations. The analytical approach model is used to predict the energy that a certain lift system will consume in one journey by knowing the characteristics of such a lift (e.g. drive type, motor, capacity, gearing, reeving, balancing ratio, system efficiency, etc.). It has the advantage of being able to calculate the energy consumed without having to carry out any measurements on the lift system. It can be used to calculate the energy for a new installation that has not yet been built. This model is also very useful to show the energy reduction, when upgrading a certain lift, or replacing its drive, or motor.

Modelling can be achieved using a traffic simulation program containing an energy model. Many manufacturers and some independent suppliers can offer a simulation facility for traffic analysis. Some of these simulation facilities produce data for the number of stops occurring when simulating a specific traffic pattern. Thus, with the knowledge of the Schroeder TP parameter, equation 13.1 can be applied to determine energy consumption. Some manufacturers are able to offer an energy model for their equipment (Al-Sharif et al., 2004)[4]. These can give an accurate estimation of energy usage.

# 13.7    Estimating the energy consumption of escalators

Although there are exceptions, most escalators generally operate continuously at a constant speed. Escalator energy consumption is dependent on:

— rise

— speed

— step width

— mechanical design

— direction of travel

— number of passengers

— whether passengers walk or not.

Escalator power consumption can be divided into fixed losses and variable losses. Figure 13.4 (Al-Sharif, 1998)[1] diagrammatically illustrates the relationship between the power consumption of an escalator, its rise and the number of passengers boarding per minute.

Variable losses can be positive or negative depending on the direction of travel. Whether passengers walk or not also has an effect on the variable losses and can reduce them by up to 30%.

The fixed losses ($L_f$) in kW·h per day can be calculated, using the following equation (Al-Sharif, 1998)[1]:

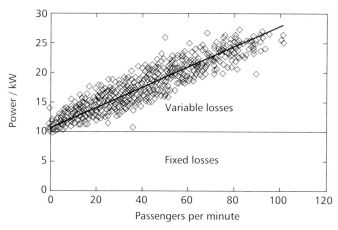

**Figure 13.4** Fixed and variable losses for an up-escalator

$$L_f = (0.55\,R + 1.95)\,H \qquad (13.2)$$

where $R$ is the rise (m) and $H$ is the number of hours of operation (h).

This equation ignores the mechanical design of the escalator. Mechanical design involves the type of bearings (plain or ball), guidance system (chain or wheel) and gearbox (involute or cavex). The majority of escalators use ball bearings, chain guidance and involute gearboxes, for which equation 13.2 applies.

The variable losses ($L_v$) in kW·h per day can be calculated using the following equation (Al-Sharif, 1996)[1]:

$$L_v = \frac{P \times W \times 9.81 \times R}{3600 \times 10^3} \times k \qquad (13.3)$$

where $P$ is the number of passengers using the escalator per day, $R$ is the rise of the escalator (m), $W$ is the average weight of a passenger (kg) and $k$ is the walking factor.

*Note*: the constant $3600 \times 10^3$ is used to convert from joules to kW·h units.

The walking factor ($k$) varies between 0.7 and 1.0 and is used to account for passengers who walk up or down the escalator. The lower value (i.e. 0.7) would apply to a high percentage of walking passengers at a fast pace. The upper value (i.e. 1.0) would apply if there are no walking passengers.

The total daily losses ($L_d$) can be found by taking the fixed daily losses ($L_f$) and adding (for an up escalator) or subtracting (for a down escalator) the variable daily losses ($L_v$).

$$L_d = L_f \pm L_v \qquad (13.4)$$

The total yearly cost can be found by multiplying the figure by the applicable number of days in the year. These could either be 365 days for escalators in public service (e.g. railway stations) or 260 working days per year for commercial premises (e.g. offices).

*Example 13.2*

Calculate the annual energy consumption for an escalator with a rise of 2.5 m running in the down direction, used by 5000 passengers per day. Assume that the average passenger weighs 75 kg and the escalator runs for 10 hours per day, 365 days per year. Ignore the mechanical design of the escalator.

The fixed daily losses energy consumption is calculated from equation 13.2 as follows:

$$L_f = (0.55 \times 2.5 + 1.95) \times 10 = 33.25 \text{ kW·h/day}$$

The variable gains are calculated from equation 13.3:

$$L_v = \frac{5000 \times 75 \times 9.81 \times 2.5}{3600 \times 10^3} \times 0.7 = 1.79 \text{ kW·h/day}$$

This is a down escalator and the net daily consumption will be the difference between the two values and the yearly consumption ($L_a$) will be:

$$L_a = 365\,(33.25 - 1.79) = 11.5 \text{ MW·h/year}$$

It can be seen in general from these examples that the dominant factor for the energy consumption is the fixed losses.

Note the variable losses are averaged over a day and are very small. The fixed daily energy consumption is the significant term. However, during periods of heavy loading this relationship reverses, when the fixed losses may be only 15–20% of the total losses.

## 13.8 Measuring the energy consumption of escalators and moving walks

The ISO working group has suggested that the energy consumption of an escalator or moving walk can be performed by running the equipment in various modes. They suggest the equipment is run in automatic mode in both directions and under no load. The standby current, peak (starting) current and high/low speed currents (if fitted) should be measured and recorded. The energy consumed for 30 minutes in each direction should also be recorded.

## 13.9 Measures to conserve energy

Vertical transportation systems should be upgraded every 10–15 years to improve passenger service, increase reliability and performance, and particularly to reduce energy consumption. The following measures should be taken into account when designing energy efficient vertical transportation systems. To take proper account of some of these measures requires specialist knowledge applied to the specific application.

### 13.9.1 Lifts

Lift motors do not work continuously, nor at constant load. The following measures will help to reduce energy consumption:

— Group lifts together in order to minimise the number of journeys by collecting passengers to travel together.

— Locate lifts in the most appropriate positions and locate stairs before lifts. If passengers pass a well signposted staircase on the way to the lift, the demand for the lift may be less.

— Review the traffic patterns and consider the suitability of the lift traffic controls to the demand. Select the lift control strategy to minimise the number of journeys.

— Select lift speeds that are appropriate to the task, e.g. slower speeds for goods lifts.

— Replace older drives with energy efficient motors. In particular, old Ward-Leonard systems are very inefficient and lead to high energy consumption.

— Select an energy efficient drive for the lift and consider regeneration systems where the energy can be used on site.

— Recover waste heat from lift motor rooms if the lifts are used intensely. Typically the heat generated into the machine space from an electric traction lift is 30% and from an hydraulic lift is 50%. See Table 12.5.

— In some multiple lift installations, it may be advantageous to omit the parking feature, whereby idle lifts are directed to specific floors.

— Consider the possibility of shutting-down some lifts at the end of the working day, when they are idle. This avoids more lifts being in service than are required and eliminates the controller standby consumption.

— Consider reducing car lighting and ventilation, when passengers are not being carried.

## 13.9.2    Escalators and moving walks

Unlike lifts, most escalators and passenger conveyors operate continuously once they have been started up. The following measures will help to reduce energy consumption:

— Delay starting escalators for as long as is practicable at the beginning of the working day.

— Stop some escalators, when convenient, after peak periods (tidal flow).

— Stop some escalators, when convenient, after normal working hours.

— Use automatic start up switches, or programme multiple escalators, to ensure they only operate when there is a demand.

— Use variable speed escalators and passenger conveyors (see section 10.3.4(b)).

# References

1    Al-Sharif L R The general theory of escalator energy consumption with calculations and examples *Elevator World* (May 1998)

2    Al-Sharif L R Lift safety gear testing without weights: critique and overview *Elevator Technology 12* (ed. A. Lustig) (Tel Aviv: International Association of Elevator Engineers) (2002)

3    Al-Sharif L R Lift energy consumption — general overview 1974-2001 *Elevator Technology 14* (ed. A.Lustig) (Tel Aviv: International Association of Elevator Engineers) (2004)

4    Al-Sharif L R, Peters R D and Smith R Elevator Energy Simulation Model *Elevator Technology 14* (ed. A.Lustig) (Tel Aviv: International Association of Elevator Engineers) (2004)

5    Council Directive 93/76/EEC of 13 September 1993 to limit carbon dioxide emissions by improving energy efficiency (SAVE) *Official J. of the European Communities* L237 22/09/1993 28–30 (1993)

6    CIBSE Guide F: *Energy efficiency in buildings* (London: Chartered Institution of Building Services Engineers) (2004)

7    Doolaard D A Energy consumption of different types of lift drive system *Elevator Technology 4* (ed. G.C. Barney) (Stockport: IAEE Publications) (1992)

8    Electrical and Mechanical Services Department *Guidelines on energy efficiency of lift and escalator installations* (Hong Kong: Electrical and Mechanical Services Department) (2000) (www.emsd.gov.hk)

9    Electrical and Mechanical Services Department *Code of practice for energy efficiency of lift and escalator installations* (Hong Kong: Electrical and Mechanical Services Department (2000) (www.emsd.gov.hk)

10    Proposal for a Directive of the European Parliament and of the Council on the energy performance of buildings (COM(2001) 226 final — 2001/0098(COD)) *Official J. of the European Communities* C231E 31/07/2001 266 (2001)

13    *V3F — The green power* (Hounslow: Kone Ltd) (date unknown)

11    Schroeder J The energy consumption of elevators *Elevator Technology I* (ed. G.C. Barney) (Chichester: Ellis Horwood) (1986)

12    Stawinoga R Designing for reduced energy elevator costs *Lift Technology I* (ed. G.C.Barney) (Stockport: IAEE Publications) (1994)

# 14    Remote monitoring and alarms

## Principal authors

Dennis Burrell (TVC Monitoring)
Charles Salter (ACE Lifts Ltd.)
Dr Gina Barney (Gina Barney Associates)

## Section contents

| | | |
|---|---|---|
| 14.1 | The reason for monitoring and alarms | 14-3 |
| 14.2 | General features of lift monitoring systems | 14-3 |
| 14.3 | Benefits of remote monitoring | 14-4 |
| 14.4 | Definitions | 14-5 |
| 14.5 | Estate management | 14-5 |
| | 14.5.1   General outstation features | 14-5 |
| | 14.5.2   Basic outstation signals | 14-6 |
| | 14.5.3   Management system | 14-6 |
| | 14.5.4   Bureau or third party management | 14-7 |
| | 14.5.5   Reduced monitoring and basic monitoring | 14-7 |
| 14.6 | Group systems | 14-7 |
| 14.7 | Interfacing with building management systems (BMS) | 14-8 |
| | 14.7.1   BMS systems | 14-8 |
| | 14.7.2   Benefits of connection with a BMS | 14-8 |
| | 14.7.3   Linking into a BMS | 14-9 |
| 14.8 | Remote alarms | 14-9 |
| 14.9 | Communications systems and interconnection protocols | 14-11 |
| 14.10 | Escalators and moving walks | 14-11 |
| References | | 14-11 |

# 14      Remote monitoring and alarms

## 14.1      The reason for monitoring and alarms

Microprocessors provide an inexpensive means of monitoring vertical transportation systems and accumulating data for immediate or later analysis. This chapter offers some guidelines on remote monitoring and remote alarms and suggests ways in which the resulting data can be used to improve the efficiency of vertical transportation systems, reduce their costs and allow them to be interfaced with other systems within the building and increase the safety of all users.

The term 'remote monitoring' has been used to cover a wide variety of systems ranging from simple alarm pushes, through manually initiated voice calls to fully automated computerised systems. This wide variety of systems arises in an attempt to meet the three different and distinct market sectors: estate management, group management and passenger safety (alarm) systems. These requirements can overlap for specific applications and may require a degree of integration between systems.

The first sector, which is dealt with in section 14.5, arises from the need to manage a large volume of dispersed lifts of varying manufacture owned by local authorities, private housing associations, airports etc. The primary requirement being that of fault indication coupled with the gathering of extensive management information and the transfer of this detailed data back to a central computer system, or third party bureau application.

The second sector, section 14.6, is applicable to group systems, generally from the same manufacture, operating in a form of campus situation. In addition to the remote monitoring described in the first sector above, these systems are more closely integrated with the lifts being monitored, being from the same manufacturer, and can offer technical optimisation, configuration and remote control of the lifts.

The third sector is based on the requirements to comply with the provision of alarm systems to ensure passenger safety, for instance the trapped persons within a lift car. These systems connect to a fully attended rescue service.

The first and second market sectors are optional, whereas the third is a mandatory requirement to ensure compliance with the Lifts Regulations[5] for all lifts first put into service after July 2003. The applicable standard is BS EN 81-28: 2003: *Remote alarm on passenger and goods passenger lifts*[2]. Section 14.8 gives details.

Although lift and escalator/moving walk monitoring systems enable building owners to self-manage lift systems, not all building managers want or need this facility. Most major suppliers offer a monitoring service which simply reports the main facts.

In summary remote monitoring and remote alarms can provide:

— *Fault monitoring*: informing the building owner or service company immediately the equipment has broken down; faster response, less down-time

— *Condition based monitoring*: monitoring the number of starts and hours in service remotely allows data to be processed for efficient, selective, planned, maintenance.

— *Video monitoring*: use of a small camera to record and transmit compressed images.

— *Data logging*: graphical analysis of types of faults, fault comparisons on a unit by unit basis.

— *Monitoring site personnel safety*: for example, logging-in during attendance, service personnel could periodically reset a 'watchdog' alarm.

— *Alarms and vandalism*: locations such as the machine room, car top, inside of a lift car etc. can be event-triggered and monitored for an unauthorised entry.

Although much of this chapter is based around lift remote monitoring the similar principles can be applied to the monitoring of escalators and other passenger sensitive equipment. Section 14.10 gives some guidance.

## 14.2      General features of lift monitoring systems

A remote monitoring system for a lift or escalator/moving walk comprises monitoring units, communication systems and management systems. The overall system may be designed to monitor one or more data sources: alarms, faults, events and information.

Figure 14.1 provides an outline of a computerised lift monitoring system. The general features of such a system should include:

— indication of lift-in-service status

— trapped passenger alarms

— lift alarm integrity check

— performance indication

— early transmission of alarms and status to the lift maintenance contractor's monitoring and control centre

— automatic collection of lift performance data

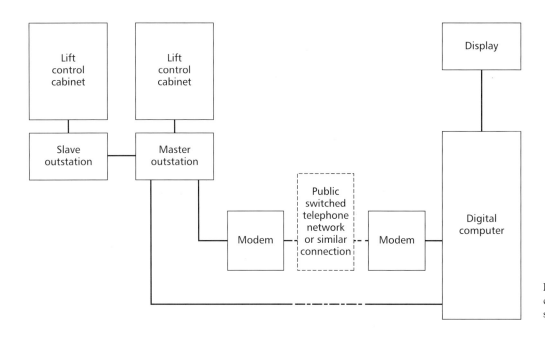

**Figure 14.1** Outline of a computerised lift monitoring system

— two-way voice communication with trapped passengers

— remote configuration of field units

— ability to conduct 'on-line' investigation and analysis of lift activity

— optional measurement of levelling performance

— statistical report generation.

# 14.3 Benefits of remote monitoring

There are benefits of remote monitoring to the users (passengers), building owner/operator, maintainers and design and development teams.

Benefits to passengers:

— increased safety and security

— increased availability and reliability

— quicker action in the event of complaints.

Benefits to the building owner/operator:

— increased safety and security

— increased availability and reliability

— faster response to callbacks

— achievement of maximum performance

— establishment of condition maintenance programmes

— provides information to enable owner personnel to determine the status of their equipment

— 24-hour assistance for trapped passengers

— 24-hour protection against accidental or deliberate damage

— direct communication with: lift maintenance contractor's monitoring control centre; call centre; bureau etc.

Benefits to the lift maintainer:

— provides protection to service base

— provides information to enable field service personnel to correct faults more quickly

— faster response to problems

— assists in identifying genuine call-backs where a performance related contract is in operation

— elimination of repetitive breakdowns

— detection and reduction of intermittent fault conditions

— anticipation of breakdown

— achievement of maximum performance

— improved fault detection and monitoring of maintenance procedures.

Benefits to design engineers and research and development teams:

— provides feedback from the field to assist with future development

— provides feedback from the field to improve and develop computer-based traffic analysis programs and simulation software.

There is a danger of collecting so much data that it cannot be assessed and therefore will not be acted upon. A clearly defined management approach is necessary if this is to be avoided.

# 14.4 Definitions

The only standard available which addresses the monitoring of lifts, escalators and moving walks is BS EN 617: 1995: *Data logging and monitoring of lifts, escalators and passenger conveyors*[3]. This standard has not been widely accepted and many lift companies and component suppliers have developed their own standards. BS EN 617 does, however, provide some definitions. These are paraphrased below.

— *Alarm*: alarm device specified in BS EN 81-1/2: 1998[1] and BS EN 81-28: 2003[2]; e.g. an alarm could be a passenger entrapment. This is an urgent category.

— *Fault*: malfunction within the installation which may cause a degradation of, or interruption to, the normal operation of the installation, e.g. a fault could be lock circuit interrupted. This is an urgent category.

— *Event*: occurrence within an installation, envisaged in the installation design, which is not a malfunction, but which may cause a degradation of, or interruption to, the normal operation of the installation, e.g. an event could be equipment on inspection control. This is not an urgent category.

— *Data logging equipment*: equipment which extracts and records by time and date, either permanently or temporarily, data relating to the operation of an installation, e.g. an outstation.

— *Monitoring equipment*: equipment connected to, and which interrogates the data logging equipment for the purpose of displaying fault and/or event information derived from the data recorded by the data logging equipment, e.g. a remote monitoring station.

## 14.5 Estate management

These systems are provided to owners, who have management responsibilities but little technical involvement over the lift stock. Generally the range and volume of lifts include lifts of varying manufacture, type and age. The remote monitoring system is required to integrate these lifts, provide a basic set of information to indicate faults, status and performance. The receiving central system should perform data acquisition, statistical calculations from site history files, alarm management, operator display and control. This enables the lift owner or operator to maintain the equipment to a high standard, offer immediate response to equipment failure, economically plan repair and refurbishment work and predict potential equipment failure.

### 14.5.1 General outstation features

The on-site remote monitoring outstation should be configured by means of digital logic and a decision table of dependencies to detect fault conditions and determine other status conditions. The transitory nature of many of the important lift signals means that simple signal monitoring is insufficient to successfully monitor all fault conditions. The application of conditional logic is required to transform the changing lift signals into deduced fault conditions; for example, the monitoring of the door lock circuit signal. This is only available at certain stages of the lifts operation and the on/off operation of the signal is therefore dependent on the stage of the lift cycle. To detect a fault with this signal it is therefore necessary to take into account the current stage of the lift cycle. Another example is the monitoring of a signal such as the landing push feed and the loss of this signal should be disregarded in times of the lift being isolated, on test control etc.

The outstation software should be configurable to meet the varying operational features of different manufacturers lift controllers. The outstation should also be capable of recording and storing this data in real time. The outstation should also act as a diagnostic tool for the on site service personnel offering access to the most recent fault conditions and the events leading up to it. This can provide a common form of logging regardless of the type of lift installed.

The outstation should offer a means of downloading the stored information locally, or more generally, to be able to transmit the data back to the central processing management system. The outstation should support various means of data transmission appropriate to the site installation. Typically this would be an autodial modem connection for estate type installations and a network connection for the more compact type of campus installation.

Data transmission should be filtered between alarm, fault and events with only defined alarms and faults causing the initiation of a transmission. This filtering of data reduces the volume of transmissions to the essential minimum.

The main outstation features, which should be available are given below:

— Realisation by logical sequence of lift fault conditions.

— Alarm, fault and event data classification.

— Data defined and recorded with actual time and date.

— Transmission of trapped passenger alarms, filtered to reduce false alarms, but with safety override.

— Operator configuration of the data transmission priority.

— Various means of transmission appropriate to the installation.

— Outstation to offer opto-isolated signal protection or similar.

— Operation to be fully battery backed (at least one hour).

— Indication of main power supply lost.

— Service personnel log-on to outstation facility.

— Service personnel offered access to recent event log via keypad or lap-top etc..

— Basic traffic analysis.

— Remote access and configuration.

— Access protection (password) for both local and remote interrogation.

— An ability to suspend recording when service personnel have logged onto site in order to inhibit false event generation whilst working on the lift.

— Capable of expansion to incorporate additional lift signals to enable targeted monitoring to the users specific requirements.

— Indication of communication failure.

## 14.5.2    Basic outstation signals

The number of input signal points monitored is not directly related to the number of events that can be generated. Event generation is determined by signals that are monitored in both stationary and in-motion conditions. The list below indicates some of the signals that should be monitored.

— alarm signal
— safety circuit chain
— door opening and closing signals and associated timing requirements
— car and landing door safety circuits
— door zone
— landing push feed
— direction signals.
— mains and controller supplies
— test, fire and independent control
— service personnel on site
— total power cut.

In addition some outstation defined events should be included:

— outstation supply lost
— back-up battery condition
— detection of an excessive number of events being generated by an outstation
— indication of transmission interruptions or failures.

There are some output signals:

— top and bottom landing floor call generation.

These signals are necessary to determine whether a lift is in an operational condition. This can only be determined by causing the lift to move and open and shut its doors. These calls can be generated to assess this and also used to verify alarm trappings etc. These calls must be only operational when the lift is in normal operating condition and inhibited at all other times.

Examples of the conditions that an outstation should deduce are:

— doors failed to open on journey completion
— alarm trapping detected
— doors not closed in predetermined time
— number of journey and door operations
— motor run time exceeded
— primary safety circuit failure
— controller supply failure
— logic supply failure.

## 14.5.3    Management system

These can be found in varying forms and configurations, but should be capable of receiving outstation data transmissions and also provide remote access to them. The system should support screens to offer an immediate indication of fault conditions, an ability to review and analyse past history both to the screen and in report form and a means of connecting directly to a selected outstation to monitor the current operation condition and movement of each lift.

The general system requirements should include the following:

— The system should support various user connections both local and remote (see Figure 14.2). This can include connection to a bureau or third party system.
— Fault monitors to provide immediate indication of fault conditions (see Figure 14.3).
— Additional screens indicating fault and status indication.

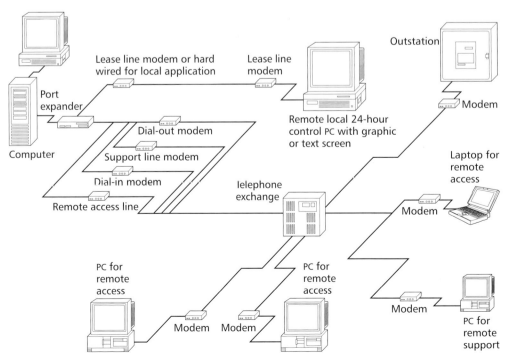

**Figure 14.2** Example of an extensive monitoring system

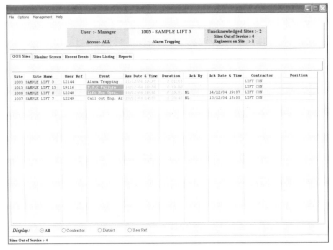

**Figure 14.3** Typical fault indication

— Dynamic on-line, real-time display of lift operations.

— Fault acknowledgement to alert other system users that action has been taken on a current fault.

— Raw data configured by system and displayed on various screens and individual site files.

— Statistical report functions where data is configured into readily available user reports.

— Dynamic on-line interrogation of the outstations.

— Determining of outstation communications integrity.

— Battery back up and associated clean system shutdown in event of power failure.

— Automatic restart on power return.

— System back-up.

Statistical reports are by user specification, but it is recommended that the minimum should include:

— Equipment availability analysis and percentage of time out of service (see Figure 14.4).

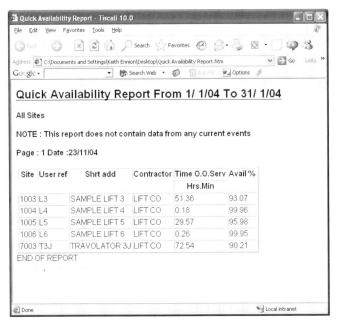

**Figure 14.4** Equipment availability analysis

— Determining and totalling of fault conditions per site to assist repair programmes.

— Breakdown reports for worst performing sites.

— Individual event logs and analysis.

The ownership of and access to some monitored data can be contentious or commercially sensitive. As lift systems provide more detailed reports of their operation, monitoring data become an indication of the performance of both the installation and of its maintenance. The lift supplier may consider that the data are provided only for the purposes of design and maintenance. Naturally, the owner and the consultant may want to review the extent of these data. Many owners are capable of generating reports and graphs using spreadsheets, word processors and mathematical analysis application programs. All the necessary data for an owner to do this should be provided by the lift monitoring system.

### 14.5.4 Bureau or third party management

In this section based on 'estate management' the central management system would generally be managed and operated by the owner. However in some instances a bureau or third party connection may be required. Variations on this can include:

— remote digital connection to the management system for 24-hour, or out-of-hours call centre, maintenance company etc.

— bureau or call centre managing the system offering fault condition activation and generation of management information

— links to other services management systems

— web based applications.

### 14.5.5 Reduced monitoring and basic monitoring

In some instances it is more applicable, especially for smaller equipment volume applications, to use a form of reduced monitoring. This would, determine the true lift operational condition by monitoring the same signal configuration as for the full system above. This is necessary in order to achieve the all required inputs and maintain safety requirements. The outstation can then offer reduced event indication of operational conditions but without defined fault information. Reduced monitoring that does not meet the signal input requirements would basically offer only input failures without any conditional logic applied.

## 14.6 Grouped systems

Lift remote monitoring can also be defined for use with grouped control systems. However there is a requirement to differentiate between this and the above 'estate management', which represents true lift monitoring. Grouped systems are generally installed in a campus situation with the lift controllers and the lift monitoring system from the same manufacture. These systems are generally managed by building occupiers. The 'monitoring' interface is generally an always on connection. The actual fault monitoring relates to loss of power supplies, alarms operated etc., but with no logical determination of other running fault conditions. In these circumstances it is possible for the controller based fault logger to pass events directly to the outstation. However, this technique is only suitable for group systems as in an estate management system it would lead to varying and non-standard monitoring.

Group systems do provide some extra advantages:

— traffic reports: response times, percentiles, number of calls, etc.

— security feature to enable/disable access to specified landings

— examples of real time display of lift activity (see Figure 14.5).

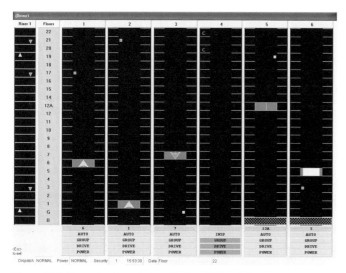

**Figure 14.5** Example of a real time display of lift activity

# 14.7 Interfacing with building management systems

## 14.7.1 Building management systems

Most building management system (BMS) manufacturers promote themselves as supporters of the philosophy of open architecture and increasingly, building management systems are being used to integrate the operation of systems other than heating, ventilation and air conditioning within buildings, and interfaces are being installed for lift systems, fire, security and lighting control. Information from the various systems is then presented in a co-ordinated manner via the BMS supervisor.

In some lift monitoring systems the possibilities for the lift data to reach the end user (e.g. the building owner) is limited. The lift and escalator industry can take advantage of the considerable success and widespread application of building management systems, which are now almost a standard item of equipment within the heating, ventilation, refrigeration and air conditioning industry.

Generally, a building management system consists of one or more microprocessor-based outstations (or network

control units). Outstations are equipped with input and output points which control and monitor the operation of the heating, ventilation and air conditioning plant etc, see Figure 14.6.

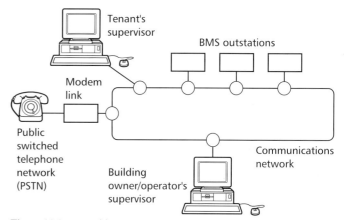

**Figure 14.6** BMS architecture

Outstations are distributed throughout the building in close proximity to the items of plant under control. They can work independently and are usually supplied from uninterruptible power supplies (UPS) to ensure they can operate during a power failure.

The whole system can be managed from a digital computer loaded with the BMS operating system, known as a supervisor (or operator workstation). Through the supervisor, the user can gain access to any equipment within the whole BMS to accomplish the tasks of monitoring, control and statistics retrieval. There can be as many BMS supervisors as are required, e.g. one in the shift duty control room, one in the building management manager's office and one inside the maintenance workshop.

The outstations and management systems are linked by a high speed local area network (LAN), allowing them to communicate continuously with each other. Remote outstations and the management systems can be connected over the public switched telephone network (PSTN) via a modem link.

## 14.7.2 Benefits of connection with a BMS

There are considerable benefits to be gained by connecting any service into a BMS and the following advantages should be noted:

— *Common user interface*: the lift system may be accessed using a standard interface, which is common to other services within the building, e.g. fire and security.

— *Cost savings*: a standard interconnection between the lift monitoring system and the BMS.

— *Space savings*: often there is insufficient space for more than one display terminal and keyboard. High-resolution monitors and multiple-task software allows a single display terminal to be used.

— *Multiple access point*: the BMS communications network may be used to access the lift monitoring system from more than one supervisor computer within the building, e.g. security office, facilities manager's office etc. In such cases the lift system must connect into the BMS network and not directly to the BMS control station.

— *Use of common software packages*: software for BMS is often integrated with other software such as word-processing, spreadsheets, graphics, databases and statistical packages. These may be used to aid the processing and improve the presentation of lift system data.

Co-ordination between the BMS and lift manufacturers often takes place after contracts have been awarded. Thus, the possibilities of linking into a BMS are frequently considered too late in the design process.

### 14.7.3 Linking into a BMS

The two main methods of interconnecting the BMS and the lift system are either at outstation or central system end. The lift monitoring outstation can be linked to the other services outstation by:

— 'no volt' relay contacts and hard wire connection

— digital inputs

— serial link connection

— outstation integration.

A schematic of such a system is shown in Figure 14.7.

Alternatively a central system link can be achieved by:

— Connecting the lift monitoring outstation onto an existing other service or BMS network by means of interface or integrator with associated a software programme loaded onto central digital computer.

— Establish a link between the two central systems with appropriate data transfer programme.

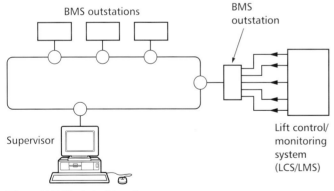

**Figure 14.7** Hardwired interface

## 14.8    Remote alarms

Clause 14.2.3 of BS EN 81-1/2: 1998[1] requires the provision of an emergency alarm device to ensure compliance with the Lifts Regulations 1997[5]. These requirements are sparse and have given rise to ambiguity. To clarify this, BS EN 81-28: 2003[2] was published to replace clause 14.2.3 *in toto*. Although this standard is relatively short its requirements are complex.

Basically the standard requires that an alarm system is provided at all times that a lift is in service, in order to ensure the rescue of trapped persons This is regarded as a foreseeable event. The alarm system is to be permanently connected to a permanently available rescue service, who must respond within five minutes (under normal circumstances) by a voice communication with the entrapped persons. The rescue service is to intervene on site within one hour (under normal circumstances) of the alarm being raised.

The standard also states that trapped person is required to 'be released within the shortest possible time.' However, an integrity check of the equipment is only required 'by the safety of the users ... at least every three days'. This latter requirement means that a person could be trapped for three days before the system is checked. And then they will need to be discovered and released. It is recommended that owners instigate an integrity check more frequently than this and should the test fail that a positive intervention on site is initiated.

Figure 14.8 illustrates by means of a flow chart and accompanying text the sequence of operations, when an alarm is being processed. The numbers in parenthesis indicate clauses in BS EN 81-28.

When an alarm system is installed there should be an exchange of information between the installer, the owner, the rescue service and the user.

After the completion of the lift installation, the following information should be given to the building owner (the numbers in parenthesis indicate clauses in BS EN 81-28):

— that they must ensure that the lift is connected to a rescue service (5.2)

— all the site information is passed to the rescue service (5.2)

— the need to keep the equipment in working order, and to remove the lift from service when the equipment is out of order (5.2)

— minimum maintenance requirements of the alarm system (5.2)

— how to change dialling parameters, e.g. telephone numbers (5.2).

Information, which should be provided by the owner to the rescue service includes:

— general information of the system with reference to BS EN 81-28 (5.3)

— the need to establish a continuous 2-way communication with trapped users (5.3)

— the address & location of the lift (5.3)

— building organisation, and availability of on-site rescue service (5.3)

— access details for the building and lift (5.3)

— special risks for entering building and lift (5.3)

— compatibility between equipment. (5.3)

— time limit of emergency power supply unit (5.3)

A sign provided in the lift to provide passenger information:

'This lift is equipped with an alarm system and linked with a rescue service' (7)

**To be read in conjunction with flowchart, Figure 14.8**

- Alarm button pressed by passenger (once) to initiate an alarm call.

- No further action is required by passenger.

- The alarm equipment checks that it is a valid alarm before dialling rescue service. *Note*: the rescue service reception equipment must be compatible with site alarm equipment.

- Filter alarm (4.1.5):
  —　Is the lift in door zone, e.g. with the doors fully open?
  —　Is the lift is moving and doors will open at the next landing stop?

- Alarm Call filtering inhibited during maintenance, repair and/or manual test. (4.1.1, 5.2)

- Alarm Call filtering void when between acknowledgement and end of alarm. (4.1.1)

- Once the alarm equipment verifies a valid alarm call (4.1.5) the unit immediately places itself into alarm mode.

- The alarm equipment can then put out a message in the lift car to the passenger(s), e.g:
  'Your call has been accepted please wait while we connect you'

- Yellow indicator to illuminate (4.1.4 and BS EN 81-70:2003, 5.4.4.3)

- The alarm equipment dials the rescue service reception equipment. If the first number is unobtainable then alternative number(s) would immediately be called (4.2.1). *Note*: each of these numbers must be connect to the reception equipment, not only the telephone handset.

- The rescue service will answer the call.

- The reception equipment identifies and records the site and location of the lift.

- Acknowledgement to the alarm equipment that the call has been received.

- Green indicator to illuminate.

- The rescue service will contact the rescuer and inform them of any relevant information (5.3).

- Whilst the rescue service is travelling to site, the rescue service reception speak regularly with the trapped passenger(s) to inform them of the status of the rescue operation.

- The rescue service arrives on site.

- The rescue service promptly releases the trapped passenger(s).

- After releasing all the passengers, the rescue service reception is informed using the voice unit in the lift car.

- The alarm system is reset. *Note*: the reset button/switch/key is located on the lift installation, inaccessible to unauthorised persons.

- The button/switch/key will generate an end of alarm message before hanging up (4.1.2).

**Automatic checks to be made by alarm unit**

- Where a rechargeable emergency electrical power supply is used, the reception equipment will be informed automatically that the alarm system has less than one hour of function remaining (4.1.3).

- The alarm equipment must check the system automatically with a simulated input signal at least every 3 days (4.2.1).

**Manual checks**

- Manual tests should be carried out periodically by the maintenance company or building owner.

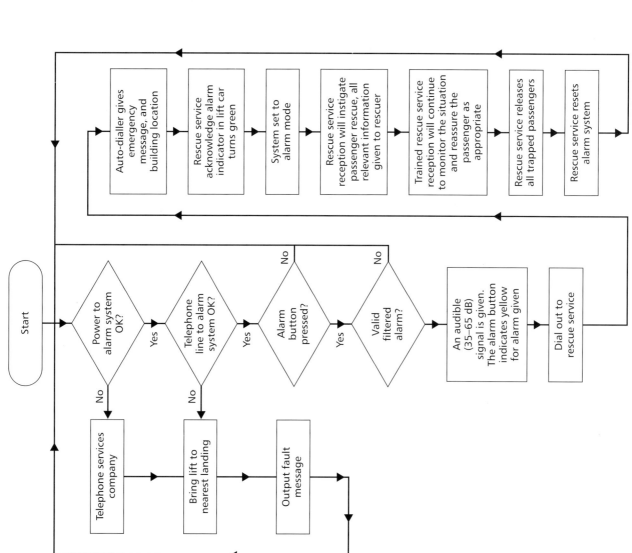

**Figure 14.8** Operation of a remote alarm: flowchart and description (figures in parenthesis refer to BS EN 81-28[2])

## 14.9 Communication systems and interconnection protocols

The outstation and the central management unit must be connected together to form the complete system. Often this uses the public switched telephone network (PSTN) via a modem link (see section 14.7.1). In other cases a network connection is used.

The protocol by which two computer systems inter-communicate consists of a comprehensive definition of all aspects of the connection including both the electrical and mechanical features of the connectors. Manufacturers often state that their protocol complies with the ISO 7-layer model[4]. In no way does this imply that such a system will communicate with any other system, although it may aid the design of communications interfaces between systems. Therefore, it is recommended that the remote monitoring equipment manufacturers agree the level of functionality with the owner, which is to be achieved by their interconnection. This must be based on a written protocol specification.

There are a number of competing systems offering network protocols which aim to provide a standard communications protocol. The ISO 7-layer model provides only a framework for the implementation of network standards. Commercial systems implementing standardised protocols defined by standards organisations include: BACnet, BITBUS, CANopen, CEBus, IEC Fieldbus, Interbus, LonWorks, P-NET, Profibus and WorldFIP.

Such standards may eventually lead to the full integration of all building services with the internal transportation systems. Adoption of standard communications or open communications protocols is a contentious issue within the lift industry, although it has been difficult to accomplish in the BMS industry. Standard systems will give the customer a choice of suppliers for the same components, ranging from push buttons to control systems. Some consultants see standard protocols as the means by which they can provide an integrated system without restricting their clients to a single supplier. Understandably, many lift manufacturers are wary of standard protocols. apart from commercial considerations, the integrity of systems may fall outside their control.

## 14.10 Escalators and moving walks

Many escalators and moving walks suffer from being out of service as a result of not being reset after a nuisance operation of the emergency stop button. Such a delay accumulates down time. Remote monitoring brings many advantages to all operators of such equipment, e.g. railway, underground, retail etc. Escalator and moving walk monitoring is included briefly within BS EN 627[3]. Much of the guidance above is applicable.

## References

1     BS EN 81-1: 1998: *Safety rules for the construction and installation of lifts. Electric lifts*; BS EN 81-2: 1998: *Safety rules for the construction and installation of lifts. Hydraulic lifts* (London: British Standards Institution) (1998)

2     BS EN 81-28: 2003: *Remote alarm on passenger and goods passenger lifts* (London: British Standards Institution) (2003)

3     BS EN 627: 1996: *Specification for data logging and monitoring of lifts, escalators and passenger conveyors* (London: British Standards Institution) (1996)

4     BS EN ISO/IEC 7498: *Information technology. Open systems interconnection. Basic reference model*: BS EN ISO/IEC 7498-1: 1995: *The basic model*; BS EN ISO/IEC 7498-2: 1989: *Security architecture*; BS EN ISO/IEC 7498-3: 1989: *Naming and addressing*; BS EN ISO/IEC 7498-4: 1989: *Management framework* (London: British Standards Institution) (dates as indicated)

5     The Lifts Regulations 1997 Statutory Instrument 1997 No. 831 (London: The Stationery Office) (1997)

# 15 Commissioning, preventative maintenance, testing and thorough examination of lifts, escalators and moving walks

## Principal authors

David Cooper (LECS (UK) Ltd.)
Dr Gina Barney (Gina Barney Associates)

## Section contents

| | | |
|---|---|---|
| 15.1 | Introduction | 15-3 |
| 15.2 | Commissioning | 15-3 |
| | 15.2.1 General conditions | 15-3 |
| | 15.2.2 Off-site checks during manufacture | 15-4 |
| | 15.2.3 On-site checks during installation | 15-4 |
| | 15.2.4 Commissioning of lifts | 15-4 |
| | 15.2.5 Commissioning of escalators and moving walks | 15-5 |
| | 15.2.6 On-site checks after completion | 15-6 |
| 15.3 | Preventative maintenance | 15-6 |
| | 15.3.1 Why maintain? | 15-6 |
| | 15.3.2 Maintenance contracts | 15-8 |
| 15.4 | Thorough examination and testing | 15-8 |
| | 15.4.1 General | 15-8 |
| | 15.4.2 Thorough examination of lifts | 15-9 |
| | 15.4.3 Periodic testing of lifts | 15-9 |
| | 15.4.4 Thorough examination of escalators and moving walks | 15-11 |
| 15.5 | Documentation | 15-11 |
| References | | 15-11 |

# 15     Commissioning, preventative maintenance, testing and thorough examination of lifts, escalators and moving walks

## 15.1     Introduction

The proper commissioning, thorough examination, inspection and preventive maintenance of lifts, escalators and moving walks is critical to ensure that they are correctly installed and are then inspected and maintained in order to achieve longevity, reliability and safety. The capital cost of such equipment is high. Ensuring that it gives the maximum service life possible, considering its design and quality of manufacture, is essential. The purchaser of any installation should bear in mind that quality differs from manufacturer to manufacturer and the life expectancy of any installation is directly linked to this as well as to correct maintenance and inspection. This chapter outlines the concepts behind the commissioning of new and modernised, or upgraded, equipment and details the subsequent preventative maintenance requirements during their operational life. It identifies the various regulatory requirements with regard to thorough examination/inspection and explains their role in the safe operation of lift, escalator and moving walk systems.

It should be understood that the roles of commissioning, thorough examination, inspection and maintenance are often undertaken by different persons. Many people are confused by these different aspects. The free Health and Safety Executive publication *Simple guidance for lift owners*[20] (available from www.hsebooks.co.uk) gives a layperson's interpretation of these aspects and valuable guidance to dutyholders.

For the purposes of this Guide, the main terms are defined as follows:

—     *Commissioning*: final work on an installation prior to putting into service of a new or upgraded installation.

—     *Thorough examination*: systematic and detailed examination to detect any defects which are or might become dangerous.

—     *Inspection*: visual and functional checks to determine that the equipment is operating correctly. *Note*: the extent of the inspection is dependent on the potential risk that could arise from the equipment.

—     *Preventative maintenance*: making of routine adjustments, replacing worn or damaged parts, topping up fluids, etc. to ensure the equipment is in an efficient and safe working condition

All these aspects include some element of *testing*, which includes checking the correct operation of various components, often to their maximum ratings.

A final important note to remember is that all the operations discussed in this chapter require persons to work on equipment. At all times they should work safely.

Attention is therefore drawn to the requirements of the Provision and Use of Work Equipment Regulations 1998[24] ('PUWER Regulations'), the Management of Health and Safety at Work Regulations 1999[23] ('MHSAW Regulations') and the guidance given in BS 7255: *Safe working on lifts*[15] and in BS 7801: *Safe working on escalators and moving walks*[16].

## 15.2     Commissioning

### 15.2.1     General conditions

Commissioning is the process of testing an installation to ensure that it meets its specification and complies with recognised standards and legislation. Various types of building services require to be commissioned to simulate the conditions which they will meet when they enter service. Lifts, escalators and moving walks are no different and the early detection of possible defects can be critical to ensuring that the design life expectancy is achieved. Guidance to achieve a successful installation can be found in two Codes of Practice: BS 5655: Part 6: *Selection and installation of new lifts*[8] and BS 5656: Part 2: *Selection, installation and location of new escalators and moving walks*[14].

Commissioning covers those activities undertaken to ensure compliance with the specified requirements. Within the framework of the Health and Safety at Work Act 1974[18], the Lifts Regulations 1997[22] and the Supply of Machinery (Safety) Regulations 1992[26], a supplier has a responsibility to ensure that supplied goods are suitable for the stated intended purpose and in compliance with the relevant Essential Health and Safety Requirements (EHSRs) as endorsed by the CE-marking of a complete system or safety components.

This is in addition to the contractual responsibility to ensure that the goods are in accordance with the contract specification. Therefore lift and escalator manufacturers normally undertake their own systems of checks at various stages within the contract. The relevant design standard for the equipment (e.g. the BS EN 81-1/2[3,4] series of harmonised standards or BS EN 115[6]) may also recommend certain site tests to be undertaken on completion of the installation work.

The client may also supplement these systems with inspections by their personnel or by a third party. Such third parties may be insurance companies, inspection organisations or consultancies which specialise in lift and/or escalator/moving walk systems. The intention to carry out such inspections should be specified in the early stages of the contract negotiation so that adequate provisions can be incorporated.

A prerequisite to commissioning is the possession of the relevant contract documents including dimensioned drawings and specifications, together with details of all agreed changes effected since origination, together with access to the technical file required by the Lifts Regulations 1997 and Supply of Machinery (Safety) Regulations 1992. In practice, even final installation drawings are commonly amended on site by agreement with those present at the time.

Specifications provide the contractual means by which specific requirements are recorded by the parties involved. In their most basic form, they may be based on a manufacturer's catalogue or a standard such as the BS EN 81 series or BS EN 115. Specifications are also used to define particular requirements such as the desired performance or the handling characteristics. In some cases it may be necessary to define the environmental standards required, which are described in Chapter 12 of this Guide.

The documentation prepared by the supplier should be checked to ensure compliance with the purchaser's requirements. Often this stage reveals oversights of detail known only to the client, or the innocent inclusion of minor variations by the supplier in order to match a standard product item.

The preliminaries having been duly agreed, the manufacture of the lift, escalator or moving walk unit commences in the knowledge of the client's requirements. There are a number of intermediate checks that can be undertaken during manufacture, including manufacturing base visits and site inspections. However, the main check is generally the commissioning test undertaken upon completion of the unit. Broadly the sequence is:

— off-site checks, during manufacture

— on-site checks, during installation

— on-site commissioning

— on-site checks on completion.

## 15.2.2    Off-site checks during manufacture

For all supply organisations, the manufacture of a lift, escalator or moving walk involves a combination of buying-in manufactured components and producing components from raw materials. Reputable manufacturers will have systems of tests and controls, within the production cycle, to ensure compliance with specified requirements. These may relate to the purchase of materials, components or subassemblies, machining or fabricating processes, packaging, storage, transportation, installation etc. The systems are tailored to the organisation's general production requirements but may be supplemented by special conditions to meet the purchaser's requirements.

For standard lift units, the benefits of imposing additional or special tests during this stage of supply rarely justify the expenditure involved. Such tests are normally recommended only where the unit is beyond the manufacturer's normal range, e.g. some special configuration, or where significant development risks are involved.

Many manufacturers have quality management systems. Where these are in place, it is common to find 'manufacturing quality plans' which cover materials, drawings, processes, equipment etc. and the manufacturing interfaces during production. Such systems, if developed within a quality conscious manufacturing environment, afford increased assurance to the purchaser.

## 15.2.3    On-site checks during installation

After factory testing, pre-assembled lift components and escalator/moving walk units will be transported, perhaps over long distances, transferred across a building site or through a building and hauled into position, all of which may result in the need for adjustment or realignment. Pre-assembled components will then be connected to other components, structures and a power supply to produce the final installation.

Lifts are generally supplied to the site as consignments of components for assembly/reassembly in the lift well. Prior to the commencement of the installation, the manufacturer should carry out checks on the lift well within which the equipment is to be installed to verify its general alignment, finish, dimensions, location of fixings etc. Additionally, manufacturers normally undertake intermediate tests and checks at various stages during installation.

Alignment tolerances for lifts are becoming increasingly critical due to the increased emphasis on quality of ride, the tendency towards higher running speeds, and the development of steel framed buildings and 'fast-track' building techniques. This is particularly true for car and counterweight guide rails and the relative positions of the machine. Manufacturers have developed schedules for checking these items since errors left undetected until completion are expensive and time consuming to correct. Similarly, alignment and fixing of landing door equipment, door locks, fixings for lift well switches and other internal equipment will be checked at appropriate stages during installation when the respective items are easily accessible. It is normal practice to document these checks, together with the relevant documentation (i.e. drawings, specification, procedures etc.).

The majority of escalators and moving walks are supplied to site preassembled. Accordingly, checks on standard units during the installation process are generally confined to structural alignment and positional accuracy of fixings. Usually it is only special units that require extensive site assembly, such as the unusually long units required in transportation facilities such as airports and underground railway systems. In this case the installer will carry out various checks and tests prior to final commissioning.

## 15.2.4    Commissioning of lifts

### 15.2.4.1    New electric traction lifts

For new traction lifts specified to the BS EN 81 series of harmonised standards there is a requirement under Annex D (normative) for examinations and tests before putting into service and the CE-marking applied. In that document, a number of tests are defined which need to be undertaken to ensure that the lift is functioning properly and has been installed to a satisfactory standard which complies with the specification and meets the requirements of current standards and legislation. These tests include:

— landing door locking devices

— electrical safety devices/systems

— suspension elements

— braking system

— measurement of speed and current (or power)

— insulation resistance and earth continuity

— limit switches

— traction and balance

— overspeed governor

— car safety gear

— counterweight safety gear (if fitted)

— buffers

— alarm devices

— functional tests

— ascending car overspeed protection device.

The tests can be reported using the pro-forma PAS 32-1[1] document published by the British Standards Institution. There may be additional tests applied by the installer. The client may also require supplementary tests, which should be agreed at the time the contract is awarded as these may involve extra time and expense to carry out. These tests are often termed 'witness tests', when carried out and witnessed by the client or their representative.

### 15.2.4.2    New hydraulic lifts

For new hydraulic lifts specified to the BS EN 81 series of harmonised standards there is a requirement under Annex D (normative) for examinations and tests before putting into service and the CE marking applied. In that document, a number of tests are defined which need to be undertaken to ensure that the lift is functioning properly and has been installed to a satisfactory standard which complies with the specification and meets the requirements of current standards and legislation. These tests include the same requirements as the traction tests above, except the braking system, traction and balance, but additionally including the following:

— limitation of piston stroke

— measurement of full load pressure

— relief valve

— rupture valve

— restrictor device

— system pressure test

— creeping and anti-creep devices

— emergency lowering systems

— motor run time limiter

— fluid temperature detecting device.

The tests can be reported using the pro-forma PAS 32-2[2] document published by the British Standards Institution. There may be additional tests applied by the installer. The client may also require supplementary tests, which should be agreed at the time the contract is awarded as these may involve extra time and expense to carry out. These tests are often termed 'witness tests', when carried out and witnessed by the client or their representative.

### 15.2.4.3    Lifts subject to important modifications (modernised lifts)

During the lifetime of any lift there may be modifications to the equipment, or it may be modernised (see Chapter 16).

For lifts installed before 1 July 1999 the earlier versions of BS EN 81[3,4], BS 5655[11,12] and even BS 2655[7] apply. Any modernisation should attempt to comply to the latest standards. However, in some instances this is not possible. BS 5655: Part 11: 1989: *Installation of and modernisation of traction lifts in existing buildings*[11], BS 5655: Part 12: 1989: *Installation of and modernisation of hydraulic lifts in existing buildings*[12] (currently under review) and BS EN 81-80: *Rules for improvements to existing lifts*[5] give guidance.

For lifts installed after 1 July 1999 they should continue to be in full compliance with the EHSRs of the Lifts Regulations 1997[22] or the current version of the relevant harmonised BS EN 81 standard. Any commissioning and testing should therefore be to those parts of PAS 32-1[1] or PAS 32-2[2] which apply to the changed equipment.

No test documents have been published by BSI for modernised lifts. BS 5655: Part 10.1.1[9] and BS 5655: Part 10.2.1[10] are available, but apply to the commissioning tests for new traction and new hydraulic lifts, respectively. These documents can be used as a basis for the testing of modernised lifts.

### 15.2.5    Commissioning of escalators and moving walks

There are two generic types of escalators and moving walks: those which are built on site and those which leave the factory as a pre-constructed package. The type which are pre-constructed are generally commissioned prior to leaving the factory. This allows any defects found to be rectified before the unit reaches the site. Clearly, units that are built on site need to be commissioned on site. New escalators should be built to conform to BS EN 115[6] and are generally commissioned to the manufacturer's specification. Chapter 16 of BS EN 115 requires a constructional inspection and acceptance inspection and test before placing in service that includes the following:

— safety devices

— braking systems

— insulation resistance and earth continuity

— functional test.

These tests can be documented using BS 5656: Part 1: *Specification and pro forma for test and examination of new installations*[13].

## 15.2.6    On-site checks after completion

Following testing of the installed units, the applicable standards recommend inspection as an integral part of the test procedure. This inspection usually involves examining the completed installation for conformity with the specification and with regard to proper workmanship. Although usually carried out by the manufacturer, third party inspection is often specified at this crucial stage of the client acceptance process.

This inspection generally results in a report, commonly known as a 'snagging list', which identifies items requiring attention by either the manufacturer or other parties involved in final installation (e.g. electrical supply contractor, builder etc.). These items may be minor and rectifiable immediately or if of a more serious nature may involve protracted contractual negotiations and/or delay to the programme.

## 15.3    Preventative maintenance

### 15.3.1    Why maintain?

Lifts, escalators and moving walks are expensive items of equipment. It would be foolish to think that a piece of equipment could operate for long without adequate maintenance being undertaken. In this context, preventative maintenance refers to adjustment, cleaning, lubrication, replacement of worn components etc. Maintenance should neither be regarded as an optional extra, nor should a 'breakdown only' approach be adopted. Statutory provisions in Regulation 5 of PUWER[24] mentions the requirement that the equipment be properly maintained. Failure to maintain equipment would lead to its safety and reliability being compromised and would be in contravention of the statutory provisions.

BS EN 13015: *Maintenance for lifts and escalators. Rules for maintenance instructions*[17] set out the basic requirements for maintenance, and its provisions should be used to form the basis of a maintenance contract. Annex A (informative) of this standard provides check lists of typical maintenance operations. Table 15.1(a) to (c) provides a summary of these check lists.

**Table 15.1(a)**  Maintenance check list for electric lifts from BS EN 13015: 2001

| Area | Equipment | Check |
|---|---|---|
| General | Housekeeping | — all components are clean; free from dust and corrosion |
|  | Electric wiring | — insulation |
| Pit | Pit area | — for excess oil/grease at bottom of guides; area is clean, dry and free from debris |
|  | Anti-rebound device and switch | — for free movement and operation; for equal tension of ropes; switch (where fitted); lubrication |
|  | Buffers | — oil level; lubrication; switch (where fitted); fixings; operation |
|  | Electric safety devices | — operation |
| Machine room | Drive motor/generator | — bearings for wear; lubrication; commutator condition |
|  | Gear box | — gear for wear; lubrication |
|  | Traction sheave | — condition and grooves for wear |
|  | Brake | — braking system; parts for wear; stopping accuracy |
|  | Controller | — cabinet is clean, dry and free from dust |
|  | Overspeed governor and tension pulley | — moving parts for free movement and wear; operation; switch |
|  | Main rope and diverter pulley(s) | — condition and grooves for wear; bearings for abnormal noise and/or vibrations; guarding; lubrication |
|  | Suspension ropes/chains | — for wear, elongation and tension; lubrication only where intended |
|  | Rope/chains terminations | — for deterioration and wear; fixings |
|  | Safety gear(s)/ascending car overspeed protection means | — moving parts for free movement and wear; lubrication; fixings; operation; switch |
|  | Motor run-time limiter | — operation |
|  | Electric safety devices | — operation; electric safety chain; correct fuses are fitted |
| Well | Car/counterweight guides | — for film of oil where required on all guide surfaces; fixings |
|  | Car/counterweight guide shoes | — guide shoes/rollers for wear; fixings; lubrication where necessary |
|  | Suspension ropes/chains | — for wear, elongation and tension; lubrication only where intended |
|  | Rope/chains terminations | — for deterioration and wear; fixings |
|  | Final limit switches | — operation |
|  | Well lighting | — operation |
|  | Electric safety devices | — operation; electric safety chain |
| External | Lift car | — emergency lighting, car buttons, key switches; fixings of panels and ceiling |
|  | Landing entrances | — operation of landing locks; doors for free running; door guiding; door gaps; wire rope, chain or belt when used, for integrity; emergency unlocking device; lubrication |
|  | Car door | — 'door closed' contact or lock; doors for free running; door guiding; door gaps; wire rope or chain when used for integrity; passenger door protective device; lubrication |
|  | Floor level | — stopping accuracy at landing |
|  | Emergency alarm device | — operation |
|  | Landing controls and indicators | — operation |

**Table 15.1(b)** Maintenance check list for hydraulic lifts from BS EN 13015: 2001

| Area | Equipment | Check |
|---|---|---|
| General | Housekeeping | — all components are clean; free from dust and corrosion |
| | Electric wiring | — insulation |
| Pit | Pit area | — for excess oil/grease at bottom of guides; the pit area is clean, dry and free from debris |
| | Buffers | — oil level; lubrication; switch where fitted; fixings |
| | Electric safety devices | — operation |
| Machine room | Tank unit | — hydraulic fluid level; tank and valve unit for leakage |
| | Controller | — cabinet is clean, dry and free from dust |
| | Pressure relief valve | — operation |
| | Manual lowering valve | — operation |
| | Hand pump | — operation |
| | Motor run time limiter | — operation |
| | Electric safety devices | — operation; electric safety chain; correct fuses are fitted |
| | Hose/pipe work | — for damage and leakage |
| Well | Jack | — for oil leakage |
| | Telescopic jack | — for synchronisation |
| | Overspeed governor and tension pulley | — moving parts for free movement and wear; operation; switch |
| | Main rope pulley(s) | — condition and grooves for wear; bearings for abnormal noise and/or vibrations; guarding; lubrication |
| | Car/balancing weight/jack guides | — for film of oil where required on all guide surfaces; fixings |
| | Car/balancing weight/jack shoes | — guide shoes/rollers for wear; fixings |
| | Safety gear/pawl/clamping devices | — moving parts for free movement and wear; fixings; operation; switch |
| | Suspension ropes/Chains | — for wear, elongation and tension; lubrication only where intended |
| | Ropes/chains terminations | — for deterioration and wear; fixings |
| | Well lighting | — operation |
| | Final limit switch | — operation |
| | Electric safety devices | — operation; electric safety chain |
| | Anti-creep device | — operation |
| | Rupture valve/one way restrictor | — operation |
| | Hose/pipe work | — for damage and leakage |
| External | Lift car | — emergency lighting, car buttons, key switches; fixing of panels and ceiling |
| | Landing entrances | — operation of landing locks; doors for free running; door guiding; door gaps; wire rope, chain or belt when used, for integrity; emergency unlocking device; lubrication |
| rope or | Car door | — door closed contact or lock; doors for free running; door guiding; door gaps; wire chain when used for integrity; passenger door protective device; lubrication |
| | Floor level | — stopping accuracy at landing |
| | Emergency alarm device | — operation |
| | Landing controls and indicators | — operation |

**Table 15.1(c)** Maintenance check list for escalators and moving walks from BS EN 13015: 2001

| Area | Equipment | Check |
|---|---|---|
| Machine space | Controller | — cabinet is clean, dry and free from dust |
| | Gear box | — gear and associated parts; lubrication |
| | Drive motor | — bearings for wear; lubrication |
| | Brake | — braking system; parts for wear |
| | Auxiliary brake | — braking system; parts for wear |
| | Intermediate gear box | — gear and associated parts; lubrication |
| | Main drive chain | — for tension and wear; lubrication |
| | Step/pallet chain | — for tension and wear; lubrication |
| | Step/pallet | — step/pallet and step/pallet wheels for integrity |
| | Conveyor belt | — for condition and tension |
| | Drive belt | — for condition and tension |
| | Track system | — for condition and wear; fixings |
| | Safety devices | — operation |
| External | Clearances | — step to step and step to skirting clearances |
| | Combs | — condition; meshing with steps, pallets or belt |
| | Comb plate | — clearances and operation |
| | Handrails | — for free running and condition; tension; synchronisation between step/pallet band and the handrail |
| | Safety devices | — operation |
| | Deflector devices | — condition |
| | Lighting | — operation |
| | Display | — operation |
| | Signs/pictograms | — condition |
| | Balustrade | — condition of panels; fixings of interior claddings |
| | Controls | — operation |
| | Unobstructed access | — availability |

An important requirement of the standard is the provision of a maintenance instruction handbook to be supplied by the installer to the owner of each installation.

## 15.3.2 Maintenance contracts

Maintenance contracts vary from contractor to contractor, but in general there are two types of contract within the lift and escalator industry:

— contracts which provide for checking and lubrication only, repairs being subject to agreed further costs (these are more aptly called 'oil and grease' contracts)

— contracts which provide for fully comprehensive preventative maintenance cover all parts, labour and call-out fees.

With the 'oil and grease' contract, an operative from the lift maintenance company will attend and check lubrication levels, adjust anything that requires attention and clean the unit. Any further labour attendances or component replacement(s) etc. will normally attract an additional cost.

The fully comprehensive preventative maintenance contract usually includes for all activity described in the 'oil and grease' contract, but the labour and component costs in the event of a breakdown are met by the maintenance contractor. The small print of such contracts needs to be read carefully to avoid misunderstandings regarding exclusions. It is normal to exclude vandalism and misuse but, in addition, some companies will exclude major items such as hydraulic ram seals, gear box repairs, etc.

Fully comprehensive maintenance contracts allow for a regular budgeted cost and should secure a predetermined performance level throughout the life of the installation. The on-going maintenance costs of lift/escalator systems must be considered an integral part of the operating costs of the building. In most cases, they are negotiable with the equipment manufacturer in the form of a long-term agreement. The longer the agreement period, the greater is the incentive for the contractor to develop effective programmes for maintenance work. Contracting the equipment manufacturer to provide the maintenance beyond the initial warranty period has inherent advantages in respect of product familiarity, particularly in terms of design, development and training.

The overall costs of both forms of contract over the life cycle of the equipment should be similar. Unfortunately, the low initial cost of the 'oil and grease' contract is often a deciding factor in their selection. The total budget for lift/escalator maintenance is then sometimes determined solely on the cost of the 'oil and grease' contract and non-essential preventative works are regarded as unnecessary expenditure. This inevitably leads to poor performance, accelerated deterioration of equipment and premature failure.

The level of activity undertaken by the maintenance contractor varies according to the age and complexity of each installation, the equipment usage and the performance requirements. These factors determine not only the number of visits per year (which may range from two to twenty) but also the scope of work undertaken at each visit over, say, a five- or eight-year programme.

The installation of performance data loggers, to either new, or existing lift control systems, makes it feasible to specify maintenance requirements in terms of quantitative performance criteria. With such equipment, it is now comparatively simple to record and analyse performance data such as service and usage characteristics, number of failures over a specified period, mean time between failures, average/maximum service response time and system downtime/percentage system availability.

## 15.4 Thorough examinations and tests

### 15.4.1 General

A thorough examination of an installation is a systematic and detailed examination performed by a competent person. The purpose is to determine the condition of the installation and report on its suitability for its continued safe use.

Thorough examinations are generally required to be carried out so that the dutyholder complies with various legislation. The principal applicable legislation is the Health and Safety at Work etc. Act 1974[18]. Specifically:

— *Section 3*: the duty of employers and self employed to conduct their undertakings in such a way that people they do not employ are not put at risk.

— *Section 4*: the duty of owners of premises to maintain safe conditions for persons other than employees who may use or come into contact with equipment within premises.

— *Section 6*: the duty of suppliers, importers and/or manufacturers to ensure equipment is safe for its intended use (including incorporation of safe means of cleaning, maintenance, setting and inspection) and is supplied with adequate information regarding safe use.

All these provisions must be complied with insofar as is reasonably practicable.

A competent person according to BS 7255: *Safe working on lifts*[15] is:

[a] person, suitably trained and qualified by knowledge and practical experience, and provided with the necessary instructions, to enable the required work to be safely carried out

It is important that the competent person is independent and impartial so that an objective assessment can be made. For example, it is not appropriate to engage someone employed by the maintainer of the equipment to be examined, as they could be responsible for assessing their company's work. Few organisations have such competencies in-house and must use an external third party. An inspection body accredited by the United Kingdom Accreditation Service (UKAS) would be a suitable organisation to carry out thorough examinations. Insurance companies, who do not themselves carry out thorough examinations, or the Safety Assessment

Federation[25] (a trade organisation) can also recommend inspection bodies.

## 15.4.2 Thorough examination of lifts

The Lifting Operations and Lifting Equipment Regulations 1998[21] (LOLER) introduced new requirements for the safe provision and use of lifting equipment and applies to lifts and hoists used to lift people and loads. Regulation 9 of these regulations requires that in-service thorough examinations take place to ensure the continued safe use of the equipment. These examinations are required to take place every six months for passenger lifts and annually for goods lifts, unless a risk assessment shows the frequency should be reduced or increased in accordance to an examination scheme drawn up by a competent person. The examination should include as a minimum:

— landing door locking devices

— main drive system components

— worm and other gearing

— electrical safety devices/systems

— suspension elements

— braking system

— governors

— safety gear

— overload detection devices

— hydraulics.

Following an examination a report should be issued by the competent person, see Figure 15.1 (page 15-10), the requirements of such a report are detailed in Regulation 10 of the regulations. Many people still know this report as an 'insurance inspection'. This is incorrect as it is a statutory inspection. A LOLER examination must also be carried out after substantial or significant changes have occurred, e.g. modernisation, major repair or after an exceptional circumstance, e.g. an accident. LOLER applies to workplaces and not to domestic dwellings, although a similar examination regime is recommended.

## 15.4.3 Periodic testing of lifts

Generally thorough examinations do not involve any extensive testing. However periodic tests are required to be carried out under section 16.3.3 of the BS EN 81-1[3] and BS EN 81-2[4] standards. To meet these requirements in the UK, guidelines have been issued by the Safety Assessment Federation in consultation with the HSE. These guidelines are known as the LG1 Lifts Guidelines[25] (currently under review). They recommend a series of tests are undertaken at yearly, five-yearly and ten-yearly intervals. See Table 15.2 for a summary. These tests include:

For both electric and hydraulic lifts:

— earth continuity

— electrical safety devices

— terminal speed reduction systems

— landing door interlocks

— main drive system

— overspeed governors and safety gear

— overspeeding of ascending car

— car overload detection devices

— levelling

For traction lifts only:

— traction, brake

— geared machines.

For hydraulic lifts only:

— hydraulic systems

— hydraulic rupture/ restrictor valves

— hydraulic cylinders

**Table 15.2** Summary of tests recommended to be undertaken at yearly, 5-yearly and 10-yearly intervals

| Examination/test | Electric lifts | | | Hydraulic lifts | | |
|---|---|---|---|---|---|---|
| | Every year | Every 5 years | Every 10 years | Every year | Every 5 years | Every 10 years |
| Earth continuity | — | ● | ● | — | ● | ● |
| Electric safety devices | ● | ● | ● | ● | ● | ● |
| Terminal speed reduction system | — | ● | ● | — | — | — |
| Landing door interlocks | ● | ● | ● | ● | ● | ● |
| Main drive system | As necessary | As necessary | As necessary | As necessary | As necessary | As necessary |
| Safety system | — | ● | ● | — | ● | ● |
| Overspeed of ascending car | — | ● | ● | — | — | — |
| Energy dissipation buffers | ●* | ● | ● | ●* | ● | ● |
| Suspension | ● | ● | ● | ● | ● | ● |
| Car overload detection devices | ● | ● | ● | ● | ● | ● |
| Hydraulic system | — | — | — | — | ● | ● |
| rupture/restrictor valves | — | — | — | — | ● | ● |
| Hydraulic cylinder | — | — | — | ●† | ● | ● |
| Electrical anti-creep device | — | — | — | ● | ● | ● |
| Low pressure detection devices | — | — | — | ● | ● | ● |
| Traction, brake | ● | ● | ● | — | — | — |
| Levelling | — | ● | ● | ● | ● | ● |
| Balancing check | As necessary | As necessary | As necessary | As necessary | As necessary | As necessary |

* if no buffer return switch    † after 5 years in service

## REPORT OF THOROUGH IN-SERVICE EXAMINATION OF LIFTING EQUIPMENT

Type: (P) — periodic; (PS) — periodic, following a scheme of examination;

(O) — examination after the occurrence of exceptional circumstances

Owner/occupier of premises: Anytown Borough Council

Address: Town Hall
         Bishop's Place
         Anytown
         GC4 6PQ

Type of lift and description: Electro-hydraulic passenger lift

Owner's identification number: TH/01

Manufacturer: Essex Lift Co. Ltd.

Manufacturer's serial number: CE0037/1459

Location of lift: Town Hall foyer

| | |
|---|---|
| Report type, periodicity and when applicable: | (P), 6-monthly |
| S.W.L. for the configuration examined: | 8 persons (630 kg) |
| Test certificate date and no: | Not required |
| (A) Defects that are, or could become a danger to persons, remedial actions required, and date by which defects are to be remedied: | (A) That the car-top 13 A socket outlet be earthed before 19/10/2002 (1 month) |
| (B) Other defects: | (B) The suspension rope tensions should be equalised |
| (C) Observations: | (C) The following recommendations are made:<br>1. That an approved type rubber mat, to BS 921, be provided at the control panel.<br>2. That emergency lighting be installed within the machine room.<br>3. That ventilation be provided within the machine room.<br>4. That a safety barrier be provided in accordance with BS 7255<br>Lift Guidelines (LG1) Tests/ Examinations. Internal lock examination (PSL): 19/09/02.<br>Levels 1 to 3 internally examined. Observation: the shaft-top lifting beam (S.W.L. 1 tonne) was included within the scope of this examination. |

Last examination:                          Next examination due before: 19/03/2003

I confirm that the equipment was thoroughly examined on 19/09/2002 and that, subject to the remedial action noted in section (A) being completed, is safe to operate.

Name: Michael Jones                    Address: Webster & Booth,
                                                47 Canal Street,
Signature: M Jones                              Manchester, M1 3HF

Date of issue of report: 19/09/2002

**Figure 15.1** Example report of thorough examination of a lift

— electrical anti-creep systems

— low pressure detection devices.

These tests are required to be no more severe than those carried out at commissioning. They should be undertaken by a competent person, who may be employed by the maintenance company or by a third party. It is again important that the competent person is independent and impartial so that an objective assessment can be made. It may not be appropriate for the maintainer of the equipment to use one of their staff. Certificates are issued following each successful test, an example is shown in Figure 15.2 (see page 15-13).

### 15.4.4 Thorough examination of escalators and moving walks

There is no specific legislation requiring the thorough examination of escalators and moving walks. However, The Health and Safety at Work etc. Act 1974[18] applies generally together with the Management of Health and Safety at Work Regulation 1999[23]. Section 19 of the Workplace (Health, Safety and Welfare) Regulations 1992[27] makes reference to escalators and that regular inspections should be made. Previous Health and Safety Executive Guidance Note PM45[19] (now withdrawn) recommended a basic six-monthly examination by a competent person, which is still regarded as good practice, including:

— check on running clearances

— check on general operation

— visual examination of exterior of the complete unit

— examination of step/pallet chains and guides

— examination of the main drive system and gearing

— operational check of all safety devices

— check of lighting and warning notices.

Such an examination should be documented and reported to the dutyholder.

Clause 16.2.3 of BS EN 115: 1995[6] recommends that a 'periodic inspection and test should ascertain whether the escalator or moving walk is safe in operation and should bear on:

(*a*)  safety devices, with regard to their effective operation;

(*b*)  brake(s);

(*c*)  driving elements for visible signs or wear and tear, and for sufficient tension of belts and chains;

(*d*)  steps, pallets or the belt, for defects, true run and guidance;

(*e*)  dimensions and tolerances specified in the standard;

(*f*)  combs, for proper condition and adjustment;

(*g*)  balustrade interior panelling and the skirting;

(*h*)  handrails;

(*i*)  test of the electrical continuity, etc.'

Table 15.1(c) summarises Table A.3 of BS EN 13015: 2001[17] and provides a maintenance check list, which gives guidance of checks to be carried out under a maintenance contract.

At the present time work is being carried out by an industry working party to provide a guidance note on the thorough examination of escalators and moving walks, which will indicate the areas for examination and the periodicity.

Figure 15.3 (see page 15-14) illustrates the type of report that might be issued following the thorough examination of an escalator or moving walk. The table is based on the proforma provided in PM45[19] (1984), which in turn was based on a 1970 document, and could be used as an aide memoire in the event of a thorough examination being undertaken.

## 15.5 Documentation

Owners of lift, escalator and moving walk equipment should maintain documentation detailing their commissioning, preventive maintenance, testing and thorough examination. Besides the requirements to keep the statutory thorough examination documents ('LOLER-lifts' only), it is recommended that copies of the following information should be retained:

— the commissioning certificate and declaration of conformity (signed and dated)

— the test documents

— past and current maintenance contract documentation

— maintenance attendances (machine room log cards)

— breakdown attendances

— LG1 reports (lifts only)

These documents will provide a valuable source of information in the event of the equipment becoming unreliable, upgraded, involved in an accident, etc.

## References

1    BS PAS 32-1: 1999: *Specification for examination and test of new lifts before putting into service. Electric traction lifts* (London: British Standards Institution) (1999)

2    BS PAS 32-2: 1999: *Specification for examination and test of new lifts before putting into service. Hydraulic lifts* (London: British Standards Institution) (1999)

3    BS EN 81-1: 1998: *Safety rules for the construction and installation of lifts. Electric lifts* (London: British Standards Institution) (1998)

4    BS EN 81-2: 1998: *Safety rules for the construction and installation of lifts. Hydraulic lifts* (London: British Standards Institution) (1998)

5    BS EN 81-80: 2003: *Safety rules for the construction and installation of lifts. Rules for improvement of safety of existing passenger and goods passenger lifts* (London: British Standards Institution) (2003)

6       BS EN 115: 1995: *Safety rules for the construction and installation of escalators and passenger conveyors* (London: British Standards Institution) (1995)

7       BS 2655: *Specification for lifts, escalators, passenger conveyors and paternosters*: Part 8: 1971: *Modernization or reconstruction of lifts, escalators and paternosters* (London: British Standards Institution) (1971)

8       BS 5655: *Lifts and service lifts*: Part 6: 2002: *Selection and installation of new lifts* (London: British Standards Institution) (2002)

9       BS 5655: *Lifts and service lifts*: Part 10.1.1: 1995: *Commissioning tests for new electric lifts* (London: British Standards Institution) (1995)

10      BS 5655: *Lifts and service lifts*: Part 10.2.1: 1995: *Commissioning tests for new hydraulic lifts* (London: British Standards Institution) (1995)

11      BS 5655: *Lifts and service lifts*: Part 11: 1989: *Recommendations for the installation of new, and the modernisation of, electric lifts in existing buildings* (London: British Standards Institution) (1989)

12      BS 5655: *Lifts and service lifts*: Part 12: 1989: *Recommendations for the installation of new, and the modernisation of, hydraulic lifts in existing buildings* (London: British Standards Institution) (1989)

13      BS5656: *Safety rules for the construction and installation of escalators and passenger conveyors*: Part 1: 1997: *Specification and pro forma for test and examination of new installations* (London: British Standards Institution) (1997)

14      BS 5656: *Safety rules for the construction and installation of escalators and passenger conveyors*: Part 2: *Code of practice for the selection, installation and location of new escalators and moving walks* (London: British Standards Institution) (2004)

15      BS 7255: 2001 (Amd 1: 2002): *Code of practice for safe working on lifts* (London: British Standards Institution) (2001)

16      BS 7801: 1995: *Code of practice for safe working on escalators and passenger conveyors in use* (London: British Standards Institution) (1995)

17      BS EN 13015: 2001: *Maintenance for lifts and escalators. Rules for maintenance instructions* (London: British Standards Institution) (2001)

18      Heath and Safety at Work etc. Act 1974 (London: Her Majesty's Stationery Office) (1974)

19      HSE PM45: *Thorough examination of escalators and passenger conveyors* (London: Health and Safety Executive) (1984)

20      HSE INDG 339: *Thorough examination and testing of lifts — Simple guidance for lift owners* (London: Health and Safety Executive) (2001)

21      Lifting Operations and Lifting Equipment Regulations 1998 Statutory Instrument 1998 No. 2307 (London: The Stationery Office) (1998)

22      The Lifts Regulations 1997 Statutory Instrument 1997 No. 831 (London: The Stationery Office) (1997)

23      Management of Health and Safety at Work Regulations 1999 Statutory Instrument 1999 No. 3242 (London: The Stationery Office) (1999)

24      Provision and Use of Work Equipment Regulations 1998 Statutory Instrument 1998 No. 2306 (London: The Stationery Office) (1998)

25      SAFed *Guidelines to the thorough examination and testing of lifts* (London: Safety Assessment Federation) (1998)

26      Supply of Machinery (Safety) Regulations 1992 Statutory Instrument 1992 No. 3073 (Amended 1994) (London, The Stationary Office) (1994)

27      The Workplace (Health, Safety and Welfare) Regulations 1992 Statutory Instruments 1992 No. 3004 (London: The Stationary Office) (1992)

---

## ELECTRIC LIFT

This form details ALL the examinations and tests recommended to be undertaken at intervals not exceeding ONE YEAR. It addresses the most common lift arrangements. Where non-standard arrangements have been adopted, the most appropriate tests should be carried out and documented.

Owner/occupier of premises:

Address:

**CIBSE LIFTS GROUP**

Type of lift and description:

Owner's identification number:

Manufacturer's serial number:

Location of lift:

### 1 ELECTRICAL SAFETY DEVICES

If separate terminal stopping switches are fitted, do they operate satisfactorily?

| N/A | YES | NO |

Comments:

### 2 LANDING DOOR INTERLOCKS

Are all landing door interlocks in good condition and do they operate satisfactorily?

| YES | NO |

Comments:

### 3 ENERGY DISSIPATION BUFFERS

Do the buffers return to their fully extended position after they have been compressed?

| N/A | YES | NO |

Comments:

### 4 CAR OVERLOAD DETECTION DEVICE

Does the overload detection device operate satisfactorily?

| N/A | YES | NO |

State method of test:

Load at which the device was tested: _____ kg

Comments:

### 5 BRAKE

Are all gripping components within the brake in a satisfactory condition?

| YES | NO |

Comments:

### DECLARATION OF EXAMINATION AND TEST

Date of examination and test:

Person responsible for undertaking examination and/or test:

Name:

Job title:

Signature:

Employer name:

Address:

**Figure 15.2** Example (blank) certificate for the one year tests under LG1

# EXAMINATION REPORT

| Owner/occupier of premises:<br><br>Address:<br><br>Contact person: | Type of installation, identification number and description: |
|---|---|

| Numbers refer to visual verification, functional tests, etc. in PM45 Chapter 4 ||
|---|---|
| ITEM | CONDITION |
| 4.1.1  Do all automatic electrical safety devices function correctly? | Yes/No/see observation .... below |
| 4.1.2  Do all manually operated emergency stop devices function correctly? | Yes/No/see observation .... below |
| 4.2.1  Does the operational brake operate satisfactorily? | Running up:              metres<br>Running down:          metres<br>Yes/No/see observation .... below |
| 4.2.2  Does the auxiliary brake operate satisfactorily? | Yes/No/see observation .... below |
| 4.3     Is the condition of the steps/pallets satisfactory? | Yes/No/see observation .... below |
| 4.4     Are the step-to-step and step-to-skirt clearances satisfactory? | Yes/No/see observation .... below |
| 4.5     Are the combs in a satisfactory condition ? | Yes/No/see observation .... below |
| 4.6     Are the balustrade interior paneling and the skirting in a satisfactory condition? | Yes/No/see observation .... below |
| 4.7     Are the handrails in a satisfactory condition? | Yes/No/see observation .... below |
| 4.8     Is the earth continuity less than 0.5 $\Omega$ ? | Yes/No/see observation .... below; ....... $\Omega$ |
| 4.9     Are the surrounds, lighting and notices in a satisfactory condition? | Yes/No/see observation .... below |
| 4.10   Is a separate report on the driving elements being submitted? | Yes/No/see observation .... below |

| Observation | Detail of observation |
|---|---|
| A |  |
| B |  |
| C |  |
| D |  |

Continue on a separate sheet if necessary

## ADDITIONAL INFORMATION

Which parts (if any) were inaccessible? Repairs, renewals, alterations or additions required to enable the installation to continue to be used with safety: (a) immediately or (b) within a specified time, the time to be stated.

| Classification (a) or (b) | Detail of repairs, renewals, alterations or additions required (Continue on a separate sheet if necessary) |
|---|---|
|  |  |
|  |  |
|  |  |
|  |  |

If no repairs, renewals, alterations or additions are required enter 'None'

Defects, other than those specified above, which require attention:

Other observations:

I certify that on _____ I examined this installation and that the foregoing is a correct report of the result.

Signature: _____ Qualification:

Address:

Date:

Date of next thorough examination:

Notes:

**Figure 15.3** Suggested format for a report of a thorough examination of an escalator or moving walk; the details shown should form the minimum content of a report of a periodic thorough examination of an escalator or moving walk

# 16     Undertaking modifications to existing lifts

## Lead author

Dr Gina Barney (Gina Barney Associates)

## Chapter contents

| | | |
|---|---|---|
| 16.1 | Introduction | 16-3 |
| 16.2 | Life cycle considerations | 16-3 |
| 16.3 | Influencing factors to upgrading | 16-3 |
| 16.4 | Relevant legislation, standards and codes of practice | 16-4 |
| 16.5 | Undertaking modifications to an existing lift installed before 1 July 1999 | 16-4 |
| 16.6 | Undertaking modifications to an existing lift installed after 1 July 1999 | 16-4 |
| 16.7 | Important considerations when undertaking modifications to existing lifts | 16-5 |
| | 16.7.1   Improving performance | 16-5 |
| | 16.7.2   Replacement | 16-5 |
| | 16.7.3   Summary of modifications undertaken to existing lifts | 16-5 |
| 16.8 | Improving the safety of existing lifts | 16-6 |
| 16.9 | Step-by-step approach to improving the safety of existing lifts | 16-6 |
| 16.10 | Tests and records | 16-7 |
| References | | 16-7 |

# 16 Undertaking modifications to existing lifts

## 16.1 Introduction

In the UK there are over 207 000 passenger and passenger/goods lifts in service — 50% of which were installed before 1979 — these are all candidates for some level of upgrading (see Figure 16.1).

## 16.2 Lift cycle considerations

Some reasons for upgrading a lift are that as time progresses it becomes less reliable, probably less aesthetically pleasing and technologically backward. A more important reason for upgrading is to ensure that the owners* fulfil their duty to provide a safe environment.

---

\* Natural or legal entity having right of possession. *Note*: the natural or legal entity can be the owner, lessee, tenant, operator of the equipment, etc.

Upgrading may be undertaken to improve the performance in terms of its traffic handling, ride quality or energy consumption or to improve the equipment. Often this type of upgrading is termed 'modernisation'.

A lift is often refurbished to restore it to a 'good as new condition'. Then the worn out equipment and components are simply replaced. A like-for-like replacement of any equipment or any component is not considered to be upgrading. Some replacements can occur during routine maintenance operations, e.g. the replacement of a burnt-out motor. The status quo of the installation is unchanged and the same level of safety is maintained.

Owners of lifts are conscious of the life cycle of their equipment with regard to the capital expenditure and recurrent costs. Most are concerned with the economic life cycle defined as the estimated number of years until an item no longer represents the least expensive method of

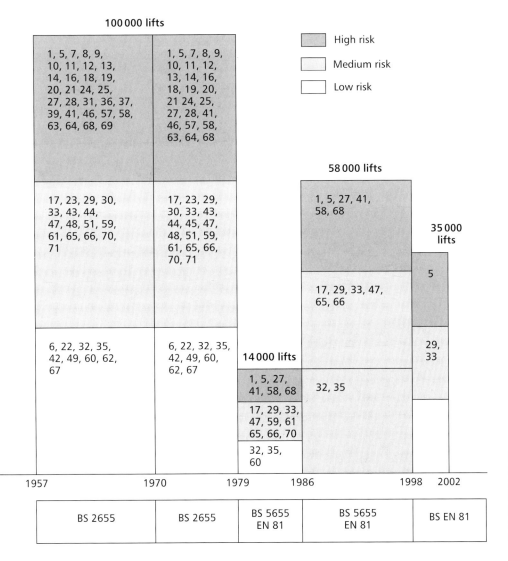

Figure 16.1 Approximate number of UK lift installations; the numbers refer to significant hazards identified in BS EN 81-80: 2003 and give guidance on those hazards likely to require consideration

performing its function. However, some owners may consider the technological life of their equipment important, i.e. when it becomes obsolete. These owners may chose to upgrade their equipment in order that their building is attractive to its tenants or prospective tenants. Other owners consider the useful life of their equipment, i.e. when it no longer performs its function to some established performance standard. For example, passengers now expect the lift ride quality to be better than that provided a decade ago.

## 16.3 Influencing factors to upgrading

The formulation of a lift upgrading scheme should be undertaken by a competent person in conjunction with the client in order to ensure that the client's needs are fully satisfied. During the lifetime of a lift, taken as 20–25 years for an electric lift and 15 years for an hydraulic lift, it may have two changes of car interior and landing doors, one change of drive system and one change of traffic dispatcher. Each upgrading scheme will vary from one lift installation to another.

The type of installation often dictates whether an upgrading scheme is practicable and/or economic. A low-budget lift installed ten years ago may not be a viable proposition for upgrading as the equipment was not designed for a prolonged life. Conversely, a high quality lift installed 25 years ago may be upgraded to provide a further decade of useful life. Upgrading can be undertaken as a step-by-step process in order to spread the financial costs.

A refurbishment is usually less expensive than a full upgrading, but may not extend the life of the lift by more than a few years. In the long term it could be more expensive.

Future plans for the building in which the lift is installed may influence the decision regarding the type of upgrading. A building purchased as an investment may only be prepared for re-sale. A building situated in an area selected for re-development would warrant little expenditure

Compliance with the latest safety standards is an important factor. It would be unwise for a building owner to ignore changes in legislation and safety standards. In the event of an incident, ignorance would be no defence.

## 16.4 Relevant legislation, standards and codes of practice

The following will be referred to in the following sections. An owner contemplating the upgrading of a lift should be familiar with, or engage someone who is familiar with the following minimum legislation, standards and codes of practice.

The main legislation applying to lifts is the Lifts Regulations 1997[20], which enact the European Lifts Directive. It requires new lifts to be installed, either to a harmonised European standard, or to have design certification from a notified body to ensure that the Essential Health and Safety Requirements (EHSRs) are met.

The two main harmonised standards for the construction and installation of lifts are BS EN 81-1: 1998[2] for electric lifts and BS EN81-2: 1998[3] for hydraulic lifts. These two safety standards are applied to all lifts installed after 1 July 1999. Other standards in the EN 81 series may be applicable to meet some of the Lift Directive's Essential Health and Safety Requirements, e.g. accessibility, fire testing, etc., see section 16.6.

Recommendations for the modernisation of lifts in existing buildings are given in BS 5655: Part 11: 1989[6] for electric lifts and BS 5655: Part 12: 1989[4] for hydraulic lifts. These standards are now over 15 years old in concept, and have fallen significantly behind recent changes. Revised versions are expected from BSI during 2006. These two standards deal with the upgrading of, and modifications to existing lifts.

BS 5655: Part 6: 2002[4] is a Code of Practice for the installation of new lifts. It does suggest, however, that its recommendations may be used as guidance when making alterations to existing lift installations. Reference will be made to this standard.

Code of Practice BS 7255: 2001[8] indicates the environment for safe working on lifts. It is divided into two main sections. Section 4 deals with the responsibilities of the owner and section 5 deals with the responsibilities of the worker towards safe working on lifts. Annex B of BS 7255 offers suggested improvements for consideration by an owner to improve safe working.

BS EN 81-80: 2003[16] provides guidance to the progressive improvement to the safety of existing lifts. This standard is not a harmonised standard but represents the considered thinking of a number of European experts and it has been approved by all the standards institutions (including BSI) in Europe.

## 16.5 Undertaking modifications to an existing lift installed before 1 July 1999

A lift installed before 1 July 1999, when the Lifts Regulations 1997 came into force, should have been installed to the safety rules for the construction and installation current at the time it was put into service. The standards could have been to the BS 2655 series dating back to 1957, or the BS 5655 series dating back to 1979. Some lifts may have been upgraded from, for example, a BS 2655 standard, to a BS 5655 standard over a period of time.

When upgrading an existing lift it does not have to comply with the latest standard, BS EN 81-1/2: 1998, but only to the standard applying at the time of the original installation. However the opportunity should be taken to upgrade it to the latest state of the art for technology and safety to maximise the improvements.

There is no compulsion on an owner, or operator, to bring a lift up to the latest level of safety; this is voluntary. However, in the event of an incident it is likely that their attention will be drawn to the best practice contained in the latest safety standards. This situation can be avoided by carrying out a safety audit from time to time and upgrading all lifts to the latest safety standard in order to ensure the highest currently perceived level of safety is obtained. It is not always reasonable and practicable to carry out all the recommendations resulting from an audit. In deciding what is reasonably practicable (HSE, 1987)[19] the seriousness of a risk to injury should be weighed against the difficulty and cost of removing or reducing that risk. In considering the cost no allowance should be made for the size, nature or profitability of the business concerned. Where the difficulty and costs are high, and a careful assessment of the risk shows it to be comparatively unimportant, action may not need to be taken. However, where the risk is high, action should be taken at whatever cost.

An owner contemplating the complete removal* of an existing lift may not be able to install a lift that fully meets the ESHRs of the Lift Directive. For example, it may not be possible to provide refuge spaces at the extremes of travel to EHSR 2.2. However, if the existing lift is completely removed then the upgrading becomes the installation of a new lift in an existing building and the ESHRs of the Lifts Directive applies.

## 16.6 Undertaking modifications to an existing lift installed after 1 July 1999

When a lift installed after 1 July 1999 is upgraded it must continue to comply with the ESHRs of the Lift Regulations[20]. The upgrading should also take note of any revisions to BS EN 81-1: 1998, e.g. the corrigenda dated March 2000, and any published interpretations in DD CEN TS 81-29[10], published by BSI. In addition other amendments that may apply include:

— BS EN 81-1/2: 1998 plus prA1 (Amendment 1) with regard to electronic safety systems.

— BS EN 81-1/2: 1998 plus A2 (Amendment 2) with regard to machine room-less lifts.

— BS EN 81-1/2: 1998 plus BS EN 81-28: 2003[9] with regard to remote alarms.

— BS EN 81-1/2: 1998 plus BS EN 81-72: 2003[14] with regard to firefighting lifts.

— BS EN 81-1/2: 1998 plus BS EN 81-70: 2003[12] with regard to provision of lifts for the use of persons with disabilities.

— BS EN 81-1/2: 1998 plus BS EN 81-58: 2003[11] with regard to the fire testing of landing doors.

— BS EN 81-1/2: 1998 plus BS EN 81-71[13] with regard to vandal resistant lifts.

— BS EN 81-1/2: 1998 plus BS EN 81-73[15] with regard to the behaviour of lifts in the event of a fire.

It is again important to emphasise that an owner, or operator, of a lift is competent, or engages someone who is, to be vigilant and is aware of any changes to the standards and codes of practice.

## 16.7 Important considerations when undertaking modifications to existing lifts

### 16.7.1 Improving performance

The performance of existing lifts can deteriorate in service as the equipment ages and wears. The requirements of the building in which the lift equipment is installed may also change, either in terms of the quantity of service, i.e. an extra traffic handling demand, or in terms of quality of service, i.e. improved passenger service times. These factors inspire the upgrading of the installation to meet these new requirements.

As an example, consider increasing the rated speed. This will almost certainly require changing the drive system as the principal alteration. A consequential alteration may be to ensure the electrical power supply to the new equipment is sufficient to meet the changed electrical loading. A check might also need to be made that the traction provided at the new speed is adequate. Consideration might also be given to upgrading the machine room lighting for safety reasons.

### 16.7.2 Replacement

Sometimes less significant work is carried out to improve the major components without any improvement in performance. This work often involves fewer changes.

For example, a traction drive motor may be changed for one with different electrical characteristics, but the same mechanical characteristics, or a relay based drive controller may be upgraded to a solid state controller with the same performance characteristics, but a different interface to the installation.

### 16.7.3 Summary of modifications undertaken to existing lifts

At the time of publication (September 2005), draft revisions to BS 5655: Part 11[6] and draft BS 5655: Part 12[7] list the following changes or replacements:

[1] Change of rated speed *

[2] Change of rated load *

[3] Change of travel *

[4] Change of mass *

[5] Change of complete controller including door operations

[6] Change of drive control system

---

* Complete removal is considered to have occurred if only the guide rails and their fixings remain.

* see section 16.10

[7] Change of traffic control system

[8] Change from manual to power-operated doors

[9] Change of entrances

    [9.1] Alteration to existing landing entrances

    [9.2] Change in the number of landing entrances

    [9.3] Addition of car entrances

[10] Change of a safety component

    [10.1] Landing door locking devices

    [10.2] Safety gear

    [10.3] Overspeed governors

    [10.4] Buffers

    [10.5] Electronic safety device

    [E10.6] (Electric) Ascending car overspeed protection

    [H10.6] (Hydraulic) Rupture valves and one-way restrictors

    [H10.7] (Hydraulic) Clamping and pawl devices

[11] Change of electric safety devices

    [11.1] Electric safety devices; manually operated

    [11.2] Electric safety devices; non-manually operated

[E12] (Electric) Change of the drive components

    [E12.1] Lift machine

    [E12.2] Brake

[H12] (Hydraulic) Change of the jack and lift machine

    [H12.1] Change of jack

    [H12.2] Pump and pump motor

    [H12.3] Hydraulic control block

    [H12.4] Change of pressure relief valve

[13] Change of a car enclosure and/or interior finishes

[14] Change of door operator

[15] Change from gates to doors

[16] Change of guide rails or type of guide rails

The reference numbers shown in square brackets refer to Table 16.1 (pages 16-8 to 16-15), where the definitions of the change/alteration, the motivation and the main resulting actions are summarised. Cross references are given in Table 16.1 to the relevant clauses in BS 5655-11, BS 5655-12, BS EN 81-1, BS EN 81-2 and BS EN 81-80. Users of Table 16.1 should note that it provides guidance only and they must carefully consider each cross reference, in order to identify any other relevant clauses and then to determine if any consequential alterations are required or if other factors need to be checked.

## 16.8     Improving the safety of existing lifts

Owners and operators of lifts have duties under various regulations to ensure the safety of persons transported in a lift, persons working on it and persons in its vicinity. To show due diligence it would be wise periodically to carry out, or have carried out, by a technically competent and sufficiently trained person, a safety audit to determine the level of safety of the installation.

The improvement of the safety of lifts is a continual process. It results from expert considerations of any risk assessments carried out, experience of serious events occurring to lifts in service and the adoption of various directives, acts, regulations, standards, codes, etc. that are issued from time to time. Lifts installed to the latest published British, European and International safety standards reflect the state of the art for safety that can be achieved today according to the experts who have developed these standards and to the technology available. This is not to say that lifts cannot be made safer.

When installed, a lift will provide levels of safety deemed sufficient by the safety standard current at that time. As a lift ages it moves further and further from the currently applicable safety standards and thus its level of safety is likely to be lower than that provided by a newly installed lift. For example, consider a pair of lifts operating as a duplex, one installed in 1998 and the other in 2000. The newer lift will be provided with an emergency alarm permanently connected to a rescue service, which the slightly older lift may not have.

It is important for an owner, or operator, of a lift to be aware of the changes in safety requirements. This is illustrated by three examples from the current harmonised safety standard BS EN 81-1: 1998:

(1) To protect passengers, clause 14.2.3 requires an emergency alarm device to be permanently connected to a rescue service, to enable trapped passengers to be released.

(2) To protect workers, clause 5.9 requires that adequate lighting be provided in the well, to enable work activities to be conducted safely.

(3) To protect passers-by, clause 5.2.1.2 requires that partially enclosed wells be provided with a sufficiently high enclosure, to prevent human contact or interference.

The UK has adopted BS EN 81-80: 2003: *Safety rules for the construction and the installation of lifts. Existing lifts*: Part 80: *Rules for the improvement of safety of existing passenger and goods passenger lifts*. This safety standard does not have the status of a harmonised standard under the European Directives and in the UK will not be enacted in law. The BS EN 81-80 safety standard does, however, provide the rules for the upgrading of existing lifts with the aim of providing an equivalent level of safety to that of a newly installed lift. This not always possible, but measures should be put in place to reduce all hazards to the smallest residual risk.

There is no duty on an owner, or operator, to bring a lift up to the latest level of safety, it is voluntary. However, in the event of an incident it is likely that their attention will be drawn to the best practice contained in the latest safety standards. This situation can be avoided by carrying out a safety audit from time to time and upgrading all lifts to the recommendations of BS EN 81-80, in order to ensure the highest currently perceived level of safety is obtained.

It is not always reasonable and practicable to carry out all the recommendations resulting from an audit. In deciding what is reasonably practicable (HSE, 1987)[19] the seriousness of a risk to injury should be weighed against the difficulty and cost of removing or reducing that risk. Where the difficulty and costs are high, and a careful assessment of the risk shows it to be comparatively unimportant, action may not need to be taken. However, where the risk is high, action should be taken at whatever cost.

## 16.9 Step-by-step approach to improving the safety of existing lifts

The best approach is to apply a step-by-step improvement to the safety of existing lifts by tracking the improvements, which are required as the standards develop. This is illustrated in Figure 16.2.

BS EN 81-80 identifies 74 significant hazards. These are listed in Table 16.2 (page 16-16). In the examples above, (1) is no. 71, (2) is no.17 and (3) is no.7. Table 16.2 can be used as an aide memoire to determine the number and short description of each hazard present. The 'Remedial action' column indicates the remedial action to be taken by reference to a current safety standard. These are mostly taken from BS EN 81-1: 1998 (electric lifts) and BS EN 81-2: 1998 (hydraulic lifts). Some remedial actions that are specific to electric lifts and are shown (indicated by {1}) and others that are specific to hydraulic lifts and are shown (indicated by {2}). Some hazards have a number of options that can be applied, i.e. (a), (b), (c), etc. Table 16.2 is necessarily succinct and should only be applied with appropriate reference to BS EN 81-1, BS EN 81-2, BS EN 81-28, BS EN 81-70 and BS EN 81-80.

BS EN 81-80 was written as a European safety standard and as such has had to allow for the wide range of situations in all the CEN member states. To accommodate this range, the standard proposes a filtering method to identify the priority of each risk. This procedure is particularly useful in the UK as it permits each installation to be accessed individually. What is a high priority hazard in one installation may be low priority in another. Considering example 2, a lift with no well lighting would be at a higher priority than a lift installed to BS EN 81-1: 1985, which had some well lighting.

Applying the filtering process in the UK results in the 74 significant hazards being allocated high, medium or low priority as shown by the numbers in the boxes of Figure 16.1. This priority allocation is for guidance only as each installation must be examined individually (by a competent person) in order to determine its particular risks. It will be noted that there are three significant hazards that require attention on post 1 July 1999 installations.

Table 16.1 also includes a remark 'Checks to BS EN 81-80' in the second column. This remark refers to the significant hazards listed in BS EN 81-80 and summarised in Table 16.2.

## 16.10 Tests and records

Where any changes listed in 16.7.3 which are indicated by a star (⋆) are made, a full test of the complete lift installation should be carried out.

Where any of other changes or replacements listed in 16.7.3 are made, there might be consequential changes and it is essential that appropriate tests be selected and conducted to ensure a safe installation. The tests indicated in the BS 5655-10[5] and PAS 32[17,18] series of standards are likely to be appropriate and these documents can also be used to make a suitable record. The document used will depend on when the lift installation was first put into service.

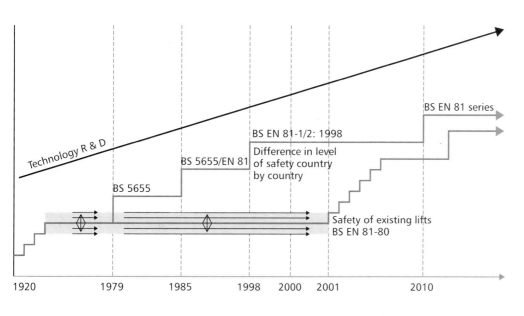

**Figure 16.2** Step-by-step improvement of the safety of existing lifts

**Table 16.1** Undertaking modifications to existing lifts (users of this table should note that it provides guidance only and they must carefully consider each cross reference, in order to identify any other relevant clauses and then to determine if any consequential alterations are required or if other factors need to be checked together with appropriate reference to BS 5655-11, BS 5655-12, BS EN 81-1, BS EN 81-2, BS EN 81-28, BS EN 8 1-70 and BS EN 81-80

| **1 Change of rated speed** | **Major modification — full tests and records required.** |
| --- | --- |
| **Definition**<br>For electric lifts a change in rated speed is any increase greater than 5% or decrease greater than 8% (see BS EN 81-1, Section 12.6).<br><br>For hydraulic lifts a change in rated speed is any increase in rated speed greater than 8% (see BS EN 81-2, Section 12.8).<br><br>**Motivation**<br>An increase in rated speed can occur, for example, where it is desired to improve performance. A decrease in rated speed can occur, for example, as the result of change of use from passenger to goods service. | **Checks to clauses of BS EN 81-1/2 (detailed in BS 5655-11/12), include:**<br>Dimensions at the well ceiling and pit (5)<br>Safety gear (9.8)<br>Buffers (10.3–10.4)<br>Guide system (10.2)<br>The limits of the unlocking zone (7.7.1)<br>Power supply and switchgear (13)<br>Inspection speed (14.2.1.3)<br>Security of the counterweight/balancing weights (8.18)<br>The safe working spaces and equipment clearances (6)<br><br>**Electric only:**<br>Suspension (9.1) and traction (9.3)<br>Tripping means for safety gears (9.9)<br>Overspeed governor, ascending car overspeed protection device (9.10)<br><br>**Hydraulic only:**<br>Suspension (9.1–9.3)<br>The tripping means for safety gears and clamping devices (9.10)<br>Rupture/restrictor valves (12.5)<br><br>**Checks to BS EN 81-80 (see Table 16.2 and BS EN 81-80 for details), include:**<br>Electric: 3, 6–18, 19–24, 40, 47–53, 60, 62–64, 66–72, 74<br>Hydraulic: 3, 6–18, 19–24, 40, 47–49, 51, 54, 60–72, 74 |
| **2 Change of rated load** | **Major modification — full tests and record required** |
| **Definition**<br>A change in rated load is a change greater than 5%, or 75 kg (whichever is the greater).<br><br>**Motivation**<br>A change in rated load can occur as the result of a need to transport heavier loads or can result from changes to the available size of the platform area of the car. | **Checks to clauses of BS EN 81-1/2 (detailed in BS 5655-11/12), include:**<br>Verification of the well structure (5)<br>Drive supports, guide rail fixings, buffer supports (10)<br>Safety gear (9.8)<br>Overspeed governor (9.9)<br>Guidance system (10.2)<br>Buffers (10.3–10.4)<br>Drive system (12)<br>The available car area and the new rated load (8, Table 1)<br>Load weighing detection system (14.2.5)<br>The load plate (15)<br>The safe working spaces and equipment clearances (6)<br><br>**Electric only:**<br>Suspension (9.1–9.3) and traction (9.3)<br>Ascending car overspeed protection device (9.10)<br><br>Hydraulic only<br>Suspension (9.1, 9.3)<br>Compatibility of the pressure relief valve (12.5.3)<br><br>**Checks to BS EN 81-80 (see Table 16.2 and BS EN 81-80 for details), include:**<br>Electric: 38-46, 50-53, 55-57, 60, 66, 70, 73, 74<br>Hydraulic: 38-46, 51, 54-57, 60-66, 70, 73, 74 |

*Table continues*

**Table 16.1** Undertaking modifications to existing lifts — *continued*

| 3 Change of travel | Increase in travel is a major modification — full tests and record required<br>Decrease in travel is a modification — appropriate tests and records required |
|---|---|
| **Definition**<br>A change of travel is any increase or decrease of the travel distance between the highest and lowest finished floor levels.<br><br>*Note*: a small change may cause refuge spaces and over-travel distances to be insufficient.<br><br>**Motivation**<br>A change in travel can occur where a lowest, or highest, finished floor level is raised, e.g. to accommodate a suspended floor, or lowered, e.g. to accommodate access for persons with disabilities. A change in travel can also occur where higher or lower floors are no longer served, e.g. service to a basement level is no longer required or higher floors are removed from a traffic zone.<br><br>*Note*: the provision of additional entrances may be required. | **Checks to clauses of BS EN 81-1/2 (detailed in BS 5655-11/12), include:**<br>Dimensions at the well ceiling and pit (5)<br>System of guiding (10.2)<br>Final limit switches (10.5)<br>Changes to the wiring (13) should be checked<br>Access (5.2.2, 5.5, 5.7.3.2) and rescue (5.10)<br>Machine room/pulley room requirements (6)<br>Structural and fire integrity (5.3)<br>Pit depth (5.7.2.2)<br>Stopping devices (5.7.2.5)<br>Buffering characteristics (10.4)<br>Top/bottom clearances (5.7)<br><br>**Electric only:**<br>Suspension system and traction (9.1–9.6)<br><br>**Hydraulic only:**<br>Suspension system (9.1–9.3)<br>Hydraulic jack (12.2)<br><br>**Checks to BS EN 81-80 (see Table 16.2 and BS EN 81-80 for details), include:**<br>Electric:  6-18, 19–37, 40, 66<br>Hydraulic:  6-18, 19–37, 40, 66 |
| **4 Change of mass** | **Major modification — full tests and record required** |
| **Definition**<br>A change of suspended or driven mass of either empty car, or suspended mass, or mass of a jack is any increase, or decrease, greater than 5%.<br><br>**Motivation**<br>A change in mass can occur as the result of a larger or smaller car being installed, changes to the linings (car refurbishment), changes to the car doors/operators (manual to power doors, adding car doors, change of operator type), addition or changes of other equipment; and attachments carried on the car (car top balustrades, guarding, canopies, traps, etc.).<br><br>*Note*: changes to the mass has similar effects to changing the rated load. | **Checks to clauses of BS EN 81-1/2 (detailed in BS 5655-11/12), include:**<br>Verification of well structure (5)<br>Guidance system (10.2)<br>Suspension (9.1–9.3)<br>Buffers (10.3–10.4)<br>Safety gear (9.8)<br><br>**Electric only:**<br>Drive system (12)<br>Traction (9.3)<br>Governor (9.9)<br>Ascending car overspeed protection (9.10)<br><br>**Hydraulic only:**<br>Tripping means (9.10)<br>Balancing weight (8.18)<br>Compatibility of the pressure relief valve (12.5.3)<br><br>**Checks to BS EN 81-80 (see Table 16.2 and BS EN 81-80 for details), include:**<br>Electric:  38–46, 50-53, 55-57, 60, 66, 70, 73, 74<br>Hydraulic:  38–46, 54–57, 60, 66, 70, 73, 74 |
| **5 Change of complete controller including door operations** | |
| **Definition**<br>A change of all or part of a controller.<br><br>*Note*: a complete controller comprises the drive control system, the traffic controller and the door operator. | For details see drive control system (change 6); traffic controller (change 7); door operator (see change 14). |

*Table continues*

**Table 16.1** Undertaking modifications to existing lifts — *continued*

| 6  Change of drive control system | Appropriate tests and records required |
|---|---|
| **Definition**<br>A change in the drive control system, which is the system controlling and monitoring the running of the lift machine (but not door operations), sometimes called motion control (see BS 5655-6:2002, 9.2 and Chapter 8).<br><br>*Note*: for electric lifts the drive system comprises the hoist motor, any gear (if installed), brake, sheave, bearing, bedplate, drive controller and signal interface. For hydraulic lifts the drive system comprises the pump unit, control valves, jack, piping, drive controller and signal interface.<br><br>**Motivation**<br>A change in the drive system might be required to improve the ride comfort to passengers, improve passenger handling, the accuracy of floor levelling, reduce the number of breakdowns, reduce energy consumption, or provide a greater level of safety to the operation of the lift.<br><br>*Note*: a new electric motor (see BS 5655-6:2002, 9.2) or pump motor (see BS 5655-6:2002, 9.2.2) might be required to match the drive technology employed (see change 12). | **Checks to clauses of BS EN 81-1/2 (detailed in BS 5655-11/12), include:**<br>Earthing (13)<br>Wiring (13)<br>Safe working spaces and equipment clearances (6.3.2)<br>Rated voltage, current, power (13)<br>Electromagnetic compatibility (EMC) (BS EN 12015/12016)<br>Inspection control (14.2.1.3)<br>Ventilation (6.3.5)<br>Auxiliary supplies (13.4.1)<br><br>**Hydraulic only:**<br>Anti-creep devices (9.12)<br><br>**Checks to BS EN 81-80 (see Table 16.2 and BS EN 81-80 for details), include:**<br>Electric: 53, 60, 62-64, 66-69, 74<br>Hydraulic:  54, 60-69, 74 |
| **7  Change of traffic control system** | **Appropriate tests and records required** |
| **Definition**<br>A change of the traffic control system, which supervises and distributes landing and car calls to specific lift car(s) in order to handle the calls in an efficient manner (see BS 5655-6:2002, clause 7, Chapter 9, Barney[1]).<br><br>**Motivation**<br>A change of traffic control system might be required to reduce passenger waiting and journey times, increase the number of passengers served, provide special features to increase accessibility for disabled persons, reduce lift group failures by the replacement of relays with solid state technology, improve the behaviour of the lift in the event of fire, reduce<br><br>any risks owing to the poor condition of wiring, etc. | **Checks to clauses of BS EN 81-1/2 (detailed in BS 5655-11/12), include:**<br>Earthing (13)<br>Wiring (13)<br>Safe working spaces and equipment clearances (6.3.2)<br>Rated voltage, current, power (13)<br>Electromagnetic compatibility (EMC) (BS EN 12015/12016)<br>Ventilation (6.3.5)<br>Auxiliary supplies (13.4.1)<br><br>**Checks to BS EN 81-80 (see Table 16.2 and BS EN 81-80 for details), include:**<br>Electric/hydraulic:  23, 66, 68, 74 |
| **8  Change from manual to power-operated doors** | **Appropriate tests and records required** |
| **Definition**<br>This change involves the addition of powered devices to drive (operate) the car and/or the landing doors.<br><br>**Motivation**<br>A change from manual to power-operated doors might be required to improve the service to the passengers (traffic handling) or to reduce the burden on passengers to open and close the doors by hand, e.g. to assist persons with disabilities. | **Checks to clauses of BS EN 81-1/2 (detailed in BS 5655-11/12), include:**<br>Verification of the well structure (5)<br>Adequate clearances (11)<br>Hazards on the car roof (5.7.1.1)<br>Change the mass of the car (see change 4)<br>Capability of the drive system (see change 6)<br>Child hand protection (7.2.3.6)<br>Protection against electric shock (13.5.3.2 and 13.5.3.5)<br>Dynamic requirements (8.7.2.1.1)<br>Fire integrity of the landing entrance (7.2.2)<br><br>**Electric only:**<br>Traction (9)<br><br>**Checks to BS EN 81-80 (see Table 16.2 and BS EN 81-80 for details), include:**<br>Electric/hydraulic:  4, 6-18, 25–44, 58, 59, 66, 68, 70 |

*Table continues*

**Table 16.1** Undertaking modifications to existing lifts — *continued*

### 9 Change of entrances

| 9.1 Alteration to existing landing entrances | Appropriate tests and records required |
|---|---|
| **Definition**<br>This change involves alterations to the landing entrances which can occur when they are refurbished by the addition of new panel skins or when they are completely replaced by different components not of the same specification as the original, e.g. heavier.<br><br>*Note*: the type of operation, manual or powered, is not changed (see change 8).<br><br>**Motivation**<br>To replace damaged or distressed door panels or complete doors. | **Checks to clauses of BS EN 81-1/2 (detailed in BS 5655-11/12), include:**<br>Conformity (7)<br>Fire integrity (7.2.2)<br><br>**Checks to BS EN 81-80 (see Table 16.2 and BS EN 81-80 for details), include:**<br>Electric/hydraulic: 6–18, 25–37, 58, 59, 66, 74 |

| 9.2 Change in the number of landing entrances | Appropriate tests and records required |
|---|---|
| **Definition**<br>This change involves the provision of additional entrances or the reduction in the number of entrances.<br><br>*Note*: see change 3 for change of travel.<br><br>**Motivation**<br>Additional landing entrances might be required where an existing lift does not serve all floors throughout its existing travel, e.g. skip/stop arrangements, or where a mezzanine floor is introduced. There might also be occasions when entrances are to be removed, e.g. at the extremes of travel. | **Checks to clauses of BS EN 81-1/2 (detailed in BS 5655-11/12), include:**<br>Structural integrity (5.3)<br>Fire integrity (7.2.2)<br>Clearances (11)<br>Safe working spaces (5.7.1)<br>Compatibility with door operator (7)<br><br>*Note*: new locks to be a 'CE' type-tested design.<br><br>**Checks to BS EN 81-80 (see Table 16.2 and BS EN 81-80 for details), include:**<br>Electric/hydraulic: 6–18, 25–37, 50–53, 58, 59, 66, 73, 74 |

| 9.3 Addition of car entrances | Appropriate tests and records required |
|---|---|
| **Definition**<br>This change involves the provision of additional car entrances.<br><br>**Motivation**<br>An additional car entrance may be added to service landings at the rear or side of the well. | **Checks to clauses of BS EN 81-1/2 (detailed in BS 5655-11/12), include:**<br>Hazards on the car top (8.15)<br>Car structural integrity (8.3)<br>Refuge spaces (5.7.1, 5.7.2)<br>Clear working areas (8.13.2)<br><br>*Note*: if floor area changes, see change 2. If suspended mass changes see change 4.<br><br>**Checks to BS EN 81-80 (see Table 16.2 and BS EN 81-80 for details), include:**<br>Electric/hydraulic: 25, 27, 28, 30, 33, 37, 58, 59 |

### 10 Change of a safety component

| 10.1 Landing door locking devices | Appropriate tests and records required |
|---|---|
| **Definition**<br><br>This change involves the changing or replacement of a landing door locking device.<br><br>**Motivation**<br>Landing door locking devices can be changed or replaced by a more modern device, as the result of the unavailability of an identical equipment. New landing door locking devices might be fitted as the result of the change in the number of entrances (see change 9). | **Checks to clauses of BS EN 81-1/2 (detailed in BS 5655-11/12), include:**<br>Conformity (7.7)<br>Fire integrity of landing door (7.2.2)<br>Fire integrity of locking device<br><br>*Note*: new locks to be a 'CE' type-tested design.<br><br>**Checks to BS EN 81-80 (see Table 16.2 and BS EN 81-80 for details), include:**<br>Electric/hydraulic: 1, 4, 29 to 37, 40, 58, 59 |

| 10.2 Safety gear | Appropriate tests and records required |
|---|---|
| **Definition**<br>Safety gear can be of an instantaneous or progressive type.<br><br>**Motivation**<br>A change can occur when a replacement is required or another change requires a different device. | **Checks to clauses of BS EN 81-1/2 (detailed in BS 5655-11/12), include:**<br>Conformity (9.8)<br>Energy absorption (F 3.2.4.1)<br>Compatibility with associated safety system (see change 10.3)<br>Soundness of the mountings.<br><br>**Checks to BS EN 81-80 (see Table 16.2 and BS EN 81-80 for details), include:**<br>Electric/hydraulic: 1, 10, 50a or 50b |

*Table continues*

**Table 16.1** Undertaking modifications to existing lifts — *continued*

| 10.3 Overspeed governors | Appropriate tests and records required |
|---|---|
| **Definition**<br>This change involves the changing or replacement of an overspeed governor.<br><br>**Motivation**<br>A change can occur when a replacement is required or another change requires a different device. | **Checks to clauses of BS EN 81-1/2 (detailed in BS 5655-11/12), include:**<br>Conformity (9.9)<br>Calibration<br>Compatibility with associated safety system (see change 10.2)<br>Clear working space (6.3.2)<br><br>**Checks to BS EN 81-80 (see Table 16.2 and BS EN 81-80 for details), include:**<br>Electric/hydraulic: 1, 50a or 50b |

| 10.4 Buffers | Appropriate tests and records required |
|---|---|
| **Definition**<br>Buffers can be of energy accumulation or energy dissipation types.<br><br>**Motivation**<br>A change can occur when a replacement is required or another change requires a different device. | **Checks to clauses of BS EN 81-1/2 (detailed in BS 5655-11/12), include:**<br>Conformity (10.3–10.4)<br>Safe working spaces (5.7.3) and equipment clearances<br>Pit strength (5.3.2)<br><br>**Checks to BS EN 81-80 (see Table 16.2 and BS EN 81-80 for details), include:**<br>Electric/hydraulic: 14–18, 56–57 |

| 10.5 Electronic safety devices | Appropriate tests and records required |
|---|---|
| **Definition**<br>Electronic safety devices, replacing the functions of devices listed in BS EN 81-1/2:1998, Annex A.<br><br>**Motivation**<br>A change can occur when a replacement is required or another change requires a different device. | **Checks to clauses of BS EN 81-1/2 (detailed in BS 5655-11/12), include:**<br>Conformity (14, F.6, Annex H) |

| E10.6 (Electric) Ascending car overspeed protection | Appropriate tests and records required |
|---|---|
| **Definition**<br>Ascending car overspeed protection comprises speed monitoring and speed reducing elements.<br><br>**Motivation**<br>A change can occur when a replacement is required or another change requires a different device. Ascending car overspeed protection may be added, as it was first required by the Lift Regulations 1997. | **Checks to clauses of BS EN 81-1 (detailed in BS 5655-11), include:**<br>Conformity (9.10)<br>Integration with other equipment<br>Integration with building structure<br><br>**Checks to BS EN 81-80 (see Table 16.2 and BS EN 81-80 for details), include:**<br>Electric: 10, 50a or 50b, 52 |

| H10.6 (Hydraulic) Rupture valves and one-way restrictors | Appropriate tests and records required |
|---|---|
| **Definition**<br>A rupture valve is a device that is capable of stopping a downward moving car and holding it stationary. A restrictor is a device that is capable of restricting the downward speed of a car in the case of a major leakage.<br><br>**Motivation**<br>A change can occur when a replacement is required or another change requires a different device. | **Checks to clauses of BS EN 81-2 (detailed in BS 5655-12), include:**<br>Conformity (12.5.5, 12.5.6)<br><br>**Checks to BS EN 81-80 (see Table 16.2 and BS EN 81-80 for details), include:**<br>Hydraulic: 54, 65 |

| H10.7 (Hydraulic) Clamping and pawl devices | Appropriate tests and records required |
|---|---|
| **Definition**<br>A clamping device is a device that is capable of stopping a downward moving car and holding it stationary, and can be of a progressive or instantaneous type.<br><br>**Motivation**<br>A change can occur when a replacement is required or another change requires a different device. | **Checks to clauses of BS EN 81-2 (detailed in BS 5655-12), include:**<br>Well structure (5)<br>Conformity (9.9, 9.11)<br>Compatibility with tripping system (9.10)<br><br>**Checks to BS EN 81-80 (see Table 16.2 and BS EN 81-80 for details), include:**<br>Hydraulic: 54, 56 |

| 11 Change of electric safety devices | |
|---|---|

| 11.1 Electric safety devices — manually operated | Appropriate tests and records required |
|---|---|
| **Definition**<br>Electric safety devices — manually operated are one of the seven manually operated stopping devices listed in Annex A of BS EN 81-1/2 (incorporating A2) e.g. pit switch stopping device.<br><br>**Motivation**<br>A change can occur when a replacement is required or another change requires a different device. | **Checks to clauses of BS EN 81-1/2 (detailed in BS 5655-11/12), include:**<br>Conformity (14.1.2, 14.2.2)<br>Location (Annex A)<br>Prevent involuntary release (14.2.2.2)<br><br>**Checks to BS EN 81-80 (see Table 16.2 and BS EN 81-80 for details), include:**<br>Electric/hydraulic: 16, 70a, 70b |

*Table continues*

**Table 16.1** Undertaking modifications to existing lifts — *continued*

| 11.2 Electric safety devices — non-manually operated | Appropriate tests and records required |
|---|---|
| **Definition**<br>Electric safety devices — non-manually operated are one of the 37 non-manual devices listed in Annex A of BS EN 81-1 (incorporating A2) and 30 non-manual devices listed in Annex A of BS EN 81-2 (incorporating A2), e.g. buffer switch.<br><br>**Motivation**<br>A change can occur when a replacement is required or another change requires a different device. | **Checks to clauses of BS EN 81-1/2 (detailed in BS 5655-11/12), include:**<br>Conformity (14.1.2)<br>Location (Annex A)<br><br>**Checks to BS EN 81-80 (see Table 16.2 and BS EN 81-80 for details), include:**<br>Electric/hydraulic: 8, 31, 41, 51, 57, 6 |

### E12 (Electric) Change of the drive components

| E12.1 Lift machine | Appropriate tests and records required |
|---|---|
| **Definition**<br>The lift machine comprises the hoist motor, gear (if installed), sheave, pulley, bearing and bedplate are changed.<br><br>**Motivation**<br>This change can occur for many reasons, including where excessive wear has taken place, fatigue of the main components is suspected, change of speed, change of levelling accuracy, etc. A traction sheave might be changed as the result of wear or other damage. | **Checks to clauses of BS EN 81-1 (detailed in BS 5655-11), include:**<br>Safe working spaces and equipment clearances (6.3.2)<br>Integration with other equipment<br>Rated voltage, current, power (13)<br>Electromagnetic compatibility (EMC) (BS EN 12015/12016)<br>Ventilation (6.3.5)<br>Rated voltage, current, power (13)<br>Guarding (9.7)<br>Traction (9.3).<br><br>**Checks to BS EN 81-80 (see Table 16.2 and BS EN 81-80 for details), include:**<br>Electric: 21–24, 47–49, 53, 60, 62–64, 66–68, 69, 74 |

| E12.2 Brake | Appropriate tests and records required |
|---|---|
| **Definition**<br>Device which can operate automatically and hold a car stationary.<br><br>**Motivation**<br>A change can occur when a replacement is required or another change requires a different device. | **Checks to clauses of BS EN 81-1 (detailed in BS 5655-11), include:**<br>Conformity (12.4.2.1)<br>Safe working spaces and equipment clearances (6.3.2)<br>Integration with other equipment<br>Rated voltage, current, power (13)<br>Electromagnetic compatibility (EMC) (BS EN 12015/12016)<br>Ventilation (6.3.5)<br>Rated voltage, current, power (13)<br>Guarding (9.7)<br><br>**Checks to BS EN 81-80 (see Table 16.2 and BS EN 81-80 for details), include:**<br>Electric: 1, 21, 47, 60, 66, 74 |

### H12 (Hydraulic) Change of the jack and lift machine

| H12.1 Change of jack | Appropriate tests and records required |
|---|---|
| **Definition**<br>A jack comprises a cylinder and ram (piston) and its connecting pipework.<br><br>**Motivation**<br>A change of jack might be required as the result of damage or wear or as the result of another modification, such as a change in travel or rated load. | **Checks to clauses of BS EN 81-2 (detailed in BS 5655-12), include:**<br>Compatibility of hydraulic fluid<br>Potential fire hazards<br>Well structure (5)<br>Pressure and buckling calculations (12.2.1–12.2.2)<br>Compatibility with building structure<br>Guarding (9.4)<br>Safe working spaces and equipment clearances (6.3.2)<br>Top/bottom clearances (5.7)<br><br>**Checks to BS EN 81-80 (see Table 16.2 and BS EN 81-80 for details), include:**<br>Hydraulic: 3, 6–18, 54, 61, 65 |

*Table continues*

**Table 16.1** Undertaking modifications to existing lifts — *continued*

| H12.2 Pump and pump motor | Appropriate tests and records required |
|---|---|
| **Definition**<br>Unit comprising an electric motor and attached pump which circulates the hydraulic fluid.<br><br>**Motivation**<br>A change in the pump/pump motor can occur when the capacity and/or the control characteristics of the system has been changed, or a like-for-like replacement cannot be found. | **Checks to clauses of BS EN 81-2 (detailed in BS 5655-12), include:**<br>Compatibility of hydraulic fluid<br>Potential fire hazards<br>Integration with other equipment<br>Rated voltage, current, power (13)<br>Electromagnetic compatibility (EMC) (BS EN 12015/12016)<br>Ventilation (6.3.5)<br>Rated voltage, current, power (13)<br>Guarding (9.4)<br>Safe working spaces and equipment clearances (6)<br>Cooling (12.14)<br>Wiring (13)<br><br>**Checks to BS EN 8 1-80 (see Table 16.2 and BS EN 81-80 for details), include:**<br>Hydraulic:  19–24, 61, 62, and 64–69 |
| **H12.3 Hydraulic control block** | **Appropriate tests and records required** |
| **Definition**<br>A hydraulic control block controls the hydraulic fluid in and out of the jack and provides control of rated, inspection and emergency lowering speeds.<br><br>**Motivation**<br>A change might be required as the result of damage or wear or as the result of another modification, such as a change in travel or rated load. | **Checks to clauses of BS EN 81-2 (detailed in BS 5655-12), include:**<br>Compatibility of hydraulic fluid<br>Potential fire hazards<br>Integration with other equipment<br>Rated voltage, current, power (13)<br>Electromagnetic compatibility (EMC) (BS EN 12015/12016)<br>Ventilation (6.3.5)<br>Rated voltage, current, power (13)<br>Inspection speed (14.2.1.3d)<br>Emergency lowering (12.9.1.2)<br>Non-return valve (12.9)<br>Wiring (13)<br><br>**Checks to BS EN 81-80 (see Table 16.2 and BS EN 81-80 for details), include:**<br>Hydraulic:  3, 5, 19-24, 54, 60, 61, 65 |
| **H12.4 Change of pressure relief valve** | **Appropriate tests and records required** |
| **Definition**<br>A pressure relief valve is needed to limit the system pressure to 1.4 times the full load pressure (exceptionally to 1.7 times).<br><br>**Motivation**<br>A change might be required as the result of damage or wear or as the result of another modification, such as a change in travel or rated load. | **Checks to clauses of BS EN 81-2 (detailed in BS 5655-12), include:**<br>Compatibility of hydraulic fluid<br>Potential fire hazards<br><br>**Checks to BS EN 81-80 (see Table 16.2 and BS EN 81-80 for details), include:**<br>Hydraulic:  54, 61, 65 |
| **13  Change of a car enclosure and/or interior finishes** | **Appropriate tests and records required** |
| **Definition**<br>The car enclosure is the passenger/goods carrying unit, including the car frame, car interior and fit out.<br><br>**Motivation**<br>From time to time the car interiors begin to look tired and dated and require a new fit out. Sometimes the car enclosure requires change to accommodate a change in landing doors or change of rated load. At this time consideration should be given to increasing the platform area to include the floor area of any extensions or recesses (BS EN 81-1:1998, 8.2.1), e.g. stretcher extensions, or they should be removed. (*Note*: a car with a stretcher extension (see BS 5655-6:2002, 9.1.4) is one where the extension is available for the transport of stretchers under controlled conditions.) | **Checks to clauses of BS EN 81-1/2 (detailed in BS 5655-11/12), include:**<br>Disability access (BS EN 81-70)<br>Platform area, see change 2 (15)<br>Load change, see change 4<br><br>**Checks to BS EN 81-80 (see Table 16.2 and BS EN 81-80 for details), include:**<br>Electric:  38–40, 44 to 46, 58, 59, 73<br>Hydraulic:  38–40, 44 to 46, 58, 59, 73 |

*Table continues*

**Table 16.1** Undertaking modifications to existing lifts — *continued*

| 14  Change of door operator | Appropriate tests and records required |
|---|---|
| **Definition**<br>Mechanism for opening and closing the landing and car doors.<br><br>**Motivation**<br>The door operator is changed to one with a different specification. A change in positional performance might be desired from open loop to closed loop control, or the dynamic performance might require improvement. | **Checks to clauses of BS EN 81-1/2 (detailed in BS 5655-11/12), include:**<br>Structural compatibility with car/car frame<br>Compatibility with locking devices<br>Unlocking zone (7.7.1)<br>Apron (8.4)<br>Adequate clearances (5.7, 11)<br>Hazards on the car roof (5.7.1.1)<br>Change the mass of the car (see change 4)<br>Protection against electric shock (13.5.3.2 and 13.5.3.5).<br>Dynamic requirements (8.7.2.1.1)<br><br>**Checks to BS EN 81-80 (see Table 16.2 and BS EN 81-80 for details), include:**<br>Electric:  34, 35, 66, 74<br>Hydraulic:  34, 35, 66, 74 |
| **15  Change from gates to doors** | **Appropriate tests and records required** |
| **Definition**<br>Gates are used to protect the access to a lift car and are perforate.<br><br>**Motivation**<br>In order to improve safety the gates can be replaced by doors. The change might retain manual operation or the opportunity might be taken to fit power-operated doors. | **Checks to clauses of BS EN 81-1/2 (detailed in BS 5655-11/12), include:**<br>Conformity (7, 8)<br>Well structure (5)<br>Clearances (11)<br>Change the mass of the car (see change 4)<br><br>**Electric only:**<br>Traction (9.3)<br><br>**Checks to BS EN 81-80 (see Table 16.2 and BS EN 81-80 for details), include:**<br>Electric/hydraulic:  25 to 37, 40, 58, 59, 66, 74 |
| **16  Change of guide rails or type of guide rails** | **Appropriate tests and records required** |
| **Definition**<br><br>Guidance system for the lift car and counterweight/balancing weight.<br><br>**Motivation**<br>A change of guide rails or type of guide rails can occur when an installation is upgraded or modified. | **Checks to clauses of BS EN 81-1/2 (detailed in BS 5655-11/12), include:**<br>Guidance system (10, Annex G)<br>Well structure (5)<br>Clearances (5.7)<br>Compatibility with fixings<br>Compatibility with safety gear (9.8)<br>Compatibility with governor (9.9)<br><br>**Checks to BS EN 81-80 (see Table 16.2 and BS EN 81-80 for details), include:**<br>Electric:  11-13, 50, 55<br>Hydraulic:  11-13, 50, 55 |

**Table 16.2** Summary of significant hazards from BS EN 81-80: 2003 that might be encountered while undertaking modifications to existing lifts; column 1 is hazard number, column 2 is a summary, column 3 refers to the relevant clause number in BS EN 81-80: 2003 and column 4 offers remedial action (references are to BS EN 81-1/2: 1998 unless indicated otherwise, see sections 16.8 and 16.9)

| No. | Description | BS EN 81-80 clause | Remedial action to BS EN 81-1/2* |
|---|---|---|---|
| **General** | | | |
| 1 | Presence of harmful materials | 5.1.4 | 0.3.1 |
| **Accessibility** | | | |
| 2 | No or limited accessibility for disabled persons | 5.2.1 | Measures to BS EN 81-70 |
| 3 | Drive system with bad stopping/levelling accuracy | 5.2.2 | BS EN 81-70, 5.3.3 |
| **Vandalism** | | | |
| 4 | No or inadequate vandal resistance | 5.3 | Measures to prEN 81-71 |
| **Behaviour in the event of fire** | | | |
| 5 | No or inadequate control functions in case of fire | 5.4 | Measures to BS EN 81-73 |
| **Lift well** (Section 5 of BS EN 81-1: 1998, BS EN 81-2: 1998) | | | |
| 6 | Well enclosures with perforate walls | 5.5.1.1 | (a) fit imperforate well enclosure, or (b) fit perforate enclosure to BS EN 294: 1992, 4.5.2 |
| 7 | Partially enclosed well with too low enclosure | 5.5.1.2 | 5.2.1.2 |
| 8 | (a) Inadequate locking devices on access doors to well and pit | 5.5.2 | 5.2.2.2.1 |
|  | (b) Car does not stop when access doors to well and pit are opened | 5.5.2 | 5.2.2.2.2 |
| 9 | Inadequate vertical surface below landing door sills | 5.5.3 | 5.4.3 |
| 10 | Counterweight/balancing weight without safety gear in case of accessible spaces below well | 5.5.4 | (a) provide solid pier, or (b) fit safety gear to counterweight/balance weight |
| 11 | No or inadequate partition of counterweight/balancing weight travel path | 5.5.5 | 5.6.1 |
| 12 | No or inadequate pit screen for several lifts in the same well | 5.5.6.1 | 5.6.2.1 |
| 13 | No or inadequate partition for several lifts in the same well | 5.5.6.2 | 5.6.2.2 |
| 14 | Insufficient safety spaces in headroom and pit | 5.5.7 | {1} 5.7.1–5.7.3 {2} 5.7.1–5.7.2 |
| 15 | Unsafe pit access | 5.5.8 | {1} 5.7.3.2 {2} 5.7.2.2 |
| 16 | No or inadequate stopping devices in the pit or in the pulley room | 5.5.9 | {1} 5.7.3.4, 6.4.5 {2} 5.7.2.5, 6.4.5 |
| 17 | No or inadequate lighting of the well | 5.5.10 | 5.9 |
| 18 | No alarm system in pit and on car top | 5.5.11 | 5.10 (14.2.3, BS EN 81-28) |

| No. | Description | BS EN 81-80 clause | Remedial action to BS EN 81-1/2* |
|---|---|---|---|
| **Machine and pulley rooms** (Section 6 of BS EN 81-1: 1998, BS EN 81-2: 1998) | | | |
| 19 | No or unsafe means of access to machine and pulley room | 5.6.1 | 6.2 |
| 20 | Slippery floor in machine or pulley room | 5.6.2 | 6.3.1.2, 6.4.1.2 |
| 21 | Insufficient clearances in machine room | 5.6.3 | Guard to BS EN 294: 1992, Table 4 |
| 22 | No or inadequate protection on different levels in machine pulley room | 5.6.4 | 6.3.2.4–6.3.2.5 |
| 23 | Inadequate lighting in machine or pulley room | 5.6.5 | 6.3.6, 6.4.7 |
| 24 | Inadequate lifting means for handling equipment | 5.6.6 | Test and display SWL of lifting means and check suitability of position |
| **Landing doors and car doors** (Section 7 of BS EN 81-1: 1998, BS EN 81-2: 1998) | | | |
| 25 | Perforate landing doors and car doors | 5.7.1 | 7.1, 8.6.1 |
| 26 | Inadequate strength of landing door fixings | 5.7.2 | 7.2.3.1, 7.4.2.1 |
| 27 | Inadequate provision of glass in doors | 5.7.3 | (a) 7.2.3.2–7.2.3.4, 8.6.7.2–8.6.7.4, or (b) Annex J, or (c) 7.6.2, or (d) remove, add signal |
| 28 | No or inadequate protection against dragging of a child's hands on a horizontal sliding car or a landing doors with glass | 5.7.4 | 7.2.3.6, 8.6.7.5 |
| 29 | No or inadequate lighting on landing | 5.7.5 | 7.6.1 |
| 30a | No or inadequate protective devices on power operated car and landing doors (not intended for disabled use) | 5.7.6 | (a) 7.5.2.1.1, 8.7.2.1.1, or (b) BS EN 81-70, 5.2.3–5.2.4 |
| 30b | No or inadequate protective devices on power operated car and landing doors (intended for disabled use) | 5.7.6 | BS EN 81-70, 5.2.3–5.2.4 |
| 31 | Unsafe or inadequate locking device of landing door | 5.7.7 | 7.7.3.1 |
| 32 | Unlocking of landing door without using a special tool | 5.7.8.1 | 7.7.3.2 |
| 33 | Access to door locks through perforate well enclosure | 5.7.8.2 | (a) fit imperforate well enclosure, or (b) fit protection around door locks |
| 34 | No automatic closing device on horizontal sliding doors | 5.7.9 | 7.7.3.2 |
| 35 | Inadequate link between panels of landing doors | 5.7.10 | 7.7.6 |

* {1} indicates BS EN 81-1 only, {2} indicates BS EN 81-2 only

**Table 16.2** Summary of significant hazards from BS EN 81-80: 2003 that might be encountered while undertaking modifications to existing lifts — *continued*

| No. | Description | BS EN 81-80 clause | Remedial action to BS EN 81-1/2* | No. | Description | BS EN 81-80 clause | Remedial action to BS EN 81-1/2* |
|---|---|---|---|---|---|---|---|
| 36 | Inadequate fire resistance of landing doors | 5.7.11 | Fit doors to specified fire regulations | 52 | No protection means against ascending car overspeed on electric lifts with counter-weight {electric lifts} | 5.9.4 | {1} 9.10 |
| 37 | Power operated car door moving with open hinged landing door | 5.7.12 | Ensure: the landing door is not unlocked until the car door is fully open AND the car door cannot close until the landing door is fully closed | 53 | Inadequate design of lift machine to prevent uncontrolled movement with open doors {electric lifts} | 5.9.4, 5.12.1 | {1} (a) change to BS EN 81-1: 1998 machine, or (b) install protective means to BS EN 81-80, 5.9.4, Note 2, and/or (c) fit double acting brake to 12.4.2 |

**Car, counterweight and balancing weight**
(Section 8 of BS EN 81-1: 1998, BS EN 81-2: 1998)

| No. | Description | BS EN 81-80 clause | Remedial action to BS EN 81-1/2* | No. | Description | BS EN 81-80 clause | Remedial action to BS EN 81-1/2* |
|---|---|---|---|---|---|---|---|
| 38 | Large car area in relation to rated load | 5.8.1 | (a) reduce the available car floor area, or (b) restrict use of lift to instructed users only, or (c) verify the intended use | 54a | No or inadequate protection against free fall, overspeed and creeping {hydraulic lifts} | 5.9.5 | {2} 9.5 and Table 3 |
| 39 | Inadequate length of car apron | 5.8.2 | 8.4 | 54b | Automatic return to lowest floor when anti-creep used {hydraulic lifts} | 5.9.5 | {2} 14.2.1.5 |
| 40 | No car doors | 5.8.3 | (a) fit power operated car doors to 8.6–8.10, or (b) fit manual car doors to 8.6–8.7.1, 8.9–8.10 | | | | |

**Guide rails, buffers, final limit switches**
(Section 10 of BS EN 81-1: 1998, BS EN 81-2: 1998)

| No. | Description | BS EN 81-80 clause | Remedial action to BS EN 81-1/2* |
|---|---|---|---|
| 41 | Unsafe locking of car top emergency trap door | 5.8.4 | 8.12.4.2 |
| 42 | Insufficient strength of car top and emergency trap door | 5.8.5 | 8.13.1 |
| 43 | No or inadequate balustrade on car to protect against falling | 5.8.6 | (a) reduce free distance to less than 0.3 m, or (b) fit balustrade to 8.13.3, or (c) fit full height partition to reduce free distance to less than 0.3 m |

| No. | Description | BS EN 81-80 clause | Remedial action to BS EN 81-1/2* |
|---|---|---|---|
| 55 | Counterweight or balancing weight guided by 2 wire ropes {electric lifts} | 5.10.1 | {1} (a) 10.2.1, or (b) fit 4 wire ropes |
| 56 | No or inadequate buffers | 5.10.2 | 10.3 |
| 57 | No or inadequate final limit switches | 5.10.3 | 10.5 |

**Distances car/landing doors**
(Section 11 of BS EN 81-1: 1998, BS EN 81-2: 1998)

| No. | Description | BS EN 81-80 clause | Remedial action to BS EN 81-1/2* |
|---|---|---|---|
| 44 | Insufficient ventilation in car | 5.8.7 | 8.16 |
| 45 | Inadequate lighting in car | 5.8.8.1 | 8.17.1–8.17.3 |
| 46 | No or inadequate emergency lighting in car | 5.8.8.2 | 8.17.4 AND illuminate alarm button |

| No. | Description | BS EN 81-80 clause | Remedial action to BS EN 81-1/2* |
|---|---|---|---|
| 58 | Large horizontal gap between car and wall facing the car entrance | 5.11.1 | (a) reduce distance to 11.2.1, or (b) fit car door locking device to 8.9.3 |
| 59 | Excessive horizontal distance between car door and landing door | 5.11.2 | 11.2.3 |

**Suspension, compensation, overspeed**
(Section 9 of BS EN 81-1: 1998, BS EN 81-2: 1998)

**Lift machine**
(Section 12 of BS EN 81-1: 1998, BS EN 81-2: 1998)

| No. | Description | BS EN 81-80 clause | Remedial action to BS EN 81-1/2* |
|---|---|---|---|
| 47 | No or inadequate protection against injury on sheaves, pulleys and sprockets | 5.9.1 | {1} 9.7 {2} 9.4 |
| 48 | No or inadequate protection against rope/chains leaving the sheaves, pulleys or sprockets | 5.9.1 | {1} 9.7 {2} 9.4 |
| 49 | No or inadequate protection against introduction of objects on sheaves, pulleys or sprockets | 5.9.1 | {1} 9.7 {2} 9.4 |
| 50a | No safety gear and/or over-speed governor {electric lifts} | 5.9.2 | {1} 9.8–9.9 |
| 50b | Incorrect functioning of safety gear {electric lifts} | 5.9.2 | {1} (a) adjust system, or and/or overspeed governor (b) 9.8–9.9 |
| 51 | No or inadequate slack rope switch for governor rope | 5.9.3 | {1} 9.9.11.3 {2} 9.10.2.10.3 |

| No. | Description | BS EN 81-80 clause | Remedial action to BS EN 81-1/2* |
|---|---|---|---|
| 60a | No or inadequate emergency operation system {electric lifts} | 5.12.2 | {1} 12.5, 16.3.1 |
| 60b | No or inadequate emergency operation system {hydraulic lifts} | 5.12.2 | {2} 12.9, 16.3.1 |
| 61 | No shut-off valve {hydraulic lifts} | 5.12.3 | {2} 12.5.1 |
| 62 | No or inadequate means of stopping the machine and checking its position | 5.12.4 | {1} 12.7 {2} 12.4 |
| 63 | No or inadequate slack rope/chain device | 5.12.5 | {1} 9.5.3, 12.9 {2} 12.13 |
| 64 | No run-time limiter | 5.12.6 | {1} 12.10 {2} 12.12 |
| 65a | No or inadequate low pressure device {indirect hydraulic lifts} | 5.12.7 | {2} 12.9.1.5 |

* {1} indicates BS EN 81-1 only, {2} indicates BS EN 81-2 only

**Table 16.2** Summary of significant hazards from BS EN 81-80: 2003 that might be encountered while undertaking modifications to existing lifts — *continued*

| No. | Description | BS EN 81-80 clause | Remedial action to BS EN 81-1/2★ | No. | Description | BS EN 81-80 clause | Remedial action to BS EN 81-1/2★ |
|---|---|---|---|---|---|---|---|
| 65b | No or inadequate low pressure device, jack not rigidly fastened to the car {direct acting hydraulic lifts} | 5.12.7 | {2} 12.9.1.5 | 70a | No or inadequate inspection control station on car top | 5.14.2 | 14.2.1.3 |
| **Electric installation/appliances** (Section 13 of BS EN 81-1: 1998, BS EN 81-2: 1998) | | | | 70b | No or inadequate stopping device on car top | 5.14.2 | 14.2.2 |
| 66 | Insufficient protection against electric shock and/or marking of electrical equipment; missing notices | 5.13.1 | (*a*) 13.1.2 and (*b*) 13.5.3.3 and (*c*) fit warning notice to group controllers | 71 | No or inadequate emergency alarm device | 5.14.3 | 14.2.3, measures to BS EN 81-28 |
| 67 | No or inadequate protection on lift machine motor | 5.13.2 | 13.3.1–13.3.3 | 72 | No or inadequate communication system between machine room and car (travel height ≥ 30 m) | 5.14.4 | 14.2.3.4 |
| 68 | No lockable main switch | 5.13.3 | 13.4.2 | 73 | No or inadequate load control on car | 5.14.5 | 14.2.5 |
| **Protection against electric faults, etc.** (Section 14 of BS EN 81-1: 1998, BS EN 81-2: 1998) | | | | **Notices, markings, operating instructions** (Section 15 of BS EN 81-1: 1998, BS EN 81-2: 1998) | | | |
| 69 | No protection against phase reversal | 5.14.1 | 14.1.1.1.j | 74 | Missing notices, markings and operating instructions for safe use and maintenance | 5.15 | {1} 15.2.1, 15.3, 15.4, 15.5.1, 15.5.3, 15.7, 15.11, 15.15 {2} 15.2.1, 15.2.5, 15.3, 15.4, 15.5.1, 15.5.3, 15.7, 15.11, 15.15, 15.17, 15.18 |

★ {1} indicates BS EN 81-1 only, {2} indicates BS EN 81-2 only

# References

1      Barney G C *Elevator traffic handbook* (London: Spon) (2003)

2      BS EN 81-1: 1998: *Safety rules for the construction and installation of lifts*: Part 1: *Electric lifts* (London: British Standards Institution) (1998)

3      BS EN 81-2: 1998: *Safety rules for the construction and installation of lifts*: Part 2: *Hydraulic lifts* (London: British Standards Institution) (1998)

4      BS 5655-6: 2002: *Lifts and service lifts. Code of practice for selection and installation* (London: British Standards Institution) (2002)

5      BS 5655-10: 1986: *Lifts and service lifts. Specification for the testing and inspection of electric and hydraulic lifts* (London: British Standards Institution) (1986)

6      BS 5655-11: 1989: *Recommendations for the installation of new, and the modernization of, electric lifts in existing buildings* (London: British Standards Institution) (1989) (under revision)

7      BS 5655-12: 1989: *Recommendations for the installations of new, and the modernization of, hydraulic lifts in existing buildings* (London: British Standards Institution) (1989) (under revision)

8      BS 7255: 2001: *Code of practice for safe working on lifts* (London: British Standards Institution) (2001)

9      BS EN 81-28: 2003: *Remote alarms on passenger and goods passenger lifts* (London: British Standards Institution) (2003)

10     DD CEN/TS 81-29: 2004: *Safety rules for the construction and installation of lifts. Safety rules for the construction and installation of lifts. Lifts for the transport of persons and goods. Interpretations related to EN 81-20 up to EN 81-28* (London: British Standards Institution) (2004)

11     BS EN 81-58: 2003: *Lift landing doors, fire resistance testing* (London: British Standards Institution) (2003)

12     BS EN 81-70: 2003: *Safety rules for the construction and installation of lifts. Particular applications for passenger and goods passenger lifts*: Part 70: *Accessibility to lifts for persons including persons with disability* (London: British Standards Institution) (2003)

13     BS EN 81-71: 2005: *Safety rules for the construction and installation of lifts*: Part 71: *Vandal resistant lifts* (London: British Standards Institution) (2005)

14     BS EN 81-72:2003: *Rules for lifts which remain in use in case of fire (Firefighters lifts)* (London: British Standards Institution) (2003)

15     BS EN 81-73: 2005: *Behaviour of lifts in the event of fire* (London: British Standards Institution) (2005)

16     BS EN 81-80: 2003: *Existing lifts. Rules for the improvement of safety of existing passenger and goods passenger lifts* (London: British Standards Institution) (2003)

17     PAS 32-1: 1999: *Specification for examination and test of new lifts before putting into service. Electric traction lifts* (London: British Standards Institution) (1999)

18     PAS 32-2: 1999: *Specification for examination and test of new lifts before putting into service. Hydraulic lifts* (London: British Standards Institution) (1999)

19     HSE leaflet IND(G)1(L) Rev. 1987 (London: Health and Safety Executive) (1987)

20     The Lifts Regulations 1997. Statutory Instrument 1997 No. 831 (London: The Stationery Office) (1997)

# 17    Legislation, standards and codes of practice

## Principal authors

John Snowball (Steven Morris Associates)
Dr Gina Barney (Gina Barney Associates)

## Chapter contents

| | | |
|---|---|---|
| 17.1 | Legislation | 17-3 |
| | 17.1.1 Construction (Design and Management) Regulations 1994 (CDM) | 17-3 |
| | 17.1.2 Control of Asbestos at Work Regulations 1987 | 17-3 |
| | 17.1.3 Control of Substances Hazardous to Health Regulations 1999 (COSHH) | 17-3 |
| | 17.1.4 Disability Discrimination Act 1995 (DDA) | 17-3 |
| | 17.1.5 Electricity at Work Regulations 1989 | 17-4 |
| | 17.1.6 Electrical Equipment (Safety) Regulations 1994 | 17-4 |
| | 17.1.7 Electromagnetic Compatibility Directive (EMC) | 17-4 |
| | 17.1.8 Framework Directive | |
| | 17.1.9 Health and Safety at Work etc. Act 1974 (HSWA) | 17-4 |
| | 17.1.10 Lifting Operations and Lifting Equipment Regulations 1998 (LOLER) | 17-5 |
| | 17.1.11 Lifts Regulations 1997 | 17-5 |
| | 17.1.12 Low Voltage Directive | 17-6 |
| | 17.1.13 Machinery Directive | 17-6 |
| | 17.1.14 Management of Health and Safety at Work Regulations 1999 (MHSWR) | 17-6 |
| | 17.1.15 Provision and Use of Work Equipment Regulations 1998 (PUWER) | 17-6 |
| | 17.1.16 Personal Protection Equipment at Work Regulations 1992 (PPE) | 17-7 |
| | 17.1.17 Supply of Machinery (Safety) Regulations 1992 (as amended 1994) | 17-7 |
| | 17.1.18 Workplace (Health, Safety and Welfare) Regulations 1992 | 17-7 |
| 17.2 | Standards and Codes of Practice | 17-7 |
| | 17.2.1 British Standards Institution | 17-7 |
| | 17.2.2 Standards and Codes of Practice | 17-8 |
| References | | 17-8 |

# 17    Legislation, standards and codes of practice

## 17.1    Legislation

*Important note*: this section is provided for information only. Of necessity it is brief, may not include all possible information and may or may not be applicable to all activities in the vertical transportation field. Responsible persons must review the contents and decide applicability. CIBSE cannot be held responsible for any loss or injury resulting from the use of this information. Other sources of information include:

— British Standards Institution (BSI): http://bsonline.techindex.co.uk

— Chartered Institution of Building Services Engineers (CIBSE): www.cibse.org

— Her Majesty's Stationery Office (HMSO): www.hmso.gov.uk

— Health and Safety Executive (HSE): www.hse.gov.uk

— Office of the Deputy Prime Minister (ODPM): www.odpm.gov.uk

— The Stationery Office (TSO): www.tso.co.uk

The legislation is listed alphabetically by title to avoid any presumption of relative importance.

### 17.1.1    Construction (Design and Management) Regulations 1994

The Construction (Design and Management) Regulations 1994 (CDM) place duties on clients and their agents (where appointed), designers and contractors to coordinate and manage the health and safety aspects of a construction project with the aim to control and reduce the risks involved.

These Regulations are extensively covered in Chapter 18 of this Guide.

### 17.1.2    Control of Asbestos at Work Regulations 1987

The Control of Asbestos at Work Regulations 1987 require employers to prevent the exposure of employees to asbestos or, if this is not reasonably practicable, to control such exposure to the lowest possible level. Before any work with asbestos is carried out, the Regulations require employers to make an assessment of the likely exposure of employees to asbestos dust, which can include a description of the precautions that are taken to control dust release and to protect workers and others who may be affected by that work.

These Regulations are superior to the PUWER Regulations (see section 17.1.14), COSHH Regulations (see section 17.1.3) and the CDM Regulations (see section 17.1.1), which rely on them.

### 17.1.3    Control of Substances Hazardous to Health Regulations 1999

The Control of Substances Hazardous to Health Regulations 1994 (COSHH) and subsequent amendments set out a framework of action for employers and self-employed persons to follow, which aims to protect the health of all people who might be exposed to hazardous substances at work. Employers must protect employees and others who may effected by:

— carrying out a risk assessment

— identifying and implementing control measures

— ensuring that the control measures are used

— ensuring that employees are properly informed, trained and supervised.

Hazardous substances include chemicals, dust, gases and fumes. Asbestos is excluded from the Control of Substances Hazardous to Health Regulations as it is covered by separate regulations (see section 17.1.2).

These Regulations resulted from European Directive 80/1107/EEC and first came into force in 1988. The latest version includes provisions required by the European Biological Agents Directive (90/679/EEC) and came into force on 25 March 1999.

### 17.1.4    Disability Discrimination Act 1995

The Act gives disabled people new rights in access to goods, facilities and services, buying and renting land and employment. The right of non discrimination came into force in December 1996 requiring goods, facilities and services to be accessible to disabled people; this can include the removal of physical barriers, but does not impose specific requirements.

Service providers have had to change their policies and provide auxiliary aids from October 1999. Businesses and service providers have had a duty, from 1 October 2004, to make 'reasonable adjustments' to the 'physical features' of both old and new buildings, in order to overcome barriers to access. These reasonable adjustments must consider a range of disabilities such as people with mobility, visual, hearing, speech and dexterity impairments as well as those with learning difficulties and mental health disabilities.

'Reasonable adjustments' take account of:

— practicality

— financial and other costs

— disruption

— resources available

— availability of financial assistance.

Lifts, escalators and moving walks are examples of 'physical features'.

*Note*: the Disability Rights Commission★ has published a number of codes of practice relating to duties applicable under the Disability Discrimination Act 1995.

## 17.1.5 Electricity at Work Regulations 1989

These Regulations came into force on 1 April 1990 and introduce a control framework incorporating fundamental principles of electrical safety applying to a wide range of plant systems and work activities. They apply to all places of work, and electrical systems at all voltages. They apply to employers and self-employed persons and set out requirements for all electrical systems, including construction, integrity, maintenance and isolation.

## 17.1.6 Electrical Equipment (Safety) Regulations 1994

The Electrical Equipment (Safety) Regulations 1994 implement the requirements of composite Directive 93/68/EEC and cover the supply of electrical equipment which, when properly installed, does not endanger persons, domestic animals or property and provides safe operation of the equipment by users, free from electric shock. Low voltage is defined as 50 to 100 V AC or 75 to 1500 V DC.

Schedule 2 of these Regulations excludes parts for escalators and passenger conveyors, as these are considered to be a factory-built assembly.

## 17.1.7 Electromagnetic Compatibility Directive (EMC)

This Directive was first enacted as the Electromagnetic Compatibility Directive (89/336/EEC) and amended by 92/31/EEC and 93/68/EEC. This Directive deals with the two elements of EMC, i.e. emission and immunity.

The emission requirements of the Directive are specified so as to ensure a level of electromagnetic emission which will cause minimal disturbance to other equipment.

The immunity requirements of the Directive are specified so as to ensure a level of electromagnetic immunity which will allow minimal disturbance to vertical transportation equipment.

★ Information is available from DRC Helpline, Freepost MID02164, Stratford-upon-Avon, CV37 9BR (tel. +44 (0)8457 622633), or from the Disability Rights Commission website at www.drc-gb.org

Generic immunity and emission standards that support the Electromagnetic Compatibility Regulations 1992 are the BS EN 61000[6] series. Industry standards for lifts, escalators and passenger conveyors are BS EN 12015[4] and BS EN 12016[5].

## 17.1.8 Framework Directive

European Directive 89/391/EEC deals with 'the introduction of measures to encourage improvements in the health and safety of workers at work.' The Directive is largely implemented in the Management of Health and Safety at Work Regulations 1992 (MHSWR) (see section 17.1.13).

## 17.1.9 Health and Safety at Work etc. Act 1974 (HSWA)

This is a primary piece of legislation, also used to enact other safety regulations. Introduces the duty that everyone is their own safety officer.

(a) It applies to all employers, who must, as far as reasonably practical, safeguard the health, safety and welfare of employees. In particular the provision and maintaining of:

— safe plant and safe systems of work

— safe handling, storage, maintenance and transport of (work) articles and substances

— necessary information, instruction, training and supervision

— a safe place of work, safe access and egress

— a safe working environment with adequate welfare facilities.

Employers of five or more employees must prepare and revise a written statement of safety policy. Employees must read, understand and apply the employer's safety policy.

(b) Employers, the self-employed and employees have a duty to conduct their undertakings in such a way as to ensure, so far as is reasonably practicable, that all persons who might be affected by the work activity are not exposed to risks to their health and safety.

(c) Manufacturers, suppliers etc. of articles for use at work have a duty to ensure, so far as is reasonably practicable, that the articles are so designed and constructed that they will be safe and without risk to health when they are being set, used, cleaned or maintained.

(d) Erectors and installers of articles for use at work have a duty to ensure, so far as is reasonably practicable, that nothing about the way articles are erected or installed is unsafe or a risk to health.

(e) Persons concerned with premises have a duty to persons other than employees who use non-domestic premises made available to them as a place of work. It is the duty of the person who controls the premises to take such measures as it is reasonable for them to take to ensure, so far as is reasonably practicable, that the premises, the means of access and egress to and from the premises, and any plant of substance in the premises, are safe and without risk to health.

## 17.1.10 Lifting Operations and Lifting Equipment Regulations 1998 (LOLER)

The Regulations give effect to Directive 89/655/EEC on the health and safety requirements for the use of work equipment by persons at work, as amended by Directive 95/63/EC, and came into force on 5 December 1998.

Lifting operations mean an operation concerned with the lifting or lowering of a load. Lifting equipment means work equipment for lifting or lowering loads and includes its attachments for anchoring, fixing or supporting it. An accessory for lifting means work equipment for attaching loads to machinery for lifting. Work equipment means any machinery, appliance, tool or installation for use at work. Load includes a person and the Regulations include passenger lifts.

LOLER applies to lifting equipment for lifting persons, but does apply to escalators and passenger conveyors.

LOLER requires that a 'thorough examination'* be carried out every six months (or as determined by risk assessment) by a competent person and a report issued. The report should notify any defect which in the opinion of the competent person could be, or become, a danger to persons. Where there a serious risk of personnel injury a report should be sent as soon as reasonably practical to the relevant enforcing authority (HSE or Local Authority).

PUWER, see section 17.1.14, applies to lifting equipment.

## 17.1.11 Lifts Regulations 1997

These Regulations implement Directive 95/16/EC ('the Lift Directive') in order to meet the 'essential health and safety requirements' (ESHRs) defined in the Directive. The Regulations came into full force on 1 July 1999. The Regulations contain fifteen complex schedules setting out the arrangements. The most important of these is Schedule 1, which sets out the ESHRs relating to the design and construction of lifts and safety components. Among the terms defined are: lift, harmonised standard, installer, safe, placing on the market, Essential Health and Safety Requirements, responsible person. 'Putting into service' is not specifically defined.

The Lifts Regulations 1997 require new lift installations to comply with the ESHRs laid down in Schedule 1 of the Regulations. These requirements apply to the entire lift installation including the building fabric and supporting building services. Compliant installations will carry a 'CE' mark in the lift car. The CE-marking denotes that either (a) the entire installation complies in full to harmonised standards or to a pre-approved 'model' standard, or (b) the installation meets the minimum essential health and safety requirements approved by a 'notified body'. These

are known as the 'Routes to Conformity'. The most common routes to conformity are the installation of 'model' lifts and lift installations meeting harmonised standards. Schedule 1 is summarised below.

1 General:

1.2(*a*) Car to be designed for adequate space and strength for rated load.

1.2(*b*) Provide (if possible) unimpeded access to disabled persons.

1.3(*a*) Provide adequate means of suspension.

1.3(*b*) Provide at least two ropes or chains.

1.4.1 Provide an overload device.

1.4.2 Provide overspeed limitation.

1.4.3 Provide speed monitoring and speed limiting on fast lifts.

1.4.4 Adequate traction is required.

1.5.1 Each lift has its own machine.

1.5.2 Machinery is inaccessible to public.

1.6.1 Controls for use of disabled may be provided.

1.6.2 Function of controls to be clearly indicated.

1.6.3 Group call circuit interconnections provided.

1.6.4(*a*) No confusion with lift supply.

1.6.4(*b*) Possible to switch off lift under load.

1.6.4(*c*) Movement dependent on an electrical safety circuit.

1.6.4(*d*) A fault in the electrical system not dangerous.

2 Hazards to persons outside the car:

2.1(*a*) Adequate well size.

2.1(*b*) Entering well stops lift.

2.2 Provision of refuge spaces.

2.3(*a*) Provide strong landing doors.

2.3(*b*) Provide landing door interlocks

3 Hazards to persons in the car:

3.1(*a*) Fully enclosed cars.

3.1(*b*) Doors cannot open between floors.

3.2(*a*) Prevention of free fall/uncontrolled upward movement.

3.2(*b*) The device is capable of stopping lift with rated load and speed.

3.3 Buffers to be provided.

3.4 If device in 3.2 set then lift cannot move.

4 Other hazards:

4.1 Power doors not to crush passengers.

4.2 Doors to have fire resistance.

4.3 Counterweights to be guided.

---

* The Safety Federation (SaFed) provides guidance in its *Guidelines on the thorough examination and testing of lifts*, known as LG1 examinations. (www.safed.co.uk)

4.4     Provision of equipment to release trapped passengers.

4.5     Two-way permanent communication with rescue service.

4.6     Lift machine over-temperature detection.

4.7     Car ventilation to be provided.

4.8     Car lighting (normal and emergency) to be provided.

4.9     Alternative power for communication and lighting.

4.10    Fire control.

5       Marking:

5.1     Car rating plate.

5.2     Release of trapped passengers without outside help (if so designed).

6       Instructions for use:

6.1     Provide instruction manual for safety components.

6.2(a)  User instruction manual to be provided.

6.2(b)  Log book to be provided.

For installations where conformity is to be obtained other than by installing to harmonised standards, the specific requirements for the lift installation's environment should be sought. This is defined in the model lift's technical documentation, or otherwise approved by a Notified Body. The harmonised standards which satisfy the EHSRs are the BS EN 81[1] series of safety standards.

For lift modernisations where the lift is not deemed to be new, the installation falls outside of the scope of the Lifts Regulations and BS 5655[3] etc. still applies.

The Regulations do not apply to lifts installed and put into service before 1 July 1999 and a number of specialist lifts listed in Schedule 14 of the Regulations.

## 17.1.12    Low Voltage Directive

This European Directive (72/23/EEC) is concerned that electrical equipment, when properly installed, shall not endanger persons, domestic animals or property and shall provide safe operation of the equipment by users free from risk of electric shock. Low voltage is defined as 50–1000 V AC or 75–1500 V DC.

Lifts are excluded in Annex II of the Directive, as lifts can be treated for the purpose of the Directive as a factory-built assembly. Escalators and passenger conveyors are not excluded from the Directive.

## 17.1.13    Machinery Directive

This Directive was first enacted as 89/392/EEC and amended by Directives 91/368/EEC, 93/44/EEC and 93/68/EEC.

It applies to escalators and applies to other vertical transportation equipment not appropriate to be regulated by the Lifts Directive, e.g. lifting platforms, stairlifts, domestic lifts.

## 17.1.14    Management of Health and Safety at Work Regulations 1999 (MHSWR)

These Regulations implement most of the European Directive 89/391/EEC and European Directive 91/383/EEC dealing with the health and safety of persons employed on a fixed term or temporary basis. Regulation 3 requires:

> 'Every employer and self employed person to make a suitable and sufficient assessment of safety risks to employees and others not directly employed, but who are affected by the employers undertakings, in order to put in place appropriate control measures. Reviews of the assessments shall be made and significant findings recorded if more than five people are employed.'

The purpose of the assessment is to identify and quantify the risk. Employers are required to implement preventative and protective measures to eliminate risk, and to put in place effective control measures to address residual risks and hazards.

The employer is required to appoint competent persons to assist the employer in order to develop controls and procedures for health and safety management. The regulations include requirements for training, health and safety assistance, information, organisation, control, monitoring and review.

## 17.1.15    Provision and Use of Work Equipment Regulations 1998 (PUWER)

The Regulations revoke and re-enact the Provisions and Use of Work Equipment Regulations 1992, which gave effect to Directive 89/655/EEC on the minimum health and safety requirements for the use of work equipment by workers at work, and came into force on 5 December 1998.

The Regulations require risks to the health and safety of persons from equipment they use at work, to be prevented or controlled by ensuring that it is:

—       suitable for use;

—       maintained in a safe condition; and

—       inspected in certain circumstances.

'Use of work equipment' means any activity involving work equipment and includes starting, stopping, programming, setting, transporting, repairing, modifying, maintaining, servicing and cleaning.

'Work equipment' covers all machinery, appliance, tool, equipment or installation used by an employee or a self-employed person at work and includes static and mobile machinery, installations, lifts, escalator and passenger conveyor equipment. It includes hoists and elevating work platforms.

The regulations cover also cover: thorough examination, guarding, controlling, provision of information, training in the use of work equipment.

LOLER (see section 17.1.10) additionally applies to lifting equipment.

## 17.1.16 Personal Protection Equipment at Work Regulations 1992

Implements some of the requirements of the Workplace Directive (89/656/EEC).

Personal protective equipment (PPE) means:

'All equipment designed to be worn or held by a person at work to protect against one or more risks, and any addition or accessory designed to meet this objective.'

Personal protective equipment includes:

— helmets

— eye protection

— ear protection

— safety footwear

— gloves

— safety harness

— protective clothing

— high visibility clothing etc.

Employers are required to provide suitable personal protective equipment to each of their employees who might be exposed to risk.

Personal protective equipment is to be used as a last resort after all measures to prevent or control risks at source are exhausted.

The Regulations cover: suitability, compatibility, maintenance, replacement, information, loss, defect, etc.

## 17.1.17 Supply of Machinery (Safety) Regulations 1992 (as amended 1994)

The Supply of Machinery (Safety) Regulations 1992 and subsequent amendments implement the requirements of the Machinery Directive (98/37/EC). The Machinery Directive applies to a wide range of machines that include chain saws, power presses, tractors etc., but it is also applicable to escalators and moving walks. Annex 1 of the Machinery Directive lists the essential health and safety requirements (ESHRs) that apply to all machines.

The harmonised standard that supports the Machinery Directive and the Supply of Machinery (Safety) Regulations is BS EN 115[2].

## 17.1.18 Workplace (Health, Safety and Welfare) Regulations 1992

These regulations implement most of the requirements of the Workplace Directive (89/654/EEC) and are concerned with the minimum standards for workplace health and safety and the reduction of risk. The Regulations have been applied in full since 1 January 1996. The provisions have long been part of UK law but their application was not. Areas covered include: maintenance of workplace, maintenance of workplace equipment, ventilation, temperature, lighting, cleanliness, traffic routes, fall protection, doors and gates, sanitary and washing facilities, etc.

Regulation 19 requires lifts, passenger conveyors and escalators to function safely, be equipped with any necessary safety devices and have one or more identifiable and accessible emergency stop controls.

## 17.1.19 Other legislation

In addition to the above the following statutory provisions might be applicable to the construction, installation, service, maintenance and use of vertical transportation equipment:

— Building Regulations 2000 (e.g. Part M) and subsequent amendments

— Confined Spaces Regulations 1997

— Construction (Head Protection) Regulations 1989

— Construction (Health, Safety and Welfare) Regulations 1996 (CHSWR)

— Fire Precautions Act 1971

— Fire Precautions (Workplace) Regulations 1997

— Health and Safety (First Aid) Regulations 1991

— Health and Safety (Safety Signs and Signals) Regulations 1996

— Health and Safety (Display Screen Equipment) Regulations 1992

— Manual Handling Operations Regulations 1992

— Noise at Work Regulations 1989

— Reporting of Injuries, Diseases and Dangerous occurrences Regulations 1995 (RIDDOR)

## 17.2 Standards and codes of practice

This section is provided to indicate some of the standards and codes of practice pertinent to vertical transportation equipment.

### 17.2.1 British Standards Institution

The British Standards Institution (BSI) was founded in 1908 and incorporated by Royal Charter in 1929. It is an independent organisation that works with industry, trade associates and government to produce British, European and International standards. BSI is also involved in product testing and certification and quality assurance management systems. BSI's aim is 'to help British business become more efficient and competitive'.

The Mechanical Handling Equipment technical committee for lifts, escalators and passenger conveyors (MHE/4) is responsible for the production of standards and provides experts for the various CEN and ISO committees in developing harmonised standards.

In the production of national standards, BSI aims to ensure that they are consistent in content and format. For some time now this has included international work which is eventually either produced as a national standard or, more usually now, as a BS EN or BS ISO. BSI is now heavily involved in the work of the International Organisation for Standardisation (ISO), the International Electro-technical Commission (IEC), the European Committee for Standardisation (CEN) and the European Committee for Electro-technical Standardisation (CENELEC) in the harmonisation of standards.

Technical committee MHE/4 is made up of members from trade associations, professional institutions, user groups, government departments, notified bodies and local authorities representing the many different requirements and opinions.

The technical committee is large and to deal with the work efficiently and speed-up the decision making process, the MHE/4 technical committee has delegated particular tasks to an Advisory Panel (standing committee) and a number of subcommittees and panels.

The Advisory Panel includes in its terms of reference the possibility to 'take executive decisions on the behalf of MHE/4 where agreed by the chairman'.

The subcommittees and panels include members from the main MHE/4 committee, with a direct interest and specialist knowledge in the particular tasks and it is possible to co-opt persons with a particular expertise, when required. Each subcommittee and panel has its terms of reference and reports back to MHE/4 and its advisory panel on progress and for guidance on policy matters. Chairmen of sub-committees are usually nominated by MHE/4, although it can be left to the subcommittee members to elect their own chairman.

Generally, the sub-committees and panels are not permanently constituted and once they have completed their task(s) they are either disbanded or retained to deal with future amendments.

Once national work has been approved by MHE/4 it is edited by BSI and the draft standard or code of practice is circulated as a draft for public comment (DPC). Comments received are collated by the secretary, circulated to the originating sub-committee or panel for resolution. One this process is complete the draft can be signed off by the chairman.

Draft CEN standards (prEN) and draft international standards (DIS) are circulated for comment and dealt with in a similar manner.

It is becoming increasingly clear that purely national work is diminishing and being superseded by international and European harmonised standards work.

## 17.2.2 Standards and codes of practice

An up-to-date list (at the time of publication) is provide in Appendix A2. Responsible persons must review the list and decide their applicability.

# References

1    BS EN 81: *Safety rules for the construction and installation of lifts* (various parts) (London: British Standards Institution) (various dates)

2    BS EN 115: 1995: *Safety rules for the construction and installation of escalators and passenger conveyors* (various parts) (London: British Standards Institution) (various dates)

3    BS 5655: *Lifts and service lifts* (various parts) (London: British Standards Institution) (various dates)

4    BS EN 12015: 1998: *Electromagnetic compatibility. Product family standard for lifts, escalators and passenger conveyors. Emission* (London: British Standards Institution) (1998)

5    BS EN 12016: 2004: *Electromagnetic compatibility. Product family standard for lifts, escalators and moving walks. Immunity* (London: British Standards Institution) (2004)

6    BS EN 61000: *Electromagnetic compatibility (EMC)* (various parts) (London: British Standards Institution) (various dates)

# 18 Construction (Design and Management) Regulations 1994

## Principal author

Lift and Escalator Industry Association

## Chapter contents

| | | |
|---|---|---|
| 18.1 | Introduction | 18-3 |
| 18.2 | Definitions | 18-3 |
| 18.3 | General | 18-4 |
| 18.4 | Requirements of the CDM Regulations | 18-5 |
| 18.5 | Compliance with the CDM Regulations in relation to lift and escalator work | 18-7 |
| 18.6 | Roles and responsibilities | 18-8 |
| | 18.6.1 Client | 18-8 |
| | 18.6.2 Planning supervisor | 18-9 |
| | 18.6.3 Designer | 18-10 |
| | 18.6.4 Principal contractor | 18-11 |
| | 18.6.5 Contractors and self-employed persons | 18-11 |
| 18.7 | Penalties for failure to observe the CDM Regulations | 18-12 |
| References | | 18-12 |
| Bibliography | | 18-12 |

*Note*: At the time of publication (September 2005) the Construction (Design and Management) Regulations 1994 are under review and are likely to be amended within the lifetime of this Guide.

# 18    Construction (Design and Management) Regulations 1994

## 18.1    Introduction

The Construction (Design and Management) Regulations 1994[1] (CDM Regulations) were introduced against a background of improving safety in the construction industry.

The National Association of Lift Makers (NALM) published guidance to its members on the CDM Regulations and the CIBSE is indebted to its successor, the Lift and Escalator Industry Association (LEIA), for permission to reproduce this guidance[2]. LEIA was formed from the combined resources of NALM and the British Lift Association (BLA).

The published guidance concentrates on lifts and escalators but it is equally important to consider the wider picture especially the role of the planning supervisor. The Association of Planning Supervisor's publication EP1/96[3] is essential reading. Cooper[4] sets out key tasks for client, planning supervisor, designers, principal contractor and contractor/subcontractor.

## 18.2    Definitions

These definitions are important not only for their content but for the reason that certain of the expressions in the CDM Regulations are used in a different context to that in which they have been traditionally applied in the lift/escalator industry.

—    *Agent*: any person who acts as agent for a client in connection with the carrying on by the person of a trade, business or other undertaking, whether for profit or not.

—    *Client*: any person for whom a project is carried out, whether the project is carried out in-house or by another person. One of a number of clients, or the agent of a client can volunteer to accept the duties of Regulations 6 and 8–12. This acceptance has to be made by way of a declaration to the HSE when the project is notified.

—    *Cleaning work*: the cleaning of any window or transparent/translucent wall, ceiling or roof in or on a structure where the cleaning involves a risk of falling more than 2 m.

—    *Construction work*: the carrying out of any building, civil engineering or engineering construction work, and includes any of the following:

(a)    construction, alteration, conversion, fitting-out, commissioning, renovation, repair, upkeep, redecoration or other maintenance (including cleaning which involves the use of water or an abrasive at high pressure or the use of corrosive or toxic substances), decommissioning, demolition or dismantling of a structure

(b)    preparation for an intended structure including site clearance, exploration, investigation (but not site survey) and excavation, and laying or installing the foundations of the structure

(c)    assembly or disassembly of prefabricated elements of a structure; removal of a structure or part of a structure, or of any product or waste resulting from demolition or dismantling or a structure or disassembly of prefabricated elements of a structure; installation, commissioning, maintenance, repair or removal of mechanical, electrical, gas, compressed air, hydraulic, telecommunications, computer or similar services which are normally fixed within or to a structure, but does not include mineral resource exploration or extraction activities.

—    *Contractor*: any person who carries on a trade or business or other undertaking, whether for profit or not, in connection with which he/she undertakes to or does manage construction work, or arranges for any person at work under his/her control (including any employee, where he/she is an employer) to carry out or manage construction work. This definition can therefore be applied to the self-employed.

—    *Design*: in relation to any structure; includes drawing, design details, specification and bill of quantities (including specification of articles or substances) in relation to the structure

—    *Designer*: any person who carries on a trade, business or other undertaking in connection with which he/she prepares a design or arranges for any person under his/her control to prepare a design relating to a structure or part of a structure.

—    *Health and safety file*: a file or other record in permanent form containing the information required by Regulation 14(d), about the design, methods and materials used in the construction of a structure which it may be necessary for appropriate third parties to know about for their health and safety.

—    *Health and safety plan*: that which provides the health and safety focus for the construction phase of a project. The pre-tender health and safety plan should be prepared in time so that it is available for contractors tendering or making similar arrangements to carry out or manage construction work. The pre-tender plan should include:

(a)     a general description of the works

(b)     details of timings within the project

(c)     details of risks to workers as far as possible
        at that stage

(d)     information required by potential princi-
        pal contractors to demonstrate competence
        or adequacy of resources

(e)     information for preparing a health and
        safety plan for the construction phase and
        information for welfare provision.

The health and safety plan for the construction
phase should include:

(a)     arrangements for ensuring the health and
        safety of all who may be affected by the
        construction work

(b)     arrangements for the management of
        health and safety of construction work and
        monitoring of compliance with health and
        safety law

(c)     information about welfare arrangements.

— *Planning supervisor*: any person who has overall
   responsibility for co-ordinating the health and
   safety aspects of the design and planning phase
   and for the early stages of the health and safety
   plan and the health and safety file.

— *Principal contractor*: means the person who should
   take account of health and safety issues when
   preparing and presenting tenders or similar
   documents. The principal contractor also has to
   develop the health and safety plan and co-ordinate
   the activities of all contractors to ensure they
   comply with health and safety legislation.
   Principal contractors also have duties to check on
   the provision of information and training for
   employees and for consulting with employees, and
   the self-employed on health and safety.

— *Project*: a project which includes or is intended to
   include construction work.

— *Structure*: any building, steel or reinforced concrete
   structure (not being a building), railway line or
   siding, tramway line, dock, harbour, inland
   navigation, tunnel, shaft, bridge, viaduct, water-
   works, reservoir, pipe or pipeline (regardless of
   intended or actual contents), cable aqueduct,
   sewer, sewage works, gasholder, road, airfield, sea
   defence works, river works, drainage works,
   earthworks, lagoon, dam, wall, caisson, mast,
   tower, pylon, underground tank, earth retaining
   structure or structure designed to preserve or alter
   any natural feature, and any similar structure to
   these, and any formwork, falsework, scaffold or
   other structure designed or used to provide support or means of access during construction work,
   and any fixed plant in respect of work which is
   installation, commissioning, decommissioning or
   dismantling and where that work involves a risk of
   falling more than 2 m.

## 18.3     General

The Construction (Design and Management) Regulations
1994[1] implement the design and management content of
the Temporary or Mobile Construction Sites Directive[5]
of the EC, which was adopted on 24th June 1992. The
Directive contains two parts; the first applies the
Framework Directive provisions to construction sites, the
second refers the Workplace Directive to sites. Future
Regulations will implement the second part of the
Directive; the consequence will be that four main
Construction Regulations[6–9], dating from 1961 and 1966,
will be modified to contain the new requirements, or
replaced entirely by new material.

The Temporary or Mobile Construction Sites Directive
was required to be implemented in EC Member States by
local Regulations by 1st January 1994. After substantial
consultation, the UK regulations implementing the first
part of the Directive were made on 19th December 1994,
and laid before Parliament on 10th January 1995. They
came into effect from 31st March 1995.

Recognising that the construction 'system' in the UK has
characteristics not anticipated by the Directive, the CDM
Regulations simplify it by requiring the client to appoint
two central figures for the planning and the carrying out
of construction work within the scope of the Regulations.
These are the planning supervisor and the principal
contractor. The link between them is the safety plan,
initiated by the planning supervisor and adjusted by the
principal contractor to provide health and safety details
relevant to the work — risks, timings, information,
arrangements — which together make up a comprehensive
'how to do it safely' document for the work to be done.
There is also a requirement for a health and safety file to
be kept and given to the eventual owner of the construction work — a 'how we built it' collection of relevant
information which will be of use if future modification is
required. The Regulations give detailed job descriptions
for identified parties to the contract, in addition to duties
placed on them under the Management of Health and
Safety at Work Regulations 1992[10](MHSWR).

The CDM Regulations apply to work in territorial waters,
but not offshore, nor to the drilling and extractive
industries except indirectly.

Application of the CDM Regulations is not universal.
Generally, the Regulations apply to construction work
which lasts for more than 30 days or will involve more
than 500 person-days of work includes any demolition
work (regardless of duration or size)involves five or more
workers being on site at any one time.

CDM Regulations always apply to any design work for the
construction process. The Regulations do not apply where
the work is minor and carried out in premises normally
inspected by the local authority.

Minor work is done by people who normally work on the
premises and is (a) not notifiable or (b) entirely internal or
(c) it is carried out in an area which is not physically
segregated, normal work has not been suspended, the
contractor has no authority to exclude people, and the
work does not involve maintaining or removing insulation
on pipes, boilers or other parts of heating and hot water
systems.

Premises normally inspected by the local authority include where goods are stored for retail or wholesale distribution or sold (including car windscreens, tyres and exhaust replacement operations), exhibition displays, offices, catering services, caravan and temporary residential accommodation, animal care except vets, farms and stables, churches, undertakers, consumer services, launderettes and sports premises.

## 18.4 Requirements of the CDM Regulations

Regulation 4 covers circumstances where a number of clients (or their agents — persons acting with the client's authority) are about to be involved in a project. One of the clients, or the agent of a client, can take on the responsibilities of the effective sole client. Clients appointing agents must be reasonably satisfied about their competence to carry out the duties given to clients by the Regulations. To appoint, a declaration is sent to the HSE, which is required to acknowledge and date the receipt of it.

Regulation 5 applied CDM to the developer of land transferred to a domestic client and which will include premises intended to be occupied as a residence. Where this happens, the developer is subject to Regulations 6 and 8–12 as if he/she were the client.

Regulation 6 requires every client to appoint a planning supervisor and principal contractor in respect of each project. These appointments must be changed or renewed as necessary so that they remain filled at all times until the end of the construction phase. The planning supervisor has to be appointed as soon as is practicable after the client has enough information about the project and the construction work to enable him/her to comply with Regulations 8(1) and 9(1). The principal contractor, who must be a contractor, has to be appointed as soon as practicable after the client has enough information to enable him/her to comply with Regulations 8(3) and 9(3). The same person can be appointed as both planning supervisor and principal contractor, provided he/she is competent to fulfil both roles, and the client can appoint him/herself to either or both positions provided he/she is similarly competent.

Regulation 7 requires the planning supervisor to give written notice of notifiable projects to the HSE, as soon as practicable after his/her appointment as planning supervisor and as soon as practicable after the appointment of the principal contractor, and in any event before the start of the construction work. Where work which is notifiable is done for a domestic client and a developer is not involved, then the contractor(s) doing the work have the responsibility of notifying the HSE, and one of these can notify on behalf of any others. Again, notification must be made before any work starts. Notifiable work is construction work where the construction part lasts for more than 30 days, or will involve more than 500 person-days of construction work. A 'working day' is any day on which construction work is carried out, regardless of the duration of the work and whether a weekend or holiday is involved. A 'person day' is one individual, including supervisor and specialists, carrying out construction work

for one normal working shift. Where there is any doubt about qualification for notification, projects should be notified.

Particulars to be notified to the HSE include details of the planning supervisor and principal contractor, and declarations signed on their behalf accepting the appointment, the planned number of contractors on the site and the name and address of any contractors already chosen. The remainder of the particulars include familiar details such as the date of commencement of work, and the address of the site.

Regulation 8 covers the requirements for competence of planning supervisor, designers and contractors. The client must be reasonably satisfied that a potential planning supervisor is competent to perform the functions required by these Regulations, before any person is appointed to the role, Regulation 8(1) states that no designer can be hired by any person to prepare a design unless that person is reasonably satisfied the designer is competent to do so, and similarly no contractor can be employed by anyone to carry out or manage construction work unless the person employing the contractor is reasonably satisfied as to the contractor's competence, Regulation 8(3). Those under a duty to satisfy themselves about competence will only discharge that duty when they have taken 'such steps as it is reasonable for a person in their position to take', which include making reasonable enquiries or seeking advice where necessary to satisfy themselves as to the competence.

'Competence' in this sense refers only to competence to carry out requirement, and not to contravene any prohibition placed on the person by any relevant regulation or provision.

Provision for health and safety in a wide sense is covered by Regulation 9. Clients must not appoint any person as planning supervisor unless they are reasonably satisfied that the potential appointee has allocated or will allocate adequate resources to enable the functions of planning supervisor to be carried out. Similarly, anyone arranging for a designer to prepare a design must be reasonably satisfied the potential designer has allocated or will allocate adequate resources to comply with Regulation 13. No-one is allowed to appoint a contractor to carry out or manage construction work unless reasonably satisfied that the contractor has allocated or will allocate adequate resources to enable compliance with statutory requirements.

The client is required by Regulation 10 to ensure so far as is reasonably practicable that a health and safety plan which complies with Regulation 15(4) has been prepared in respect of the project before the construction phase starts. There is no duty on either the client or the planning supervisor to ensure that the plan continues to be in compliance with Regulation 15 once work has begun; this duty to keep it up to date is laid on the principal contractor by Regulation 15(4).

Regulation 11 obliges the client to ensure that the planning supervisor is provided with information relevant to his/her functions about the state or condition of any premises where relevant construction work will be carried out. This will be information which the client has, or which the client could obtain by making reasonable enquiries, and it has to be provided as soon as reasonably practicable but certainly before work starts to which the information relates. The client is required by Regulation 12 to take reasonable steps to ensure that the information in any health and safety file which is given to him/her is kept available for inspection by anyone who may need the information in the file to comply with any law. A client who sells the entire interest in the property of the structure can satisfy this requirement by handing over the file to the purchaser and ensures the purchaser is aware of the significance and contents of the file.

Designers are covered by Regulation 13. Except where the design is prepared in-house, employers cannot allow employees to prepare a design, unless the employer has taken reasonable steps to ensure that the client for the project is aware of the duties to which the client is subject by virtue of these Regulations and any practical guidance issued by the HSC on how to comply.

The designer is to ensure that any design he/she prepares and which he/she knows will be used for construction work includes adequate regard to three needs:

(a)   to avoid foreseeable risks to health and safety of those constructing or cleaning the structure at any time and anyone who may be affected by that work

(b)   to ensure that risks to constructors or cleaners of the structure at any time, or to anyone who may be affected by that work, are combated at source, and

(c)   to ensure that priority is given to measures which will protect all such persons over measures which only protect each person at work.

Secondly, the designer is to ensure the design includes adequate information about any aspect of the project, structure or material to be used which might affect the health or safety of constructors, cleaners or anyone who may be affected by their work.

Thirdly, a stronger duty to co-operate with the planning supervisor and any other designer is placed on a designer, so far as is necessary to enable each of them to comply with health and safety laws.

The duties are then qualified by Regulation 13(3), which allows the first two of them to include the required matters only to the extent that it is reasonable to expect the designer to deal with them at the time the design is prepared, and as far as reasonably practicable.

Regulation 14 details the duties of the planning supervisor. This duty holder must:

(a)   ensure as far as is reasonably practicable that the design of any structure in the project complies with the needs specified in Regulation 13 and includes adequate information

(b)   take reasonable steps to ensure co-operation between designers to enable each to comply with Regulation 13

(c)   be in a position to advise any client and any contractor to enable them to comply with Regulation 8(2) and 9(2) competence of designer, and to advise any client on compliance with Regulations 8(3), 9(3) and 10 (competence of contractor and readiness of the health and safety plan, and

(d)   ensure that a health and safety file is prepared in respect of each structure in the project, reviewing and amending it over time, and finally delivering it to the client on completion of construction work on each structure.

Regulation 15 sets out the specific requirements for the health and safety plan. This is to be prepared by the appointed planning supervisor so as to contain the required information and be available for provision to any contractor to carry out or manage construction work on the project.

The information required to go into the plan is as follows:

—   a general description of the construction work

—   details of the intended timescale for the project and any intermediate stages

—   details of any risks known to the planning supervisor or which are reasonably foreseeable risks to the health and safety of constructors

—   any other information which the planning supervisor has or could reasonably get which a contractor would need in order to show that he/she has the necessary competence or has or will get the adequate resources required by Regulation 9

—   information which the principal contractor and other contractors could reasonably need to satisfy their own duties under the Regulations.

The principal contractor must take reasonable steps, until the end of the construction phase, to ensure the plan contains the required features, which:

—   are arrangements for the project which will ensure so far as is reasonably practicable the health and safety of all constructors and those who may be affected by the work, taking account of the risks involved in the work and any activity in the premises where the work takes place which could put any people at risk

—   enable any contractor to understand how he/she can comply with any duties placed on him/her in respect of welfare

—   arrangements which will include where necessary the method of managing the construction work and monitoring of compliance with health and safety regulations.

Regulation 16 specifies the duties and powers of the principal contractor. These are, firstly, to take reasonable steps to ensure co-operation between contractors so far as is necessary to enable each to comply with requirements imposed. This includes, but is not limited to, those sharing the construction site for the purposes of Regulation 9 of the Management of Health and Safety at Work Regulations 1992[10] (MHSWR).

Secondly, the principal contractor must ensure so far as is reasonably practicable that every contractor and every employee complies with any rules in the health and safety plan. The principal contractor can make any reasonable written rules and include them in the plan, and give reasonable directions to any contractor.

Thirdly, the principal contractor must take reasonable steps to ensure that only authorised persons are allowed where construction work is being carried out. Fourth, he/she must ensure that required particulars are displayed in any notice covered by Regulation 7, and are displayed in a readable condition where they can be read by any person at work on the project.

Finally under this Regulation, he/she must provide the planning supervisor promptly with any information he/she possesses or could reasonably find out from a contractor which the planning supervisor does not already possess and which could reasonably be believed necessary for inclusion in the health and safety plan.

Duties on the giving of information and training requirements are set out in Regulation 18. The principal contractor must (as far as is reasonably practicable) ensure that every contractor is provided with comprehensible information on the risks to him/herself and any employees or persons under his/her control which are present as a result of the work. In the same terms, the principal contractor must ensure that every contractor who employs people on the work provides his/her employees with the information and training required by Regulations 8 and 11(2)(b) of the MHSWR.

Provision is made by Regulation 18 for the receipt of advice from employees and the self-employed by the principal contractor, who must ensure that there is a suitable mechanism in place for discussing and conveying their advice on health and safety matters affecting their work. Arrangements for the co-ordination of these views of employees or their representatives are to be made having regard to the nature of the work and the size of the premises concerned.

Contractors' duties are covered by Regulation19(1), where in relation to a project they must co-operate with the principal contractor as necessary, provide the principal contractor with any relevant information which might affect anyone's health or safety while on the project or who could be affected by it. This information includes relevant risk assessments, and information which might prompt a review of the safety plan for the project. Contractors must also comply with any directions of the principal contractor, and any applicable rules in the safety plan. The Regulation requires contractors to provide the principal contractor with any information which is notifiable by the contractor to the enforcing authority under the Reporting of Injuries, Diseases and Dangerous Occurrences Regulations 1985[11] (RIDDOR) — details of injuries, diseases and dangerous occurrences as defined which are related to the project.

Other information to be supplied by the contractor to the principal contractor includes anything which he/she knows or could reasonably find out which the principal contractor does not know and would reasonably be expected to pass to the planning supervisor if he/she did know, in order to comply with Regulation 16(1)(e) to amend the health and safety file.

Regulation 19 contains in parts (2), (3) and (4) general requirements to be observed by employers with employees working on construction work, and the self-employed.

No employer can allow his/her employees to work on construction work, and no self-employed person can work, unless the workers have been given specific pieces of information. These are:

— the names of the planning supervisor and principal contractor

— the health and safety plan or relevant parts of it.

A defence is provided against prosecution in part (5), which allows that this duty can be satisfied by showing that all reasonable enquiries had been made and the employer or self-employed person reasonably believed either that the Regulations did not apply to the particular work being done or that he/she had in fact been given the information required.

The Regulations have the same coverage as the Health and Safety at Work etc Act 1974[12] by Regulation 20, and except for Regulations 10 and 16(1)(e), they do not confer a right of civil action (Regulation 21). This means that breach of the Regulations can only result in criminal prosecution, and cannot be used in civil claims by injured people. This provision is the same as that contained in the MHSWR. The enforcing authority for the Regulations is exclusively the Health and Safety Executive (Regulation 22). Appropriate Sections of the Factories Act 1961[13] and the Construction Regulations[6–9] (regarding notification requirements) are revoked, as are Regulations 5 and 6 of the Construction (General Provisions) Regulations 1961[6] which deal with the appointment of safety supervisors in larger firms and their duties.

## 18.5 Compliance with the CDM Regulations in relation to lift and escalator work

The main steps to complying with the CDM Regulations can be summarised as follows:

(1)  Establish the probable impact of the Regulations on your organisation according to the nature of work to be undertaken:

(a)  *New lifts for installation in new buildings*: for all new construction work involving lifts and/or escalators the Health and Safety Executive (HSE) will be the enforcing authority. The construction work will be notifiable where it lasts for more than 30 days or involves more than 500 person days of work. But CDM also applies to non-notifiable work which involves five people or more on site at any one time. On this basis CDM will apply to almost all new lift work.

(b)  *Work of alteration or renovation*: these are the terms used in the Regulations, they include refurbishment, modernisation, upgrading etc but not demolition or dismantling which will be covered later.

CDM will apply where work involves the criteria detailed above, see 18.3, i.e. 30 days, 500 person-days or five people on site providing HSE is the enforcing authority. As virtually all such work will be classified as work of construction HSE will be the enforcing authority even where the premises are normally inspected by local authority inspectors. In addition, CDM will apply to any design work no matter how long the work lasts or how many workers are involved, always providing HSE is the enforcement authority.

Subject to the above criteria much work of alteration or renovation will fall within the scope of CDM.

(c)   *Maintenance*: this expression will include servicing and work carried out as part of a service contract as well as that undertaken for comprehensive maintenance. CDM will not normally apply to fixed term contracts involving maintenance or emergency work on a frequent or irregular basis. However, in the case of work undertaken as part of a maintenance contract with five or more persons on site at any one time and where the work is work for which HSE will be the enforcing authority then CDM will apply.

In addition, such work will require notification where it lasts for more than 30 days or involves more than 500 person days of construction work. Examples of such work might be the re-roping of a large installation or replacement of major component parts.

(d)   *Demolition or dismantling*: demolition is not defined in the Regulations but the expression can be taken to include the removal of a lift installation. CDM applies to all demolition or dismantling work, regardless of the length of time or number of workers involved, except where the work is inspected by local authorities or is carried out for a domestic client.

(2)   Ensure that senior management are aware of the Regulations and what will be required to comply with them. Project management staff in particular need to know that reportable injuries and dangerous occurrences must be reported to the principal contractor on site, as well as to the HSE in the usual way.

(3)   Check the safety policy statement and risk assessments to ensure that clients, the principal contractor and other contractors can be satisfied as to ones competence to carry out work in health and safety. (Employers with less than five employees in total are not required by law to have written safety policies and risk assessments, but in practice may find that they will be excluded from work unless they can provide them).

(4)   It is especially important to make sure that clients understand the obligations placed upon them. At the time of tender ensure that all duties have been considered which relate to your role under CDM.

(5)   Be prepared to provide detailed method statements for ones own work or for work which involves

liaison with other contractors. It may be found helpful to use a standard format.

(6)   Ensure that your employees have received adequate health and safety training and that this can be shown to have taken place. It may not be sufficient to rely upon the possession of trade qualifications alone to establish this, as many of the requirements are relatively recent.

(7)   It is illegal for any employee to work on construction work unless they have been given the names of the planning supervisor and the principal contractor for the project, and the parts of the site health and safety plan which are relevant to the work to be done. Failure to comply with this requirement is punishable by a fine of up to £5000 in the first instance. A formal means of recording that the information has been provided should be set up.

(8)   Ensure that information about the work is given to the planning supervisor, and that any modifications agreed later are copied to the planning supervisor for use in the health and safety file.

(9)   Determine what procedures are available on site for consultation with the principal contractor about health and safety matters. Make sure your employees know about them, and encourage them to report any problems they may find or suggestions they may have.

(10)   Determine what site rules have been made by the principal contractor, which will apply in addition to the CDM Regulations. Ensure your employees are all aware of those which affect them.

## 18.6   Roles and responsibilities

### 18.6.1   Client

The client's main duties are to appoint a planning supervisor and a principal contractor for each project. The client must be 'reasonably satisfied' that the person to be appointed as planning supervisor has the competence and resources to perform his/her functions under the CDM Regulations. Such competence and resources are to be measured against the project concerned, i.e. the more complex the project the greater degree of competence and resources required. The principal contractor cannot be anyone other than a 'contractor' i.e. someone who carries out or manages construction work as a trade or in a business capacity, whether for profit or not. The client's duty to be reasonably satisfied as to the principal contractor's competence and resources apply equally if he/she directly appoints any other contractor(s).

The appointments are to be made 'as soon as is practicable' after the client has the information about the project and the construction work so as to enable him/her to be reasonably satisfied as to the competence and the resources of the person to be so appointed.

The client can appoint the same person as the planning supervisor and the principal contractor provided the competence and resource requirements are satisfied. The client may also be the approved planning supervisor, principal contractor or both, provided he/she is competent to perform the relevant functions.

The client is permitted to appoint an agent or another client to carry out his/her function in respect of the project. This obviously allows for the less well-informed clients to delegate their duties to those more experienced. These duties include the following:

— To ensure that the planning supervisor is provided with all the information relevant to his/her responsibilities under the CDM Regulations. The information must be that already in the clients possession or which it is reasonable to obtain.

— To ensure that he/she is 'reasonably satisfied' as to the competence and resources of a designer (i.e. a person who in pursuit of a trade, business or undertaking prepares a design) who he/she intends to appoint. Such competence is measured against the design to be prepared and the resources against the ability to comply with his/her functions under the CDM Regulations.

— To ensure 'as far as is reasonably practicable' that the 'construction phase' of any project does not start unless a health and safety plan has been prepared. The phrase 'construction phase' means the period of time starting when the construction work in any project starts and ending when construction work in that project is completed. Once the construction phase has commenced then neither the client nor the planning supervisor are under a duty to check that the plan meets its requirements. This duty falls to the principal contractor.

In conclusion, although the lift or escalator maker will probably never assume the role of client, he/she should be aware of what the client's duties are. They are, as far as is reasonably practicable, to:

— select and appoint a competent planning supervisor, and principal contractor

— be satisfied that the planning supervisor and principal contractor are competent and allocate adequate resources for health and safety

— be satisfied that designers and contractors are also competent and will allocate adequate resources when making arrangements for them to work on the project

— provide the planning supervisor with information relevant to health and safety on the project; ensure construction work does not start until the principal contractor has prepared a satisfactory health and safety plan

— ensure the health and safety file is available for inspection after the project is completed.

## 18.6.2    Planning supervisor

The planning supervisor is a creation of the CDM Regulations. His/her duties are as follows:

— To ensure 'as far as is reasonably practicable' that the design of any structure in a project includes

among the design considerations adequate regard to the need to avoid foreseeable risks, to combat risks at source and to give priority to measures to protect all persons as opposed to particular individuals. He/she must also ensure that the design includes adequate information regarding potential risks to all persons. It is his/her duty to co-ordinate the health and safety aspects of project design and planning. Further information in this respect is given in Appendix 2 of the *Approved Code of Practice*[14] (ACoP).

— To ensure co-operation between the designers. The extent of the duty will depend upon the number and the nature of the designer(s). If many, then the planning supervisor will have to resolve any interface problems between the designs. If a contractor is concerned then the planning supervisor will have to discuss with the principal contractor the inclusion of the design within the health and safety plan. To give advice to the client to enable him/her to appoint designers and contractors.

— To give advice to contractors to enable them to appoint designers.

— To ensure that the health and safety file is kept in respect of each structure within a project and to review, amend and add to it prior to delivery to the client.

— To see that the health and safety plan for each project is prepared so as to allow it to be given to the principal contractor prior to the carrying out of the construction work. This duty overlaps with that of the client to ensure that the construction phase does not start until the health and safety plan has been prepared. The plan is to contain a variety of information, for example, details of risks to health and safety which are known or 'reasonably foreseeable', and information as will permit the principal contractor to comply with his/her duties in respect of the plan and with his/her statutory duties generally. For further information on the health and safety plan see Appendix 4 of the *Approved Code of Practice* (ACoP). The aim is to make the plan specific for the project itself and the planning supervisor may have to be pro-active and make decisions as to the best options within the constraints of the project. It is intended the plan be available to the HSE during routine inspections or accident investigations.

— To notify the HSE in writing of the project. The particulars of that notice are set out in Schedule 1 to the CDM Regulations. Such notice is required to be given 'as soon as is practicable' after the planning supervisor's appointment.

The planning supervisor has overall responsibility for co-ordinating the health and safety aspects of the design and planning phase and for the early stages of the health and safety plan and the health and safety file.

The planning supervisor therefore assumes certain responsibilities which means he/she could face a personal liability in addition to there being a corporate liability.

The company as a corporate entity must examine its insurance cover, particularly as regards the need for professional indemnity cover. Product liability insurance will not normally be sufficient without an extension of the design element.

Where a lift or escalator maker accepts the role of planning supervisor it will be in addition to that of the Contractor, or possibly the principal contractor, and he/she will often have a design function. As planning supervisor he/she will therefore be required to co-ordinate the health and safety aspects involved with all these activities and those for the project as a whole. He/she will need to ensure that:

— designers comply with their duties, in particular the avoidance and reduction of risks

— designers co-operate with each other for the purpose of health and safety

— a health and safety plan is prepared before arrangements are made for a principal contractor to be appointed

— the project is notified to the HSE

— the health and safety file is prepared and delivered to the client at the end of the project.

In addition to the above the planning supervisor must be able to give advice to the client on the competence and allocation of resources by designers and all contractors; and:

— advise contractors appointing designers

— advise the client on the health and safety plan before the construction phase starts.

Lift and escalator makers will need to consider carefully the implications of these obligations, though they may not often arise in the case of new construction, they could quite often for alteration and renovation work.

Where the extent of the work requires a significant knowledge of other trades' expertise, then it would be unwise for any company who does not have the breadth of expert knowledge to take on the role of planning supervisor. In any event companies must have regard for their insurance provisions and the extent to which these provide cover against the prospect of a criminal liability.

## 18.6.3    Designer

From the definition of designer it will be apparent that this includes architects, engineers and quantity surveyors. However, also included are: principal contractors, contractors and self-employed contractors who carry out design. The designers duties are:

— To alert the client of his/her duties under the CDM Regulations and of the guidance given in the ACoP. When preparing his/her design he/she must give adequate consideration to avoiding foreseeable risks, to combating risks at source and to giving priority to all those who carry out or may be affected by the construction work.

— To ensure that the design contains adequate information as to any aspect of the project,

structure or materials which might affect health and safety.

— To co-operate with the planning supervisor and other designers so as to enable each of them to comply with all relevant statutory requirements.

The duty owed by the designer is to anyone carrying out construction work on the project and anyone who might be affected by such work. The second and third duties above extend only to those matters which it is reasonable to expect the designer to address at the time the design is prepared and to the extent that it is otherwise 'reasonably practicable' to do so. The ACoP states that in this context 'reasonably practicable' means weighing the risk to health and safety created by a feature of the design against designing to avoid risks, tackling the causes of risks at source and reducing and controlling the effects of risk.

By way of guidance, the ACoP states that as the design develops, the designer needs to examine methods by which the structure might be built and to analyse the hazards and risks associated with these methods. The choice between methods of construction extends to the choice between materials. The designer needs also to consider the safety of the maintenance of the structure when built. It is stated that if the client wishes to specify design standards or principals he/she will, in effect, be taking on part of the designers functions. If a client does so there will be a need to clarify the limits of everyone's function within the design process.

In conclusion, whilst the lift or escalator maker will almost always have a design role there will be cases where under CDM he/she may be asked to assume the role of 'designer, and as such his/her duties will be to:

— alert clients as to their duties

— consider during the development of designs the hazards and risks which may arise to those constructing and maintaining the structure

— design to avoid risks to health and safety so far as is reasonably practicable

— reduce risks at source if avoidance is not possible

— consider measures which will protect all workers if neither avoidance nor reduction to a safe level is possible

— ensure that the design includes adequate information on health and safety

— pass this information on to the planning supervisor so that it can be included in the health and safety plan and ensure that it is given on drawings or in specifications etc.

— co-operate with the planning supervisor and, where necessary other designers involved in the project.

A lift or escalator maker would normally only be involved as the 'designer' in CDM terms in the case of alteration or renovation work where a substantial part of the work and the design involved relates to the lift or escalator. Nevertheless, there will be a need to review the company's insurance provisions bearing in mind there will be an element of design involving other trades whose insurance cover will also need to be considered.

## 18.6.4 Principal contractor

The principal contractor's duties are as follows:

— To take 'reasonable steps' to ensure co-operation between contractors so as to enable each contractor to comply with the relevant statutory provisions, not only the CDM Regulations.

— To ensure 'as far as it is reasonably practicable' that contractors and employees comply with the health and safety plan. The principal contractor has to examine the health and safety plan and the other contractors assessments to ensure that risks have been properly evaluated. It may prove necessary for the principal contractor to produce a co-ordinated approach to risk assessments. Such a co-ordinated approach does not relieve individual contractors of their legal duties; they are still required to monitor the co-ordinated arrangements and to co-operate with the principal contractor so as to ensure the arrangements are compatible with the health and safety plan.

The health and safety plan should be available at the tender stage. This is to allow contractors to determine the allocation of sufficient resources. Once the principal contractor has been appointed the responsibility for the development, implementation and monitoring of the plan should be transferred to him/her.

— To take 'reasonable steps' to ensure that only 'authorised persons' are allowed on the site. The ACoP states that the measures taken to exclude an unauthorised-authorised person need to be related to what is 'foreseeable'. For example, they will need to be greater if the site is adjacent to a school than if located in a remote country area.

— To ensure that notice of the project is displayed in a reasonable condition. The ACoP suggests this be at the site entrance or in the site office.

— Promptly to provide the planning supervisor with information in connection with the health and safety file.

— To provide each contractor with comprehensible information as to health and safety risks to that contractor and his/her employees.

— To ensure that each contractor provides its employees with information and training.

— To ensure that all employees and self-employed contractors are able to give the principal contractor advice regarding health and safety matters affecting them.

The principal contractor is permitted to give reasonable directions to other contractors so as to enable the principal contractor to comply with his/her duties under the CDM Regulations.

In conclusion, the principal contractor has to take reasonable steps to ensure co-operation between contractors and that contractors and their employees comply with the health and safety plan and that all risks have been properly evaluated. The principal contractor's key duties are to:

— develop and implement the health and safety plans

— arrange for competent and adequately resourced contractors to carry out sub-contracted work

— ensure the co-ordination and co-operation of all contractors

— obtain from contractors risk assessments and details of how they intend to carry out high risk operations

— ensure that contractors have information about risks on site

— ensure that workers on site have been given adequate training

— ensure that contractors and workers comply with site rules set out in the health and safety plan

— monitor health and safety performance

— ensure that all workers are properly informed and consulted

— make sure only authorised people are allowed on site

— display the notification of the project to HSE

— pass information to the planning supervisor for the health and safety plan.

Again, it will be necessary to review companies' insurance provisions due to the principal contractor having a responsibility for other sub-contractors on site and for ensuring they also have adequate cover.

In addition, there will inevitably be extra costs to be accounted for in terms of time and manpower for ensuring that all the key duties listed above are complied with.

Whereas the lift or escalator maker may not often find him/herself being asked to assume the role of principal contractor on new construction work, this could often be the case on alteration or renovation work.

## 18.6.5 Contractors and self-employed persons

The duties of contractors and self-employed persons are:

— To co-operate with the principal contractor that is necessary to allow the principal contractor or any contractor or self-employed person to comply with their duties under the relevant statutory provisions, not only the CDM Regulations.

— Promptly to provide the principal contractor with information which might affect the health and safety of persons.

— To comply with directions given by the principal contractor necessary to enable him/her to comply with his/her duties under the CDM Regulations.

— To comply with the health and safety plan.

— Promptly to provide the principal contractor with information regarding an event notifiable under the Reporting of Injuries, Diseases and Dangerous Occurrences Regulations 1985[11] (RIDDOR).

— Promptly to provide the principal contractor with information which he/she in turn has to provide to the planning supervisor for inclusion within the health and safety file.

— To provide its employees with information and training. Employees of contractors and the Self-employed must be informed of the name of the planning supervisor, the name of the principal contractor, and of the contents of the health and safety plan before commencing work on site.

The ACoP states that duties on a principal contractor, any contractor and the self-employed are complimentary and the flow of information between them is essential for the effective implementation of the health and safety plan.

Contractors have duties to play their part in the successful management of health and safety during the construction work. Their duties are to:

— provide information for the health and safety plan about risks to health and safety arising from their work and the steps they will take to control and manage the risks

— manage their work so that they comply with the rules in the health and safety plan and directions from the principal contractor

— provide information for the health and safety file, and about injuries, dangerous occurrences and ill health

— provide information to their employees.

However the lift or escalator maker is employed in contractual terms, i.e. as a sub-contractor, he/she will be a Contractor under CDM.

## 18.7     Penalties for failure to observe the CDM Regulations

Failure to comply with the duties under the CDM Regulations may give rise to a criminal and civil liability. The former is more important and is likely to be more common. Any attempt by those involved in administering the CDM Regulations to exclude criminal liability will be ineffective.

Save as in respect of (a) the client's duty to ensure that the health and safety plan is prepared prior to the construction phase, and (b) the principal contractor's duty only to allow 'authorised' persons onto the site, the CDM Regulations contain a general exclusion in respect of civil liability. However, a conviction under the CDM Regulations is admissible in evidence in the subsequent civil proceedings. Attempts to exclude all limits of a liability by way of provisions in contracts of appointment are also likely to prove ineffective. This is particularly so where, as is likely, the civil action arises out of a claim for negligence in respect of injury or death.

The HSE has other powers to combat non-compliance. These include prohibition notices (i.e. notices to stop work) and improvement notices. Such powers are likely to be an economic incentive on the party at fault to comply.

## References

1      Construction (Design and Management) Regulations 1994 Statutory Instrument 1994 No 3140 (London: The Stationery Office) (1994)

2      *Construction (Design and Management) Regulations 1994* NALM Guidelines (London: Lift and Escalator Industry Association) (1996)

3      *General and Specific References – For Planning Supervisors* EP1/96 (Edinburgh: Association of Planning Supervisors) (1996)

4      Cooper D   Safety Matters — Construction (Design and Management) Regulations *Elevation* Winter 95/96 (1995)

5      Council Directive 92/57/EEC of 24 June 1992 on the implementation of minimum safety and health requirements at temporary or mobile construction sites ('Temporary or Mobile Construction Sites Directive') *Official J. of the European Communities* (26.08.1992) L 245 (1992)

6      Construction (General Provisions) Regulations 1961 Statutory Instrument 1961 No. 1580 (London: The Stationery Office) (1961)

7      Construction (Lifting Operations) Regulations 1961 Statutory Instrument 1961 No. 1581 (London: The Stationery Office) (1961)

8      Construction (Health and Welfare) Regulations 1966 Statutory Instrument 1966 No. 93 (London: The Stationery Office) (1966)

9      Construction (Working Places) Regulations 1966 Statutory Instrument 1966 No. 94 (London: The Stationery Office) (1966)

10     Management of Health and Safety at Work Regulations 1992 Statutory Instrument 1992 No. 2051 (London: The Stationery Office) (1994)

11     Reporting of Injuries, Diseases and Dangerous Occurences Regulations 1985 Statutory Instrument 1985 No. 2023 (London: The Stationery Office) (1985)

12     Health and Safety at Work etc Act 1974 (London: The Stationery Office) (1974)

13     Factories Act 1961 (London: The Stationery Office) (1961)

14     *Managing construction for health and safety: Construction (Design and Management) Regulations 1994* Approved Code of Practice L54 (Bootle: Health and Safety Executive) (1994)

## Bibliography

*Designing for health and safety in construction* ISBN 0 7176 0807 7 (Bootle: Health and Safety Executive) (1995)

*A guide to managing health and safety in construction* ISBN 0 7176 0755 0 (Bootle: Health and Safety Executive) (1995)

*Health and safety for small construction sites* Guidance Note HS(G) 130 ISBN 0 7176 0806 9 (Bootle: Health and Safety Executive) (1995)

# A1    Glossary of terms

## Principal authors

Dr Gina Barney (Gina Barney Associates)
David Cooper (Lecs UK Ltd.)
John Inglis (Amron Resources)

## Introduction

The following glossary of terms has been reproduced by kind permission, from the *Elevator and Escalator Micropedia* by G C Barney, D A Cooper and J Inglis, published by the International Association of Elevator Engineers, PO Box 7, Sedburgh, LA10 5GE. It contains a glossary defining some 1950 terms and cross references used in the vertical transportation industry, i.e. lifts (*sic.* elevators), escalators and passenger conveyors. These include approximately 1100 electric traction, 250 hydraulic and 500 escalator entries, specific to their speciality, all extensively cross referenced.

The individual entries do not constitute a dictionary definition, as characteristics such as pronunciation and word etymology are not given. Owing to the desire for preciseness and conciseness, the entries are very terse, being the minimum to give a term an authoritative meaning. Nevertheless there are over 35 000 words needed to achieve this objective.

Entries are generally arranged in noun order so that an entry such as:

**bail type governor** See governor: bail type.

will be found under 'governor' with the definitions for twelve other governor related entries. Occasionally this arrangement is not appropriate, e.g:

**inspection unit**

where a single entry is made in the normal word order. There should be no difficulty finding a term, owing to the extensive cross referencing.

The entries have been prepared using a number of authoritative sources. The source of each entry is given at the end of the entry, usually in the form of a letter code and a page/chapter reference number. The sources used are as follows:

AS    Donoghue: ANSI/ASME Handbook A17.1[1]

BA    Author (Barney) generated definition

BE    Barney and dos Santos; *Elevator Traffic*[2]

BO    British Standard, BS 2655 series[3]

BS    British Standard, BS 5655 series[4]

BS70    British/European Standard, BS EN 115[5]

BS78    British Standard, BS 7801[6]

CO    Author (Cooper) generated definition

ET    *Elevator Technology*[7]

HH    *Hydraulic Handbook*[8]

J    Janovsky; *Elevator Mechanical Design*[9]

JI    Author (Inglis) generated definition.

LO    London Underground Glossary of Terms (private publication)

N    *Elevator Terms*; NEIEP (private publication); 1980

O    *Shorter Oxford English Dictionary*[10]

P    Phillips; *Electric Lifts*[11]

S    Strakosch; *Vertical Transportation*[12]

## References

1    Donoghue E A *Safety Code for Elevators and Escalators* ANSI/ASME Handbook A17.1 (New York NY: American Society of Mechanical Engineers) (1984)

2    Barney G C and dos Santos S M *Elevator Traffic* (2nd. ed.) (London: Peter Peregrinus) (1985)

3    BS 2655: *Specification for lifts, escalators, passenger conveyors and paternosters* (largely superseded by BS 5655) (London: British Standards Institution) (various dates)

4    BS 5655: *Lifts and service lifts* (London: British Standards Institution) (various dates)

5    BS EN 115: 1995: *Safety rules for the construction and installation of escalators and passenger conveyors* (London: British Standards Institution) (1995)

6    BS 7801: 1995: *Safe working on escalators and passenger conveyors in use* (London: British Standards Institution) (1995)

7    *Elevator Technology* (Chichester: Ellis Horwood) (1986)

8    *Hydraulic Handbook* (1st. ed.) (Trade and Technical Press) (date unknown)

9    Janovsky L *Elevator Mechanical Design* (Chichester: Ellis Horwood) (1993)

10    *Shorter Oxford English Dictionary* (Oxford: Oxford University Press) (1973)

11    Phillips R S *Electric Lifts* (London: Pitman) (1973)

12    Strakosch G *Vertical Transportation* (London: Wiley) (1983)

# A1 Glossary of terms

**A-side.** The left side of an elevator car or hoistway, when viewed by standing in front of the entrance and facing the hoistway. AS12

**abstract.** A general order or sales summary sheet that indicates duty, control, power supply, machine, signals and all other major features of an escalator or passenger conveyor installation. NE1

**AC control.** See control: AC

**acceptance test.** See test: acceptance.

**acceptance.** A form signed by the owner or his agent which indicates that the contract for installation is essentially complete, and that the customer accepts the equipment. NE1

**access door.** See doors: access.

**accidents.** Unintentional incidents, which may cause injury or damage. CO

**accumulator.** A device that stores hydraulic fluid under pressure so that it can be available immediately for use when required. HH

**acoustic noise.** See noise: acoustic.

**active oil.** The amount of oil available in a tank of a hydraulic elevator that can be circulated into a system. JI

**actuator.** Any hydraulic device which applies force: e.g. a cylinder or motor. HH

**adaptor rings.** The top and bottom ring in a vee packing assembly. JI

**addendum.** A change to a previously written specification or proposal, usually published prior to the bid date. NE1

**adjacent entrance.** An arrangement where an elevator car has two entrances arranged at 90° to each other.

**adjunct.** An applied section of architectural metal fastened to the edge of the escalator or passenger conveyor decking for the purpose of increasing the effective width. CO

**adjustable chain tension device.** A carriage usually mounted on rollers located in the lower head which, through springs or weights, maintains proper tension on the step chain of an escalator. CO

**adjustable flow control.** A valve used to restrict the flow of hydraulic oil whose setting is adjustable, generally from shut off to no restriction. Jl

**adjustable resistor.** See resistor: adjustable.

**adjustable track.** See track: adjustable.

**adjuster.** An elevator, escalator or passenger conveyor technician, who carries out the final inspection of new and modernised installations to ensure that all the equipment has been properly installed and set up according to specification. N1

**adsil.** See anti-friction coating.

**advance door opening.** See door: advance opening.

**air bleed.** A device which allows the release of trapped air in the fluid system of an hydraulic elevator. BOpt9

**air bleed cock.** Enables air to be expelled from the upper parts of the hydraulic system. JI

**air bleed line.** The small diameter line that is connected to a waste oil container allowing the collection of oil as the air is bled from the system, usually at the cylinder. JI

**air bleed screw.** See air bleed cock.

**air breather.** The device usually placed on the tank lid to allow the entry of air into the tank as the oil is discharged and allows the discharge of air to atmosphere as the oil returns to the tank. JI

**air cord.** Part of the driving mechanism of a door operator, which is made from a small diameter wire rope. N2

**air entrapment.** Refers to pockets of air that can be left in a system when charging the system with oil. JI

**air temperature differential.** Is the difference between the ambient air outside the machine room and the air temperature inside the machine room. JI

**airborne noise.** see noise: acoustic.

**alarm bell.** See bell: alarm.

**alarm system.** An emergency system installed on all cars, which comprises a bell, a pushbutton in the car and an uninterruptible source of power, usually a battery. SS145

**algorithm.** A set of rules, to which a system (often a control system) must conform. BE94

**algorithm: group supervisory control.** A set of rules defining the control policy that must be obeyed by an elevator supervisory control system in order that it may pick up passengers from their arrival floors and transport them to their desired destination floors. BE94

**alteration.** Any change to equipment other than maintenance, repair or replacement. CO

**ambient temperature.** The temperature of the surrounding air at a particular point in time. JI

**AND gate.** A solid state logic device, where the output value is true, if both the input values are true; and is false, if either, or both, the input values are false. BA

**angle bracket.** See bracket: angle.

**angle of contact.** See angle of wrap.

**angle of inclination.** The maximum angle to the horizontal in which the steps move on the inclined part of an escalator. LO5/32

**angle of traction.** See angle of wrap.

**angle of wrap.** The proportion of a sheave, which is in contact with the suspension ropes, measured in degrees of contact. P68

**annular space.** In the case of a ram and cylinder is the space between the outside of the ram and the inside of the cylinder. JI

**annunciator.** A signalling device, which provides to passengers information regarding elevator car position etc by means of indicator lamps, audio announcements etc. AS2

**anode.** A positive terminal. NE4

**anti-creep.** A feature found on hydraulic elevators, which prevents the car from changing its relative position with respect to the landing floor by compensating for any leakage of oil etc. N4

**anti-extrusion rings.** A ring of material usually harder than the packing and placed on the side of the packing away from the pressure, which prevents the pressure on the softer packing being extruded through the gap between the ram and gland head. JI

**anti-friction coating.** An application applied to the skirt panels of escalators and passenger conveyors to reduce the likelihood of static electricity. CO

**anti-nuisance device.** A device found on some supervisory control systems, whereby the number of passengers in the car are determined, and compared to the number of calls registered, in order that unnecessary trips are prevented. BE97

**anti-reversal device.** A device provided to prevent the unintentional reversal of an escalator. CO

**anti-slide knobs.** Material, usually metal, of various shapes and sizes, depending upon manufacture, mounted on the deck boards to prevent riding passengers from sliding packages or baggage on top of the deck boards as they ride the unit. CO

**apron: car.** A guard installed onto the underside of an elevator car, which employs advance opening doors, to prevent the trapping of objects or passenger limbs, whilst a descending car is levelling at a landing. BOpt9

**apron: landing.** A guard installed onto the underside of a landing sill to protect against entrapments should a car stop below the landing level. BA

**arc.** A flame formed by the passage of an electric current between two conductors. NE4

**arc quencher.** Any device used to eliminate or reduce the arc formed when current carrying contacts are opened. NE5

**architect's drawings.** Drawings made to show the necessary features of the entire construction of a building. NE5

**architrave.** The various parts surrounding a doorway, in order to present a neat appearance; a moulding. O59

**armature.** The member of an electric machine in which an alternating voltage is generated by virtue of relative motion with respect to a magnetic field flux. NE5

**arrangement: criss-cross.** An escalator installation where the adjacent units have boarding and alighting at opposite ends from each other. CO

**arrangement: multiple parallel.** An arrangement of escalators where a number of installations running in both directions are located parallel to each other. CO

**arrangement: zig-zag.** An escalator installation where the adjacent units have boarding and alighting at opposite ends from each other. CO

**arrival bell.** See bell: arrival.

**arrival gong.** See bell: arrival.

**arrival rate: down peak passenger.** The number of passengers arriving at an elevator system for service during a five minute peak period, when traffic is predominately in the down direction. BE220

**arrival rate: interfloor passenger.** The number of passengers arriving at an elevator system for service during any five minute period, with no dominant traffic pattern. BE238

**arrival rate: up peak passenger.** The number of passengers arriving at an elevator system for service during a five minute peak period, when traffic is predominately in the up direction. BE11

**arrival rate: up peak percentage.** The number of passengers arriving at the main floor of an elevator system for service during the worst five minute period during an up peak traffic condition expressed as a percentage of the total building population. BE11

**arrow: direction.** An illuminated arrival symbol to indicate the direction of travel; see arrow: down and arrow: up. BA

**arrow: down.** An illuminated arrow symbol either mounted in the rear of an elevator car, or mounted above or alongside the car entrance, or both, which indicates to intending passengers that the direction of travel of the arriving car is to be in the downward direction. AS16

**arrow: up.** An illuminated arrow indicating an up travelling car in a similar fashion to a down arrow. AS16

**astragal.** A moulding, usually made of rubber or metal, on the leading edge of hoistway and car doors and extending the full height on centre opening doors or the full width of bi-parting doors, in order to reduce the effects of injury should the doors touch a passenger and to quieten door operation. AS12

**astragal: safety.** A resilient, incompressible safe edge mounted onto the bottom of the upper section of a bi-parting hoistway door of a freight elevator. AS22

**asymmetric relay.** See relay: asymmetric.

**atmospheric pressure tank.** A tank that has an air breather allowing the air in the tank to pass into or out of the tank to atmosphere freely and so preventing pressure build up in the tank as the oil volume varies. JI

**attendant.** A person who is permanently located in the elevator car in order that passengers do not need to operate the controls, such as the car switch (in older systems), destination pushbuttons and car/hoistway doors (in manual systems). N6

**authorised persons/personnel.** An individual who has (a) received general elevator, escalator or passenger conveyor awareness/training and competency appropriate to their job function, and (b) been instructed on the detail of the work to be undertaken, and (c) received authority from the client for the work to be undertaken. BS78p1

**automatic by-pass.** A feature of an elevator supervisory control system, which causes the elevator car to automatically by-pass landing calls under certain circumstances, such as when a car is fully loaded and has no room for further passengers, or a car is making a special trip to serve a demand at a distant floor e.g. lobby service, heavy demand call etc. SS77

**automatic closer.** See closer: car door.

**automatic control.** A generic term, which is used to define any error activated, power amplifying, negative feedback, closed loop control system. BI1.2

**automatic lubricator.** See lubricator: automatic.

**automatic pushbutton control.** A term used to define the simplest means of automatically controlling a single car, where a car may be called to a floor by the pushing of a landing pushbutton (provided it is not already busy) and commanded to travel to a destination floor by the operation of a car call pushbutton. BE86

**automatic remote monitoring system.** See system: automatic remote monitoring.

**auxiliary brake.** See brake: auxiliary.

**auxiliary drive chain.** See chain: auxiliary drive.

**auxiliary isolating switch.** See switch: auxiliary isolating.

**auxiliary motor.** See motor: auxiliary.

**auxiliary ram guides.** The guiding system attached to the moving heads on telescopic cylinders, designed to prevent buckling of the ram assemblies. JI

**auxiliary supply.** An alternative supply to the main power supply source. CO

**average car load.** The total number of passengers carried in one direction of travel, divided by the number of trips in that direction, averaged over a certain time period, usually taken as five minutes, hence up peak or down peak average car load. BE14

**axle.** A pin or rod in the nave of a wheel(s) on which the wheel turns. LO6/32

**B-side.** The right side of an elevator car or hoistway, when viewed by standing in front of the entrance and facing the hoistway. AS14

**babbit.** Soft alloy of tin, antimony and copper used as an anti-friction material for the socketing of wire ropes for elevators. J34

**backlash.** Excessive clearance between the teeth of the worm and worm gear of a geared machine; it permits a rocking action of the gear when the worm is held stationery. NE8

**baggage stops.** Protuberances mounted on deck boards of an escalator to prevent passengers from sliding packages or baggage on top of the deckboards as they ride the escalator. NE8

**bail type governor.** See governor: bail type.

**balance line.** Is required on twin ram systems where each ram and cylinder has its own pipe rupture valve fitted, which is arranged to balance the pressure between cylinders and ensure both valves close at the same time. JI

**balanced traffic.** A term used in connection with the interfloor traffic condition to indicate that the traffic flows in both up and down directions are substantially equal. BE9

**ball valve.** See valve: ball.

**balustrade.** The side of an escalator extending above the steps, which includes skirt panels, interior panels, decks and handrails. NE8

**balustrade bracket.** See bracket: balustrade.

**balustrade decking.** See decking: balustrade.

**balustrade lighting.** See lighting: balustrade.

**balustrade supportwork.** The bolted fabricated steel framework that supports the balustrade. LO6/32

**bank (1).** A number of groups of cars placed physically together, with each group serving a particular zone of a building, where more than one group may serve the same zone and it is possible to have a bank comprising one group only. BE92

**bank (2).** A number of escalators in close proximity. CO

**bar lock.** Type of interlock used with manually operated doors. AS13

**barney.** A small car attached to a rope and used to push cars up a slope. O159

**basement service.** Service provided to a floor or floors below the main terminal in a building, which may be restricted at times in order to improve the service to other parts of the building. BE95

**bearing.** A device that supports and minimises the friction between moving and static surfaces. LO6/32

**bearing plate.** The building support member on which the truss of an escalator is mounted. CO

**bed lift.** See elevator: bed.

**bed-plate.** The foundation or support to which the hoist machine is attached, usually made of steel beams: a pedestal. AS13

**bell: arrival.** A bell either mounted on the elevator car or as part of a fixture on the landing, which signals the arrival of the car at a floor, where it is to pick-up passengers. BA

**bell: alarm.** A bell, located either in the hoistway, or on a suitable landing, or on the car, which when operated by a passenger pressing a pushbutton inside the car, is used to call attention and assistance. N2

**bi-directional.** The ability to operate in two directions. CO

**bi-parting doors.** Consist of two counterweighted panels, which slide vertically, one in the upward direction and one in the downward direction, interconnected so as to move in synchronism, and strongly constructed to facilitate their use in freight elevators (goods lifts). P220

**borehole.** A vertical hole bored in the elevator pit to accommodate the cylinder assembly of a direct acting hydraulic elevator. BOpt9

**borehole liner.** See liner: borehole.

**bottle cylinder.** A cylinder in the shape of a bottle, the displacement ram passes through the gland packing at the top or neck of the bottle. JI

**bottom landing.** The lower end of an escalator where passengers board or exit. CO

**bottom terminal floor.** See bottom terminal landing.

**bottom terminal landing.** The lowest landing in a building, which an elevator serves, where passengers may enter and leave the car. N13

**bottom runby: car.** See runby: bottom — elevator car.

**bottom runby: counterweight.** When an elevator car is level with the upper terminal landing, the counterweight bottom runby is the distance between the striking surface of the counterweight buffer and the counterweight buffer striker plate. AS10

**box: halfway (1).** A junction box mounted in the hoistway near the halfway point of the elevator car travel to which the stationary ends of the travelling cables(s) are attached. AS18

**box: halfway (2).** A terminal box provided in an escalator installation to run wiring to for onward connection to the controller. CO

**bracket: angle.** Formed steel mechanical component used to securely attach guide-rails to the building structure or to securely attach two or more components together. N4

**bracket: balustrade.** One of the several structural steel members which support the escalator balustrade. NE9

**bracket: guide-rail.** Formed steel mechanical components to which guide-rails are attached. AS18

**bracket: spreader.** A U-shaped bracket fastened to two counterweight rails in order to strengthen them. AS23

**brake.** An electro-mechanical device, consisting of a spring assembly, which is held in compression by the energising of an electro-magnet, and which holds the friction shoes from contact with the brake drum or disc, thus allowing the elevator car or escalator step band to move. See also brake: elevator and brake: escalator and passenger conveyors. J86/CO

**brake arm.** The lever that supports and transfers movement to the brake shoes. LO6/32

**brake armature.** The magnetic part of the brake mechanism which, when attracted to the brake coil, moves the levers and linkages to release the brake. LO6/32

**brake callipers.** An assembly of two pivoted levers, linked by a tie rod at one end and fitted with brake pad carriers at the other, released by an electromagnet or hydraulic pressure assembly and applied by compression springs. LO6/32

**brake coil.** The coil that when energised provides the force to cause the brake to lift, either by movement of the solenoid core or the brake armature. LO7/32

**brake cooling switch.** See switch: brake cooling.

**brake dashpot.** The dashpot that dampens the braking action of an electromagnetic brake. LO7/32

**brake drum.** A smooth surface usually mounted on the hoist machine drive shaft, with which the brake shoes make contact whenever the brake magnet is de-energised, in order to absorb the energy of motion. AS13

**brake: elevator.** In the event of the elevator car exceeding its rated speed, or a power failure, or a control system demand to hold the

car stationary, the brake is de-energised and the brake operated, thus stopping the car in safe distance or holding the car in position. J86/CO

**brake: escalator and passenger conveyors.** In the event of the operation of any one of a number of safety devices and/or a power failure, the brake operates and stops the escalator in a safe distance. J86/CO

**brake lift detector.** The switch used to detected mechanically that the escalator brake has fully released (lifted). LO7/32

**brake lining.** Material used to line brake shoes, which has a high coefficient of friction. AS13

**brake magnet.** A magnet usually provided in the form of a solenoid, which is used to cause the brake shoes to move away from the brake drum, whenever it is energised. J87

**brake motor.** See motor: brake.

**brake pad.** The high friction replaceable material that acts on the brake disc comprising two pads held in carriers to act on either side of the disc when applied. LO7/32

**brake release lever.** A lever used to automatically release the brake during handwinding. LO7/32

**brake shoes.** See shoes: brake.

**brake solenoid.** The solenoid whose core moves to operate the levers and linkages to release the brake. LO7/32

**brake-stopping distance.** The distance taken for the escalator to stop upon application of the brake. CO

**brake: auxiliary.** A fail safe brake, which is used to stop an escalator under all normal conditions or under certain fault conditions only. It is typically situated on one side of the main drive shaft. LO6/32

**brake: disc.** An assembly where lined pads slow, by friction, a disc mounted on a rotating shaft, which is spring applied, or electro-magnetically or hydraulically released and is only used as an auxiliary brake at present. LO11/32

**brake: emergency.** An auxiliary mechanically automatically operated brake, which will stop a fully loaded escalator, if the drive chain breaks. NE48

**brake: main.** A fail safe brake sometimes provided which is used to stop an escalator under all normal conditions or under certain fault conditions only, typically situated on one side of the main drive shaft. LO6/32

**brake: operational.** See brake: service.

**brake: rated load.** The load which the brake of the escalator must be designed to stop and hold. CO

**brake: service.** An electro-mechanical device, consisting of a spring assembly, which is held in compression by the energising of an electromagnet and which holds the friction shoes from contact with the brake drum or disc, thus allowing the escalator step band to move. In the event of the operation of any one of a number of safety detection devices and/or a power failure, the brake is de-energised and the brake automatically operates, thus stopping the escalator in a safe distance and holding the step chain in position. CO

**bridge rectifier.** A type of full wave rectifier using four diodes. NE14

**broken handrail switch.** See switch: broken handrail.

**broken step chain safety switch.** See switch: broken step chain safety.

**broken drive chain switch.** See switch: broken drive chain.

**brush applicator.** Attached the end of feed pipes these apply lubricant to a chain by means of light contact. LO7/32

**brush: deflector.** A brush provided above the escalator steps and affixed to the skirt panels which is designed to keep passengers feet away from the gap between the edge of the steps and the skirt panels. CO

**brush: newel entry.** A brush provided at the newel end of an escalator to cover the internal components of the newel entry switch and to prevent passengers fingers entering this space. CO

**buffer.** Device capable of absorbing the kinetic energy of motion of a descending car or counterweight, when they have passed a normal limit of travel by providing a resilient stop, and comprising a means of braking using fluids or springs (or similar means). AS3/BSpt1

**buffer return spring.** Spring used to return an energy dissipation type of buffer back to its operating position. J143

**buffer switch (1).** A switch which is activated should a buffer be operated, which removes power to the elevator drive system. AS14

**buffer switch (2).** A switch, which is activated should the oil in an oil buffer fall below a minimum allowable level and which prevents further operation of the elevator. AS14

**buffer: car.** A final emergency device to bring an elevator car to rest by absorbing the energy of motion should the car pass the normal downward limit of travel. J134

**buffer: counterweight.** A final emergency device to bring a counterweight to rest by absorbing the energy of motion should the counterweight pass the normal downward limit of travel. J134

**buffer: energy accumulation type.** A buffer where the kinetic energy of motion is stored in the gradual compression of a spring, which provides a progressive retarding force. J135

**buffer: energy dissipation type.** A buffer where the kinetic energy of motion is dissipated, by converting the energy into heat by the flow of oil through a series of holes, and hence applying a constant force of retardation. J142

**buffer: oil.** An energy dissipation type of buffer. J142

**buffer: spring.** An energy accumulation type of buffer. J135

**buffer: stroke.** The distance that a buffer can be compressed. N15

**building population.** See population: building.

**building: commercial.** A building in which people work; such as offices, stores, industrial. BE55

**building: institutional.** A building in which people receive a service; such as hospitals, school, universities, public buildings. BE55

**building: residential.** Buildings in which people live; such as houses, hotels, flats, hostels. BE55

**building: retail.** A building from which a product or service is sold. CO

**bulkhead.** See safety bulkhead.

**bumper.** Device other than a spring or oil buffer capable of absorbing the kinetic energy of motion of a descending car or counterweight, when they have passed a normal limit of travel. AS3

**bunching.** A traffic pattern, where a number of elevators move around a building together, instead of being evenly separated about the building, often caused by a sudden heavy traffic demand or to an inadequate traffic supervisory system. SS446

**burst pressure.** See rupturing pressure.

**busbar.** A heavy, rigid metallic conductor usually insulated and used to carry a high current and make a common connection between several circuits. LO7/32

**bush.** A cylinder sleeve forming a bearing surface for a shaft or pin, usually as a lining. It has two diameters and the cylindrical length is usually greater than the larger diameter. LO8/32

**button.** See pushbutton.

**button: car call.** See pushbutton: car call.

**button: door close.** See pushbutton: door close.

**button: door open.** See pushbutton: door open.

**button: landing call.** See pushbutton: landing call.

**button: push.** See pushbutton.

**button: stop.** See pushbutton: stop.

**by-pass floors.** Floors, which are by-passed in a building, as a result of a supervisory control action or because the car is fully loaded. SS77

**by-pass valve.** See valve: by-pass.

**cab.** That part of an elevator car, comprising a self contained enclosure, mounted on an elevator platform, in which passengers or goods are carried. N17

**cabin.** See car.

**cable.** A wire for carrying electric current. CO

**cable end box.** The junction box used for the connection of the incoming electrical supply prior to distribution to each switchboard. LO8/32

**cable: trailing.** See cable: travelling.

**cable: travelling.** A cable made up of electrical conductors, which trails behind the car of an elevator, dumbwaiter or material lift to provide an electrical connection between the car and a fixed outlet in the hoistway or machine room. AS11

**CAD.** See computer aided design.

**call.** A demand for service by a passenger, which is entered into an elevator supervisory control system, by the passenger pressing either a landing or car call pushbutton. AS14

**call accepted.** The acceptance of a landing or car call by an elevator's supervisory control system. BA

**call accepted indicator.** An indicator contained within or adjacent to a landing or car call pushbutton, which is illuminated by an elevators supervisory control system when it accepts a call. AS14

**call allocation.** The action of an elevator supervisory control system, when allocating a landing call to a specific car for service. BE112

**call button.** See call pushbutton.

**call back.** A service visit, at the request of an elevator, escalator or passenger conveyor operator, made by a maintenance technician, which is not scheduled, and which arises because the equipment has gone out of service owing to a fault condition. N17

**call memory.** Part of an elevator supervisory control system, where all landing and car calls are stored before being serviced. BA

**call pushbutton.** A pushbutton situated either in car or on a landing, on which passengers may indicate their travelling intentions. BA

**call registration.** The action of registering a call. BA

**call registration indicator.** See call accepted indicator.

**call: car.** A passenger demand registered from within a car requesting that the car stop at a specified landing. N18

**call: down.** A passenger demand registered on a landing, requesting transportation by an elevator in the down direction. BA

**call: hall.** See call: landing.

**call: heavy duty.** In some circumstances a landing call is given extra emphasis by the elevator supervisory control system, when either (1) a new landing call is registered within a short predefined time, or (2) several cars have left the floor fully loaded, or (3) too many landing and car calls have been assigned to a single car, thus requiring the supervisory control system to take special priority action. BE106

**call: highest reversal.** The highest landing that an elevator visits during a trip in the upward direction before reversing its direction of travel. BE88

**call: landing.** A passenger demand registered on a pushbutton on a landing for transportation to other floors in a building. N63

**call: lowest reversal.** The lowest landing an elevator visits during a trip in the downward direction before reversing its direction of travel. BA

**call: registered.** See call accepted.

**call: up.** A passenger demand registered on a landing, requesting transportation by an elevator in the up direction. BA

**cam.** Piece of machinery used to convert linear motion into circular motion employed in elevator installations to operate (1) hoistway door interlocks (2) hoistway floor selectors (3) car mounted terminal switches (4) hoistway mounted terminal switches. AS14

**cam: door.** [syn: vane] Device mounted on a car door and used to unlock and drive the landing doors. AS16

**cam: retiring.** A cam mounted on an elevator car, which remains in a retracted or retired position, whilst the car is moving, until the car is about to stop, when it drops, in order to unlock the landing door interlock. AS21

**canopy.** The top of an elevator cab, which is supported by the walls and contains the ceiling. AS14

**canopy: car.** See canopy.

**cantilevered car frame.** See frame: cantilevered car.

**capacitor.** An electrical device made of two flat conductors separated by a thin insulator capable of retaining or storing electrical energy after the charging voltage is disconnected. NE18

**capacity: contract.** See capacity: rated.

**capacity: handling (elevator).** The total number of passengers that an elevator system can transport in a period of five minutes during the up peak traffic condition with a specified car loading, usually taken as 80% of rated capacity. BE12

**capacity: rated.** The maximum legal load, which an elevator car is permitted to carry measured in a number of passengers or a specific weight in kg. BOpt9

**capacity: theoretical escalator handling.** The total number of passengers that an escalator system can transport in theory in the knowledge of factors such as step width, speed, rise, etc. CO

**car.** The load carrying unit comprising enclosure (cab), car frame, platform and door(s). AS3

**car allocation.** The action of an elevator supervisory control system, when allocating a specific car to a set of landing calls for service. BE94

**car apron.** See apron: car.

**car bounce.** Where the ride in the car of an hydraulic elevator is not smooth, but exhibits an irregular motion (bounce) often caused by air entrapped in the system being compressed and expanded as the pressure in the system changes. See also stick-slip. JI

**car buffer.** See buffer: car.

**car button.** See pushbutton: car call.

**car call.** See pushbutton: car call.

**car call panel.** See panel: car operating.

**car call stop.** See stop: car.

**car canopy.** See canopy.

**car control panel.** See panel: car operating.

**car coming indicator.** See indicator: car coming.

**car counterweight.** A counterweight roped directly to the elevator car in a drum drive installation and approximately equal to 70% of the weight of the car. AS14

**car despatch.** A term used to indicate the type of supervisory control system employed, where cars are despatched from terminal floors in a building at scheduled intervals. BE97

**car door.** See door: car.

**car door closer.** See closer: car door.

**car door lock.** See lock: door.

**car door interlock.** See interlock: car door.

**car enclosure.** See enclosure: car.

**car entrance.** See entrance: car.

**car fan.** See fan: car.

**car floor.** See floor: car.

**car frame.** See frame: car.

**car isolation.** The isolation of the car platform by means of rubber or other sound absorbing

**material** in order to reduce or absorb the transmission of vibration and noise. N73

**car operating panel.** See panel: car operating.

**car panel.** See panel: car operating.

**car platform.** See platform: car.

**car position indicator.** See indicator: car position.

**car preference.** A system used on simple traffic controllers, where for a period of time a car call can be registered preferentially before a landing call. Also see service: independent.

**car push button.** See pushbutton: car call.

**car safety gear.** See safety gear.

**car sling.** See frame: door.

**car stop.** See stop: car.

**car switch.** See switch: car.

**car top.** The top of the car enclosure. AS146

**car top clearance.** See clearance: car top.

**car top control station.** See station: car top inspection.

**car top inspection station.** See station: car top inspection.

**car travel distance.** The distance that the car of an hydraulic elevator travels from the lowest landing to the top landing, excluding overruns or ram travel. JI

**car ventilation.** See ventilation: car.

**car: free.** A car to which the supervisory control system has not allocated any further calls and is therefore free to be given a new assignment. BE131

**car: next.** Usually the next car to leave a main floor as defined by the group supervisory control system. BE37/95

**car: rear opening.** Where the car is furnished with doors at the rear of the car in addition to the normal doors provided at the front. SS192

**car: side opening.** Where the car is furnished with doors at the side of the car in addition to the normal doors provided at the front. SS48

**car: through.** A car which is fitted with doors to the front entrance and a further set to the rear of the car. BA

**carriage.** A carriage usually mounted on rollers located in the lower head which through springs or weights maintains proper tension on the escalator step chain. CO

**carriage gap.** The smallest gap between a fixed member of the escalator truss and the carriage frame. LO8/32

**carriage rollers.** The four vertically mounted rollers that support the weight of the tension carriage and permit its longitudinal movement within the escalator truss. LO8/32

**carriage shaft.** The driven shaft in the tension carriage carrying two sprockets that tension and reverse the direction of the escalator step chains. LO17/32

**carriage switch.** See switch: carriage.

**carriage tensioners.** Compression springs or weighted levers linked to the carriage to provide the tension on the escalator step chains. LO8/32

**carriage track.** The tracks that support and give lateral and horizontal restraint to the tension on the escalator step chains. LO8/32

**carriage: return.** A carriage usually mounted on rollers located in the lower head which though springs or weights maintains proper tension on the escalator step chain. CO

**carriage: sliding lower.** A carriage usually mounted on rollers located in the lower head which though springs or weights maintains proper tension on the escalator step chain. CO

**carriage: tension.** The mobile assembly (carriage) in which the running track is mounted to guide the escalator steps around return sprockets mounted on the idler shaft within it comprising two carriage tensioners within the assembly provide the tension on the step chains which is mobile to account for the elongation of the step chains over time. LO28/32

**carrying capacity.** See capacity: rated.

**castell key.** The unique key that operates the castell lock often provided at the escalator switch. LO p8/32

**castell lock.** See lock: castell.

**catenary roller.** One of a series of rollers fitted in the roller bow of an escalator. LO9/32

**cathode.** A negative terminal. NE18

**caution signs.** Signs provided to draw attention to risks and/or hazards. CO

**cavitation.** A noise created when the available oil at the pump intake is less than the nominal pump output, thus creating a vacuum condition and a very loud noise. HH

**central ram.** A ram and cylinder placed under the car platform in a central location. JI

**centre decking.** The decking between escalators. LO9/32

**centre opening doors.** See doors: centre opening.

**centrelines.** A basic reference line used in the erection of elevators and escalators. NE21

**centrifugal governor.** See governor: centrifugal.

**chain.** Connected flexible series of metal or other links. O309

**chain anchors.** Devices to allow the step chains to be locked by providing a physical link between the chain and a fixed part of the escalator. LO9/32

**chain anchor switch.** See switch: chain anchor.

**chain drive (elevator).** Alternative means of suspension to wire ropes for electric and hydraulic elevators. S464/P96

**chain drive machine.** An indirect drive machine having a chain connecting the driving motor to the drive sheave. N21

**chain guide.** A solid strip that sits within the step chain link plates to give lateral (side) guidance to the escalator step band. LO9/32

**chain lubrication.** An application applied to a chain for the purposes of lubrication to prevent premature wear and also to achieve noise reduction. CO

**chain roller.** The wheel mounted on either side of the escalator step on the chain wheel axle used to support the weight of the step band and passenger loading. LO9/32

**chain sheave.** See sheave: chain.

**chain stretch switch.** See switch: chain stretch.

**chain wheel.** The wheel mounted on either side of the escalator step on the chain wheel axle used to support the weight of the step band and passenger loading. LO9/32

**chain wheel axle.** Generally the common axle that links the escalator step frame with the two step chains and is supported at either end by a chain wheel; on some machines separate stub axles are used instead of a common axle. LO9/32

**chain wheel track.** The chain wheel running and upthrust track. LO9/32

**chain: auxiliary drive.** A chain driving an auxiliary piece of equipment such as a countershaft, handrail, lubricator, governor, etc especially on an escalator. LO6/32

**chain: compensating.** A chain used to offset the varying effect of the hoisting ropes, one end of which is attached to the underside of the elevator car and the other to the counterweight or to a fixed point in the hoistway. AS15

**chain: drive (escalator).** The chain provided to transmit power from the worm reduction unit to the escalator step band and thus cause rotation. CO

**chain: handrail.** A chain provided to drive the handrail. CO

**chain: ladder.** Left and right hand sections of an escalator step chain that are supplied joined at every three pitches by a step axle. LO18/32

**chain: step band drive.** The chain provided to transmit power from the worm reduction unit to the escalator step band and thus cause rotation. CO

**check valve.** See valve: check.

**chevron packing.** See vee packing seal.

**choke line.** A restriction or hydraulic resistance deliberately introduced to restrict the flow. JI

**chord members.** The longitudinal members of the escalator truss assembly. NE22

**cill.** See sill.

**circuit.** The path of an electric current. NE22

**circuit breaker.** A device designed to open a circuit when excessive current flows in that circuit. NE23

**circuit protective conductor (CPC).** An earthing cable connecting an exposed conductive part of an installation to the main earth terminal. LO9/32

**circulation.** The process by which persons in a building move around the building in both horizontal and vertical modes. G

**cladding.** A covering. CO

**clearance.** The space by which one object avoids contact with another object. G

**clearance: bottom car.** When the elevator car rests on its fully compressed buffers the bottom car clearance is the clear vertical distance from the pit floor to the lowest structural part, mechanical part, equipment or device installed beneath the car platform, with the exception of guide shoes, guide rollers, safety jaw assemblies, platform aprons and platform guards. AS3

**clearance: counterweight top.** When the elevator car floor is level with the bottom landing floor the top counterweight clearance is the shortest distance between any part of the counterweight structure and the nearest part of the overhead structure or any other obstruction. AS3

**clearance: running.** The clearance between fixed and moving or rotating components, e.g. the distance between the elevator car sill and the hoistway entrance sill. AS22

**clearance: step to comb.** The gap between the tread of an escalator step or pallet and the underside of a comb plate. CO

**clearance: step to balustrade.** The gap between the edge of a step or pallet and the escalator skirt panel. CO

**clearance: step to step.** The gap between the escalator steps or pallets. CO

**clearance: top car.** When the car floor is level with the top terminal landing floor, the top car clearance is the shortest vertical distance between the top of the car crosshead, or car top if no crosshead is provided, and the nearest part of the overhead structure or any other obstruction. AS3

**cleat.** The tread section teeth or the slats. LO9/32

**cleated riser.** See riser: cleated.

**closed pilot valve.** See valve: closed pilot.

**closer: car door.** A mechanical device attached to a car door whose function is to ensure the car door automatically closes after use, using the stored energy in a set of weights or a spring. AS4

**closer: landing door.** A mechanical device attached to a landing door whose function is to ensure the landing door automatically closes after use, using the stored energy in a set of weights or a spring. AS4

**code.** [syn: standard] A system of rules or regulations. O361

**coil.** A number of turns of insulated wire on a former, typically used in relays and contactors, solenoids, transformers and chokes. LO9/32

**collective control.** See control: simplex collective.

**collective selective control.** See control: directional collective.

**comb.** The aluminium sections, or steel plates with teeth that mesh with the escalator step tread as the step passes underneath. LO9/32

**comb assembly.** The assembly of aluminium comb sections (or steel plate type comb) and treadplate, mounted upon the comb plate. LO9/32

**comb light.** See light: comb.

**comb lighting.** See lighting: comb.

**comb plate switch.** See switch: comb plate.

**comb plate.** The section of floor plate on which the comb teeth segments are mounted at the upper and lower landings of an escalator where the teeth are mounted on the inner edge while the outer edge butts against the floor plate. NE25

**comb release tool.** A special tool or screwdriver that is used to release and/or lift the comb or comb sections. LO9/32

**comb section.** A replaceable section of the comb. LO9/32

**comb switch.** See switch: comb plate.

**comb teeth.** A series of teeth which ride the grooves of the escalator step tread as the step passes underneath and are designed to be extremely brittle which allows them to break off if a wedging action should occur at their point of contact with the step tread. CO

**commercial building.** See building: commercial.

**common sector.** See sector: common.

**compact escalator.** See escalator: compact.

**compatibility.** The compatibility characteristics of hydraulic oils such that they can be mixed. JI

**compensating chain.** See chain: compensating.

**compensating rope.** See rope: compensating.

**compensating rope sheave.** See sheave: compensating rope.

**competent person.** A person with enough theoretical and practical knowledge to be able to detect defects and their seriousness. CO

**compound motor.** See motor: compound.

**comprehensive maintenance contract.** See maintenance: comprehensive.

**compression line fitting.** A fitting designed to join or terminate solid pipe lines using a special compression ring that cuts into the pipe due to the tapered fitting compressing the ring as it is tightened. JI

**computer aided design (CAD).** A system where a digital computer carries out the tedious and time consuming aspects of an engineering design. BE152

**concentric newel.** See newel: concentric.

**conduit.** Part of a closed system, of connecting tubes and junctions forming an enclosure for the protection of cables. Usually of circular cross section. LO10/32

**constant flow rate.** Where the oil flow from a pump or through a valve in a hydraulic system remains substantially constant, despite any changes in pressure and oil temperature. The acceptable variation should be specified at the time of selecting the components. JI

**constant velocity ram.** See telescopic ram.

**contact angle.** See angle of wrap.

**contact: door.** An electric switch device operated by a door panel, which is closed when the door panel is in the closed position, allowing the operation of the elevator car. N38

**contact: gate.** A mechanically operated switch, which prevents the operation of the elevator unless the elevator gate is closed. N58

**contactor.** An electromagnetic device for making and breaking a power circuit. NE28

**contactor: directional.** A contactor with its contacts arranged so as to provide power to the main motor in a pre-set direction (i.e. up or down) CO

**contactor: down.** A contactor with its contacts arranged so as to provide power to the main motor to rotate the escalator step band in a down direction. CO

**contactor: main.** A contactor provided to supplement a directional contactor in the motor circuit. CO

**contactor: up.** A contactor with its contacts arranged so as to provide power to the main motor to rotate the escalator step band in an up direction. CO

**contaminated oil.** Oil that has been over heated; used at excessive pressure for long periods of time; has previously been used and has not been filtered; contains dirt or other foreign matter; or condensation in the tank has introduced water into the oil (which creates a bacteria that causes odours when heated). JI

**contract speed (escalator).** See speed: rated (escalator).

**contract speed (elevator).** See speed: rated (elevator).

**contract capacity.** See capacity: rated.

**contract load.** See capacity: rated.

**contraction of oil.** Changes in oil temperature which cause a change in the volume of oil, and in the case of an hydraulic elevator can cause the car to move a short distance. JI

**control component.** An electrical device used to control elements of escalator operation; either by the switching of circuits or the altering of supplies. LO10/32

**control logic.** The defined sequence and precedence of escalator operations, both manually and automatically initiated for normal, maintenance and fault conditions. LO10/32

**control: AC.** A form of motion control achieved by the use of an AC motor to drive the hoist machine or escalator step band. N1

**control: attendant.** Where the direction of travel, door closing and car starting are under the control of an attendant. N6

**control: automatic pushbutton.** Where the travelling passengers are able to command an elevator car to move from floor to floor without the need of an attendant, as door control and car direction and starting are all automatic. BE86

**control: collective.** See control: simplex collective.

**control: DC.** A form of motion control achieved by the use of a DC motor to drive the hoist machine or escalator step band. N33

**control: directional collective.** Where landing calls are registered on a set of up and down landing call push buttons, the landing and car calls being registered in any order but are answered strictly in floor sequence in the direction of travel, taking account of the direction of travel of the registered landing calls. BE88

**control: door.** The control system which opens and closes the car and landing doors of an elevator installation. BA

**control: down collective.** See control: up-distributive, down-collective.

**control: drive.** The system which controls the starting, stopping, direction of motion, acceleration, retardation, and speed of the elevator car or escalator. AS4

**control: full collective.** See control: directional collective.

**control: group supervisory.** A control system which commands a group of interconnected elevator cars with the aim of improving the elevator system performance. BE93

**control: group collective.** A simple form of group control system, where two (duplex) or three (triplex) cars are interconnected and collectively controlled, but providing a means of allocation of the best placed car to each landing call. BSpt6

**control: non-collective.** The simplest form of control whereby a car will only answer a landing call if it is available. BSpt6

**control: on-call.** An elevator supervisory control system where cars are despatched to serve landing calls according to a fixed or tunable algorithm. BE97

**control: scheduled.** An elevator supervisory control system where cars are despatched to serve landing calls according to a fixed schedule from terminal floors. BE97

**control: simplex collective.** [syn: non-selective] Where landing calls are registered on a single set of landing call push buttons, and landing and car calls may be registered in any order, but are answered strictly in floor sequence in the direction of travel, passengers being unable to indicate their desired direction of travel. BE87

**control: supervisory.** An open loop control system which is used to manage a plant or process, such as an elevator traffic control system. G

**control: up-distributive, down-collective.** Where a single set of landing push buttons indicate a down demand on floors within a building, thus allowing the elevator system to distribute upward going passengers when travelling in the up direction and to collect downward going passengers when travelling in the down direction. BE87

**controller.** A controlling device in the form of an electrical panel, normally located in the upper head of a compact escalator and consisting of the electrical devices required to assure proper operation of the drive mechanism. CO

**controller: programmable.** A controlling device which can have its operating rules altered by means of a program. G

**conveyor.** An endless moving belt for the movement of goods or people. CO

**cooler.** See heat exchanger.

**cooling core.** A core constructed with metal fins arranged around the pipes carrying the oil, similar in design to a car radiator. JI

**cooling switch.** See switch: cooling.

**cooper.** A maker of wooden vessels. O421

**cord: air.** [syn: aircraft cable] A small diameter wire rope frequently used as part of the driving mechanism on door operators, door hangers, gates and selector devices. AS12

**corridor.** A passage or covered way between two places. O431

**countershaft drive chain switch.** See switch: countershaft drive chain.

**countershaft.** The intermediate shaft used to transmit power from main drive or idler shaft to the handrail drive. LO10/32

**counterweight.** A component which is employed to ensure traction between the drive sheave and the suspension ropes and which comprises a set of weights to balance the weight of the car and a proportion of the load in the car often taken as 50% of the rated load. AS15

**counterweight buffer.** See buffer: counterweight.

**counterweight filler.** A metal component of predetermined size and weight which when stacked with other fillers in the counterweight frame forms the counterweight assembly. AS15

**counterweight guard.** A screen installed in the pit, and sometimes at the mid point of the hoistway, to prevent persons from encroaching into the counterweight runway space. AS15

**counterweight header.** A weight component larger than a standard filler, which extends around the counterweight guide-rails and guides the counterweight. AS15

**counterweight safety.** A mechanical device attached to the counterweight frame designed to stop and hold the counterweight in the event of an overspeed or free fall or the slackening of the suspension ropes. AS10

**counterweight: car.** A counterweight, which is directly roped to the elevator car on a winding drum installation, and which is approximately 70% of the car weight. AS14

**counterweight: guide-rails.** Steel T-shaped sections which guide the counterweight in its vertical travel in the hoistway. N31

**cover: plates.** The cover plate at top and bottom landings of an escalator, which is flush with the building floor and the comb plate and is removable for access to the equipment. NE55

**cranked link.** A step chain link that can be incorporated to enable the escalator to be installed with an odd number of steps (and odd number of chain links). LO11/32

**creep.** The small downward movement of a hydraulic elevator owing oil leakages or temperature changes. BA

**criss cross arrangement.** See arrangement: criss cross.

**cross beam.** See crown bar.

**crown bar.** The upper member of the car frame of an elevator car. AS15

**curved track.** See track: curved.

**cushioned stop.** See stop: cushioned.

**cylinder.** The outermost lining of a hydraulic jack. AS15

**cylinder (displacement type).** A single-acting cylinder where the cylinder ram is sealed at the cylinder gland against fluid losses and where the output force is proportional to the ram area. BOpt9

**cylinder (piston type).** A single-acting or double-acting cylinder, where the piston, which is attached to the cylinder ram, seals against the inside of the bore of the cylinder tube and where the output force is proportional to the piston area in one direction and to the piston area minus the ram area in the other direction. BOpt9

**cylinder: double acting.** A cylinder in which pressure can be applied at either end, so giving complete hydraulic control. HH

**cylinder gland.** The seal used to prevent loss of fluid. BOpt9

**cylinder head.** The part of the cylinder that holds the seal and guiding rings that make contact with the ram as it moves in and out of the cylinder. JI

**cylinder head guide yoke.** The guide fitted to intermediate stages of telescopic cylinders to maintain the alignment and prevent the

buckling of the ram and cylinder assembly when extended. JI

**cylinder ram.** The smooth circular moving part of a hydraulic jack, which is forced out of the cylinder by fluid pressure. BOpt9

**cylinder tube.** See cylinder.

**dado.** A decorative moulding or facing on the lower part of a cab wall. O305

**dashpot.** A mechanical device comprising a piston moving in a cylinder against air or oil, used to control or cushion the movement of an arm, lever or rod particularly those used to prevent the slamming of doors. AS16

**data-logging.** The process of logging (acquiring) and analysing data automatically using a digital computer based equipment. BE

**DC control.** See control: DC.

**deck board.** The capping member of the balustrade of an escalator, usually considered as that portion of the balustrade extending from the handrail outward to the exterior line of the escalator. NE34

**deck.** The transverse members of the balustrade with a high deck located immediately below the handrail stand and a low deck located immediately above the skirt panel and having an interior and/or exterior section. CO

**deck: inner.** A second deck of glass balustrade escalator covering from the glass inward to the inner face of the skirts. CO

**deck: outer.** The deck of a glass balustrade escalator covering from the glass to the outermost edge of the escalator. CO

**decking.** The top cover to the balustrade beneath handrail level. LO11/32

**decking: balustrade.** The cladding affixed to the balustrade. CO

**decking cover strip.** A strip or moulding joining the balustrade decking of two adjacent escalators. LO11/32

**dee track.** See track: dee.

**deflector.** A metal plate fitted to each dust tray access. It deflects dust and debris into the dust tray. LO11/32

**deflector device.** An additional device to minimise the risk of trapping between the escalator steps and the skirting. BS95p5

**deflector sheave.** See sheave: deflector.

**demand sector.** See sector: demand.

**demarcation lights.** See lights: demarcation.

**demarcation line.** Located near the edge of the step tread, consisting of a machined groove or contrasting material provided to assist passengers in boarding the escalator by designating the step outline as the step band profile unfolds. CO

**despatch floor.** See floor: despatch.

**despatch interval time.** See time: despatch interval.

**despatch signal.** See signal: despatch.

**despatcher panel.** See panel: despatcher.

**detector: passenger.** An automatic electronic device, which causes door re-opening whenever a passenger is detected in the threshold using photo-electric, electromagnetic, electrostatic or ultrasonic detection methods. AS20

**detritus.** A flammable accumulation of oil and grease, which can easily accumulate in an escalator truss. CO

**device: anti-nuisance.** A device which attempts to reduce the effect of mischievous or malicious passengers registering more car calls than there are passengers in the car or attempting to send a car away when no passengers are present in the car. BE138

**device: door re-opening.** A device which detects the obstruction of automatic power doors and causes them to either re-open or go into another mode of operation such as nudging. AS16

**device: hoistway door locking.** Means of securing the closed hoistway door and preventing it from being opened from the landing except under specified conditions. AS6

**device: levelling.** A mechanism, which will move an elevator car, when it is in the levelling zone, at a reduced speed towards a landing and stop it there. BOpt9

**device: signalling.** An annunciator (light, indicator, bell, buzzer, etc), which provides information to passengers about car direction, car position, car arrival, call acceptance etc. AS10/11

**devices: earthquake protection.** A device or group of devices which regulate the operation of an elevator or group of elevators during or after an earthquake. AS499

**diamond stop.** See stop diamond.

**die cast step.** See step: die cast.

**differential pressure valve.** See valve: differential pressure.

**dip stick.** The measuring stick or rod usually fitted to the filler cap, which allows the depth of oil in the tank to be measured. JI

**direct coupled pump.** See pump: direct coupled.

**direct drive.** See drive: direct.

**direct drive machine.** See machine: direct drive.

**direct on line start (DOL).** Motors that are connected directly to the full voltage without some form of resistance or other current or voltage limiting device in the circuit. JI

**direct plunger driving machine.** See machine: direct plunger driving.

**direction arrow.** See arrow: direction.

**direction indicator.** See indicator: landing direction.

**directional contactor.** See contactor: directional.

**directional collective control.** See control: full collective.

**directional limit switch.** See switch: directional limit.

**directional sector.** See sector: directional.

**directional start switch.** See switch: directional start.

**disc brake.** See brake: disc.

**discrete electrical components.** Devices such as diodes, capacitors or resistors used as distinct control elements in electrical circuits. LO11/32

**displacement piston.** See displacement ram.

**displacement type governor.** See governor: displacement type.

**diversity factor.** A factor which may be applied to reduce the sizing of services, for example electric power cables, on the basis of a mathematical probability that not all connected equipment will require serving at the same time. SS179

**diverter.** See pulley: diverting.

**dividing screen.** Screen installed between the paths of travel of two elevators sharing the same hoistway to enable the safe working on one elevator whilst the other elevator is still operational. BA

**door.** The movable portions of the car or hoistway entrance, which control the safe access to and from the moving car. AN4

**door cam.** See cam: door.

**door close button.** See button: door close.

**door close limit.** See limit: door close.

**door closed time.** See time: door closed.

**door closer: car.** See closer: car door.

**door closing time.** See time: door closing.

**door contact.** See contact: door.

**door control.** See control: door.

**door dwell time.** See time: door dwell.

**door gib.** See gib: door

**door guide.** See gib: door.

**door guide-rails.** See guide-rails: door.

**door hanger.** See hanger: door.

**door hanger sheave.** See sheave: door hanger.

**door hanger track.** See track: door hanger.

**door header.** See header: door.

**door holding time.** See time: car call dwell and time: landing call dwell.

**door interlock.** See interlock: door.

**door interlock zone.** See zone: door.

**door limit switch.** See switch: door limit.

**door linkage.** See linkage: door.

**door lock.** See lock: door.

**door open time.** See time: door open.

**door open button.** See push button: door open.

**door operator.** See operator: door.

**door power operator.** See operator: door.

**door premature opening.** See door: advance opening.

**door re-opening device.** See device: door re-opening.

**door sill (cill).** See sill: door.

**door switch.** See switch: door.

**door track.** See track: door.

**door vane.** See vane: door.

**door zone.** See zone: door.

**door: access.** Means of access to equipment areas and other spaces pertaining to an elevator or escalator installation such as machine rooms, overhead machine spaces, etc and with access usually restricted to authorised persons. AS12/NE1

**door: advance opening.** The initiation of door opening whilst a car is slowing into a floor, under normal operating conditions, usually when the car is in a door zone of plus or minus 200 mm of floor level and such that the car is substantially level at the floor before passengers can attempt to exit. AS16

**door: car.** The door, which is part of the passenger carrying enclosure, and serves to protect passengers from contact with the hoistway walls and equipment. BA

**door: hoistway.** The door sealing access to the hoistway from the landing floors. AS4

**door: inspection.** Means of access to equipment areas and other spaces pertaining to an escalator installation such as machinery spaces etc and with access usually restricted to authorised persons. CO

**door: landing.** See door: hoistway.

**door: multiple panel (leaf).** Door(s) comprising two or more panels which are arranged to telescope behind each other as the door(s) opens. P219

**door: pre-opening.** See door: advance opening.

**door: side opening.** A single or multiple panel, horizontally sliding door. P216

**door: single panel (leaf).** A horizontally sliding, side opening door comprising a single leaf. P216

**door: slide up-down.** See doors: bi-parting.

**door: two speed.** An arrangement, for either side or centre opening doors, where one panel slides behind the other panel at twice the speed, in order that both panels arrive at the opening position simultaneously. P216

**doors: bi-parting.** A vertically sliding door, often found on freight elevators, which consists of two sections, so interconnected that they open simultaneously away from each other. AS4

**doors: centre opening.** A horizontally sliding door, with two or more panels, so interconnected that they open simultaneously away from each other. AS4

**double acting cylinder.** See double acting rams.

**double acting rams.** Rams which incorporate a piston head and two cylinder connections one at each end, where connecting the pressure line to one and the exhaust line to the other causes the piston and ram to move in one direction; and reversing the oil connections causes the piston and ram to move in the opposite direction. JI

**double acting seal.** See seal: double acting.

**double deck(er) elevator.** See elevator: double deck(er).

**double wrap.** See wrap: double.

**down peak.** A down peak traffic condition exists, when the dominant or only traffic flow is in the downward direction, with all or the majority of the passengers leaving the building at the main terminal floor of the building. BE7

**down peak interval.** See interval: down peak.

**down peak passenger arrival-rate.** See arrival-rate: down peak passenger.

**down peak traffic.** See traffic: down peak.

**down arrow.** See arrow: down.

**down collective control.** See control: up-distributive, down-collective.

**down contactor.** See contactor: down.

**down stop.** See stop: down.

**drain line.** See oil drain line.

**dress guard.** See guard: skirt.

**drip pan.** See drip tray.

**drip tray.** A pan which is welded or bolted to the truss of an escalator along its full length and width. NE42

**drive chain.** See chain: drive.

**drive control.** See control: drive.

**drive controller.** A separate controller provided on some larger escalators containing electrical and/or electronic components or devices which interpret the outputs from the logic controller and set the drive motors speed and direction. CO

**drive machine (elevator).** A power unit which provides the means for raising and lowering the car and which comprises: the electric motor or hydraulic power unit; gearing, brake; sheave or drum; couplings and bedplate. J14

**drive machine (escalator).** The combination of motor and gear reduction unit which forms the drive mechanism for all moving parts on an escalator. NE42

**drive sheave.** See sheave: drive.

**drive unit.** See drive machine.

**drive wheels.** The sprockets over which the escalator drive chain or chains and step chain(s) pass. CO

**drive: direct.** A drive where the driving part is directly connected to the driven part, either with or without intermediate gears. AS7

**drive: drum.** A positive elevator drive system whereby the car and the counterweight are secured to a multi-grooved drum, such that as one set of ropes unwind from the drum the other set of ropes wind on. J71

**drive: indirect.** A drive system where the driving part is connected to the driven part by means of V-belts, tooth drive belts, or drive chains. AS181

**drive: linear.** A drive which utilises the electromagnetic propulsion, provided by a linear motor, between a fixed part (often the guides) and a moving part (often the car) with or without a counterweight. BA

**driving station.** The area of free space within the truss at the top/drive end of the escalator or passenger conveyor for use by maintenance and inspection personnel. BS78p2

**dropped step support.** The ramps that act on the escalator trailer wheel axle or step frame and step chain and support the steps through the comb in the event of one or more wheels or their tyres becoming detached. LO12/32

**dropped step switch.** See switch: dropped step.

**drum.** The cylinder of a drum type driving machine, on which the hoisting ropes wind and unwind, when raising or lowering the elevator car. AS17

**drum brake.** See brake drum.

**drum drive.** See drive: drum.

**duck board.** An insulated platform/stand for raising operative personnel above floor level,

and provide insulation protection to earth. (Used in machine room areas where there is a possibility of moisture or water ingress). LO12/32

**dumbwaiter.** An elevator used for the vertical transportation of materials only and comprising a car whose dimensions are such as prevent the transportation of passengers, and which moves in guides, often situated beneath a counter or sited at counter top level. AS4/BSpt9

**duplex.** Two interconnected cars, sharing a common signalling system, controlled under a simple group control system operating under directional collective principles. BE88

**dust tray.** A metal tray supported under the main drive and tension carriages that catches any small objects and dust that falls from the steps as they return under the escalator. LO13/32

**duty range.** The designed performance range of an escalator or passenger conveyor. CO

**dwell time.** See time: door dwell.

**dynamic oil pressure.** The oil pressure during the starting and/or running of the system, which (owing to system friction) will always be higher than the static oil pressure. JI

**dynamic seal.** See seal: dynamic.

**dynamic sector.** See sector: dynamic.

**earth.** The main terminal used to connect the installations earthing and bonding system to the conductive mass of earth normally by a conductor provided as part of the power distribution. LO13/32

**earth leakage circuit breaker.** A circuit breaker designed to break the supply in the event of a current flowing to earth. LO13/32

**earthing.** The act of connecting the exposed conductive parts of an installation to earth. LO13/32

**earthquake protection devices.** See devices: earthquake protection.

**earthquake sensors.** Sensors which can detect the incidence of earthquake ground waves prior to the actual earthquake shock and which are used to operate control devices in order to bring the elevator safely to rest. S391

**eccentric ram loading.** The loading on the ram, which occurs when the load does not press directly on the centre of the ram, or when the direction of the load is not in-line with the axes of the ram. JI

**electrical drawings.** Plans showing electrical circuits. CO

**electrical interference.** See interference: electrical.

**electrical noise.** See noise: electrical.

**electro-mechanical brake.** See brake.

**electronic valve.** See valve: electronic.

**elephant ear.** The 'ear-shaped' replaceable rubber insert that forms part of the handrail entry guard on some escalators. LO13/32

**elevator.** [syn: lift] A permanent lifting equipment, serving two or more landing levels, provided with a car or platform for the transportation of passengers and/or freight, running at least partially in rigid guides either vertical or inclined to the vertical by less than 15 degrees. J13

**elevator: bed.** Elevators for the conveyance of patients being moved on beds or stretchers in hospitals, clinics, nursing homes etc with a platform shape which is narrow and deep, capable of carrying a load of 20 persons or more and equipped with solid doors of a width of at least 1300 mm and capable of excellent levelling accuracy. P52

**elevator: direct-plunger hydraulic.** A hydraulic elevator having a plunger or cylinder directly attached to the platform or car frame. AS5

**elevator: direct acting.** See elevator: direct-plunger hydraulic.

**elevator: double decker.** An elevator having two compartments located one above the other. SS337

**elevator: electric.** A power elevator, which uses an electrical drive machine to provide energy for the movement of the car. AS5

**elevator: electro-hydraulic.** A direct plunger machine, where liquid is directly pumped under pressure into the cylinder by a pump driven by an electric motor. AS5

**elevator: firefighting.** An elevator, which may be supplied with additional fire resistant protection, installed in a fire protected zone and designated to have controls that enable it to be used under the direct control of the firefighting services for emergency purposes. BA

**elevator: fireman's.** An elevator, which may or may not be supplied with additional fire resistant protection, designated to have controls that enable it to be used under the direct control of the firefighting services for emergency purposes. BSpt6

**elevator: freight.** An elevator primarily used to transport freight and goods, where only the operator and persons necessary to load and unload the freight are permitted to travel. AS5

**elevator: gravity.** An elevator where gravity is used as the motive force to move the car. AS5

**elevator: hand.** An elevator where manual energy is used to move the car. AS5

**elevator: hydraulic.** A power elevator, which uses the energy stored in a liquid under pressure to provide the energy for the movement of the car. AS5

**elevator: inclined.** An elevator which travels at an inclination to the vertical of 15° or more. BSpt1

**elevator: indirect acting.** A hydraulic elevator where the plunger or cylinder is indirectly connected to the platform or car frame by ropes or chains. BA

**elevator: maintained-pressure hydraulic.** A direct plunger elevator where liquid under pressure is available for application to the cylinder at all times. AS5

**elevator: multideck.** An elevator having two or more compartments located above each other to form a multi-level stack. AS5

**elevator: observation.** An elevator designed as an architectural feature to give passengers a panoramic view while travelling in a partially enclosed well. BSpt6

**elevator: passenger.** An elevator primarily used to carry passengers other than the operator (if any). AS5

**elevator: passenger/freight.** An elevator of such dimensions that only goods and restricted classes of passengers (such as freight handlers, employees) may be carried. AS175

**elevator: power.** An elevator utilising energy other than gravitational or manual to provide motion for the car. AS5

**elevator: roped-hydraulic.** A hydraulic elevator where the piston is connected to the car by means or wire ropes. AS5

**elevator: service.** A passenger elevator used to transport materials, which conforms to the standards for passenger conveyance, but is often specially strengthened to carry freight or goods. SS307

**elevator: sidewalk.** An elevator of the freight type used to carry materials, except automobiles, between a street level and a level or levels below AS5

**elevator: stair.** Elevators provided for persons with impaired mobility, which can be permanently or temporarily installed on a stairway, which provide a seat for the person to ride on. SS351

**elevator: wheelchair.** A platform elevator, which can be fitted to a stairway for the transportation of wheelchairs and which generally can be folded away when not in use. SS350

**elongated newel.** See newel: elongated.

**EMC.** Electromagnetic compatibility: comprises immunity and emission. BA

**emergency brake.** See brake: emergency.

**emergency coils.** See emergency solenoids. JI

**emergency hand pump.** See pump: emergency hand.

**emergency lighting.** See lighting: emergency.

**emergency solenoids.** Solenoids provided with two coils in the one housing, with one coil for normal operation and a low voltage coil for emergency operation from a battery in the event of a mains supply failure. JI

**emergency stop switch.** See switch: emergency stop.

**enclosure: car.** The top and the walls of the car resting on and attached to the car platform. AS5

**encoder shaft.** A rotary digital encoder, which when rotated by a toothed tape attached to the car can provide a very accurate value for the position of a car in a hoistway, as a binary number. BI115

**energy accumulation type buffer.** See buffer: energy accumulation type.

**engineer.** A person who is capable of innovation and possesses graduate academic qualifications and subsequent responsible experience in the industry. BA.

**engineer surveyor.** A person who undertakes a periodic thorough examination of equipment. CO

**entrance: car.** The protective assembly which closes the hoistway enclosure openings normally used for entrance to and exit from the car. AS5

**entrance floor.** See floor: main.

**entrapped air.** See air entrapment.

**EPROM** A device of storing computer data in a semi permanent form, erased using an electrical signal. LO13/32

**equal lay.** See lay: equal.

**erection working line.** The theoretical line parallel to the escalator step nose line between erection working points. LO14/32

**erection working point.** The theoretical point on the intersection of escalator centre line, finish floor level and erection working line. LO14/32

**escalator.** A power driven endless moving stairway inclined at between 28° and 35° for the short range upward and downward transportation of passengers. AS5/BS70p5

**escalator: compact.** An escalator with the drive machine incorporated within the bounds of the truss and typically without separate machine areas. LO10/32

**escalator flight time.** See time: escalator flight time.

**escalator: heavy duty public service.** A public service escalator with major non wearing components suitable for operating for 40 years in an underground railway environment. LO17/32

**escalator: spiral.** An escalator that can follow a curved path. BA

**escalator: wheelchair.** An escalator designed to transport a wheelchair. BA.

**escutcheon rubber.** The 'ear-shaped' replaceable rubber insert that forms part of the handrail entry guard on some escalators. Also known as the elephants ear. LO13/32

**excess load indicator.** See indicator: excess load.

**exhaust flow.** The oil being drained back to the tank from cylinders, actuators or other parts of the system usually via a valve. JI

**expansion of oil.** See oil expansion.

**expansion chamber.** [syn: muffler] A large chamber placed in the pressure line, usually close to the pumping unit, which allows the pulsation waves in the pipeline to expand when entering the chamber and which causes their amplitude and frequency not to revert to the original form on leaving the chamber. JI

**express jump.** The distance between the main terminal floor of a building and an express zone terminal floor. BA

**express lobby.** See lobby: express.

**express zone.** See zone: high rise.

**express zone lobby.** See floor: express zone terminal.

**express zone terminal floor.** See floor: express zone terminal.

**express-run.** When a car makes an non stop run from its current floor to a destination floor ignoring any possible stopping floors on the trip. BE17

**extended heads.** Extensions of the truss proper at either the lower or upper head to reach the building support steel when it is located beyond the standard dimensional requirements of the escalator. CO

**extended newel.** See newel: extended.

**exterior panels.** Covering on the escalator truss on the exterior side of the balustrading. CO

**external pump.** See pump: external.

**fan: car.** A means of mechanically ventilating the passenger car enclosure of an elevator, aiding the air movement through the vent openings provided. AS147

**fault condition switch.** See switch: fault condition.

**fender casting.** The casting that forms a corner piece at the end of the skirting, on some escalators, and to which the handrail entry guard is fitted. LO14/32

**filter.** A fine mesh panel or tube located in the oil or air flow path to prevent the entry or expelling of foreign or unwanted materials that could damage the system moving parts. HH

**filter contamination detection.** The detection of the contamination of hydraulic oil by means of a pressure gauge or other method of detecting a pressure increase at the inlet side of the filter. JI

**final limit switch.** See switch: final limit.

**finish floor level.** The level of the floor adjacent to the escalator landing. LO14/32

**fire shutter.** An automatic or manual fireproof horizontal rolling steel curtain completely enclosing the escalator wellway in case of fire within the building and to eliminate the stack effect created by the wellways in the event of fire. CO

**fire shutter switch.** See switch: fire shutter.

**fireman's elevator.** See elevator: fireman's.

**fireman's lift.** See elevator: fireman's.

**fireman's service.** See service: fireman's.

**fireman's switch.** See switch: fireman's.

**fishplate.** A flat steel plate, which is machined on one side, used to connect together, in rigid alignment, two end to end sections of elevator guide-rail or sections of escalator tracking. AS17

**fixed flow control.** Pumps or valves designed to transfer fluid at a fixed flow either by the design characteristics or pressure and/or temperature compensation. JI

**fixed sector.** See sector: static.

**fixture.** Term used to denote a variety of signalling and indicating devices, such as landing and car call pushbuttons, position indicators, direction indicators, card access devices etc. BA

**fixture: intelligent.** A fixture commonly the car operating panel or lobby call registration panel, which has the ability to present information to passengers in an interactive manner and which may be able to process its input-output via a computer communication bus instead of via a multi pair travelling cable. BA

**fixture: talking.** A fixture which is programmed to provide passengers with information by means of a simulated speech output. BA

**flared joint.** A system designed to prevent a hydraulic pipe and its fitting from separating under pressure, where the ends of pipes are flared to match the pipe fitting. JI

**fleet angle.** Angle of deviation at which the rope leaves the centre of the sheave groove, usually less than two degrees. BA

**flexible conduit.** A pliable conduit which can be bent by hand with a reasonable small force, but without other assistance, and which is intended to flex frequently throughout its life. LO15/32

**flexible guide clamp safety.** See safety: flexible guide clamp.

**flexible pressure line.** See hose, flexible.

**flight.** A number of escalators, and/or stairs within the same shaft. LO15/32

**flight time.** See time: flight.

**float switch.** See switch: float.

**floor.** The layer of boards, brick, stone etc, on which people tread; the under surface of the interior of a room. O771

**floor plate.** A removable steel plate finished with a hard wearing floor material, typically situated above the escalator trusswork, where there is insufficient clearance for floor trays. LO15/32

**floor population.** See population: floor.

**floor selector.** See selector: floor.

**floor stopping switch.** See switch: floor stopping.

**floor to floor cycle time.** See time: cycle.

**floor to floor height.** See interfloor distance.

**floor to floor time.** See time: flight.

**floor tray.** The removable steel tray infilled with concrete or ribbed aluminium and finished with a hard wearing floor material. LO15/32

**floor: bottom terminal.** Lowest floor in a building zone from which elevator cars can load and unload passengers. AS7

**floor: bypass.** Floors at which a landing call has been registered, but which are passed by the elevator car under circumstances when the car is fully loaded (load bypass) or when the car has other higher priority duties to perform (control bypass). SS77/103

**floor: car.** The under surface of the interior of an elevator car, on which passengers stand. BA

**floor: dispatch.** Floors in an elevator zone, often the terminal floors, from which cars were dispatched under the control of the scheduling supervisory control system. BE97

**floor: entrance.** See floor: main.

**floor: express zone terminal.** The lowest floor of a high rise zone in a building which is served by an elevator car after it leaves the main terminal floor. BE92

**floor: heavy duty.** A floor at which a considerably larger than average number of passengers are demanding service often detected by successive cars leaving the floor fully loaded or the immediate re-registration of a landing call as soon as a car has left a floor. BE133/340

**floor: highest.** The highest, occupied or otherwise, floor within a building. CO

**floor: highest reversal.** The floor at which a car reverses direction, when travelling in an upward direction having completed its last car call, in preparation to serve registered down landing calls. BSpt6

**floor: lowest.** The lowest, occupied or otherwise, floor within a building. CO

**floor: lowest reversal.** The floor at which a car reverses direction, when travelling in a downward direction having completed its last car call, in preparation to serve registered up

landing calls, particularly during an interfloor traffic condition. BA

**floor: lowest terminal.** See floor: bottom terminal.

**floor: main.** The main or principal floor of a building. BA

**floor: main terminal.** See floor: main.

**floor: parking.** A floor at which an elevator car is parked when it has completed serving its car calls and the supervisory control system does not reallocate it to serve further landing calls. BE96

**floor: terminal.** The highest and lowest floors at the extremities of travel of an elevator car within a building zone. AS7

**floor: top terminal.** Highest floor in a building zone from which elevator cars can load and unload passengers. AS7

**floor: upper terminal.** See floor: top terminal.

**flow fuse.** See pipe rupture valve.

**flow restriction valve.** See valve: pipe rupture.

**flow divider.** Where the oil line is divided into two or more lines either through branching pipe fittings or a manifold. JI

**fluid level switch.** See switch: float.

**flyball governor.** See governor: flyball.

**flywheel.** A rotating mass usually attached to the electric motor shaft, sized to provide inertia in the system sufficient to prevent a sudden stop of the low inertia motor rotor, if the power is removed from the motor when running full speed. JI

**flywheel (1).** A disc located on the motor shaft of an elevator and normally used for hand winding. CO

**flywheel (2).** A disc located on the motor shaft of an escalator. CO

**footlight.** See light: foot.

**foundation.** The reinforced concrete base on which the escalator truss supports are mounted. LO15/32

**four way traffic.** See traffic: four way.

**frame: cantilevered car.** The type of frame that is only guided or supported on one side, with the cabin support beams cantilevered out from the uprights. See also rucksack elevators. JI

**frame: car.** [syn: sling] A supporting frame consisting of stiles, cross beam, safety plank and platform to which the guide shoes, car safety and hoisting ropes or hydraulic plunger or cylinder is attached. AS3

**frame-size.** Commonly used to indicate the size of an electrical drive motor. BA

**free car.** See car: free.

**freight elevator.** See elevator: freight.

**front.** The front (of an elevator car) is the side in which the entrance is situated or in the case of multiple entrances the side containing the entrance nearest to the car operating panel. N57

**frothing (of oil).** The condition of hydraulic oil that has air entrapped in it (aeration), due to the bad design of the components and their piping often where air bleeding is inadequate or air bleeding systems are not installed, which seriously effects system performance. JI

**full collective control.** See control: directional collective.

**full load current.** Maximum continuous operating current. LO15/32

**full wave rectifier.** A rectifier that allows current to pass in one direction through the load during the full cycle of AC. NE57

**fuse.** A safety device that opens the electrical feed line to a circuit of more than the designated amount of current should flow through it. NE57

**gate.** See door.

**gate closer.** See closer: car door.

**gate contact.** See contact: gate.

**gate operator.** See operator: door.

**gate power operator.** See operator: door.

**gear pump.** See pump: gear.

**gear.** Wheels working one upon another, by means of teeth (or otherwise) for transmitting or changing motion and power. O838

**gear: helical.** Gear wheels running on parallel axes with the teeth twisted obliquely to the gear wheel axles. BA

**gear: safety.** A mechanical device attached to the car frame or to the counterweight designed to stop and hold the elevator car in the event of free fall or of a predetermined overspeed or rope slackening. BOpt9

**gear: worm.** A gear, used to connect non-parallel, non-intersecting shafts, with the teeth of the intersecting wheels cut on an angle. BA

**gearbox.** Wheels working one upon another, by means of teeth (or otherwise) for transmitting or changing motion, power and/or speed (often called a worm reduction unit). CO

**geared machine.** See machine: geared traction drive.

**geared traction machine.** See machine: geared traction drive.

**gearless traction machine.** See machine: gearless traction drive.

**generator.** An electromechanical device which converts mechanical energy in the form of motion into electrical energy strictly as DC power. BA

**gib: door.** A door component fixed to the bottom edge of a sliding door panel which runs in a machined groove in the sill to guide and correctly hold the door panel in position. AS18

**gib: guide shoes.** A liner for car or counterweight guide shoes. AS18

**gland.** A mechanical component which is used to hold the sealing material, that prevents oil leakage between the ram and cylinder, but still allows the ram to move freely into or out of the cylinder. JI

**gland packing.** The sealing material that forms a seal between a fixed and moving part, i.e. the seal between the cylinder and ram. JI

**gland seal.** See gland packing.

**gong.** See hall lantern and gong.

**goods lift.** See: elevator: freight.

**governor drive chain switch.** See switch: governor drive chain.

**governor rope.** See rope: governor.

**governor switch.** See switch: governor.

**governor.** Strictly a mechanical device which is a closed loop, error activated means of automatically controlling the speed of a machine, but in the elevator context it is used to detect an overspeed situation. BA

**governor: bail type.** Horizontal shaft type governor. AS165

**governor: centrifugal.** A mechanical device which utilises the effects of centrifugal forces operating on weights rotating in a horizontal or vertical plane to provide a movement which can in turn be used to operate a control device. BA

**governor: displacement type.** Horizontal shaft centrifugal type governor, which uses the movement of weights mounted on the governor sheave to operate the rope gripping device. AS165

**governor: flyball.** Vertical shaft centrifugal type governor, which utilises the movement of a pair of flyballs, driven by the vertical shaft, to lift a collar or sleeve, which in turn operates the rope gripping device. AS165

**governor: horizontal shaft.** Governor where the activating shaft rotates in the horizontal plane. BA

**governor: overspeed.** A governor used to detect the occurrence of a predetermined speed. BA

**governor: pull through.** Governors of any type where the rope is gripped by spring loaded jaws and can 'pull through' rather than being solidly locked to the rope gripping jaws thus preventing damage to the rope. AS165

**governor: vertical shaft.** Governor where the activating shaft rotates in the vertical plane. BA

**groove.** A long narrow channel machined into a surface. BA

**groove: 'U'-profile.** A groove cut into a drive sheave, which is semi circular in shape, and of a radius which is approximately equal to the diameter of the suspension rope. P66/7

**groove: undercut.** A groove cut into a drive sheave, which is a modified 'V'-groove having the lower sides cut in the shape of a 'U'. N152

**groove: 'V'-cut.** A groove cut into a drive sheave in the shape of a 'V'. N155

**group supervisory control.** See control: group supervisory.

**group supervisory control algorithm.** See algorithm: group supervisory control.

**group.** A group of cars is a number of cars placed physically together, using a common signalling system and under the control of a supervisory control system. BE89

**guard.** A device placed over or enclosing an item where access is to be prevented for reasons of safety or security. CO

**guard: counterweight.** Unperforated metal guards installed, whenever necessary, in the pit, on all open sides of a counterweight runway AS49

**guard: dress.** See guard: skirt.

**guard: handrail.** A guard usually made of brush or rubber, that fits over the outside of the handrail where it enters or leaves the balustrade and designed to keep a person's fingers out of the handrail opening. CO

**guard: intersection.** A triangular shaped piece, usually plastic, located at the point where the escalator decking intersects the horizontal underside portion of the ceiling in the well-way, in order to prevent injury to passengers if they are looking over the side of the escalator and a part of their body should enter this intersecting angle. CO

**guard: sheave.** A protective guard around a rope carrying sheave. N128

**guard: sight.** A vertical strip of material, which is mounted adjacent to the leading edge of a side sliding landing door and used to block out any view of the hoistway space, whenever the elevator doors are in the open position. N130

**guard: sill.** [syn: toe guard] A smooth often bevelled apron, extending downwards from the sill of the landing or car entrance, with the intention of removing shear hazards to passengers from structural members projecting into the hoistway. BS/ENpt1

**guard: skirt.** A continuous rubber strip attached to the escalator skirt panel to deflect feet and long clothing away from the edge of a step. CO

**guard: toe.** See guard: sill.

**guard: wedge.** A piece of triangular shaped material located at the point where the decking on an escalator intersects the underside of a wellway ceiling. NE158

**guide bracket.** See bracket: guide-rail.

**guide: door.** See gib: door.

**guides.** See guide-rail.

**guides: handrail.** Polished metal guides on which the handrail runs throughout its entire travel. CO

**guide-rail.** A set of vertical machined surfaces installed in the hoistway to guide the travel of an elevator car or counterweight. AS18

**guide-rail: car.** Guide-rails used to direct the travel of an elevator car in a hoistway. AS18

**guide-rail: counterweight.** Guide-rails used to direct the travel of a counterweight in a hoistway. AS18

**guide-rail: door.** Vertical tracks used to guide the travel of bi-parting freight doors. N38

**guide-shoes.** Devices used to guide the movement of doors, cars and counterweights along their associated guide-rails. N61

**guide-shoes: door.** Guiding devices mounted on both horizontal and vertically moving doors to guide their travel. N62

**guide-shoes: slipper.** Guide-shoes used to guide an elevator car or counterweight, which are 'U' shaped so that the gibs surround and bear onto the machined surfaces of the tongue part section of the guide-rails. AS132

**guide-shoes: roller.** Guide-shoes used to guide an elevator car or counterweight, which are constructed of a set of rollers (three or six) which run on the machined surfaces of the guide-rails. AS131

**half track.** See track: half.

**halfway box.** See box halfway.

**hall.** [syn: floor, e.g. floor call; landing, e.g. landing push-button; corridor, e.g. corridor call.]

**hall call.** See call: landing.

**hall direction indicator.** See indicator: landing direction.

**hall lantern and gong.** Unit providing a visual and acoustic indication of the availability of an elevator car to accept passengers for a specific direction of travel, which is mounted adjacent to each elevator. BA

**hall push button.** See push button: landing.

**hall stop.** See stop: landing call.

**hallway.** The lobby or entrance passage to a building and other floors a corridor or passage. O917

**hand lowering.** The action of lowering an hydraulic elevator in the event of an emergency. BA

**hand powered lift.** See lift: hand powered.

**hand pump.** See pump: hand.

**hand pumping.** The action of raising an hydraulic elevator in the event of an emergency. BA

**hand rope.** See rope: hand.

**handling capacity.** See capacity: handling (elevator).

**handrail.** The moving handhold provided for escalator passengers which moves over the top of the balustrade and newel. NE63

**handrail brush.** A brush provided at the newel end to cover the internal components of the newel entry switch. CO

**handrail drive.** The mechanism including sprockets, chains and wheels which drives and directs the travel of an escalator handrail. NE63

**handrail entry switch.** See switch: handrail entry.

**handrail guard.** See guard: handrail.

**handrail guides.** See guides: handrail.

**handrail spacers.** Inserts of contrasting colour to indicate direction and speed of the handrail. CO

**handrail speed detector.** A device that measures the handrail speed and in the event of underspeed or overspeed opens a switch in the safety circuit. LO16/32

**handrail support moulding.** The extruded section of the balustrading that connects the vertical interior panelling to the horizontal decking and supports the handrail track. LO16/32

**handrail tensioning device.** The assembly of components, and their adjustable fixing, used to tension handrails. LO16/32

**handrail track.** See track: handrail.

**handwinding.** The action of using a manual device to permit the emergency movement of an electric traction elevator or the manual movement of an escalator. BOpt9

**handwinding device.** The mechanical means provided to manually rotate the escalator step band or to wind an elevator up or down. CO

**handwinding instructions.** A notice showing instructions how to operate the handwinding equipment in the event of an elevator or escalator failure. LO17/32

**handwinding ratchet.** A ratchet that is fitted to the end of the drive motor shaft and turned by hand to move the escalator. LO17/32

**hanger: door.** An assembly, which is fastened to the top of a door panel, supporting and permitting the sliding movement of the door panel(s), comprising the hanger sheave and hanger track. AS18

**hanger sheave.** See sheave: door hanger.

**hanger track.** See track: door hanger.

**hatch.** See hatchway.

**hatchway.** An obsolete term used to describe the elevator hoistway, derived from the use of a framed and covered opening in a floor; a miniature access door. AS19

**hauling rope.** See rope: hauling.

**head.** The area under the landing plates at either end of an escalator. NE65

**head jamb.** See jamb: head.

**head room.** The dimension from the escalator step tread to the underside of the wellway opening immediately above. CO

**header: door.** A horizontal structural member located on the hoistway side of an elevator entrance used to support the door hanger. AS16

**headroom.** Clear working space provided above machinery. N65

**heat dissipation.** Is the ability of the tank housing and cylinder to lower the temperature by natural or artificial means. JI

**heat exchanger.** Device that causes hot oil to be cooled to the desirable working temperature by circulating the oil through pipes fitted with cooling fins, or through a form of radiator core, sometimes assisted by a fan to increase the efficiency of the cooling system. JI

**heat transfer.** The transfer of heat between the equipment and the air, to ensure good hydraulic performance, where in some cases additional items such as heat exchangers and cooling systems may be required. JI

**heavy duty call.** See call: heavy duty.

**heavy duty floor.** See floor: heavy duty.

**heavy duty public service escalator.** See escalator: heavy duty public service.

**helical gear.** See gear: helical.

**helper.** In USA the lowest classification of an employee working in an elevator company. N65

**high call reversal.** See call: highest reversal.

**high chord truss.** See truss: high chord.

**high rise zone.** See zone: high rise.

**highest floor.** See floor: highest.

**highest reversal floor.** See floor: highest reversal.

**hoist machine.** See machine.

**hoistway.** A vertical opening through a building or structure in which elevators, material lifts, dumbwaiters etc travel extending from the pit at the bottom to the underside of the roof or machinery space above. AS6

**hoistway door.** See door: hoistway.

**hoistway door combination mechanical lock and electrical contact.** A device with two functions where (*a*) the operation of the driving machine is prevented unless the hoistway doors are in the closed position and (*b*) the hoistway doors are locked in the closed position to prevent them being opened from

the landing side unless the car is in the landing zone. AS6

**hoistway door (electrical) contact.** See contact: door.

**hoistway door interlock.** See interlock: hoistway door.

**hoistway door mechanical lock.** See lock: door.

**holding time.** See time: door dwell.

**hollow rams.** Rams manufactured from tubes compared with solid round material. JI

**honed finish.** A machining system that improves the surface finish of rams or the bores of cylinders. JI

**hood.** The solid protective screen projecting upwards from the roof of a paternoster car, which continues with the apron of the paternoster car above, to form a continuous cover over the space between cars. BOpt9

**horizontal shaft governor.** See governor: horizontal shaft.

**hose, flexible.** Hoses used to transmit fluid between parts, which move relatively to each other, sometimes made of synthetic rubber reinforced with wire or canvas to give strength and provided with union-type end fittings, often fitted by the hose manufacturers. HH

**hydraulic lift.** See elevator: hydraulic.

**hydraulic lift: direct acting.** See machine: direct plunger driving.

**hydraulic lift: suspended type.** See machine: roped hydraulic drive.

**hydraulic power unit.** Part of the elevator drive system and comprising pump, pump motor, control valves and fluid storage tank. BOpt9

**hydraulic synchronised rams.** See telescopic rams.

**idler shaft.** The driven shaft in the tension carriage carrying two sprockets that tension and reverse the direction of the escalator step chains. LO17/32

**idler sheave.** See sheave: idler.

**idler sprocket.** A sprocket used to change the direction of chain movement. LO17/32

**inch.** To move an escalator at maintenance speed. LO17/32

**inch directional contactors.** The up and down interlocking contactors that connect the escalator power supply to the drive motor for maintenance, permit inching speed and fix the mode of rotation. LO17/32

**inch speed.** The escalator speed used for inspection and maintenance purposes, typically a quarter of rated speed. LO17/32

**inching (1).** A manual operation, usually carried out on freight elevators, where a car switch or a push button is used to cause the car platform to move in small increments until it is level with the landing sill. AS19

**inching (2).** A manual operation carried out under maintenance situations, where the escalator step band is rotated in small increments. CO

**inclination.** The angle to which the escalator is manufactured. CO

**incline.** The sloped area between the upper and the lower landings/machine rooms. LO17/32

**inclined section.** The portion of an escalator which is inclined, in general trigonometric terms could be referred to as the hypotenuse. CO

**inclined transportation.** Means of moving people or goods which is not on a level plane. CO

**independent service.** See service: independent.

**index: performance.** Term used in control engineering where a variable is selected and its performance is maximised. BA

**indicator: call accepted.** An indicator adjacent to or contained within a landing call or car call push button, which is illuminated when the elevator supervisory control system has accepted the call into its memory. BA

**indicator: call registration.** See indicator: call accepted.

**indicator: car coming.** An indicator adjacent to or contained within a landing call push button, fitted on installations which are controlled by very simple supervisory control systems, and which is illuminated whenever the elevator car is coming to the calling landing. BA

**indicator: car position.** An indicator adjacent to or above a car or landing entrance, which is illuminated to indicate the position of the elevator car in the hoistway. BA

**indicator: direction.** See indicator: landing direction.

**indicator: direction landing.** An indicator adjacent to or above a car entrance, which is illuminated whenever that car is to stop at that landing and which indicates the intended direction of travel for the car. BA

**indicator: excess load.** An indicator located on the car operating panel, which is illuminated whenever the passenger load in the car exceeds the rated value. BA

**indicator: lift in use.** An indicator adjacent to or contained within a landing call push button, which is illuminated whenever the elevator is busy serving a demand, usually fitted on installations controlled by a very simple supervisory control system. BA

**indicator: lift coming.** See indicator: car coming.

**indicator: next car.** An indicator adjacent to a car entrance or installed inside an elevator car, which illuminates to indicate the next car, in a sequence, to leave a specific floor. BA

**indicator: overload.** An indicator, usually installed inside an elevator car, which indicates by an acoustic alarm together with an illuminated sign, that the passenger load in the car is in excess of the rated value. BA

**indicator: position.** See indicator: car position.

**indirect coupled pumps.** See pumps: indirect coupled.

**indirect drive.** See drive: indirect.

**indirect drive machine.** See machine: indirect drive.

**inductor.** An electrical device made of a coil of wire on a former, which is capable of storing energy and which tends to oppose the current flowing in it. BA

**in-line filter.** A filter assembly mounted in the main piping system to prevent foreign material passing into the valve or cylinder usually of the high pressure type. JI

**inner deck.** The second deck of a glass balustrade escalator; covering from the glass inward to the inner face of the skirts. NE71

**inspection door.** See door: access.

**inspection outlet.** A hard wired socket provided in various locations of an elevator or an escalator for the connection of the inspection unit. CO

**inspection unit.** A portable plug-in unit used to control the inching of an escalator during inspection and maintenance. LO17/32

**institutional building.** See building: institutional.

**insulation resistance.** The electrical resistance between a conductor and earth. CO

**integrated rupture valve.** See valve: integrated rupture.

**intensive duty traffic.** See traffic: intensive duty.

**interface: mechanical.** Resistance to motion provided by friction and/or mechanical means or devices. CO

**interference: electrical.** Unwanted signals transmitted via the electrical supplies or as electromagnetic radiation, which can interact with properly generated signal sequences to produce incorrect or hazardous operation of equipment. BA

**interfloor distance.** The vertical distance between two adjacent landing floors. BA

**interfloor flight time.** See time: flight.

**interfloor jump time.** See time: flight.

**interfloor passenger arrival-rate.** See arrival-rate: interfloor passenger.

**interfloor traffic.** See traffic: (balanced) interfloor.

**interior panel.** The major panel portion of the balustrade located immediately above the skirt panel, canted outwards and extending from the skirt panel to the deck boards. CO

**interlock: car door.** A device which prevents the operation of the driving machine unless the hoistway doors are closed. BA(EITB)

**interlock: door.** A switch provided to mechanically and/or electrically lock a door, generally fitted to a car or hoistway door, usually a mechanically operated electrical contact, which prevents the operation of the driving machine unless certain conditions are satisfied. BA

**interlock: hoistway door.** A device having two functions, where the operation of the driving machine is prevented unless the hoistway doors are in the closed position *and* the hoistway doors are locked in the closed position and prevented from being opened unless the elevator car is within the landing zone. AS6

**interlock: landing door.** See interlock: hoistway door.

**intermediate support.** Often required on escalators with extreme rises to give additional support at a point near the centre of the longitudinal length of the truss thus reducing

the loading on the building members at each end of the escalator. CO

**internal pump.** See pump: internal.

**internal ram pressure.** A pressure created when hollow rams are used and the oil either flows through the ram as in the case of telescopic rams or is allowed to fill the inside of the ram of the displacement type. JI

**intersection guard.** See guard: intersection.

**interval.** The average time between successive car arrivals at the main terminal (or other defined) floor with no specified level of car loading or traffic condition. BE14

**interval: down peak.** The average time between successive car arrivals at the main terminal (or other defined) floor with no specified level of car loading during a down peak traffic condition. BE213

**interval: loading time.** See time: passenger loading.

**interval: loading.** The minimum time an elevator car is held at the main terminal (or other defined) floor, under the up peak traffic condition, after the first passenger has registered a call, before it is allowed to depart. BE163

**interval: up peak.** The average time between successive car arrivals at the main (or other defined) floor with cars assumed to be loaded to 80 percent of rated capacity during the up peak traffic condition. BE15

**interval: waiting.** A term sometimes used to designate the up peak interval and at other times to designate the time a passenger waits for service. BE14

**isolation: car.** Means of isolating the passenger cabin from vibration and sound borne noise. BA(fem)

**isolator.** A manually operated mechanical switch used to open or close electrical circuits under no load conditions. LO17/32

**jack.** The plunger and cylinder of a hydraulic elevator. AS19

**jamb.** The two vertical side posts of an elevator entrance, strike jamb and return jamb, plus the 'lintel' or head jamb. AS19

**jamb: head.** The horizontal member of the three members constituting an elevator entrance, which connects to the side vertical members. AS19

**jamb: return.** A vertical member of the three members constituting an elevator entrance, behind which the sliding portion of the door passes, whenever it opens and closes. AS21

**jamb: slide.** See return jamb.

**jamb: strike.** A vertical member of the three members constituting an elevator entrance, against which a side sliding door closes. AS23

**jaws.** Parts of overspeed safety gear, which grip the governor rope (in the case of an overspeed governor) and grip the machined surfaces of the guide-rails (in the case of car or counterweight safeties). N75

**jewel.** A coloured or translucent, lens or protective cover, which is placed in front of a signal indicator. BA

**joint moulding.** Metal extrusion used to cover and support the joint between two panels. LO17/32

**jointed ram.** See ram joint.

**journey time.** See time: passenger journey.

**jump time.** See time: flight.

**junction box.** An enclosure for the protection of electrical terminals and conductors. LO17/32

**key switch.** See switch: key.

**kick(er) plate.** See plate: kicker.

**kinked link detector.** The switch that detects kinked escalator step chain links and provides either alarm or protection. LO18/32

**ladder chain.** See chain: ladder.

**laminar flow.** The flow of fluids, where the original stratification of the fluid is not disturbed and which occurs below certain critical velocities, usually where the Reynolds number is less than 1500. See also Reynolds number. HH

**landing.** A portion of floor or corridor adjacent to elevator car entrances or escalator terminal end, where passengers may board or exit. BA

**landing apron.** See apron: landing.

**landing call.** See call: landing.

**landing door.** See door: hoistway.

**landing door closer.** See closer: landing door.

**landing door combination mechanical lock and electrical contact.** See contact: landing door combination mechanical and electrical.

**landing door electrical contact.** See contact: door.

**landing door interlock.** See interlock: hoistway door.

**landing door locking device.** See device: hoistway door locking.

**landing door mechanical lock.** See lock: door.

**landing lantern and gong.** See hall lantern and gong.

**landing plates.** See floor plate.

**landing push button.** See push button: landing call.

**landing stop.** See stop: landing call.

**landing zone.** See zone: door.

**landing: bottom terminal.** See floor: bottom terminal.

**landing: direction indicator.** See indicator: landing direction.

**landing: terminal.** See floor: terminal.

**landing: top terminal.** See floor: top terminal.

**Lang's lay.** See lay: Lang's.

**lay.** The twisting of yarn (wires) to form a strand or the twisting of strands to form a rope. O1187

**lay: equal.** The wires in the strand are so spun that they all have an equal lay length. J21

**lay: Lang's.** The direction of the lay of the wires in the strand is the same as the direction of the lay of the strands in the rope. J21

**lay: left.** The strands of a rope are spun in an anticlockwise direction. J22

**lay: ordinary.** The direction of the lay of the wires in the strand is opposite to the direction of the lay of the strands in the rope. J21

**lay: regular.** See lay: ordinary.

**lay: right.** The strands of a rope are spun in a clockwise direction. J22

**lay: rope.** See lay.

**leakage.** The amount of fluid lost out of a system due to faulty joints or seals designed to contain the fluid under specific pressures and temperatures. JI

**levelling.** An operation which improves the accuracy of stopping at a landing, and which ensures the car platform is level with floor. BS/ENpt1

**levelling device.** See device: levelling.

**levelling zone.** See zone: levelling.

**lift.** [syn: elevator.] See elevator.

**lift car.** See car.

**lift coming indicator.** See indicator: car coming.

**lift in use indicator.** See indicator: lift in use.

**lift machine: drum machine.** See machine: winding drum.

**lift machine: geared machine.** See machine: geared traction drive.

**lift machine: gearless machine.** See machine: gearless traction drive.

**lift management.** The management of elevator systems to provide in-service indication, equipment diagnosis, traffic monitoring and supervisory controller optimisation. BE361

**lift well.** See well.

**lift: bed.** See elevator: bed.

**lift: firemans.** See elevator: fireman's.

**lift: goods.** See elevator: freight.

**lift: hand powered.** See elevator: hand.

**lift: hydraulic.** See elevator: hydraulic.

**lift: passenger.** See elevator: passenger.

**lift: passenger/goods.** See elevator: passenger/freight.

**lift: service.** See elevator: service.

**lift: wheelchair.** See elevator: wheelchair.

**lifting lug.** A point provided from which to lift or raise the escalator, normally only used during installation. CO

**lifting beam.** A iron or steel beam that is suitable for attaching lifting tackle and that has been certified for a safe working load (SWL). LO18/32

**light duty traffic.** See traffic: light duty.

**light emitting diode.** A device consisting of a semiconductor junction enclosed in a plastic case, which emits light when an electric current is passed through it, in one direction only. LO18/32

**light: comb.** Small flush type light panels located in the skirt panels on both sides of the unit at both upper and lower head and immediately adjacent to the comb teeth. These lights illuminate the comb and step tread to assist in boarding and alighting the escalator. CO

**light: foot.** Small flush type light panels located in the skirt panels on both sides of the unit at both upper and lower head and immediately adjacent to the comb teeth, which illuminate the comb and step tread to assist in boarding and alighting the escalator. CO

**lighting: balustrade.** A lighted panel running the length of the balustrade, newel to newel, located parallel to immediately above the skirt panel, or full height plastic panels with lighting systems located behind them. NE9

**lighting: comb.** Lighting provided at comb level at a terminal end of an escalator or passenger conveyor. CO

**lighting: emergency.** Lighting provided in an elevator car in the event the car becomes stationary between floors and supplied from a standby generator or emergency batteries. S145

**lighting: step demarcation.** The illumination provided by multiple light fixtures located under the steps at the lower and upper landing of an escalator or at the entrance and exit of a moving walk, which provide demarcation between the step treads as the light shines up through the steps. CO

**lighting: under step.** The illumination provided by multiple light fixtures located under the steps at the lower and upper landing of an escalator or at the entrance and exit of a moving walk which provide demarcation between the step treads as the light shines up through the steps. CO

**lights: demarcation.** Green fluorescent lamps mounted under the escalator steps in front of the comb teeth at both landings, which are visible between the leading edge of one step and the riser of the adjacent step. CO

**limit switch.** See switch: limit.

**limit: door close.** A contact mounted on the door operator, which is actuated when the doors are fully closed and reduces or removes the power from the door operator. AS16

**limit: door open.** A contact mounted on the door operator, which is actuated when the doors are fully opened and reduces or removes the power from the door operator. AS16

**line: pilot.** A line for fluid actuating a control. HH

**linear drive.** See drive: linear.

**liner: borehole.** A rigid capped tube inserted into the borehole of a hydraulic elevator to prevent its collapse or the ingress of water. BOpt9

**liner: guide shoe.** The replaceable part of a sliding guide shoe, sometimes called a gib, which slides against the guide-rails and steadies the car in its travel. AS18

**liner: hydraulic.** An insert placed inside the original cylinder of a hydraulic jack to stop leaks. N82

**lining: brake.** The lining of the brake shoes of an elevator made of material possessing a high coefficient of friction. J87

**linkage: door.** Connecting links controlling the motion of the doors and associated with the door operator or the door closer. AS16

**lintel.** The horizontal member of an entrance frame used to support the load above the entrance. O1219

**load.** The weight of passengers inside an elevator car. BA

**load chord truss.** A truss design where most of the supporting steel is located below the escalator step line. CO

**load relieving ramp.** A ramp with low friction insert that acts on the step chains to reduce the load on the chain wheels as they move round the upper curves of the escalator. LO18/32

**load weighing.** Process of determining the number of passengers in an elevator car by weighing the load of the car and passengers. BE277

**load: average.** The weight of passengers carried in an elevator car averaged over the number of trips made in a five minute period. BE14

**load: brake.** The load which the brake of the escalator must be designed to stop and hold. CO

**load: contract.** See load: rated.

**load: percentage.** The weight of passengers carried in an elevator car expressed as a percentage of the rated capacity. BA

**load: rated.** The weight of passengers which the elevator car is certified to carry. BE14

**loading interval.** See interval: loading.

**loading supports.** Points upon which the load of an escalator or passenger conveyor are imposed, normally at or close to the terminal ends of the unit. CO

**loading time.** See time: passenger loading.

**lobby.** [syn: main terminal (floor), foyer, ground (UK), first (USA).] An entrance or corridor used as a waiting place. O1228

**lobby panel.** See panel: despatcher.

**lobby: express.** See floor: express zone terminal.

**lobby: sky.** A terminal floor at the highest floor served by a low zone group of elevators, where passengers may wait for service by a high rise group of elevators. S331

**local zone.** See zone: local.

**lock: bar.** A form of door lock used on manually operated doors. AS13

**lock: car door.** See lock: door.

**lock: castell.** A mechanical interlock that ensures that when the key is removed the circuit breaker and isolator cannot be closed. LO8/32

**lock: door.** A mechanical lock of any type which is used to prevent the opening of a car or hoistway door, unless the car is in the door zone. BOpt9

**lock: hoistway door.** See lock: door.

**loom: wiring.** A group of wires cut to pre determined lengths and running parallel to each other. CO

**low oil level protection.** Generally an electrical float switch used to signal a low level of oil in the hydraulic reservoir. JI

**low pressure switch.** See switch: low pressure.

**low step switch.** See switch: low step.

**lower head.** The horizontal portion of the truss at the lower end of the escalator. CO

**lower landing.** The area at the bottom end of an escalator or passenger conveyor. CO

**low(est) call reversal.** See call: low(est) reversal.

**lowest floor.** The bottom floor of a building. CO

**lowest reversal floor.** See floor: lowest reversal.

**lubrication.** A fluid or grease applied to moving components for the purpose of noise reduction, friction reduction and to reduce operating temperatures. CO

**lubrication float switch.** See switch: lubrication float.

**lubricator: automatic.** A device to supply lubricant through non-corrosive seamless metallic feed pipes to various parts of an escalator or passenger conveyor. It is normally located in a readily accessible position in the upper tank or machine room. LO5/32

**lubricators.** Applicators located to assure proper lubrication by depositing oil on the various moving mechanisms located within the escalator. CO

**M-G set.** See motor generator set.

**machine.** A device for doing work. CO

**machine room.** A room or space in which the machine(s) and associated equipment are located. BS/ENpt1

**machine room stop.** A manually operated switch used to stop an escalator from the machine room area. CO

**machine: basement drive.** Where the elevator drive machine is located at the bottom of the elevator hoistway. BA

**machine: belt drive.** An indirect drive machine using a belt as the means of connection. AS8

**machine: chain drive.** An indirect drive machine using a chain as the means of connection. AS8

**machine: direct drive.** An electric driving machine where the motor is directly connected mechanically in elevators to the driving sheave, drum or shaft and in escalators to the step band, without intermediate mechanical gearing. AS7

**machine: direct plunger driving.** A hydraulic driving machine, where the cylinder is directly connected to the car. AS8

**machine: driving.** The power unit which provides the energy necessary to rotate the escalator step band or to raise and lower an elevator, material lift or dumbwaiter comprising some or all of: an electric motor or hydraulic motor; mechanical gearing; brake; sheave, drum or chain sprockets; couplings, shafts, journals and bearings; machine frame. J14

**machine: drum.** See machine: winding drum.

**machine: electric drive.** A driving machine where the energy is supplied by an electric motor. AS7

**machine: geared.** A machine utilising a gear for energy transmission. CO

**machine: geared traction drive.** A traction drive machine utilising a gear for energy transmission. AS8

**machine: gearless traction drive.** A traction drive machine with no intermediate gearing. AS8

**machine: hydraulic drive.** A driving machine where the energy is supplied by the stored energy in a hydraulic fluid applied by means of a moving ram in a cylinder. AS8

**machine: indirect drive.** An electric driving machine, where the motor is connected indirectly by means of belts, chains etc to the sheave, shaft or gearing. AS8

**machine: overhead.** Where the elevator drive machine is located at the top of the elevator hoistway. N101

**machine: rack and pinion drive.** An electric drive machine, where the movement of the car is achieved by power driven pinions mounted on the car travelling on a stationary rack fixed in the hoistway. AS8

**machine: rated load.** The load which the machine of the escalator, passenger conveyor or elevator must be designed to move. CO

**machine: roped hydraulic drive.** A hydraulic driving machine where the cylinder is connected to the car by roping. AS8

**machine: screw.** An electric driving machine where the motor drives a screw assembly to raise and lower the car. AS8

**machine: traction.** A direct drive machine, where the motion of the car is obtained through friction between the suspension ropes and the driving sheave. AS8

**machine: winding drum.** A geared drive machine, where the suspension ropes are fastened to a winding drum. AS8

**machine: worm geared.** A direct drive machine where the energy is transmitted to the elevator sheave or drum, or escalator step band, via worm gearing. AS8

**machinery space.** Space available for the various components required which form the escalator or passenger conveyor. CO

**magnet: brake.** A solenoid which, when energised, causes the brake shoes to move away from the brake drum. AS13

**main brake.** See brake: main.

**main circuit breaker.** The circuit breaker used to switch the main electrical supply for each elevator or escalator. LO19/32

**main contactor.** A contactor with its contacts arranged so as to provide power to the main motor to back up the directional contactors. CO

**main directional contactors.** The interlocking changeover contactors used for final connection of the drive motor to the incoming supply and directional control. CO

**main floor.** See floor: main.

**main isolator.** The isolator used to open or close the main electrical supply for each escalator or elevator. CO

**main motor.** The prime mover. CO

**main supply.** Power provided from which the prime mover power is derived. CO

**maintenance.** The action of preservation without impairment or the keeping in being. O1261

**maintenance: breakdown.** Maintenance undertaken in order that components and equipment may be returned to satisfactory operation. ET197

**maintenance: comprehensive.** A form of maintenance contract, where the system is inspected, oiled and greased, adjusted and breakdowns repaired during normal working hours, but excluding call backs outside normal working hours, repairs due to vandalism and work arising from legislation. ET201

**maintenance: full (FM).** See maintenance: comprehensive.

**maintenance: performance guaranteed.** A contract offered to an elevator, escalator or passenger conveyor owner, which guarantees certain performance, (for example: no of elevators simultaneously in service, high mean time between failures (MTBF), low periods of down time) and on the failure to perform results, in the lowering of the premium paid to the maintainer. ET201

**maintenance: planned.** Preventative maintenance scheduled to be performed at specified intervals of time or for specified numbers of operations. ET197

**maintenance: preventative.** Maintenance provided to ensure the satisfactory operation of components and equipment by delaying or preventing or reducing the severity of any breakdown that may occur. ET199

**maintenance: replacement.** The replacement of components and materials, which have worn out or reached the end of their useful life. ET198

**maintenance: scheduled.** See maintenance: planned.

**manifold.** A metal block in which passages are formed and on which valves are mounted permitting the elimination of many, but not all, interconnecting pipes and shortening the length of the fluid passages. HH

**manual control switch.** See switch: manual control.

**manual lowering device.** See handwinding: device.

**mechanic.** A person who is capable of maintaining the status quo, but not of innovation (engineer); a skilled elevator operative who has followed a prescribed plan of training and education. N88

**mechanical interference.** Resistance to motion provided by friction and/or mechanical means or devices. CO

**mechanically synchronised.** Hydraulic elevators which use a telescopic ram assembly to maintain constant velocity due to the rope or chain synchronising external to the cylinder. JI

**medium duty traffic.** See traffic: medium duty.

**micron filter.** Filters, where the size of the particles that the filter will reject is determined in microns. JI

**microprocessor.** An electronic device which provides methods of control by reacting to input signals in accordance with an algorithm to provide predetermined output signals. CO

**modernisation.** The process of improving an existing system by bringing it 'up to date'. BA

**modernisation overlay.** See overlay: modernisation.

**monitoring: remote.** The signalling over a distance of the events (faults, passenger activity, elevator activity etc) occurring in an elevator installation. BE361

**motor.** A device which can convert electrical energy into mechanical energy. BA

**motor generator set.** A device comprising an AC motor driving a DC generator and therefore capable of converting one form of electrical energy to another using a mechanical coupling. BA

**motor overload.** An automatic device to protect a motor against damage as a result of electrical overload. CO

**motor protection.** An automatic device to protect a motor against damage as a result of electrical overload. CO

**motor thermistor protection.** Is where the electric motor is protected from overheating by thermistor junctions being placed on the winding of the motor, allowing the temperature to be monitored very accurately and without delay. JI

**motor: auxiliary.** A motor used for driving parts of an escalator, but not the main drive. LO6/32

**motor: brake.** A motor sometimes provided to open the brake shoes. CO

**motor: compound.** A motor with shunt and serious coils giving combined characteristics of shunt and series type motors (e.g. high starting torque and limited maximum speed). LO10/32

**motor: main.** The prime mover. CO

**mouldings.** Extruded aluminium shapes which through hidden fasteners position and lock in place the interior panels of an escalator. CO

**moving walkway.** A type of passenger carrying device on which passengers stand or walk, and in which the passenger carrying surface remains parallel to its direction of motion and uninterrupted. NE90

**moving walkway: belt pallet type.** A moving walkway with a series of connected and power driven pallets, which form a continuous belt treadway. NE91

**moving walkway: edge supported belt type.** A moving walkway with the treadway supported near its edges by succession of rollers. NE91

**moving walkway: pallet type.** A moving walkway with a series of connected and power driven pallets which together constitute the treadway. NE91

**moving walkway: roller bed type.** A moving walkway with the treadway supported throughout its width by a succession of rollers. NE91

**muffler.** See expansion chamber.

**multi stage cylinders.** See telescopic ram and cylinder.

**multiple leaf door.** See door: multiple (panel) leaf.

**multiple parallel arrangement.** See arrangement: multiple parallel.

**multiplying pulley.** See pulley: multiplying.

**needle valve.** See valve: needle.

**newel base.** The flat vertical portion of the newel assembly supporting the newel overhang. CO

**newel entry switch.** See switch: newel entry.

**newel entry brush.** A brush provided at the newel end to cover the internal components of the newel entry switch and to prevent passengers fingers entering this space. CO

**newel wheel.** A cast iron or steel wheel that carries the handrail around the top and bottom end of an escalator or terminal ends of a passenger conveyor. NE93

**newel.** Extensions of the balustrade of an escalator at both the lower and upper limits of travel located to assist passengers in boarding and alighting the escalator. NE93

**newel: concentric.** A newel configuration which utilises a semi-circle as its basic shape. CO

**newel: elongated.** A newel configuration which utilises a parabolic shape for its design, not to be confused with the extended newel which is required by the ANSI/ASME code. CO

**newel: extended.** A newel design, not associated with the shape of the newel, where the outer end of the newel extends beyond the comb teeth of the escalators. CO

**newel: stand.** An upright metal mounting that supports the newel wheels on an escalator or passenger conveyor. NE93

**next car.** See car: next.

**next car indicator.** See indicator: next car.

**nib.** See nosing.

**no load start.** A procedure whereby a hydraulic elevator motor can start under no load condition, by allowing the pump flow to pass direct to the tank during motor stating until the motor has reached nominal full speed, when the control valve closes to slowly cause the flow to be directed to the cylinder. JI

**noise: acoustic.** Noise which is transmitted through air and which may be generated by parts of: either an elevator installation, such as the machine, car movement, ropes and chains in the hoistway; or of an escalator installation, such as the machine, and transmitted via parts of the structure to remote parts of a building. P42

**noise: electrical.** Noise generated in power devices such as M-G sets, thyristor (SCR) controllers, etc and which is transmitted by electromagnetic radiation. See also interference: electrical. BA

**non reversal device.** A device provided to prevent the sudden reversal of an escalator or passenger conveyor. CO

**nose line.** The line formed by the intersection of the escalator step of the riser with the step tread. CO

**nosing.** Rounded edge of a step or cover for the edge of a step. O1415

**notices.** Written or pictographic signs placed on or near an escalator to warn of hazards. CO

**nudging.** With automatic door operation should the doors remain open for longer than a specified time then the doors are compulsorily closed at reduced speed, with the intention of removing any obstruction. AS20

**'O'-ring.** An endless packing ring of circular cross-section (toroidal ring) normally mounted in a groove in such a manner that the effectiveness of sealing increases with the pressure. HH

**observation elevator.** See elevator: observation.

**oil buffer.** See buffer: oil.

**oil cooler.** See heat exchanger.

**oil cushion stop.** See stop: cushioned.

**oil drain line.** The line that carries overflow oil, oil leakage from gland and exhaust oil from the valve pilot system back to a container but not to the tank if the oil is likely to be contaminated. JI

**oil drip pan.** See drip tray.

**oil level indicator.** The means to monitor the oil level in the tank of a hydraulic elevator to ensure that there is sufficient oil for the elevator car to reach the top floor, which can be in the form of a sight glass or dip stick. JI

**oil temperature detection.** The detection of unacceptable oil temperature rises by detection devices which are usually either thermistor or bi-metal sensors placed in the oil tank. JI

**on-call control.** See control: on-call.

**one-to-one roping.** See roping: one-to-one.

**open pilot valve.** See valve: open pilot.

**opening: door advance.** See opening: door pre-opening.

**opening: door premature.** See opening: door pre-opening.

**opening: door pre-opening.** The initiation of the door opening sequence, whenever the elevator car is within the door zone, in order to reduce the floor to floor cycle time. S129

**operational brake.** See brake: service.

**operator.** Person who rides in the elevator car and controls the movement of the car and the opening and closing of the doors. N100

**operator: door.** A power operated device which opens and closes the hoistway and/or the car doors, where the power is not derived from springs, car movement or manual means. AS4

**OR gate.** A solid state logic device, where the output value is true, when any input is true and is only false when both inputs are false. BA

**ordinary lay.** See lay: ordinary.

**outer deck.** The deck of a glass balustrade escalator covering from the glass to the outermost edge of the escalator. NE100

**overhead.** The upper end of the hoistway. N101

**overhead beam.** The steelwork and reinforced concrete located at the top of the elevator well, which supports the elevator equipment. BOpt9

**overhead machine.** See machine: overhead.

**overhead structure.** See overhead beam.

**overlay: modernisation.** Where a new control system is installed over the top of the existing control system and which takes over the function of the original controller. BA

**overload.** A condition where the rated capacity of a piece of equipment has been exceeded. BA

**overload indicator.** See indicator: overload.

**overspeed.** A condition which is said to occur when an elevator exceeds it rated speed by a specified amount or the step band or treadway of an escalator or passenger conveyor exceeds the nominal rated speed. CO

**overspeed governor.** See governor: overspeed.

**overspeed governor switch.** See switch: governor overspeed.

**overtravel.** The safe distance that a moving object may travel past its normal point of movement, without hitting any fixed objects. (See clearance.) N102

**packing.** The wearing material fitted into a gland assembly to provide an oil seal between the ram and cylinder. JI

**pads: sound insulating.** See pads: sound isolating.

**pads: sound isolating.** Pads made of a dense resilient material, which can be inserted between a noise/vibration producing equipment such as a machine, control cabinet or electrical transformer and their fastenings with the building structure, to reduce the intensity of the noise transmitted into a building structure and the air. S402

**pallet.** One of the series of rigid platforms which together form an articulated treadway or the support for a continuous treadway on a moving walkway. CO

**panel: car call.** See panel: car operating.

**panel: car operating.** An assembly of push buttons and indicators mounted on a panel inside an elevator car including, amongst other things: car call, door open/close, alarm and mechanics control push buttons; car call, position, direction and information indicators, together with a number of key operated switches for use by authorised persons. PXII

**panel: despatcher.** Combined starters' and building supervisors' panel comprising, amongst other things, indication of up/down car and landing calls, car position, direction and status together with a number of key operated switches for use by authorised persons. P262

**panel: exterior.** The panel enclosing the exterior side of the balustrade. CO

**panel: vision.** Small window located in elevator doors fitted with safety glass which permits passengers to see when a car has reached a landing. AS24

**parallel installation.** An escalator installation where the units are mounted directly parallel and in line with each other. CO

**parking.** Action of moving an elevator car to a specified floor or leaving it at its current floor, whenever the car has no further calls (landing or car) assigned to it for service. AS20

**parking floor.** See floor: parking.

**parking zone.** See zone: parking.

**passenger.** Any person transported by an elevator car. BS/ENpt1

**passenger arrival rate.** The rate at which passengers arrive for service by an elevator system. BE47

**passenger average time to destination.** See time: passenger average to destination.

**passenger conveyor.** A power driven installation with endless moving walkway (e.g. pallets, belts) for the conveyance of passengers either on the same or between different traffic levels. BS70p5

**passenger elevator.** See elevator: passenger.

**passenger emergency stop switch.** See switch: emergency stop.

**passenger/freight elevator.** See elevator: passenger/freight.

**passenger/goods lift.** See elevator: passenger/freight.

**passenger journey time.** See time: passenger journey.

**passenger lift.** See elevator: passenger.

**passenger loading time.** See time: passenger loading.

**passenger transfer time.** See time: passenger transfer.

**passenger transit time.** See time: transit.

**passenger unloading time.** See time: passenger unloading.

**passenger waiting time.** See time: passenger waiting.

**paternoster.** Form of lift machine, available in Europe but now obsolete, where a low speed (0.4 m/s) loop of continuously moving horizontal platforms, running in a dual hoistway, allow agile passengers to enter and leave the cars through open entrances. PXVIII

**pawl device.** A mechanical device used in hydraulic elevators to prevent creep. BA.

**peak oil pressure.** The maximum pressure developed in a system, usually caused by sudden stops and starts of the system, shock loading and/or waterhammer. JI

**peek-a-boo.** A method of door operation during firefighting service, where a constant pressure is required on the door open button, in order to cause the doors to open at a landing; the release of the pressure causing an immediate closure of the doors. CO

**percentage load.** See load: percentage.

**performance guaranteed maintenance.** See maintenance: performance guaranteed.

**performance index.** See index: performance.

**personal protective equipment (PPE).** Equipment provided to or purchased by maintenance or other personnel for protection, such as safety helmets, goggles etc. CO

**PRFF.** See relay: phase failure or reversal.

**phase failure relay.** See relay: phase failure.

**phase reversal relay.** See relay: phase reversal.

**photo-electric passenger detector.** See detector: passenger.

**pilot line.** Small lines or passages that carry the oil that controls larger valves. JI

**pilot line filter.** A fine mesh that prevents small particles of foreign matter entering and or blocking the pilot lines and valves. JI

**pilot valve.** A small valve that controls the fluid flow in the pilot lines. JI

**pipe coupling.** The connection between lengths of pipe. JI

**pipe rupture valve.** See valve: pipe rupture.

**piston rod.** The rod that moves in and out of the gland packing, and is attached to the piston head inside the cylinder. See ram, for large diameter rods. JI

**piston seal.** A plastic or composition material with good wearing properties, suitable for the fluid being used in the cylinder, fitted to the piston and to prevents oil passing the piston head during operation. JI

**piston stroke.** There are two different strokes associated with hydraulic elevators, (1) the total stroke of the cylinder, (2) the working stroke of the cylinder. See car travel distance. JI

**piston type cylinder.** See cylinder: piston type.

**pit (1).** That part of the hoistway or well situated below the lowest landing served by the elevator car. BSpt5

**pit (2).** A recess in the floor to receive that portion of the lower head and the lower end of the incline section which occurs below the floor line when there is no floor under the escalator such as in a basement. CO

**pit stop switch.** See switch: pit.

**pit switch.** See switch: pit.

**pit tanking.** Means of preventing the ingress of water into the pit area, which is normally situated at the lowest level in a building. BA

**plastic flow.** When excessive pressure is placed on a seal the seal is extruded through (plastic flow) the small space between the ram and the gland housing. JI

**plate: kick(er).** Plate used at the bottom of doors, cabinets and risers of steps and car enclosures to protect them from shoe marks. BA(EITB)

**platform: car.** Load bearing floor of the car enclosure. AS3

**plunger.** See ram.

**plunger joint.** See ram joint.

**plunger stop.** See stop: plunger.

**police circuit.** A circuit which maintains the directional contactors after the brakes have been lifted and the starting sequence is complete. CO

**poppet valve.** See valve: poppet.

**population: building.** Total population of a building. BE43

**population: floor.** Population of a specific floor in a building. BE161

**position indicator.** See indicator: car position.

**positive head.** Where the oil level in the tank is sufficiently above the pump intake, to ensure the pump is always supplied with enough oil to avoid cavitation. JI

**PPE.** See personnel protective equipment.

**pre-formed groove.** See groove: 'U'-profile, and groove: 'V'-profile.

**pre-load on seals.** Where the space provided for the seal or 'O'-rings is always slightly smaller in the direction of sealing than the dimension of the seal; the other dimension has to be slightly larger than the seal to allow expansion of the seal under pressure. JI

**pressure compensated valve.** See valve: pressure compensated.

**pressure hose.** See hose, flexible.

**pressure line filter.** The filter, usually of the high pressure type, placed in the main pressure line to filter oil in one or both directions. JI

**pressure line.** A line that carries the fluid at system pressure, which can be either metal tube or flexible hose, selected to suit the highest system plus a factor of safety. JI

**pressure tank.** A tank that does not open to atmosphere, and uses the fluid to build up pressure in the tank. JI

**pressure: differential.** Where a hydraulic component has a different pressure on either side; this difference is often referred to as pressure drop or pressure loss. JI

**pressure: relief.** See relief valve.

**preventative maintenance.** See maintenance: preventative.

**probable stops.** [syn: expected stops] See stops: probable .

**process switch.** An electromechanical device used to detect a physical condition as part of a control sequence. CO

**profiled groove.** See groove: 'U'-profile, and groove: 'V'-profile.

**progressive safety gear.** See safety-gear: progressive.

**public service type.** A type of escalator generally forming part of a public traffic system and of a more sturdy construction that a standard store type escalator. CO

**pull down cylinder.** An arrangement used on hydraulic elevators fitted with a counterweight whereby the counterweight is pulled down by a piston rod in tension operated by a ram unit installed in the pit. To allow space for a pull down cylinder to be installed under the counterweight the car is roped 1:1 and the counterweight roped 3:1 or 4:1. JI

**pull through governor.** See governor: pull through.

**pulley.** Simple mechanical device consisting of a grooved wheel over which a rope or similar may pass for the purpose of changing the direction of applied power. O1705

**pulley: diverting (1).** An idler pulley used to change the direction of the rope lead where the drive sheave diameter is less than the distance between the pick up points of the car and counterweight. BOpt9

**pulley: diverting (2).** An idler pulley used to change the direction of an escalator chain. CO

**pulley: governor.** The pulley, located with the overspeed governor in the machine room around, which the governor rope passes. J118

**pulley: multiplying.** A pulley mounted on the car frame or counterweight round which the suspension ropes pass in order to gain a 2:1 mechanical advantage. BOpt9

**pulley: overhead.** Pulleys used to alter the pick up points for the car and counterweight where the machine room is positioned other than directly above the hoistway. BA(EITB)

**pulley: tension.** The pulley, which is part of the governor tension sheave assembly located in the pit, around which the governor rope passes. J118

**pulsation.** The throbbing or vibrating effect set up in fluids, often induced by the design of the pump, and which can cause damage to the system, if not damped. JI

**pump: direct coupled.** A type of hydraulic pump arranged to be directly connected to the electric motor by either a solid or a resilient in-line coupling. JI

**pump: emergency hand.** Fitted to hydraulic elevators of the indirect type to enable the car to be lifted out of the safety gear during a power failure or to other types of hydraulic elevators to enable a car to be raised to a landing, in order to rescue trapped passengers. JI

**pump: external.** A pump located outside the oil tank where both the suction and pressure ports of the pump are connected to the system by pipelines or flexible hoses. JI

**pump: gear.** A pump which has two intermeshing gears inside a housing such that the oil is transported around the gear in the cavity formed between the teeth and the housing. JI

**pump: hand.** A pump that is operated by hand. See also pump: emergency hand. JI

**pump: internal.** A pump, which is submerged in the oil tank and is always covered with oil, thus allowing the direct entry of oil into the suction filter mounted on the end of the pump. JI

**pump: screw.** A pump where two or three intermeshing screws mounted parallel to each other in a casing impel the liquid along the thread as they rotate, the screws also acting as mutual seals to prevent leakage. HH

**pump: vane.** A rotary pump where the oil is moved by axially sliding vanes set eccentrically on the rotating part. JI

**pumps: indirect coupled.** Pumps connected to an electric motor via a belt drive or gear system. JI

**pushbutton.** An insulated button which operates electrical contacts when pushed. BA

**pushbutton: car call.** A pushbutton which generates a car call, when pushed. BA

**pushbutton: door close.** A pushbutton which causes the car doors to close, when pushed. BA

**pushbutton: door open.** A pushbutton which causes the car doors to open, when pushed. BA

**pushbutton: landing call.** A pushbutton which generates a landing call, when pushed. BA

**pushbutton: stop (1).** A pushbutton which causes the elevator car to stop, when pushed. BA

**pushbutton: stop (2).** A push button, normally located in the same place as the escalator directional start switches, as part of the stop/start switch assembly. CO

**quadruplex.** A group of four cars sharing a common signalling system. BE88

**quality of service.** The passengers perception of the efficiency of an elevator installation measured in terms of passenger waiting time. BE14

**quantity of service.** The handling capacity of an elevator installation. BE14

**queue.** An orderly line of persons waiting their turn. O1729

**rail.** See guide-rails

**ram.** The male member of a substantial cylinder assembly. HH

**ram coupling.** See ram joint.

**ram cushion stop.** See stop: cushioned.

**ram follower.** The guide fitted to the ram and guided to prevent the ram buckling when it is extended and arranged to follow the ram at half the extended length. JI

**ram joint.** The screwed connection between sections of a ram allowing shorter sections to be assembled, thus forming one long ram. JI

**ram stop.** See stop: ram.

**rated load.** See load: rated.

**rated load: brake.** The load which the brake of the escalator must be designed to stop and hold. CO

**rated load: machinery.** The load which the machine of the escalator must be designed to move. CO

**rated load: step.** The load which the escalator step must be designed to support. CO

**rated load: structural.** The total stated load imposed on the structure of the building. CO

**rated load: truss.** The load which the truss of an escalator must be designed to support. CO

**rated speed: elevator.** See speed: rated (elevator).

**rated speed: escalator.** See speed: rated (escalator).

**rated speed: moving walkway.** See speed: (rated moving walkway).

**RCD.** See residual current device.

**re-levelling.** After an elevator car has stopped level at a floor, an operation permitting the stopping position to be corrected (if necessary) during unloading and unloading, by successive car movements. BS/ENpt1

**reaction.** Signifies the load imposed on the building structure by the escalator. CO

**recessed floor pans.** Pan type construction being used as a substitute for floor and landing plates, This construction allows the consumer to fill the pans with another material duplicating the floor surrounding. CO

**registered call.** See call accepted.

**registration: call.** Action of the passenger in the registration of a car or landing call. BA

**regular lay.** See lay: ordinary.

**relay.** An electromechanical device that is operated by a change in one electric circuit and serves to make or break one or more connections in the same or other electrical circuit. CO

**relay: asymmetric.** A relay provided to detect the failure of one or more supply phases and/or the incorrect sequencing of those phases. CO

**relay: phase failure.** Relay which detects a failure of a phase of an incoming electrical supply and which causes the elevator system to be shut down. BA

**relay: phase failure or reversal.** A relay provided to detect the failure of one or more supply phases and/or the incorrect sequencing of those phases. CO

**relay: phase reversal.** Relay which detects a phase reversal of an incoming electrical supply and, which causes the elevator system to be shut down. BA

**relay: time delay.** A relay which acts as a timing device by delaying the application of a control signal. BA

**relief valve.** See valve: relief.

**remote monitoring.** See monitoring: remote.

**reserve oil.** The oil in a tank that is in excess of the minimum oil required to operate the system. JI

**residential building.** See building: residential.

**residual current device.** A circuit breaker designed to break the supply in the event of a current flow to earth. LO13/32

**resistor: adjustable.** A resistor that has taps, sliding bands or a wiper which, when moved, allows all or part of the resistor to be used. NE1

**retail building.** See building: retail.

**retiring cam.** See cam: retiring.

**return.** To take or lead back at an angle, often 90 degrees, upon a former direction. O1818

**return carriage.** See carriage: return.

**return jamb.** See jamb: return.

**reverse phase relay.** See relay: phase reversal.

**reversible.** An escalator or passenger conveyor which has the ability to run in either direction. CO

**Reynolds number.** A dimensionless number used in considerations of fluid flow and given by the relationship: fluid velocity multiplied by pipe diameter divided by kinematic viscosity. HH

**right hand lay.** See lay: right.

**rise.** The vertical distance between two steps in a stair; the vertical distance between boarding and alighting levels of an escalator. BACO

**riser.** The upright part of a step; the vertical piece connecting two treads in a stair. O1837

**riser: cleated.** Vertical cleats on an escalator step riser, which mesh with slots on the adjacent step tread as the steps move from incline to the horizontal. NE23

**riser: electrical.** A vertical enclosed space in a building from which electrical distribution is made. BA

**riser: step.** The vertical portion or front of a step. NE139

**roller guide shoes.** See shoes: roller guide.

**roller: step.** The roller fitted to the escalator step which runs on a track to determine the profile of the escalator. CO

**rope lay.** See lay.

**rope.** A construction of twisted fibres or wire (wire rope) to form continuous load bearing element. N120

**rope: compensating.** Wire rope used to counterbalance or partially counterbalance the weight of the suspension ropes as the elevator car moves up and down the hoistway. AS10

**rope: governor.** A wire rope attached to the elevator car, which drives the governor. J117

**rope: hand.** A control rope passing through an elevator car allowing the travelling passenger to start and stop the car; now obsolescent. N64

**rope: hauling.** An endless rope used to manually raise and lower a hand powered elevator. BOpt9

**rope: safety.** A rope used on hydraulic elevators to actuate the safety gear, where one end is connected to the safety gear actuating arm at the car end, passing over a sheave mounted on the main ram sheave assembly to the pit equipment at the other end. JI

**rope: shipper.** See rope: hand.

**rope: suspension.** The ropes in an elevator system used to suspend the car and counterweight in the hoistway. BA

**rope: tail.** See rope; safety.

**rope: wire.** Rope made by twisting wires around an inner core. AS21

**roping: one-to-one.** An arrangement of ropes, where the mechanical advantage is one and hence the suspension ropes, car and

counterweight all travel at the same speed. Jcp3

**roping: two-to-one.** An arrangement of ropes, where the mechanical advantage is two and hence the rope speed is twice that of the car and counterweight. Jcp3

**rotary selector switch.** See switch: rotary selector.

**round trip time.** See time: round trip.

**rucksack elevators.** The name given to elevators, where the car is only supported on one side. JI

**runby.** The unobstructed distance a car or counterweight may travel at the extremes of the hoistway before an obstruction is encountered. BA

**runby: bottom — elevator car.** The distance between the car buffer-striker-plate and the car-buffer striking-surface, when the elevator car floor is level with the bottom landing. AS10

**runby: top — direct-plunger hydraulic elevator.** The distance the elevator car can run above the highest terminal landing, before it strikes the mechanical stop. AS10

**running clearance.** See clearance: running.

**rupture valve.** See pipe rupture valve.

**rupturing pressure.** The pressure at which a hydraulic component bursts or leaks through fault cracks, when subjected to pressure test. JI

**safe-edge.** A mechanically actuated door re-opening device mounted on the leading edge of a car door which on colliding with a passenger or other object causes the car and landing doors to re-open. AS22

**safety.** A generic term used to describe the safety features employed in elevator installations. BA

**safety astragal.** See astragal: safety.

**safety bulkhead.** A second base or bulkhead welded inside the bottom of the cylinder of a hydraulic elevator (which is buried in the ground and could suffer corrosion) to prevent the sudden loss of oil in the event of a failure of the lowest bottom plate of the cylinder. JI

**safety circuit switches.** See switches: safety circuit.

**safety edge.** See safe-edge.

**safety-gear.** Mechanical devices used to stop a car or counterweight under specific conditions. Jcp8

**safety-gear: instantaneous.** A safety gear which applies a rapidly increasing pressure on the guide-rails during the stopping period. J117

**safety-gear: instantaneous with buffered effect.** A safety gear which applies a rapidly increasing pressure on the guide-rails during the stopping period, but with a buffered effect provided by oil buffers interposed between the lower members of the car frame and the safety plank. J117

**safety-gear: progressive.** A safety gear which applies a limited pressure on the guide-rails during the stopping period. J117

**safety plank.** Bottom member of the car frame supporting the car guide shoes and safety gear. AS22

**safety rope.** See rope: safety.

**safety test.** See test: safety.

**safety: car.** Mechanical device attached to the car frame to stop and hold the car should any of three conditions, free fall, predetermined overspeed or rope slackening, occur. AS10

**safety: counterweight.** Mechanical device attached to the counterweight frame to stop and hold the counterweight should any of three conditions, free fall, predetermined overspeed or rope slackening, occur. AS10

**safety: flexible guide clamp.** A form of car safety where a pair of wedge shaped jaws are actuated under unsafe conditions and grip the guide-rails to bring the car to a safe stop. J128

**SAPB.** See single automatic push button.

**scheduled control.** See control: scheduled.

**SCR.** See thyristor.

**screw machine.** See machine: screw.

**screw pump.** See pump: screw.

**seal: double acting.** Seals which are required to retain the oil pressure on either side, e.g. on the piston head of a double acting cylinder. JI

**seal: dynamic.** A seal placed between a fixed and moving part for example: a gland seal for a ram or piston. JI

**seal: gland.** See gland packing.

**seal: ring.** See 'O'-ring.

**seal: static.** A seal between two static parts to prevent oil leakage for example: a cover plate or mounting components together. JI

**secondary sheave.** See sheave: secondary.

**sector.** A group of landings or of landing calls considered together for elevator car allocation or parking purposes. BE94

**sector: common.** Static sector defined for both up and down landing calls originating from a number of contiguous landings. BE98

**sector: demand.** A sector in which there is a demand for service indicated by the registration of landing calls. BE98

**sector: directional.** Static sector that includes a number of contiguous landings defined for one landing call direction only. BE99

**sector: dynamic.** Sector whose boundaries are defined by the position of the cars and hence are continually changing. BE100

**sector: static.** Fixed number of landings grouped together. BE98

**segments.** The radius portions of the escalator assembly. CO

**seismic sensor.** See sensor: seismic.

**seismic switch.** See switch: seismic.

**selector: floor.** Part of the control system of some elevators which determines the position of the car in the hoistway and automatically stops it at the required landing. BOpt9

**self re-levelling.** See re-levelling.

**sensor: seismic.** Sensor capable of detecting the onset of an earthquake. BA

**service brake.** See brake: service.

**service elevator.** See elevator: service.

**service switch.** See switch: service.

**service: basement.** The provision of passenger service to the basement or basements of buildings on a special or regular basis. BE95

**service: fireman's.** Elevator, which serves all floors in a building, and which can come under the sole command of a fireman in the event of a fire in the building. P61

**service: independent.** Operation of an elevator such that it only answers car calls and which is brought into operation by the use of a special key switch located in the car. AS19

**service: intensive duty.** Where an elevator system makes 180 or more starts per hour. PcpVI

**service: light duty.** Where an elevator system makes 90 or less starts per hour. PcpVI

**service: medium duty.** Where an elevator system makes from 90 to 180 starts per hour. PcpVI

**service: quality.** See quality of service.

**service: quantity.** See quantity of service.

**shaft encoder.** See encoder: shaft.

**shaft.** See hoistway.

**shaftway.** See hoistway.

**sheave.** A wheel having a groove or grooves in its circumference, in order to receive a rope or ropes; a pulley. O1969

**sheave guard.** See guard: sheave.

**sheave guide.** A guide attached to the sheave located on the top of the ram of hydraulic elevators of the indirect type for diverting the ropes; the guide prevents lateral movement of the sheave assembly. JI

**sheave: chain.** Sheave with rectangular shaped groove over which a chain may run. AS15

**sheave: compensating rope.** A pit-mounted grooved sheave which guides and maintains the tension on the compensating ropes. AS15

**sheave: deflector.** Grooved sheave used to deflect ropes in order to place them in the correct lifting positions. AS16

**sheave: door hanger.** Small grooved sheave which runs on the door track and which allows the door to slide easily. N64

**sheave: drive.** A wheel, the rim of which is grooved to receive the suspension ropes, and which allows the motion of the driving machine to be transmitted to the ropes by friction. BOpt9

**sheave: governor tension rope.** A weighted pit-mounted sheave used to maintain tension on a governor control rope. AS23

**sheave: hanger.** See sheave: door hanger.

**sheave: idler.** Grooved sheave used to guide, to change direction or to apply tension to a rope. N70

**sheave: secondary.** A groove used to permit the double wrapping of the suspension ropes in order to increase traction. AS22

**sheave: tension.** A sheave used to maintain tension on a rope. BA

**shim.** A piece of metal or other material used to fill out a space. NE129

**shim: kicker.** Small slotted plate used to pack out, align or square-up guide-rails. N77

**shim: trouser leg.** A small slotted plate used to pack out, align or square up manufactured in the shape of the pair of trousers. CO

**shipper rope.** See rope: hand.

**shock loads.** See peak oil pressure.

**shoes: brake.** The moving component of a brake, to which the brake linings of high coefficient of friction material are fixed and which when in contact with the brake drum causes an elevator car, escalator or passenger conveyor step band to be held in a stationary position or brought to rest. AS13/J87

**shoes: roller guide.** Component used to guide an elevator car or counterweight along the guide-rails comprising a set of three (or six) spring loaded rubber tyred rollers. J114

**shoes: slide.** See shoes: slipper guide.

**shoes: slipper guide.** Component used to guide an elevator car or counterweight along the guide-rails comprising a set of swivel shoes lined with a low coefficient of friction material running against greased guide-rails. J112

**side opening door.** See door: side opening.

**side ram.** Rams installed at the side instead of under the car platform, in order to reduce or eliminate the need to drill bore holes in the case of long ram and cylinder units. JI

**side stile.** See stile.

**sight glass.** A small glass or plastic panel placed on the side of oil tank, in order to observe the oil level is sufficient. JI

**sight guard.** See guard: sight.

**signal: despatch.** Signal given to the elevator power control system to cause the elevator car to move. BA

**signalling device.** See device: signalling.

**signalling system.** See system: signalling.

**silencer.** See expansion chamber.

**silicon controlled-rectifier.** See thryistor.

**sill.** Lower horizontal part of a doorway. O1996

**sill guard.** See guard: sill.

**sill-stop.** Support member fastened to the guide-rails of vertical bi-parting doors. AS22

**sill: door.** Lower horizontal member of a landing entrance. AS16

**simplex collective control.** See control: simplex collective.

**simulation.** The development and use of models to aid in the evaluation of ideas and the study of dynamic systems or situations. BE151

**single automatic push button.** An automatic push button control system, where only one button is provided on the landing to indicate both directions of travel. BE87

**single leaf door.** See door: single panel (leaf).

**skip-stop operation.** Where a duplex pair of elevators in a building share a common lobby but one car serves even floors and the other serves odd floors. BA

**single stage ram.** A tube or solid column that has a constant diameter for the full length of its travel or stroke. JI

**single wrap.** Roping arrangement, where one end of the suspension rope is fastened to the car, passes over the drive sheave and is then fastened to the counterweight. J44

**skirt.** The panels located immediately adjacent to the escalator steps or treadway. CO

**skirt guard.** See guard: skirt.

**skirt panel.** The lowest panel within the balustrade, located immediately adjacent to the escalator steps and running parallel to the step travel on both sides. CO

**skirt switches.** See switches: skirt.

**skirting (board).** Narrow boarding placed at the base of a wall. O2011

**sky lobby.** See lobby: sky.

**slack rope switch.** See switch: slack rope.

**slenderness ratio.** A dimensionless number given by the relationship: the length of a column or ram divided by the radius of gyration of the member. JI

**slide jamb.** See jamb: return.

**slide up-down door.** See door: slide up-down.

**sliding lower carriage.** See carriage: sliding lower.

**sling.** Device for hoisting bulky or heavy articles. O2019

**sling: car.** See frame: car.

**slipper guide shoes.** See shoes: slipper guide.

**slope: moving walkway.** The angle which the treadway makes to the horizontal. CO

**socketing.** The preparation of suspension rope end fastenings. J33

**soffit.** The under horizontal surface of an architrave, cornice, lintel, arch or escalator truss. O2041

**soft start.** Uses a form of electrical control equipment that limits the current and/or voltage during the starting cycle of the motor, to reduce the starting current and provide a smooth acceleration. JI

**solenoid.** An electromagnetic device consisting of a movable iron core (or cores) surrounded by a coil, where the core (often referred to as plunger) is magnetically attracted to the centre of the coil when the coil is energised. CO

**solenoid valve.** See valve solenoid.

**solid rams.** A ram or piston made from solid bar not tube. JI

**solid state.** Electronic circuits making use of semiconductor physics. BA

**sound isolating pads.** See pads: sound isolating.

**speed governor.** A device provided to detect an overspeed condition of the escalator step band. CO

**speed reduction unit.** Wheels working one upon the other, by means of teeth (or otherwise) for transmitting or changing motion, power and/or speed (often called a worm reduction unit). CO

**speed: contract (elevator).** See speed: rated (elevator).

**speed: contract (escalator).** See speed: rated (escalator).

**speed: rated (elevator).** The linear car speed in the hoistway, which the elevator manufacturer contracts to supply. BOpt9

**speed: rated (escalator).** The rate of travel of the steps measured along the angle of inclination, with rated load on the steps, but in the case of reversible escalator the rated speed shall be the rate of travel of the steps in the 'up' direction. CO

**speed: rated (moving walkway).** The rate of travel of the treadway measured along the angle of inclination, with rated load on the treadway. In the case of the reversible inclined moving walkway the rated speed shall be the rate of travel of the treadway in the 'up' direction. CO

**split seal.** A circular shaped seal, which assists jack assembly as it has been cut to allow the placing of the seal around a ram or piston so that the two ends can come together. JI

**spool valve.** See valve: spool.

**spreader bracket.** See bracket: spreader.

**spring buffer.** See buffer: spring.

**spring: buffer return.** Spring used to return an energy dissipation type of buffer back to its operating position. J143

**spud.** See gib: door.

**stair climber.** A form of stair climbing elevator on which a mobility impaired person can sit in order to reach another floor. S351

**stanchions.** The vertical members of the truss assembly. CO

**stand: newel.** See newel: stand.

**standard.** An authoritative or recognised exemplar of correctness, perfection, or some definite degree of any quality. 02107

**star delta starter.** The interlocking changeover contactors used to start two speed AC drive motors. CO

**starter.** Originally a person who manually operated and despatched elevators, supervised attendants and directed passengers, but now is a piece of control equipment to stop and start the M-G set. AS23

**starter switching solenoid (Watford starter).** An accelerating rheostat unit that shorts out resistance in a stepped operation by means of solenoid operated actuation. CO

**starts per hour: electric traction elevator.** For an electric traction elevator the number of starts per hour is the number of motor starts per hour and is the sum of starts in both up and down directions. BA

**starts per hour: hydraulic elevator.** For a hydraulic elevator the starts per hour is the number of pump motor starts per hour, i.e. to move the elevator in the up direction. JI

**static friction (stiction).** Is the friction or holding power between parts that move during the operation of the hydraulic elevator e.g. ram and cylinder packing is the major example of static friction. See also dynamic friction and stick-slip. JI

**static oil pressure.** The oil pressure in a stationary ram holding a load, when the elevator is not moving and in a standby or holding position ready to be operated. JI

**static seal.** See seal: static.

**station: car-top inspection.** Control panel situated on the top of the car which allows the elevator to be removed from service and controlled from the car top. AS14

**station: mechanics.** A control panel, very often plugged in, situated in the ends of an escalator allowing the step band to be rotated under controlled conditions by a mechanic. CO

**stationary switch.** See switch: stationary.

**steel tape.** See tape: steel.

**step.** The moving platform on which an escalator passenger rides. NE139

**step axle.** A shaft connecting the escalator step chains on each side and fastened to the step at the front end of the step frame and on which the chain wheels are installed. NE27/32

**step band.** The mobile assembly of steps and two loops of step chains within the escalator. LO27/32

**step chain.** Heavy section steel roller chain, through which step axles pass, linking the main drive at the top of the escalator and the lower (tension) carriage at the bottom of the escalator and comprising two chains to each escalator handed for each side of the steps. LO27/32

**step chain wheel.** The wheel mounted on either side of the escalator step on the chain wheel axle used to support the weight of the step band and passenger loading. LO9/32

**step demarcation lighting.** See lighting: step demarcation.

**step frame.** The escalator steel framework upon which axles, wheels, riser and treads are mounted to form the step assembly. LO27/32

**step journey time.** See time: escalator flight time.

**step nose line.** The theoretical line that intersects the nose of each step on the useable part of an escalator or in a stairway. LO27/32

**step plan.** The pressed steel escalator frame that forms the tread and the riser which combined with the step yokes forms the step frame. LO27/32

**step riser.** See riser: step.

**step roller.** See roller: step.

**step tracks.** See tracks: step.

**step tread.** The cleated surface of the escalator step assembly that meshes with the comb. LO27/32

**step upthrust switch.** See switch: step upthrust.

**step wheels.** The wheels of an escalator step which are secured to and driven by the step chain. NE139

**step yoke.** The side of the escalator step frame that may be integral with the frame or a separate steel forging or pressing. LO27/32

**step: die cast.** A type of escalator step thus called due to its manufacturing process. CO

**step: rated load.** The load which the escalator step must be designed to support. CO

**stick-slip.** A phenomenon caused when rams are operating through the gland packing, particularly at slow speed, when the difference between the static friction and the sliding friction causes a gripping and then a release effect on the ram movement. JI

**stile.** Vertical member of the car frame. AS23

**stop diamond.** A design of passenger emergency stop device used principally on London Underground escalators. CO

**stop push.** A latching push button and switch used to interrupt the safety circuit, and stop the escalator. LO27/32

**stop push button.** See push button: stop.

**stop switch.** Switch: stop.

**stop: car call.** See stop: car.

**stop: car.** A stop by an elevator car at a floor resulting from a car call. BA

**stop: cushioned.** A stop fitted to the end of ram stroke inside the cylinder, which prevents the ram stop hitting the end of the cylinder. JI

**stop: down.** A stop by an elevator car whilst travelling in the down direction. BA

**stop: hall call.** See stop: landing call.

**stop: landing call.** A stop by an elevator car resulting from a landing call. BA

**stop: plunger.** A fixed stop fitted at the end of the plunger inside the cylinder of hydraulic elevators thus preventing the plunger being forced out of the gland and packing. JI

**stop: ram.** The internal or external stop on a ram to prevent the ram being pushed out of a cylinder at the end of its stroke. JI

**stop: up.** A stop by an elevator car whilst travelling in the up direction. BA

**stops: probable.** The average number of stops an elevator car makes, during a round trip under up peak traffic conditions, calculated using statistical methods. BE18

**stretcher gear.** The pair of wheels and system of weights used to tension the handrails on some escalators. LO27/32

**strike jamb.** See jamb: strike.

**stroke: oil buffer.** Distance the buffer piston or plunger moves, excluding the travel of the buffer plunger accelerating device. AS3

**stroke: spring buffer.** Distance the contact end of the spring moves, before all the coils are in contact or a fixed stop is reached. AS3

**submersible electric motor.** See under oil motor.

**suction intake.** The common term for the oil being sucked into the pump. JI

**suction line.** The pipe line that is used to supply the pump with sufficient oil. JI

**supervisory control.** See control: supervisory.

**supervisory panel.** See panel: despatcher.

**supply distribution.** A system comprising busbar trunking and a cable end box used to feed individual switch boards. CO

**supply switch gear.** The group of switchboards electrically connected to the supply distribution systems and to individual escalator controllers. LO27/32

**suspension rope.** See rope: suspension.

**sweep track.** See track: curved.

**switch.** A device which makes, breaks or changed connections in an electrical circuit. LO28/32

**switch: auxiliary isolating.** A switch located in the vicinity of the escalator machine, or in the return station, or in the vicinity of the control devices, which interrupts the supply to the motor without cutting the supply to the socket outlets needed for maintenance and inspection purposes. BS78p2

**switch: brake cooling.** The switch which causes a reduction in the brake coil current to prevent overheating of electromagnetic brakes. LO p7/32

**switch: broken drive chain.** A switch provided to detect the failure of the escalator drive chain being also activated under slack chain or sudden impact conditions. CO

**switch: broken handrail.** A switch in the safety circuit that opens when a break in the escalator handrail is detected. LO7/32

**switch: broken step chain safety.** A switch in the safety circuit that opens when a break in the escalator step chain is detected. NE14

**switch: buffer.** A mechanically operated switch, which removes power from the elevator drive system, whenever the oil buffer is compressed. AS14

**switch: car.** An attendant operated switch mounted in the elevator car used to control the motion (starting and stopping) of the car. P249

**switch: carriage.** One of a pair of switches in the safety circuit which open when the escalator tension carriage moves beyond set limits. LO8/32

**switch: chain anchor.** The switch in the safety circuit which detects that the chain anchors have been removed prior to the starting of an escalator. CO

**switch: chain stretch.** A switch provided to detect the stretch of an escalator chain or chains. CO

**switch: collision.** See switch: displacement.

**switch: comb plate.** A switch in the safety circuit that opens when excessive force or deflection is detected on the escalator comb or combplate. LO9/32

**switch: cooling.** The switch that causes a reduction in brake coil current to prevent over heating on electromagnetic brakes. LO10/32

**switch: countershaft drive chain.** A switch in the safety circuit that opens when a break in the countershaft drive chain is detected. LO10/32

**switch: derailment.** See switch: displacement.

**switch: directional start.** A key operated switch located generally in the newel bases at both upper and lower landings, which allows the designated authority to select the movement of the stairs for up and down direction and is sometimes located in the adjacent walls or columns. CO

**switch: displacement.** Switch actuated by the displacement of the counterweight used to signal to the control system that a collision is possible. AS499

**switch: door.** Switch operated by the movement of a door. BOpt9

**switch: door limit.** Switch which limits the travel of a door. AS16

**switch: dropped step.** A switch provided to detect a dropped escalator step situation. CO

**switch: emergency stop (1).** Switch located in the elevator car which when operated causes the power to be removed from drive machine and brake. AS6

**switch: emergency stop (2).** A separate stop button usually located in adjacent walls, columns or within the balustrading providing the facility for a passenger or observer to stop the escalator, in the event of an emergency. CO

**switch: fault condition.** A solid state/electro mechanical device used to detect faults in an escalator and to provide either protection or warning. CO

**switch: final limit.** Emergency switch used to stop an elevator automatically, in the event that the car travels a predetermined distance past the terminal landing. BOpt9

**switch: final terminal stopping.** A mechanically operated switch, which automatically causes the power to be removed from the elevator drive machine and brake, independent of the normal terminal stopping switch, car switch, push button or any other control device. AS182

**switch: fire shutter.** A switch fitted to detect the release of a fire shutter and to stop the escalator. CO

**switch: fireman's.** Switch which when operated brings the designated elevator car under the control of the fire fighting service. BSpt6

**switch: float.** The combined arrangement of a float that moves with the change in oil level in the tank, and operates a switch at pre-adjusted levels. JI

**switch: floor stopping.** Switch or switches used to bring a elevator car to rest at or near a designated floor. BOpt9

**switch: governor.** A mechanically operated switch mounted on the governor that removes power from the escalator motor and brake when an escalator overspeed condition occurs. NEp60

**switch: governor drive chain.** A switch on the safety circuit that opens when a break in the governor drive chain is detected. LO16/32

**switch: governor overspeed.** Mechanically operated switch located on the governor, which removes the power from the elevator drive machine and brake, whenever an overspeed condition occurs. AS18

**switch: handrail entry.** A switch provided at the newel entry aperture where the handrail passes through and designed to trip and cut off power to the main motor in the event of an obstruction being detected. CO

**switch: key.** Switch which can only be operated by means of a key. BA

**switch: limit.** Switch placed in the hoistway to indicate to the control system that a specified limit has been passed. BA

**switch: low pressure.** An electrical switch actuated by hydraulic pressure and used to signal a reduction in pressure in the hydraulic system. JI

**switch: low step.** The switches in the safety circuit, that open when a low escalator step is detected approaching or leaving either comb. LO19/32

**switch: lubrication float.** The switch that detects a low level of lubricant on an escalator and provides either alarm, or protection. CO

**switch: manual control.** A manually operated switch used to select a single escalator control option. CO

**switch: newel entry.** A switch provided at the newel entry space to stop the escalator or passenger conveyor should a passengers fingers enter this space. CO

**switch: normal terminal stopping.** Switch of any type which causes the elevator automatically to slow down and stop at or near the terminal landing, independent of the car switch, push button or any other control device. AS182

**switch: oil buffer.** Switch used to indicate the level of oil in an oil buffer is below a specified level and prevent operation of the elevator. AS14

**switch: pit.** Emergency stop switch located in the elevator or escalator pit, which when operated causes power to be removed from the drive machine and brake. AS188

**switch: rotary selector.** A device that makes, breaks or changes connections in an electrical circuit. CO

**switch: seismic.** Switch activated by ground movement to signal the possibility of an earthquake. AS499

**switch: service.** Key operated switch which is not operative whilst the elevator car is in motion, used to take the elevator out of service. BOpt9

**switch: slack rope.** Switch or switches arranged to stop the elevator should the suspension ropes slacken by a predetermined amount. BOpt9

**switch: slow down.** Hoistway mounted switch used to control the slow down sequence of a elevator car to a landing. BA

**switch: stationary.** A switch in the safety circuit forming part of some governors that opens as the escalator step band speed decreases to zero. CO

**switch: step upthrust.** A switch designed to shut down an escalator in the event of a step being forced upwards off its intended plane of travel. CO

**switch: stopping.** Switch actuated by the movement of the elevator car, at predetermined points in the hoistway, and which causes power to removed from the drive machine. BOpt9

**switch: terminal slow down.** A limit switch located at a terminal landing, which initiates a slow down sequence in the event the normal slow down system fails to function. AS24

**switch: terminal stopping.** See switch: normal terminal stopping and switch: final terminal stopping.

**switch: underspeed.** A switch in the safety circuit forming part of some governors that opens when the step band speed falls below a set limit. LO30/32

**switch: wedge breaker roller.** A switch that monitors the resetting of an escalator brake prior to restart. CO

**switchboard.** An enclosure containing the main circuit breaker, main isolator, and in some cases the mechanical locking system used to switch on and off, isolate (and lock off) the electric supply to each escalator. CO

**switches: safety circuit.** Electrical circuit switches located at various points within the unit which will cause the escalator to shut down in order to prevent accidents to passengers or damage to the escalator itself. CO

**switches: skirt.** Safety switches located immediately behind the escalator skirt panels at the lower landing, which are activated if a wedging action occurs between the steps and skirt panels. CO

**synchronised rams.** See telescopic rams.

**synchronising valve.** See valve: synchronising.

**system response time.** See time: system response.

**system: alarm.** See alarm system.

**system: automatic remote monitoring.** A system of remote monitor units on each machine, central processor, software and video display units that send, read, interpret and display operating and fault information from the monitored machines. LO6/32

**system: signalling.** Means of indicating landing calls to the supervisory control system using a common riser of landing push buttons. BA

**tail rope.** See rope: safety.

**tail shaft.** The driven shaft in the tension carriage carrying two sprockets that tension and reverse the direction of the escalator step chains. LO17/32

**tandem operation.** Escalators used in series with common intermediate landings. CO

**tangent track.** See track: adjustable.

**tank discharge.** See exhaust flow.

**tank return.** Either the exhaust line from the main valve or, the pilot valves discharging oil back to the tank. JI

**tape: steel.** Tape, usually toothed, used to drive tachometers, position sensors and governors. BA

**teagle.** Early form of British lift (c.1845) driven by a belt from line shafting in industrial premises and controlled by a hand rope. S6/8

**telescopic ram and cylinder.** An arrangement of rams and cylinders, which may be of different diameters, working in synchronism, where the synchronism may be hydraulically or mechanically arranged for constant speed. JI

**temperature compensated.** Electrical or thermal devices fitted to a hydraulic elevator control system, in order to change the valve settings, and compensate for any change in oil temperature and bring the performance back to an acceptable level. JI

**tension carriage.** See carriage: tension.

**tension pulley.** See pulley: tension.

**tension sheave.** See sheave: tension.

**terminal final stopping switch.** See switch: final terminal stopping.

**terminal floor.** See floor: terminal.

**terminal landing.** See floor: terminal.

**terminal normal stopping switch.** See switch: normal terminal stopping.

**terminal slow down switch.** See switch: terminal slow down.

**terminal stopping switch.** See switch: terminal stopping.

**terminal: express zone.** See floor: express zone terminal.

**test: acceptance.** Inspection and test of new or altered equipment to check for code/standard and contract conformance. AS7

**test: periodic.** Detailed examination and tests carried out periodically to ensure continued compliance to relevant codes/standards. AS7

**test: safety.** Procedure whereby all parts of the elevator car safety gear and governor are subjected to a rigorous visual inspection and then tested under controlled operating conditions. N124

**theoretical escalator handling capacity.** See capacity: theoretical escalator handling.

**thread seal.** A compound or plastic material painted on or wrapped around threads to form a fluid seal between two threaded parts; for example, a pipe being screwed into a valve housing. JI

**threshold comb.** The toothed portion of a threshold plate on a moving walkway designed to mesh with the grooved treadway surface of an escalator or moving walkway. NEp146

**threshold: moving walkway.** The portion of the landing adjacent to the treadway consisting of one or more stationary or slightly moveable plates. CO

**through car.** See car: through.

**thyristor.** A three terminal semiconductor rectifier, which can be controlled to turn on at a point during the positive half cycle of the AC waveform. BA

**time.** The interval between two successive events, or the period through which an action, condition, or state continues. O2308

**time delay relay.** See relay: time delay.

**time: boarding.** See time: passenger loading.

**time: car call dwell.** The time that the elevator doors are held open at a landing, after the door opening sequence has been completed, in response to a stop resulting from a car call. BE16

**time: cycle.** The time for an elevator to move from one floor to the next adjacent floor, measured from the instant that the doors start to close at the departure floor to the instant the doors start to close at the arrival floor, provided that no passengers have entered or left the car. ET267

**time: despatch interval.** The period of time between successive car departures from a terminal floor for a group of elevators controlled by a scheduling supervisory control system. BE37

**time: door closed.** The period of time which elevator doors remain closed. BA

**time: door closing.** The period of time measured from the instant that the elevator door close push button is pressed (or the first visible door movement) until the door interlocks are made up. BE16

**time: door hold(ing).** See time: car call dwell and time: landing call dwell time.

**time: door open.** The period of time that the elevator doors remain open. BA

**time: door opening.** The period of time measured from the instant of the elevator car being level at a floor and when the doors are open 800 mm. BE16

**time: entry.** See time: passenger loading.

**time: escalator flight time.** The time taken for an escalator step to travel between floor levels. CO

**time: flight.** See time: single floor flight and time: multiple floor flight.

**time: floor to floor.** See time: single floor flight or multiple floor flight.

**time: interfloor.** The period of time for an elevator car travelling at rated speed to pass between two adjacent floors. BE16

**time: journey.** See time: passenger journey.

**time: landing call dwell.** The time that the elevator doors are held open at a landing, after the door opening sequence has been

completed, in response to a stop resulting from a landing call. BE16

**time: loading.** See time: passenger loading.

**time: loading interval.** The period of time that a car may be held at the main terminal after the first passenger has registered a car call. BE37

**time: multiple floor flight.** The period of time measured from the instant when the door interlocks are made up at the departure floor until the instant that the elevator car is level at the next stopping floor, which can be more than two floors distant. BE16

**time: passenger average to destination.** The average time that a passenger takes to reach the mid point of travel, including average waiting time. BA

**time: passenger journey.** The period of time that a passenger spends travelling to a destination floor measured from the instant that the passenger registers a landing call at the departure floor until the instant the passenger alights at the destination floor. BE165

**time: passenger loading.** The average period of time required for a single passenger to enter an elevator car. BE16

**time: passenger transfer.** The average period of time required for a single passenger to enter or leave an elevator car. BE16

**time: passenger transit.** See time: transit.

**time: passenger unloading.** The average period of time required for a single passenger to leave an elevator car. BE16

**time: passenger waiting.** The period of time that a passenger spends waiting for an elevator car measured from the instant that the passenger registers a landing call until the instant the passenger enters the car. BE165

**time: performance.** The time for an elevator to move from one floor to the next adjacent floor, measured from the instant that the doors start to close at the departure floor to the instant the doors are open 800 mm at the arrival floor. BA

**time: round trip.** The average period of time for a single elevator car trip around a building, usually during up peak traffic conditions, measured from the time the car doors open at the main terminal, until the car doors reopen at the main terminal, when the car returns to the main terminal, after its trip around the building. BE13

**time: running.** The total period of time during a round trip, when the elevator is moving. S66

**time: single floor flight.** The period of time measured from the instant when the door interlocks are made up at the departure floor until the instant that the elevator car is level at the next adjacent landing. BE16

**time: standing.** The total period of time during a round trip, when the elevator is not moving. S70

**time: stop.** A composite time period which represents the 'penalty' time introduced by the elevator car stopping at a floor and which comprises the sum of door opening, door closing and single floor flight times minus the transit time to pass between two floors at rated speed (interfloor time). BE16

**time: system response.** The period of time that it takes an elevator group to respond to the first registered landing call at a floor. BE273

**time: transfer.** See time: passenger transfer.

**time: transit.** The period of time that a passenger spends travelling in an elevator car measured, from the instant that the passenger boards the car, until the instant that the passenger alights at the destination floor. BE4

**time: unloading.** See time: passenger unloading.

**time: waiting.** See time: passenger waiting.

**toe guard.** See guard: sill.

**top runby.** See runby: top — direct plunger hydraulic elevator.

**top terminal floor.** See floor: top terminal.

**top terminal landing.** See floor: top terminal.

**track bracket.** A bracket used to fix the position and secure the track to the trusswork. LO28/32

**track insert.** Replaceable steel track that is secured into cast track. LO28/32

**track section.** A length of track. LO28/32

**track supports.** Brackets fastened to the vertical stanchion members. CO

**track: adjustable.** The horizontal track section that leads onto and off of the escalator main drive and idler sprockets (also known as the tangent track). LO5/32

**track: curved.** The curved track that guides the escalator step band between the horizontal and the incline. LO11/32

**track: dee.** The semicircular track that guides the trailer wheels around the main drive and idler sprockets, and where the upthrust changes to running track and vice versa. CO

**track: door.** A rail on which the door hanger rolls and which allows the horizontal sliding movement of the doors. AS16

**track: door hanger.** An assembly, which is fastened to the top of a door panel and which allows the horizontal sliding movement of the door. AS16

**track: half.** The half width track section that forms part of the slide track on the tension carriage side. LO16/32

**track: handrail.** The track that guides the handrail on the passenger side between the newel wheels at each end. LO16/32

**track: hanger.** See track: door.

**track: tangent.** See track: adjustable.

**track: upper line.** The track between the main drive and idler sprockets on the passenger side of the escalator. LO30/32

**track: upthrust.** The track that ensures that the possible lifting of wheels from the running track is restricted. LO30/32

**track: variable.** The track section that is of special length for different escalator rises, fitted at the head of the incline. LO31/32

**tracks: step.** A series of tracks which support and guide the escalator steps through both the exposed and return portions of step travel, where the chain leading wheels and the trailing wheels have separate track systems and where changes in the vertical height between the chain wheel track and the trailing wheel track cause the step profile to change. CO

**traction machine.** See machine: traction.

**traffic analysis.** Determination of the statistical characteristics of passenger movements (average passenger waiting and journey times, percentiles, etc) in an elevator and escalator systems. BA

**traffic controller.** See control: group supervisory.

**traffic: (balanced) interfloor.** A traffic condition where there is no discernable pattern of calls and a random traffic pattern can be said to exist. BE9

**traffic: down peak.** A down peak traffic condition exists when the dominant or only traffic flow is in a downward direction with all or the majority of passengers leaving the lift system at the main terminal of the building. BE7

**traffic: four way.** A four way traffic condition exists when the dominant traffic flows to and from two specific floors, one of which may be the main floor. BE8

**traffic: heavy duty.** See traffic: intensive duty.

**traffic: intensive duty.** Where an individual lift car is expected to undertake more than 180 starts per hour. PcpVI

**traffic: light duty.** Where an individual lift car is expected to undertake 90 or less starts per hour. PcpVI

**traffic: medium duty.** Where an individual lift car is expected to undertake between 90 and 180 starts per hour. PcpVI

**traffic: two way.** A two way traffic condition exists when the dominant traffic flow is to and from one specific floor, which is not the main floor. BE8

**traffic: up peak.** An up peak traffic condition exists when the dominant or only traffic flow is in the upward direction with all or the majority of the passengers entering the lift system at the main floor of the building. BE6

**trailer wheel.** The wheel mounted on either side of the escalator step on the trailer wheel axle used to set the inclination of the step. LO29/32

**trailer wheel axle.** The common axle that links the escalator step frame with the trailer wheels mounted at either end. LO29/32

**trailer wheel track.** The escalator trailer wheel running and upthrust track. LO29/32

**trailing cable.** See cable: travelling.

**trailing wheel.** Idler wheels which support the riser end of an escalator step. NE148

**transformer.** An electrical device which by electro magnetic induction transfers AC voltage and current between two or more windings at the same frequency and at different values of voltage and current. LO9/32

**transportation: horizontal.** Where the movement of people and materials is in the horizontal plane. BA

**transportation: vertical.** Where the movement of people and materials is in the vertical plane. BA

**travel (1).** The vertical distance an elevator can move, measured between the bottom terminal floor and the top terminal floor of building zone. AS11

**travel (2).** The vertical distance an escalator serves between two levels. CO

**travelling cable.** See cable: travelling.

**tread board.** The wooden board onto which slats are mounted to form the escalator step tread. LO29

**tread former.** A roller assembly (or skid) placed on both sides in the escalator comb region to ensure that the step treads align with the comb in the event of lateral step movement. LO29/32

**tread section.** The aluminium cleated die casting that when mounted together in the step frame form the escalator step tread. LO29/32

**treadplate.** The moveable steel plate that forms a wearing surface and interfaces between the comb level and finished floor level. LO29/32

**treadway.** The passenger carrying member of a moving walkway. CO

**trip counter.** See counter: journey.

**trip: express (run).** The distance an elevator travels without stopping during a movement between terminal floors or when crossing an unserved building zone. BA

**triplex.** Three interconnected cars, sharing a common signalling system, controlled under a simple group control system operating under directional collective principles. BE88

**trouser leg shim.** See shim: trouser leg.

**truss.** An assembly of structural steel or tubular steel shapes which forms the supporting structure for the escalator. NE150

**truss module.** A section of the truss manufactured as one assembly and joined to adjacent modules on site. LO29/32

**truss supports.** Concrete walls, steel structures or a combination of both used to support the truss work. LO29/32

**truss work.** The steelwork forming part of the escalator truss. LO29/32

**truss: high chord.** A design where most of the truss steel structure is located above the escalator step line. CO

**truss: rated load.** The load which the truss of an escalator must be designed to support. CO

**turbulent flow.** Where the particles within the fluid cannot negotiate the pipe and valve configuration at an increased velocity, causing the flow to change from laminar to turbulent flow. HH

**twin rams.** Two rams arranged to support the load, where both can be under the elevator car or one ram can be on either side of the car in order to avoid deep excavation work. JI

**two point suspension.** Relates to an escalator unit in which the total load is supported at two points: the upper head and the lower head. CO

**two speed door.** See door two speed.

**two speed drive.** A switching system used for the speed control and star/delta starting of alternating current motors. CO

**two-to-one roping.** See roping: two-to-one.

**two way traffic.** See traffic: two way.

**'U'-groove.** See groove: 'U'.

**under oil motor.** A squirrel cage motor, in open frame construction, fully immersed in the oil and directly coupled to a pump, where the oil is in contact with the windings and in the space between the stator and rotor. JI

**under step lighting.** See lighting: under step.

**undercut groove.** See groove: undercut.

**underspeed switch.** See switch: underspeed.

**unloaded start.** See no load start.

**unloading ramp.** The ramp with low friction insert that acts on the step chains to reduce the load on the chain wheels as they move round the upper curves of the escalator. LO18/32

**up peak.** See traffic: up peak.

**up peak interval.** See interval: up peak.

**up peak passenger arrival rate.** See arrival-rate: up peak passenger.

**up peak traffic.** See traffic: up peak.

**up arrow.** See arrow: up.

**up call.** See call: up.

**up contactor.** A contactor with its contacts arranged so as to provide power to the main motor to rotate in an up direction. CO

**up stop.** See stop: up.

**uplighting.** Luminaries that reflects light upward, where used on some escalators they consist of bowl shaped lamp fitting/reflector mounted upon a pole protruding from the balustrade decking. LO30/32

**upper head.** The horizontal portion of the truss at the upper end of the escalator where the drive unit, connecting sprockets and controller are normally mounted. CO

**upper line track.** See track: upper line.

**upper machine room.** The compartment beneath the upper landing passenger concourse, forming the upper section of the machine room, which contains the escalator control, and drive machinery. LO30/32

**upper terminal floor.** See floor: top terminal.

**upper zone.** See zone: high rise.

**upside down cylinder.** An arrangement for hydraulic elevators where the cylinder assembly can be inverted, so the piston is extended from or retracted into the bottom of the cylinder, so that the piston rods are in tension. Sometimes referred to as 'boot strap' type. JI

**upthrust angle.** The angle track that ensures that the possible lifting of wheels from the incline and curved running tracks is restricted by means of the upthrust pin. LO30/32

**upthrust pin.** The lug or pin integral with the escalator step, located either on both or one side only and positioned to engage with the upthrust angle and restrict the upward movement of the step. LO30/32

**upthrust system.** The upthrust track, upthrust angle and other methods that combine and ensure that the possible lifting of wheels from the running track is restricted on all areas of the escalator. LO30/32

**upthrust track.** See track: upthrust.

**vacuum.** Strictly zero pressure, but used loosely to denote a pressure, which is negative compared to atmospheric pressure. See also cavitation. JI

**valve coil.** See valve solenoid.

**valve solenoid.** A valve that has its pilot system operated by solenoids. JI

**valve: ball.** Where the moving part of the valve is spherical shaped and has a hole through its centre. The ball is held in between seals, and by rotating the ball the flow can be controlled. JI

**valve: bypass.** Valve, which is used to divert fluid into an alternative path, for example: the pump output from the fluid power line to the fluid storage tank, of a hydraulic elevator. BOpt9

**valve: check.** A one way valve that is installed to prevent the reverse flow of oil back to the pump, or to prevent a reverse flow in a hydraulic circuit. JI

**valve: closed pilot.** A pilot valve system that is normally closed with the power to the solenoid turned off. JI

**valve: differential pressure.** A valve, where the spool, or piston, is moved by fluid pressure (for example a pipe rupture valve), where the valve closes, when there is a loss of pressure on one side of the valve due to line failure. JI

**valve: electronic.** Typically the electronic circuit that monitors the temperature and/or pressure and which in turn varies the flow rate of the valve in accordance with the design parameters. JI

**valve: integrated rupture.** A pipe rupture valve mounted inside the cylinder base of a telescopic ram and cylinder. JI

**valve: needle.** A type of valve usually fitted in the pilot lines of hydraulic valve systems for controlling small oil flow, which can be either manually or solenoid operated. JI

**valve: open pilot.** A pilot valve that is normally open when the power to the solenoid is turned off. JI

**valve: pipe rupture.** A valve designed to close in the event of the pressure line from a cylinder failing or bursting by detecting the sudden increase in differential pressure across the valve and where in the case of high inertia systems the valve may have a cushioned closure to avoid high pressure peaks. JI

**valve: poppet.** A cylindrical piston approximately the same length as its diameter, where the movement of the poppet longitudinally, controls the fluid flow at its end, where the seal is made. JI

**valve: pressure compensated.** A valve which has in-built controls or components, that detect pressure changes and vary the valve operation either directly or indirectly to compensate for the change in pressure. JI

**valve: relief.** A valve that opens, when a set pressure is reached, or to maintain a constant pressure in a system. JI

**valve: shut off.** A valve that can be either electrically or manually operated to close off the fluid flow in a system. JI

**valve: spool.** A long cylindrical plunger inside a valve assembly, that moves longitudinally and controls fluid flow by ports and seals positioned along its length. JI

**valve: synchronising.** A small valve located at the bottom of each stage of a telescopic cylinder of the hydraulically synchronised type, which allows oil to be transferred from one stage to another in cases where the synchronisation needs correction. JI

**vane pump.** See pump: vane.

**vane.** A thin piece of metal, positioned in the hoistway, which operates as the actuating part of a magnetically operated switch. AS24

**vane: door.** A mechanism mounted on a car door transmitting operating power to the hoistway doors. AS24

**variable flow.** A hydraulic pump, whose displacement can be changed for any constant drive speed. JI

**variable track.** See track: variable.

**variable resistance drive.** A drive system used to control the starting current of direct current motor by varying the series resistance of the motor armature. Typically incorporates a bank of switched fixed resistors housed in a separate enclosure. CO

**vee groove.** See groove: 'V'-cut.

**vee packing seal.** The name given to a seal, which when viewed in cross section is vee shaped, sometimes called chevron seal. JI

**velocity fuse.** See pipe rupture valve.

**velocity valve.** See valve: pipe rupture.

**ventilation: car.** Means of removal of heat, generated inside the car, by natural or mechanical means, via suitable vents placed in the car enclosure. AS147

**vertical transportation.** See transportation: vertical.

**vibration.** Vibration in a hydraulic system caused by pressure pulses from pumps and relief valve flutter, which may cause damage to the more vulnerable parts of a system. HH

**viscosity.** The internal friction or resistance to the relative motion of parts of a fluid. JI

**vision panel.** See panel: vision.

**wainscot.** The walls of an elevator car extending from the floor to (usually) the ceiling. AS24

**waiting interval.** See interval: waiting.

**waterhammer.** A term used in conjunction with a pressure surge in any liquid, which is caused by sudden interruption of flow, whose magnitude depends on the amount of liquid, its velocity and the speed of the interruption. HH

**Watford starter.** An accelerating rheostat unit that shorts out resistance in a stepped operation by means of solenoid operated actuation. CO

**wedge breaker roller switch.** See switch: wedge breaker roller.

**weighing: load.** A means of determining the weight (but not the number) of passengers being carried in an elevator car. BE277

**well.** The space bounded by the bottom of the pit and the walls and roof of the hoistway in which the car and counterweight travel. BSpt5

**wellway.** The portion of the building which receives and supports the escalator truss. NE158

**wellway railing.** A balustrade located around the escalator wellway opening to prevent people falling into it. CO

**wellway railing capping.** The capping member of the wellway railing to match the capping member with the escalator decking. CO

**wheel newel.** See newel wheel.

**wheel: worm.** Part of a worm gear. J75

**wheelchair lift.** See elevator: wheelchair.

**width.** The normal dimension measured between the escalator balustrade panels. CO

**winding.** See handwinding.

**winding drum machine.** See machine: winding drum.

**wiper ring.** Ring arranged so that they grip a piston rod and scrape off any foreign matter. HH

**wire rope.** See rope: wire.

**wiper seal.** See wiper ring.

**wiring diagram.** A drawing that shows the connections between the controller and all switches, contacts etc. NE159

**wiring loom.** A group of wires cut to predetermined lengths and running parallel to each other. CO

**working point.** A point used by escalator manufacturers to determine the relationship of the unit to the building structure to assure proper erection. CO

**working pressure.** The pressure measured at the cylinder entry of an hydraulic lift, when lifting the car and its rated load at rated speed. JI

**worm gear.** See gear: worm.

**worm reduction gear.** See gear.

**worm wheel.** See wheel: worm.

**wrap angle.** See angle of wrap.

**wrap: single (1:1).** A roping arrangement where the rope joining the car and the counterweight passes over the sheave once. J44

**wrap: double.** A roping arrangement where, in order to increase the traction, the rope joining the car and the counterweight passes over the drive sheave twice. J44

**yoke attachment.** A fixing arrangement on the cylinder head of an intermediate ram stage on a telescopic ram of a hydraulic elevator. JI

**yokes.** See cylinder head guide yoke.

**zig zag arrangement.** See arrangement: zig zag.

**zone.** A number of floors, usually adjacent, in a building served by a group or groups of cars. BE91

**zone: door.** A distance (about 200 mm) measured from the landing floor, in both directions, in which it is permitted for the car doors to be opened, when a car is levelling at a floor. BA

**zone: express.** See zone: high rise.

**zone: high rise.** A building zone situated in the middle or top of the building. BE92

**zone: landing.** See zone: door.

**zone: levelling.** A distance near to each landing floor in which an elevator car slows and 'inches' towards the floor level. BA

**zone: local.** A building zone adjacent to and including the main floor. BE91

**zone: parking.** An area designated for the parking of cars when they have served their last car call. BA

**zone: upper.** See zone: high rise.

# A2    Lift kinematics

## Principal author

Dr Gina Barney (Gina Barney Associates)

## A2.1    Fundamentals

Lift kinematics is the study of the motion of a lift in a shaft without reference to mass or force. This motion is described in terms of velocity (speed), acceleration and jerk (rate of change of acceleration). The maximum values of these parameters is limited by what passengers perceive as a comfortable ride. Speed has no influence on comfort and can be any practical value. However, the maximum values of acceleration and jerk are typically limited to 1.2–1.5 m/s$^2$ and 1.5–1.8 m/s$^3$ to meet passenger expectations.

Modern drives kinematics can be controlled precisely to match speed reference profiles. An example of a speed reference curve is shown in Figure A2.1. Curves similar to these are often presented in manufacturers literature as a demonstration of a fast, comfortable and efficient drive system.

The analysis of lift kinematics cannot be made using the three familiar equations:

$$s = u t + \tfrac{1}{2} a t^2 \qquad v = u + a t \qquad v^2 = u^2 + 2 a s \qquad \text{(A2.1)}$$

These equation assume, for simplicity, that the stated value of acceleration ($a$) is reached instantaneously. This is not true which make the mathematical analysis more complex. Figure A2.2 illustrates the complex nature of ideal lift motion.

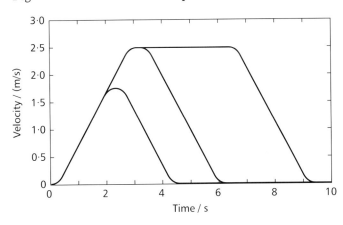

**Figure A2.1** Example of a speed reference curve

## A2.2    Ideal kinematics of a lift system

H.D. Motz published an exact analysis of the ideal kinematics of lifts in 1976[1]. The equations most relevant to the motion of practical lift systems are presented below.

Distance ($s_a$) to reach rated acceleration ($a$):

$$s_a = \frac{a^3}{6 j^2} \qquad \text{(A2.2)}$$

Time ($t_a$) to reach rated acceleration:

$$t_a = \frac{a}{j} \qquad \text{(A2.3)}$$

**Figure A2.2** Lift dynamics;
(a) rated speed reached before
rated acceleration, (b) rated
acceleration reached, rated speed
not reached, (c) both rated
acceleration and rated speed
reached

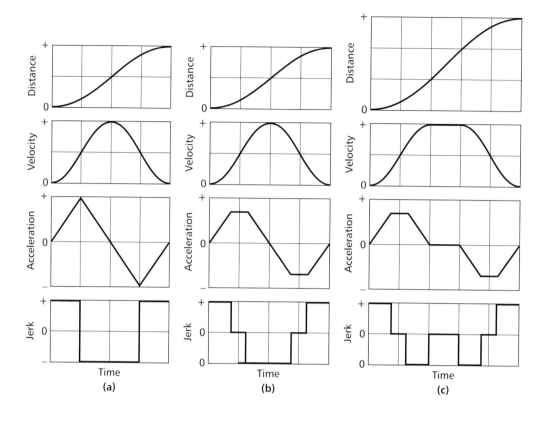

Speed ($v_a$) at rated acceleration:

$$v_a = \frac{a^2}{2j}$$ (A2.4)

Distance ($s_{vm}$) to reach rated speed ($v_m$):

$$s_{vm} = \frac{v_m^2}{2a} + \frac{a \times v_m}{2j}$$ (A2.5)

Time ($t_{vm}$) to reach rated speed:

$$t_{vm} = \frac{v_m}{a} + \frac{a}{j}$$ (A2.6)

Maximum speed ($v$) reached for a single floor jump of ($d_f$):

$$v = -\frac{a^2}{2j} + \sqrt{\left(a \times d_f\right) + \left(\frac{a^2}{j}\right)^2}$$ (A2.7)

Flight time ($t_f(1)$) for a single floor jump if rated speed $v_m$ is reached:

$$t_f(1) = \frac{d_f}{v_m} + \frac{a}{j} + \frac{v_m}{a}$$ (A2.8)

Flight time ($t_f(1)$) for a single floor jump of $d_f$ if speed ($v$) is less than rated speed $v_m$:

$$t_f(1) = \frac{a}{j} + \sqrt{\frac{4d_f}{a} + \left(\frac{a}{2j}\right)^2}$$ (A2.9)

The flight times given by equations A2.8 and A2.9 are most important times when carrying out traffic calculations.

## A2.3    Worked example

Using the equations above consider a gearless system with the following parameters:

$$v_m = 5.0 \text{ m/s}; \ a = 1.0 \text{ m/s}^2; \ j = 1.5 \text{ m/s}^3; \ d_f = 5.0 \text{ m}$$

Distance ($s_a$) to reach rated acceleration ($a$), using equation A2.2:

$$s_a = \frac{1.0^3}{6 \times 1.5^2} = 0.074 \text{ m}$$

Time ($t_a$) to reach rated acceleration using equation A2.3:

$$t_a = 1.0 / 1.5 = 0.67 \text{ s}$$

Speed ($v_a$) at rated acceleration using equation A2.4:

$$v_a = \frac{1.0^2}{2 \times 1.5} = 0.33 \text{ m/s}$$

Distance ($s_{vm}$) to reach rated speed ($v_m$) using equation A2.5:

$$s_{vm} = \frac{5.0^2}{2 \times 1.0} + \frac{1.0 \times 5.0}{2 \times 1.5} = 14.17 \text{ m}$$

Time ($t_{vm}$) to reach rated speed using equation A2.6:

$$t_{vm} = \frac{5.0}{1.0} + \frac{1.0}{1.5} = 5.67 \text{ s}$$

Maximum speed ($v$) reached for a single floor jump of $d_f$ using equation A2.7:

$$v = -\frac{1.0^2}{2 \times 1.5} + \sqrt{\left(1.0 \times 5.0\right) + \left(\frac{1.0^2}{2 \times 1.5}\right)^2} = 1.93 \text{ m/s}$$

Flight time ($t_f(1)$) for a single floor jump if $v$ is less than $v_m$ using equation A2.9:

$$t_f(1) = \frac{1.0}{1.5} + \sqrt{\frac{4 \times 5.0}{1.0} + \left(\frac{1.0}{1.5}\right)^2} = 5.19 \text{ s}$$

## A2.4    Data and results for three typical lift systems

Table A2.1 (page A-32) gives the results for three systems. The first is typical of a geared system, the second is typical of a high speed gearless system (examined in section A2.3 above) and the third is for a super fast system. All the results are for ideal kinematics and do not include any start delays, levelling times, which must be added.

The geared and the gearless systems do not reach the rated speed over a trip distance of 5.0 m. To achieve this the geared system requires a minimum distance of 5.46 m (2 × 2.73) and the gearless system requires a minimum distance of 28.34 m (2 × 14.17), i.e. a 5-floor jump.

The super fast system requires a trip of some 250 m, in order to reach its rated speed mid flight and will take at least 30 s for the trip.

**Table A2.1** Data and results for three lift systems

| Parameter | | Geared | Gearless | Super fast |
|---|---|---|---|---|
| $d_f$ | Trip distance (m) | 5.0 | 5.0 | 400 |
| $v_m$ | Speed (m/s) | 1.6 | 5.0 | 16.8 |
| $a$ | Acceleration (m/s²) | 0.6 | 1.0 | 1.2 |
| $j$ | Jerk (m/s?) | 0.8 | 1.5 | 1.8 |
| $t_f(1)$ | Flight time for trip distance (s) | 6.57 | 5.19 | 38.5 |
| $v$ | Maximum speed reached during trip (m/s) | 1.52 | 1.93 | 16.8 |
| $s_a$ | Distance to reach rated acceleration (m) | 0.06 | 0.07 | 0.09 |
| $t_a$ | Time to reach rated acceleration (s) | 0.75 | 0.67 | 0.67 |
| $v_a$ | Speed at rated acceleration (m/s) | 0.22 | 0.33 | 0.40 |
| $s_{vm}$ | Distance to reach rated speed (m) | 2.73 | 14.17 | 123.20 |
| $t_{vm}$ | Time to reach rated speed (s) | 3.42 | 5.67 | 14.67 |

## A2.5    Computer programs

Most major lift companies can provide the data derived above using computer programs. Independent industry design programs are also available.

## Reference

1    Motz H D On the kinematics of the ideal motion of lifts *Foerden und haben* 26 (1976) (in German) and *Elevatori* (January 1991) (in English and Italian)

# A3 Legislation and standards related to lifts, escalators and moving walks

## Principal authors

Dr Gina Barney (Gina Barney Associates)
John Snowball (Steven Morris Associates)

## Warning

Sections A3.1–A3.5 of this appendix list legislation and standards relevant to lifts, escalators and moving walks (passenger conveyors). The lists were as comprehensive and up-to-date as possible at the time of publication (September 2005). The entries are arranged in numerical and date order. They include entries which are now not current. These may be useful when dealing with equipment not installed to the current requirements. For the latest information readers should consult government websites regarding current legislation and BSI on-line (http://www.bsonline.bsi-global.com) regarding current standards.

## A3.1 Legislation related to lifts, escalators and moving walks

### A3.1.1 Relevant European Directives and related documents

86/312/EWG 86/312/EEC 86/312/CEE Commission Directive of 18 June 1986 adapting to technical progress Council Directive 84/529/EEC on the approximation of the laws of the Member States relating to electrically operated lifts

89/392/EEC Council Directive of 14 June 1989 on the approximation of the laws of Member States relating to machinery

90/486/EWG 90/486/EEC 90/486/CEE Council Directive of 17 September 1990 amending Directive 84/529/EEC on the approximation of the laws of the Member States relating to electrically operated lifts (90/486/EEC)

95/16/EG 95/16/EC 95/16/CE European Parliament and Council Directive 95/16/EC of 29 June 1995 on the approximation of the laws of the Member States relating to lifts

95/16/EGVerz 2000 95/16/ECVerz 2000 95/16/CEVerz 2000 00/C292/01 List of notified bodies designated by the Member States and the EFTA countries (EEA Members) under the new approach Directives

### A3.1.2 Relevant UK legislation

The Supply of Machinery (Safety) Regulations 1992 Statutory Instruments 1992 No. 3073, as amended by the Supply of Machinery (Safety) (Amendment) Regulations 1994 Statutory Instruments 1994 No. 2063, and Supply of Machinery (Safety) (Amendment) Regulations 2005 Statutory Instruments 2005 No. 831

The Lifts Regulations 1997 Statutory Instruments 1997 No. 831

## A3.2 British national standards related to lifts, escalators and moving walks

PAS 32-1: 1999: *Specification for examination and test of new lifts before putting into service. Electric traction lifts*

PAS 32-2: 1999: *Specification for examination and test of new lifts before putting into service. Hydraulic lifts*

DD 176: 1988: *Data logging and remote monitoring equipment for lifts, escalators and passenger conveyors*

DD 197: 1990: *Recommendations for vandal resistant lifts*

DD 222: 1996: *Rack and pinion lifts*

BS 302-4: 1987: *Stranded steel wire ropes. Specification for ropes for lifts*

BS 329: 1968: *Specification for steel wire ropes for electric lifts*

CP 407: 1972: *Electric, hydraulic and hand-powered lifts*

BS 2655: *Specification for lifts, escalators, passenger conveyors and paternosters*:

— BS 2655-1: 1970: *General requirements for electric, hydraulic and hand powered lifts*

— BS 2655-2: 1959: *Single-speed poly-phase induction motors for driving lifts*

— BS 2655-3: 1971: *Arrangements of standard electric lifts*

— BS 2655-4: 1969: *General requirements for escalators and passenger conveyors*

— BS 2655-5: 1970: *General requirements for paternosters*

— BS 2655-6: 1970: *Building construction requirements*

— BS 2655-7: 1970: *Testing and inspection*

— BS 2655-8: 1971: *Modernization or reconstruction of lifts, escalators and paternosters*

— BS 2655-9: 1970: *Definitions*

— BS 2655-10: 1972: *General requirements for guarding*

BS 3810-8: 1975: *Glossary of terms used in materials handling*

BS ISO 4190-1: 1999: *Lift (US: Elevator) installation. Class I, II, III and VI lifts*

BS ISO 4190-1: 2001: *Lift (US: Elevator) installation. Class IV lifts*

BS 5323: 1980: *Code of practice for scissor lifts*

BS 5588: *Fire precautions in the design and construction of buildings*:

— BS 5588-5: 1986: *Code of practice for firefighting stairways and lifts*

— BS 5588-5: 1991: *Code of practice for firefighting stairs and lifts*

— BS 5588-8: 1988: *Code of practice for means of escape for disabled people*

— BS 5588-8: 1999: *Code of practice for means of escape for disabled people*

BS 5655: *Lifts and service lifts*:

— BS 5655-1: *Explanatory Supplement: 1981: Explanatory supplement to BS 5655 Lifts and service lifts Part 1 Safety rules for the construction and installation of electric lifts (EN 81:Part 1)*

— BS 5655-1: 1979, EN 81-1: 1977: *Safety rules for the construction and installation of electric lifts*

— BS 5655-1: 1986, EN 81-1: 1985: *Safety rules for the construction and installation of electric lifts*

— BS 5655-2: 1983: *Lifts and service lifts. Specification for hydraulic lifts*

— BS 5655-2: 1988, EN 81-2: 1987: *Safety rules for the construction and installation of hydraulic lifts*

— BS 5655-3: 1989: *Lifts and service lifts. Specification for electric service lifts*

— BS 5655-5: 1989: *Specification for dimensions of standard lift arrangements*

— BS 5655-6: 1985: *Lifts and service lifts. Code of practice for selection and installation*

— BS 5655-6: 1990: *Lifts and service lifts. Code of practice for selection and installation*

— BS 5655-6: 2002: *Lifts and service lifts. Code of practice for the selection and installation of new lifts*

— BS 5655-7: 1983: *Specification for manual control devices, indicators and additional fittings*

— BS 5655-8: 1983: *Specification for eyebolts for lift suspension*

— BS 5655-9: 1985: *Specification for guide rails*

— BS 5655-10: 1986: *Specification for the testing and inspection of electric and hydraulic lifts*

— BS 5655-10.1.1: 1995: *Specification for the testing and examination of lifts and service. Electric lifts Commissioning test for new lifts*

— BS 5655-10.2.1: 1995: *Specification for the testing and examination of lifts and service. Hydraulic lifts. Commissioning tests for new lifts*

— BS 5655-10.1.2 (draft): *Specification for the testing and examination of lifts and service lifts. Electric lifts Commissioning tests for modernised lifts*

— BS 5655-10.2.2 (draft): *Specification for the testing and examination of lifts and service lifts. Hydraulic lifts. Commissioning tests for modernised lifts*

— BS 5655-11: 1989: *Recommendations for the installation of new, and the modernization of, electric lifts in existing buildings*

— BS 5655-12: 1989: *Recommendations for the installations of new, and the modernization of, hydraulic lifts in existing buildings*

— BS 5655-13: 1995: *Recommendations for vandal resistant lifts*

— BS 5655-14: 1995: *Specification for hand powered service lifts and platform hoists*

BS 5656: 1983: *Safety rules for the construction and installation of escalators and passenger conveyors*

BS 5656-1: 1997: *Safety rules for the construction and installation of escalators and passenger conveyors. Specification and proformas for test and examination of new installations*

BS 5656-2: 2004: *Safety rules for the construction and installation of escalators and moving walks. Code of practice for the selection, installation and location of new escalators and moving walks*

BS 5776: 1996: *Specification for powered stairlifts*

BS 5810: 1979: *Code of practice for access for the disabled to buildings*

BS 5900: 1980: *Specification for powered home lifts*

BS 5900: 1991: *Specification for powered domestic lifts*

BS 5900: 1999: *Specification for powered domestic lifts with partially enclosed cars and no lift well enclosures*

BS 5965: 1980: *Specification for manually driven balanced personal home lifts*

BS 6440: 1983: *Code of practice for powered lifting platforms for use by disabled persons*

BS 6440: 1999: *Power lifting platforms for use by disabled persons. Code of practice*

PD 6523: 1989: *Information on access to and movement within and around buildings and on certain facilities for disabled people*

PD 6500: 1984: *Explanatory supplement to BS 5655 'Lifts and service lifts' Part 1 'Safety rules for the construction and installation of electric lifts' (EN 81:Part 1)*

PD 6500: 1986: *Explanatory supplement to BS 5655 'Lifts and service lifts' Part 1 'Safety rules for the construction and installation of electric lifts' (EN 81:Part 1)*

BS 6977: 1981: *Specification for insulated flexible cables for lifts and for other flexible connections*

BS 6977: 1991: *Specification for insulated flexible cables for lifts and for other flexible connections*

BS 7255: 1989: *Code of practice for safe working on lifts*

BS 7255: 2001: *Code of practice for safe working on lifts*

BS 7801: 1995: *Code of practice for safe working on escalators and passenger conveyors in use*

BS 7801: 2004: *Code of practice for safe working on escalators and moving walks*

BS ISO 18738: 2003: *Lifts (elevators).Measurement of lift ride quality*

# A3.3 European standards related to lifts, escalators and moving walks

BS EN 81: *Safety rules for the construction and installation of lifts and service lifts*:

— BS EN 81 1: 1998: *Electric lifts*

— EN 81-1/prA1: *Electric lifts*; A1: *Programmable electronic systems*

— EN 81-1/A2: *Electric lifts*; A2: *Machinery and pulley spaces*

— BS EN 81-1/AC: 2000: *Electric lifts*; *Amendment AC*

— BS EN 81-2: 1998: *Hydraulic lifts*

— EN 81-2/prA1: *Hydraulic lifts*; A1: *Programmable electronic systems*

— EN 81-2/A2: *Hydraulic lifts*; A2: *Machinery and pulley spaces*

— BS EN 81-2/AC: 2000: *Hydraulic lifts*; *Amendment AC*

— BS EN 81-3: 2001: *Electric and hydraulic service lifts*

— prEN 81-5: *Screw lifts*

— prEN 81-6: *Guided chain lifts*

— prEN 81-7: *Rack and pinion lifts*

— prEN 81-8: see prEN 81-58

— TR 81-10: *CEN guide*

— prEN 81-11: see prEN 81-21

— prEN 81-21: *New lifts in existing buildings* (previously EN 81-11)

— prEN 81-22: *Inclined lifts*

— BS EN 81-28: 2003: *Remote alarms on passenger and goods passenger lifts*

— DD CEN/TS 81-29: 2004: *Interpretations*

— prEN 81-31: *Electric and hydraulic goods lifts (accessible to persons)*

— prEN 81-32: see prEN81-40

— prEN 81-33: see prEN81-41

— prEN 81-40: *Powered stairlifts for seated, standing and wheelchair users moving in an inclined plane* (previously EN 81-32)

— prEN 81-41: *Vertical lifting platforms* (previously EN 81-33)

— prEN 81-43: *Special purpose lifts for cranes*

— BS EN 81-58: 2003: *Lift landing doors, fire resistance testing* (previously EN 81-8)

— BS EN 81-70: 2003: *Rules for accessibility of disabled people to lifts*

— BS EN 81-71: 2005: *Vandal resistant lifts*

— BS EN 81-72: 2003: *Rules for lifts which remain in use in case of fire (Firefighters lifts)*

— EN 81-73: *Behaviour of lifts in the event of fire*

— BS EN 81-80: 2003: *Existing lifts. Rules for the improvement of safety of existing passenger and goods passenger lifts*

BS EN 115: 1995: *Safety rules for the construction and installation of escalators and passenger conveyors*

BS EN 115/prA1: 1998: *Safety rules for the construction and installation of escalators and passenger conveyors; Amendment A1*

BS EN 292-1: 1991: *Safety of machinery. Basic concepts, general principles for design. Basic terminology, methodology*

BS EN 292-2: 1991: *Safety of machinery. Basic concepts, general principles for design. Technical principles and specifications*

BS EN 627: 1996: *Specification for data logging and monitoring of lifts, escalators and passengers conveyors*

EN 1050: 1996: *Safety of machinery. Principles for risk assessment*

BS EN ISO 10535: 1998: *Hoists for the transfer of disabled persons. Requirements and test methods*

BS EN 12015: 1998: *Electromagnetic compatibility Product family standard for lifts, escalators and passenger conveyors. Emission*

BS EN 12015: 2004: *Electromagnetic compatibility Product family standard for lifts, escalators and passenger conveyors. Emission*

BS EN 12016: 1998: *Electromagnetic compatibility Product family standard for lifts, escalators and passenger conveyors. Immunity*

BS EN 12016: 2004: *Electromagnetic compatibility Product family standard for lifts, escalators and passenger conveyors. Immunity*

BS EN ISO 12100-1: 2003: *Safety of machinery. Basic concepts, general principles for design*

BS EN 12158-1: 2000: *Builders hoists for goods. Hoists with accessible platforms*

BS EN 12158-2: 2000: *Builders hoists for goods. Inclined hoists with non-accessible load carrying devices*

BS EN 12159: 2000: *Building hoists for persons and goods*

BS EN 12385-5: 2002: *Steel wire ropes. Safety. Stranded ropes for lifts*

BS EN 13015: 2001: *Maintenance for lifts and escalators Rules for maintenance instructions*

BS EN 50214: 1998: *Flexible cables for lifts*

# A3.4 International standards related to lifts, escalators and moving walks

ISO 4190-3: 1982: *Passenger lift installations. Service lifts class V*

ISO 4190-5: 1987: *Lifts and service lifts (USA: Elevators and dumbwaiters). Control devices, signals and additional fittings*

ISO 4190-6: 1984: *Lifts and service lifts (USA : elevators and dumbwaiters). Passenger lifts to be installed in residential buildings. Planning and selection*

ISO 7465: 2001: *Passenger lifts and service lifts. Guide rails for lift cars and counterweights. T-type*

ISO 8383: 1985: *Lifts on ships. Specific requirements*

ISO 9386-1: 2000: *Power-operated lifting platforms for persons with impaired mobility. Rules for safety, dimensions and functional operation. Vertical lifting platforms*

ISO 9386-2: 2000: *Power-operated lifting platforms for persons with impaired mobility. Rules for safety, dimensions and functional operation. Powered stairlifts for seated, standing and wheelchair users moving in an inclined plane*

ISO 9589: 1994: *Escalators. Building dimensions*

ISO/TR 11071-1: 1990: *Comparison of worldwide lift safety standards. Electric lifts (elevators)*

ISO/TR 11071-1: 1990: Amd 1: 1999

ISO/TR 11071-1: 1990: Amd 2: 2001: References to Australian standards

ISO/TR 11071-2: 1996: *Comparison of worldwide lift safety standards. Hydraulic lifts (elevators)*

ISO/TR 11071-2: 1996: Amd 1: 1999: *Reference to Japanese and Australian standards*

ISO/TS 14798: 2000: *Lifts (elevators), escalators and passenger conveyors. Risk analysis methodology*

ISO/TR 16764: 2003: *Lifts, escalators and passenger conveyors. Comparison of worldwide standards on electromagnetic interference/electromagnetic compatibility*

ISO/TR 16765: 2003: *Comparison of worldwide safety standards on lifts for firefighters*

# A3.5 Current standards related to access and movement of people with disabilities in buildings

prEN 81-40, ISO/FDIS 9386-2: *Powered stairlifts for seated, standing and wheelchair users moving in an inclined plane*

prEN 81-41, ISO/FDIS 9386-1: *Vertical lifting platforms*

BS EN 81-70: 2003: *Rules for accessibility of disabled people to lifts*

EN 81-72: *Rules for lifts which remain in use in case of fire (Firefighters lifts)*

BS EN 81-73: 2005: *Behaviour of lifts in the event of fire*

EP 230: 2001: *BSI Electronic Book. Disability Access (BS 8300:2001)* (CD-ROM)

BS 5588-8: 1999: *Fire precautions in the design, construction and use of buildings. Code of practice for means of escape for disabled people*

BS 5776: 1996: *Specification for powered stairlifts*

BS 5900: 1999: *Specification for powered domestic lifts with partially enclosed cars and no lift well enclosures*

BS 5965: 1980: *Specification for manually driven balanced personal home lifts*

BS 6440: 1999: *Power lifting platforms for use by disabled persons. Code of practice*

PD 6523: 1989: *Information on access to and movement within and around buildings and on certain facilities for disabled people*

BS 8300: 2001: *Design of buildings and their approaches to meet the needs of disabled people. Code of practice*

BS EN ISO 10535: 1998: *Hoists for the transfer of disabled persons. Requirements and test methods*

BS EN 12182: 1999: *Technical aids for disabled persons General requirements and test methods*

# A3.6 Interpretations to BS EN 81-1/2

Safety standards are very necessary, but the documents that describe them require detailed study. The same applies to interpretations to the standards until there is a difficulty, when every word is analysed. It is very important that designers, manufacturers, installers, maintainers, owners, inspectors and consultants keep up-to-date with such interpretations. BSI has published DD CEN/TS 81-29: *Safety rules for the construction and installation of lifts. Lifts for the transport of persons and goods. Interpretations.* This contains a complete listing and description of interpretations to the current 1998 versions of EN 81-1/2 (series 500–572) and a cross reference to those interpretations still relevant made to the earlier EN 81-1/2 standards (series 1-272). These latter interpretations were published by BSI in BS HB 10105: 2000 as the *Lifts Handbook: An explanatory supplement to BS 5655: Parts 1 and 2*. However, this publication no longer appears in the BSI catalogue.

Table A3.1 gives the interpretation number on a clause-by-clause basis with a 'X' in the column of the standards relevant to the clause. Only a brief description is given, so it will necessary to examine the actual text of each interpretation to understand the full meaning.

New interpretations are issued on an *ad hoc* time scale. Eventually these are collected together and published. This means that a practitioner's knowledge of current interpretations may be out-of-date without it being realised. *Elevatori* publishes the basic text of each new interpretation shortly after it becomes available. A supplementary table (Table A3.2, page A-42) is provided at the end of the 'Part 29' series showing interpretations 573–580, the abstracts of which have been recently published in *Elevatori*.

*Warning*: interpretations do not have the same status as the standards to which they are related. However the application of interpretations should give to the interested parties confidence that the relevant standard has not been wrongly applied.

**Table A3.1** List of interpretations to BS EN 81-1/2

| Clause | No. | Brief description | EN 81-1 | | | EN 81-2 | |
|---|---|---|---|---|---|---|---|
| | | | 1978 | 1985 | 1998 | 1987 | 1998 |
| 0.1.2.1 | 249 | Diverter pulleys made of plastic | | X | X | X | X |
| 1.2 | 532 | Maximum allowable pressure | | | | | X |
| 1.3 | 532 | Maximum allowable pressure | | | | | X |
| 1.3(g) | 524 | Speeds less than 1 m/s | | | | | X |
| 3 | 140 | Clear height of car | X | X | X | X | X |
| 3 | 166 | Definition of permanent lifting equipment | X | X | X | X | X |
| 3 | 553 | Electric safety chain | | | X | | X |
| 5.2.2.1.1 | 58 | Signs on inspection traps | X | X | X | X | X |
| 5.2.2.1.2 | 216 | Requirement of emergency doors | | X | X | X | X |
| 5.3.1.2 | 518 | Use of glass in partially enclosed wells | | | | X | X |
| 5.3.1.2 | 567 | Glass walls, floor and ceiling of well | | | | X | X |
| 5.3.2.2 | 517 | Strength of floor under buffers | | | | X | X |
| 5.3.2.3 | 517 | Strength of floor under buffers | | | | X | X |
| 5.4.3.2.1(a) | 156 | Distances to walls (entrance sides) | X | X | X | X | X |
| 5.4.3.2.2 | 25 | Prevention of misuse of car door locking mechanism | X | X | X | X | X |
| 5.6.1 | 501 | Protection in well | | | | X | X |
| 5.6.1 | 568 | Counterweight screen | | | X | | X |
| 5.6.2 | 568 | Counterweight screen | | | X | | X |
| 5.7 | 565 | Clearances in the headroom and the pit | | | | X | X |
| 5.7.1.1 | 251 | Distance between the guides of yoke and car at the same guide rail | | | | X | X |
| 5.7.1.1(c) | 212 | Free vertical distance above diverter pulleys on the car | | X | X | X | X |
| 5.7.1.1(d) | 122 | Standing area, location on car roof | | X | X | X | X |
| 5.7.2.1 | 229 | Distance between counterweight and bottom of the pit | | | | X | X |
| 5.7.2.2 | 539 | Accessibility of pit | | | | X | X |
| 5.7.2.3(b)(2) | 157 | Clearances in pit | | | | X | X |
| 5.7.2.3 | 229 | Distance between counterweight and bottom of the pit | | | | X | X |
| 5.7.2.5(a) | 121 | Types of stop switch | | | | X | X |
| 5.7.3.2 | 539 | Accessibility of pit | | | | X | X |
| 5.7.3.3(b)(2) | 157 | Clearances in pit | X | X | X | | |
| 5.7.3.4 | 121 | Types of stop switch | X | X | X | | |
| 5.8 | 22 | Use of sprinkler systems | X | X | X | X | X |
| 5.8 | 231 | Main earth cables inside the well | X | X | X | X | X |
| 5.9 | 516 | 50 lux well lighting | | | X | | X |
| 5.9 | 551 | Well lighting | | | | X | X |
| 5.10 | 534 | Alarm devices in pit | | | | X | X |
| 6.1.2 | 566 | Diverter pulleys in the headroom | | | | X | X |
| 6.1.2 | 272 | Diverter pulleys in the well, location at the pedestal of the jack | | | | X | X |
| 6.1.2.1.1 | 73 | Pulleys at top of well | | X | X | X | X |
| 6.1.2.1.1 | 239 | Protection of diverter pulleys in the pit | | X | X | | |
| 6.1.2.1.1 | 248 | Maintenance on rope terminations | | X | X | X | X |

**Table A3.1** — *continued*

| Clause | No. | Brief description | EN 81-1 | | | EN 81-2 | |
|---|---|---|---|---|---|---|---|
| | | | 1978 | 1985 | 1998 | 1987 | 1998 |
| 6.1.2.1.2(b) | 113 | Dimensioning of openings between machine room and well | X | X | X | | |
| 6.1.2.1.4(c) | 271 | Protection at pulleys, introduction of objects, dimension of objects | | X | X | | |
| 6.1.2.3 | 234 | Maintenance of air conditioners inside machine room | | X | X | X | X |
| 6.2.2(b) | 536 | Access to the interior of machine room | | | | X | X |
| 6.3.2.1 | 3 | Machine room, maintenance areas | X | X | X | X | X |
| 6.3.3.2 | 105 | Protective measures on trapdoors | X | X | X | X | X |
| 6.3 | 569 | Machine rooms and overhead pulleys | | | | X | X |
| 6.3.5.2 | 234 | Maintenance of air conditioners inside the machine room | | X | X | X | X |
| 6.3.6 | 550 | Machine room lighting | | | | X | X |
| 6.3.7 | 220 | Installation for heavy equipment hoisting | | X | X | X | X |
| 6.4 | 569 | Machine rooms and overhead pulleys | | | | X | |
| 6.4.3.1 | 105 | Protective measures on trapdoors | X | X | X | X | X |
| 6.7.3.3(b)(2) | 547 | Pit depth | | | X | | |
| 6.7.2.3(b)(2) | 547 | Pit depth | | | | | X |
| 7 | 269 | Additional means for security locking at landing doors | | X | X | X | X |
| 7.1.1 | 50 | Handles on sliding doors | X | X | X | X | X |
| 7.1.1 | 170 | Design of edges of doors | X | X | X | X | X |
| 7.1.1 | 192 A | Design of closing edges of doors | X | X | X | X | X |
| 7.4.3.1 | 132 | Suspension for vertically sliding doors | X | X | X | X | X |
| 7.5.1 | 192 A | Design of closing edges of doors | X | X | X | X | X |
| 7.5.2 | 171 | Design of large landing and car doors | | X | X | X | X |
| 7.5.2.1.1.1 | 49A | Closing force limiter | X | X | X | X | X |
| 7.5.2.1.1.1 | 187 | Solutions of closing-force limitations | X | X | X | X | X |
| 7.5.2.1.1.1 | 197 | Measurement of the closing force | | X | X | X | X |
| 7.5.2.1.1.3 | 49A | Closing force limiter | X | X | X | X | X |
| 7.5.2.1.1.3 | 106 | Protective devices on doors | X | X | X | X | X |
| 7.5.2.1.1.3 | 128 | Protective device arrangement on centre opening doors | X | X | X | X | X |
| 7.5.2.1.1.3 | 158 | Actuating force for door protective devices | X | X | X | X | X |
| 7.5.2.1.1.3 | 187 | Solutions of closing-force limitations | X | X | X | X | X |
| 7.5.2.1.2 | 171 | Design of large car doors and landing doors | | X | X | X | X |
| 7.5.2.2 | 23 | Requirements for vertically-sliding doors | X | X | X | X | X |
| 7.5.2.2 | 172 | Design of vertically sliding car and landing doors | | X | X | X | X |
| 7.7.2.1 | 196 | Energising the brake | | X | X | X | X |
| 7.7.2.1 | 207 | Preliminary operations | | | | X | X |
| 7.7.2.2 | 196 | Energising the brake | | X | X | X | X |
| 7.7.3 | 222 | Type examination of door locking devices | | X | X | X | X |
| 7.7.3 | 227 | Power operated opening of car door | | X | X | X | X |
| 7.7.3.2 | 50 | Handles on sliding doors | X | X | X | X | X |
| 7.7.3.2 | 171 | Design of large landing and car doors | | X | X | X | X |
| 7.7.4.1 | 222 | Type examination of door locking devices | | X | X | X | X |
| 7.7.5.1 | 222 | Type examination of door locking devices | | X | X | X | X |
| 7.7.6 | 99 | Linkage of door panels (strength) | X | X | X | X | X |
| 7.7.6.1 | 100 | Linkage of door panels (fire resistance) | X | X | X | X | X |
| 8.1.1 | 140 | Clear height of car | X | X | X | X | X |
| 8.2.1 | 544 | Available car area | | | | X | X |
| 8.2.1 | 131 | Recesses in lift car | X | X | X | X | X |
| 8.2.1 | 191 | Available car area | X | X | X | X | X |
| 8.2.2 | 63 | Loading devices and rated load | X | X | X | | |
| 8.2.2 | 191 | Available car area | | | | X | X |
| 8.2.2 | 206 | Use of handling devices, calculation | | X | X | | |
| 8.2.2.3 | 226 | Calculation of the jack | | | | X | X |
| 8.2.2.4 | 523 | Good lift rated load | | | | | X |
| 8.2.3 | 63 | Loading devices and rated load | | | | X | X |
| 8.2.3 | 206 | Use of handling devices, calculation | | | | X | X |
| 8.3 | 202 | Cars made of wood | | X | X | X | X |
| 8.3 | 211 | Advertising message in the car | | X | X | X | X |
| 8.3 | 261 | Mirrors at the walls of the car | | X | X | X | X |
| 8.3.2.1 | 24 | Defined area for door strength calculations | X | X | X | X | X |
| 8.4.1 | 193 | Reduction of the distance between car sill and landing door sill | X | X | X | X | X |
| 8.6.1 | 32 | Mesh width of mesh panel doors | X | X | X | X | X |
| 8.6.1 | 172 | Design of vertically sliding car- and landing doors | | X | X | X | X |
| 8.6.6 | 132 | Suspension for vertically sliding doors | X | X | X | X | X |

*Table continues*

**Table A3.1** — *continued*

| Clause | No. | Brief description | EN 81-1 | | | EN 81-2 | |
|---|---|---|---|---|---|---|---|
| | | | 1978 | 1985 | 1998 | 1987 | 1998 |
| 8.7.2.1.1.1 | 187 | Solutions of closing-force limitations | X | X | X | X | X |
| 8.7.2.1.1.1 | 197 | Measurement of the closing force | | X | X | X | X |
| 8.7.2.1.1.3 | 158 | Actuating force for door protective devices | X | X | X | X | X |
| 8.7.2.1.1.3 | 180 | Protective device on car folding doors | X | X | X | X | X |
| 8.7.2.1.1.3 | 187 | Solutions of closing-force limitations | X | X | X | X | X |
| 8.12.4 | 31 | Emergency car doors | X | X | X | X | X |
| 8.13 | 571 | Balustrade height, etc. | | | X | | X |
| 8.13.3 | 572 | Balustrade height, etc. | | | | | X |
| 8.17.1 | 260 | Switching off the car lighting | | X | X | X | X |
| 8.17.3 | 130 | Emergency lighting in lift car | | X | X | X | X |
| 8.17.4 | 549 | Car lighting | | | | X | X |
| 8.18.2(a) | 141 | Rope restraint on counterweight pulleys | X | X | X | | |
| 8.18.3 | 164 | Emergency machine for traction drive lifts | X | X | X | | |
| 9.1.2 | 561 | Suspension ropes | | | X | | X |
| 9.3 | 33 | Traction sheave with groove inserts | X | X | X | | |
| 9.3.1 | 165 | Traction examination | X | X | X | | |
| 9.3.1(a) | 270 | Traction, lifting of the empty car, duration of the test | | X | X | | |
| 9.3.3 | 70 | Safety switch for suspension ropes | | | | X | X |
| 9.4.1 | 56 | Guards for chain pulleys | | | | X | X |
| 9.4.4 | 264 | Fleet angle of suspension ropes | | X | X | | |
| 9.5.3 | 70 | Safety switch for suspension ropes | X | X | X | | |
| 9.6 | 561 | Suspension ropes | | | X | | |
| 9.6.2 | 537 | Anti rebound device operation | | | | X | |
| 9.7 | 56 | Guards for chain pulleys | X | X | X | | |
| 9.8.2.1(d) | 525 | Instantaneous safety gear 0.63–1.00 ms | | | | | X |
| 9.8.3.1 | 520 | Safety gear operation activation | | | | X | X |
| 9.8.3.1 | 235 | Tripping of the safety gear of the car | | X | X | | |
| 9.8.5.1 | 230 | Release of a tripped safety gear | | | | X | X |
| 9.8.5.3 | 230 | Release of a tripped safety gear | | X | X | | |
| 9.8.7 | 48 | Car floor inclination | X | X | X | X | X |
| 9.8.8 | 230 | Release of a tripped safety gear | | X | X | X | X |
| 9.8.8 | 237 | Slack rope/chain and safety gear contract | | | | X | X |
| 9.8.8 | 252 | Electric safety device at the safety gear | | | | X | X |
| 9.9 | 148 | Overspeed governor in pit | X | X | X | | |
| 9.9.1 | 149 | Indication of rated speeds for overspeed | X | X | X | | |
| 9.9.1 | 160 | Governor tripping speed check | X | X | X | | |
| 9.9.2 | 559 | Limit switches heavy rated loads, low speeds | | | | X | |
| 9.9.2.1 | 526 | Text revised for clamping device | | | | | X |
| 9.9.5.1 | 527 | Release of clamping device | | | | | X |
| 9.9.5.2 | 527 | Release of clamping device | | | | | X |
| 9.9.6 | 561 | Suspension ropes | | | X | | |
| 9.9.6.1 | 71 | Overspeed governor drive | X | X | X | | |
| 9.9.6.5 | 159 | Tensioning of governor rope | X | X | X | | |
| 9.9.7 | 228 | Response time | | X | X | | |
| 9.9.9 | 72 | Manual checking of safety gear | X | X | X | | |
| 9.9.11 | 177 | Electric safety device at the overspeed governor | X | X | X | | |
| 9.9.11.1 | 266 | Operation of the electric safety device at the overspeed governor | | X | X | | |
| 9.9.11.2 | 241 | Electric safety device on overspeed governor | | X | X | | |
| 9.10.1 | 555 | Safety gear | | | X | | |
| 9.10.2 | 160 | Governor tripping speed check | | | | X | X |
| 9.10.2.1 | 149 | Indication of rated speeds for overspeed governor | | | | X | X |
| 9.10.2.2 | 559 | Limit switches heavy rated loads, low speeds | | | | | X |
| 9.10.2.5.1 | 71 | Overspeed governor drive | | | | X | X |
| 9.10.2.5.2 | 148 | Overspeed governor in pit | | | | X | X |
| 9.10.2.5.2 | 159 | Tensioning of governor rope | | | | X | X |
| 9.10.2.6 | 228 | Response time | | | | X | X |
| 9.10.2.8 | 72 | Manual checking of safety gear | | | | X | X |
| 9.10.2.10.2 | 177 | Electric safety device at the overspeed governor | | | | X | X |
| 9.10.2.10.2 | 241 | Electric safety device on overspeed governor | | | | X | X |
| 9.10.3 | 535 | Ascending car retardation | | | | X | |
| 9.10.3.2 | 256 | Tripping the safety gear by suspension failure | | | | X | X |
| 9.10.4 | 555 | Safety gear | | | X | | |
| 9.10.5 | 555 | Safety gear | | | X | | |

*Table continues*

**Table A3.1** — *continued*

| Clause | No. | Brief description | EN 81-1 | | | EN 81-2 | |
|--------|-----|-------------------|---------|------|------|---------|------|
| | | | 1978 | 1985 | 1998 | 1987 | 1998 |
| 9.10.6 | 561 | Suspension ropes | | | | | X |
| 9.11.7 | 210 | Buffering system in pawl devices | | | | X | X |
| 10.1.2 | 94 | Fixing of guide rails | X | X | X | X | X |
| 10.1.2.1 | 542 | Guide rails, yield point, tensile strength | | | | X | X |
| 10.3 | 127 | Impact speed on buffers | X | X | X | X | X |
| 10.3.1 | 103 | Buffer arrangements | X | X | X | X | X |
| 10.3.1 | 111 | Possible design of instantaneous safety gear with buffered effect | X | X | X | | |
| 10.3.1 | 521 | Moving buffers | | | | X | X |
| 10.3.2 | 111 | Possible design of instantaneous safety gear with buffered effect | | | | X | X |
| 10.3.3 | 557 | Car buffer requirements | | | | | X |
| 10.3.3 | 194 | Buffers underneath the car | | | | X | X |
| 10.3.4 | 236 | Touch between the ram and the bottom of the cylinder | | | | X | X |
| 10.4.1.2.2 | 564 | Energy accumulation buffers | | | | X | X |
| 10.4.2.1 | 560 | Electromechanical brake | | | | X | |
| 10.4.3.2 | 533 | Striking speed on buffers | | | | X | |
| 10.5.2.3(a) | 134 | Final limit switch | X | X | X | X | X |
| 10.5.2.3(a) | 224 | Tripping of the final limit switch | | | | X | X |
| 10.5.3 | 201 | Effects after operation of the final limit switch | | | | X | X |
| 10.5.3.1 | 545 | Limit switches | | | | X | |
| 10.5.3.1 | 512 | Final limit switch usage | | | | | X |
| 10.5.3.1 | 513 | Final limit switch usage | | | | | X |
| 10.5.3.1(a) | 219 | Final limit switches for drum drive lifts | | X | X | | |
| 10.5.3.2 | 512 | Final limit switch usage | | | | | X |
| 10.5.3.2 | 513 | Final limit switch usage | | | | | X |
| 10.5.3.2 | 238 | Return to normal service from operation of the final limit switch | | | | X | X |
| 10.5.3.2 | 245 | Realisation of non response to calls | | | | X | X |
| 10.6 | 182 | Combination of slack-rope switch and safety gear switch | | | | X | X |
| 10.6 | 237 | Slack rope/chain and safety gear contact | | | | X | X |
| 11 | 250 | Distances between car and installation inside the well | | X | X | X | X |
| 11.4 | 217 | Distance between car and counterweight | | X | X | X | X |
| 12.2.1(b) | 164 | Emergency machine for traction drive lifts | X | X | X | | |
| 12.4.1(a) | 108 | Interruption of motor power supply | | | | X | X |
| 12.4.1(b) | 207 | Preliminary operations | | | | X | X |
| 12.4.2.1 | 244 | Minimum retardation of the brake | | X | X | | |
| 12.4.2.3 | 196 | Energising the brake | | X | X | | |
| 12.5 | 147 | Removable hand wheel | X | X | X | | |
| 12.5.5.2 | 538 | Accessibility of rupture valve | | | | | X |
| 12.5.6.2 | 538 | Accessibility of rupture valve | | | | | X |
| 12.5.7 | 502 | Hydraulic control | | | | | X |
| 12.5.7 | 178 | Filter | | | | X | X |
| 12.7.1 | 552 | Monitoring device, main contactors | | | | X | |
| 12.7.1 | 108 | Interruption of motor power supply | X | X | X | | |
| 12.7.3(a) | 552 | Monitoring device, main contactors | | | | X | |
| 12.7.3 | 259 | Combination of control- and monitoring device | | X | X | | |
| 12.8 | 533 | Striking speed on buffers | | | | X | |
| 12.9 | 118 | Protective measures in machine room | X | X | X | | |
| 12.9.1.5 | 175 | Design of the manually operated emergency lowering valve | | | | X | X |
| 12.9.1.5 | 225 | Safety against slack rope/chain at the manual emergency lowering valve | | | | X | X |
| 12.11 | 118 | Protective measures in machine room | | | | X | X |
| 12.12.4 | 554 | Motor run time limiter | | | | | X |
| 12.13 | 268 | Operation of the temperature detecting device | | | | X | X |
| 13 | 18 | Printed circuits | X | X | X | X | X |
| 13.1.1.2 | 541 | Electric installations, wiring, method | | | | X | X |
| 13.1.2 | 519 | Degree of protection — IP codes | | | | X | X |
| 13.1.2 | 263 | IP-degree in the well | | X | X | X | X |
| 13.1.4 | 255 | Power supply of automatic doors | | X | X | X | X |
| 13.1.4 | 257 | Application of BS EN 60204 | | X | X | X | X |
| 13.3.2 | 505 | Door motor protection | | | | X | X |

*Table continues*

**Table A3.1** — *continued*

| Clause | No. | Brief description | EN 81-1 | | | EN 81-2 | |
|---|---|---|---|---|---|---|---|
| | | | 1978 | 1985 | 1998 | 1987 | 1998 |
| 13.3.2 | 186 | Motor protection | | X | X | X | X |
| 13.3.3 | 186 | Motor protection | | X | X | X | X |
| 13.4.2 | 506 | Main switch — multiple | | | | X | X |
| 13.5.1.3 | 541 | Electric installations, wiring, method | | | | X | X |
| 13.5.3.3 | 119 | Light switch | X | X | X | X | X |
| 13.5.3.6 | 541 | Electric installations, wiring, method | | | | X | X |
| 13.6.1 | 563 | Electric supply of the lift | | | | X | X |
| 13.6.2 | 173 | Socket outlets and switches for lighting | X | X | X | X | X |
| 14.1.1 | 213 | Failure analysis for inspection operation | | X | X | X | X |
| 14.1.1.3 | 240 | Position of contacts of contactors | | X | X | X | X |
| 14.1.2.1.2 | 123 | Electric safety devices in neutral conductor | | X | X | X | X |
| 14.1.2.1.3 | 510 | Electrical safety circuit monitoring | | | | X | X |
| 14.1.2.1.3 | 515 | Bypass of landing/car door contacts | | | | X | X |
| 14.1.2.1.3 | 548 | Safety circuits | | | | X | X |
| 14.1.2.1.3 | 540 | Inspection controls in relation to glass lifts | | | | X | X |
| 14.1.2.1.4 | 507 | Emergency electrical operation | | | | X | |
| 14.1.2.4 | 196 | Energising the brake | | X | X | X | X |
| 14.1.2.4 | 553 | Electric safety chain | | | X | | X |
| 14.2 | 267 | Use of emergency electrical operation | | | | X | X |
| 14.2 | 558 | Emergency electrical control | | | | | X |
| 14.2.1.2 | 196 | Energising the brake | | X | X | X | X |
| 14.2.1.2 | 263 | IP-degree in the well | | X | X | X | X |
| 14.2.1.3 | 101A | Inspection control station arrangements | X | X | X | X | X |
| 14.2.1.3 | 120 | Inspection control | X | X | X | X | X |
| 14.2.1.3 | 133 | Timer in inspection operation circuit | X | X | X | X | X |
| 14.2.1.3 | 183 | Inspection controls and door movements | X | X | X | X | X |
| 14.2.1.3 | 265 | Inspection control and door movements | | X | X | X | X |
| 14.2.1.3 | 570 | Inspection control | | | X | | X |
| 14.2.1.4 | 136 | Emergency electrical arrangements | X | X | X | | |
| 14.2.1.4 | 267 | Use of emergency electrical operation | | X | X | | |
| 14.2.1.5 | 200 | Protection against phase reversal | | | | X | X |
| 14.2.1.5.1 | 258 | Activation of the re-levelling device | | | | X | X |
| 14.2.2 | 223 | Failure analysis for inspection operation | | X | X | X | X |
| 14.2.2.1 | 98 | Car stop switch in docking operation | X | X | X | X | X |
| 14.2.2.2 | 531 | In car stopping device | | | | X | X |
| 14.2.2.3(a) | 101A | Inspection control station arrangements | X | X | X | X | X |
| 14.2.3.3 | 514 | Duplex voice operation | | | | X | X |
| 14.2.4.3 | 126 | Car direction indicators | X | X | X | X | X |
| 14.2.4.3 | 215 | Signal indicating the direction of the car | | X | X | X | X |
| 15 | 511 | type certificates, safety devices | | | | X | X |
| 15 | 522 | marking electronic components | | | | X | X |
| 15.2 | 211 | advertising message in the car | | X | X | X | X |
| 15.2.3.1 | 125 | push button for alarm signal | X | X | X | X | X |
| 15.2.3.2 | 198 | identification of controls in the car | | X | X | X | X |
| 15.9 | 218 | indication of the level of car stop | | X | X | X | X |
| 16.1.3 | 543 | type examination certificate | | | | X | X |
| 16.2(a)(6) | 519 | degree of protection — IP codes | | | | X | X |
| Annex A | 137 | combination of electric safety devices | X | X | X | X | X |
| Annex D | 242 | verification: phase reversal, motor run time limiter, speed control device | | X | X | X | X |
| Annex D2 | 556 | safety gear test, suspension failure | | | | | X |
| Annex D2 | 560 | electro mechanical brake | | | | X | |
| Annex D2(g)(1) | 160 | governor tripping speed check | | | | X | X |
| Annex D2(h)(2) | 138 | traction tests | X | X | X | | |
| Annex D2(h)(2) | 165 | traction examination | X | X | X | | |
| Annex D2(i)(1) | 160 | governor tripping speed check | X | X | X | | |
| Annex D2(n)(1) | 528 | check rope slackening | | | | | X |
| Annex E | 242 | verification: phase reversal, motor run time limiter, speed control device | | X | X | X | X |
| Annex F0.2 | 543 | type examination certificate | | | | X | X |
| Annex F1.1.2 | 154 | extent of type tests on door locks | X | X | X | X | X |
| Annex F4.3.2 | 149 | indication of rated speeds for overspeed governor | X | X | X | X | X |

*Table continues*

**Table A3.1** — *continued*

| Clause | No. | Brief description | EN 81-1 | | | EN 81-2 | |
|--------|-----|------------------|---------|------|------|---------|------|
| | | | 1978 | 1985 | 1998 | 1987 | 1998 |
| Annex F6 | 508 | tests — safety chain | | | | X | X |
| Annex F6 | 548 | safety circuits | | | | X | X |
| Annex H1 | 509 | PCB safety circuits | | | | X | X |
| Annex H1 | 510 | electrical safety circuit monitoring | | | | X | X |
| Annex J1 | 504 | dimensions of glass | | | | X | |
| Annex J7 | 530 | hinged glass doors | | | | X | X |
| Annex J7 | 529 | delete reference to national regulations | | | | X | X |
| Annex J7 | 503 | fixing glass | | | | X | X |
| Annex N | 546 | sheave equivalent number evaluation | | | | X | |

**Table A3.2** Supplementary list of interpretations to EN 81-29

| Clause | No. | Brief description | *Elevatori* issue no. | EN 81-1: 1998 | EN 81-2: 1998 |
|--------|-----|------------------|-----------------------|---------------|---------------|
| | 562 | NOT YET AVAILABLE | | | |
| 7.2.3.1 | 573 | Doors panels | 5/04 | X | X |
| 8.3.2.1 | 573 | Doors panels | 5/04 | X | X |
| 8.6.7.1 | 573 | Doors panels | 5/04 | X | X |
| 7.2.3.1 | 574 | Mechanical strength of car/landing doors and car walls | 4/04 | X | X |
| 8.3.2.1 | 574 | Mechanical strength of car/landing doors and car walls | 4/04 | X | X |
| 8.6.7.1 | 574 | Mechanical strength of car/landing doors and car walls | 4/04 | X | X |
| 7.5.2.1.1 | 575 | Kinetic energy of closing doors | 1/05 | X | X |
| 7.7.3.2 | 576 | Automatic closing and locking of landing doors | 5/04 | X | X |
| 8.7.2.1.1 | 575 | Kinetic energy of closing doors | 1/05 | X | X |
| 8.7.2.1.1.3 | 577 | Car door re-opening device | 1/05 | X | X |
| 12.1 | 578 | Levelling and stopping accuracy | 5/04 | X | X |
| 14.2.3 | 579 | Emergency alarm device | 2/05 | X | X |
| 10.3.4 | 580 | Energy accumulation buffers with non linear characteristics | 2/05 | X | X |
| 10.3.6 | 580 | Energy accumulation buffers with non linear characteristics | 2/05 | X | X |

# Index

(G) indicates that the term is defined in Appendix A1: Glossary of terms

AC motors   1-3, 7-3 to 7-4, 7-18, 8-8, 8-11, 8-13
AC variable voltage drives   5-18, 8-11, 8-16, 13-5
acceleration
    drives   8-7 to 8-8, 8-11, 8-13, 8-16
    energy   13-4 to 13-5, A-29 to A-32
    equipment   5-4, 5-6, 5-18, 5-29 to 5-30
    escalator   10-9
    monitoring   12-11 to 12-12, 12-15
    traffic   3-9, 4.3 to 4.5
    — see also ride comfort
ACoP — see Approved Code of Practice
advanced door opening   3-10, 4-3 to 4-4, 9-11, 11-12
AI — see artificial intelligence
air conditioning   5-11, 5-15, 5-19, 7-10, 12-8 to 12-10, 12-13, 13-4, 14-8
airports   2-8, 2-11 to 2-13, 2-15, 3-16 to 3-18, 4-5, 5-5, 5-8, 5-11, 5-17, 8-3, 10-3, 10-4, 14-3, 15-4
alarms — see remote alarm, emergency alarm
algorithm, lift group control   (G), 3-11, 3-14, 4-7 to 4-8, 4-11, 9-4 to 9-14
alighting, escalators and moving walks   2-7, 2-11, 2-14 to 2-15, 10-4, 10-6
alteration   (G), 5-4, 15-13
    CDM   18-3, 18-7 to 18-8, 18-10 to 18-11
    upgrading   16-4 to 16-6, 16-8, 16-11
    — see also modernisation
ANSI Standard Z65-1   3-19
anti-creep devices, hydraulic drives   (G), 7-9, 8-13, 15-5, 15-7, 15-9, 15-11, 16-10, 16-17
Approved Code of Practice   18-9 to 18-12
arrival rate   (G), 3-5 to 3-6, 3-11 to 3-12, 3-14, 3-21
    control   9-13
    simulation   4-6, 4-13 to 4-14, 4-16
artificial intelligence, lift group control   9-4 to 9-8, 9-13
automatic push button control   (G), 8-3
average highest call reversal floor   3-7 to 3-8, 4-3 to 4-6, 4-14 to 4-15
average number of passengers   3-3, 3-7, 3-20, 4-3, 4-5 to 4-6
    — see also loading factor, capacity factor
average number of stops   3-3, 3-7 to 3-8, 4-3 to 4-6
average passenger times — see passenger

back-up
    battery   12-11, 14-8
    system   14-7
    to lift group control   9-8, 9-10
balustrade, escalator and moving walk   (G), 10-5, 10-6, 15-7
basement service   3-15, 3-17
bedplates   5-10, 7-4 to 7-5, 7-7, 16-10, 16-13
bi-parting doors   (G), 5-20, 5-22 to 5-23, 7-21
blind people   7-30
boarding, escalators and moving walks   2-7, 2-11, 2-14 to 2-15, 10-4
bottom drive systems   5-10, 5-15, 5-19, 5-23, 7-7 to 7-8, 7-28
Braille markings, lift controls   7-29, 11-12
brakes   (G),
    lift   3-9, 5-25, 7-4 to 7-9, 7-22, 7-25, 8-7, 13-2, 15-8 to 15-9, 15-12, 16-6, 16-10, 16-13

brakes (continued)
    escalator, moving walk   10-3 to 10-5, 10-10, 15-8, 15-11
British Council for Offices   3-5
British Standards Institution   17-7
British Standards and Codes of Practice
    — see Appendix A3
BS 302   A-33
BS 476   7-21
BS 721   7-8
BS 2655   6-3, 11-8, 15-5, 16-3 to16-4,
BS 5499   6-6
BS 5588   5-25 to 5-26, 6-3 to 6-10
BS 5655   5-8, 6-1, 12-1, 16-1, 16-2
BS 5655-1   12-3
BS 5655-6   2-15, 3-6, 3-9, 5-3, 5-10, 7-3, 8-7, 9-3, 12-5 to 12-6, 15-3, 16-4, 16-10, 16-14,
BS 5655-10   7-23, 15-5, 16-7
BS 5655-11/12   12-3, 16-6, 16-8 to 16-15
BS 5776   5-28, 11-8, 11-10
BS 5900   5-27, 8-4 to 8-5, 11-8
BS 6440   5-27 to 5-28, 11-7 to 11-8
BS 6472   12-12
BS 6841   12-12
BS 7255   5-3, 12-12, 15-3, 15-8, 15-10, 16-4
BS 7671   10-8, 12-3, 12-6 to 12-7
BS 7801   10-3, 15-3
BS EN 81-1
    (156 instances, see chapter end references)
BS EN 81-2
    (92 instances, see chapter end references)
BS EN 81-3   5-19 to 5-20
BS EN 81-28   7-30, 8-3, 11-6, 11-10, 11-12, 14-3, 14-5, 14-9 to 14-10, 16-5, 16-7 to 16.8
BS EN 81-58   7-21, 16-5
BS EN 81-70   2-11, 2-16, 5-5 to 5-8, 5-17, 5-26 to 5-27
BS EN 81-71   5-5, 16-5
BS EN 81-72   5-25, 6-3 to 6-4, 6-6 to 6-8, 9-11, 11-10, 12-3, 12-6 to 12-7, 16-5
BS EN 81-80   11-7, 12-3, 15-5, 15-11, 16-3, 16-4, 16-7 to 16-18
BS EN 115   2-7, 2-14, 10-3 to10-6, 10-8, 10-10, 15-3 to 15-5, 15-11,17-7
BS EN 627   14-11
BS EN 1570   5-28 to 5-29
BS EN 12015-16   8-18, 10-8, 12-5 to 12-6, 16-10, 16-13 to 16-14, 17-4
BS EN 50014   5-28
BS EN 60529   6-8
BS ISO 4190-1   3-8, 5-4, 5-6, 5-8, 5-10, 5-17 to 5-19, 5-24, 5-32 to 5-34, 7-7, 11-6
BS ISO 4190-2   5-4, 5-8, 5-10 to 5-15, 5-24, 5-33
buffer zones, human personal space   2-4
buffers   (G), 5-19, 7-3, 7-13, 7-16, 7-23 to 7-25, 7-27, 12-10, 15-5, 16-6, 17-5
    accumulation   7-24, A-40, A-42
    dissipation   7-24 to 7-2515-9, 16-12
building
    management systems   9-6, 11-12, 12-7, 12-15, 14-8
    population — see population
Building Regulations   2-16, 5-4 to 5-6, 5-25, 6-3, 11-4, 11-12, 12-3, 12-10, 13-3, 17-7
building types
    airports   2-8, 2-11 to 2-13, 2-15, 3-16 to 3-18, 4-5, 5-5, 5-8, 5-11, 5-17, 7-19, 8-3, 10-33, 10-4, 14-3, 15-4
    car parks   2-10, 2-12, 2-15, 3-15 to 3-17, 3-19, 4-5 to 4-6, 5-5, 5-11, 5-17, 8-11, 9-3, 94, 12-9
    commercial   3-4 to 3-5, 3-8, 3-10, 3-18, 4-13, 5-6, 5-8, 5-21, 7-6, 7-9 to 7-10, 11-6, 11-8, 13-7 to 13-9

building types (continued)
    department stores   2-12, 3-17, 5-5, 5-11, 5-17, 5-19, 10-4
    entertainment centres, cinemas, theatres, sports centres, stadia and concert halls   2-12, 3-18, 5-5, 5-11, 5-17, 5-19
    hospitals   2-4, 2-6 to 2-7, 2-12 to 2-13, 2-15, 3-5, 3-9, 3-16, 3-18, 4-5, 5-5 to 5-6, 5-8, 5-11 to 5-12, 5-14, 5-17, 5-19, 7-19, 8-3 to 8-4, 9-11, 11-12, 12-11
    hotels   2-12, 2-13, 3-5, 3-9, 3-15, 3-18 to 3-19, 4-5 to 4-6, 5-6, 5-8, 5-12, 5-17, 5-19, 5-29, 7-29, 9-3, 9-4, 12-11, 13-7, 13-8
    institutional   2-13, 3-5, 3-10, 3-17, 3-19, 5-21
    offices   2-3, 2-7, 2-11 to 2-13, 2-15, 3-5 to 3-6, 3-9 to 3-10, 3-17 to 3-19, 4-6, 5-6, 5-8, 5-11 to 5-12, 5-16 to 5-19, 5-27, 6-4, 6-10, 9-3, 12-11, 13-3, 13-9, 18-5
    railway stations   2-7 to 2-9, 2-11 to 2-13, 2-15, 3-15 to 3-18, 5-6, 5-12, 5-17, 9-3, 10-4, 13-9
    residential   2-13, 3-5, 3-9, 3-11, 3-18 to 3-19, 4-5 to 4-6, 5-7 to 5-8, 5-12, 5-17, 5-19, 5-21, 5-24, 6-4, 6-10, 7-10, 9-3
    residential care homes and nursing homes   2-13, 3-19, 5-7, 5-12, 5-17, 5-19, 5-27
    shopping centres   2-7 to 2-13, 2-15, 3-16 to 3-19, 4-5 to 4-6, 5-7 to 5-8, 5-12, 5-17, 5-19, 10-4, 11-5
    universities and other education buildings   2-13, 3-19, 5-8, 5-12, 5-17, 5-19
bulk queues, interior circulation design   2-4
bulk transit systems   2-8, 3-6
bunching, lift group control   (G), 4-8, 9-3


cables, cabling, sizing   10.8, 12-3, 12-6 to 12-7, 18.4
capacity — see rated capacity
capacity factor   3-8, 4-5 to 4-6, 4-9
car
    capacity factor   3-8, 4-5 to 4-6, 4-9
    environmental conditions   12-10
    firefighting lifts   6-8
    fixtures   5-7, 7-29, 9-8
    goods lift   5-13
    loading factor   3-7 to 3-8, 3-11, 3-21
    motor vehicle lift   5-22
    observation lift   5-16
    operating panel   6-6, 7-29 to 7-30, 9-14, 11-6 to 11-7
    service lifts   5-20
car frame   (G), 3-10, 5-25, 7-16 to 7-17, 7-19, 7-22 to 7-23
car parks   2-10, 2-12, 2-15, 3-15 to 3-17, 3-19, 4-5 to 4-6, 5-5, 5-11, 5-17, 8-11, 9-3, 9-4, 12-9
care homes — see nursing homes
CDM— see Construction (Design and Management) Regulations 1994
centre-opening doors   (G), 3-9, 5-8, 5-18, 5-22, 7-18, 7-20 to 7-21
chain stores   2-12, 3-17
    — see also shopping centres
change-over supply   6-8
CIBSE Guide A: Environmental design   12-11
CIBSE Guide F: Energy efficiency in buildings   13-3
cinemas   2-12, 3-18, 5-5, 5-11, 5-17, 5-19
circulation   (G), 2-2, 2-4 to 2-5, 2-7, 2-9, 2-11 to 2-13, 2-15
cleaning, observation lifts   5-19, 18-3

clearance (G), 5-10, 5-14, 5-18, 5-20, 7-7, 7-10, 7-13, 7-20, 15-11, 16-8 to16-16
closed-loop
    door operator 7-18, 8-16, 16-15
    drive systems 8-8
comfort, ride 5-6, 7-3, 8-7, 8-12, 12-10 to 12-12, 13-5
    — see also acceleration, deceleration, environmental conditions, jerk, noise, ride quality, vibration
commercial buildings — see offices
commissioning
    controllers 8-4
    lifts 15-3 to 15-5, 15-7, 15-9, 15-11, 18-3 to 18-4
communication
    acoustic 5-11, 5-15
    systems 5-26, 6-3, 6-6, 6-8, 6-10, 8-3
    — see also remote alarms, emergency alarm
compensating and ropes 7-16, 7-27, 13-4, 13-8,16-17
computer software up-peak calculation 4-3
condensation, controller cabinets 8-5, 12-9, 12-16
Construction (Design and Management) Regulations 1994 18-3 to 18-12
contactors (G), 8-6, 10-9
contractors
    — see Construction (Design and Management) Regulations
contraflows, shopping centres 2-10
control — see traffic, drive control
control valves, hydraulic drives 7-12, 8-6, 8-13
controllers — see traffic, drive control
controller cabinet 5-11, 15-15, 5-25, 7-13, 8-4 to 8-5, 8-16, 9-3, 12-9, 12-13,14-4, 15-6 to 15-7
cooling 5-9, 5-11, 5-14, 5-15, 5-19, 5-25, 7-9, 7-10, 7-12, 8-6, 8-12, 12-8 to 12-11, 12-13, 12-15, 13-4 to 13-5, 16-14
    — see also heating, ventilation
corridors 2-5 to 2-6, 5-7, 6-4
counterweights (G),
    hydraulic drives 5-9, 8-6
    lifts 5-19, 5-21, 5-25, 5-29, 5-31, 7-3 to 7-5, 7-7 to 7-9, 7-11, 7-13 to 7-16, 7-22 to 7-25, 7-27, 7-28, 8-8, 8-13, 13-5, 13-7, 15-4 to 15-6, 16-8, 16-15 to 16-17
cross-over escalator configuration (G), 2-14
crowded density 2-9
cycle time 3-11, 7-18, 8-3

data logging, lift group control (G), 9-7, 9-9, 14-3, 14-4, 14-5, 14-11
DC motors 7-3, 7-18, 8-8 to 8-9
DC thyristor (SCR) drives, regenerated energy 13-6
deceleration 3-6, 3-9, 5-18, 5-29, 5-30, 7-25, 8-7 to 8-9, 8-11, 8-12, 8-16, 10-9, 12-12, 13-4
decking (G), 10-8
density (of occupation) 2-3, 2-5, 8-3, 9-13
    escalators 2-7
    lifts 2-15, 3-9, 3-10
    malls 2-10
    moving walks and ramps 2-8
    shopping centres 2-12
    stairways 2-6, 2-7, 2-10,
department stores 2-11 to 2-12, 3-17, 5-5, 5-11, 5-17, 5-19, 10-4
    — see also shopping centres
design capacity
    lift cars 4-9
    — see also handling capacity

despatch interval (G), 3-12, 3-16, 6-10
direct-acting jacks, hydraulic drives 5-22, 7-10 to 7-11, 7-13, 16-18
direction indicators, lifts (G), 7-30, 9-14
directional collective control 9-4
disabled people 2-18, 7-20, 11-3, 11-4, 11-5, 11-6, 11-10, 11-12
    evacuation lifts 5-28, 6-3, 6-4, 6-9,
discrete digital simulation 3-3
diversity factor, electrical (G), 12-3, 12-6
documentation 5-28, 15-4, 15-11, 17-6
domestic buildings — see residential buildings
Doolard's method, energy consumption calculation 13-5
door
    dwell times — see dwell times
    lock (G), 3-9, 14-5, 15-6 to 15-7, 15-10
    opening/closing times — see door operating times
    operating times 3-9 to 3-10, 4-4, 4-7, 7-18, 9-14
    operators (G), 3-10, 7-17 to 7-20, 8-4, 8-15 to 8-16, 9-14, 12-11, 16-6, 16-9
doors
    bi-parting (G), 5-20, 5-22 to 5-23, 7-21
    centre-opening (G), 3-9, 5-8, 5-18, 5-22, 7-18, 7-20 to 7-21
    hinged 5-20, 7-20
    side opening (G), 3-9, 5-8, 7-18, 7-20 to 7-21
double deck(er) lifts 2-15, 3-14, 3-16, 4-6, 4-8, 5-30
double wrap roping systems 7-4, 7-5, 7-27 to 7-28, 13-5
down-peak traffic
    calculation and simulation 4-6 to 4-8, 4-13, 4-16
    control 9-3, 9-5, 9-6 to 9-8, 9-10 to 9-11, 9-14
    design 3-4 to 3-5, 3-11, 3-13 to 3-14, 3-18
    — see also traffic, down-peak
drive control (G), 5-6, 8-4, 9-3, 9-7, 13-5, 16-5, 16-9 to 16-10
drive sheave — see sheaves
drives
    electric traction 5-9 to 5-10, 5-14 to 5-15, 5-18, 5-22, 7-3, 8-6 to 8-7, 12-8
    escalator 10-5
        goods 5-13
    hydraulic 5-9 to 5-10, 5-14 to 5-15, 5-18, 7-9, 7-10, 8-13 to 8-14, 11-7
    motor vehicle 5-22
    observation 5-18
    passenger, goods/passenger 5-9
    rack and pinion 5-24
    service 5-20
    variable voltage, variable frequency (VVVF) 5-9, 5-18, 7-3, 8-11 to 8-13, 10-9 to 10-10, 13-5
dwell times 2-10, 2-15, 3-11, 3-16, 4-4, 4-7 to 4-9, 5-5 to 5-6, 7-19, 7-30, 9-9, 9-11, 9-14, 11-12
Dyform ropes 7-26
dynamic sector (G), 3-14, 9-5 to 9-7,
dynamics 2-10, 3-9, 3-21, A-30
    — see also kinematics

earthing (G), 8-6, 8-9, 8-16, 10-1012-3, 12-7, 12-15 to 12-16, 15-5, 15-9, 16-10
electric traction drives 5-9 to 5-10, 5-14 to 5-15, 5-18, 5-22, 7-3, 8-6 to 8-7, 12-8
electrical equipment 5-26, 6-7, 12-9, 17-4, 17-6
electrical systems 12-3, 12-15, 17-4
electromagnetic compatibility 8-16, 10-8, 16-10, 17-4

electronic safety device 16-6, 16-12
electronic safety edges 5-5 to 5-8, 7-19, 11-12
EMC— see electromagnetic compatibility
emergency alarm 14-9, 15-6 to 15-7, 16-6
emergency escape routes 2-14, 3-16
emergency lighting (G), 12-12 to 12-13, 12-15 to 12-16, 15-6 to 15-7
energy
    accumulation buffers 7-24, A-40, A-42
    consumption 8-8, 8-14, 9-4, 10-9, 13-3 to 13-10, 16-3, 16-10
    dissipation buffers 7-24 to 7-25, 15-9, 16-12
    efficiency 5-9, 13-3, 13-5, 13-7
    escalator 10-9, 13-8
    lifts 13-4, 13-6 to 13-8
    regeneration 8-7, 8-8, 8-9, 8-12, 12-4, 12-5, 13-4, 13-6
entertainment centres, cinemas, theatres, sports centres, stadia and concert halls 2-12, 3-18, 5-5, 5-11, 5-17, 5-19
entrance bias, lifts 3-16
entrances — see lift doors, portals
environmental aspects, escalators and moving walks 10-4
environmental conditions 2-4, 7-12, 7-13, 8-5, 12-9, 12-10, 13-8
    — see also comfort
Equipment and protection systems intended for use in potentially explosive atmospheres (EXAT Directive) 5-28
escalator
    alighting 2-7, 2-11, 2-14 to 2-15, 10-4, 10-6
    boarding 2-7, 2-11, 2-14 to 2-15, 10-4
    bulk transit systems 2-8
    commissioning 15-5
    configuration 2-14
    drives 10-8
    energy consumption 13-8 to 13-9
    handling capacity 2-7 to 2-8, 2-10
    handrail 2-14, 10-3 to 10-8, 10-10
    in hotels 2-12
    in railway stations 2-13
    in shopping centres 2-9 to 2-11, 3-19
    inspection 15-11
    location and layout 2-13, 2-14, 10-3
escape lifts 6-9 to 6-10
escape routes 2-3, 2-12, 2-14, 3-5, 3-16, 6-4 to 6-5, 6-9
EHSR — see Essential Health and Safety Requirements
Essential Health and Safety Requirements 5-3, 5-16, 7-9, 7-25, 11-6, 12-10, 15-3, 16-4, 17-5, 17-8
estimated time of arrival, lift group control 9-7
ETA — see estimated time of arrival
EXAT Directive 5-28
explosion protected (Ex) lifts 5-28
express zones, round trip time calculation (G), 3-17, 4-4 to 4-5
external installations 5-16, 5-19, 5-22, 5-24, 12-11

fail-safe operation, lifts 8-4
fan 8-5, 12-8 to 12-11, 13-4
feedback devices, systems, techniques 5-9, 7-3, 8-7 to 8-11, 8-13, 8-16
fire protection 10-8, 12-8
fire rating 5-26, 6-6, 7-21
firefighter's switch 6-8
firefighting
    lifts 3-9, 3-14, 3-15, 3-18, 5-25, 5-26, 6-3 to 6-10
    stairs/stairways 5-25, 6-4 to 6-7

fireman's lift   (G), 5-26, 6-3, 9-11
fixtures   (G), 5-3, 5-5, 5-7, 5-27, 7-3,
        7-29 to 7-30, 9-8
flat construction ropes   7-26, 7-28
flat-bed motors   7-9, 8-13
    — see also linear induction drives
flats — see residential buildings
flight times   (G), 3-9, 3-11, 3-17, 4-4 to 4-5,
        5-18, 8-3, 9-14, A-30
floor cycle time   3-11, 7-18, 8-3
floor plates, building   3-14 to 3-16
flow rate, oil   8-13
flow rate, pedestrian   2-5 to 2-8, 2-10
flow rate, water   6-7
flux vector control   8-12 to 8-13
folding seat   5-7, 11-12
folding shutter gates, lifts   5-13, 5-22 to 5-23,
        A-39
formula
        design   4-14
        down-peak   3-13
        energy   13-6
        interfloor   3-14
        H and S   3-10, 3-11,
        machine room   5-33 to 5-34
        mid-day   3-14
        up-peak   3-7
free flow design   2-3, 2-5 to 2-6, 2-9
    — see also uncrowded density
full collective control, landing call collection
        5-4, 9-4
full flow design   2-5 to 2-7, 2-9
    — see also crowded density
funicular railways   5-24, 5-29


gates, collapsible, folding, leaf, shutter   (G),
        2-3, 5-13, 5-14, 5-20, 5-22, 5-27, 5-29,
        7-21, 16-6, 16-15
gear life   7-6
geared traction drives   (G), 5-3, 7-3, 7-5 to 7-6,
        8-6, 12-8, 13-7, 15-9, A-31 to A-32
gearless traction drives   (G), 5-3, 5-11, 5-16,
        5-18, 7-3 to 7-6, 8-6, 8-8, 8-11 to 8-12,
        12-8, 13-7
general analysis planning technique   4-3,
        4-5 to 4-6
generators, lift drive control   (G), 7-3,
        8-8 to 8-9, 13-5,15-6
generator, standby   5-9, 6-8, 12-7
glass   5-16 to 5-19, A-37
glass lifts   3-15, 5-16, 5-19, 10-6
    — see observation lifts
Glossary of terms   A1-1 to A1-31
going   2-6 to 2-7
goods lifts   2-12, 3-15, 3-18, 5-3, 5-11 to 5-14,
        5-21, 6-5
governor rope   5-25, 7-22 to 7-24, 16-17, A-39
governors   7-22, 15-9, 16-8, 16-12
Greater London Council   3-6
group (supervisory) control — see traffic
group layouts   2-15, 5-16
groups — see lift groups
groove   (G), 7-5 to 7-6, 7-22, 7-28 to 7-29,
        15-6 to 15-7
guard, guarding (G)
        escalator   10-6 to 10-7, 10-10
        lift   5-29, 7-15, 12-13, 15-6 to 15-7, 16-9,
        16-13 to 16-14
guide rails   (G), 5-10, 5-14, 5-19, 5-24 to 5-25,
        5-29, 7-3, 7-13 to 7-15, 7-17,
        7-22 to 7-24, 12-16, 13-5, 15-4, 16-6,
        16-8, 16-15, 16-17
guide shoes   (G), 5-19, 7-14 to 7-17, 8-8, 13-5,
        15-6 to 15-7
Guidelines to the thorough examination and
        testing of lifts   — see LG1

hall call   (G), 3-18, 4-10, 4-12, 9-8,
        allocation   5-4, 9-5, 9-7, 9-12, 9-13, 13-5
    — see also landing calls
hall lanterns   (G), 7-16, 7-30, 9-8
halls
        concert   2-12, 3-18, 5-5, 5-11, 5-17, 5-19
        of residence   2-14, 3-19, 5-8, 5-12,
handling capacity   (G), 2-3, 3-4, 3-21, 4-3
        basement service   3-15
        control   9-4 to 9-5, 9-8, 9-12 to 9-14
        corridors   2-5 to 2-4
        door operating   7-18, 11-12
        drives   8-3, 8-7, 8-12, 8-13, 8-16
        energy   13-5
        escalators   2-7, 2-8
        exit ramp   2-12, 3-17
        firefighting lifts   3-15
        landing call allocation systems   3-13
        lifts   2-8, 2-10, 3-3 to 3-7, 3-9 to 3-10,
        3-12 to 3-16, 4-5 to 4-9, 4-13, 4-15
        moving walks and ramps   2-8
        observation lifts   5-16 to 5-17
        portals   2-4
        stairways   2-6, 2-7
handrail, escalator   (G), 2-14, 10-3 to 10-8,
        10-10
harmonic distortion, electrical systems
        8-9 to 8-11, 12-5 to 12-6
headroom   (G), 5-9 to 5-11, 5-14 to 5-16, 5-18,
        5-22 to 5-23, 5-27, 5-31, 7-7 to 7-8,
        7-28, 16-16, A-37
Health and Safety Executive Approved Code of
        Practice L54   18-9 to 18-12
Health and Safety Executive Guidance Note
        PM 45: Escalators: periodic thorough
        examination   15-11
health and safety file, CDM Regulations
        18-1 to 18-12
health and safety plan, CDM Regulations
        18-1 to 18-12
heating, cooling, ventilation   8-9, 8-11,
        12-8 to 12-13, 12-15, 13-4 to 13-5, 14-8
highest call reversal floor   (G), 3-7 to 3-8,
        4-3 to 4-6, 4-14 to 4-15
home
        lifts   8-4
        residential care   2-13, 3-19, 5-7, 5-12,
        5-17, 5-19, 5-27
hospitals   2-4, 2-6 to 2-7, 2-12 to 2-13, 2-15, 3-5,
        3-9, 3-16, 3-18, 4-5, 5-5 to 5-6, 5-8,
        5-11 to 5-12, 5-14, 5-17, 5-19, 7-19,
        8-3 to 8-4, 9-11, 11-12, 12-11
hotels   2-12, 2-13, 3-5, 3-9, 3-15, 3-18 to 3-19,
        4-5 to 4-6, 5-6, 5-8, 5-12, 5-17, 5-19,
        5-29, 7-29, 9-3, 9-4, 12-11, 13-7, 13-8
human factors, interior circulation design   2-4
hydraulic   5-10, 5-29
        commissioning   15-5
        control   8-4, 8-6 to 8-7
        control valves   7-12, 8-6, 8-13
        drives   5-9, 5-14, 7-9 to 7-10
        goods   5-11, 5-15
        machine room   5-34, 12-8 to 12-10
        maintenance   15-7
        modernisation   16-4, 16-7
        motor vehicle   5-21
        MRL   5-10 to 5-11, 5-14
        observation   5-18
        ram   (G), 5-22, 7-12, 8-13 to 8-14, 16-13
        testing   15-9


IEC   14-11, 17-8
imaging systems   9-9
in-car noise   12-11
    — see also noise

in-car surveys, passenger traffic measurement
        4-12
inclination
        escalators   2-7, 2-14, 10-3, 10-4,
        10-7 to 10-8
        lifts   5-29 to 5-30,
        moving walks and ramps   2-8, 2-10, 2-13
        stairlifts   11-8
        stairways   2-6
indicators   2-18, 5-27, 6-10, 7-3, 7-29, 8-4,
        9-13, 15-6
        direction   7-30, A-41
        position   5-6, 5-26, 6-6, 7-29, 8-5, 9-11
indirect-acting jacks, hydraulic drives   7-11,
        7-13
inspection   5-27, 6-6, 6-8 to 6-9, 7-8, 7-11, 10-9,
        15-3, 15-4 to 15-6, 15-8
instantaneous safety gear   (G), 7-15, 7-22 to 23,
        16-11 to 16-12
intercoms   5-11, 5-15, 5-26, 12-7, 12-15
        firefighting lifts   6-6, 6-10
    — see also communications systems
interfaces
        control   8-5 to 8-6, 10-4, 10-8
        electrical wiring   12-3, 12-7,
        12-15 to 12-16
        fire   10-8
        lift monitoring systems   14-3,
        14-8 to 14-11
interference, electrical systems   (G), 8-5, 8-10,
        8-16, 12-8
interfloor distance   (G), 3-8 to 3-9, 3-11, 3-15,
        3-21, 4-5, 8-7 to 8-8
interfloor traffic   (G), 3-5, 3-10, 3-14,
        4-6 to 4-7, 4-12 to 4-13, 4-16, 9-3 to 9-8
interior circulation   2-3 to 2-4, 2-12
interleaved zones, tall buildings   3-17, 3-19
interpersonal distances, interior circulation
        design   2-4 to 2-5
interval   (G), 5-4, 5-6, 8-3, 9-10, 9-12 to 9-14
        calculation   2-15, 3-5 to 3-7, 3-11 to 3-14,
        3-19, 3-21
        computer   4-5 to 4-6
        simulation   4-7 to 4-10, 4-12, 4-15, 4-17
inverter drives   8-12, 12-4
inverter starters, escalators and passenger
        conveyors   10-9
isolation
        mechanical   7-5, 7-77-16, 7-17, 7-19
        power supplies   6-9, 8-6, 12-7, 12-13,
        12-15
isolator   (G), 12-5, 12-7


jacks, hydraulic drives   (G), 5-10, 5-15, 5-24,
        7-11 to 7-12, 8-13, 15-7
        upgrading   16-6, 16-9 to 16-10,
        16-13 to 16-14
jerk   3-9, 4-4 to 4-5, 5-4, 5-6, 8-7 to 8-8, 8-11,
        10-9, 12-12, A-29
    — see also comfort


kinematics   4-4, A-29, A-31
    — see also dynamics


landing calls   3-4 to 3-6, 3-11 to 3-14, 4-7, 4-11,
        6-8, 6-10, 7-29, 8-4, 8-6, 9-3 to 9-11,
        9-14
landing fixtures   7-29
lay, rope   (G)
        Lang's   7-26
        ordinary   7-26
layout
        building   2-9, 2-15, 5-5 to 5-7, 6-4 to 6-5,
        9-13, 13-3

layout (continued)
    equipment   2-9, 2-11, 2-15, 5-3 to 5-4,
      5-16, 5-19, 5-21, 6-4 to 6-5, 7-7, 7-10
legislation   17-3 to 17-7
LEIA (Lift and Escalator Industry Association)
    18-1
LG1   15-9, 15-11, 17-5
Lift and Escalator Industry Association   18-1
lift types
    disabled   5-26
    evacuation   5-26
    explosion proof   5-28
    firefighting   5-25
    goods   5-11 to 5-15
    inclined   5-29
    lifting platforms   5-27, 11-7
    motor vehicle   5-21 to 5-23
    observation   2-10 to 2-11, 3-4, 3-15, 5-7,
      5-16 to 5-19, 7-9 to 7-10, 12-11, 12-13
    passenger, goods/passenger   5-4 to 5-11,
      11-6
    rack and pinion   5-3, 5-9, 5-14, 5-16, 5-23,
      5-25
    scissor   5-28
    service   5-19 to 5-20
    stairlifts   5-27, 11-8
lift monitoring   8-3 to 8-4, 14-3 to 14-4,
    14-7 to 14-9
lift selectors   8-5
lift shaft — see well
lift traffic analysis software   4-8
lift well — see well
Lifting Operations and Lifting Equipment
    Regulations 1998   15-9, 15-11, 17-5
Lifts Directive   17-5
Lifts Regulations 1997   17-5
lighting   (G), 6-9, 7-13, 10-6, 11-5, 13-6, 14-8,
    16-5 to 16-7, 16-16 to 16-17
    car   7-30, 12-5, 12-7, 12-15, 13-4, 13-5,
      13-10, 17-6
    machine room   5-10, 5-15, 8-5, 12-10,
      12-13
linear induction drives   (G), 7-3, 7-9, 7-7, 8-13
load — see rated load
load weighing   (G), 4-12, 9-9 to 9-10, 9-14, 16-8
loading factor   3-7 to 3-8, 3-11, 3-21
lobbies   (G)
    control aspects   9-5, 9-8, 9-10 to 9-11, 9-14
    design aspects   2-3, 2-12 to 2-15, 3-4, 3-8,
      3-11, 3-14 to 3-18
    fire   5-25 to 5-26, 6-3 to 6-10,
    lift   4-4, 4-7, 4-11 to 4-12, 5-4, 5-6, 5-9,
      5-12, 5-16, 7-17, 12-13
    sky   (G), 3-15, 3-17, 5-9
lock, door   (G), 3-9, 14-5, 15-6 to 15-7, 15-10
LOLER — see Lifting Operations and Lifting
    Equipment Regulations 1998
loss of
    phase   12-4, 16-8
    supply   6-7 to 6-8, 14-8
lunch time traffic   3-4, 3-14, 4-6, 4-12 to 4-13
    — see also mid-day


machine room-less lifts   5-4, 5-10 to 5-11,
    5-14 to 5-15, 5-18, 5-25 to 5-26, 7-8,
    8-4
    environment   12-8, 12-13
    firefighting   6-6 to 6-7
machine room
    cooling   12-9
    electrical requirements   12-3 to 12-5
    goods lifts   5-14 to 5-15
    heating   12-9
    lighting   12-10
    maintenance   12-13
    motor vehicle lifts   5-23

machine room (continued)
    noise   12-11
    observation   5-18
    passenger and passenger/goods
      5-10 to 5-11
    rack and pinion   5-25
    service lifts   5-20
    temperature   12-8
    ventilation   12-8
main switches, lifts   (G), 12-5
    — see also isolator
maintenance   (G), 5-3 to 5-4, 5-10 to 5-11,
    5-13 to 5-15, 5-19, 5-21, 5-25 to 5-28,
    12-13
    components   7-6, 7-11, 7-13, 7-30
    drives   8-3 to 8-7, 8-9
    data logging   9-9, 14-4, 14-7
    escalator   10-5 to 10-6, 10-9
    electrical systems   12-7, 12-12
    firefighting lifts   6-7 to 6-9
    preventative   15-3, 15-6 to 15-8
mall widths, shopping centres   2-10
malls — see shopping centres
manual doors   5-10, 5-13 to 5-14, 7-20
mechanical lift selectors   8-5
mechanical safety edges   7-19, 8-15
mechanical ventilation, machine rooms   12-4
mid-day   3-4, 3-14 to 3-15, 4-6 to 4-7, 4-13,
    4-16 to 4-17, 9-3, 9-8, 9-12, 9-14, 13-7
modelling — see simulation
modernisation   5-3, 7-6, 8-9, 16-3, 16-4, 17-6
    CDM Regulations   18-7
    commissioning   15-5, 15-9
    energy   13-4, 13-7
    environmental conditions   12-3
    simulation   4-7, 4-11 to 4-12, 4-16
modular drives, escalators and moving walks
    10-9
monitoring — see remote monitoring
motor speed reference   8-7
motor vehicle lifts   5-21 to 5-23
motors   (G)
    AC   1-3, 7-3 to 7-4, 7-18, 8-8, 8-11, 8-13
    control techniques   7-6, 8-8, 8-11 to 8-12,
      8-16
    DC   7-3, 7-18, 8-8 to 8-9
    door operator   7-18, 8-16, A-40
    moving walks and escalators
      10-8 to 10-10
moving walks and ramps
    commissioning   15-3 to 15-5
    disabled use   11-3, 11-9
    equipment   10-3 to 10-10
    examination   15-11
    interior circulation   2-3, 2-8, 2-10,
      2-13 to 2-15
    maintenance   15-6 to 15-7
    monitoring   14-3 to 14-4, 14-11
MRL   5-10 to 5-11, 5-15 to 5-16, 7-8, 12-8
multi-leaf gates   (G), 7-21
multiple entry levels, lifts   3-15


natural ventilation, machine rooms
    12-8 to 12-10
network protocol, building energy management
    systems   14-11
neural networks, lift group control   9-8
noise   8-10
    acoustic   (G), 12-11
    bedplate   7-7
    car   7-16, 12-12
    comfort   12-11
    door   7-19
    escalators and passenger conveyors   10-5,
      10-8
    hydraulic drives   7-12

noise (continued)
    lobbies   3-16
    machine rooms   7-7, 15-6
    rack and pinion drives   5-25
    travel   5-4, 7-15, 7-26, 7-28, 12-10
non-directional collective control, landing call
    collection   9-4
non-metallic ropes   7-28
notifiable work, CDM Regulations
    18-4 to 18-5, 18-7, 18-11
numbers of passengers   5-8, 9-9, 10-4
    calculation ,simulation   4-3, 4-5 to 4-6,
      4-12
    round trip time   3-4, 3-6 to 3-8,
      3-11 to 3-14, 3-20
nursing homes   2-18, 3-9, 3-19, 5-7, 5-12, 5-17,
    5-19, 11-12


observation lifts   (G), 2-10 to 2-11, 3-4, 3-15,
    5-7, 5-16 to 5-19, 7-9 to 7-10, 12-11,
    12-13
obstructions, corridor handling capacity   2-6
obstruction, passenger   7-19
occupancy — see density (of occupation)
offices
    circulation   2-3, 2-4, 2-12
    control   9-4, 9-9, 9-13 to 9-14
    electrical   12-11
    energy   13-3, 13-9
    lift types   5-6, 5-8, 5-11 to 5-12,
      5-16 to 5-19, 5-27
    traffic design   3-5 to 3-6, 3-9 to 3-10,
      3-17 to 3-19, 3-21, 4-5 to 4-7,
      4-12 to 4-13
offshore lifts   5-24 to 5-25
on call traffic control   (G), 3-12, 8-3
operating panel, car   6-6, 7-30, 9-14,
    11-6 to 11-7
operational tests, firefighting lifts   6-9
optical passenger detectors   7-19, 8-15
outdoor installation — see external installation
overspeed governors   (G), 5-25, 7-22 to 7-23,
    7-24, 15-5 to 15-7, 15-9, 16-6, 16-8,
    16-12, 16-17


pallet   (G), 2-8, 2-10, 10-3 to 10-4, 10-6 to 10-8,
    15-7, 15-11
panoramic lifts — see observation lifts
parallel escalator configuration   (G), 2-14
parking   (G)
    lifts   4-13, 7-6, 8-6, 9-5, 9-7, 9-10 to 9-11,
      13-3, 13-5, 13-10
    spaces   2-9 to 2-10, 2-12, 3-17, 3-19, 5-21
PAS 32-1   7-22, 7-23, 7-24, 7-25, 11-7, 15-5,
    16-2
PAS 32-2   7-23, 7-24, 7-25, 11-7, 15-5, 16-7
passageways, handling capacity   2-5
passenger
    communication devices
      — see communication systems
    conveyors — see moving walks
    definition   2-3
    densities — see density (of occupation)
    detection devices   3-12, 7-16 to 7-17, 8-11
    journey time   3-12 to 3-13, 3-16, 5-25, 9-4,
      9-7 to 9-8
    lifts and goods/passenger   5-4 to 5-11, 11-6
      — see also lift types
    numbers of   3-4, 3-6 to 3-8, 3-11 to 3-14,
      3-20, 4-3, 4-5 to 4-6, 4-12, 5-8, 9-9,
      10-4
      — see also capacity factor, loading
      factor
    time to destination   3-12 to 3-13, 4-10 to
      4-11, 9-7 to 9-8

passenger (*continued*)
    traffic measurement 4-12
    transfer time 3-10 to 3-11, 3-16, 4-3, 4-15, 7-17
    transit time 3-12 to 3-13, 3-15, 4-4, 4-7, 4-10 to 4-11, 4-15
    waiting time 2-15, 3-4, 3-6, 3-12 to 3-15, 3-16, 4-5, 4-8, 4-10 to 4-11, 4-17, 5-4, 5-6, 9-3 to 9-5, 9-8, 9-12, 13-5
Paternoster systems (G), 5-3
payloads 5-8, 5-12, 5-17, 5-19, 5-21, 5-24
pedestrian
    definition of 2-3
    flow rates 2-5 to 2-8, 2-10
    speed 2-5, 2-7 to 2-8
    waiting areas, design 2-4
pedestrian density
    corridors 2-5
    escalator 2-7
    moving walk 2-8
    shopping centres 2-9
    space 2-5
    stairway 2-6 to 2-7, 2-10
percentage population served 3-7, 3-21, 9-13
performance — *see* quality of service
performance monitoring 14-3 to 14-5, 14-7
performance parameters, drives 8-3, 9-3
    — *see also* quality of service
performance time 3-7, 3-9 to 3-11, 3-15, 4-3, 4-5 to 4-6
personal space 2-4
phase
    failure 12-4, 16-8
    reversal 12-4
photocell detectors 7-19, 8-15, 9-9, 10-9 to 10-10
pistons, hydraulic jacks 7-9, 7-11 to 7-13, 15-5, 16-13
pit depth 5-10 to 5-11, 5-15, 5-21, 5-23, 5-31, 5-32, 5-33, 7-13, 7-25, 16-9, A-38
platform/enclosure assembly, lift cars 3-8, 4-5, 4-9, 7-16 to 7-17
population (G), 2-5, 2-8, 3-7, 3-11, 5-6 to 5-7, 8-3, 9-9,
    estimation 3-4 to 3-6
    percentage served 3-7, 3-21, 9-13
portals 2-3, 2-6, 2-13
    — *see also* doors, gates
position indicators (G), 5-6, 5-26, 6-6, 7-29 to 7-30, 8-3, 8-5, 9-11
power distribution, machine rooms 12-3 to 12-7
power-operated doors 5-13, 5-20, 5-22 to 5-24, 5-26, 6-6, 6-9, 7-17, 7-19 to 7-21, 16-6, 16-10, 16-15
power supplies 5-30, 6-8 to 6-9, 8-5, 12-3 to 12-4, 12-6, 14-8
power supply monitoring 14-8
power units, hydraulic drives 7-11, 12-9
pressure sensitive pads 9-9
pressurisation, firefighting shafts 6-5
primary power supplies, firefighting lifts 6-9
programs 8-6, 9-6 to 9-8, 9-9, 13-8
    logging 14-4, 14-7, 14-9
    simulation 4-3 to 4-9
progressive safety gear (G), 7-15, 7-22 to 7-24, 7-29, 16-11 to 16-12
project, CDM Regulations 18-4
protection
    fire 3-15, 5-26, 6-7 to 6-9, 10-8, 12-6
    power supplies 6-10, 12-4
pulley rooms 7-8, 12-9 to 12-10, 12-12 to 12-13, 16-16
pump motors, hydraulic drives 7-12, 8-13 to 8-14, 16-6, 16-10, 16-14
pump rooms, hydraulic drives 5-18, 5-25, 6-7, 7-10

push buttons 2-15, 5-22, 7-29, 8-3, 11-12, 14-11
push chairs 2-10 to 2-11, 3-19, 5-5, 5-7

quality of service (G), 3-4 to 3-6, 3-10, 4-7, 5-4, 5-6, 5-14, 16-5
quantity of service (G), 3-4 to 3-6, 16-5
queues (G), 2-4, 2-6, 3-6, 3-11 to 3-12, 4-7 to 4-8, 4-10 to 4-13, 5-6

rack and pinion lifts 5-3, 5-9, 5-14, 5-16, 5-23, 5-25
radio equipment, interference 12-8
railway stations 2-7 to 2-9, 2-11 to 2-13, 2-15, 3-15 to 3-18, 5-6, 5-12, 5-17, 9-3, 10-4, 13-9
ram (G), 5-22, 7-12, 8-13 to 8-14, 16-13
ramps
    exit 2-12, 3-17
    moving 2-8, 3-17 to 3-19
rated capacity
    lifts 2-11, 3-7 to 3-9, 3-15, 3-21, 4-14, 9-10
    stairlifts 11-9
    — *see also* design capacity, handling capacity, loading factor
rated speed 7-9 to 7-10, 7-22, 12-8, 16-5
    disabled lifts 11-6 to 11-10
    energy 13-4, 13-7 to 13-8
    escalator 2-7, 10-4, 10-8
    lifts, traffic design 3-8 to 3-9, 3-11, 3-15, 4-3, 4-5, 4-7
    lifts, type 5-9 to 5-11, 5-14, 5-17, 5-21, 5-27 to 5-28
records 12-7, 14-5, 16-7 to 16-15
    — *see also* documentation
refuge
    areas for disabled people 5-26, 6-9, 11-10
    space, safety 7-7, 7-10, 16-5, 16-9, 16-11, 17-5
refurbishment — *see* modernisation
regulations 17-3 to 17-7
regeneration 8-7 to 8-8, 13-6
relay controllers 8-5, 10-10
re-levelling 4-4, 5-9, 5-14, 7-27, 8-11
remote alarm 1-4, 7-30, 11-5 to 11-6, 12-9, 12-16, 14-3, 14-9 to 14-10
remote monitoring 12-7, 12-15, 14-3 to 14-11
renovation — *see* modernisation
rentable area 3-5, 9-13
resetting, safety gear 7-22 to 7-23
residential buildings 6-4, 6-10, 7-10, 9-3
    circulation 2-13
    equipment 5-7 to 5-8, 5-12, 5-17, 5-19, 5-21, 5-24
    traffic design 3-5, 3-9, 3-11, 3-18 to 3-19, 4-5 to 4-6
    — *see also* home lifts, nursing homes
residential care homes and nursing homes 2-13, 3-19, 5-7, 5-12, 5-17, 5-19, 5-27
reversal, phase 12-4
RICS — *see* Royal Institution of Chartered Surveyors
ride comfort 5-6, 7-3, 8-7, 8-12, 12-10, 12-12, 13-5
ride quality 5-6, 7-3, 8-7, 8-12, 12-10, 12-12, 13-5
    — *see also* acceleration, deceleration, jerk
riser heights
    escalators 10-5, 10-8
    stairways 2-6, 2-11
roller guide shoes 5-19, 7-15 to 7-16, 8-8
    — *see also* guide shoes
rope
    compensating 7-28
    governor 5-25, 7-22 to 7-24, 16-17, A-39

rope (*continued*)
    suspension 5-3, 5-18, 7-27, 15-6 to 15-7
    types, construction 7-25 to 7-26
    wear, life 3-9, 5-10, 5-15, 15-6 to 15-7
roping systems 7-28 to 7-29
round trip time 3-7, 3-10 to 3-17, 3-21, 4-3 to 4-8, 5-4, 8-3, 8-13, 9-12
Royal Institution of Chartered Surveyors 3-3
RTT — *see* round trip time

SAFed — *see* Safety Assessment Federation
safety 5-1, 7-20 to 7-22
    anti-creep devices, hydraulic drives 7-8, 8-10 to 8-11
    clearances 5-11
    counterweights 7-6, 7-13, 7-21
    escalators and passenger conveyors 10-1 to 10-3
    home and stair lifts 5-20
    hospital passenger lifts 5-2
    hydraulic lifts 7-9, 7-13 to 7-14
    lift cars 7-13 to 7-14
    lift door operators 3-8, 7-16 to 7-17
    maintenance 11-6
    obstruction detectors 7-17, 8-11
    overspeed governors
    rack and pinion lifts 5-15 to 5-16
    scissor lifts 5-20
    — *see also* brakes, health and safety,
Safety Assessment Federation 15-2, 15-3, 16-2
safety devices
    escalator and moving walk 10-5, 10-8, 10-10, 15-11
    lifts 5-4, 7-18 to 7-19, 8-4, 8-16, 15-5 to 15-7, 15-9, 16-6, 16-12 to 16-13
safety edges (G)
    electronic 5-5 to 5-8, 7-19, 11-12
    mechanical 7-19, 8-15
safety factor, ropes 7-26
safety file, health and 18-1 to 18-12
safety gear (G)
    activating devices 7-23
    instantaneous 7-15, 7-22 to 23, 16-11 to 16-12
    progressive 7-15, 7-22 to 7-24, 7-29, 16-11 to 16-12
safety plan, health and 18-1 to 18-12
scenic lifts — *see* observation lifts
scheduled traffic controllers 3-11 to 3-12
schedules for electrical systems 12-15 to 12-16
Schroeder
    calculation of *H* 3-8, 3-10
    method, energy consumption calculation 13-4, 13-6 to 13-8
scissor lifts 5-28
secondary power supplies, firefighting lifts 5-26, 6-7 to 6-8
sectoring, lift group control 3-12, 3-14, 9-5 to 9-7, 9-12
sectors, and zoning, tall buildings 3-16 to 3-17
sensorless flux vector control 8-13
service lifts 5-19 to 5-20
service quality — *see* quality of service
sheave shaft load 7-4, 7-6, 7-28
sheaves (G), 7-8 to 7-9, 7-15 to 7-16, 7-26, 7-28, 16-17
shoes — *see* guide shoes
shopping centres 2-15, 5-12, 10-4, 11-5
    chain stores 2-12, 3-17
    goods lifts 5-12
    interior circulation 2-8 to 2-11
    mall 2-3, 2-9 to 2-10, 2-12, 3-17
    mall widths 2-10
    observation lifts 2-10, 3-15, 5-7, 5-17
    passenger lifts 2-10, 3-19, 4-6, 5-7
    service lifts 5-19
    traffic planning 3-19

shutter gates, lifts — *see* gates, collapsible, folding, leaf, shutter

shuttle lifts 3-15, 3-17

side-acting jacks, hydraulic drives 5-9, 5-14, 7-11

side-opening doors 3-9, 5-8, 7-18, 7-20

signals, lift monitoring systems 14-5 to 14-6

simulation 3-3, 3-8, 4-3, 4-5 to 4-7, 5-4, 9-11
    down-peak traffic control 3-13, 4-16
    energy consumption 13-8
    interfloor 3-14, 4-16
    mid-day traffic 3-14, 4-16
    planning technique 4-7
    templates 4-7, 4-16
    up-peak 4-9, 4-16

single bridge static converter drives 8-10

single floor flight time 3-9, 3-11, 3-17, 4-4 to 4-5, 5-18, 8-3, 9-14, A-30 to A-32

single floor transit time 3-8, 8-3, 8-6

single hinged manual doors 7-20

single side-acting jacks, hydraulic drives 5-9, 5-14, 7-11

single speed drives 7-8, 7-12, 8-11 to 8-12

single wrap roping systems 7-5, 7-27 to 7-28

sizing electrical cables 12-6

sky lobbies 3-15, 3-17, 5-9

sliding doors 5-13, 5-22 to 5-23, 5-33, 7-20

soft master–slave control 9-9

soft starters 10-9

solar gain 5-19, 12-8 to 12-9, 12-11, 12-15

solid-state controllers 5-9, 7-3, 12-5, 16-5

speed
    escalators and moving walks 2-7, 10-8
    escape lifts 6-9
    firefighting lifts 6-6
    hydraulic 5-9
    inclined lifts 5-30
    lifting platforms 5-27, 11-7
    motor vehicle 5-21
    lifts 3-9, 3-11, 4-4
    pedestrians 2-5, 2-7 to 2-8
    rack and pinion lifts 5-24
    stairlifts 5-28, 11-9

speed control
    escalator 10-9
    lifts 5-9, 7-4, 7-12, 7-18, 8-8 to 8-9, 8-13, 8-16
    — *see also* overspeed governors

speed reference, lift drives 8-7 to 8-10, 8-12, 8-16, A-29

sports centres 2-12, 3-18, 5-5, 5-11, 5-17

sprinklers 5-25, 6-4, 6-7, 10-8

stacked zones, tall buildings 3-16 to 3-17

stairlifts 5-27 to 5-28, 11-8 to 11-9

stairways
    and escalators 2-15
    and lifts 2-14
    contraflows 2-10
    design and location 2-9, 3-15
    evacuation 6-9 to 6-10
    firefighting 3-15, 6-3, 6-7
    handling capacity 2-6 to 2-7
    inclination 2-6
    riser heights 2-6
    shopping centres 2-10
    tread depth 2-6

standard communications protocols 14-11

standards — *see* British Standards

standby power supplies 5-9, 6-8, 12-4 to 12-7, 12-15

starters (G), 8-9, 10-9

static converter drives 7-3, 8-8 to 8-11

static sectoring algorithms — *see* sectoring, lift group control

step utilisation, escalators 2-10

step width, escalators 2-7 to 2-8, 2-11, 13-8

stops — *see* average number of stops

supervisory control algorithms 9-4, 9-6, 9-8, 12-5

surveys, passenger traffic measurement 3-4 to 3-5, 4-11 to 4-12 to 4-14, 8-8

system response time (G), 3-13, 9-4, 9-9

system utilisation — *see* capacity factor, loading factor

tall buildings 2-13, 3-9, 3-14 to 3-19, 5-14, 5-30

telephones, PSTN 5-23, 6-10, 7-30, 11-12, 12-7, 14-8 to 14-11
    — *see also* communications systems

temperature — *see* cooling, heating, ventilation

testing 6-8 to 6-9, 15-9
    — *see also* commissioning, PAS 32

theatres 2-12, 3-18, 5-5, 5-11, 5-17, 5-19, 5-26

thyristors 8-9 to 8-12, 10-9, 13-5

tied-down compensation 7-16, 7-28

top drive systems 5-10, 5-15, 7-7 to 7-8, 7-28

tracer gas method, lift door fire rating 7-21

traction drives — *see* drives, electric traction

traffic (G)
    analysis 4-3, 4-8, 4-11 to 4-12, 9-11, 13-8, 14-4
    describing 4-13
    down-peak 3-4, 3-13 to 3-14, 4-16, 9-6 to 9-8, 9-10, 9-14
    group control 4-12, 5-4, 8-4, 8-8, 8-18, 9-4 to 9-6, 9-9 to 9-11
    group control algorithms 3-11, 3-14, 4-7 to 4-8, 4-11, 9-4 to 9-14
    measurement 4-12
    measuring 4-11
    patterns 3-4 to 3-5, 3-10 to 3-13, 3-14 to 3-15, 3-18, 4-6, 4-16, 5-4, 9-5, 9-8 to 9-9, 13-8
    planning 3-3 to 3-21
    reports, lift monitoring 14-8
    interfloor 3-5, 3-10, 3-14 to 3-15, 4-6 to 4-7, 4-12 to 4-13, 4-16, 9-3 to 9-8
    mid-day 3-4, 3-14 to 3-15, 4-6, , 4-16, 9-8
    up-peak 3-3 to 3-7, 3-10, 3-12 to 3-14, 4-5 to 4-6, 4-9, 4-16, 9-10, 9-12, 13-7

transit time, single floor 3-8, 8-3, 8-6

travel time, terminal floors 3-9

tread depth 2-6

turnstiles — *see* portals

twin cylinder (jack), hydraulic drives 7-11

two-bridge static converter drives 8-9 to 8-11

two-speed drives 2-9, 7-3, 7-6, 8-12, 10-9, 13-5

two-stop hydraulic escape lifts 6-9

two-way pedestrian traffic 2-6, 3-18

U-groove — *see* groove

uncrowded density
    shopping centres 2-9
    — *see also* free flow design

undercut groove — *see* groove

underlying handling capacity 3-14

underslung car systems 5-18, 7-8, 7-27 to 7-28

unidirectional flows, shopping centres 2-4, 2-10

universities and other education buildings 2-13, 3-19, 5-8, 5-12, 5-17, 5-19

up-distributive/down-collective control 9-4

upgrading — *see* modernisation

up-peak
    boosters 9-12
    handling capacity — *see* handling capacity

up-peak (*continued*)
    calculation — *see* interval, calculation
    interval — *see* interval
    sectoring — *see* sectoring, lift group control
    simulation — *see* simulation
    traffic — *see* traffic, up-peak
    zoning, subzoning 3-12, 9-12

usable area 3-5, 4-13, 9-13

user interface, lift monitoring systems 14-8

V-groove — *see* groove

valve, hydraulic control (G), 7-12, 8-6, 8-13

variable speed AC drives 5-9, 5-14, 5-18, 13-4, 13-10

variable voltage, variable frequency (VVVF) 5-9, 5-18, 7-3, 8-11 to 8-13, 10-9 to 10-10, 13-5

vector control 5-30, 8-13

ventilation (G)
    car 12-5, 12-10
    controller cabinet 8-5
    machine room 12-8
    machine-room-less 5-11, 5-16
    pump room 7-10, 12-9
    well 6-6, 12-10
    — *see also* cooling, heating

vertical bi-parting doors, goods lifts 5-20, 5-22 to 5-23, 7-21

very tall buildings 3-9, 3-14 to 3-15, 3-17

vibration (G)
    equipment 7-7, 7-15 to 7-16
    escalator 10-8
    human comfort 5-4, 12-11 to 12-12
    — *see also* comfort

visual impact 2-10, 3-15

visually impaired people 10-8, 11-5, 11-12

voice synthesisers 11-12

voltage drops 10-8, 12-4, 12-6

waiting areas 2-4, to 2-5, 2-15, 3-5
    — *see also* lobbies

waiting times — *see* passenger, waiting time

walk round escalator configuration 2-14

walking speeds 2-5 to 2-6, 2-9 to 2-10

walkways 2-5, 2-14, 3-19, 5-6, 5-12
    — *see also* corridors

wall climber lifts 5-16, 5-18
    — *see also* observation lifts

Ward Leonard lift drive control 8-8 to 8-9, 13-5 to 13-6, 13-10

Ward Leonard systems, regenerated energy 13-6

waste heat 12-8, 13-6, 13-10

well 5-10, 5-14, 5-18, 5-20, 5-22, 5-27, 5-31 to 5-34, 12-10, 12-12, 13-4, 15-7
    ventilation 6-6, 12-10

wheelchair 2-6, 5-4 to 5-9, 5-26 to 5-27 to 5-33, 6-9, 7-20, 7-29, 10-3, 11-4, 11-5 to 11-10, 11-12

wheelchair users — *see* disabled people

wiring interfaces, electrical systems 12-7

worm reduction gear 7-3, 7-5, 12-8

zone
    building 3-9, 3-13, 3-17, 9-6, 9-11 to 9-12
    door 3-10, 8-16, 14-6, 14-10
    express 3-17, 4-4 to 4-5
    human buffer 2-4 to 2-5